# NEW National Curriculum Mathematics A/A*

## K. M. Vickers
## M. J. Tipler
### H. L. van Hiele

© K. M. Vickers, M. J. Tipler and H. L. van Hiele 1993, 1996

First published in 1993 by Canterbury Educational Ltd
Revised edition published in 1996 by:
Stanley Thornes (Publishers) Ltd
Ellenborough House, Wellington Street
CHELTENHAM, Glos. GL50 1YW
England

96  97  98  99  00  /  10  9  8  7  6  5  4  3  2  1

The right of K. M. Vickers, M. J. Tipler and H. L. van Hiele to be
identified  as authors of this work has been asserted by them in
accordance with the Copyright, Designs and Patents Act 1988

A catalogue record for this book is available from the British Library

ISBN 0 7487 2794 9

Printed and bound in Great Britain by
BPC Paulton Books Ltd, Paulton

# PREFACE

**New National Curriculum Mathematics** by K. M. Vickers and M. J. Tipler is a complete mathematics course, carefully designed and now updated to ensure full coverage of the revised 1995 National Curriculum. This book completes the Higher Tier GCSE and covers all the material in Key Stage 4 (and KS3 Exceptional Performance.)

Although this book is more academic in content and style than the previous books in this series it still retains many of the features of the previous books. As well as skill developing exercises there are many discussion exercises, investigations and practical exercises. In addition there are research projects for very able pupils.

There is a good balance between tasks which develop knowledge, skills and understanding, and those which develop the ability to tackle and solve problems. Many activities do both. There is a thorough and careful development of each topic. Questions within each exercise or activity are carefully graded to build pupil confidence.

Throughout each topic, relevance to everyday life is emphasised. The acquisition of knowledge and skills is integrated with their use and application.

Each section begins with revision printed on pink paper for ease of identification. Each section ends with a review chapter which contains revision questions on the material developed in this book. In each of the other chapters, every skill developing exercise finishes with review questions and there is a review at the end of these chapters.

Many questions from GCSE examinations are included; in the Revision, in the Reviews at the end of each chapter and in the four Review Chapters.

This book does not replace the teacher. Rather, it is a resource for both the pupil and the teacher. The teacher can be flexible about what is taught and when.

This book takes into consideration:
    pupils' needs
    pupils' interests
    pupils' experiences
    the need for pupils to explore mathematics
    the use of technology
    both independent and co-operative work habits

This book encourages pupils to:
    use a wide range of mathematics
    discuss mathematical ideas
    undertake investigations
    participate in practical activities
    use reference material
    relate mathematics to everyday life
    select appropriate methods for a task
    analyse and communicate information
    discuss difficulties
    ask questions

It is hoped that the pupil who uses this book will:

develop a real interest in mathematics

become well motivated

gain much enjoyment from mathematics

develop a fascination with mathematics

develop an ability to use mathematics in other subjects

become confident in the use of the calculator and computer

gain a firm foundation for further study

become proficient at applying mathematics to everyday life

develop both independent and co-operative work habits

become aware of the power and purpose of mathematics

develop an ability to communicate mathematics

develop an appreciation of the relevance of mathematics

develop an ability to think precisely, logically and creatively

become confident at mathematics

gain a sense of satisfaction

Calculator keying sequences are for the Casio *fx–82*LB. Some slight variation may be needed for other models and makes.

The version of LOGO used is LOGOTRON — standard LOGO for the BBC. The version of BASIC used is BBC BASIC.

K.M. Vickers
1996

Acknowledgements

The author wishes to thank all those firms and enterprises who have so kindly given permission to reproduce tables and other material. A special thanks to S.P.R. Coxon, I. Kelderman, S.C. Lees-Jeffries, J.A. Ogilvie and S. Napier for their valuable contributions and to F. Tunnicliffe for the illustrations. The author is grateful to the Examination Boards for allowing questions from past GCSE papers to be included.

Every effort has been made to trace all the copyright holders. If any have been inadvertently overlooked the publishers will be pleased to make the necessary arrangements at the first opportunity.

# Contents

## NUMBER

## ALGEBRA

# SHAPE, SPACE AND MEASURES

# HANDLING DATA

# Level Descriptions for Exceptional Performance

## Attainment Target 1 : Using and Applying Mathematics

### ■ Exceptional performance

Pupils give reasons for the choices they make when investigating within mathematics itself or when using mathematics to analyse tasks; these reasons explain why particular lines of enquiry are followed and others rejected. Pupils apply the mathematics they know in familiar and unfamiliar contexts. Pupils use mathematical language and symbols effectively in presenting a convincing reasoned argument. Their reports include mathematical justifications, explaining their solutions to problems involving a number of features or variables.

## Attainment Target 2 : Number and Algebra

### ■ Exceptional performance

Pupils understand and use rational and irrational numbers. They determine the bounds of intervals. Pupils understand and use direct and inverse proportion. In simplifying algebraic expressions, they use rules of indices for negative and fractional values. In finding formulae that approximately connect data, pupils express general laws in symbolic form. They solve problems using intersections and gradients of graphs.

## Attainment Target 3 : Shape, Space and Measures

### ■ Exceptional performance

Pupils sketch the graphs of sine, cosine and tangent functions for any angle, and generate and interpret graphs based on these functions. Pupils use sine, cosine and tangent of angles of any size, Pythagoras' theorem, and the conditions for congruent triangles, when solving problems in two and three dimensions. They calculate lengths of circular arcs and areas of sectors, and calculate the surface area of cylinders and volumes of cones and spheres.

## Attainment Target 4 : Handling Data

### ■ Exceptional performance

Pupils interpret and construct histograms. They understand how different methods of sampling and different sample sizes may affect the reliability of conclusions drawn; they select and justify a sample and method to investigate a population. They recognise when and how to use conditional probability.

# Key Stage 4: Further Material

Using mathematics, communicating mathematically and reasoning should be set in the context of the other areas of mathematics. The study of areas under graphs should apply to work on analysing data, work involving velocity and time, and probability. Trigonometric functions should be considered from the standpoint of the behaviour of functions, as well as a tool for solving problems in two and three dimensions.

## ■ 1. Pupils should be given opportunities to:

**a** apply their knowledge, understanding and skills to solving problems of increasing complexity in a wider range of contexts.

Pupils should be taught to:

## ■ 2. Using and Applying Mathematics

**a** explain and evaluate their choice of approach to solving problems set in contexts or areas of mathematics that are new to them;

**b** express mathematical ideas unambiguously through the efficient use of conventional mathematical notations;

**c** understand the necessary and sufficient conditions under which generalisations, inferences and solutions to problems remain valid;

**d** extend their mathematical reasoning into understanding and using more rigorous argument, leading to notions of proof.

## ■ 3. Number

**a** understand and use direct and inverse proportion;

**b** distinguish between rational and irrational numbers, and appreciate that irrational numbers complete the real-number system;

**c** understand and calculate the upper and lower bounds of numerical solutions, particularly in the context of measurement;

**d** simplify numerical expressions involving roots; understand and use roots and reciprocals expressed in index form.

Pupils should be taught to:

## ■ 4. Algebra

**a** simplify algebraic expressions; solve equations and inequalities by algebraic and graphical methods, selecting the most appropriate method for the problem concerned;

**b** construct and use tangents to curves to estimate rates of change for non-linear functions, and use appropriate compound measures to express results;

**c** interpret the meaning of the area under a graph and apply this to the solution of numerical and statistical problems;

**d** interpret and apply the transformation of functions in the context of their graphical representation, including $y = f(x + a), y = f(kx)$ and $y = f(x) + a$, applied to $y = f(x)$;

**e** select mathematical functions, *eg exponential or trigonometric functions*, to fit sets of data that model increasingly complex situations, and use them to solve problems;

## ■ 5. Shape, Space and Measures

**a** extend measurement, including distances and angles, to more complex plane shapes and solids, including circular arcs, cylinders, cones and spheres; understand and use relationships between similar figures and solids;

**b** apply simple vector methods to the solution of problems;

**c** extend their understanding of trigonometry to angles of any size, the graphs and behaviour of trigonometric functions, and the application of these to the solution of problems in two and three dimensions, including appropriate use of the sine and cosine rules;

**d** use angle and tangent properties of circles.

## ■ 6. Handling Data

**a** use sampling methods, considering their reliability;

**b** extend skills in handling data into constructing and interpreting histograms;

**c** describe the dispersion of a set of data; find and interpret the standard deviation of a set of data;

**d** understand when and how to estimate conditional probabilities.

# NUMBER

# Number Revision

**Writing a Number as a Product of Prime Factors. HCF, LCM.**

This "factor tree" can be used to rewrite
90 as $2 \times 3 \times 3 \times 5$.

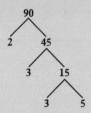

The **highest common factor (HCF)** of two numbers is the greatest number that is a factor
of both of the given numbers.
For instance, since $36 = \underline{2} \times 2 \times \underline{3} \times \underline{3}$ and $90 = \underline{2} \times \underline{3} \times \underline{3} \times 5$, the HCF of 36 and
90 is $2 \times 3 \times 3$ i.e. 18.

The **lowest common multiple (LCM)** of two numbers is the smallest number that is a
multiple of both of the given numbers. The lowest common multiple is sometimes called
the **least common multiple**.
For instance, since $36 = \underline{2} \times \underline{2} \times \underline{3} \times \underline{3}$ and $90 = 2 \times 3 \times 3 \times \underline{5}$, the LCM of 36 and
90 is $2 \times 2 \times 3 \times 3 \times 5$ i.e. 180.

**Number Lines. Negative Numbers**

$<$ means "is less than"     $>$ means "is greater than".
On a number line, the smaller a number the further to the left it is placed.
For instance, since $2 \cdot 1 < 2 \cdot 8$, $2 \cdot 1$ is to the left of $2 \cdot 8$ on a number line; since $\frac{4}{5} > \frac{2}{5}$, $\frac{4}{5}$ is to
the right of $\frac{2}{5}$ on a number line.

The [+/−] key on the calculator is pressed to display a negative number.
Positive numbers, such as $+2$, may be written without any sign.
Negative numbers, such as $-2$, are always written with the negative sign.
The negative numbers are shown on a number line, or scale, as numbers that are less than
zero.

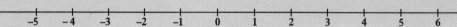

**Calculating with Positive and Negative Numbers**

We may use a number line to **add** or **subtract**.
To add a positive number, move to the right; e.g. $-2 + 3 = 1$.
To add a negative number, move to the left; e.g. $-2 + (-3) = -5$.
To subtract a positive number, move to the left; e.g. $-2 - 3 = -5$.
To subtract a negative number, move to the right; e.g. $-2 - (-3) = 1$.

*continued . . .*

... *from previous page*

To multiply or divide, firstly multiply (or divide) the numbers, disregarding the signs, then find the sign for the answer using:     two like signs give positive
two unlike signs give negative

For instance:     $3 \times (-6) = -18$     $\dfrac{-16}{8} = -2$     $2 \times (-8) \times (-3) = 48$

## Decimals

A decimal such as $0 \cdot 166666 \ldots$, in which the digit 6 repeats, is called a recurring decimal; it is written as $0 \cdot 1\dot{6}$. Recurring decimals are sometimes called repeating decimals.

Multiplying a given number by a number greater than 1 will increase the given number.
Multiplying by a number smaller than 1 will decrease the given number.
For instance, $12 \cdot 8 \times 2 \cdot 4$ has an answer larger than $12 \cdot 8$; $12 \cdot 8 \times 0 \cdot 4$ has an answer smaller than $12 \cdot 8$.

Dividing a given number by a number larger than 1 will decrease the given number.
Dividing by a number smaller than 1 will increase the given number.
For instance, $12 \cdot 8 \div 2 \cdot 4$ has an answer smaller than $12 \cdot 8$; $12 \cdot 8 \div 0 \cdot 4$ has an answer larger than $12 \cdot 8$.

## Index Notation and Standard Form

The numbers $10, 100, 1000, 10000, \ldots$ can be rewritten as $10^1, 10^2, 10^3, 10^4, \ldots$
The numbers $\frac{1}{10}, \frac{1}{100}, \frac{1}{1000}, \ldots$ can be rewritten as $\frac{1}{10^1}, \frac{1}{10^2}, \frac{1}{10^3}, \ldots$ or as $10^{-1}, 10^{-2}, 10^{-3}, \ldots$
The numbers $7 \cdot 0 \times 10^4$, $7 \cdot 36 \times 10^2$, $8 \cdot 6 \times 10^{-2}$ are written in Standard Form.
Standard Form is also called Standard Index Notation or Scientific Notation.

**Standard form is $a \times 10^n$ where $1 \le a < 10$ and n is an integer.**

Take the following steps to rewrite a number given in standard form as a number in decimal form.
   *Step 1*   Move the decimal point. The index with the 10 gives the number of places and the direction in which the point is to be moved.
   *Step 2*   Omit the multiplication sign and the power of 10.

*Examples*   1.   $2 \cdot 47 \times 10^4 = 24700$   (move the point 4 places in the positive direction)
   2.   $3 \cdot 0 \times 10^{-4} = 0 \cdot 0003$   (move the point 4 places in the negative direction)
   3.   $4 \cdot 5 \times 10^0 = 4 \cdot 5$   (move the point 0 places)

Take the following steps to rewrite a number given in decimal form as a number in standard form.
   *Step 1*   Write the decimal point after the first non-zero digit.
   *Step 2*   Insert a multiplication sign and a power of 10. The index with the 10 is found by considering the number of places, and the direction, the point would need to be moved to get back to the original number.

*Examples*   1.   $8957 = 8 \cdot 957 \times 10^3$   (the point in $8 \cdot 957$ needs to be moved 3 places in the positive direction to get 8957)
   2.   $5 = 5 \cdot 0 \times 10^0$   (the point in $5 \cdot 0$ needs to be moved zero places to get 5)
   3.   $0 \cdot 0903 = 9 \cdot 03 \times 10^{-2}$   (the point in $9 \cdot 03$ needs to be moved 2 places in the negative direction to get $0 \cdot 0903$)

*continued* ...

## Approximation and Estimation

To approximate (round) to d.p. (decimal places), decide how many figures are wanted after the decimal point. Omit all the following figures with the proviso that, if the first figure omitted is 5 or larger, increase the last figure kept by 1.
For instance, 34·548 rounded to 1 d.p. is 34·5, 34·548 rounded to 2 d.p. is 34·55.

To approximate to s.f. (significant figures), count from the first non-zero figure. Zeros may need to be inserted so the size of the number is unchanged.
For instance, 34·548 rounded to 3 s.f. is 34·5; 34·548 rounded to 1 s.f. is 30; 0·03458 rounded to 2 s.f. is 0·035.

A guideline to the accuracy with which we should give an answer to a calculation is:
Count how many d.p. (or s.f.) there are in the number with the fewest d.p. (or s.f.). Round the answer to this many, or just one more, d.p. (or s.f.).

For instance, acceptable answers for $\frac{28 \cdot 1}{0 \cdot 89}$ are 31·6 (1 d.p.), 31·57 (2 d.p.), 32 (2 s.f.), 31·6 (3 s.f.).

The symbol $\approx$ means "is approximately equal to".

To estimate an answer to a calculation, replace each number with a simpler number.
For instance, $\frac{8 \cdot 81 \times 74 \cdot 85}{0 \cdot 46} \approx \frac{10 \times 75}{\frac{1}{2}}$ giving an estimate of 1500.

Some useful **guidelines** on which numbers to choose for the replacement numbers are:
- Wherever possible, approximate to numbers such as 1, 2, 5, 10, 50, 100 etc. that are easy to work with mentally.
- Look for numbers which will cancel.
- Replace decimals between 0 and 1 with simple fractions.
- When multiplying or dividing, never approximate a number with 0.
- Remember, it is an estimate. The approximations don't need to be very accurate.

## Calculation with the Calculator

The scientific calculator does operations in the correct order. An expression such as
$14 - 2(5 + 1)$ is keyed in as $\boxed{14}$ $\boxed{-}$ $\boxed{2}$ $\boxed{\times}$ $\boxed{(}$ $\boxed{5}$ $\boxed{+}$ $\boxed{1}$ $\boxed{)}$ $\boxed{=}$ to get the correct answer of 2. (Some calculators do not need the $\times$ pressed before the ( sign.)

We sometimes need to insert brackets or use the memory function.
For instance, $\frac{29 + 6}{4 + 3}$ can be worked out in one of the following ways.

Either **Key** $\boxed{(}$ $\boxed{29}$ $\boxed{+}$ $\boxed{6}$ $\boxed{)}$ $\boxed{\div}$ $\boxed{(}$ $\boxed{4}$ $\boxed{+}$ $\boxed{3}$ $\boxed{)}$ $\boxed{=}$
or **Key** $\boxed{29}$ $\boxed{+}$ $\boxed{6}$ $\boxed{=}$ $\boxed{\text{Min}}$ $\boxed{4}$ $\boxed{+}$ $\boxed{3}$ $\boxed{=}$ $\boxed{\text{SHIFT}}$ $\boxed{\text{X}{\leftarrow}\text{M}}$ $\boxed{\div}$ $\boxed{\text{MR}}$ $\boxed{=}$

The $\boxed{x^y}$ key is used to calculate powers.
For instance, $2^7$ is found by keying $\boxed{2}$ $\boxed{\text{SHIFT}}$ $\boxed{x^y}$ $\boxed{7}$ $\boxed{=}$ .
$1 \cdot 8^{-1}$ may be found by keying $\boxed{1 \cdot 8}$ $\boxed{\text{SHIFT}}$ $\boxed{x^y}$ $\boxed{1}$ $\boxed{+/-}$ $\boxed{=}$ or since $1 \cdot 8^{-1} = \frac{1}{1 \cdot 8}$ it may be found by keying $\boxed{1}$ $\boxed{\div}$ $\boxed{1 \cdot 8}$ $\boxed{=}$ or by keying $\boxed{1 \cdot 8}$ $\boxed{\text{SHIFT}}$ $\boxed{\frac{1}{x}}$ .

*continued . . .*

. . . *from previous page*

Very large numbers and very small numbers cannot be keyed directly into an 8 digit calculator. If numbers such as these are part of a calculation, they may be keyed into the calculator in standard form using the EXP key.

For instance, $34\,820\,000\,000 \times 734\,000\,000$ can be rewritten as $(3{\cdot}482 \times 10^{10}) \times (7{\cdot}34 \times 10^8)$. The keying sequence $\boxed{3{\cdot}482}$ $\boxed{\text{EXP}}$ $\boxed{10}$ $\boxed{\times}$ $\boxed{7{\cdot}34}$ $\boxed{\text{EXP}}$ $\boxed{8}$ $\boxed{=}$ gives a screen display of $2{\cdot}555788^{19}$, which may be rounded sensibly as $2{\cdot}56 \times 10^{19}$ to 3 s.f.

Note  An alternative keying sequence is:
$\boxed{\text{MODE}}$ $\boxed{8}$ $\boxed{3}$ $\boxed{3{\cdot}482}$ $\boxed{\text{EXP}}$ $\boxed{10}$ $\boxed{\times}$ $\boxed{7{\cdot}34}$ $\boxed{\text{EXP}}$ $\boxed{8}$ $\boxed{=}$ which gives a screen display of $2{\cdot}56^{19}$.

Mode 8 is the Scientific mode on the Casio calculator. Keying $\boxed{\text{MODE}}$ $\boxed{8}$ $\boxed{3}$ converts all the numbers keyed in, and the answer, to standard form rounded to 3 significant figures.

Mode 7 is the Fix mode. Keying $\boxed{\text{MODE}}$ $\boxed{7}$ $\boxed{4}$ rounds all the numbers keyed in, and the answer, to 4 decimal places.

Mode 9 is the Normal mode; decimals are displayed exactly as they are keyed in.

**Fractions and Ratio**

In the fraction $\frac{4}{9}$, 4 is called the numerator; 9 is called the denominator.

The fraction $\frac{4}{9}$ is called a proper fraction since the numerator is less than the denominator.

The fraction $\frac{7}{3}$ is called an improper fraction since the numerator is greater than the denominator. An improper fraction is sometimes called a vulgar fraction.

A mixed number consists of a whole number and a proper fraction. Examples are $2\frac{3}{4}, 5\frac{1}{2}$.

The fraction $\frac{4}{9}$ may be written as the ratio 4 : 9.
The ratio of two quantities x and y is written as x : y and is read as "the ratio of x to y". A ratio compares quantities of the same kind.
For instance, if A = 3cm and B = 7mm then the ratio A : B is 3cm : 7mm which is 30mm : 7mm or simply 30 : 7.

Equivalent fractions (equal fractions) may be formed by multiplying (or dividing) both the numerator and denominator by the same number.
For instance, since  $\frac{16}{24} = \frac{32}{48}$ (multiplying top and bottom by 2)

and  $\frac{16}{24} = \frac{2}{3}$ (dividing top and bottom by 8)

then  $\frac{2}{3}, \frac{16}{24}, \frac{32}{48}$ are equivalent fractions.

Equivalent ratios (equal ratios) may be formed by multiplying (or dividing) both parts of a ratio by the same number.
For instance, the ratios 2 : 3, 16 : 24 and 32 : 48 are equivalent ratios.

*continued* . . .

*. . . from previous page*

A fraction (or ratio) is written as the **simplest fraction** (or **simplest ratio**) if the numbers in the fraction (or ratio) are the smallest possible whole numbers. A fraction written in its simplest form is said to be written in its **lowest terms**.

For instance, since $\frac{16}{24} = \frac{2}{3}$ we say that, in its lowest terms the fraction $\frac{16}{24}$ is $\frac{2}{3}$.

For instance, since $1\cdot2 : 3 = 12 : 30 = 2 : 5$, we say that $1\cdot2 : 3$ written as the simplest ratio is $2 : 5$.

To **increase** (or decrease) a quantity **by a given fraction** firstly work out the actual increase (or decrease).

For instance, to decrease 720cm by $\frac{1}{3}$ proceed as follows:

> ***Step 1***    $\frac{1}{3}$ of 720cm = 240cm
>
> ***Step 2***    Decrease 720cm by 240cm to get the answer of 480cm.

To **increase** (or decrease) a quantity **in a given ratio** firstly rewrite the ratio as a fraction. For instance, to increase 100g in the ratio 5 : 4 proceed as follows:

> ***Step 1***    Rewrite 5 : 4 as $\frac{5}{4}$
>
> ***Step 2***    Find $\frac{5}{4} \times 100g = 125g$.

To **share in a given ratio** proceed as shown in the following example.

*Example*    To share £600 between two people in the ratio 2 : 3 take the following steps:

> ***Step 1***    For every £2 that the first person gets, the second person gets £3. That is, from every £5, the first person gets £2 and the second person gets £3.
>
>         Hence the first person gets $\frac{2}{5}$ of the money; the second person gets $\frac{3}{5}$.
>
> ***Step 2***    $\frac{2}{5}$ of £600 = £240; $\frac{3}{5}$ of £600 = £360.
>
>         Hence one person gets £240 and the other gets £360.

To **multiply fractions** take the following steps.

> ***Step 1***    Write any whole numbers or mixed numbers as improper fractions.
> ***Step 2***    Cancel if possible.
> ***Step 3***    Multiply the numerators; multiply the denominators.
> ***Step 4***    If the answer is an improper fraction, write it as a mixed number.

*Examples*    $\frac{1\,\cancel{2}}{8} \times \frac{5}{\cancel{9}_3} = \frac{5}{24}$
                
$$2\tfrac{2}{3} \times 2\tfrac{1}{2} = \frac{4\,\cancel{8}}{3} \times \frac{5}{\cancel{2}_1}$$
$$= \frac{20}{3}$$
$$= 6\tfrac{2}{3}$$

To **divide** by a fraction, multiply by the reciprocal.
Remember: to find the reciprocal of a fraction, invert the fraction. That is, turn the fraction "upside down".

*Examples*    $\frac{2}{3} \div 4 = \frac{1\,\cancel{2}}{3} \times \frac{1}{\cancel{4}_2}$
             
$$2\tfrac{2}{5} \div 2\tfrac{1}{10} = \frac{12}{5} \div \frac{21}{10}$$
$$\frac{2}{3} \div 4 \quad = \frac{1}{6}$$
$$= \frac{4\,\cancel{12}}{1\,\cancel{5}} \times \frac{\cancel{10}^2}{\cancel{21}_7}$$
$$= \frac{8}{7}$$
$$= 1\tfrac{1}{7}$$

*continued . . .*

...*from previous page*

For fractions to be added or subtracted they must have the same denominator.
To add or subtract mixed numbers we may use one of the methods shown in the following
example.

*Example*   $2\frac{1}{3} + 3\frac{4}{5} = \frac{7}{3} + \frac{19}{5}$     **or**     $2\frac{1}{3} + 3\frac{4}{5} = 2\frac{5}{15} + 3\frac{12}{15}$

$\qquad\qquad\qquad = \frac{35}{15} + \frac{57}{15}$ $\qquad\qquad\qquad = 5\frac{17}{15}$

$\qquad\qquad\qquad = \frac{92}{15}$ $\qquad\qquad\qquad\quad = 6\frac{2}{15}$

$\qquad\qquad\qquad = 6\frac{2}{15}$

## Percentages

7% means 7 parts in every 100. That is, 7% means $\frac{7}{100}$.

Any percentage, decimal, fraction or ratio may be written in one of the other forms.

For instance, $\frac{2}{5}$ may be rewritten as 0·4 or 40% or 2 : 5.

In percentage calculations we usually rewrite the percentage as either a fraction or a
decimal.

For instance, to find 15% of £5 we may begin with $\frac{15}{100} \times £5$ or $0\cdot15 \times £5$ to get answer of 75p.

To increase 600 by 5% we can find 5% of 600 and add this to 600 or we may find

$\qquad$ 105% of 600 $= \frac{105}{100} \times 600$

$\qquad\qquad\qquad\quad = 1\cdot05 \times 600$

$\qquad\qquad\qquad\quad = 630$

To write a given quantity as a percentage of another quantity proceed as follows:
$\quad$ ***Step 1***$\quad$ Write the given quantity as a fraction of the other quantity.
$\quad$ ***Step 2***$\quad$ Rewrite this fraction as a percentage.

For instance, £5 as a fraction of £8 is $\frac{5}{8} = \frac{5}{8} \times 100\%$

$\qquad\qquad\qquad\qquad\qquad\qquad = 62\cdot5\%$

To find a percentage increase (or **decrease**) we compare the actual increase (or decrease)
with the initial value.

$\qquad$ % Increase (Decrease) $= \dfrac{\text{Actual Increase (Decrease)}}{\text{Initial Value}} \times 100\%$

For instance, to find the percentage reduction in price of a jersey which was priced at £39
and which is reduced to £26 in a sale:

$\qquad$ % decrease $= \frac{13}{39} \times 100\% = 33\%$ (to the nearest percentage)

## REVISION EXERCISE

1. Dana's family, of 3 adults, plan to fly to Madrid on July 2nd, returning on July 9th. They have booked to stay in a Triple room at the Tryp Plaza. They will hire a Renault Clio for 7 days. Use the given information to find the total cost, to the nearest pound, of Dana's family accommodation at the Tryp Plaza and their rental car costs.

Tryp Plaza

| Costs per person in UK£ | | |
|---|---|---|
| | **3 Day Ministay** | **Extra Nights** |
| **1 Nov 92-31 Mar 93** | | |
| Twin | £ 99.00 | £ 49.50 |
| Single | £132.50 | £ 65.50 |
| Triple | £ 94.00 | £ 47.00 |
| **01 Apr-31 Oct 93** | | |
| Twin | £117.50 | £ 58.50 |
| Single | £179.00 | £ 89.00 |
| Triple | £111.50 | £ 56.00 |

**All 3 day ministays include 2 nights accommodation, continental breakfast daily, all hotel taxes and service charges. Plus a half day sightseeing tour of the city (sightseeing not included in the cities indicated by a # next to the hotel name). Extra nights include continental breakfast, hotel taxes and services charges.**

**Exchange Rate:** 175 peseta = £1

### Rental Car Charges

| | | Rates are per car per day in Spanish Peseta | | | | |
|---|---|---|---|---|---|---|
| **Group** | **Car Model** | **1-6 Day hire per day** | **7-13 Day hire per day** | **14-20 Day hire per day** | **21-28 Day hire per day** | **29+ Day hire per day** |
| A | Opel Corsa Swing | 6462 | 5553 | 5553 | 4673 | 3991 |
| B | Renault Clio | 7343 | 6306 | 6306 | 5298 | 4531 |
| C | Opel Astra | 8366 | 7513 | 7513 | 6803 | 5838 |
| D | Renault GTS | 11334 | 10084 | 10084 | 9601 | 8238 |
| E | Ford Orion | 17980 | 15410 | 15410 | 12953 | 11092 |
| F | Renault Chamade TXE | 18222 | 15623 | 15623 | 13123 | 11249 |

**Valid:** 01 April - 30 June and 01 October 1993 - 31 March 1994
For travel 01 July - 30 September 1993 (High Season) a surcharge will apply, please ask your consultant for full details.

High Season surcharge: 15%

2. (a) Write 80 as a product of prime factors.
   (b) Find the highest common factor of 80 and 32.

3. Mary's school is raising money to buy computers. The school needs a total of £8000.
   (a) In the first week of fund-raising, 30% of the amount needed is collected. How much money does the school still need to raise?
   (b) In the second week Mary's class raises £400. What percentage is this of the total of £8000?

4. Evaluate.
   (a) $-12 + 6$         (b) $5 - (-3)$         (c) $-8 + (-3)$
   (d) $-5 \times (-3)$  (e) $\frac{-48}{8}$    (f) $-6 \times [3 - (-1)]$
   (g) $(-4)^2 \div (-2)$ (h) $2 + (-6) \times 8$ (i) $4 + (-2)[5 + (-4)]$

5. In a holiday camp in Spain, cabins are spaced evenly around a circle and are numbered consecutively, starting with 1. If the cabin with number 18 is directly opposite cabin number 40, how many cabins are there in the circle?

6. On Monday the water level at the Cheddar Gorge was 1·2m below normal. On Tuesday it rose 4·5m, then it dropped gradually until on Saturday it was 0·6m above normal level. By how many metres did the water level drop from Wednesday till Saturday?

7. Write these in standard form.
   (a) 15·8     (b) 8     (c) 0·00041     (d) 348 590 000

8. 250 is to be divided by $2·4 \times 10^{-3}$.
   Aaron claims the answer will be larger than 250; Diana claims it will be smaller. Who is right? Explain your answer.

9. Write these ratios in their simplest form.
   (a) £3·50 : 70p     (b) 45 sec : $2\frac{1}{3}$ min

10. (i) Estimate the answer to   (a) $0·49 \times 321$   (b) $\frac{42·8 + 16·4}{0·021}$   (c) $\frac{18·4 + 7·25}{16·83 - 9·04}$
    (d) $\frac{7\sqrt{10}}{5(3·7 - 0·54)}$
    (ii) Use your calculator to find the answers correct to 2 s.f. Use your estimates as a check.

11. At the beginning of a game of cards Amy, Belinda and Carmen had counters in the ratio 5 : 8 : 12. At the end of the game the same number of counters was distributed in the ratio 3 : 5 : 7.
    (a) Who had won counters; who had lost?
    (b) What is the smallest number of counters the girls could have had for this game?

12. (i) Write these as fractions       (a) $0·12$        (b) $3\%$            (c) $\sqrt[3]{\frac{1}{8}}$
    (ii) Write these as percentages   (a) $\frac{17}{40}$  (b) $2·3 \times 10^{-3}$  (c) $5^{-1}$
    (iii) Write these as decimals      (a) $0·3\%$        (b) $\sqrt{0·25}$    (c) $3\frac{3}{16}$

13. The Earth is not a perfect sphere. Measured to the nearest kilometre, the radius towards the poles is $6·357 \times 10^3$ km and the radius towards the equator is $6·378 \times 10^3$ km. How much larger is the equatorial radius than the polar radius? (Answer in metres.)

14. Calculate.   (a) $\frac{2}{5} \times \frac{3}{8}$      (b) $2\frac{1}{4} \times 4$      (c) $3\frac{3}{4} \times 1\frac{3}{5}$

(d) $\frac{2}{3} \div \frac{5}{6}$      (e) $4\frac{1}{5} \div 2\frac{1}{3}$      (f) $\frac{2}{3} - \frac{5}{9}$

(g) $3\frac{1}{2} + 2\frac{5}{6}$      (h) $\frac{3}{5} + \frac{1}{4} - \frac{1}{2}$      (i) $5\frac{1}{3} - 2\frac{1}{2}$

(j) $\frac{5}{6}(2\frac{2}{3} - 1\frac{2}{5})$      (k) $\frac{4}{9} + 5 \times 1\frac{2}{3}$

15. Calculate, showing all your working. (Give the answers in standard form.)

(a) $(4\cdot3 \times 10^5) \times (6\cdot0 \times 10^3)$      (b) $\dfrac{8\cdot24 \times 10^4}{4\cdot0 \times 10^{-2}}$      (c) $(5\cdot1 \times 10^4) - (3\cdot6 \times 10^3)$

16.

### Seats Won in General Elections

|  | Conservative | Labour | Liberal | Communist | Plaid Cymru | SNP | Others (GB) | Others (NI) |
|---|---|---|---|---|---|---|---|---|
| 1918 | 383 | 73 | 161 | 0 | 0 | 0 | 9 | 81 |
| 1922 | 344 | 142 | 115 | 1 | 0 | 0 | 10 | 3 |
| 1923 | 258 | 191 | 158 | 0 | 0 | 0 | 5 | 3 |
| 1924 | 412 | 151 | 40 | 1 | 0 | 0 | 10 | 1 |
| 1929 | 260 | 287 | 59 | 0 | 0 | 0 | 6 | 3 |
| 1931 | 521 | 52 | 37 | 0 | 0 | 0 | 3 | 2 |
| 1935 | 429 | 154 | 21 | 1 | 0 | 0 | 8 | 2 |
| 1945 | 213 | 393 | 12 | 2 | 0 | 0 | 16 | 4 |
| 1950 | 299 | 315 | 9 | 0 | 0 | 0 | 0 | 2 |
| 1951 | 321 | 295 | 6 | 0 | 0 | 0 | 0 | 3 |
| 1955 | 345 | 277 | 6 | 0 | 0 | 0 | 0 | 2 |
| 1959 | 365 | 258 | 6 | 0 | 0 | 0 | 1 | 0 |
| 1964 | 304 | 317 | 9 | 0 | 0 | 0 | 0 | 0 |
| 1966 | 253 | 364 | 12 | 0 | 0 | 0 | 0 | 1 |
| 1970 | 330 | 288 | 6 | 0 | 0 | 1 | 1 | 4 |
| 1974 (Feb.) | 297 | 301 | 14 | 0 | 2 | 7 | 2 | 12 |
| 1974 (Oct.) | 277 | 319 | 13 | 0 | 3 | 11 | 0 | 12 |
| 1979 | 339 | 269 | 11 | 0 | 2 | 2 | 0 | 12 |
| 1983 | 397 | 209 | 23 | 0 | 2 | 2 | 0 | 17 |
| 1987 | 376 | 229 | 22 | 0 | 3 | 3 | 0 | 17 |

(a) In 1950, what percentage of seats was won by the Conservative Party?
(b) What was the percentage decrease in the number of seats between the 1945 and 1950 elections?
(c) Between which two consecutive elections did Labour gain the most seats?
(d) Between which two consecutive elections did Labour increase the seats won by the greatest percentage?

17. Use your calculator to find the answer to these. (Give the answers to 3 s.f. where rounding is necessary.)

(a) $253\,000\,000 \times 6\,630\,000\,000$      (b) $0\cdot000\,082\,9 \div 0\cdot000\,000\,773$      (c) $5^{-2}$

18. A builder knows from experience that 4% of bricks will be damaged when they reach the building site. How many bricks should the builder order, if 5000 are needed to finish a job?

19. $s = \sqrt{b^2 - 4ac}$    $a = -3.7$, $b = 6.8$, $c = 1.9$

    (a) Estimate the value of s.

    (b) Calculate the value of s, rounding sensibly.

20. Joseph needs $6\frac{1}{2}$ cups of cooked rice for a recipe of Nasi Goreng. If 2 cups of uncooked rice with $2\frac{1}{2}$ cups of water make $4\frac{1}{3}$ cups of cooked rice, how many cups of uncooked rice does Joseph need for his recipe? How much water should he add?

21. $s = \frac{1}{2}(u + v)t$. Find s if $u = \frac{3}{5}$, $v = 2\frac{1}{4}$, $t = 3$.

22. A chocolate factory is considering two options for a special deal on its 250g chocolate bars.
Option 1: adding an extra 20% of chocolate to the bars, at no extra cost.
Option 2: giving a discount of 20% on the 250g bars.
Which option would give the customer the best value for money? Explain your answer.

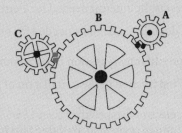

23. A transmission system consists of three cog-wheels. Cog-wheel A has 10 teeth, one of which is black. Of the 30 teeth of cog-wheel B, one is black and one is red. Cog-wheel C has 12 teeth, one of which is red.

    (a) The wheels are in a position where the two black teeth and the two red teeth touch. How many full revolutions does cog-wheel A need to make before the system is in exactly the same position again?

    (b) If cog-wheel C makes one full revolution, what fraction of a revolution do the other two cog-wheels make?

24. All 72 ladies attending a garden party were wearing gloves. After the party 29 gloves were found. Some ladies had lost one glove, some had lost both gloves.
The ratio of ladies who lost gloves to ladies who did not lose any gloves was 5 : 13.
How many ladies lost only one glove?

25.

| | | |
|---|---|---|
| 0·4 | $\frac{4}{5}$ | $\frac{5}{8}$ |
| 0·7 | 1·2 | |

    (a) Which two of these numbers, when multiplied together, will give the **largest** answer?

    (b) Which two of these numbers, when multiplied together, will give the **smallest** answer?

                                                        SEG

26. The plan of a house has been drawn using a scale of 1 : 20.

    (a) (i) On the plan, the length of the lounge is 25cm.
             What is the actual length of the lounge in metres?

        (ii) The actual lounge is 3·2m wide.
            How wide is the lounge on the plan?

    (b) The actual kitchen is 2·6m wide.
        Estimate, in feet, the width of the actual kitchen.

                                                          SEG

**27.**

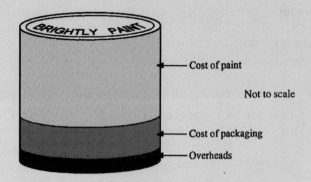

Selling price of a tin of paint = Cost of paint + Cost of packaging + Overheads.
When buying a tin of **BRIGHTLY PAINT** $\frac{2}{3}$ of the price is the actual cost of the paint and $\frac{1}{4}$ of the cost is packaging.

The rest is the amount needed for Fermats overheads.

**(a)** Calculate the amount needed for overheads on a $2\frac{1}{2}$ litre tin of paint which sells at £5·40.

Storage and transportation costs account for $\frac{2}{5}$ of Fermats overheads on any product.

**(b)** What fraction of the cost of a tin of paint goes towards transportation and storage?   **SEG**

**28.** A new electronic typewriter costs £86·53.
At the end of every year, its value falls by 15% of its value at the start of the year.
Calculate the value of the typewriter at the end of 3 years.   **ULEAC**

**29.** The water trough has a semicircular cross-section.

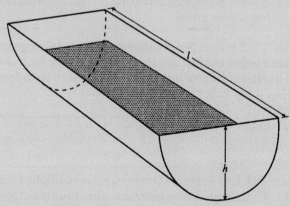

The capacity of the trough is given by the formula $C = \frac{1}{2}\pi h^2 l$.

$h = 800$mm and $l = 2000$mm.

**(a)** Write these measurements in standard form.

**(b)** Calculate the capacity (in mm³) of this trough, giving your answer in standard form.

**NEAB**

**30.** The weights of two tins of fruit are in the ratio 3 : 5.
Find the weight of the smaller tin as a percentage of the weight of the larger tin.   **SEG**

31. The current price for scrap metal is £4 per kilogram.
A particular bundle of scrap metal weighs 27 kilograms, to the nearest kilogram.
Find the price range for this bundle of scrap metal.                                    **SEG**

32.

KILLICK BANK

MONTHLY REPORT JUNE
147 million pounds was used
to buy 2100 houses.
Average cost of a house is £

(a) Write the number 147 million in standard form.

(b) Write the number 2100 in standard form.

The corner of the page showing the average cost of a house is missing.
(c) Use your answers to (a) and (b) to calculate the average cost of a house. Give your answer in
standard form.                                                                         **ULEAC**

33.

The manager of a carpet shop has made a mistake in writing the advertisement above.
The prices are correct, but the 'percentage off' is NOT correct.

(a) Find, correct to one decimal place, the true 'percentage off'.

(b) In another shop, where a genuine reduction of 20% had been made, the sale price of a
carpet was also £6·39. What was the original price in this shop?                      **NICCEA**

34. (a) The formula for the volume, $V$ cm$^3$, of a square-based pyramid is

$V = \frac{1}{3}x^2h$     where $x$ is the length of the base and $h$ is the height.

Calculate the volume of a square-based pyramid if $x = 7·5$ cm and $h = 5·2$ cm.

(b) A formula to calculate the surface area, $A$ cm$^2$, of a square-based pyramid is given by

$$A = x^2 + x\sqrt{(4y^2 - x^2)}$$

where $x$ cm is the length of the base and $y$ cm is the length of the slant edge.
Show how, without using a calculator, you would make a rough estimate of the surface area
if $x = 6·2$ and $y = 4·9$.                                                            **NEAB**

23

**35.**

## PINE TIMBER SHELVING

Widths: 15 cm / 20 cm / 25 cm.

Lengths: 120 cm / 136 cm . . . . increasing
to 200 cm in multiples of 16 cm.

Priced at 2p per cm of length for 15 cm width.

Other widths proportionally priced.

### SPECIAL OFFER

7½% discount on 200 cm lengths while stocks last.

Peter has to produce a ready reckoner for Pine Shelving costs.
He started the table below but did not finish it.

| length \ width | PINE SHELVING Prices in £s | | |
|---|---|---|---|
| | 15cm | 20cm | 25cm |
| 120cm | 2·40 | 3·20 | 4·00 |
| 136cm | 2·72 | | 4·53 |
| 152cm | 3·04 | 4·05 | 5·07 |
| 168cm | 3·36 | 4·48 | 5·60 |
| 184cm | 3·68 | 4·91 | 6·13 |
| 200cm | Out of Stock | Out of Stock | |

Calculate the two numbers missing from the table.
You **must** show all your working.

**SEG**

**36.** A light year is the distance travelled by light in 365 days.
The speed of light is $3 \cdot 0 \times 10^5$ kilometres per second.

**(a)** Calculate the number of kilometres in one light year.
Give your answer in standard form.

**(b)** The distance to the nearest star is $4 \cdot 0 \times 10^{13}$ kilometres.
How many light years is this?

**(c)** One kilometre = 0·625 miles.
Calculate the speed of light in miles per second.

**SEG**

**37.** Work out $4 \times 10^8 - 4 \times 10^6$.
Give your answer in standard form.

**ULEAC**

**38.** Part of a bus timetable is shown.

| | am | | | | | am | | pm | | | pm |
|---|---|---|---|---|---|---|---|---|---|---|---|
| Baiter | 7·02 | 7·22 | 7·42 | 8·02 | 8·22 | 8·32 | then every 10 minutes | 6·12 | 6·32 | then every 20 minutes | 10·32 |
| Recreation Road | 7·12 | 7·32 | 7·52 | 8·12 | 8·32 | 8·42 | | 6·22 | 6·42 | | 10·42 |
| Landscape Gardens | 7·19 | 7·39 | 7·59 | 8·19 | 8·39 | 8·49 | | 6·29 | 6·49 | | 10·49 |
| Centre Row | 7·24 | 7·44 | 8·04 | 8·24 | 8·44 | 8·54 | | 6·34 | 6·54 | | 10·54 |

**(a)** How long does the journey take from Baiter to Centre Row?

**(b)** John needs to be in Centre Row at 10.00am.
What is the latest time he can catch a bus from Baiter?

**(c)** To estimate the amount of money collected in fares for each journey, the driver uses the formula

$$\text{Amount (£)} = 5 \times \sqrt{\frac{p^2}{100}}$$

where $p$ is the number of passengers.

**(i)** Use your calculator to estimate the amount collected when 26 passengers use the bus.

**(ii)** Write down the order in which you used the keys on your calculator.     **SEG**

**39. (i)** A Jumbo flies $2·1 \times 10^6$ miles in a year.
It flies on 300 days of each year.
What is the average number of miles it flies each day?

**(ii)** The airline uses this formula to work out its cost per passenger for a flight:

$$c = \frac{pf}{315m}$$

Where     £$c$ = the cost of the flight per passenger,
           £$p$ = the annual running cost of the plane,
       $f$ miles = the length of the flight,
and     $m$ miles = the annual mileage of the plane.

$p = 14$ million.

**(a)** Write the value of $p$ in standard form.

**(b)** $m = 1·6 \times 10^6$.
Calculate $c$ when $f = 1500$.     **NEAB**

**40.** The value of the two-digit number $xy$ is $10x + y$.
For example 25 is $10 \times 2 + 5$.
$p, q$ and $r$ are also digits.

**(a)** What is the value of the three-digit number $pqr$?

**(b)** Show that $pqr - rqp$ is divisible by 11.     **NEAB**

**41.** Ann finds this information about 'The Lagoons'.

> Last year:
>
> 380 000 people visited 'The Lagoons';
>
> 'The Lagoons' was open for 3248 hours.

One of 'The Lagoons' staff spoke to Karen.

> It is very busy for 20% of the time we are open. At these times, between 160 and 200 people enter each hour. For 50% of the time we are open, between 100 and 120 people enter each hour.

Use Ann and Karen's data to estimate the number of people per hour entering 'The Lagoons' during the remaining 30% of the time.                    **NEAB**

# Approximation. Accuracy. Errors

## UPPER and LOWER BOUNDS

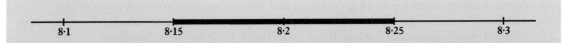

Suppose a measurement is given as 8·2m, to the nearest tenth of a metre. Any measurement between 8·15m and 8·25m would be given, to the nearest tenth of a metre, as 8·2m.
A measurement a little less than 8·15m, e.g. 8·14m, would be given as 8·1m to the nearest tenth of a metre. A measurement a little greater than 8·25m, e.g. 8·27m, would be given as 8·3m to the nearest tenth of a metre; as would a measurement of 8·25m. This can be summarized as follows.

If a measurement $l$ is given as $l = 8 \cdot 2$m, correct to one decimal place, then $8 \cdot 15$m $\leq l < 8 \cdot 25$m.

We say that 8·15m is the lower bound of 8·2m and 8·25 is the upper bound.

We can also write the measurement of 8·2m, to the nearest tenth of a metre, as $8 \cdot 2 \pm 0 \cdot 05$m.
This means the measurement lies between $8 \cdot 2 - 0 \cdot 05$m and $8 \cdot 2 + 0 \cdot 05$m.
That is, the measurement lies between 8·15m and 8·25m.

*Worked Example*  The area of a park is given as 1·27 hectares, correct to two decimal places. Find the upper and lower bounds for the area of this park.

*Answer*  Any measurement between 1·265 hectares and 1·275 hectares would be given to two decimal places as 1·27 hectares.
That is    1·265 hectares $\leq$ Area $<$ 1·275 hectares.
Hence, the lower bound is 1·265 hectares and the upper bound is 1·275 hectares.

*Worked Example*  The 'weight' of a Rolls Royce is given as 2400kg. Find the greatest and least possible 'weight' of this car if 2400kg is given correct to (a)  2 significant figures.
(b)  3 significant figures.

*Answer*      (a)  If 2350kg $\leq$ w $<$ 2450kg then w = 2400kg to 2 s.f.
Hence greatest possible weight = 2450kg; least possible weight = 2350kg.
(b)  If 2395kg $\leq$ w $<$ 2405kg then w = 2400kg to 3 s.f.
Hence greatest possible weight = 2405kg; least possible weight = 2395kg.

*Worked Example*  Dale's weight was recorded on her hospital chart as 62kg, to the nearest kilogram. Write this weight as  62 ± . . .kg.

*Answer*  62 ± 0·5kg.

---

## DISCUSSION EXERCISE 1:1

• Nuria made up a rule for finding the upper and lower bounds of numbers given to any number of decimal places. She told her friends the rule was "add and subtract 5 into the next decimal place". When her friends didn't understand, she gave these examples.

$$
\begin{array}{r} 8\cdot2 \\ +\ 0\cdot05 \\ \hline 8\cdot25 \end{array}
\qquad
\begin{array}{r} 8\cdot2 \\ -\ 0\cdot05 \\ \hline 8\cdot15 \end{array}
$$
Lower bound of 8·2 is 8·15;
upper bound is 8·25

$$
\begin{array}{r} 1\cdot27 \\ +\ 0\cdot005 \\ \hline 1\cdot275 \end{array}
\qquad
\begin{array}{r} 1\cdot27 \\ -\ 0\cdot005 \\ \hline 1\cdot265 \end{array}
$$
Lower bound of 1·27 is 1·265;
upper bound is 1·275

Discuss  Nuria's rule.

• Nuria made up a similar rule for finding the upper and lower bounds of numbers given correct to any number of significant figures. She gave the following examples to support her rule.

$$
\begin{array}{r} 2400 \\ +\ \ 50 \\ \hline 2450 \end{array}
\quad
\begin{array}{r} 2400 \\ -\ \ 50 \\ \hline 2350 \end{array}
\quad
\begin{array}{r} 16240 \\ +\ \ \ 5 \\ \hline 16245 \end{array}
\quad
\begin{array}{r} 16240 \\ -\ \ \ 5 \\ \hline 16235 \end{array}
\quad
\begin{array}{r} 800000 \\ +\ 50000 \\ \hline 850000 \end{array}
\quad
\begin{array}{r} 800000 \\ -\ 50000 \\ \hline 750000 \end{array}
$$

What is Nuria's rule? Does this rule always work?  Discuss.

---

The **decimals  8·2, 8·20, 8·200 are** *not* the same.  The decimal 8·200 is given to three decimal places (i.e. to the nearest thousandth) while 8·20 is given to two decimal places (i.e. to the nearest hundredth) and 8·2 is given to one decimal place (i.e. to the nearest tenth).
 A measurement given as 8·200m is more accurate than a measurement given as 8·20m; 8·20m is more accurate than 8·2m.

Unless we are told otherwise, we assume a measurement given as 8·2m is given to the nearest tenth of a metre. The upper bound is 8·25m and the lower bound is 8·15m.
Similarly, we assume a measurement given as 8·20m is given to the nearest hundredth of a metre; upper bound is 8·205m and lower bound is 8·195m.
Similarly, we assume a measurement given as 8·200m is given to the nearest thousandth of a metre; upper bound is 8·2005m and lower bound is 8·1995m.

---

*Worked Example*  The length of a rod is measured as 42·83cm.
Copy and complete this inequality for the length.

$$. . . \text{cm} \ \le \ \text{length of rod} < . . . \text{cm}$$

*Answer*  42·825cm ≤ length of rod < 42·835cm

*Worked Example* This label is on a bottle of coke.
What is the minimum and maximum
amount of coke in this bottle?

*Answer*   We assume that the measurement 1·2 litres is given to the nearest tenth of a litre.
Then amount of coke = 1·2 ± 0·05 litres.
That is,  minimum amount = 1·15 litres
maximum amount = 1·25 litres

## EXERCISE 1:2

1.  Nigel used a trundle wheel to measure the length of a corridor. His measurement was 27·3m.
    Anne used a tape. Her measurement was 27·30m. Explain the difference between a
    measurement of 27·3m and 27·30m.

2.  A pencil is measured as 17·3cm to the nearest mm. Which of the following gives the range for
    the possible length of this pencil?
    **A.** 17·2cm $\leq l <$ 17·4cm      **B.** 16·8cm $\leq l <$ 17·8cm      **C.** 17·25cm $\leq l <$ 17·35cm

3.  The weight of a full suitcase is given as 12·78kg correct to 2 d.p. Which of the following gives
    the set of possible values for the weight of this suitcase?
    **A.** 12·77kg $\leq$ w < 12·79kg    **B.** 12·775kg $\leq$ w < 12·785kg    **C.** 12·73kg $\leq$ w < 12·83kg

4.  Which of the following gives the range of possible values of a number given as 3·1 correct to
    two significant figures?
    **A.** 3·05 < n $\leq$ 3·15      **B.** 3·05 < n < 3·15      **C.** 3·05 $\leq$ n < 3·15      **D.** 3·05 $\leq$ n $\leq$ 3·15

5.  The mass of a parcel is given as 1·4kg, to the nearest tenth of a kilogram.
    (a) Find the upper bound of the mass of this parcel.
    (b) Find the lower bound.

6.  A racing car was timed at 50·73 seconds, to the nearest hundredth of a second, for one circuit
    of a racing track.
    (a) What is the lower bound for the true time?
    (b) As an inequality, write down the range of possible values for the true time.

7.  The weight of a box of chocolates is given as 250 ± 10g.
    (a) What is the upper bound of this weight?
    (b) What is the lower bound?

8.  In an experiment, the temperature of a liquid was taken at 1 minute intervals. One of these
    measurements was given as 45·6°C.
    Between what bounds does the true temperature lie?

9.  Deon measured the distance between two points as 46·8cm.
    Write the true distance as  46·8 ± . . .cm.

10. Beth measured the length and the width of the spine of this book. Her measurements, shown
    on the diagram, are accurate to the nearest mm.
    (a) What is the greatest possible length of the spine of this book?
    (b) Find the least possible length of this spine.
    (c) Between what bounds must the true width of the spine lie?

2·9cm

25·0cm

11. The area of a field is given as 3547m², to the nearest square metre. Which of the following gives the possible values for this area?

    **A.** 3542m² ≤ A < 3552m²  **B.** 3546m² ≤ A < 3548m²  **C.** 3546·5m² ≤ A < 3547·5m²

12. The capacity of an ice-cream container is given as 1020m*l*, to the nearest ten millilitres. What are the upper and lower bounds for the capacity of this container?

13. In a newspaper article it was stated that, in Wales, there are 262 400 girls under the age of 15.
    (a) If this figure is correct to the nearest 100, what is the greatest and least number of girls under the age of 15?
    (b) If this figure is correct to the nearest 10, find the upper and lower bounds of the true number of girls of this age.

14. Elizabeth measures the length and width of a hockey field. She wrote these dimensions as: length = 91m, width = 55m.
    (a) What is the range of possible values for the true length?
    (b) What are the upper and lower bounds for the true width?

15. To the nearest half of a metre, the length of a field is given as 42·5m. What are the upper and lower bounds of the length of this field?

Review 1 (a) Richard measured the length of his desk as 1·234m, to the nearest mm. What are the upper and lower bounds of the length of this desk?
    (b) Richard measured the volume of a jar as 1·2 litres to the nearest tenth of a litre. Which of the following gives the set of all possible values for the volume of this jar?
       **A.** 1·1*l* ≤ V < 1·3*l*     **B.** 0·7*l* ≤ V < 1·7*l*     **C.** 1·15*l* ≤ V < 1·25*l*
    (c) Richard gave his height as 1·71metres.
       Copy and complete this inequality.   . . .m ≤ Height < . . .m
    (d) Richard wrote a measurement as 0·36 ± 0·005kg.
       Between what bounds does this measurement lie?

Review 2 Sandra used an electronic balance to measure the mass of a chemical. Her measurement was 28·60 grams, accurate to 2 d.p. As an inequality, write down the range of possible values for the mass of this chemical.

Review 3 Tandia used her watch to find the time it took to complete a maths. test. She wrote this time as 27 minutes. Between what bounds does Tandia's true time for this test lie?

## DISCUSSION EXERCISE 1:3

A distance given as 10m correct to 2 s.f. has upper bound of 10·5m. **Discuss** why the lower bound is 9·95m rather than 9·5m. As part of your discussion consider what 9·5m, 9·6m, 9·7m, 9·73m, 9·748m, 9·88m, 9·9m, 9·94m, 9·95m, 9·953m, 9·96m, 9·981m would be given as, correct to 2 s.f.

Angela claimed that "there is a similar problem" with a measurement of 100m correct to 3 s.f. and 1000m correct to 4 s.f. **Discuss** Angela's claim.

# UPPER and LOWER BOUNDS in CALCULATIONS

## DISCUSSION EXERCISE 1:4

- Kate measured the front cover of a book. Her measurements, shown
  on the diagram, were to the nearest mm.
  Kate calculated the perimeter as $2(18\cdot4 + 24\cdot5) = 85\cdot8$cm.
  Since her measurements were approximate, Kate also calculated the
  upper and lower bounds for this perimeter. She did this as follows.

  Greatest value for $18\cdot4$cm = $18\cdot45$cm. Greatest value for $24\cdot5$cm = $24\cdot55$cm.

  Hence, greatest value for perimeter = $2(18\cdot45 + 24\cdot55)$
  $$= 86\text{cm}.$$
  Least value for $18\cdot4$cm = $18\cdot35$cm. Least value for $24\cdot5$cm = $24\cdot45$cm.

  Hence, least value for perimeter = $2(18\cdot35 + 24\cdot45)$
  $$= 85\cdot6\text{cm}$$
  Kate concluded that the perimeter must lie between $85\cdot6$cm and 86cm.

  Kate then calculated the upper and lower bounds for the area of the front cover of this book.
  Her calculations gave her the following: lower bound = $448\cdot6575$cm$^2$,
  upper bound = $452\cdot9475$cm$^2$.
  What calculations did Kate do to get these results? What conclusion could Kate make from
  these results? **Discuss.**

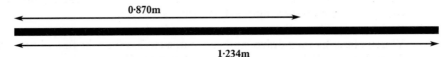

  Brian measures the length of a metal bar as $1\cdot234$m to the nearest mm. He then measured
  and cut off a piece that was $0\cdot870$m long.
  Brian's calculation for the length of metal left was $1\cdot234 - 0\cdot870 = 0\cdot364$m.
  Brian's calculations for the upper and lower bounds of metal left were:

  Greatest value for $1\cdot234$m = $1\cdot2345$m. Least value for $1\cdot234$m = $1\cdot2335$m.

  Greatest value for $0\cdot870$m = $0\cdot8705$m. Least value for $0\cdot870$m = $0\cdot8695$m.

  Hence, greatest length of metal left = $1\cdot2345 - 0\cdot8705$
  $$= 0\cdot364\text{m}.$$
  least length of metal left = $1\cdot2335 - 0\cdot8695$
  $$= 0\cdot364\text{m}.$$
  Anne said that Brian's calculations should have been:

  Greatest length of metal left = $1\cdot2345 - 0\cdot8695$
  $$= 0\cdot365\text{m}.$$
  Least length of metal left = $1\cdot2335 - 0\cdot8705$
  $$= 0\cdot363\text{m}.$$

  Anne explained her reasoning. What might Anne's explanation have been? Whose
  calculations are correct, Brian's or Anne's? **Discuss.**

- Maths. books are packed into boxes, each with 20 books. If the weight of one of these books is
  540g, to the nearest ten grams, find the minimum weight of one book and the maximum
  weight of one book. **Discuss** how to find the minimum and maximum weight of a box of
  these books.

- Linda used the formula $s = \dfrac{d}{t}$ to find her average speed for an 80m hurdle race. Her time for this race was 10·54 seconds, correct to 2 d.p.

  Linda's calculation for her average speed was $s = \dfrac{80}{10\cdot54}$
  $$= 7\cdot59\text{m/sec} \quad (2 \text{ d.p.})$$

  Linda began her calculation for the upper and lower bounds by assuming that the distance 80m was accurate to two significant figures.

  | | |
  |---|---|
  | Greatest distance = 80·5m. | Least distance = 79·5m. |
  | Greatest time = 10·545sec. | Least time = 10·535sec. |

  Should Linda now use the calculation $s = \dfrac{80}{10\cdot545}$ or $s = \dfrac{80\cdot5}{10\cdot535}$ or some other calculation to find the upper bound? **Discuss.**

  What calculation should Linda use to find the lower bound? **Discuss.**

- Make a summary of your discoveries. This summary should include finding upper and lower bounds for calculations involving addition, subtraction, multiplication or division.

*Worked Example* Jayne measures the length and width of a sheet of A4 paper. These dimensions are shown on the diagram. She then draws, and cuts out, a circle of radius 7cm. If all Jayne's measurements are to the nearest cm find
(a) the greatest possible area of paper left
(b) the least possible area of paper left.

30cm

21cm

*Answer*  For the sheet of paper:  Greatest length = 21·5cm    Least length = 20·5cm
Greatest width = 30·5cm    Least width = 29·5cm
Greatest area = greatest length × greatest width
$$= 21\cdot5 \times 30\cdot5$$
$$= 655\cdot75\text{cm}^2$$
Least area = least length × least width
$$= 20\cdot5 \times 29\cdot5$$
$$= 604\cdot75\text{cm}^2$$
For the circle: Greatest radius = 7·5cm    Least Radius = 6·5cm
Hence, greatest area = $\pi\,(7\cdot5)^2$
$$= 176\cdot71\text{cm}^2 \,(5 \text{ s.f.})$$
least area = $\pi\,(6\cdot5)^2$
$$= 132\cdot73\text{cm}^2 \,(5 \text{ s.f.})$$
(a) Greatest area of paper left = greatest area of sheet − least area of circle
$$= 655\cdot75 - 132\cdot73$$
$$= 523\text{cm}^2 \,(3 \text{ s.f.})$$
(b) Least area of paper left = least area of sheet − greatest area of circle
$$= 604\cdot75 - 176\cdot71$$
$$= 428\text{cm}^2 \,(3 \text{ s.f.})$$

*Worked Example*  The mass of a piece of cork is measured as 150g; the volume is measured as 620cm³. Both of these measurements are correct to 2 significant figures. Find the range of possible values for the density of this cork.

*Answer*  Greatest mass = 155g   Least mass = 145g
Greatest volume = 625cm³   Least volume = 615cm³
The relationship between density, mass and volume is $d = \frac{m}{v}$.

Greatest density $= \dfrac{\text{greatest mass}}{\text{least volume}}$          Least density $= \dfrac{\text{least mass}}{\text{greatest volume}}$

$= \dfrac{155}{615}$                                                $= \dfrac{145}{625}$

$= 0{\cdot}25\text{g/cm}^3$ (2 s.f.)                       $= 0{\cdot}23\text{g/cm}^3$ (2 s.f.)

To 2 s.f., $0{\cdot}23\text{g/cm}^3 \le d < 0{\cdot}25\text{g/cm}^3$ gives the range of possible values for the density of this cork.

*Worked Example*  The volume of a cube is given as 34·7cm³. Find the upper and lower bounds for the length of an edge of this cube.

*Answer*  Assuming 34·7cm³ is accurate to the nearest tenth of a cm³, upper bound for the volume = 34·75cm³, lower bound = 34·65cm³.
The relationship between the length of an edge and the volume is $V = l^3$
When $V = 34{\cdot}75$, $l = \sqrt[3]{34{\cdot}75}$          When $V = 34{\cdot}65$, $l = \sqrt[3]{34{\cdot}65}$
$= 3{\cdot}263\text{cm}$ (3 d.p.)                         $= 3{\cdot}260\text{cm}$ (3 d.p.)
Hence, upper bound for $l = 3{\cdot}263\text{cm}$ (3 d.p.); lower bound $= 3{\cdot}260\text{cm}$ (3 d.p.).

## EXERCISE 1:5

1. One hundred booklets are stacked in one pile. If the height of one booklet is measured as 6mm, to the nearest mm, what is the maximum height of the pile?

2. Sharon drew this sketch of the floor of a room in her home.
   The measurements are correct to one decimal place.
   (a) What is the greatest possible perimeter?
   (b) What is the least possible perimeter?
   (c) Within what range of values does the true floor area of this room lie?

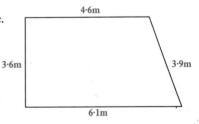

3. The area of a rugby field is given as 6900m², correct to three significant figures. The length of this field is 100m, correct to three significant figures.
   Find   (a) the upper and lower bounds for the area of this field
          (b) the greatest possible length of this field
          (c) the least possible width of this field.

4. (a) Measure the length and breadth of this rectangle, to the nearest mm.
   (b) Calculate the upper and lower bounds for the area.
   (c) What are the bounds for the perimeter?

5.  The formula $A = 4\pi r^2$ gives the surface area of a sphere. The surface area of one sphere is given as $82{\cdot}4\,cm^2$, correct to 3 s.f. Find the set of possible values for the radius of this sphere.

6.  A chocolate bar is wrapped in the package shown.
    The dimensions are given correct to the nearest $0{\cdot}2cm$.
    (a) Between what values does the true area of a triangular face lie?
    (b) What is the minimum volume of this package?

3·6cm   4cm   9·2cm

7.  (a) The formula $I = \frac{V}{R}$ can be used to calculate the current, I, in an electrical circuit.
    In a circuit that Jayne set up, she measured V as $6{\cdot}6$ and R as $3{\cdot}8$; both measurements correct to 2 s.f. Jayne then calculated maximum and minimum values for I. What answers should she get?
    (b) Jayne also calculated the range of possible values for the power, P, using the formula $P = \frac{V^2}{R}$ What answers should she get?

8.  (a) Use the formula $a = \frac{v^2 - u^2}{2s}$ to find **a** when $v = 35, u = 20, s = 8{\cdot}7$.
    (b) Assuming the values of $v$, u and s are correct to 2 s.f. find the least possible value for **a**.

9.  The formula $f = \frac{uv}{u+v}$ is used in a Physics experiment.
    Find the greatest possible value for f if $u = 6{\cdot}2 \pm 0{\cdot}05cm$ and $v = 8{\cdot}8 \pm 0{\cdot}05cm$.

10. (i) The upper bound of 10 given correct to 2 s.f. is $10{\cdot}5$. Explain why the lower bound is not $9{\cdot}5$. What is the lower bound?
    (ii) Find the upper and lower bounds for the following calculations, given the numbers 34, 25, 18 and 10 are correct to 2 s.f.
    (a) $34 + 18$  (b) $25 - 10$  (c) $34 + 18 - 25$  (d) $25 \times 10$
    (e) $\frac{34}{10}$  (f) $(18)^2$  (g) $\frac{25+18}{10}$  (h) $\frac{10^2 - 25}{18 + 34}$

Review 1  Barbara measured the dimensions of a tennis court. Her measurements were:
    length $23{\cdot}77m$, width $10{\cdot}97m$.
    (a) Between what values does the true width lie?
    (b) What is the maximum area of this tennis court?

Review 2  $V = \frac{4}{3}\pi r^3$ is a formula for the volume of a sphere.
    (i) The radius of a sphere is given as $8{\cdot}2cm$, correct to 1 d.p.
        (a) Between what bounds must the true radius lie?
        (b) Find the set of possible values for the volume of this sphere.
    (ii) The volume of a sphere is given as $520\,cm^3$, correct to 2 significant figures.
        Calculate the greatest and least values for the radius of this sphere.

Review 3  The formula $t = \frac{v-u}{a}$ gives the time, t, for an object to increase its speed from u to v, under constant acceleration, a.
    (a) Find t when $v = 95, u = 60, a = 5{\cdot}0$.
    (b) Assuming the values of $v$, u and a are correct to two significant figures, find the upper and lower bounds for t.

## ACCURACY of CALCULATIONS

*Worked Example*  The area of a circle is given as 121cm², correct to 3 significant figures. Find the radius of this circle, giving the answer to as many significant figures as can be justified.

*Answer*  The upper bound of the area of the circle is 121·5cm²; the lower bound is 120·5cm².

$A = \pi r^2$ may be rearranged as $r = \sqrt{\frac{A}{\pi}}$, to find the radius.

If $A = 121\cdot5\text{cm}^2$, $r = \sqrt{\frac{121\cdot5}{\pi}}$ $\qquad\qquad$ If $A = 120\cdot5\text{cm}^2$, $r = \sqrt{\frac{120\cdot5}{\pi}}$
$\qquad\qquad\qquad\qquad = 6\cdot219\text{cm to 4 s.f.}$ $\qquad\qquad\qquad\qquad\qquad\qquad = 6\cdot193\text{cm to 4 s.f.}$

Since 6·219 and 6·193 agree to just two significant figures the answer for the radius should be given to two significant figures. (To 4 s.f. the figures are 6·219 and 6·193; to 3 s.f. the figures are 6·22 and 6·19; to 2 s.f. the figures are 6·2 and 6·2.) That is, radius = 6·2cm to 2 s.f.

## EXERCISE 1:6

1. Aisha measured the length of a rectangular field as 101m, to the nearest metre. She measured the width as 43m, to the nearest metre.
   (a) Aisha calculated the greatest and least possible values for the area of the field. What answers should she get?
   (b) Aisha then wrote the area, accurate to 1 s.f. What did she write?

2. Correct to 3 s.f., the area of a triangle is 17·6cm². The height is 6·1cm, correct to 2 s.f.
   (a) Write down the upper and lower bounds for the area.
   (b) Write down the upper and lower bounds for the height.
   (c) Using your answers to (a) and (b) calculate the greatest and smallest length of the base of the triangle. Copy and complete the inequality . . .cm ≤ length of base < . . .cm.
   (d) How many significant figures is it appropriate to give for the length of the base?

3. The area of a volleyball court is given as 162 square metres, correct to three significant figures. The width is given as 9·0m, to the nearest tenth of a metre.
   (a) Find the greatest and least possible values for the area.
   (b) Find the upper and lower bounds for the width.
   (c) Find the length of this court, giving the answer as accurately as can be justified.

4. The circumference of a circle is given as 17·8cm, correct to the nearest mm.
   (a) As an inequality, write down the range of possible values for this circumference.
   (b) Calculate the radius of this circle, giving the answer as accurately as can be justified.

5. Thomas measures the length of the top of his calculator as 15·1cm and the width as 7·9cm. Calculate the area of the top of Thomas's calculator, giving the answer to as many significant figures as can be justified.

6. The volume of a cube is given as 270mm³ correct to 3 s.f. Calculate the length of an edge of this cube, giving the answer as accurately as can be justified.

*Review*  To the nearest tenth of a second, Anna was timed as running the 100m in 12·3 seconds.
   (a) Find Anna's greatest and least possible time for this race.
   (b) Assuming that the distance is correct to 3 significant figures, calculate Anna's average speed as accurately as can be justified.

## PERCENTAGE ERROR

An error of 0·5m in a measurement of 234m is much less important than an error of 0·5m in a measurement of 4m.

The **percentage error** for the 234m measurement is $\frac{0.5}{234} \times 100\% = 0.2\%$ (1 d.p.) while the percentage error for the 4m measurement is $\frac{0.5}{4} \times 100\% = 12.5\%$

*Worked Example* The length of a patio is given as 27m, to the nearest metre.
  (a) What is the maximum error in this measurement?
  (b) What is the maximum percentage error?

*Answer* (a) Maximum error = 0·5m.
  (b) Maximum % error $= \frac{0.5}{27} \times 100\%$
    $= 1.9\%$ (2 s.f.)

*Worked Example* Nell calculated the area of a circle. She used r = 6·4cm when in fact the radius was 4·6cm.
  Find the percentage error in Nell's answer.

*Answer* If r = 6·4cm, A = πr²        If r = 4·6cm, A = πr²
    $= \pi (6.4)^2$            $= \pi (4.6)^2$
    $= 128.7 \text{cm}^2$ (1 d.p.)      $= 66.5 \text{cm}^2$ (1 d.p.)
        Actual error in Nell's answer = 62·2cm²
        % error $= \frac{62.2}{66.5} \times 100\%$
          $= 93.5\%$ (1 d.p.)

*Worked Example* To 1 significant figure, the radius of a cylinder is 9cm and the height 30cm.
  (a) Find the maximum and minimum possible values for the volume of the cylinder.
  (b) Calculate the greatest percentage error in the value of the volume when using r = 9cm and h = 30cm.

*Answer* (a) Maximum radius = 9·5cm        Minimum radius = 8·5cm
      Maximum height = 35cm        Minimum height = 25cm

    Using V = πr²h, maximum volume = π × 9·5² × 35
              $= 9923.5 \text{cm}^3$ (5 s.f.)

        minimum volume = π × 8·5² × 25
              $= 5674.5 \text{cm}^3$ (5 s.f.)

  (b) Using r = 9, h = 30,  V = π × 9² × 30
          $= 7634.1 \text{cm}^3$ (5 s.f.)
    Difference between 7634·1 and 5674·5 = 1959·6
    % error $= \frac{1959.6}{5674.5} \times 100\%$
      $= 34.5\%$ (3 s.f.)
    Difference between 7634·1 and 9923·5 = 2289·4
    % error $= \frac{2289.4}{9923.5} \times 100\%$
      $= 23.1\%$ (3 s.f.)
    Hence greatest percentage error = 34·5% (3.s.f.)

## EXERCISE 1:7

1. A pumpkin was weighed as 2·4kg, to the nearest tenth of a kilogram.
   (a) What is the maximum possible error in this weight?
   (b) What is the maximum percentage error?

2. Derek measured out 28m*l* of oil, for an experiment.
   (a) If this measurement is accurate to the nearest millilitre, find the maximum error.
   (b) Calculate the maximum percentage error in the measurement.

3. The distance of the earth from the sun is measured as 150 100 000 km to 4 significant figures.
   What is the greatest possible percentage error in this measurement?

4. An advertisement on TV was timed as 40·6 seconds, to the nearest tenth of a second.
   Find the maximum percentage error in this measurement.

5. The diameter of a wheel is measured as 32·4cm ± 0·05cm.
   Find the maximum percentage error in this measurement.

6. Evan calculated the volume of a cube. He used 34mm for the length when he should have used 43mm.
   Find the percentage error in Evan's answer.

7. A car travelled 344miles in 8 hours.
   Find the percentage error in the calculation for the average speed if the distance is taken as 334 miles rather than 344 miles.

8. Marsala won a 1600m race in 55·4 seconds.
   Both of these numbers are accurate to
   3 significant figures.
   (a) Find the greatest and least possible values
       for Marsala's speed.
   (b) Marsala's trainer calculated her speed
       using 1600m and 55·4 seconds. What is the greatest percentage error this trainer could have made?

9. Sita measured the length and width of a rectangle as length = 10·4cm, width = 6·0cm. Her measurements were to the nearest mm.
   (a) Find the maximum and minimum possible values for the area of the rectangle.
   (b) Sita calculated the area as $10·4 \times 6 = 62·4cm^2$.
       What is the maximum percentage error she could have made? Give your answer to 3 s.f.

10. The total resistance R, in an electrical circuit in which there are two resistances $R_1$ and $R_2$ in parallel is given by the formula
$$R = \frac{R_1 + R_2}{R_1 R_2}.$$
$R_1$ is measured as $4 \cdot 23 \pm 0 \cdot 005$ ohms and $R_2$ as $9 \cdot 3 \pm 0 \cdot 05$ ohms.
(a) What is the least possible value for R?
(b) What is the greatest possible value for R?
(c) Calculate the greatest percentage error in the value for R if $R_1 = 4 \cdot 23$ and $R_2 = 9 \cdot 3$ are used for the calculation.

**Review 1** The distance between two villages is measured as 15·8km, to the nearest tenth of a kilometre.
What is the greatest percentage error in this measurement?

**Review 2** Jake mistakenly used 8·98cm instead of 9·89cm for the radius when he was calculating the volume of a sphere.
(a) Use the formula $V = \frac{4}{3} \pi r^3$ to find the value Jake got.
(b) Find the volume of the sphere using the correct value of r = 9·89cm.
(c) What was the maximum percentage error Jake could have made? Round your answer sensibly.

**Review 3** A jet ski travels for 0·5 hour at a constant speed of 40mph. This time is accurate to one significant figure; the speed is accurate to two significant figures.
(a) Copy and complete the inequalities for the possible values of the time and the speed.
... hour $\leq$ time $<$ ... hour
... mph $\leq$ speed $<$ ... mph
(b) Find the greatest percentage error in the calculation of the distance travelled by the jet ski if the time is taken as exactly 0·5 hours and the speed is taken as exactly 40mph.

## CHAPTER 1   REVIEW

1. Jafar has a piece of wood that has a length of 30cm, correct to the nearest centimetre.
(a) Write down the minimum length of the piece of wood.

Fatima has a different piece of wood that has a length of 18·4cm, correct to the nearest millimetre.
(b) Write down the maximum and minimum lengths between which the length of the piece of wood must lie.                                                                 **ULEAC**

2. Anita measured her handspan with a ruler and found it was 16cm to the nearest centimetre. Julie measured her handspan more accurately and found it was 158mm to the nearest millimetre.
Use the upper and lower bounds of the measurements to show whether it is possible that Julie's handspan is **larger** than Anita's.                                       **SEG**

3. Comment on the difference between 9·9 and 9·90 as decimals.              **ULEAC**

4. (a) The mass of a plant on kitchen scales, is 2·474kg. What is the least possible mass of the plant?
   (b) The mass of another plant on scientific scales is 1·6280kg. What are the upper and lower bounds of the mass of this plant?                                    **SEG**

5. A machine makes iron bolts that must have a shaft diameter of 2·6cm correct to 1 decimal place.
   (a) What are the upper and lower bounds for the diameter of a bolt?

   A gauge is an instrument that is used to check if a bolt has a diameter within the allowed limits.
   A gauge is selected.
   It measures bolts with diameter 2·6 ± 0·1cm.
   (b) Explain why this gauge **is not** the correct one to check the diameters of these bolts.

   A different gauge is selected.
   This time the gauge is the correct one.
   (c) Write down the diameter of bolts that this gauge measures.

   A second machine produces bolts that have a shaft diameter of 2·60cm correct to 2 decimal places.
   (d) What are the upper and lower bounds for the diameter of a bolt produced by this second machine?                                         **SEG**

6. In 1988, Florence Griffith-Joyner set a world record for running exactly 200 metres. Her time, 21·34 seconds, was given correct to the nearest 0·01 second.
   Calculate her greatest possible average speed, in metres per second.           **ULEAC**

7. (a) In a practical test a teacher asks one of her students to measure a distance the teacher knows to be exactly 12 metres. She offers the student a ruler 15cm long or a tape 3m long.
       Which is the more accurate for the student to use? Give a reason for your answer.
   (b) From a metal rod 50cm long, a piece 15cm long is cut off. Each of these measurements is correct to the nearest centimetre.
       (i)   What is the greatest possible length of the metal rod?
       (ii)  What is the smallest possible length of the piece cut off?
       (iii) Find the difference between the answers to parts (i) and (ii). What information does this give about the length of rod remaining?                   **MEG**

8. The current, I amps, flowing through an electrical appliance is found by dividing the power, W watts, by the voltage, V volts, of the electricity supply.
   The power rating of Malcolm's microwave oven is 650 Watts, correct to the nearest watt. The electricity supply has a voltage of 240±20 volts.
   Calculate the maximum and minimum values of the current that flows through the microwave oven, giving your answers in amps correct to 3 significant figures.       **WJEC**

9. The weight of one tin of dog food is 500g to the nearest 10g.
   What are the bounds on the total weight of 100 tins?                            **SEG**

**10.** The measurements of a rectangular microchip are given as length 12mm and width 7mm, correct to the nearest millimetre.
  **(a)** Between what limits must the length of the microchip lie?
  **(b)** Between what limits must the area of the microchip lie?
  **(c)** The area is given as $(84 \pm x)mm^2$.
    Suggest a suitable value for x.                                     **NEAB**

**11.** The cost of a CD player from a warehouse is given as £90 to one significant figure. A retailer buys 125 of them and calculates the total cost as £11 250.
  **(a)** What is the maximum error he could have made in calculating the total price?
  **(b)** What is the minimum error he could have made?                **SEG**

**12.**                    ***BUILDING AN EXTENSION?***
  Jane is planning to build an extension on the back of her semi-detached house.
  Jane has a flat stick that she knows to be one metre long.
  Using the metre stick, she estimated, to the nearest half metre, the dimensions of the base of the extension.
  These were                Length 4·5metres          Width 4 metres
  **(a)** Use Jane's estimates to calculate the lower bound for the area of the base of the extension. Write your answer to 4 significant figures.

---

**You will need planning permission if the proposed extension**

- exceeds 70 cubic metres of volume in the case of any type of house other than a terraced house;
- is higher than the highest part of the roof of the original house;
- has any part higher than 4 metres as measured from the ground.

---

  Jane estimates the height of the extension by eye and decides that the height is 3 metres, to the nearest metre.
  **(b)** Based upon Jane's estimates, explain why she may need to apply for planning permission.
    You **must** show all your working.                                **SEG**

**13.** The volume of a cylinder is given as 880m*l* correct to 2 significant figures.
  John measures its height as 11·2cm (to the nearest mm).
  Between what limits must the radius of the cylinder lie?            **NEAB**

**14.** A small delivery van can take a load of up to 1000kg.

This van has to take the following to a supermarket:
25 large bags of potatoes, each bag weighing **25kg** to the nearest **kg,**
120 large boxes of soap powder, each box weighing **3000g** to the nearest **10g.**
Could this load be over the limit?
You **must** show all your working.                                     **SEG**

15. Damian runs 400m round a track in 68·2 seconds. This was timed by Jenny to the nearest
    tenth of a second.
    (a) State the maximum time Damian could have taken, based on Jenny's timing.
    (b) Jenny writes down Damian's time as "68·20 seconds".
        Explain why this is misleading.
    (c) Damian believes the length of the 400m track is only correct to the nearest half metre.
        Calculate his maximum and minimum possible average speeds in metres per second,
        assuming his time was 68·2 seconds (correct to 1 decimal place).
    (d) Sue wants to run exactly 400m at an average speed of at least 7 metres per second. What
        is the time by Jenny's watch (correct to the nearest tenth of a second) that Sue should
        aim to beat?                                                    **NEAB**

16. (a) A roll of dress material measures 23 metres, correct to the nearest metre. A shopkeeper
        cuts material of length 6m 40cm, correct to the nearest 10cm, from the roll. What is the
        maximum possible length of material left on the roll?
    (b) Salma is doing an environmental science project about a park in her town. She uses a
        local map with a scale of 1 : 20 000 to estimate the distance from her home to the park
        and to estimate the area of the park.
        (i) Salma measures the map distance from her home to the park gate as 16·3cm, correct
            to the nearest mm. Calculate, in kilometres, the minimum possible distance from
            Salma's home to the park gate.
        (ii) The area representing the park on the map is 7cm², correct to the nearest cm².
            Find the maximum possible area of the park in km².              **MEG**

17.

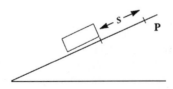

A student is studying how a sledge slides down a slope. The sledge starts from the point P.
The time, $t$ seconds, that the sledge takes to slide a distance, $s$ metres, from P is given by the
formula:–

$$a = \frac{2s}{t^2}$$

where $a$ is the acceleration in metres per second per second.

The student measures the distance from P as 50 metres to the nearest 0·5 metres and the time
as 6 seconds to the nearest 0·2 seconds.

Calculate the maximum and minimum values for $a$ using these readings.         **ULEAC**

18.

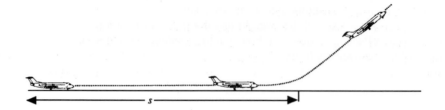

An aircraft accelerates down the runway until it reaches a sufficiently high speed, $V$, to take off.

The formula for the distance, $s$, travelled down the runway at take-off is

$$s = \frac{V^2}{2a}$$

where $V$ is the speed at take-off and $a$ is the acceleration.

For a particular aircraft $\qquad V = 72\text{m/s} \pm 5\%$

$$a = 1\cdot7\text{m/s}^2 \pm 1\%$$

Calculate the possible range of values of the distance $s$.

Express your answer in the form

$$\ldots\ldots\ldots \leq s \leq \ldots\ldots\ldots \qquad \textbf{NEAB}$$

19. The area, correct to 3 significant figures, of a large rectangular car park is 27 500 square metres. The breadth, correct to 3 significant figures, is 155 metres.
    (a) Find the possible values of the area and breadth. Use these values to calculate the greatest and smallest length of the car park and hence complete the inequality below.
       $\ldots\ldots\ldots$ metres $<$ length of car park $< \ldots\ldots\ldots$ metres
    (b) To how many significant figures are your two answers the same?   **ULEAC**

20. The length of each side of a square, correct to 2 significant figures, is 3·7cm.
    (a) Write down the least possible length of each side.
    (b) Calculate the greatest and least possible perimeters of this square.
    (c) (i) When calculating the perimeter of the square how many significant figures is it appropriate to give in the answer?
        (ii) Explain your answer.
    (d) If this question had referred to a regular octagon, instead of a square, would your answer to part (c) (i) have been the same? Explain your answer.   **ULEAC**

21. The formula $S = \frac{F}{A}$ is used in engineering.

    $F = 810$, correct to 2 significant figures.
    $A = 2\cdot93$, correct to 3 significant figures.

    (a) For the value of $F$, write down
        (i) the upper bound,      (ii) the lower bound.

(b) For the value of $A$, write down
   (i) the upper bound,          (ii) the lower bound.
(c) Calculate (i) the upper bound and (ii) the lower bound for the value of $S$ for these values of $F$ and $A$. Write down all the figures on your calculator display.
(d) Write down this value of $S$ correct to an appropriate number of significant figures.

**ULEAC**

22. The average speed of Karen's car is 60mph and she travels for 4 hours, both values being given to one significant figure.
   (a) Find  (i)  the maximum possible distance Karen has travelled,
             (ii) the minimum possible distance Karen has travelled.
   (b) Karen gives the distance she has travelled as 240 miles. What is the maximum percentage error she could be making?          **SEG**

# Proportion

## DIRECT PROPORTION

### DISCUSSION EXERCISE 2:1

- This table shows the distance travelled by a car.

  For $t = 4$, the value of the ratio $\frac{s}{t}$ is $\frac{8}{4} = 2$.

  | t (min) | 1 | 2 | 3 | 4 | 5 |
  |---------|---|---|---|---|----|
  | s (km)  | 2 | 4 | 6 | 8 | 10 |

  What is the value of the ratio $\frac{s}{t}$ for other values of t?
  Is the car travelling at constant speed?

  Can the relationship between s and t be written as $s = kt$ where k is some constant number? If so, what is the value of k?

  What does the distance/time graph look like?
  Discuss.

- To make scones, $\frac{1}{2}$ cup of milk is needed for every 2 cups of flour. How much milk is needed with 5 cups of flour?

  Can the relationship between the amount of milk (m) and flour (f) be written as $m = kf$ where k is some constant number? If so, what is the value of k?

  What does the graph of m plotted against f look like?
  Discuss.

-

  | $l$ | 2 | 4 | 5 | 8 | 10 | 15 | 20 | 30 |
  |-----|---|---|---|---|----|----|----|----|
  | P   | 8 |   |   |   |    |    |    |    |

  What values for P, the perimeter of a square, correspond to the other values of $l$, the length of the square?

  Is the value of $\frac{P}{l}$ always the same? If the relationship between P and $l$ is written as $P = kl$, where k is some constant number, what is the value of k?

  What does the graph of P plotted against $l$ look like?
  Discuss.

If two quantities increase at the same rate, so that if one is doubled so is the other, the quantities are said to be **directly proportional**.

The symbol $\propto$ is read as "is proportional to".
For instance, the statement "perimeter is proportional to length" could be written as "$P \propto l$" where $P$ stands for perimeter and $l$ stands for length.

$a \propto b$ means $a = kb$ where $k$ is some positive number. If we know one pair of values for $a$ and $b$ we can find the value of $k$.

*Worked Example*

| x | 2 | 5 | 10 | 20 | 50 |
|---|---|---|----|----|----|
| y |   |   | 15 |    |    |

Given that $y$ is proportional to $x$, find the missing values of y.

*Answer* Since $y \propto x$, then $y = kx$.
From the table, when $x = 10, y = 15$. Hence $15 = k \times 10$.
$$\frac{15}{10} = k$$
$$1 \cdot 5 = k$$
The relationship between $x$ and $y$ is then $y = 1 \cdot 5x$.
We now use $y = 1 \cdot 5x$ to find the values of $y$ for $x = 2, 5, 20$ and $50$.

| x | 2 | 5   | 10 | 20 | 50 |
|---|---|-----|----|----|----|
| y | 3 | 7·5 | 15 | 30 | 75 |

*Worked Example* The current, $I$, in a particular type of wire is proportional to the voltage, $V$. If $I = 8$ amps when $V = 5$ volts, find
(a) the current when the voltage is 8 volts
(b) the voltage if the current is 10 amps.

*Answer* Since $I \propto V$, then $I = kV$
When $I = 8, V = 5$. Hence $8 = k \times 5$ which gives $k = 1 \cdot 6$.
The relationship between $I$ and $V$ is $I = 1 \cdot 6V$.
(a) Using $I = 1 \cdot 6V$, $I = 1 \cdot 6 \times 8$
$$= 12 \cdot 8 \text{ amps.}$$
(b) Using $I = 1 \cdot 6V$, $10 = 1 \cdot 6V$
$$\frac{10}{1 \cdot 6} = V$$
$$6 \cdot 25 = V \qquad \text{That is, } V = 6 \cdot 25 \text{ volts.}$$

## EXERCISE 2:2

1. This table shows the cost of tickets to a concert.

| Number, N | 3 | 6 | 8 |
|---|---|---|---|
| Cost, C, in £ | 13·5 | 27 | 36 |

(a) Copy and complete: If C ∝ N, then ... = kN.
(b) Use one set of values for C and N to find the value of k.
(c) Replace k in C = kN to find the relationship between C and N.
(d) Use this relationship to find the cost of 19 tickets.
(e) A school party went to this concert. The total cost of the tickets was £153. How many were in this school party?

2. In each of the following y is proportional to x; that is y = kx.
For each, find the value of k then copy and complete the tables.

| x | 3 | 5 | | 20 |
|---|---|---|---|---|
| y | 18 | | 54 | |

(a)

| x | 2 | | 16 | 35 |
|---|---|---|---|---|
| y | | 35 | 56 | |

(b)

| x | 1 | 3 | 5 | |
|---|---|---|---|---|
| y | | | 2 | 2·8 |

(c)

3. Map distances, m, are proportional to distances on the ground, g.
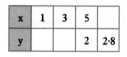
(a) Write this statement using the symbol ∝.
(b) 2mm on the map corresponds to 5km on the ground. Find the relationship between m and g.
(c) Two villages are 12km apart. How far apart are they on the map?
(d) The length of a lake on the map is 7mm. What is the actual length of this lake?

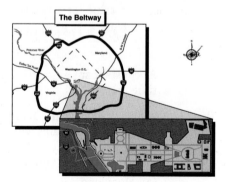

4. The distance a cyclist travels is directly proportional to the number of revolutions of the front wheel of the bicycle.
(a) Write down the relationship between the distance s, the number of revolutions r and a constant k.
(b) The cyclist travels 24m for 10 revolutions of the front wheel. Find the relationship between s and r.
(c) How far does the cyclist travel for 120 revolutions?
(d) How many revolutions are needed to travel 120m?

5. The extension, e, of a spring is proportional to the mass, m, hung from the spring.
   A mass of 2kg gives an extension of 5cm.
   (a) Find the relationship between e and m.
   (b) Use this relationship to find the mass needed to give an extension of 40mm.

6. The acceleration of a moving object is proportional to the force acting on the object. If a force
   of 150 Newtons produces an acceleration of 18 metres per sec² find
   (a) the relationship between the acceleration, a, and the force, F
   (b) the force needed to give an acceleration of 4·5m/sec²
   (c) the acceleration produced by a force of 200 Newtons.

7.

| x | 1 | 2 | 3 |
|---|---|---|---|
| y | 3 | 5 | 7 |

(a)

| x | 3 | 5 | 7 |
|---|---|---|---|
| y | 1 | -0·5 | -2 |

(b)

| x | 1 | 2 | 3 |
|---|---|---|---|
| y | 0·4 | 0·1 | -0·8 |

(c)

| x | 2 | 3 | 4 |
|---|---|---|---|
| y | 4 | 7 | 9 |

(d)

| x | 1 | 2 | 3 |
|---|---|---|---|
| y | -2 | -4 | -6 |

(e)

In which of the above relationships is y proportional to x? Explain your answer.
Plot the graphs of each relationship to help answer this question.

8. The formula v = u + at gives the velocity (v) after time (t) of an object which has initial
   velocity (u) and constant acceleration (a).
   Are there any values of u for which v is proportional to t? Explain your answer.

**Review 1** At constant speed, the distance (s) travelled by a car is directly proportional to the
   time (t).
   (a) Write this statement using the symbol ∝.
   (b) Rewrite this statement using the symbol =.
   (c) At constant speed, a car travels 160km in 2 hours.
       Find the relationship between s and t.
   (d) Use the relationship to find the distance travelled in $2\frac{1}{4}$ hours.
   (e) How long does it take to travel 280km?

**Review 2** The cost, C, of furnishing fabric is proportional
   to the width, W, of the fabric.
   (a) Write down the relationship between C, W
       and a constant k.
   (b) The cost of one yard of 45″ wide furnishing
       fabric is £13·50. What is the cost of one yard
       of 54″ wide fabric?

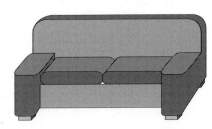

a $\propto$ b is read as "a is proportional to b". It may also be read as "a varies as b".
a $\propto$ b$^2$ is read as "a is proportional to the square of b" or as "a varies as the square of b".
a $\propto$ $\sqrt{b}$ is read as "a is proportional to the square root of b" or as "a varies as the square root of b".

Just as a $\propto$ b means a = kb, where k is some positive number, a $\propto$ b$^2$ means a = kb$^2$;
a $\propto$ b$^3$ means a = kb$^3$, a $\propto$ b$^4$ means a = kb$^4$, a $\propto$ $\sqrt{b}$ means a = k$\sqrt{b}$ etc.

k is known as the **constant of variation**.

*Worked Example* The energy of a moving object is proportional to the square of its speed. If the object has 45 units of energy when it is moving at a speed of 5 metres per second, how many units of energy does it have at a speed of 8 metres per second?

*Answer* Using E for energy and v for speed, E $\propto$ v$^2$ or E = kv$^2$.
Since v = 5 when E = 45 then $45 = k \times 5^2$
$$\frac{45}{25} = k$$
$$k = 1\cdot8$$
The relationship between E and v is E = 1·8v$^2$.
When v = 8, $E = 1\cdot8 \times 8^2$
$$= 115\cdot2 \text{ units.}$$

*Worked Example* The distance a person can see, when looking at the horizon, varies as the square root of the height of the person above sea level. A person who is 16m above sea level can see for a distance of 14km.
(a) Find the relationship between d, the distance of the horizon and h, the height of the person above sea level.
(b) Use this relationship to find the distance a person could see if the person was 46m above sea level.
(c) What height above sea level would Andrew be if he could see for 20km?

*Answer* (a) d $\propto$ $\sqrt{h}$ or d = k$\sqrt{h}$
Since d = 14 when h = 16 then $14 = k\sqrt{16}$
$$14 = 4k$$
$$k = 3\cdot5$$
The relationship between d and h is d = 3·5$\sqrt{h}$ .

(b) We have to find d when h = 46. d = 3·5$\sqrt{h}$
$$= 3\cdot5\sqrt{46}$$
$$= 24\text{km (to the nearest km)}$$

(c) We have to find h when d = 20. $20 = 3\cdot5\sqrt{h}$
$$\frac{20}{3\cdot5} = \sqrt{h}$$

$$\left(\frac{20}{3\cdot5}\right)^2 = h \text{ (squaring both sides)}$$

$$h = 33\text{m (to the nearest metre)}$$

## EXERCISE 2:3

1.  Using k as the constant of variation, write down the relationship between the following.
    (a) The area (A) of a square varies as the square of the length of a side ($l$).
    (b) The volume (V) of a sphere is proportional to the cube of the radius (r).
    (c) Total price (P) of chocolate fish is proportional to the number bought (n).
    (d) The surface area (A) of a cube varies as the square of the length of an edge ($l$).
    (e) The time (T) it takes for a pendulum to swing back and forth once is proportional to the square root of the length ($l$) of the pendulum.
    (f) The air-resistance (r) to a bullet varies as the square of the speed (v) of the bullet.

2.  It is known that **a** is proportional to the square of n.
    (a) Find k, the constant of variation.
    (b) Find the relationship between n and a.
    (c) Copy and complete the table.

| n | 2 |   | 5 | 8 | 20  |
|---|---|---|---|---|-----|
| a |   | 8 |   |   | 200 |

3.

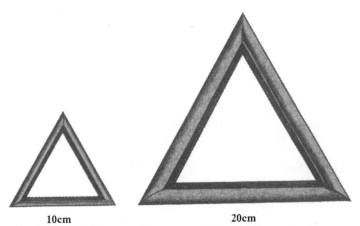

10cm         20cm

"Designer" photo frames are shaped like equilateral triangles. The mass of each frame is proportional to the square of the length of a side.
If the mass of the large photo frame is 500g find the mass of the small one.

4.  When a ball is thrown up in the air, the height it reaches varies as the square of the speed with which it is thrown.
    A ball, which was thrown with a speed of 29·4 m/sec reaches a height of 44·1m.
    With what speed must a ball be thrown if it is to reach a maximum height of 10m?

5.  The mass, m, of a cube is proportional to the cube of the length, $l$, of an edge.
    (a) Write down the relationship between m, $l$ and a constant k.
    (b) A cube of length 5cm has a mass of 400g. Use this information to find the value of k.
    (c) What is the mass of a cube which is 8cm long?

6.

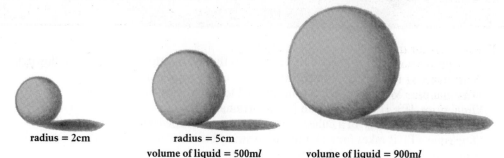

radius = 2cm      radius = 5cm

volume of liquid = 500m*l*      volume of liquid = 900m*l*

These spheres are filled with liquid.
The volume of liquid in each varies as the cube of the radius.
Find    (a) the volume of liquid in the small sphere
        (b) the radius of the large sphere.

7. It is known that $m \propto \sqrt{a}$.
   (a) Show that the value of k, the constant
   of variation, is 6·8.
   (b) Find the value of m if a = 20.
   (c) Find the value of a if m = 15.

| a | 4 | 9 | 16 | 25 |
|---|---|---|----|----|
| m | 13·6 | 20·4 | 27·2 | 34 |

8. If a stone is dropped from the top of a building, the time (t) it takes to reach the ground is
   proportional to the square root of the height (h) of the building.
   A stone takes 4·5 seconds to reach the ground after being dropped from a building 100 feet
   high.
   A stone is dropped from a building 50 feet high. How long does it take to reach the ground?

Review 1 The energy, E, stored in a spring is proportional to the square of the extension, e.
         (a) Write down the relationship between E, e, and a constant k.
         (b) If the extension is 4cm, the energy stored is 320 joules. Use this information to
             find the value of k.
         (c) How much energy is stored in the spring if the extension is 2cm?

Review 2 It is known that y is proportional to $x^3$.
         (a) Find the value of y if x = 50.
         (b) Find the value of x if y = 6·75.

| x | 10 | 20 | 30 | 40 |
|---|----|----|----|----|
| y | 2 | 16 | 54 | 128 |

Review 3 The current (I) in an electrical circuit varies as the square root of the power (P).
         If the current is 3·5 amps when the power is 25 watts, find the current when the power
         is 36 watts.

## DISCUSSION EXERCISE 2:4

● The formula for the circumference of a circle is C = πd.
  Is C proportional to d?
  What happens to C if d is doubled?
  What happens to C if d is halved?
  What effect does increasing the diameter have on the
  circumference? What effect does decreasing the diameter have?
  Discuss.

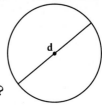

● A = πr² is the formula for the area of a circle.
  Discuss the statement "A is proportional to r²".
  What happens to A if r is doubled?
  What happens to A if r is trebled?
  What happens to A if r is halved?
  What effect does increasing the radius have on the area?
  What effect does decreasing the area have on the radius?
  Discuss.

●

Is the perimeter of a square proportional to the length of a side?
Is the area of a square proportional to the length of a side?
Is the area of a square proportional to the perimeter?
Discuss. Use formulae to justify the arguments you use in your discussion.

What happens to the perimeter if the length of a side is doubled?
What happens to the area if the length of a side is doubled?
What happens to the area if the perimeter is doubled?
Discuss.

● Discuss what happens to the volume of a cube
  if the length of an edge is doubled.
  What if the length of an edge is trebled?
  What if the length of an edge is halved?

  Each edge on a cube is five times the length of an
  edge of the cube shown. What can you say about
  the volumes of these two cubes? Discuss.

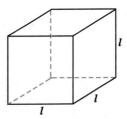

## INVERSE PROPORTION

---

### DISCUSSION EXERCISE 2:5

---

- The following table gives the time taken to complete a 200km journey for various average speeds.

| Average speed, v (km/hr) | 20 | 40 | 50 | 80 | 100 |
|---|---|---|---|---|---|
| Time, t (hours) | 10 | 5 | 4 | 2·5 | 2 |

For t = 10, the product vt = 200.
What is the product vt for other values of t?

Can the relationship between t and v be written as $t = \frac{k}{v}$ where k is some constant number? If so, what is the value of k?

What does the graph of t plotted against v look like?
Discuss.

- Simone plans to spend £60 on theatre tickets next year. All the shows she plans to see cost from £5 for the cheapest seats to £20 for the best seats. The table gives the number of shows Simone can see if she always buys the same priced tickets.

| Price, P (in £) | 20 | 15 | 12 | 10 | 5 |
|---|---|---|---|---|---|
| Number, n | 3 | 4 | 5 | 6 | 12 |

Discuss the relationship between n and P. As part of your discussion, draw a graph.

- 

| Hourly rate, r (in £) | 2 | 4 | 5 | 8 | 10 |
|---|---|---|---|---|---|
| Hours, h | 50 | 25 | 20 | 12·5 | 10 |

This table shows the time taken to earn £100 at different rates of pay.
Discuss the relationship between h and r.

- What was similar about the three examples given above? Discuss. As part of your discussion, consider the tables, the graphs and the relationships between the two variables.

If two quantities increase at opposite rates, so that if one is doubled the other is halved, the quantities are said to be indirectly proportional. Indirect proportion is usually called inverse proportion. Quantities that are indirectly proportional are usually said to be inversely proportional.

If a is inversely proportional to b, then $a \propto \frac{1}{b}$ or $a = \frac{k}{b}$ where k is some positive number.

Just as for direct proportion, where we could have a quantity directly proportional to the square of another so we can have a quantity inversely proportional to the square of another. For instance, a may be inversely proportional to the square of b. The relationship between a and b in this case is $a = \frac{k}{b^2}$, where k is some positive number. This is sometimes called the inverse square law.

## DISCUSSION EXERCISE 2:6

- For each statement, **discuss** whether the quantities are likely to be directly proportional or inversely proportional or not proportional.

  The weight of a sheet of paper and its area.
  The weight of a sheet of paper and its length.
  The number of chocolates in a box and the size of the box.
  The cost of a box of chocolates and the weight of chocolates in the box.
  The rate of pay and the earnings for a 40 hour week.
  The age of a kitten and its weight.
  The cost of a phone call and the time taken for this call.
  The area of an isosceles triangle and the length of a side.
  The size of an exterior angle and the number of sides of regular polygons.
  The base length and height of right-angled triangles which have the same area.

- Think of quantities, other than those mentioned already in this chapter, which could be directly proportional or inversely proportional. Write statements, similar to those above but include the words "is proportional to" or "is inversely proportional to".
  **Discuss** your statements.

*Worked Example*  Boyle's law states that at a constant temperature, the volume of a gas is inversely proportional to its pressure.
  (a) Find the relationship between volume V, pressure P and a constant k.
  (b) When the pressure is 400N/m², the volume is 2m³. Use this information to find the value of k.
  (c) Find the volume when the pressure is 200N/m².
  (d) Find the pressure when the volume of the gas is 2·5m³.

***Answer*** (a) Since $V \propto \frac{1}{P}$ then $V = \frac{k}{P}$.

(b) Since $V = 2$ when $P = 400$ then $2 = \frac{k}{400}$

$$800 = k$$

(c) The relationship between $V$ and $P$ is $V = \frac{800}{P}$.

When $P = 200$, $V = \frac{800}{200}$

$$= 4m^3$$

(d) When $V = 2\cdot5$, $2\cdot5 = \frac{800}{P}$

$$2\cdot5P = 800 \text{ (multiplying both sides by P)}$$

$$P = \frac{800}{2\cdot5}$$

$$= 320N/m^2$$

***Worked Example*** The intensity of a light on an object is inversely proportional to the square of the distance of the object from the light.
If the intensity of the light is 8 units at a distance of 5 metres, find the intensity at a distance of 3 metres.

***Answer*** Using $I$ for intensity and $d$ for distance, $I \propto \frac{1}{d^2}$ or $I = \frac{k}{d^2}$.

Since $I = 8$ when $d = 5$, $\quad 8 = \frac{k}{5^2}$

$$5^2 \times 8 = k$$

$$200 = k$$

Then $I = \frac{200}{d^2}$

When $d = 3$, $I = \frac{200}{3^2}$

$$= 22 \text{ units (to the nearest unit)}$$

## EXERCISE 2:7

1. Write down the relationship between the two variables using $k$ as the constant of variation.
   (a) $m$ is inversely proportional to n.
   (b) $x$ varies inversely as the square of y.
   (c) $b$ is inversely proportional to the square of d.
   (d) $l$ varies inversely as p.
   (e) $t$ varies inversely as the square root of u.
   (f) $a$ is inversely proportional to the cube of h.

2. For parallelograms of the same area, height varies inversely as the length of the base. If the height is 5cm when the base is 8cm find
   (a) the relationship between height h, length of the base $l$ and a constant k expressed as $h = \ldots$
   (b) the value of the constant k
   (c) the height when the length of the base is 2·5cm.

3. The wavelength of sound waves is inversely proportional to the frequency. If the frequency of the note G is 387 cycles per second and the wavelength is 0·853 metres find the wavelength of the note C which has frequency of 256 cycles per second.

4. It is known that y is inversely proportional to $x^2$.
   (a) Write down the relationship between y, x and a constant k.
   (b) Find the value of k.
   (c) Find the value of y when x = 2.

   | x | 0·1 | 0·2 | 0·4 | 0·5 | 1 |
   |---|-----|-----|-----|-----|---|
   | y | 200 | 50 | 12·5 | 8 | 2 |

5. The resistance R, in a fixed length of wire varies inversely as the square of the diameter d. If the diameter is 5mm the resistance is 0·08 ohms.
   Find the resistance if the diameter is 4mm.

6. The air pressure available from a bicycle pump is inversely proportional to the square of the diameter of the pump.
   If a pressure of 8 units is available from a pump of diameter 25mm find
   (a) the pressure available from a pump of diameter 14mm
   (b) the diameter of the pump which can deliver 15 units of pressure.

7. The frequency of radio waves varies inversely as the wavelength. Radio M broadcasts on a wavelength of 212 metres and frequency of $1·42 \times 10^6$ cycles per second.
   (a) Radio P broadcasts on 384m. What frequency is this?
   (b) For Radio Q, the frequency is $6·2 \times 10^5$ cycles per second. What wavelength is this?

8. At a constant temperature, the volume V of a gas is inversely proportional to its pressure P. The gas in a cylindrical container of radius 2m is at a pressure of 500N/m². The gas is transferred into another cylindrical container. This new container is the same height but twice the radius of the first one. What is the pressure of the gas in the new container?

Review 1  It is known that m is inversely proportional to n.
Copy and complete the table.

| m | | 2 | 5 | | 20 |
|---|---|---|---|---|---|
| n | 100 | | 10 | 5 | |

Review 2  The force of attraction between two bodies varies inversely as the square of their distance apart.
If the force of attraction is 2 units when the bodies are 100km apart, find the force of attraction when they are 50km apart.

## INVESTIGATION 2:8

Proportion and Graphs

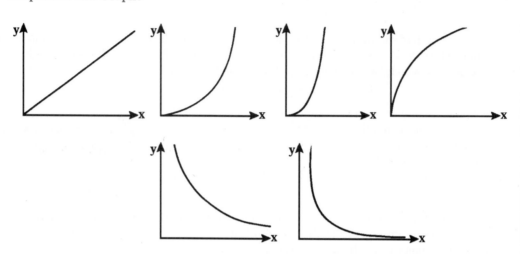

Investigate the graphs associated with proportion. You could include $y \propto x$, $y \propto x^2$, $y \propto x^3$, $y \propto x^4$, $y \propto \sqrt{x}$, $y \propto \sqrt[3]{x}$, $y \propto \frac{1}{x}$, $y \propto \frac{1}{x^2}$, $y \propto \frac{1}{x^3}$, $y \propto \frac{1}{\sqrt{x}}$.

You could include the following in your investigation.
Consider $y \propto x^2$; if $k = 3$ then $y = 3x^2$.

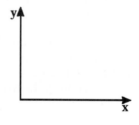

| x | 1 | 2 | 3 | 4 | 5 |
|---|---|---|---|---|---|
| y | 3 | 12 | 27 | 48 | 75 |

Now plot the graph on these axes.

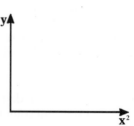

| $x^2$ | 1 | 4 | 9 | 16 | 25 |
|---|---|---|---|---|---|
| y | 3 | 12 | 27 | 48 | 75 |

Now plot the graph on these axes.

Continue by plotting similar graphs for other values of $k$ such as $k = 1$, $k = 2$, $k = 4$ etc.

Write a report on your investigation. Use tables and graphs in your report.

## PRACTICAL EXERCISE 2:9

Make a pendulum similar to that shown. You will need the following equipment.

Equipment  A piece of string about 50cm long.
Some nuts or bolts of different weights.
A stopwatch or a watch from which you
can read seconds.

As well as the above equipment you will need some way
of suspending your pendulum a little way out from a wall.

Use your pendulum to investigate the relationship between the time (T) for a complete swing
and the length of the string.
You could also investigate the relationship between T and the weight attached to the end of the
string.

Note  Start your pendulum swinging by pulling the weight to the side, keeping the string
taut. T is the time taken for the weight to move through one swing from this starting position
back to the same position.

Write a report on your investigation. Include graphs in your report. Mention proportion in your
report.

## INVESTIGATION 2:10

**Proportion and Difference Tables**

| x | 1 | 2 | 3 | 4 | 5 |
|---|---|---|---|---|---|
| y | 4 | 16 | 36 | 64 | 100 |

Which of the following is true : $y \propto x$, $y \propto x^2$, $y \propto x^3$?

Consider the following "difference table" for the y-values

| 4 | | 16 | | 36 | | 64 | | 100 | |
|---|---|----|---|----|---|----|---|-----|---|
| | 12 | | 20 | | 28 | | 36 | | ← 1st differences |
| | | 8 | | 8 | | 8 | | | ← 2nd differences |

| x | 1 | 2 | 3 | 4 | 5 |
|---|---|---|---|---|---|
| y | 2 | 16 | 54 | 128 | 250 |

Which of the following is true : $y \propto x$, $y \propto x^2$, $y \propto x^3$?
What do you think will happen if a difference table is
formed?

*continued . . .*

*. . . from previous page*

**Investigate** the relationship between proportion and difference tables. For your difference tables, you could use the following program.

```
10    MODE 3
20    INPUT  "HOW MANY Y-VALUES WILL YOU ENTER? (MINIMUM 4)"N
30    DIM Y(N), D1(N – 1), D2(N – 2), D3(N – 3)
40    PRINT "ENTER THE Y-VALUES, PRESSING< RETURN>AFTER EACH ONE"
50    FOR J = 1 TO N
60    INPUT Y(J)
70    NEXT J
80    PRINT   "Y-VALUES";
90    FOR J = 1 TO N
100   PRINT SPC(5); Y(J);
110   NEXT J
120   PRINT : PRINT   "1ST DIFF"; SPC(5);
130   FOR J = 1 TO N – 1
140   D1(J) = Y(J + 1) – Y(J)
150   PRINT SPC(5); D1(J);
160   NEXT J
170   PRINT : PRINT   "2ND DIFF"; SPC(10);
180   FOR J = 1 TO N – 2
190   D2(J) = D1(J + 1) – D1(J)
200   PRINT SPC(5); D2(J);
210   NEXT J
220   PRINT : PRINT   "3RD DIFF"; SPC(14);
230   FOR J = 1 TO N – 3
240   D3(J) = D2(J + 1) – D2(J)
250   PRINT SPC(5) ; D3(J);
260   NEXT J
270   PRINT
400   END
```

**Note** If you want to include another row of differences you must change line 30 and insert extra lines after line 270.

If you wish, you could use a spreadsheet instead of the program.

|   | A | B | C |
|---|---|---|---|
| 1 | = 2 | = A2 – A1 | = B2 – B1 |
| 2 | = 16 | = A3 – A2 | = B3 – B2 |
| 3 | = 54 | = A4 – A3 | = B4 |
| 4 | = 128 | = A5 | |
| 5 | = | | |

## CHAPTER 2   REVIEW

**1.**

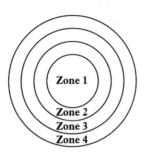

Barratts sells electrical goods.
It makes a delivery charge to deliver goods to the customers' homes.
The delivery charge depends on the zone in which the customer lives.
The diagram shows how the zones are numbered.
The delivery charge is directly proportional to the zone number.
The delivery charge for Zone 2 is £15.
£$C$ is the delivery charge. $Z$ is the zone number.

(a) Write down a formula which expresses $C$ in terms of $Z$.

(b) Calculate
   (i)  the delivery charge for Zone 4,
   (ii) the delivery charge for Zone 3.                                    **ULEAC**


**2.** The distance ($d$ metres) travelled by a stone falling vertically varies in direct proportion to the square of the time ($t$ seconds) for which it falls.

(a) Write a formula to connect $d, t$ and the constant of variation $k$.

   A stone takes 2 seconds to fall 20 metres.
(b) Find the value of $k$.

(c) How far will the stone fall in 4 seconds?

   A stone is dropped from a balloon which is 500 metres above the ground.
(d) How many seconds will the stone take to reach the ground?            **ULEAC**


**3.** The time of swing, $T$ seconds, of a pendulum is proportional to the square root of the length, $L$ centimetres, of the pendulum.

A pendulum of length 64cm has a time of swing 1·6 seconds.

Find the formula for $T$ in terms of $L$.                                  **MEG**


**4.** Two variables, $x$ and $y$, vary in such a way that $y$ is inversely proportional to the square of $x$.

(a) When $x = 4$, $y = 5$.
   Find the formula giving $y$ in terms of $x$.

(b) Find the value of $y$ when $x = 5$.                                    **WJEC**

5. The number of coins, $N$, with diameter $d$ cm and with a fixed thickness that can be made from a given volume of metal can be found by using the formula

$$N = \frac{k}{d^2}$$

where $k$ is a constant.

(a) Given that 5000 coins of diameter 2·5cm can be made from the volume of metal, find the value of $k$.

(b) Calculate how many coins of diameter 2cm can be made from an equal volume of metal.

(c) Rearrange the formula $N = \frac{k}{d^2}$ to make $d$ the subject.

(d) 2000 coins are to be made using an equal volume of metal. Calculate the diameter of these coins.

**MEG**

6.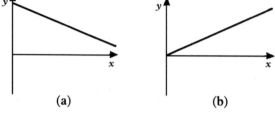

(a)        (b)        (c)

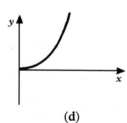
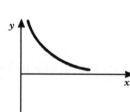
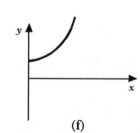

(d)        (e)        (f)

In each case select the graph which could represent the given statement.
(i) $y$ varies directly as $x$.
(ii) $y$ has constant value.
(iii) $y$ is inversely proportional to $x$.
(iv) $y$ varies as the square of $x$.

**NICCEA**

7. (a) Write the formula $y = \frac{kl}{t^2}$ ($k$ = constant) in a sentence using the two phrases 'varies directly as' and 'varies inversely as'.

(b) $y = 3$ when $l = 12$ and $t = 2$. Find the value of $y$ when $l = 20$ and $t = 5$.

**NEAB**

# 3 Rational and Irrational Numbers

## FRACTIONAL and DECIMAL FORMS of NUMBERS

Any fraction, such as $\frac{5}{8}$, may be written as a decimal by dividing the numerator by the denominator. Using the calculator for the division $5 \div 8$ gives an answer of $0.625$. The decimal, $0.625$, is said to be a **terminating decimal** since it terminates (stops) after three decimal places. Some fractions have decimal forms which are non-terminating. For instance, the decimal form of $\frac{5}{6}$ is $0.8\dot{3}$. The decimal, $0.8\dot{3}$, is said to be a **recurring decimal**, or a repeating decimal, since the digit 3 repeats.

A terminating decimal, such as $0.34$, may be written in the form $\frac{m}{n}$ (i.e. as a fraction) as follows:

$$0.34 = \frac{34}{100}$$
$$= \frac{17}{50}$$

A recurring decimal, such as $0.34\dot{1}2\dot{6}$ can be written in the form $\frac{m}{n}$ as follows:

$$0.34\dot{1}2\dot{6} \times 100\,000 = 34\,126.126\,126\,126\ldots$$
$$- \quad 0.34\dot{1}2\dot{6} \times 100 \quad = \quad 34.126\,126\,126\ldots$$

$$0.34\dot{1}2\dot{6} \times 99\,900 = 34\,092.000\,000\,000\ldots \qquad \text{Hence } 0.34\dot{1}2\dot{6} = \frac{34\,092}{99\,900}$$
$$= \frac{947}{2775}$$

---

### DISCUSSION EXERCISE 3:1

To write $0.34\dot{1}2\dot{6}$ as a fraction, we multiplied firstly by $100\,000$ then by $100$ and subtracted. Why did we choose to multiply by these numbers? **Discuss.**

As part of your discussion, write other recurring decimal as fractions. Include the following types.

- One recurring digit; e.g. $0.\dot{3}$.
- One recurring digit after one or more non-recurring digits; e.g. $0.4\dot{6}$, $0.23\dot{5}$, $0.105\dot{7}$.
- A recurring cycle of length two digits; e.g. $0.\dot{7}\dot{2}$, $0.3\dot{1}\dot{8}$, $0.20\dot{4}\dot{3}\dot{6}$.
- A recurring cycle of length three or more digits; e.g. $0.\dot{2}6\dot{1}$, $0.2\dot{1}3\dot{4}$, $0.03\dot{2}45\dot{1}$.

---

### INVESTIGATION 3:2

**Non-Terminating, Non-Recurring Decimals**
Consider the following decimal which neither terminates nor repeats: $0.41441444144441\ldots$
What are the digits in the next 6 places of this decimal?
Can this decimal be written as a fraction?
**Investigate.**

## RATIONAL and IRRATIONAL NUMBERS

A number which can be written in the form $\frac{m}{n}$ (where m and n are whole numbers) is called a **rational number**. Since all terminating and recurring decimals can be written in this way, terminating and recurring decimals are rational numbers.

It can be proven (see page 64) that numbers such as $\sqrt{2}, \sqrt{3}, \sqrt{5}, \sqrt{6}, \sqrt{7}$, etc. cannot be written as fractions; i.e. cannot be written in the form $\frac{m}{n}$. These numbers are called **irrational numbers**. The decimal form of an irrational number neither terminates nor repeats. The square root of any number, other than a square number, is irrational. Another well known irrational number is $\pi$.

*Worked Example*  Which of the following numbers are rational and which are irrational?

$$3\pi, \sqrt{9}, \tfrac{1}{3}, \sqrt{10}, 0{\cdot}99, 4{\cdot}\dot{3}$$

*Answer*  $3\pi$ is irrational since $\pi$ is irrational.

$\sqrt{9}$ can be simplified to 3 and hence is rational.

$\frac{1}{3}$ is rational since it is in the form $\frac{m}{n}$ where m and n are whole numbers.

$\sqrt{10}$ is irrational since it is the square root of a number which is not a square number.

$0{\cdot}99$ is rational since it is a terminating decimal.

$4{\cdot}\dot{3}$ is rational since it is a recurring decimal.

## EXERCISE 3:3

1.  Which of the following numbers are rational? Explain your answers.
    (a) $\frac{15}{99}$   (b) $\pi^2$   (c) $\sqrt{5}$   (d) $\sqrt{4}$   (e) $0{\cdot}6$   (f) $0{\cdot}\dot{6}$   (g) $\frac{\pi}{0{\cdot}6}$

2.  Which of the following numbers are irrational?
    (a) $\sqrt{16}$   (b) $\sqrt{8}$   (c) $0{\cdot}375$   (d) $0{\cdot}8\dot{1}\dot{2}$   (e) $\frac{1}{\pi}$   (f) $\frac{1}{\sqrt{4}}$   (g) $\frac{\sqrt{8}}{3}$

3.  State whether the following numbers are rational or irrational. Write each of the rational numbers as a fraction in its lowest terms.
    (a) $\frac{\sqrt{2}}{2}$   (b) $\frac{\pi}{2}$   (c) $\frac{2}{\sqrt{25}}$   (d) $\sqrt{3}$   (e) $0{\cdot}98$   (f) $0{\cdot}0\dot{4}$   (g) $1{\cdot}2\dot{6}$

4.  Where possible, write each of the following in the form $\frac{x}{y}$, where x and y are whole numbers with no common factor other than 1. For those numbers which cannot be written in this form, explain why not.
    (a) $0{\cdot}36$   (b) $\frac{1{\cdot}6}{4}$   (c) $\frac{1}{\pi^2}$   (d) $\frac{\sqrt{49}}{2}$   (e) $0{\cdot}\dot{7}$   (f) $0{\cdot}0\dot{3}\dot{4}$   (g) $\sqrt{11}$
    (h) $0{\cdot}2\dot{5}$   (i) $0{\cdot}34\dot{1}$   (j) $\sqrt{3}-1$   (k) $9\pi$   (l) $2{\cdot}616161...$

5.  If it is possible to do so, give an example of each of the following. Give both the fractional and decimal forms.
    (a) A rational number which can be written as a terminating decimal.
    (b) An irrational number which can be written as a terminating decimal.
    (c) A rational number which can be written as a recurring decimal, with just one digit repeating.
    (d) An irrational number which cannot be written as a terminating or recurring decimal.
    (e) A rational number which can be written as a recurring decimal, with two recurring digits and one non-recurring digit.

**Review 1**  State whether the following numbers are rational or irrational.

(a) $\frac{1}{9}$   (b) $5\pi$   (c) $\frac{1}{\sqrt{9}}$   (d) $9 \cdot 0\dot{9}$   (e) $\sqrt{99}$   (f) $\frac{3}{1 \cdot 5}$   (g) $5 + \sqrt{5}$

**Review 2**  (a)  Write down three rational numbers which lie between 3 and 4.
(b)  Write down three irrational numbers which lie between 3 and 4.

**Review 3**  Write these recurring decimals in the form $\frac{a}{b}$ where **a** and **b** are integers.

(a) $0 \cdot 05\dot{3}$      (b) $0 \cdot 5\dot{1}\dot{2}$      (c) $1 \cdot 309\dot{4}$      (d) $0 \cdot 242424 \ldots$

## DISCUSSION EXERCISE 3:4

- What is the length of a diagonal of this rectangle?

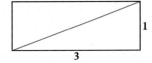

  What is the value of the ratio $\dfrac{\text{circumference}}{\text{diameter}}$ for this circle?

Can all irrational numbers be represented geometrically?  **Discuss.**

-

Victoria claimed that all irrational numbers can be represented by a point on the number line, as can all rational numbers. She supported this claim with a good argument.
What argument might Victoria have used?  **Discuss.**

### OPERATIONS with IRRATIONAL NUMBERS

Remember that squaring and square rooting are inverse operations. That is, one of these operations "undoes" the other. For instance, $(\sqrt{5})^2 = 5$ and $\sqrt{7^2} = 7$.

## INVESTIGATION 3:5

**Operations with Irrational Numbers**

**Investigate**  multiplying, dividing, adding and subtracting irrational numbers. As part of your investigation, make and test statements such as "the sum of any two irrational numbers is also an irrational number". You may wish to use the following.

Consider the irrational number $\sqrt{8}$ .
$\sqrt{8}$ may be rewritten as $\sqrt{2 \times 2 \times 2} = \sqrt{2} \times \sqrt{2} \times \sqrt{2}$
$$= (\sqrt{2})^2 \times \sqrt{2}$$
$$= 2\sqrt{2}$$

*continued . . .*

*. . . from previous page*

What happens if you multiply the irrational numbers $\sqrt{2}$ and $\sqrt{8}$?

What if $\sqrt{8}$ was divided by $\sqrt{2}$?

What if $\sqrt{8}$ was replaced by $\sqrt{6}$?

What if . . .

Consider the numbers $3 + \sqrt{5}$ and $2 - \sqrt{5}$. Are these two numbers irrational?

What happens if you add $3 + \sqrt{5}$ and $2 - \sqrt{5}$?

What if you subtracted $2 - \sqrt{5}$ from $3 + \sqrt{5}$?

What if the numbers were $5 + \sqrt{3}$ and $5 - \sqrt{2}$?

What if . . .

Make a summary of your discoveries in this investigation. In this summary include statements such as "the product of two irrational numbers may be rational". Give examples to support the statements you make.

## PROVING $\sqrt{2}$ is IRRATIONAL: proof by contradiction

In a **proof by contradiction,** we assume a statement is true then show that this statement *cannot* be true. An example is given in the following discussion exercise.

## DISCUSSION EXERCISE 3:6

- The following proof uses the fact that if $x^2$ is an even number, so also is x. Why is this so? Discuss.

- Discuss each step of the following proof by contradiction.
  Assume $\sqrt{2}$ is rational. That is, assume $\sqrt{2}$ may be written as $\frac{m}{n}$ where m and n are whole numbers with no common factor other than 1.

$$\text{If } \sqrt{2} = \frac{m}{n}$$
$$\text{then } 2 = \frac{m^2}{n^2} \text{ (squaring both sides)}$$
$$2n^2 = m^2 \text{ (multiplying both sides by } n^2\text{)}$$

Since $2n^2$ is divisible by 2, so also is $m^2$. That is, $m^2$ is an even number. Since $m^2$ is an even number so also is m. Then m may be replaced by a number 2p, where $p = \frac{1}{2}$ m.

$$2n^2 = (2p)^2 \text{ (replacing m by 2p)}$$
$$2n^2 = 4p^2 \text{ (expanding } (2p)^2\text{)}$$
$$n^2 = 2p^2 \text{ (dividing both sides by 2)}$$

Since $2p^2$ is divisible by 2, so also is $n^2$. That is, $n^2$ is an even number. Since $n^2$ is an even number, so also is n.

We have now shown that both m and n are even numbers. Since m and n are both even numbers, they both have a factor of 2. This contradicts the assumption that $\sqrt{2} = \frac{m}{n}$ where m and n are whole numbers with no common factor other than 1. Hence, the assumption is false. Hence $\sqrt{2}$ is not rational; that is, $\sqrt{2}$ is irrational.

- Prove by contradiction that $\sqrt{3}$ is irrational.

- Is $\sqrt{4}$ irrational? What happens if you attempt to prove, by contradiction, that $\sqrt{4}$ is irrational? Discuss.

## SIMPLIFYING SURDS

Irrational numbers such as $\sqrt{2}$, $1 - \sqrt{5}$, $\frac{3}{\sqrt{3}}$ which involve square roots are often called **surds**. Surds are written in their simplest form when there is no surd on the denominator and when the smallest possible whole number is under the $\sqrt{\phantom{x}}$ sign.

*Worked Example*  Simplify.  (a) $\frac{4}{\sqrt{5}}$   (b) $\frac{3}{\sqrt{3}}$   (c) $\sqrt{\frac{2}{5}}$   (d) $\frac{1+\sqrt{3}}{\sqrt{7}}$

*Answer*  (a) $\frac{4}{\sqrt{5}} = \frac{4}{\sqrt{5}} \times \frac{\sqrt{5}}{\sqrt{5}}$ (multiplying top and bottom by $\sqrt{5}$)

$\qquad = \frac{4\sqrt{5}}{(\sqrt{5})^2}$

$\qquad = \frac{4\sqrt{5}}{5}$

(b) $\frac{3}{\sqrt{3}} = \frac{3}{\sqrt{3}} \times \frac{\sqrt{3}}{\sqrt{3}}$ (multiplying top and bottom by $\sqrt{3}$)

$\qquad = \frac{3\sqrt{3}}{(\sqrt{3})^2}$

$\qquad = \frac{3\sqrt{3}}{3}$

$\qquad = \sqrt{3}$

(c) $\sqrt{\frac{2}{5}} = \frac{\sqrt{2}}{\sqrt{5}}$

$\qquad = \frac{\sqrt{2}}{\sqrt{5}} \times \frac{\sqrt{5}}{\sqrt{5}}$ (multiplying top and bottom by $\sqrt{5}$)

$\qquad = \frac{\sqrt{2} \times \sqrt{5}}{(\sqrt{5})^2}$

$\qquad = \frac{\sqrt{10}}{5}$

(d) $\frac{1+\sqrt{3}}{\sqrt{7}} = \frac{(1+\sqrt{3})}{\sqrt{7}} \times \frac{\sqrt{7}}{\sqrt{7}}$ (multiplying top and bottom by $\sqrt{7}$)

$\qquad = \frac{\sqrt{7}(1+\sqrt{3})}{(\sqrt{7})^2}$

$\qquad = \frac{\sqrt{7} + \sqrt{7} \times \sqrt{3}}{7}$

$\qquad = \frac{\sqrt{7}}{7} + \frac{\sqrt{21}}{7}$

*Worked Example*  Simplify.  (a) $\sqrt{32}$   (b) $\sqrt{8} \times \sqrt{24}$   (c) $\frac{3}{\sqrt{2}} + \sqrt{8}$   (d) $(2 + \sqrt{5})^2$   (e) $\sqrt{8} - \sqrt{18}$

*Answer*  (a) $\sqrt{32} = \sqrt{16 \times 2}$

$\qquad = \sqrt{16} \times \sqrt{2}$

$\qquad = \sqrt{4^2} \times \sqrt{2}$

$\qquad = 4\sqrt{2}$

(b) $\sqrt{8} \times \sqrt{24} = \sqrt{8 \times 24}$

$\qquad = \sqrt{8 \times 8 \times 3}$

$\qquad = \sqrt{8^2 \times 3}$

$\qquad = \sqrt{8^2} \times \sqrt{3}$

$\qquad = 8\sqrt{3}$

(c) $\frac{3}{\sqrt{2}} + \sqrt{8} = \frac{3}{\sqrt{2}} \times \frac{\sqrt{2}}{\sqrt{2}} + \sqrt{4 \times 2}$

$\qquad = \frac{3\sqrt{2}}{2} + \sqrt{4} \times \sqrt{2}$

$\qquad = \frac{3\sqrt{2}}{2} + 2\sqrt{2}$

$\qquad = \frac{3\sqrt{2} + 4\sqrt{2}}{2}$

$\qquad = \frac{7\sqrt{2}}{2}$

(d) $(2 + \sqrt{5})^2 = (2 + \sqrt{5})(2 + \sqrt{5})$

$\qquad = 4 + 4\sqrt{5} + (\sqrt{5})^2$

$\qquad = 4 + 4\sqrt{5} + 5$

$\qquad = 9 + 4\sqrt{5}$

(e) $\sqrt{8} - \sqrt{18} = \sqrt{4 \times 2} - \sqrt{9 \times 2}$

$\qquad = 2\sqrt{2} - 3\sqrt{2}$

$\qquad = -\sqrt{2}$

## EXERCISE 3:7

1. Simplify.    (a) $\frac{1}{\sqrt{2}}$    (b) $\frac{6}{\sqrt{3}}$    (c) $\frac{5}{\sqrt{5}}$    (d) $\sqrt{\frac{2}{3}}$    (e) $\frac{2-\sqrt{2}}{\sqrt{3}}$    (f) $\frac{\sqrt{3}+\sqrt{2}}{\sqrt{3}}$

2. Simplify.    (a) $\sqrt{18}$    (b) $\sqrt{12}$    (c) $\sqrt{75}$    (d) $\sqrt{72}$    (e) $3\sqrt{8}$    (f) $5\sqrt{27}$

3. Simplify.    (a) $\sqrt{3} \times \sqrt{12}$    (b) $\sqrt{3} \times \sqrt{27}$    (c) $\sqrt{5} \times \sqrt{8}$    (d) $\sqrt{24} \times \sqrt{32}$
        (e) $2\sqrt{3} \times 3\sqrt{2}$    (f) $4\sqrt{18} \times \sqrt{6}$    (g) $3\sqrt{5} \times 5\sqrt{75}$

4. Simplify.    (a) $3\sqrt{5} + 2\sqrt{5}$    (b) $5\sqrt{2} - 3\sqrt{2}$    (c) $2\sqrt{3} + \sqrt{12}$    (d) $\sqrt{2} - \sqrt{8}$
        (e) $\sqrt{27} + 5\sqrt{3}$    (f) $\sqrt{12} - 2\sqrt{3}$    (g) $\sqrt{32} - \sqrt{8}$

5. Expand and simplify.
   (a) $(3 + \sqrt{2})^2$    (b) $(1 - \sqrt{5})^2$    (c) $(\sqrt{2} + \sqrt{3})^2$    (d) $(\sqrt{3} - \sqrt{2})^2$
   (e) $(3 + \sqrt{2})(1 - \sqrt{2})$    (f) $(4 + \sqrt{3})(1 - \sqrt{2})$    (g) $(2 + \sqrt{2})(2 - \sqrt{2})$

6. Write these without a surd on the denominator. Simplify as much as possible.
   (a) $\frac{2}{\sqrt{3}} + 3\sqrt{3}$    (b) $5\sqrt{2} - \frac{3}{\sqrt{2}}$    (c) $\frac{\sqrt{3}}{2} + \frac{5}{\sqrt{3}}$    (d) $\sqrt{20} + \frac{2}{\sqrt{5}}$

**Review 1**   Simplify.    (a) $\sqrt{60}$    (b) $\sqrt{48}$    (c) $2\sqrt{45}$    (d) $\sqrt{15} \times \sqrt{6}$
     (e) $2\sqrt{5} \times 5\sqrt{2}$    (f) $3\sqrt{20} \times \sqrt{50}$    (g) $\sqrt{2} + \sqrt{18}$    (h) $\sqrt{50} - \sqrt{8}$

**Review 2**   Expand and simplify.    (a) $(\sqrt{3} + 5)^2$    (b) $(\sqrt{2} - \sqrt{5})^2$    (c) $(3 + \sqrt{5})(3 - \sqrt{5})$

**Review 3**   Simplify as much as possible.    (a) $\sqrt{3} + \frac{5}{\sqrt{3}}$    (b) $\sqrt{32} - \frac{3}{\sqrt{2}}$

## RESEARCH PROJECT 3:8

**Complex Numbers**

If we define $\sqrt{-1}$ as $i$, we are then able to say that every equation has a solution. For instance, the equation $x^2 = -4$ is solved as follows.

$$x^2 = -4$$
$$x = \pm\sqrt{-4} \text{ (taking the square root of both sides)}$$
$$= \pm\sqrt{4 \times -1}$$
$$= \pm(\sqrt{4} \times \sqrt{-1})$$
$$= \pm(2 \times i)$$
$$= \pm 2i \quad \text{That is, } x = 2i \text{ or } x = -2i.$$

Numbers such as $2i$ and $-2i$ are called "imaginary numbers".
Numbers such as $3 + 2i$, which are the sum of a real number (a real number is a number which can be plotted on a number line and is therefore either a rational or irrational number) and an imaginary number, are called "complex numbers".
Research this area of mathematics.

## CHAPTER 3 REVIEW

1. **(a)** Explain why $0.\dot{1}4285\dot{7}$ is a rational number.

$$\sqrt{1}\,,\ \sqrt{2}\,,\ \sqrt{3}\,,\ \sqrt{4}\,,\ \sqrt{5}\,,\ \sqrt{6}\,,\ \sqrt{7}\,,\ \sqrt{8}\,,\ \sqrt{9}\,,\ \sqrt{10}$$

   **(b)** Which of these square roots are rational numbers?                                   **ULEAC**

2. **(a)** Complete the following table, writing YES if true and NO if false. The first line has been completed for you.

|            | Rational | Irrational |
|------------|----------|------------|
| $\sqrt{2}$ | NO       | YES        |
| $\frac{7}{3}$ | ....  | ....       |
| $\pi$      | ....     | ....       |
| $4\sqrt{2}$ | ....    | ....       |

   **(b)** Write down an irrational number between 6 and 7.

   **(c)** $p$ is a non-zero rational number and $q$ is an irrational number.

      **(i)** Is $p \times q$ irrational or rational?

      **(ii)** Is $p + q$ irrational or rational?                               **SEG**

3. An irrational number is multiplied by another irrational number.

   **(a)** Write down an example to show that the answer could be a rational number.

   **(b)** Give an example of two different irrational numbers $a$ and $b$, where $\frac{a}{b}$ is a rational number.                                                                          **ULEAC**

4. **(a)** State for the following types of numbers whether they are **always rational, possibly rational** or **never rational**.

      **(i)** Finite decimal
        (one that ends).

      **(ii)** Infinite decimal
        (one that does not end).

      **(iii)** Square root of a
        whole number.

      **(iv)** Square of a
        rational number

   **(b)** For **one** of the types of numbers which you decided was **possibly rational**, give an example which is **rational**, and an example which is **not rational**.                    **SEG**

5.  Which of these expressions can be written as recurring decimals, and which can be written as non-recurring decimals?

$$\frac{2}{7}, \quad \pi, \quad \frac{1}{17}, \quad \sqrt{7}, \quad \frac{6}{47}.$$

**SEG**

6.  **(a)** Which of these numbers can be written as non-recurring decimals?

$$\tfrac{1}{7}, \quad \tfrac{1}{9}, \quad \sqrt{3}, \quad \tfrac{1}{2}, \quad \sqrt[3]{3}$$

**(b)** Write down two irrational numbers that multiply together to give a rational answer.

**(c)** Ali works out the answers to these expressions.
Write down whether the answer is rational or irrational in each case.

| | |
|---|---|
| $2+\sqrt{3}$ | |
| $2\sqrt{3}$ | |
| $(\sqrt{3})^2$ | |

**SEG**

7.  **(a)** Look at the following example which shows how to turn the recurring decimal 0·75757575. . . into a fraction.

$$x = 0·75757575\ldots$$

Step 1: Multiply by 100 $\quad 100x = 75·75757575\ldots$
Step 2: Subtract $x$ $\quad\quad 99x = 75$

Step 3: Solve the equation $\quad x = \dfrac{75}{99}$

$$x = \frac{25}{33}$$

Answer: $0·75757575\ldots = \dfrac{25}{33}$

Follow the same steps to change the recurring decimal 0·5151515151. . . into a fraction.

**(b)** Could the same method be used to change 0·123123123. . . into a fraction? Explain any amendments you would make at Steps 1, 2 or 3. **MEG**

8.  **(a)** Write down
**(i)** a rational number between $\sqrt{15}$ and $\sqrt{17}$,
**(ii)** an irrational number between 5 and 6.

**(b)** **(i)** Write down two rational numbers, each between 0 and 1, one equal to a recurring decimal and the other equal to a non-recurring decimal.
**(ii)** Show that the sum of your two numbers in (b)(i) is rational.

**(c)** Write down two irrational numbers whose product is rational. **MEG**

9. **(a)** Write down a rational number between 1·2 and 1·25.

   **(b)** Write down an irrational number between 1·2 and 1·25.                    **ULEAC**

10. **(a)** A Mathematics student attempted to define an "irrational number" as follows:
    "An irrational number is a number which, in its decimal form, goes on and on."

    **(i)** Give an example to show that this definition is not correct.
    **(ii)** What must be added to the definition to make it correct?

    **(b)** Which of the following numbers are rational and which irrational?

    $$\sqrt{4\tfrac{1}{4}}, \quad \sqrt{6\tfrac{1}{4}}, \quad \tfrac{1}{3} + \sqrt{3}, \quad (\tfrac{1}{3}\sqrt{3})^2$$

    Express each of the rational numbers in the form $\frac{p}{q}$ where $p$ and $q$ are integers.       **MEG**

11. Write the recurring decimal 0·353535. . . as a fraction in the form $\frac{x}{y}$, where $x$ and $y$ are integers.                                                                 **ULEAC**

12.

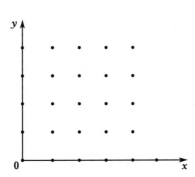

The diagram shows the first quadrant of the $xy$ plane.
The points in the plane which have integer coordinates are known as the "lattice points".

   **(a)** Write down the coordinates of 2 lattice points other than $(0, 0)$ through which the line with equation $y = \tfrac{4}{7}x$ passes.

   **(b)** Explain why the line with equation $y = \sqrt{2}x$ does not pass through any lattice points other than $(0, 0)$.

   **(c)** Hence, explain why the line with equation $y = \sqrt{2}x + K$, where $K$ is a positive integer, never passes through a lattice point other than $(0, K)$.                      **ULEAC**

13. **(a)** Write down an irrational number which lies between 4 and 5.

    **(b)** $N$ is a rational number which is not equal to zero.

    Show clearly why $\frac{1}{N}$ must also be rational.                          **NEAB**

**14.** $n$ is a positive integer such that $\sqrt{n} = 15\cdot4$ correct to 1 decimal place.

    **(a)** **(i)** Find a value of $n$.

        **(ii)** Explain why $\sqrt{n}$ is irrational.

    **(b)** Write down a number between 10 and 11 that has a rational square root.      **ULEAC**

**15.** The midpoints of the sides of a square of side 12cm are joined to form another square. The process is repeated so that a nest of five squares is formed.

Each square is labelled at one vertex only.
The area of square $B$ is half the area of square $A$.
The area of square $C$ is half the area of square $B$ and so on.

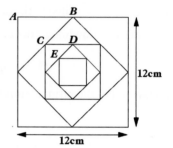

    **(i)** Calculate the perimeter of square $C$.

    **(ii)** Is the perimeter of square $D$ rational or irrational? Explain your answer.      **MEG**

**16.** When Colin was looking through a mathematics book, he read the following method for finding an approximate value for the square root of two.

> The nearest integer to $\sqrt{2}$ is 1
>
> so    $\sqrt{2} - 1 < \frac{1}{2}$          *Stage 1*
>
> Squaring both sides we get
>
> $(\sqrt{2} - 1)^2 < \left(\frac{1}{2}\right)^2$
>
> $3 - 2\sqrt{2} < \frac{1}{4}$          *Stage 2*
>
> Squaring both sides again we get
>
> $(3 - 2\sqrt{2})^2 < \left(\frac{1}{4}\right)^2$
>
> $17 - 12\sqrt{2} < \frac{1}{16}$        *Stage 3*
>
> so    $\sqrt{2} \approx \frac{17}{12}$          *Stage 4*

    **(a)** Explain each stage of the solution.

    **(b)** Use a similar method to show that an approximate value for $\sqrt{5}$ is $\frac{161}{72}$.

    **(c)** Write down Stage 1 for finding an approximate value for $\sqrt{3}$.      **NEAB**

17. (a) Write down a fraction equivalent to the recurring decimal $0.7\dot{7}$.
    (b) (i) Change $\frac{5}{6}$ into a decimal.
        (ii) Hence calculate a fraction equivalent to the recurring decimal $0.348\dot{3}$.          **SEG**

18. Simplify these.
    (a) $\sqrt{6} \times \sqrt{48}$          (b) $\frac{3}{\sqrt{2}}$          (c) $\sqrt{8} + \sqrt{2}$          (d) $(1 - \sqrt{6})^2$          (e) $\sqrt{18} - \frac{1}{\sqrt{2}}$

1. Megan and Samuel both timed Jayne's run. Samuel gave the time as 59 seconds; Megan gave it as 59·0 seconds. Explain the difference between these times.

2. Which of the following numbers are rational and which are irrational?

   For those that are rational write in the form $\frac{p}{q}$ where p and q are the smallest possible whole numbers.

   (a) $\frac{\pi}{5}$     (b) 0·38     (c) 2·4$\dot{5}$     (d) $\sqrt{3}$     (e) 0·$\dot{8}\dot{3}$     (f) $\sqrt{\frac{36}{16}}$     (g) 0·$\dot{5}$0$\dot{1}$

3. In order to improve the distance he could throw a cricketball, Jamie practised daily. Yesterday he measured his best throw as 83m, to the nearest metre.
   Find the greatest and least possible distances of this throw.

4. The volume of fruit juice in this can is given correct to 2 decimal places.
   Find the lower and upper bounds for the true volume of juice in this can.

5. $\frac{1}{11} = 0\cdot\dot{0}\dot{9}$. $\frac{1}{11}$ can be described as a rational number with a non-terminating decimal expansion; the recurring cycle is 2 digits long.
   Describe the following numbers in a similar way.

   (a) $\frac{2}{3}$     (b) $\frac{1}{6}$     (c) $\frac{7}{33}$     (d) $\frac{7}{8}$     (e) $\frac{83}{111}$     (f) $\frac{3}{7}$     (g) $\frac{3}{128}$

6. (a) The surface area of a sphere varies as the square of the diameter. A sphere of diameter 10cm has surface area of 314cm².
   Find the diameter of a sphere which has surface area of 212cm².
   (b) The volume of a sphere varies as the cube of the diameter. A sphere of diameter 10cm has a volume of 523·6cm³.
   Find the volume of a sphere with diameter of 5cm.

7. The deepest cave in England is the "Giant's Hole" in the Oxlow Caverns, Derbyshire. Its depth is 200m, correct to two significant figures. Which of the following gives the range of possible depths, d, for this cave?
   A. 199·5m ≤ d < 200·5m     B. 195m ≤ d < 205m     C. 150m ≤ d < 250m

8. If it is possible to do so, give an example of the following. If it is not possible, explain why not:
   (a) an irrational number with a non-terminating decimal expansion
   (b) an irrational number with a non-terminating decimal expansion which has a recurring cycle of 2 digits
   (c) an irrational number with a terminating decimal expansion.

9. The following masses are accurate to 2 significant figures. Write down, as an inequality, the range of possible values for the true masses.
   (a) m = 6·3kg          (b) m = 3800g          (c) m = 0·096t

10. The time for a journey varies inversely as the speed. If a journey takes 4 hours at a speed of 75km/h find
    (a) the time for this journey if the speed is 100km/h
    (b) the speed if the time for this journey is 5 hours.

11. (a) Garth claims that if the length and breadth of this rectangle are irrational numbers then so also is the area.
        Is Garth correct? Use examples or counter examples to support your answer.
    (b) Garth claims that if the length and breadth are irrational numbers then the perimeter may be either a rational or irrational number. He gave examples to support this claim. What examples might Garth have given?

12. The distances shown, taken from a roadmap, are given to the nearest kilometre.
    Using these distances, find the upper and lower bounds of the true distance by road from London to Edinburgh.

| From | To | Distance (km) |
|------|-----|---------------|
| London | Leeds | 328 |
| Leeds | Newcastle | 153 |
| Newcastle | Edinburgh | 169 |

13. The illumination from a source of light is inversely proportional to the square of the distance from the light.
    At a distance of 6m, the illumination from a particular source of light is 5 units.
    What is the illumination at a distance of 3m?

14. To the nearest foot, the height of the CN Tower in Toronto is 1815 feet.
    Using 1 foot = 0·30m, to 2 d.p., find the range (in metres) of the true height of this tower.

15. Jatinder knows that the floor area of a gym. is 150m², correct to 3 significant figures. This gym. is rectangular, with length 15m, correct to 2 significant figures.
    Jatinder calculates the greatest and least values for the width of the gym. What answers should she get?

16. Given that 4·8, 2·9 and 1·5 are given correct to 1 d.p., find the upper and lower bounds for the following calculations.

(a) $4·8^2$      (b) $4·8 - 2·9$      (c) $\dfrac{2·9}{4·8 + 1·5}$      (d) $\dfrac{2·9}{4·8 - 1·5}$

17.

| Shortest stopping distance – in metres and feet | | | | | | | |
|---|---|---|---|---|---|---|---|
| mph | Thinking distance | | Braking distance | | Overall stopping distance | | On a dry road, a good car with good brakes and tyres and an alert driver will stop in the distances shown. Remember these are shortest stopping distances. Stopping distances increase greatly with wet and slippery roads, poor brakes and tyres, and tired drivers. |
| 20 | 6 | 20 | 6 | 20 | 12 | 40 | |
| 30 | 9 | 30 | 14 | 45 | 23 | 75 | |
| 40 | 12 | 40 | 24 | 80 | 36 | 120 | |
| 50 | 15 | 50 | 38 | 125 | 53 | 175 | |
| 60 | 18 | 60 | 55 | 180 | 73 | 240 | |
| 70 | 21 | 70 | 75 | 245 | 96 | 315 | |

The table above is from the Highway Code.

(a) Which figures are in metres and which are in feet?

(b) Show that thinking distance, in metres, is proportional to speed.

(c) What thinking distance in metres, is needed if the speed is 100mph?

(d) Show that the braking distance, in feet, is proportional to the square of the speed.

(e) At what speed is the braking distance 100 feet?

18. (i) Simplify     (a) $\sqrt{96}$     (b) $\dfrac{4}{\sqrt{7}}$     (c) $\sqrt{7} \times 2\sqrt{3}$     (d) $5\sqrt{32} - 2\sqrt{8}$

(ii) Show that $(7 - \sqrt{5})^2 = 54 - 14\sqrt{5}$.

(iii) Show that $\dfrac{6}{\sqrt{2}} + \sqrt{32} = 7\sqrt{2}$.

19. Both the volume and height of this cylinder are given correct to 1 d.p.

(a) Use the formula $V = \pi r^2 h$ to find the set of possible values for the radius of this cylinder.

(b) Give the radius of the cylinder to as many significant figures as can be justified.

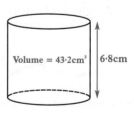

Volume = 43·2cm³    6·8cm

20. Zelma measured her handspan as 19·8cm, to the nearest mm. What is the greatest possible percentage error in Zelma's measurement? Give your answer to 2 d.p.

21. (a) The height of a tin can is recorded as 8cm to the nearest centimetre.

Let the actual height of the can be $h$ cm. Complete the inequality.

.......... $\le h <$ ..........

(b) The radius of a circular table is recorded as 1·6m to the nearest 0·1 metre.

Let the actual radius of the table be $r$ m. Complete the inequality.

.......... $\leq r <$ ..........                **ULEAC**

22. The Dome tent

    The tent is a half sphere.

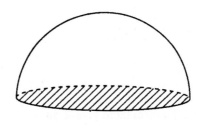

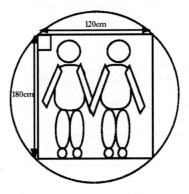

Two sleeping people need a rectangle of space 120cm wide and 180cm long.

The length of the diameter of the smallest possible tent satisfying this condition is $60\sqrt{13}$ cm.
(a) Explain why you cannot write down a decimal or fraction exactly equal to $60\sqrt{13}$.
(b) The diameter is 216cm, to the nearest centimetre.
    Using the correct inequality signs ($<$, $\leq$, $>$, $\geq$), write an expression for the range of lengths within which the diameter could lie.                **NEAB**

23. Which of the following are irrational numbers?

    $\sqrt{6}$        $\dfrac{4}{9}$        $0\cdot6$        $0\cdot\dot{4}$        $2\pi$                **ULEAC**

24. (a) The length of a post-card is 14·0cm. Between what limits does the length of this post-card lie?
    (b) The length of a steel rod is given as 14·00cm. Between what limits does the length of this steel rod lie?

(c) A recipe in a cookery book requires medium size eggs, which it says have 'mass 2 ounces/60 grams'.

Taking 16 ounces as equivalent to 454 grams and taking the '2 ounces' as exact, investigate whether the 60 grams is correct to the nearest 10 grams or correct to the nearest 5 grams.

**MEG**

25. The minimum height above sea level, $h$ metres, needed to see a ship varies as the square of the distance, $d$ kilometres, of the ship from the point of observation. When $d = 20, h = 32$.
   (a) (i) Find the formula connecting $h$ and $d$.
   (ii) Calculate $h$ when $d = 18$.
   (b) (i) Rearrange the formula to give $d$ in terms of $h$.
   (ii) Find $d$ when $h = 24$. Give the answer to the nearest kilometre.

**NICCEA**

26. Some rectangles have diagonals whose lengths are irrational.

For each of these rectangles, calculate the length of the diagonal and state whether this length is **rational** or **irrational.**

> Diagonal $= \sqrt{(a^2 + b^2)}$, where $a$ and $b$ are the lengths of the sides.

(Diagrams not to scale)

(a)

(b)

(c)

**SEG**

27. (a) 'Fitite Toys' make cubes of side 5·7cm, correct to 1 decimal place.
       Write down the range of possible values for the width of a cube.
   (b) Six of these cubes are placed side by side in a row. Calculate the range of possible values for the length of the row of six cubes.
   (c) Box A has a width of 34cm and box B has a width of 35cm, both measured to the nearest cm. Explain why you may not always be able to get the row of six cubes into box A along its width, but you should be able to get the row of six into box B.

**WJEC**

28. (a) What could be added to $3 - \sqrt{5}$ to give an answer which is a rational number?
   (b) What could be multiplied by $\sqrt{2}$ to give an answer which is a rational number? **ULEAC**

29. A child's paddling pool is in the shape of a cylinder.
Its height is **0·65m** and the radius is **2·16m**.

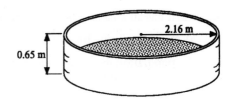

(a) The height and the radius have been measured to the **nearest centimetre.**
Complete this table to show the **lower** and **upper** bounds, in metres, for these
measurements.

|  | Lower bound | | Upper bound | |
|---|---|---|---|---|
| **Height** | | m | | m |
| **Radius** | | m | | m |

(b) Use the formula $V = \pi r^2 h$ to calculate the **lower** and **upper** bounds for the volume of the
paddling pool.

(c) The paddling pool is filled at a constant rate of 12 litres per minute to the **nearest litre.**
(There are 1000 litres in a cubic metre.)
   (i) What is the shortest possible time needed to fill the pool?
   (ii) What is the longest possible time needed to fill the pool?      **SEG**

30. Every rational number can be written as a fraction $\dfrac{a}{b}$ where $a$ and $b$ are integers.

$$\text{When} \quad x = 0 \cdot 020202020 \ldots \text{etc}$$
$$\text{then} \quad 100x = 2 \cdot 020202020 \ldots \text{etc}$$

(a) (i) Work out the value of $99x$.
   (ii) Write down $x$ as a fraction $\dfrac{a}{b}$ where $a$ and $b$ are integers.

If $y = 0 \cdot 123123123123 \ldots$ etc
(b) Find $y$ in the form $\dfrac{a}{b}$.      **ULEAC**

31. An airport baggage handler weighs each piece of luggage which he loads on to a particular
aeroplane, and records the weight correct to the nearest kilogram.
When he has loaded 233 pieces of luggage, he has recorded a total weight of 6896kg.
The maximum weight of baggage that is allowed to be loaded onto the plane is 7000kg.
(a) Could the baggage he has loaded weigh more than 7000kg? Explain your answer.

(b) Is it likely that the baggage he has loaded weighs more than 7000kg? Explain your
answer.      **MEG**

**32.** Brazil has an area of 8 500 000 km² correct to the nearest 100 000 km².

**(a)** Write down the limits between which the area of Brazil must lie.

The population density of a country is the average number of people per km² of the country. Brazil has a population of 144 million correct to the nearest million.

**(b)** Calculate the maximum and minimum values of the population density of Brazil.

ULEAC

**33.**

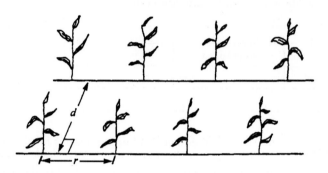

The diagram is taken from a book about growing maize.
The distance between the rows of plants is $d$ metres.
The spacing between the plants in the rows is $r$ metres.

The number, $P$, of plants per hectare, is given by the formula

$$P = \frac{10\,000}{dr}$$

$d = 0.8$ and $r = 0.45$.

**(a)** Calculate the value of $P$.
Give your answer correct to 2 significant figures.

The value of $d$ is inversely proportional to the value of $r$ and $d = 0.9$ when $r = 0.4$.
**(b) (i)** Calculate the value of $r$ when $d = 1.2$.
    **(ii)** Calculate the value of $r$ when $r = d$.

ULEAC

**34.** The power in an electrical component is given by the formula

$$P = \frac{V^2}{R}$$

where $P$ is the power in watts, $V$ the voltage in volts, and $R$ is the resistance in ohms.
$V$ and $R$ are measured experimentally and the formula is used to estimate the power.
**(a)** $V$ is measured as 2·4 volts, correct to 1 decimal place.
    Calculate the largest and smallest possible values of $V^2$.
**(b)** $R$ is measured as 1·25 ohms, correct to 2 decimal places.
    Use the formula to calculate the largest and smallest possible values of $P$.
    Give your answer correct to 2 decimal places.

SEG

**35.**

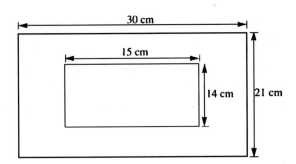

After measuring the length and width of a rectangular piece of card, Perveen draws and cuts out a smaller rectangle as shown in the diagram.
All the measurements are to the nearest cm.
Find
(i) the least possible area of card left,     (ii) the greatest possible area of card left.  **ULEAC**

**36. (a)** A square $ABCD$ of side 1 metre, contains a circle centre $O$, radius $r$.
A second circle centre $O$, radius $R$ passes through the four vertices of the square as shown.

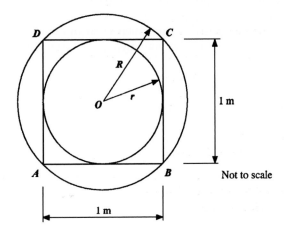

The length $AC = \sqrt{2}$ metres.
Write down answers to each of the following and say whether the true values are **rational** or **irrational.**
   (i)    The diameter of the circle radius $R$.
   (ii)   The diameter of the circle radius $r$.
   (iii)  The circumference of the circle radius $R$.
   (iv)  The area of the square $ABCD$.

  **(b)** b is a positive integer greater than 2. $\sqrt{2} \times \sqrt{b}$ is rational.
Write down a possible value for b.

  **(c)** Write the following recurring decimal as a fraction in its simplest form.

0·272727....................................................    **SEG**

**37.** The area of a rectangular field is 32 500m² and its length is 205m, both measurements being correct to three significant figures.
(a) Find
    **(i)**   the greatest possible breadth of the field, correct to one decimal place;
    **(ii)**  the smallest possible breadth of the field, correct to one decimal place.
(b) How many significant figures should be used in order to give a reliable answer for the breadth of the field?      **SEG**

**38.** In the equation

$$\frac{1}{f} = \frac{1}{u} + \frac{1}{v}$$

$u$ is the distance of an object from a lens, $v$ is the distance of the image from the lens and $f$ is the focal length of the lens.
(a) Calculate the focal length, $f$, when
    **(i)**  $u = 3$cm and $v = 6$cm,
    **(ii)**  $u = 2\cdot5$cm and $v = -3$cm.
(b) The distances $u$ and $v$ are measured to the nearest mm as $u = 4\cdot0$cm, $v = 3\cdot2$cm.
    **(i)**   Calculate the maximum possible value of $f$, giving your answer in cm to 3 decimal places.
    **(ii)**  Calculate the minimum possible value of $f$, giving your answer in cm to 3 decimal places.
    **(iii)** Calculate the greatest possible percentage error in the value of $f$ when using $u = 4\cdot0$cm and $v = 3\cdot2$cm. Give your answer to 2 decimal places.    **SEG**

# ALGEBRA

# Algebra Revision

### Prime Numbers, Factors, Multiples, Squares, Cubes, Square and Cube Roots

A prime number is divisible by just two numbers, itself and 1.

The multiples of a number are found by multiplying the number by each of 1, 2, 3, ... For instance, the multiples of 10 are 10, 20, 30, ...

A factor of a given number is a whole number that divides exactly into the given number. For instance, the factors of 10 are 1, 2, 5, 10.

A prime factor is a factor that is a prime number. For instance, the prime factors of 10 are 2 and 5.

The square numbers are $1^2, 2^2, 3^2, 4^2, \ldots$ i.e. 1, 4, 9, 16, ...

The cube numbers are $1^3, 2^3, 3^3, 4^3, \ldots$ i.e. 1, 8, 27, 64, ...

Squaring and square rooting are inverse operations, as are cubing and cube rooting. One of these operations "undoes" the other.

There are two square roots of 64, both 8 and −8. The symbol $\sqrt{\phantom{x}}$ means the positive square root, so $\sqrt{64} = 8$.

The symbol $\sqrt[3]{\phantom{x}}$ means the cube root. For instance $\sqrt[3]{64} = 4$.

### Powers. Indices.

$3^4$ is called a power of 3; 4 is called the index, 3 is called the base.

Indices is the plural of index. For instance, if we were speaking of the numbers 4 and 7 in $3^4$ and $2^7$ we would call 4 and 7 the indices.

The $x^y$ key, on the calculator, may be used to find powers.

For instance, $2^7$ is found by keying $\boxed{2}\ \boxed{\text{SHIFT}}\ \boxed{x^y}\ \boxed{7}\ \boxed{=}$

Some of the laws of indices are:
$$a^m \times a^n = a^{m+n}$$
$$\frac{a^m}{a^n} = a^{m-n}$$
$$(a^m)^n = a^{mn}$$

For instance,

$$3^4 \times 3^5 = 3^{4+5} \qquad \frac{2^9}{2^4} = 2^{9-4} \qquad (5^2)^3 = 5^{2 \times 3}$$
$$= 3^9 \qquad\qquad\qquad = 2^5 \qquad\qquad\qquad = 5^6$$

### Sequences

A sequence is a list of numbers such as 3, 7, 11, 15, ...

$t_1$ means the first term, $t_2$ means the second term and so on. For instance, for the sequence 3, 7, 11, 15, ... $t_1 = 3$, $t_2 = 7$, $t_3 = 11$ etc.

$t_n$ means the $n$th term. For instance, for the sequence 3, 7, 11, 15, ... $t_n = 4n - 1$.

Sometimes a letter other than $t$ is used. For instance $T_1$, $a_1$, $u_1$, all mean the first term.

*continued ...*

. . . *from previous page*

Sequences are sometimes based on the following special numbers – odd numbers, even numbers, squares, cubes, multiples.

The terms of a sequence are sometimes found by adding the same number to each previous term or by multiplying each previous term by the same number.

Sometimes we can continue a sequence by using the difference method. For instance, the next term in the sequence 12, 14, 22, 36, 56, . . . can be found as follows.

$$
\begin{array}{ccccccc}
12 & & 14 & & 22 & & 36 & & 56 & & 82 \\
& 2 & & 8 & & 14 & & 20 & & 26 & & \dots \text{line 1} \\
& & 6 & & 6 & & 6 & & 6 & & & \dots \text{line 2}
\end{array}
$$

The numbers on line 1 are the first differences, those on line 2 are the second differences.

3, 7, 11, 15, . . . and 5, 2, –1, –4, . . . are examples of sequences which have linear rules. The difference between any two consecutive terms is the same.
If we listed the differences as above, the numbers in the first row of differences would all be the same.

We can find the linear rule for a sequence such as 3, 7, 11, 15, . . . as follows. The difference between any two consecutive terms is 4.

The rule is $\quad t_n = 4n + a$
$\qquad\qquad t_1 = 4 \times 1 + a$ (replacing n with 1)
$\qquad\qquad\; 3 = 4 + a$ (since $t_1 = 3$)
$\qquad\qquad -1 = a$ (subtracting 4 from both sides)

The rule for the sequence 3, 7, 11, 15, . . . is then $t_n = 4n - 1$.

2, 5, 10, 17, . . . and 3, 10, 21, 36 are examples of sequences which have quadratic rules. If we listed the differences, the numbers in the second row of differences would all be the same.
We can find the quadratic rule for a sequence such as 3, 10, 21, 36, . . . as follows. Let the rule be $t_n = an^2 + bn + c$.

$$
\begin{array}{ccccc}
(a + b + c = 3) & \longleftarrow & 3 & 10 & 21 & 36 \\
\quad (3a + b = 7) & \longleftarrow & & 7 & 11 & 15 \\
\qquad (2a = 4) & \longleftarrow & & & 4 & 4
\end{array}
$$

| | | |
|---|---|---|
| $2a = 4$ | $3a + b = 7$ | $a + b + c = 3$ |
| $a = 2$ | $3 \times 2 + b = 7$ | $2 + 1 + c = 3$ |
| | $6 + b = 7$ | $3 + c = 3$ |
| | $b = 1$ | $c = 0$ |

The rule for the sequence 3, 10, 21, 36, . . . is then $t_n = 2n^2 + n$.

## Expressions, Formulae, Equations

$x + 3$ is an expression.
$p = x + 3$ is a formula. The value of $p$ depends on the value of $x$.
$2p - 4 = 1$ is an equation. Here $p$ can have only one value; $p = 2{\cdot}5$.

*continued* . . .

... *from previous page*

The expression $5a + 3b - 6a + b$ can be simplified to $4b - a$.

The expression $x - y$ may be written as $-(y - x)$.

To **expand,** we write without brackets. For instance, $3(2x - 4)$ is expanded to $6x - 12$; $(x - 2)(2x + 3)$ is expanded to $2x^2 - 4x + 3x - 6$ and simplified to $2x^2 - x - 6$.

To **factorise,** we write with brackets. For instance $6x - 15$ is factorised to $3(2x - 5)$.

A rectangle may be used to help expand. For instance, to expand $(x - 2)(2x + 3)$ we may use this rectangle to get $2x^2 - x - 6$.

|  | $2x$ | $+3$ |
|---|---|---|
| $x$ | $2x^2$ | $+3x$ |
| $-2$ | $-4x$ | $-6$ |

Three methods of **solving equations** are: trial and improvement, flowchart method, balance method. The **trial and improvement** method is particularly useful for solving polynomial equations; that is, equations which involve a square such as $x^2$ or a cube such as $x^3$.

The **flowchart method** for solving $2a - 4 = 1$ is shown below.

$$\text{Begin with a} \longrightarrow \boxed{\times 2} \longrightarrow 2a \longrightarrow \boxed{-4} \longrightarrow 2a - 4$$

$$2 \cdot 5 \longleftarrow \boxed{\div 2} \longleftarrow 5 \longleftarrow \boxed{+4} \longleftarrow \text{Begin with 1}$$

Hence $a = 2 \cdot 5$.

The **balance method** for solving $2a - 4 = 1$ is shown below.

$$2a - 4 = 1$$
$$2a = 5 \quad \text{(adding 4 to both sides)}$$
$$a = 2 \cdot 5 \quad \text{(dividing both sides by 2)}$$

The "**trial and improvement**" method for finding the solution (to 1 d.p.) for the equation $2x^3 - 1 = 9$ is shown below.

Try $x = 1$. If $x = 1$, $2x^3 - 1 = 1$ which is less than 9.

Try $x = 2$. If $x = 2$, $2x^3 - 1 = 15$ which is greater than 9.

Since 9 lies between 1 and 15, then the solution must be between 1 and 2.

Try $x = 1 \cdot 5$. If $x = 1 \cdot 5$, $2x^3 - 1 = 5 \cdot 75$ which is less than 9.

Try $x = 1 \cdot 8$. If $x = 1 \cdot 8$, $2x^3 - 1 = 10 \cdot 664$ which is greater than 9.

Try $x = 1 \cdot 7$. If $x = 1 \cdot 7$, $2x^3 - 1 = 8 \cdot 826$ which is less than 9.

The solution lies between $1 \cdot 7$ and $1 \cdot 8$. Since $8 \cdot 826$ is closer to 9 than is $10 \cdot 664$, the solution to 1 d.p. is $x = 1 \cdot 7$.

Written as $T = 2\pi \sqrt{\frac{l}{g}}$, T is said to be the **subject of the formula** since T is written, on its own, on the left-hand side.

When we rearrange a formula, such as $T = 2\pi \sqrt{\frac{l}{g}}$, so that a variable other than T is the subject, we have **transformed the formula**.

Both the balance and flowchart methods may be used to transform a formula.

For instance, to make $l$ the subject of $T = 2\pi \sqrt{\frac{l}{g}}$ the balance method may be used as shown on the next page.

*continued ...*

. . . *from previous page*

$$T = 2\pi \sqrt{\frac{l}{g}}$$

$$\frac{T}{2\pi} = \sqrt{\frac{l}{g}} \quad \text{(dividing both sides by } 2\pi)$$

$$\frac{T^2}{4\pi^2} = \frac{l}{g} \quad \text{(squaring both sides)}$$

$$\frac{gT^2}{4\pi^2} = l \quad \text{(multiplying both sides by g)}$$

That is, $l = \frac{gT^2}{4\pi^2}$.

## Reciprocals

The reciprocal of $\frac{a}{b}$ is $\frac{b}{a}$.

For instance, the reciprocal of $\frac{2}{7}$ is $\frac{7}{2}$; the reciprocal of 5 is $\frac{1}{5}$.

The $\frac{1}{x}$ key on the calculator is used to find the reciprocal of a number.

For instance, the reciprocal of 4 is found by keying $\boxed{4}$ $\boxed{\text{SHIFT}}$ $\boxed{\frac{1}{x}}$.

The operation "take the reciprocal" is needed to solve some equations by the flowchart method.
This operation is necessary if $x$ is on the bottom line of the equation.
Remember that the inverse operation for "taking the reciprocal" is also "taking the reciprocal".
For instance, $\frac{3}{x} = 5$ is solved, using the flowchart method, as follows:

Begin with x ⟶ | Take the reciprocal | ⟶ $\frac{1}{x}$ ⟶ $\boxed{\times 3}$ ⟶ $\frac{3}{x}$

$\frac{3}{5}$ ⟵ | Take the reciprocal | ⟵ $\frac{5}{3}$ ⟵ $\boxed{\div 3}$ ⟵ Begin with 5

The solution is $x = \frac{3}{5}$ or $0\cdot6$.

## Quadratic Expressions and Equations

$n^2 - 5n - 36$ may be factorised by finding the two numbers which add to $-5$ and multiply to $-36$. These are $-9$ and $4$. Hence $n^2 - 5n - 36 = (n - 9)(n + 4)$.

The quadratic equation $x^2 + 6x - 16 = 0$ may be solved by factorising then using the fact that if two expressions multiply to zero, then one of the expressions must be zero.

$$x^2 + 6x - 16 = 0$$
$$(x + 8)(x - 2) = 0$$

Either $x + 8 = 0$     or     $x - 2 = 0$
$x = -8$                    $x = 2$

*continued . . .*

*. . . from previous page*

## Graphs

$$\text{Gradient of a line} = \frac{\text{Vertical distance between 2 points on the line}}{\text{Horizontal distance between these points}}$$

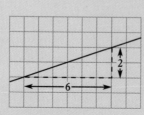

Gradient $= \frac{2}{6}$

$\qquad\qquad = \frac{1}{3}$

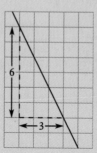

Gradient $= -\frac{6}{3}$

$\qquad\qquad = -2$

The graph of a line may be drawn by plotting points.
For instance, three points on the line $2y = 3x - 1$ are $(-1, -2)$ $(1, 1)$ $(3, 4)$. The line drawn through these points is the line $2y = 3x - 1$.
The graph of a line may also be drawn by using $y = mx + c$. When the line equation is written in this way, $m$ gives the gradient, $c$ gives the point where the line crosses the y-axis.

For instance, $2y = 3x - 1$ may be written as $y = \frac{3}{2}x - \frac{1}{2}$.

Then, gradient $= \frac{3}{2}$ and graph crosses y-axis at $-\frac{1}{2}$.

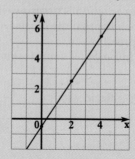

The graph of a curve may be drawn by plotting many points and joining these with a smooth curve. A summary of graphs of some special functions follows.

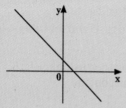
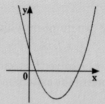
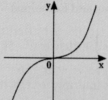

A straight line has an equation such as $y = 2 - x$ in which the highest power of $x$ is $x^1$.

A parabola has an equation such as $y = x^2 - 5x + 4$ in which the highest power of $x$ is $x^2$.

Cubic functions have equations such as $y = x^3$ or $y = 3 - 2x + 3x^2 - x^3$ in which the highest power of $x$ is $x^3$.

*continued . . .*

. . . *from previous page*

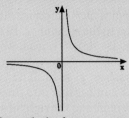

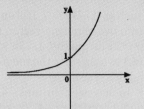

A **hyperbola** has an equation such as $y = \frac{2}{x}$ in which x is on the denominator.

An **exponential function** has an equation such as $y = 2^x$ in which x is an index.

On a **distance/time graph,** distance is on the vertical axis, time is on the horizontal axis.
The slope of the graph gives the **speed.**
The steeper the slope of the graph, the greater the speed.

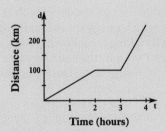

## Function Notation

f(x) means "a function of x". That is, an expression in which the variable is x.
f(3) means "the value of the function when x is replaced by 3."
For instance, if $f(x) = x^2 - 5$ then $f(3) = 3^2 - 5$
$$= 4$$

## Inequalities

**Inequalities** such as $n \leq -2$, $n > 1$, $2 \leq n < 5$ may be graphed on a number line. To display an inequality on the number line proceed as follows.

*Step 1*　Draw a line over all the values included.

*Step 2*　If the end point of the line is one of the values included, place the symbol ● on this end point; if the end point is not one of the values included, place the symbol ○ on this end point.

For instance,

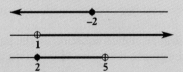

is the graph of $n \leq -2$

is the graph of $n > 1$

is the graph of $2 \leq n < 5$

The "balance method" for solving an equation may also be used to **solve an inequality.** When we use this method we must remember to change the sign of the inequality if we multiply or divide by a negative number.

*Examples*　1.　$\frac{n-2}{5} < 3$

　　　　　　　　$n - 2 < 15$　(multiplying both sides by 5)

　　　　　　　　　$n < 17$　(adding 2 to both sides)

　　　　　2.　$1 - 3n \geq 7$

　　　　　　　　$-3n \geq 6$　(subtracting 1 from both sides)

　　　　　　　　　$n \leq -2$　(dividing both sides by −3)

*continued* . . .

. . . *from previous page*

An equation such as $1 - 3n = 7$ has one solution; $n = -2$. The point $n = -2$ divides the number line into two regions, a region to the left of $-2$ and a region to the right of $-2$. In one of these regions the inequality $1 - 3n < 7$ is true and in the other $1 - 3n > 7$ is true. We may use this fact to help solve the inequality $1 - 3n \geq 7$.

We may extend this reasoning to **solve a quadratic inequality** such as $x^2 \geq 16$. The equation $x^2 = 16$ has two solutions $-4$ and $4$; $-4$ and $4$ divide the number line into three regions, a region to the left of $-4$, a region between $-4$ and $4$ and a region to the right of $4$. For numbers less than $-4$ the inequality $x^2 \geq 16$ is true, for numbers between $-4$ and $4$ the inequality is false, for numbers greater than $4$ the inequality is true. Hence the solutions for $x^2 \geq 16$ are $x \leq -4$ and $x \geq 4$.

**Inequalities in 2 variables,** such as $x + 2y < 2$, have many solutions. All the values of $x$ and $y$ which satisfy the inequality may be found by drawing the graph. The graph may be drawn by taking the following steps.

*Step 1*  Draw the boundary line $x + 2y = 2$. This line is dotted since the inequality sign is $<$. (Dotted boundary line if sign is $<$ or $>$; solid boundary line if sign is $\leq$ or $\geq$.)

*Step 2*  Test the coordinates of any point (other than a point on the boundary line) in the inequality $x + 2y < 2$. If the inequality is true for these values of $x$ and $y$ the point is in the region to be shaded.

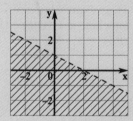

**Simultaneous Equations**

Equations such as $\begin{cases} 3x - 4y = 23 \\ 4x + 3y = 14 \end{cases}$, which need to be solved together to find the value of $x$ and $y$, are called **simultaneous equations**.

Some methods of solving these are: **trial and improvement, balance method** (also called the **elimination** method), **substitution method, graphical method.**

In the graphical method, we draw the graphs of each equation on the same set of axes. The x and y-coordinates of the point where the graphs meet give the solution of the simultaneous equations.

The balance method depends on eliminating one of the unknowns.

$$\left. \begin{array}{l} 3x - 4y = 23 \\ 4x + 3y = 14 \end{array} \right\} \quad \text{becomes} \quad \begin{cases} 9x - 12y = 69 & \text{(multiplying both sides by 3)} \\ 16x + 12y = 56 & \text{(multiplying both sides by 4)} \end{cases}$$

$$25x \qquad = 125 \quad \text{(adding the equations)}$$
$$x = 5 \quad \text{(dividing both sides by 25)}$$

When $x = 5$, $4x + 3y = 14$ becomes $20 + 3y = 14$

$$3y = -6 \quad \text{(subtracting 20 from both sides)}$$
$$y = -2 \quad \text{(dividing both sides by 3)}$$

Always check the solution by substituting the value of the unknowns into the original equations.

*continued . . .*

*. . . from previous page*

**Problem Solving**

Three methods of problem solving are: finding a pattern, solving a simpler problem first, using equations. We take the following steps to solve a problem using equations.

*Step 1*   Choose a variable such as n or x for the unknown quantity.
*Step 2*   Rewrite the statements in mathematical symbols.
*Step 3*   Combine these statements into an equation.
*Step 4*   Solve the equation.
*Step 5*   Check the answer with the information in the problem.

## REVISION EXERCISE

1.

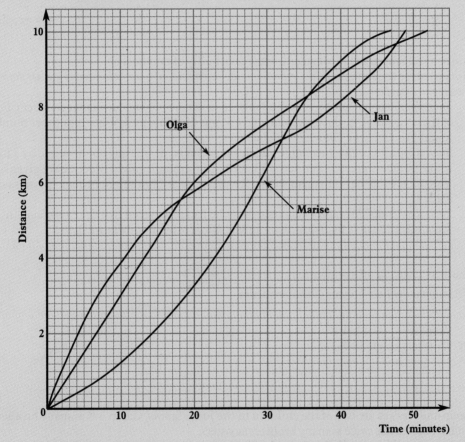

Three of the women competitors in one of the walking events in the European Championship are Olga, Marise and Jan. This graph represents the progress of these women in this event.
(a)  What distance was this event?
(b)  In what order did these three women finish?
(c)  To the nearest minute, how much faster was the fastest of these women than the slowest?
(d)  At what time did Olga overtake Jan?
(e)  How far ahead of Marise was Jan after 20 minutes?
(f)  How long did Olga take for the first half of the distance?
(g)  How far did Marise still have to go after 25 minutes?
(h)  Comment on any similarities or differences in the progress of these women in this event.

2. Match the graphs with the equations.

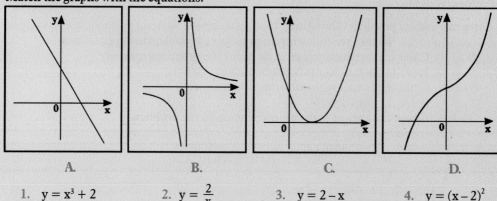

    A.                B.                C.                D.

1. $y = x^3 + 2$      2. $y = \dfrac{2}{x}$      3. $y = 2 - x$      4. $y = (x - 2)^2$

3. Minami and Steven were investigating the divisibility of numbers.
   Minami made the statement *"the expression $n^3 - n$, where $n$ is a whole number greater than zero, always gives numbers divisible by 3"*.
   (a) To support her statement, Minami replaced $n$ by 2, 5, 10 and four other numbers. For each of these values of $n$, the expression $n^3 - n$ was divisible by 3. What four other numbers might Minami have chosen?
   (b) Steven found a counter-example which showed that $n^3 - n$ was not divisible by 3 for all whole numbers greater than zero. What counter-example might Steven have given?
   (c) Minami rewrote her statement so that it was now true. How might Minami's statement now read?
   (d) Steven extended Minami's statement after he had discovered that the expression $n^3 - n$ was always divisible by two other numbers. What other numbers are these?

4. The $n$th term, $t_n$, of a sequence is given by $t_n = \dfrac{n+2}{n}$.
   Write down the first 7 terms of this sequence.

5. (i) Simplify    (a) $(2a^2b)^3$          (b) $4xy - yx$          (c) $3n - 2(1 - n)$.
   (ii) Write as a single power of 3.

   (a) $\dfrac{3^5 \times 3^4}{3^7}$          (b) $27^{-2}$          (c) $\dfrac{(3^x)^5}{9^x}$

6. Gavin and Andrea are two of the children in the Jones family. Gavin has as many brothers as sisters; Andrea has twice as many brothers as sisters.
   How many children are in this Jones family?

7. (i) Solve these equations.
   (a) $2(4 + 2x) = 13$          (b) $2a - 7 = -4$          (c) $\dfrac{3x}{-2} = 6$

   (d) $5 - 2n = n + 3$          (e) $\dfrac{9}{n} = 1\cdot5$

   (ii) Solve the inequality $15 - 2x < 1$.
   (iii) For what whole number values of $n$ is $-12 < 3n \le 6$?
   (iv) Solve the quadratic inequality $n^2 > 9$.

8. At the gym. Laura began a new training programme. Daily workout with weights and daily exercycle use were part of this programme.

   On the first day Laura was to pedal the exercycle for 8km; each day after this she was to pedal for 2km more than the day before, up to a maximum of 50 kilometres a day.

   (i) (a) How far did Laura pedal on the 5th day?

   (b) Write down, in terms of n, an expression for the distance Laura pedalled on the $n$th day during the time Laura was still increasing her "mileage".

   (c) Use your expression to find the distance pedalled on the 12th day.

   (d) Write down an equation, involving n, that could be solved to find the number of days it takes Laura to reach the maximum distance of 50km per day.
   Find this number of days.

   (ii) (a) The sequence $8, 18, 30, 44, \ldots$ gives the *total* distance Laura has pedalled after n days. Use the difference method to find the next three terms of this sequence.

   (b) What total distance does Laura pedal during the first week?

   (c) One of the following expressions gives the total distance travelled after n days. Which expression does this? Explain your choice by referring to the difference method.

   $$n + 7 \qquad n^2 + 7n \qquad n^3 + 7 \qquad n^3 + 2n + 5$$

   (d) Use the expression for the total distance to find the distance travelled during the first three weeks.

9. (i) Rearrange these line equations into the form $y = mx + c$.
   (a) $2y = x - 4$ (b) $4x + 5y - 10 = 0$ (c) $x - 2y = 0$

   (ii) A used deodorant spray can contained some deodorant in the form of a gas. Lisa measured the pressure in the can when she raised the temperature from 20°C to 160°C. She plotted the scatter diagram, then drew the line of best fit.

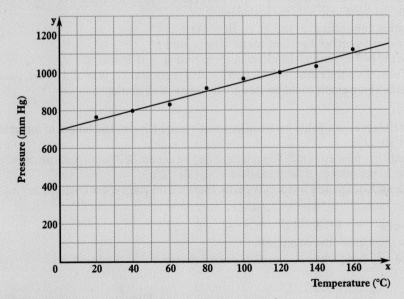

   (a) Where does this line of best fit cross the y-axis?
   (b) What is the gradient of this line?
   (c) Find the equation of this line.
   (d) If Lisa had thrown the can in a fire, raising the temperature to 500°C, the can would have exploded. Calculate the expected pressure in the can at 500°C.

10. Alkanes are molecules containing carbon atoms (C) and hydrogen atoms (H).

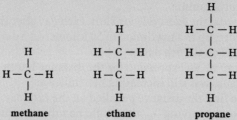

methane          ethane          propane

(a) Draw a diagram to show the structure of pentane, an alkane with five carbon atoms.

(b) The chemical formula for ethane is $C_2H_6$. Write down the chemical formula for an alkane molecule which has n carbon atoms.

(c) Explain why it is not possible to find an alkane molecule with an odd number of hydrogen atoms.

11. **Do not use graph paper for this question.**

(a) Sketch the line $2x - y = 2$, showing where it meets the x and y-axes.

(b) Find the coordinates of one point on the graph $y = \frac{1}{3}x^2$. Hence sketch this graph.

12. **(i)** Expand. Simplify if possible.
  (a) $3(1-a) - 2a(a+4)$     (b) $(x-5)(2x+3)$     (c) $(3p-q)(3p+q)$
  **(ii)** Factorise   (a) $6p + 18$     (b) $3x^2 - 4x$     (c) $a^2c + abc$.

13. The marks on a mathematics exam. ranged from 44 to 82. These marks are to be scaled so the lowest mark is 20 and the highest mark is 96. The scaling formula used is $y = ax + b$ where x is the original mark and y is the scaled mark.
One equation connecting a and b is $20 = 44a + b$.

(a) Write down another equation connecting a and b.

(b) Solve the two equations simultaneously to find a and b.

(c) Joan's mark on the exam. was 72. Ben's scaled mark was 77. Who did better, Joan or Ben?

(d) Explain how a graph could be used to find the scaled marks.

14. An approximate relationship between an adult's height, h cm, and length of forearm, f cm, is $f = \frac{1}{10}(3h - 256)$.

(a) William is 1·62 metres tall. What length do you expect William's forearm to be?

(b) Make h the subject of the formula $f = \frac{1}{10}(3h - 256)$.

(c) The length of Diane's forearm is 26cm. How tall do you expect Diane to be?

15. **(i)** Factorise.   (a) $x^2 - x - 12$     (b) $x^2 - 7x + 12$
  **(ii)** Solve these quadratic equations.
  (a) $(n-2)(n+3) = 0$     (b) $a^2 + 7a + 6 = 0$     (c) $x^2 - x = 12$

16. This graph shows the speed of a chainsaw blade during the felling of a tree. Describe what is happening.

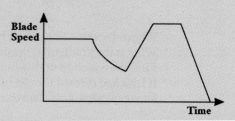

17. (a) A region  A  is defined by the inequalities  $x \geq 2$,  $y \geq 0$,  $y > 4 - x$. On a grid, shade and clearly label the region  A.

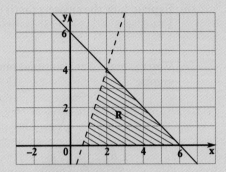

   (b) The region  R  is defined by three inequalities, one of which is  $y \leq 6 - x$.
   Write down the other two inequalities.

18. A room is 2 metres longer than it is wide.

   (i) If the length of the room is  n  metres write expressions, in terms of  n  for
   (a) the width of the room
   (b) the area of the room.

   (ii) Show that, if the area is $30m^2$ then  $n^2 - 2n = 30$.

   (iii) Using "trial and improvement", Alison found that a solution to  $n^2 - 2n = 30$  was between 6 and 7. Explain how Alison may have come to this conclusion.

   (iv) Copy and complete this table of values.

| n | 6·0 | 6·1 | 6·2 | 6·3 | 6·4 | 6·5 | 6·6 | 6·7 | 6·8 | 6·9 |
|---|-----|-----|-----|-----|-----|-----|-----|-----|-----|-----|
| $n^2 - 2n$ | 24 | 25·01 | | | | | | | | |

   Use this table of values to find a solution to  $n^2 - 2n = 30$, correct to 1 d.p.

   (v) Find the length of the room, to the nearest centimetre.

19.

|  |  |  |  |  |  |  |  | Sum | Average |
|---|---|---|---|---|---|---|---|-----|---------|
| Row 1 | | | | 1 | | | | 1 | 1 |
| Row 2 | | | 2 | 3 | 4 | | | 9 | 3 |
| Row 3 | | 5 | 6 | 7 | 8 | 9 | | 35 | 7 |
| Row 4 | 10 | 11 | 12 | 13 | 14 | 15 | 16 | 91 | 13 |

   (a) Write down the numbers on the next row of this pattern.
   (b) Write a formula connecting the row,  r,  and the number,  n,  of numbers on that row. Test your formula on the pattern given.
   (c) Use your formula to find the number of numbers on the 20th row.
   (d) On which row are there 21 numbers?
   (e) What is the average of the numbers on the 5th row?
   (f) *Without* writing down the numbers on the 6th row, find the average of these numbers. Explain your reasoning. Hence find the sum of the numbers on the 6th row.

20. Solve these simultaneous equations.
   (a)  $x - 3y = 5$      (b)  $4a + 3b = 5$
        $5x + y = 1$            $3a + 2b = 4$

21. **(i)** Find the remainder when these are divided by 7.
    (a) $1^3$  (b) $1^3 + 2^3$  (c) $1^3 + 2^3 + 3^3$  (d) $1^3 + 2^3 + 3^3 + 4^3$

    **(ii)** Explain how the answers for **(i)** can be used to help find the remainder when
    $1^3 + 2^3 + 3^3 + \ldots + 123^3$ is divided by 7.

22. **(a)** Water is poured at a constant rate into the containers. Match the containers with the graphs.

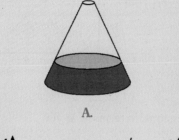

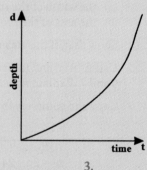

A.   B.   C.

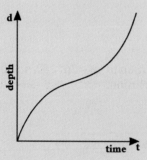

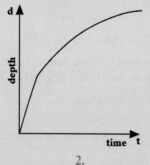

1.   2.   3.

**(b)** Sketch the shape of a container which matches this graph.

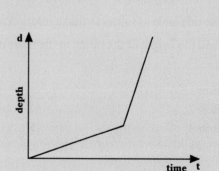

23. Write the rule for the sequence $2, 6, 12, 20, \ldots$ as $t_n = \ldots$

24. A rectangle is 2cm longer than it is wide. The area of the rectangle is 80cm².
    (a) Write a quadratic equation for $x$, the width.
    (b) Solve this equation.
    (c) Find the perimeter of the rectangle.

25. (a) Draw the graphs of $y = (x + 1)^2$ and $y = 1 - x$ for values of $x$ between $-4$ and $2$.
    (b) For what values of $x$ is $1 - x$ greater than or equal to $(x + 1)^2$?

26. A quiz consists of 10 questions. Fifty points are given for each correct answer, twenty points are deducted for each incorrect answer. Audrey has answered all questions and scored 290 points. The number of points gained by answering $x$ questions correctly is given by the expression 50x. Write and solve an equation to find the number of questions correctly answered by Audrey.

27. (a) Lucy made the statement "the expression $6n + 5$ gives prime numbers". Lucy gave three examples to support her statement. What might these have been?

   (b) Brian found a value of $n$ for which $6n + 5$ did not give a prime number. What value of $n$ might this have been?

   (c)  2    3    5    7    11    13    17    19    23    29    31    37    41    43    47

   This list gives all the prime numbers less than 50. With the exception of two of these, there is a relationship between the prime numbers and the multiples of 6.

   Explain this relationship. What are the two exceptions? Is this relationship true for the prime numbers less than 100?

   (d) Gillian wrote this number puzzle:      I think of a prime number.
   I multiply it by 5.
   I subtract 20.
   I divide by 2.
   The answer is greater than the number I thought of.
   Write and solve an inequality to find the smallest possible prime number Gillian thought of.

28. Consider this sequence of fractions: $\frac{1}{2}, \frac{2}{3}, \frac{3}{4}, \frac{4}{5}, \ldots$

   (a) Write down the next fraction in this sequence.

   (b) Write a rule for $t_n$, the $n$th term in this sequence.

   (c) $\frac{1}{2} + \frac{2}{3} = \frac{7}{6}$        $\frac{2}{3} + \frac{3}{4} = \frac{17}{12}$        $\frac{3}{4} + \frac{4}{5} = \frac{31}{20}$        $\frac{4}{5} + \frac{5}{6} = \frac{49}{30}$

   $\frac{7}{6}, \frac{17}{12}, \frac{31}{20}, \frac{49}{30}, \ldots$ is the sequence formed by adding adjacent terms of the original

   sequence. Find the next term in this new sequence.

   (d) The terms in this new sequence may be found *without* adding the fractions.
   By considering the patterns occurring in the numerators and in the denominators write down the 10th term of this new sequence.
   *Hint:*   There is a connection between the following difference table and the terms in the
   new sequence.        7            17            31            49
   10            14            18
   4            4

29. Yesterday, Kevin and Aleisha drove from their home to Stafford. Aleisha left home 10 minutes later than Kevin but drove at an average speed 20km/h faster. They both arrived in Stafford at the same time. Kevin left home at 9.10a.m. and drove at an average speed of 70km/h.
   Assuming that Kevin and Aleisha took the same route from their home to Stafford, draw a distance/time graph to illustrate. Use your graph to answer the following questions.

   (a) At what time did Kevin arrive in Stafford?

   (b) How far is Stafford from Kevin and Aleisha's home?

30. Ten metres of plastic fencing are used to form
   three sides of a rectangular sandpit placed against
   the wall of a day care centre.

   (a) If the width of the sandpit is x metres, show
       that the area is given by $A = 10x - 2x^2$ square
       metres.

   (b) Copy and complete this table.

| x | 0·5 | 1·0 | 1·5 | 2·0 | 2·5 | 3·0 | 3·5 | 4·0 | 4·5 | 5·0 |
|---|-----|-----|-----|-----|-----|-----|-----|-----|-----|-----|
| A | 4·5 | 8·0 | 10·5 | | | | | | | |

   (c) Draw the graph of A against x.
   (d) Use the graph to find the possible widths of a sandpit of area 10 square metres.
   (e) What are the dimensions of the sandpit of greatest area?

31. (i) $f(x) = 2x^2 - 10$

   (a) Find $f(-5)$.   (b) Find $f(\frac{1}{2})$.

   (c) For what values of x is $f(x) < 22$?

   (ii) $g(x) = \dfrac{3x - 6}{x + 1}$

   (a) For what value of x is $g(x) = 2$?
   (b) For what value of x has $g(x)$ no answer?

32. (a) For this parcel, the girth $g = 4x$ and the volume
       $V = x^2 l$.
       Express V in terms of g and $l$.
   (b) Make x the subject of the formula $V = x^2 l$.

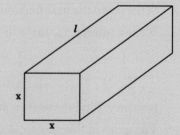

33. The diagrams below show the number of leaves grown by a plant during the first 3 years.

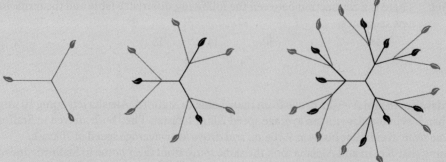

   **Year 1 : 3 leaves     Year 2 : 9 leaves         Year 3 : 21 leaves**

   (a) Draw the next diagram in this sequence. Hence show that this plant has 45 leaves in Year 4.
   (b) Explain how to *calculate* the number of leaves in Year 5.

34. The following is based on a well-known problem.
    *"The cashier who paid Amanda swapped the pounds and pence, giving Amanda pounds instead of pence and pence instead of pounds. After buying a 5p lolly, Amanda had exactly twice as much left as the cashier should have paid her."*
    How much should the cashier have paid Amanda? Is there more than one answer?

35. (i) Write each of the following expressions without brackets, in its simplest form.
    (a) $p(p^8) - p$        (b) $(p^9 + p) \div p$        (c) $p(1 + p^7)$

    (ii) If p is a whole number larger than 1, which of the expressions in (i) is the largest; which is the smallest?

36. When the temperature of a rod, of length x metres, is increased by $t°C$, the new length, y metres, is given by the formula
    $$y = x(1 + at).$$
    Calculate the value of y when $x = 2$, $t = 5$ and $a = 0.01$.                    **SEG**

37. The graph below shows the distance of an aircraft from the airport control tower.
    The aircraft starts from one end of the runway. It passes close to the control tower before taking off.

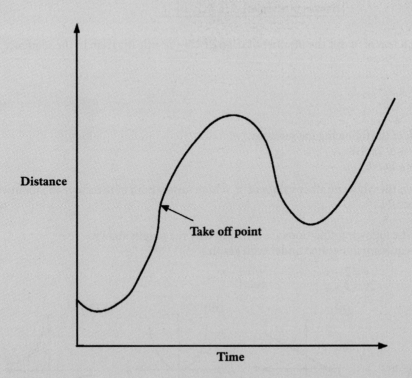

(a) Mark on the graph with a cross, the point where the aircraft passes close to the control tower.
(b) Describe what happens after the aircraft has taken off.                    **SEG**

97

38. Equilateral triangles are combined together to form shapes.
The number of triangles in the shape form a sequence.

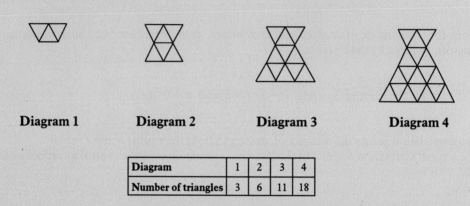

| Shape 1 | Shape 2 | Shape 3 |
|---------|---------|---------|
| 3 triangles | 7 triangles | 11 triangles |

(a) Find a rule in terms of $n$ for the number of triangles in the $n$th shape in the sequence.
(b) The triangles are now grouped together differently as shown below.

Diagram 1          Diagram 2          Diagram 3          Diagram 4

| Diagram | 1 | 2 | 3 | 4 |
|---------|---|---|---|---|
| Number of triangles | 3 | 6 | 11 | 18 |

Find a rule in terms of $n$ for the number of triangles in the $n$th diagram in the sequence.

**SEG**

39. Solve   $3x + y = 4$
$y = x + 2$

**NEAB**

40. (a) Solve each of the following inequalities.
   (i)   $5x - 4 \le 2x + 8$
   (ii)  $2(2x - 1) > 6$

(b) Write down the whole number values of $x$ which satisfy both of the above inequalities simultaneously.

**NEAB**

41. (a) Which of the following equations are illustrated by the graphs shown?
Write the equation illustrated under each graph.

$y = -x$ $\qquad$ $y = 2 - x$ $\qquad$ $y = 1 - x^2$
$y = x^2$ $\qquad$ $2y = 2 + x$ $\qquad$ $xy = 1$

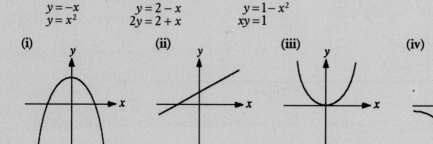

(i) $\qquad$ (ii) $\qquad$ (iii) $\qquad$ (iv)

**(b)** Sketch a graph of the equation $y = x^3 + 1$ on the graph below.

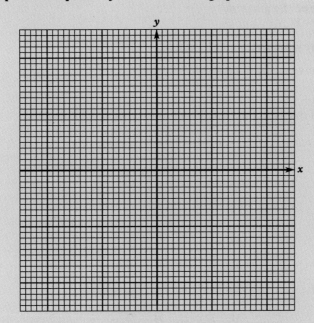

**SEG**

**42.** The formula to convert temperatures from degrees Fahrenheit (°F) into degrees Celsius (°C) is

$$C = \frac{5}{9} \ (F - 32).$$

Calculate the temperature in degrees Celsius which is equivalent to a temperature of –7°F.

**MEG**

**43.** The diagram shows a pegboard.

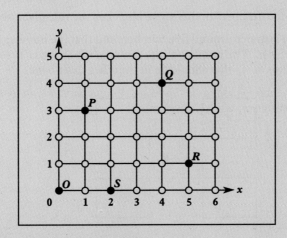

Pegs are placed in holes $O, P, Q, R$ and $S$.

**(a)** What are the co-ordinates of peg $R$?

Another peg $T$ is placed in the hole $(6, 3)$.

**(b)** Mark this hole on the diagram.
Label the hole '$T$'.

Pegs $O$ and $Q$ are joined with a straight line.

**(c)** Write down the equation of this line.                         **SEG**

**44.** The following grid consists of the numbers 1 to 40 written in 5 columns.

| 1 | 2 | 3 | 4 | 5 |
|---|---|---|---|---|
| 6 | 7 | 8 | 9 | 10 |
| 11 | 12 | 13 | 14 | 15 |
| 16 | 17 | 18 | 19 | 20 |
| 21 | 22 | 23 | 24 | 25 |
| 26 | 27 | 28 | 29 | 30 |
| 31 | 32 | 33 | 34 | 35 |
| 36 | 37 | 38 | 39 | 40 |

A shape ( ⊞ ) has been drawn to include the numbers 2, 4, 8, 12 and 14 of the grid.

The number 2 is in the top left-hand corner of the shape.
Notice that $2 + 4 + 12 + 14 = 4 \times 8$, that is,
'the sum of the four corner numbers = 4 times the centre number.'

**(a)** Draw the shape ( ⊞ ) around five numbers on the grid above so that it has 16 in its top left-hand corner.
Show clearly that the numbers in this shape also obey the rule given above.

**(b)** Suppose the shape is drawn around five numbers and that the number in the top left-hand corner is denoted by $n$. The number in the centre of the shape is $n + 6$. Fill in the expressions, in terms of $n$, that should be in the other three boxes.

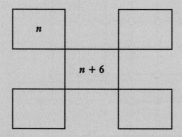

**(c)** Use your answers in **(b)** to show that the rule holds for all positions of the shape on the grid.                         **WJEC**

**45.** The distance, $d$ metres, a car travels in time $t$ seconds is given by the formula

$$d = 2 \cdot 5t^2.$$

(a) Complete the following table of values of $d$ for some values of $t$.

| Time, $t$ | 0 | 1 | 2 | 3 | 4 | 5 | 6 | 7 | 8 |
|-----------|---|-----|----|------|---|------|----|---|-----|
| Distance, $d$ | 0 | 2·5 | 10 | 22·5 | | 62·5 | 90 | | 160 |

(b) On the graph paper provided, plot the points represented in the table and draw a smooth curve through your points.

(c) Use your graph to estimate the distance travelled by the car in the first 6·5 seconds.

(d) Use your graph to estimate how long it takes the car to travel the first 50 metres.

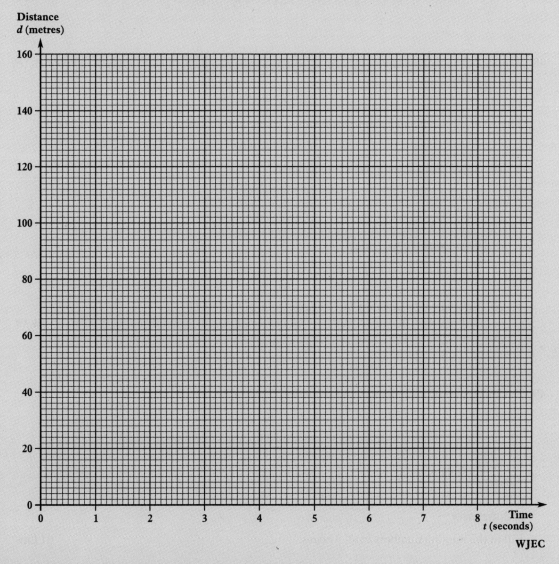

WJEC

**46. (a)** Write down **(i)** the smallest and **(ii)** the largest whole numbers which satisfy

$$-6 < x < 2.$$

**(b)** Solve the inequalities:

**(i)** $\frac{1}{2}x \geq 1$,      **(ii)** $3x - 2 > 7$,      **(iii)** $x^2 < 25$.     **MEG**

**47. (a)** Write the $n$th term for this sequence.

$$1 \quad\quad 8 \quad\quad 27 \quad\quad 64 \quad\quad 125 \quad \ldots$$

**(b)** Write the rule for this sequence below in the form $n^a$, where $a$ is an integer.

$$\frac{1}{1} \quad\quad \frac{4}{8} \quad\quad \frac{9}{27} \quad\quad \frac{16}{64} \quad\quad \frac{25}{125} \quad \ldots \quad\quad \textbf{SEG}$$

**48.** A quick but approximate rule for converting degrees Centigrade ($C$) into degrees Fahrenheit ($F$) is given below:

$$F = 2C + 30$$

The exact rule is given by this equation:

$$5F = 9C + 160$$

**(a) (i)** Solve the two simultaneous equations:

$$F = 2C + 30$$
$$5F = 9C + 160$$

**(ii)** Explain what your solution to these equations tells you about the two rules for converting temperatures.

**(b) (i)** Write the equation $5F = 9C + 160$ in the form

$$F =$$

**(ii)** Compare this equation with the equation $F = 2C + 30$.
Explain why the quick rule is a reasonable approximation for the exact rule.     **NEAB**

**49.** Neelan is investigating the number sequence

$$3, \ 4, \ 7, \ 12, \ 19, \ \ldots$$

He draws up 2 difference tables and writes down his answers under the original sequence.

| sequence | 3 | | 4 | | 7 | | 12 | | 19 | | ☐ |
|---|---|---|---|---|---|---|---|---|---|---|---|
| differences | | 1 | | 3 | | ☐ | | 7 | | | |
| differences of differences | | | ☐ | | 2 | | 2 | | | | |

Fill in the missing numbers in all 3 boxes.     **ULEAC**

**50.** Judy is using "trial and improvement" to solve the equation

$$x^2 + x = 11.$$

**Complete her working** and find a solution correct to one decimal place.

Try $x = 3.5$     $3.5^2 + 3.5 = 15.75$     too large

Try $x = 2.5$     $2.5^2 + 2.5 = 8.75$     too small

Try $x = 3.0$ ...............................................................................................

Try $x =$ ...............................................................................................      **SEG**

**51.** Two families are comparing the fare on a cross-channel ferry.
An adult fare is £$a$ and a child's fare is £$c$.
One family of two adults and five children paid £49.
The equation connecting $a$ and $c$ is $2a + 5c = 49$.
The other family of three adults and two children paid £46.
The equation connecting $a$ and $c$ is $3a + 2c = 46$.
The line on the graph represents the family with two adults and five children.

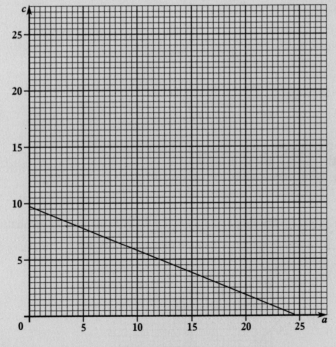

(a) Draw the line $3a + 2c = 46$ on the diagram.

(b) (i) Use your graph to find the cost of an adult fare.
    (ii) Use your graph to find the cost of a child's fare.     **SEG**

**52.** Find the whole number values of $n$ that satisfy the inequality

$$7 \leq 3n + 5 < 20.$$     **WJEC**

103

**53. (a)**

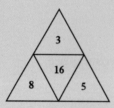 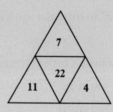 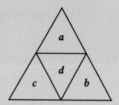

$a, b, c, d$ stand for numbers.
The numbers in each set of four triangles follow the same pattern.
Use the pattern to complete the table, in each case using one of the letters $a, b, c, d$.

| | | |
|---|---|---|
| $a + b$ | $=$ | |
| $c - a$ | $=$ | |
| $a + b + c$ | $=$ | |

**(b)** Use the same pattern to write expressions, in terms of $x$, in the two blank triangles.

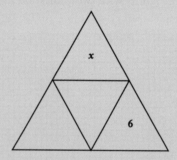

The sum of all the expressions in this set of four triangles is 60.

**(c) (i)** Write down an equation in terms of $x$.
   **(ii)** Solve this equation to find the value of $x$.

NICCEA

**54.** Label with the letter R, the single region which satisfies all of these inequalities.

$$y > 2, \qquad x + y > 4, \qquad 0 < x < 3$$

SEG

**55.**

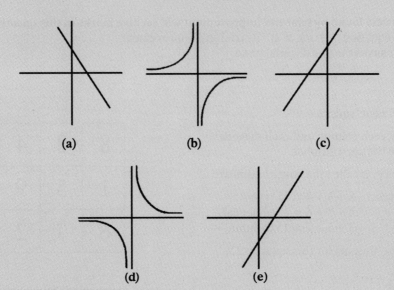

(a)          (b)          (c)

(d)          (e)

Which of the above graphs could represent the function

**(i)** $y = 2x + 3$          **(ii)** $y = \dfrac{6}{x}$          **NICCEA**

**56.** The diagram is the plan of part of the roof of a café called 'Where the Rainbow Ends', which once stood near Ashover in Derbyshire.
The lengths in feet of the cross bars are marked on the diagram.
The cross bars form a series of regular octagons.

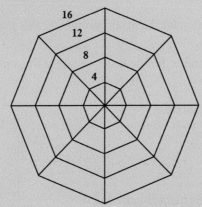

**(a)** Complete the table for each octagon from the centre:

| Octagon | Perimeter of octagon | Cumulative length |
|---------|---------------------|-------------------|
| 1 | 32 | 32 |
| 2 | 64 | 96 |
| 3 | | |
| 4 | | |

**(b)** Find a formula for the perimeter, $P$, of the $n$th octagon.
**(c)** Find a formula for the cumulative length, $B$, needed for $n$ octagons.          **MEG**

**57. Only answers found by trial and improvement will receive marks in this question.**
Solve the equation $x + \sqrt{x} = 10$ by trial and improvement.
Give your answer to one decimal place.                                    **MEG**

**58.** This is a 'magic' square.

Each row, each column and each diagonal
adds up to the same number.

This number is called the 'magic' number.

For example,   $8 + 3 + 4 = 15$ (row)
                $4 + 5 + 6 = 15$ (diagonal)
                $3 + 5 + 7 = 15$ (column)

The 'magic' number for this square is 15.

| 8 | 3 | 4 |
|---|---|---|
| 1 | 5 | 9 |
| 6 | 7 | 2 |

This is a general form of a magic square.

$a$, $b$ and $c$ represent any numbers.

| $a+b$ | $a-b+c$ | $a-c$ |
|---|---|---|
| $a-b-c$ | $a$ | $a+b+c$ |
| $a+c$ | $a+b-c$ | $a-b$ |

**(a)** Find an algebraic expression for the magic number for this magic square.
Simplify your answer.

**(b)** Find the values of $a$, $b$ and $c$ for the magic square at the top of this page.
Show your working.

Here is an incomplete magic square.

| 9 |  | 4 |
|---|---|---|
|  |  |  |
|  |  | 5 |

**(c)** Use the general form of the magic square and two
of the numbers in the square on the right to write
down two equations containing $a$ and $b$.
Find the values of $a$ and $b$.

**(d) (i)** Use the general form of the magic square and one number in the square above to write
down an equation containing $a$ and $c$.
Find the value of $c$.

**(ii)** Fill in the empty boxes in the magic square.

**(iii)** Check that it is magic.
Show your working.                                        **NEAB**

**59.** Carrie often travels from Aye to Beale and then to Cean.
When she travels at an average speed of 60mph from Aye to Beale, and 30mph from Beale to Cean, the journey takes $1\frac{1}{2}$ hours.
When she travels at an average speed of 40mph from Aye to Beale, and 50mph from Beale to Cean, the journey takes 2 hours.

  **(a)** Taking $x$ miles as the distance between Aye and Beale, and $y$ miles as the distance between Beale and Cean, show that
     **(i)** $x + 2y = 90$,     **(ii)** $5x + 4y = 400$.

  **(b)** Calculate the distance between
     **(i)** Aye and Beale,
     **(ii)** Beale and Cean.               **NICCEA**

## SEQUENCES DEFINED ITERATIVELY

**Notation**    $t_n$ is the $n$th term of a sequence.

$t_{n+1}$ is the $(n + 1)$th term i.e. the term after the $n$th term.

$t_{n+2}$ is the $(n + 2)$th term i.e. the second term after the $n$th term. This is also the term after the $(n + 1)$th term.

$t_{n-1}$ is the $(n - 1)$th term i.e. the term before the $n$th term.

Sequences may be defined by giving enough terms to establish a pattern.

For instance: 1, 2, 4, 8, 16, . . .

Sequences may be defined by giving a rule. For instance: the rule $t_n = 3n + 1$ defines the sequence 4, 7, 10, 13, . . .

Sequences may be defined by giving the first term and the relationship between consecutive terms as shown in the following worked example.

**Worked Example**    Find the first few terms of the sequence given by $t_{n+1} = t_n - 2$; $t_1 = 7$.

**Answer**    $t_{n+1} = t_n - 2$

$t_2 = t_1 - 2$   (replacing n by 1)

$= 7 - 2$   (since $t_1 = 7$)

$= 5$

$t_3 = t_2 - 2$   (replacing n by 2 in $t_{n+1} = t_n - 2$)

$= 5 - 2$   (since $t_2 = 5$)

$= 3$

$t_4 = t_3 - 2$   (replacing n by 3 in $t_{n+1} = t_n - 2$)

$= 3 - 2$   (since $t_3 = 3$)

$= 1$

$t_5 = t_4 - 2$   (replacing n by 4 in $t_{n+1} = t_n - 2$)

$= 1 - 2$   (since $t_4 = 1$)

$= -1$

The sequence is  7, 5, 3, 1, $-1$, . . .

Sequences defined by giving the relationship between consecutive terms are said to be defined **recursively** or **iteratively**. The relationship, e.g. $t_{n+1} = t_n - 2$, is said to be a recursive relationship or an iterative relationship or **an iteration**.

## DISCUSSION EXERCISE 5:1

• **Discuss** efficient calculator keying sequences to find the first few terms of the following sequences. If rounding is necessary, the terms are to be given to 3 significant figures. No intermediate working should be rounded; for instance, the calculator value for $t_2$ (not $t_2$ to 3 s.f.) should be used in the calculation for $t_3$.

$$t_{n+1} = \frac{t_n}{3}; \ t_1 = 2 \qquad t_{n+1} = 1 + \frac{1}{t_n}; \ t_1 = 1.5 \qquad t_{n+1} = \frac{2}{t_n - 3}; \ t_1 = 2.5$$

- Susan claimed that sequences given iteratively could be more easily investigated using the calculator or computer than sequences given by a rule. What reasons might Susan have given to support her claim? Is Susan correct? Discuss.

- Consider the Fibonacci sequence: 1, 1, 2, 3, 5, 8, 13, ...
  Is this sequence defined by: $t_{n+2} = t_{n+1} + t_n$; $t_1 = 1$? Discuss an efficient calculator keying sequence to give the first 100 terms of this sequence.

## DISCUSSION AND PRACTICAL EXERCISE 5:2

- 
| Program A | | Program B | |
|---|---|---|---|
| 10 | TN = 8 | 10 | DIM T(20) |
| 20 | PRINT TN | 20 | T(1) = 8 |
| 30 | FOR N = 1 TO 19 | 30 | PRINT T(1) |
| 40 | TNEXT = TN * 1·5 | 40 | FOR N = 1 TO 19 |
| 50 | PRINT TNEXT | 50 | T(N + 1) = T(N) * 1·5 |
| 60 | TN = TNEXT | 60 | PRINT T(N + 1) |
| 70 | NEXT N | 70 | NEXT N |
| 80 | END | 80 | END |

Run both of these programs. Discuss the following.

Do both programs have the same output?
How should Program A be changed to print 100 terms of the sequence given by $t_{n+1} = 1 \cdot 5 t_n$?
What two changes need to be made to Program B?
Program B stores the terms of the sequence in an *array*. Are there advantages in using an array? Discuss.

Write a program to print the first 20 terms of the sequence given by $t_{n+1} = \frac{t_n}{2} + 4$, $t_1 = 20$.

Write a program to print a number of terms of another sequence given iteratively.

- Use a spreadsheet to print many terms of some sequences defined iteratively.

## EXERCISE 5:3

1. Write down the first 5 terms of these sequences.

   (a) $t_{n+1} = t_n + 3$; $t_1 = 0$     (b) $t_{n+1} = 2t_n$; $t_1 = \frac{1}{2}$     (c) $t_{n+1} = 2t_n + 5$; $t_1 = 3$

   (d) $t_{n+1} = t_n^2$; $t_1 = 2$     (e) $\frac{t_{n+1}}{t_n} = 3$; $t_1 = 1$     (f) $\frac{t_{n+1}}{t_n} = -1$; $t_1 = 4$

2. Find the 5th term of these sequences. Give the answer to 4 s.f. if rounding is required. Do not round any intermediate calculations.

   (a) $t_{n+1} = \frac{1}{2}t_n$; $t_1 = 1$     (b) $t_{n+1} = \frac{1}{4}t_n - 1 \cdot 2$; $t_1 = 2 \cdot 3$     (c) $t_{n+1} = \frac{2}{t_n}$; $t_1 = 3$

   (d) $t_{n+1} = \frac{2}{1 + t_n}$; $t_1 = 0$     (e) $t_{n+1} = 1 - \frac{2}{t_n}$; $t_1 = 1$

3. The Antever Middle School roll is expected to rise by 2% per year for the next four years. The iteration $r_{n+1} = 1 \cdot 02 r_n$; $r_1 = 340$ gives the sequence of expected roll numbers.
   (a) What is the meaning of $r_1$?
   (b) Use the iteration to find the expected roll in four years time.

4. The iteration $v_{n+1} = (1 - \frac{1}{5}) v_n$ gives the yearly value of a car which depreciates at 20% per year. Angela pays £3000 for a car which depreciates in this way. What is Angela's car worth after 5 years? (Answer to the nearest £100.)

5. Write down the first 7 terms of these sequences.
   (a) $t_{n+2} = t_{n+1} - t_n$; $t_1 = 3, t_2 = 1$      (b) $t_{n+2} = t_{n+1} \times t_n$; $t_1 = 2, t_2 = 3$
   (c) $t_{n+2} = \frac{t_{n+1}}{t_n}$; $t_1 = 2, t_2 = 6$      (d) $t_{n+2} = 2t_{n+1} + t_n$; $t_1 = 1, t_2 = 1$

6. (a) Write down the first few terms of the sequence defined by $t_{n+1} = 3t_n$; $t_1 = 2$.
   (b) Prove that no term of this sequence is an odd number.
   *Hint:* Write down the rule for the sequence in the form $t_n = \ldots$

**Review 1** Find the first 6 terms of      (a) $t_{n+1} = 2t_n - 1 \cdot 5$; $t_1 = 4$      (b) $t_{n+1} = t_n^2 + 1$; $t_1 = 1$

**Review 2** It is predicted that the population of villages in the North East will decline at the rate of 1·5% per year for the next ten years.
Use the iteration $p_{n+1} = 0 \cdot 985 p_n$ to find the expected population in 5 years time of a village with present population of 824.

**Review 3** Find the 6th term of these sequences.
   (a) $t_{n+1} = \frac{3}{t_n} + 4$; $t_1 = 2$      (b) $t_{n+2} = t_{n+1} + 2t_n$; $t_1 = 4, t_2 = 4$

## INVESTIGATION 5:4

**Fibonacci Sequence Relationships**

The Fibonacci Sequence 1, 1, 2, 3, 5, 8, 13, 21, . . . may be generated by the iteration $t_{n+2} = t_{n+1} + t_n$; $t_1 = 1, t_2 = 1$. Consider the following proof which proves that, for the Fibonacci Sequence, $t_n + t_{n+3} = 2t_{n+2}$

$$t_{n+2} = t_{n+1} + t_n$$
$$t_{n+3} = t_{n+2} + t_{n+1} \text{ (replacing n by n + 1)}$$
$$t_{n+3} - t_{n+2} = t_{n+2} + t_{n+1} - t_{n+1} - t_n \text{ (subtracting the first line from the second)}$$
$$t_{n+3} - t_{n+2} = t_{n+2} - t_n$$
$$t_n + t_{n+3} = 2t_{n+2} \text{ (rearranging)}$$

Check this relationship, $t_n + t_{n+3} = 2t_{n+2}$, for some values of n. Write the relationship in words.

**Investigate** to find other relationships between the terms of the Fibonacci Sequence or of the related sequences given below. Prove the relationships.

| | |
|---|---|
| Fibonacci Sequence | 1, 1, 2, 3, 5, 8, 13, 21, . . . |
| Lucas Sequence | 1, 3, 4, 7, 11, 18, 29, 47, . . . |
| Tetranacci Sequence | 1, 1, 2, 4, 8, 15, 29, 56, . . . |
| Tribonacci Sequence | 1, 1, 2, 4, 7, 13, 24, 44, . . . |

## CONVERGENCE, DIVERGENCE

**DISCUSSION EXERCISE 5:5**

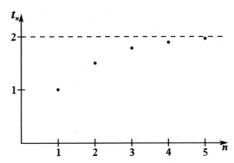

- The graph of $t_n$ against n is shown for the first five terms of the sequence $1, 1\frac{1}{2}, 1\frac{3}{4}, 1\frac{7}{8}, 1\frac{15}{16}, \ldots$
  Which number are the terms of this sequence getting closer to?
  Does any term of this sequence take this value?
  Does any term take a value greater than this?
  What will the graph look like if we graph more terms?
  **Discuss.**

- Consider the sequences $\quad 2, 4, 8, 16, 32, \ldots$
  $1, 3, 5, 7, 9, \ldots$
  $\frac{1}{2}, \frac{2}{3}, \frac{3}{4}, \frac{4}{5}, \frac{5}{6}, \ldots$
  $1, -\frac{1}{2}, \frac{1}{3}, -\frac{1}{4}, \frac{1}{5}, -\frac{1}{6}, \ldots$

  Is there a number that the terms are getting closer and closer to? **Discuss.** As part of your discussion, draw graphs of $t_n$ against $n$.

> A sequence is said to **converge** if the terms get closer and closer to a particular number. For instance: the sequence $1, 1\frac{1}{2}, 1\frac{3}{4}, 1\frac{7}{8}, 1\frac{15}{16}, \ldots$ converges since the terms get closer and closer to 2. We say that this sequence converges to 2.
> A sequence is said to **diverge** if it does not converge.

**EXERCISE 5:6**

**State whether the following sequences are convergent or divergent. For those that are convergent, find the number to which the sequence converges.**

1. $16, 15, 14, 13, \ldots$

2. $3\frac{1}{3}, 3\frac{1}{4}, 3\frac{1}{5}, 3\frac{1}{6}, \ldots$

3. $\frac{1}{6}, \frac{2}{6}, \frac{3}{6}, \frac{4}{6}, \ldots$

4. $16, 8, 4, 2, \ldots$

5. $2, 4, 8, 16, \ldots$

6. $1, -1, 1, -1, 1, \ldots$

7. $2 \cdot 02, (2 \cdot 02)^2, (2 \cdot 02)^3, (2 \cdot 02)^4, \ldots$

8. $\frac{3}{5}, \frac{5}{7}, \frac{7}{9}, \frac{9}{11}, \ldots$

9. $\frac{3}{5}, -\frac{5}{7}, \frac{7}{9}, -\frac{9}{11}, \frac{11}{13}, \ldots$

10. $t_{n+1} = t_n - 3; \ t_1 = 1$

11. $t_{n+1} = 2t_n; \ t_1 = 6$

12. $t_{n+1} = \frac{1}{2} t_n; \ t_1 = 6$

13. $t_{n+1} = \frac{1}{5}t_n; \; t_1 = 1$

14. $t_{n+1} = \frac{2}{t_n}; \; t_1 = 2$

15. $t_{n+1} = \frac{2}{1+t_n}; \; t_1 = 2$

16. $t_{n+1} = 3 + \frac{t_n}{2}; \; t_1 = 4$

Review 1 $4\frac{1}{3}, 4\frac{3}{5}, 4\frac{5}{7}, 4\frac{7}{9}, \ldots$

Review 2 $81, -27, 9, -3, \ldots$

Review 3 $t_{n+1} = \frac{4}{t_n}; \; t_1 = 5$

Review 4 $t_{n+1} = \frac{4}{3+t_n}; \; t_1 = 2$

---

## INVESTIGATION 5:7

### Convergence of Sequences

**Use a calculator or computer wherever appropriate.**

1. **Investigate** to find the numbers to which the sequences $t_{n+1} = 3 + \frac{2}{t_n}; \; t_1 = 4$ and
   $t_{n+1} = 4 - \frac{1}{t_n}; \; t_1 = 1$ converge.

2. $t_{n+2} = \frac{1}{2}(t_{n+1} + t_n); \; t_1 = 1, t_2 = 2$. **Investigate** the convergence or divergence of
   this sequence.
   **What if** different values were chosen for $t_1$ and $t_2$?
   **What if** each term is the mean of the three previous terms rather than the two
   previous terms?

3. If $t_{n+1} = t_n + d$ where d is a constant, the sequence is called an Arithmetic
   Sequence; d is called the common difference. For instance: $3, 7, 11, 15, \ldots$ is an
   Arithmetic Sequence with common difference equal to 4.
   If $t_{n+1} = r t_n$ where r is a constant, the sequence is called a Geometric Sequence; r is
   called the common ratio. For instance: $3, -6, 12, -24, \ldots$ is a Geometric Sequence
   with common ratio equal to $-2$.
   Choosing various values for $t_1$, d and r **investigate** the convergence of these
   sequences. Be sure to include fractional and negative values for d and r.

4. The sequence $1, \frac{1}{2}, \frac{1}{4}, \frac{1}{8}, \frac{1}{16}, \frac{1}{32}, \ldots$ converges to 0. The following sequences are
   formed from this sequence.

   $-1, -\frac{1}{2}, -\frac{1}{4}, -\frac{1}{8}, -\frac{1}{16}, -\frac{1}{32}, \ldots$

   $1, -\frac{1}{2}, \frac{1}{4}, -\frac{1}{8}, \frac{1}{16}, -\frac{1}{32}, \ldots$

   $10, \frac{10}{2}, \frac{10}{4}, \frac{10}{8}, \frac{10}{16}, \frac{10}{32}, \ldots$

   $1\frac{1}{2}, \frac{3}{4}, \frac{3}{8}, \ldots$

   $1\frac{1}{2}, \frac{3}{8}, \frac{3}{32}, \ldots$

   $\frac{1}{2}, \frac{1}{8}, \frac{1}{32}, \ldots$

   How are the sequences in the list related to $1, \frac{1}{2}, \frac{1}{4}, \frac{1}{8}, \frac{1}{16}, \frac{1}{32}, \ldots$? **Investigate** the

   convergence of these and other sequences related to $1, \frac{1}{2}, \frac{1}{4}, \frac{1}{8}, \frac{1}{16}, \frac{1}{32}, \ldots$
   **What if** we began with another sequence?

## RESEARCH PROJECT 5:8

**Series**

Associated with every sequence is a series.

For instance: associated with the sequence $\frac{1}{2}, \frac{1}{4}, \frac{1}{8}, \frac{1}{16}, \ldots$ is the series $\frac{1}{2} + \frac{1}{4} + \frac{1}{8} + \frac{1}{16} + \ldots$

We may talk about the sum of $n$ terms of a series or the sum to infinity.
Research series.

The following problem of Achilles and the tortoise (first considered by the Greek mathematician Zeno in the 5th century B.C.) could be investigated as part of your project: Achilles, who can run 12 times as fast as a tortoise gives a tortoise a head start of 1 standion (about 200 metres). What distance does Achilles run before overtaking the tortoise? (Zeno used a series to argue that Achilles can never overtake the tortoise.)

### CHAPTER 5 REVIEW

1.  To get a Fibonacci sequence:

| Rule | For example |
|---|---|
| Start with any two numbers. | 2<br>5 |
| To get the next number add the two numbers just before it. | $2 + 5 = 7$ |
| Continue in this way. | $5 + 7 = 12$<br>$7 + 12 = 19$<br>$12 + 19 = 31$ |

So the sequence is:

| 2 | 5 | 7 | 12 | 19 | 31 |
|---|---|---|---|---|---|

(a)  The terms in a Fibonacci sequence can be written algebraically as:

| $a$ | $b$ | $a + b$ | $a + 2b$ | $2a + 3b$ | $3a + 5b$ |
|---|---|---|---|---|---|

Below are two numbers of a Fibonacci sequence.

| | | 6 | | 17 | |
|---|---|---|---|---|---|

We can write down two equations linking the expressions and the numbers in the boxes above. These two equations are:

$$a + b = 6 \quad \text{and} \quad 2a + 3b = 17$$

By solving these two equations simultaneously, find the values of $a$ and $b$. Then fill in the empty boxes.

**(b)** A mathematician once stated:

> When you add the first six numbers of a
> Fibonacci sequence your total is always four
> times the fifth number in the sequence.

For example, using the sequence:  $1, 2, 3, 5, 8, 13, 21, \ldots$
adding the first six numbers we get  $1 + 2 + 3 + 5 + 8 + 13 = 32$
and four times the fifth number gives us  $4 \times 8 = 32$
so the statement is true in this case.

Write down the first six numbers of your own Fibonacci sequence in the boxes below.

|  |  |  |  |  |  |
|--|--|--|--|--|--|
|  |  |  |  |  |  |

**(i)** Check that the statement is true for your own Fibonacci sequence.

**(ii)** Use algebra to prove that this is always true using the Fibonacci sequence which begins:

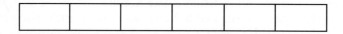

| $a$ | $b$ | $a + b$ | $a + 2b$ | $2a + 3b$ | $3a + 5b$ |
|-----|-----|---------|----------|-----------|-----------|

**(c)** Another mathematician claimed that:

> Starting with any Fibonacci sequence, for example:  $3, 2, 5, 7, 12, 19, 31, \ldots$
> - If you take any four adjacent numbers  $3, 2, 5, 7$
> - square the middle two numbers  $2^2 = 4, 5^2 = 25$
> - find the difference of these squares  $25 - 4 = 21$
> - multiply the first and fourth numbers together  $3 \times 7 = 21$
>
> your answers are the same.

Use algebra to show that this is always true using the Fibonacci sequence which begins:

| $a$ | $b$ | $a + b$ | $a + 2b$ |
|-----|-----|---------|----------|

**NEAB**

**2.** A sequence of numbers is shown below.
The first two terms are 3 and 4.
The remaining terms are found by adding together the two previous terms.

$$3, 4, 7, 11, 18, 29, \ldots$$

**(a)** Write down the next two terms in the sequence.

**(b)** The numbers from the first sequence are used to find the terms of a second sequence as shown below.
The terms are given to 2 decimal places.

$$4 \div 3 = 1 \cdot 33$$
$$7 \div 4 = 1 \cdot 75$$
$$11 \div 7 = 1 \cdot 57$$

**(i)** Calculate the next three terms of this second sequence.
**(ii)** Write down what you notice about the terms in the second sequence.        **NEAB**

3.  **(a)** Find, in terms of $n$, the $n$th term of the sequence

$$\frac{1}{3}, \ \frac{2}{5}, \ \frac{3}{7}, \ \frac{4}{9}, \ \frac{5}{11}, \ \ldots$$

**(b)** The $n$th term of a sequence is given by

$$u_{n+1} = 2u_n - 2u_n^2.$$

$$u_1 = 0 \cdot 8$$

**(i)** Calculate $u_2$.
**(ii)** What value does $u_n$ approach as $n$ gets very large?        **NEAB**

4.  **(a)** For the sequence $x_{n+1} = \sqrt{\frac{x_n + 1}{x_n}}$, set $x_1 = 1$ and use your calculator to find $x_6$.

Write each value of $x$ to 4 significant figures.

**(b)** Does the sequence converge or diverge?
Give a reason for your answer.        **SEG**

## USING GRAPHS to SOLVE EQUATIONS

The two simultaneous equations $\left.\begin{array}{l} y = x + 1 \\ y = -x + 4 \end{array}\right\}$ may be solved by finding the coordinates of the point of intersection of the graphs $y = x + 1$ and $y = -x + 4$.
This method of solving two simultaneous equations may be used with the graphs of any two functions. For instance, to solve $\left.\begin{array}{l} y = x^2 - 5 \\ y = x^3 \end{array}\right\}$ we may find the coordinates of the points of intersection of the two graphs $y = x^2 - 5$ and $y = x^3$.
This method may be adapted to solve an equation such as $x^3 + 3x - 10 = 0$ as shown in the following example.

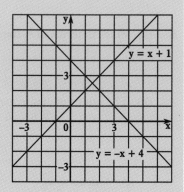

*Example*   $x^3 + 3x - 10 = 0$ may be rearranged as $x^3 = 10 - 3x$. If we draw the graphs of $y = x^3$ and $y = 10 - 3x$ then the x-coordinate of the point of intersection gives the solution of the equation $x^3 = 10 - 3x$; i.e. of the equation $x^3 + 3x - 10 = 0$.

$y = 10 - 3x$

| x | –3 | 0 | 3 |
| --- | --- | --- | --- |
| y | 19 | 10 | 1 |

$y = x^3$

| x | –3 | –2 | –1 | 0 | 1 | 2 | 3 |
| --- | --- | --- | --- | --- | --- | --- | --- |
| y | –27 | –8 | –1 | 0 | 1 | 8 | 27 |

The coordinates of the point of intersection are approximately $(1{\cdot}7, 5)$. Hence the approximate solution of the equation $x^3 + 3x - 10 = 0$ is $x = 1{\cdot}7$.

Sometimes, when solving an equation graphically, we need to rearrange the equation to make use of a graph already drawn.

For instance, if the graph of $y = x^2 + 3x - 4$ is drawn, we can use this graph to solve the equation $x^2 + 3x + 1 = 0$. The first step is to rearrange $x^2 + 3x + 1 = 0$ so that the left-hand side is $x^2 + 3x - 4$. That is, rearrange $x^2 + 3x + 1 = 0$ as $x^2 + 3x - 4 = -5$. We now find where the graphs $y = x^2 + 3x - 4$ and $y = -5$ meet.

*Worked Example*  The graph of $y = 2x^2 - 3x - 5$ is drawn below.

    (i)  Draw lines on this graph to solve the equations

        (a) $2x^2 - 3x - 2 = 0$

        (b) $2x^2 - x - 15 = 0$

        (c) $2x^2 - 3x - 5 = 0$

    (ii)  The line $y = x - 5$ meets the parabola $y = 2x^2 - 3x - 5$ at $x = 0$ and $x = 2$.

        What equation are these values of $x$ the solution of?

*Answer*  (i)  (a) $2x^2 - 3x - 2 = 0$ can be rearranged as $2x^2 - 3x - 5 = -3$.
The line $y = -3$ meets the graph $y = 2x^2 - 3x - 5$
at $x = -0.5$ and $x = 2$. Hence $x = -0.5$ and $x = 2$ are the solutions of the equation $2x^2 - 3x - 2 = 0$.

       (b) $2x^2 - x - 15 = 0$ can be rearranged as $2x^2 - 3x - 5 = -2x + 10$.
The line $y = -2x + 10$ meets the graph $y = 2x^2 - 3x - 5$
at $x = -2.5$ and $x = 3$. Hence $x = -2.5$ and $x = 3$ are the solutions of the equation $2x^2 - x - 15 = 0$.

       (c) The equation $2x^2 - 3x - 5 = 0$ does not need rearranging since the left-hand side is already $2x^2 - 3x - 5$. The solution of $2x^2 - 3x - 5 = 0$ is found where the line $y = 0$ (the x-axis) meets the graph $y = 2x^2 - 3x - 5$. The solutions are $x = -1$ and $x = 2.5$.

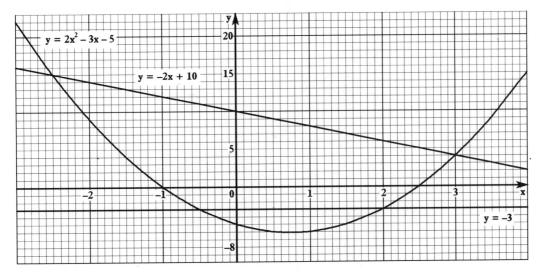

    (ii)  These values of x are the solution of the equation $2x^2 - 3x - 5 = x - 5$,
i.e. $2x^2 - 4x = 0$.

## EXERCISE 6:1

1. (a) Draw the graph of $y = x^3$ for values of $x$ between $-3$ and $3$.
   (b) On the same set of axes, draw the graph of $y = x^2 - 9$.
   (c) Use your graphs to find the approximate solution of the equation $x^3 = x^2 - 9$.

2. (a) Copy and complete this table of values for $y = 2 + x - x^2$.

   | x | −2 | −1 | 0 | 1 | 2 | 3 |
   |---|----|----|---|---|---|---|
   | y | −4 |    |   |   |   |   |

   (b) Draw the graph of $y = 2 + x - x^2$ for $x$ in the range $-2 \le x \le 3$.
   (c) On the same set of axes, draw the graph of $y = \dfrac{1}{x}$.
   (d) Use your graphs to find the approximate values of $x$ for which $\dfrac{1}{x} = 2 + x - x^2$.

3. (a) Copy and complete this table of values for $y = x^2 - 2x$. Draw the graph.

   | x | −2 | −1 | 0 | 1 | 2 | 3 | 4 |
   |---|----|----|---|---|---|---|---|
   | y | 8  |    |   |   |   |   |   |

   (b) On the same set of axes draw the line $y = 7$. Hence find approximate values for the two solutions of the equation $x^2 - 2x = 7$.

4. (i) Draw the graph of $y = x^2$ for values of $x$ between $-3$ and $3$.
   (ii) Draw lines on your graph to find solutions for
       (a) $x^2 = 5$
       (b) $x^2 = x + 3$
       (c) $x^2 = 1 - 2x$.

5.

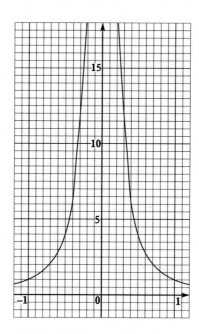

The graph of $y = \dfrac{1}{x^2}$, for values of $x$ between $-1$ and $1$, is shown.

(a) Copy and complete the following table of values for $y = \dfrac{1}{x^2}$, giving the y-values correct to 2 d.p.

| x | −3 | −2 | −1 | $-\frac{1}{2}$ | $-\frac{1}{4}$ | 0 | $\frac{1}{4}$ | $\frac{1}{2}$ | 1 | 2 | 3 |
|---|----|----|----|----------------|----------------|---|---------------|---------------|---|---|---|
| y |    |    | 1  |                | 16             | no value |         |               |   |   | 0·11 |

Draw the graph for values of x between − 3 and 3.

(b) On the same set of axes, draw the line $y = 2x + 4$.
Use the graphs to find approximate solutions to the equation $\dfrac{1}{x^2} - 2x - 4 = 0$.

(c) What line do you need to draw to solve $\dfrac{1}{x^2} - 0.5 = 0$? Draw this line. Find the solutions.

6.  The graph of $y = 4x^3 - 9x$ is shown.
What line needs to be drawn to solve
(a) $4x^3 - 9x = 2$
(b) $4x^3 - 9x + 3 = 0$
(c) $4x^3 - 9x = 0$
(d) $4x^3 - 8x = 0$
(e) $4x^3 - 11x = 4$
(f) $4x^3 - 7x - 3 = 0$?

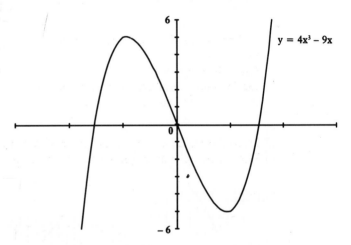

$y = 4x^3 - 9x$

7.  (i) Copy and complete this table of values for $y = x^3 - 3x^2$, rounding the y-values to 1 d.p.

| x | −1 | −0·5 | 0 | 0·5 | 1 | 1·5 | 2 | 2·5 | 3 | 3·5 |
|---|----|------|---|-----|---|-----|---|-----|---|-----|
| y |    |      |   |     |   |     |   |     |   |     |

Draw the graph of $y = x^3 - 3x^2$ for x in the range $-1 \le x \le 3.5$.

(ii) Drawing lines on your graph, if necessary, find the solutions for
(a) $x^3 - 3x^2 = 0$
(b) $x^3 - 3x^2 = 2$
(c) $x^3 - 3x^2 + 2 = 0$
(d) $x^3 - 3x^2 = x - 2$
(e) $x^3 - 3x^2 + x - 2 = 0$.

8.  (a) Draw the graph of $y = \dfrac{5}{x}$ for values of x between −5 and 5.

(b) On the same set of axes, draw the graph of $y = \dfrac{1}{10}x^2 + 2$.

(c) Show that the equation $x^3 + 20x - 50 = 0$ may be rewritten as $\dfrac{1}{10}x^2 + 2 = \dfrac{5}{x}$.

(d) Use your graphs to find the approximate solution of the equation $x^3 + 20x - 50 = 0$.

**Review 1** The graph of $y = \sqrt{x}$, for values of x between 0 and 4, is shown.

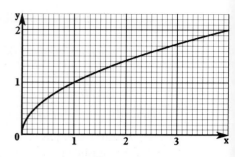

(a) Copy and complete the tables of values for $y = \sqrt{x}$ and $y = \dfrac{10}{x}$, giving the y-values rounded to 1 d.p.

$y = \sqrt{x}$

| x | 0 | 1 | 2 | 3 | 4 | 5 | 6 | 7 | 8 | 9 | 10 |
|---|---|---|---|---|---|---|---|---|---|---|----|
| y | 0 | 1 | 1·4 | | | | | | | | |

$y = \dfrac{10}{x}$

| x | 0 | 1 | 2 | 3 | 4 | 5 | 6 | 7 | 8 | 9 | 10 |
|---|---|---|---|---|---|---|---|---|---|---|----|
| y | no value | 10 | 5 | | | | | | | | |

Draw the graphs on the same set of axes.

(b) Use the graphs to find the approximate value of x for which $\dfrac{10}{x} = \sqrt{x}$.

**Review 2**

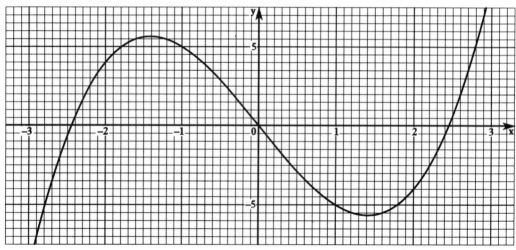

(i) The graph of $y = x^3 - 6x$ is shown.
Use this graph to find the approximate solutions of the equation $x^3 - 6x = 0$.

(ii) What line needs to be drawn on the graph to solve
  (a) $x^3 - 6x = 4$    (b) $x^3 - 6x + 3 = 0$    (c) $x^3 - 8x + 5 = 0$?

**Review 3** (a) Copy and complete this table of values for $y = (x + 2)(x - 4)$.

| x | −3 | −2 | −1 | 0 | 1 | 2 | 3 | 4 | 5 |
|---|----|----|----|---|---|---|---|---|---|
| y | 7 | 0 | | | | | | | |

Draw the graph of $y = (x + 2)(x - 4)$.

(b) Use your graph to find the approximate values of x for which $(x + 2)(x - 4) = 2$.

(c) What line do you need to draw on your graph to solve the equation $x^2 - 4x - 5 = 0$?

## USING GRAPHS and ITERATION to SOLVE EQUATIONS

In the previous section we used graphs to find solutions to equations such as $x^3 - x - 4 = 0$. These solutions were approximate solutions; at most, accurate to 1 d.p.

Solutions to equations such as $x^3 - x - 4 = 0$ can be found, as accurately as we wish, by using an iterative process. In this *iterative process* we estimate the answer, then use this estimate to find a better estimate; we then use this latest estimate to find an even better estimate and so on. To solve an equation using iteration we need an iterative formula for the equation and an estimate of the solution (or solutions). The estimate may be found by drawing a graph. The iterative formula may be found by rearranging the equation. For instance, the equation $x^2 + 2x - 7 = 0$ may be rearranged as $x = \dfrac{7}{x} - 2$ to give the iteration $x_{n+1} = \dfrac{7}{x_n} - 2$.

*Worked Example*   Find a solution, to 3 correct decimal places, for the equation $x^3 - x - 4 = 0$ using the iteration $x_{n+1} = \sqrt{1 + \frac{4}{x_n}}$ .

*Answer*   Since $x^3 - x - 4 = 0$ may be rewritten as $x^3 = x + 4$ the point (or points) of intersection of the graphs $y = x^3$ and $y = x + 4$ will give the solution (or solutions) of $x^3 - x - 4 = 0$.

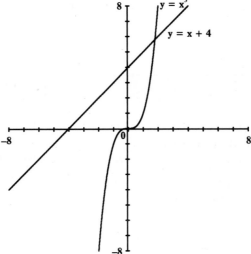

Reading from the graph, a solution is $x = 2$, to the nearest integer. $x = 2$ is the first value of $x_n$ in the iteration; that is $x_1 = 2$.

Using $x_{n+1} = \sqrt{1 + \frac{4}{x_n}}$ , and writing down each calculator value rounded to 4 d.p. we get

$$x_2 = \sqrt{1 + \tfrac{4}{x_1}} \qquad\qquad x_3 = \sqrt{1 + \tfrac{4}{x_2}} \qquad\qquad x_4 = \sqrt{1 + \tfrac{4}{x_3}}$$

$$= \sqrt{1 + \tfrac{4}{2}} \qquad\qquad = \sqrt{1 + \tfrac{4}{1.7321}} \qquad\qquad = \sqrt{1 + \tfrac{4}{1.8192}}$$

$$= 1.7321 \qquad\qquad\quad = 1.8192 \qquad\qquad\qquad = 1.7885$$

Continuing in this way we get   $x_5 = 1.7990$
$$x_6 = 1.7954$$
$$x_7 = 1.7966$$
$$x_8 = 1.7962$$

Both $x_7$, and $x_8$ have the figures 796 in the first three decimal places. Hence, to 3 correct decimal places, a solution is 1·796.

121

Notes 1. There is a difference between an answer written correct to 3 d.p. and an answer written to 3 correct d.p. An answer written correct to 3 d.p. means we round the answer to 3 d.p. whereas an answer written to 3 correct d.p. means we write the figures that actually occur in the first 3 decimal places, i.e. we do not round.

2. Leave all the figures on your calculator throughout the working. Use efficient keying sequences.

The graphics calculator can be used to reduce the amount of work in the iteration calculation. For instance, the following keying sequence can be used for the iteration $x_{n+1} = \sqrt{1 + \frac{4}{x_n}}$ with $x_1 = 2$.

2 EXE √ ( 1 + 4 ÷ ANS ) EXE EXE EXE . . .

## DISCUSSION and PRACTICAL EXERCISE 6:2

- The following program may be used to find the solution for the equation $x^3 - x - 4 = 0$ to any number of correct decimal places.
  Use this program to find the solution to 5 correct decimal places. Use $x_1 = 2$.

```
10   INPUT "TYPE IN AN ESTIMATE FOR X:" X
20   INPUT "TYPE IN THE REQUIRED NUMBER OF CORRECT DECIMAL PLACES:" D
30   E = 5 * 10 ^ - (D + 1)
40   FOR N = 1 TO 100
50   XNEXT = SQR (1 + 4/X)
60   IF ABS (XNEXT - X) < E THEN N = 100
70   PRINT XNEXT
80   X = XNEXT
90   NEXT N
100  END
```

Adapt this program to find the two solutions of $x^2 - x - 21 = 0$ to 3 correct decimal places. Use the iteration $x_{n+1} = \frac{21}{x_n} + 1$. Estimates of the solutions are $-4$ and $5$. Discuss.

Suppose we were asked to find the solutions for $x^2 - x - 21 = 0$ to 5 correct significant figures. What should the input be? Discuss.

- Use a spreadsheet, instead of the above program, to find the two solutions to $x^2 - x - 21 = 0$.

## EXERCISE 6:3

**You could use a graphics calculator or a computer for the iteration calculations.**

1.

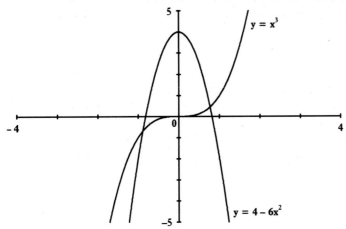

To find the solution of the equation $x^3 + 6x^2 - 4 = 0$, in the range $-3 \leq x \leq 3$, Janine began by drawing the graphs of $y = x^3$ and $y = 4 - 6x^2$.

(a) Janine estimated the negative solution to be about $-1$. Use the iteration $x_{n+1} = -\sqrt{\frac{4 - x_n^3}{6}}$, with $x_1 = -1$, to find this negative solution to two correct decimal places.

(b) Use the iteration $x_{n+1} = \sqrt{\frac{4 - x_n^3}{6}}$ to find the positive solution to three correct decimal places.

2. (a) On the same set of axes, draw the graphs of $y = x^2$ and $y = 3 - x$. Use the range $-3 \leq x \leq 3$.

(b) Use the graph to estimate, to the nearest integer, the solutions of the equation $x^2 + x - 3 = 0$.

(c) Use the iteration $x_{n+1} = \frac{3}{x_n + 1}$ to find the positive solution, to 3 correct decimal places.

(d) Use the iteration $x_{n+1} = -\sqrt{3 - x_n}$ to find the negative solution, to 4 correct decimal places.

3.

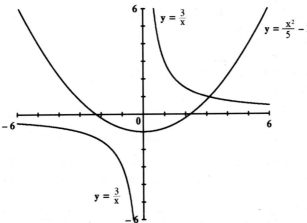

The graphs of $y = \frac{3}{x}$ and $y = \frac{x^2}{5} - 1$ are shown.

(a) Use the graph to estimate a solution to the equation $\frac{3}{x} - \frac{x^2}{5} + 1 = 0$.

(b) Use the iteration $x_{n+1} = \sqrt{\frac{15}{x_n} + 5}$ to find a solution, to 4 correct significant figures.

4.  (a) For x in the range $-2 \leq x \leq 2$, draw the graph of $y = 2x^3$.
    What line do you need to draw on this graph to be able to solve the equation
    $2x^3 + 3x - 1 = 0$?
    Draw this line on your graph.

    (b) Use your graph to estimate a solution to the equation $2x^3 + 3x - 1 = 0$.

    (c) Use the iteration $x_{n+1} = \dfrac{1}{2x_n^2 + 3}$ to find the solution to 3 correct significant figures.


5.  (a) On the same set of axes, draw the graphs of $y = x^2 - 8$ and $y = -\dfrac{1}{x}$ for values of
    x between $-3$ and $3$.

    (b) How many solutions has the equation $x^2 + \dfrac{1}{x} - 8 = 0$?

    (c) Use the iteration $x_{n+1} = \dfrac{1}{8 - x_n^2}$, with starting value $x_1 = 1$, to find one solution, to
    3 correct significant figures, for the equation $x^2 + \dfrac{1}{x} - 8 = 0$.

    (d) Use the iteration $x_{n+1} = \sqrt{8 - \frac{1}{x_n}}$ to find the other positive solution, to 4 correct
    significant figures.

    (e) Find, to 5 correct significant figures, the negative solution using the iteration
    $x_{n+1} = -\sqrt{8 - \frac{1}{x_n}}$ .


**Review**

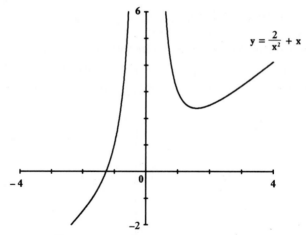

$y = \dfrac{2}{x^2} + x$

(a) The graph of $y = \dfrac{2}{x^2} + x$ is shown. What line needs to be drawn on this graph to
    solve the equation $\dfrac{2}{x^2} + x - 3 = 0$?

(b) Use the iteration $x_{n+1} = -\sqrt{\frac{2}{3 - x_n}}$ to find the negative solution, to 3 correct
    decimal places.

(c) Use the iteration $x_{n+1} = \sqrt{\frac{2}{3 - x_n}}$ with $x_1 = 1$. What happens? Explain.

(d) Use the iteration $x_{n+1} = 3 - \dfrac{2}{x_n^2}$ to find the other positive solution, to 3 correct
    decimal places.

## INVESTIGATION 6:4

Iteration: Convergence, Divergence

The equation $x^3 - x - 4 = 0$ may be rearranged as follows.

$$x^3 - x - 4 = 0$$
$$x^3 = x + 4$$
$$x^2 = 1 + \frac{4}{x} \quad \text{(dividing by x)}$$
$$x = \pm \sqrt{1 + \frac{4}{x}} \quad \text{(taking the square root)}$$

That is, if the equation $x^3 - x - 4 = 0$ is to be rearranged as $x = f(x)$ two possible rearrangements are $x = \sqrt{1 + \frac{4}{x}}$ and $x = -\sqrt{1 + \frac{4}{x}}$.

Is $x = \frac{4}{x^2 - 1}$ also a possible rearrangement of $x^3 - x - 4 = 0$? Is $x = \frac{2x^3 + 4}{3x^2 - 1}$ possible?

What other rearrangements of the type $x = f(x)$ are possible?

One possible iteration for the equation $x^3 - x - 4 = 0$ is $x_{n+1} = \sqrt{1 + \frac{4}{x_n}}$.
What other iterations are possible?
Which of these iterations converge to a solution of the equation?
Why do some iterations converge and others diverge?
Investigate.

# CHAPTER 6   REVIEW

1. (a) Alex is using "trial and improvement" to solve the equation

$$x^2 - 3x = 1.$$

Continue the working to find the solution correct to one decimal place.

Try $x = 3$      $3^2 - 3 \times 3 = 0$      too small

Try $x = 4$      $4^2 - 3 \times 4 = 4$      too large

Try $x = 3 \cdot 5$ ......................................................................................

Try ......................................................................................

(b) Multiply out the brackets and simplify your answer.

$$(x - 3 \cdot 3)(x + 0 \cdot 3)$$

**(c) (i)** Draw the graph of $y = x^2 - 3x$ on the axes provided.

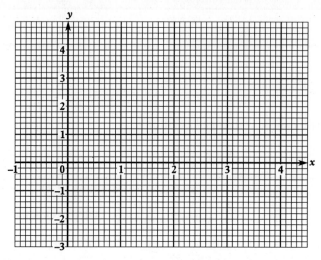

**(ii)** Use your graph to find the other solution to the equation
$$x^2 - 3x = 1.$$

**SEG**

**2.**

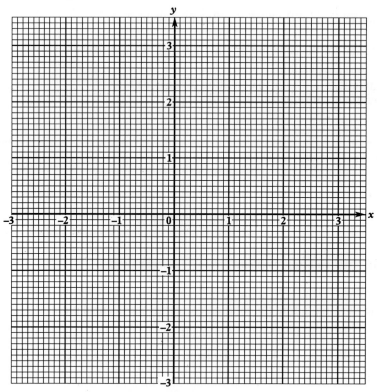

Use a **graphical method** to solve the equation

$$\frac{1}{x} = x^2 - 1.$$

You **must** show all your working.

**SEG**

**3.**

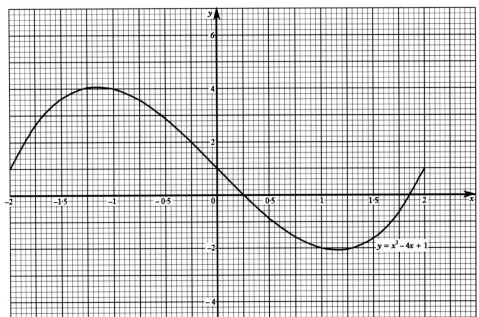

The diagram shows part of the graph of $y = x^3 - 4x + 1$.

**(a)** Use the graph to find approximate solutions in the range $-2 < x < 2$
of $\qquad x^3 - 4x + 1 = 0$

**(b)** By drawing suitable straight lines on the grid, find approximate solutions in the range $-2 < x < 2$ of the equations

(i) $x^3 - 4x - 1 = 0$,

(ii) $x^3 - 5x + 3 = 0$. **ULEAC**

**4.** The graphs of $y = x^3$ and $y = 3 - x^2$ are shown on the grid on the next page.

**(a)** Use the graphs to write down a solution of $x^3 + x^2 - 3 = 0$.

**(b)** Show that the equation

$$x = \sqrt{\frac{3}{x+1}}$$

can be rearranged to give $x^3 + x^2 - 3 = 0$.

**(c)** Use the equation

$$x = \sqrt{\frac{3}{x+1}}$$

and an iterative method to find an approximate solution of $x^3 + x^2 - 3 = 0$, giving your answer correct to 3 decimal places.

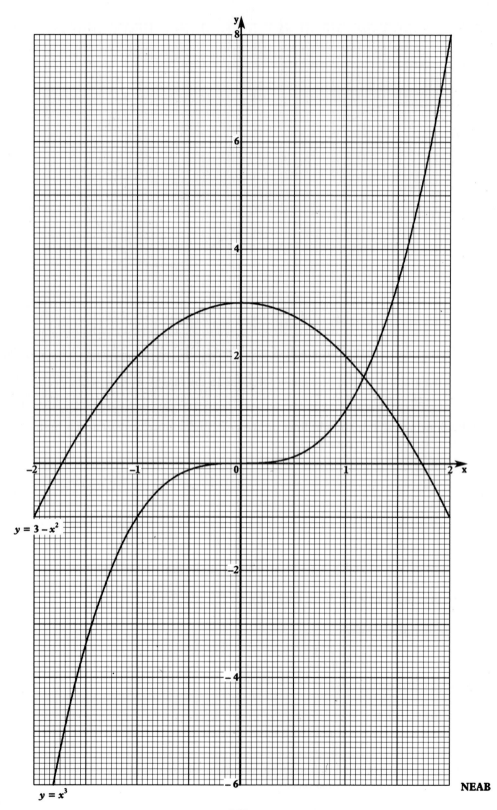

$y = 3 - x^2$

$y = x^3$

**NEAB**

## ZERO, NEGATIVE and FRACTIONAL INDICES

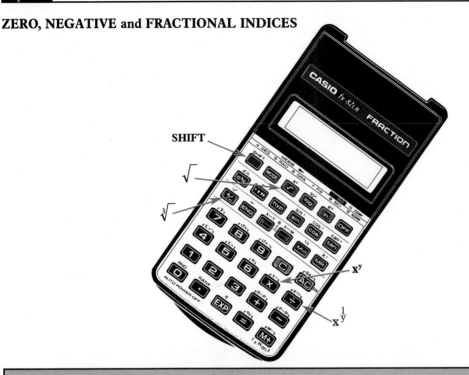

SHIFT

√

$\sqrt[3]{}$

$x^y$

$x^{\frac{1}{y}}$

---

### DISCUSSION EXERCISE 7:1

- What is the value of $\sqrt{16}$?

  Use this calculator keying sequence to find the value of $16^{\frac{1}{2}}$:   16   SHIFT   $x^{\frac{1}{y}}$   2   =

  Compare the answers for $\sqrt{16}$ and $16^{\frac{1}{2}}$.
  What if 16 was replaced with 49?
  What if 16 was replaced with 25?
  What if 16 was replaced with 7?
  What if . . .

  Make a statement about the values of $a^{\frac{1}{2}}$ and $\sqrt{a}$. Discuss.

- Use the cube root key ($\sqrt[3]{}$) on your calculator to find the value of $\sqrt[3]{8}$.

  Use this calculator keying sequence to find the value of $8^{\frac{1}{3}}$:   8   SHIFT   $x^{\frac{1}{y}}$   3   =

  Compare the answers for $8^{\frac{1}{3}}$ and $\sqrt[3]{8}$.

  Make a statement about the values of $a^{\frac{1}{3}}$ and $\sqrt[3]{a}$. Test your statement for many values of a.
  Discuss.

- How could you use the $x^{\frac{1}{y}}$ key to find the values of the following: $\sqrt[4]{16}$, $\sqrt[5]{30}$, $\sqrt[4]{20}$, . . . ?
  Discuss.

Remember:
$$a^m \times a^n = a^{m+n}$$
$$a^m \div a^n = a^{m-n}$$
$$(a^m)^n = a^{mn}$$

We can use these laws of indices to find the meaning of a zero index, a negative index and a fractional index.

Consider $\frac{2^4}{2^4}$. Since $a^m \div a^n = a^{m-n}$, then $\frac{2^4}{2^4} = 2^{4-4}$
$$= 2^0$$

But $\frac{2^4}{2^4} = \frac{2 \times 2 \times 2 \times 2}{2 \times 2 \times 2 \times 2}$
$$= 1$$

Hence, $2^0 = 1$.

The same argument is true if 2 is replaced by any other number. In general, we say that $\boxed{a^0 = 1}$.

Consider $2^3 \times 2^{-3}$. Since $a^m \times a^n = a^{m+n}$, then $2^3 \times 2^{-3} = 2^{3+(-3)}$
$$= 2^0$$
$$= 1.$$

Consider $\frac{2^3}{2^3}$. Now $\frac{2^3}{2^3} = 1$, which may be rewritten as $2^3 \times \frac{1}{2^3} = 1$.

Since both $2^3 \times 2^{-3}$ and $2^3 \times \frac{1}{2^3}$ are equal to 1, then $2^3 \times 2^{-3} = 2^3 \times \frac{1}{2^3}$.

Hence $2^{-3} = \frac{1}{2^3}$.

The same argument is true if 2 and 3 are replaced by any other numbers.

In general, we can say that $\boxed{a^{-n} = \frac{1}{a^n}}$.

Consider $(25)^{\frac{1}{2}}$; i.e. $(5^2)^{\frac{1}{2}}$. Since $(a^m)^n = a^{mn}$, then $(5^2)^{\frac{1}{2}} = 5^{2 \times \frac{1}{2}}$
$$= 5^1$$
$$= 5 \quad \text{i.e. } (25)^{\frac{1}{2}} = 5$$

We know that $\sqrt{25} = 5$. Hence $25^{\frac{1}{2}} = \sqrt{25}$.

The same argument is true if 25 is replaced by any other number.

In general, we say that $a^{\frac{1}{2}} = \sqrt{a}$.

Consider $8^{\frac{1}{3}}$. We can use reasoning similar to that above to show that $8^{\frac{1}{3}} = \sqrt[3]{8}$.

In general $a^{\frac{1}{3}} = \sqrt[3]{a}$.

We can extend the argument still further to show that $\boxed{a^{\frac{1}{n}} = \sqrt[n]{a}}$.

A meaning for $a^{\frac{m}{n}}$ can be found as follows.

$$a^{\frac{m}{n}} = (a^m)^{\frac{1}{n}} \qquad \text{Also } a^{\frac{m}{n}} = (a^{\frac{1}{n}})^m$$
$$= \sqrt[n]{a^m} \qquad\qquad\qquad = (\sqrt[n]{a})^m \qquad \text{Hence, } \boxed{a^{\frac{m}{n}} = \sqrt[n]{a^m} \text{ or } (\sqrt[n]{a})^m}.$$

## DISCUSSION EXERCISE 7:2

- The law $a^m \div a^n = a^{m-n}$ does not hold if a = 0. Why not? Which of the other laws of indices, shown "boxed" on the previous page, are true only if $a \neq 0$? ($a \neq 0$ is read as "a is not equal to zero".) Can m and n take all values?
  **Discuss.**

- **Discuss** how to prove that $8^{\frac{1}{3}} = \sqrt[3]{8}$.

*Worked Example* Without using the calculator, evaluate (a) $32^{\frac{1}{5}}$ (b) $2^{-4}$ (c) $8^{-\frac{1}{3}}$ (d) $36^{\frac{3}{2}}$.

*Answer* (a) $32^{\frac{1}{5}} = \sqrt[5]{32}$ (b) $2^{-4} = \frac{1}{2^4}$ (c) $8^{-\frac{1}{3}} = \frac{1}{8^{\frac{1}{3}}}$ (d) $36^{\frac{3}{2}} = (\sqrt{36})^3$

$\qquad = \sqrt[5]{2^5} \qquad\qquad = \frac{1}{16} \qquad\qquad = \frac{1}{\sqrt[3]{8}} \qquad\qquad = 6^3$

$\qquad = 2 \qquad\qquad\qquad\qquad\qquad\qquad = \frac{1}{\sqrt[3]{2^3}} \qquad\qquad = 216$

$\qquad\qquad\qquad\qquad\qquad\qquad\qquad\qquad = \frac{1}{2}$

*Worked Example* Evaluate $\sqrt[4]{80}$.

*Answer* Since 80 is not the 4th power of a whole number, we will use the calculator to evaluate $\sqrt[4]{80}$.

Rewrite $\sqrt[4]{80}$ as $80^{\frac{1}{4}}$. **Key** [80] [SHIFT] [$x^{\frac{1}{y}}$] [4] [=] to get answer of 2·99 to 2 d.p.

*Worked Example* Simplify (a) $\frac{x^5}{x^7}$ (b) $n^{1\cdot5} \times n^{-1}$ (c) $(a^{\frac{1}{3}})^5$ (d) $\sqrt{81x^8}$

(e) $5x^2y \times 2y^2$ (f) $5x^2y \times 2y^{-2}$

*Answer* (a) $\frac{x^5}{x^7} = x^{5-7}$ (b) $n^{1\cdot5} \times n^{-1} = n^{1\cdot5 + (-1)}$ (c) $(a^{\frac{1}{3}})^5 = a^{\frac{1}{3} \times 5}$

$\qquad\quad = x^{-2} \qquad\qquad\qquad\qquad = n^{0\cdot5} \qquad\qquad\qquad\qquad = a^{\frac{5}{3}}$

$\qquad\quad = \frac{1}{x^2} \qquad\qquad\qquad\qquad\quad = \sqrt{n}$

(d) $\sqrt{81x^8} = \sqrt{9^2 \times (x^4)^2}$ (e) $5x^2y \times 2y^2 = 10x^2y^3$ (f) $5x^2y \times 2y^{-2} = 5x^2y \times \frac{2}{y^2}$

$\qquad\qquad = 9x^4 \qquad\qquad\qquad\qquad\qquad\qquad\qquad\qquad\qquad\qquad = \frac{10x^2}{y}$

**Note** When we simplify expressions involving indices we usually give positive indices in the answers. This is illustrated in the answer to (a).

Notice that in (b) we gave the answer as $\sqrt{n}$. It is also acceptable to write the answer as $n^{\frac{1}{2}}$. We do not usually leave decimals in the indices.

## EXERCISE 7:3

1. What is the missing index?

(a) $\sqrt{36} = 36^{\cdots}$ (b) $\sqrt{28} = 28^{\cdots}$ (c) $\sqrt{100} = 100^{\cdots}$ (d) $\sqrt[3]{64} = 64^{\cdots}$

(e) $\sqrt[3]{10} = 10^{\cdots}$ (f) $\sqrt[4]{18} = 18^{\cdots}$ (g) $\sqrt[3]{94} = 94^{\cdots}$

2. Without using the calculator, evaluate these.

(a) $4^{\frac{1}{2}}$  (b) $16^{\frac{1}{2}}$  (c) $9^{\frac{1}{2}}$  (d) $64^{\frac{1}{2}}$  (e) $100^{\frac{1}{2}}$  (f) $8^{\frac{1}{3}}$

(g) $64^{\frac{1}{6}}$  (h) $125^{\frac{1}{3}}$  (i) $16^{\frac{1}{4}}$  (j) $81^{\frac{1}{4}}$  (k) $32^{\frac{1}{5}}$

3. Without using the calculator, evaluate the following.

(a) $2^4$  (b) $4^{-1}$  (c) $(\frac{1}{2})^4$  (d) $3^{-3}$  (e) $5^0$  (f) $27^{\frac{1}{3}}$  (g) $25^{\frac{1}{2}}$

(h) $16^{\frac{1}{4}}$  (i) $4^{\frac{3}{2}}$  (j) $8^{\frac{2}{3}}$  (k) $4^{-\frac{1}{2}}$  (l) $(\frac{1}{2})^{-1}$  (m) $(\frac{1}{4})^{\frac{1}{2}}$  (n) $(\frac{1}{64})^{\frac{1}{3}}$

(o) $4^{-\frac{5}{2}}$  (p) $9^{-\frac{3}{2}}$  (q) $8^{-\frac{2}{3}}$  (r) $27^{-\frac{5}{3}}$

4. Evaluate.  (a) $\sqrt[4]{30}$  (b) $\sqrt[4]{75}$  (c) $\sqrt[4]{100}$  (d) $\sqrt[4]{99}$  (e) $\sqrt[4]{120}$

5. Simplify.  (a) $(x^{\frac{2}{3}})^3$  (b) $(x^{\frac{2}{3}})^3$  (c) $(x^{-4})^{\frac{1}{2}}$  (d) $\frac{x^3}{x^2}$

(e) $\frac{x^2}{x^3}$  (f) $x^{1.5} \times x^{0.5}$  (g) $\frac{x^{-2}}{x^3}$  (h) $\frac{x^2 \times x^{0.5}}{x^{-1}}$

(i) $\frac{x^{1.5}}{x^{0.5}}$

6. Simplify.  (a) $3x^2y \times 4xy$  (b) $6xy^3 \times 2x^2y^2$  (c) $(3nm^3)^2$  (d) $4(n^4m)^2$

(e) $\frac{6nm^3}{2n^2m}$  (f) $2ab^3 \div 6a^2b$  (g) $3n^2x \div 12nx$

7. Simplify.  (a) $\sqrt{49x^6}$  (b) $\sqrt[3]{27n^6}$  (c) $\sqrt[4]{8y^{12}}$  (d) $\sqrt{100a^8}$

(e) $2n^5 \times 3n^{-2}$  (f) $5nm^2 \times 4n^{-1}$  (g) $(4n)^{-1}$  (h) $2a^2b^{-2} \times 3ab$

(i) $\frac{24x^2y}{8xy^{-1}}$  (j) $3ab^2 \div 6a^{-2}$  (k) $(4n^3)^{-2}$

8. Simplify.  (a) $\frac{x}{\sqrt{x}}$  (b) $\frac{x^2 \times \sqrt{x}}{x^{-1}}$  (c) $x^{-2} \times x^{\frac{1}{2}}$  (d) $\frac{x^2 \times x^{0.5}}{x^4}$

9. Without using the calculator, evaluate these.

(a) $(\frac{9}{25})^{\frac{1}{2}}$  (b) $(\frac{27}{64})^{\frac{1}{3}}$  (c) $(\frac{2}{3})^{-1}$  (d) $(\frac{1}{4})^{-\frac{5}{2}}$

(e) $(\frac{9}{16})^{-\frac{3}{2}}$  (f) $(\frac{8}{27})^{-\frac{2}{3}}$  (g) $(9 \times 10^{-2})^{\frac{1}{2}}$  (h) $(8 \times 4^{-3})^{\frac{1}{3}}$

**Review 1 Evaluate.**  (a) $2^0$  (b) $4^{-2}$  (c) $49^{\frac{1}{2}}$  (d) $27^{-\frac{1}{3}}$  (e) $(\frac{1}{9})^{\frac{1}{2}}$  (f) $\sqrt[4]{50}$

**Review 2 Simplify.**  (a) $(n^{\frac{3}{4}})^8$  (b) $\frac{n^4}{n^{-1}}$  (c) $\frac{x^3 \times x^{-2}}{x^4}$  (d) $\sqrt{16a^{12}}$

(e) $5x^2y \times 3x^3y^2$  (f) $3x^2 \div 6xy$  (g) $(2n^3)^{-2}$  (h) $\frac{12nm^{-1}}{4n^2m}$

(i) $\frac{\sqrt{x}}{x}$

**Review 3** Evaluate, without using the calculator.

(a) $16^{-\frac{3}{2}}$  (b) $(\frac{8}{27})^{\frac{1}{3}}$  (c) $(\frac{5}{3})^{-1}$  (d) $(\frac{1}{8})^{-\frac{5}{3}}$  (e) $(\frac{4}{9})^{-\frac{1}{2}}$

(f) $(64 \times 5^{-3})^{\frac{1}{3}}$

## EXPONENTIAL EQUATIONS

An index is also called an **exponent**. For instance, in the expression $3^5$, 5 is the index or exponent. Equations involving indices are called **exponential equations**.

*Worked Example*  Find x if $x^4 = 0.0016$.

**Answer**  $x^4 = 0.0016$

$x = \sqrt[4]{0.0016}$

$= (0.0016)^{\frac{1}{4}}$

$= 0.2$  **Keying** $\boxed{0.0016}$ $\boxed{\text{SHIFT}}$ $\boxed{x^{\frac{1}{y}}}$ $\boxed{4}$ $\boxed{=}$

*Worked Example*  Find the value of n if  (a) $a^{-2} \times a^{\frac{1}{2}} = a^n$  (b) $n^{-1} = 3^{-2}$.

**Answer**  (a) $a^{-2} \times a^{\frac{1}{2}} = a^n$  (b) $n^{-1} = 3^{-2}$

$a^{(-2+\frac{1}{2})} = a^n$  $n^{-1} = (3^2)^{-1}$

$a^{-1.5} = a^n$  $n = 3^2$

$-1.5 = n$  $n = 9$

*Worked Example*  Find the value of n if  (a) $2^n = 128$  (b) $5^n = 1$.

**Answer**  (a) $2^n = 128$  (b) $5^n = 1$

$2^n = 2^7$ (writing 128 as $2^7$)  $5^n = 5^0$ (writing 1 as $5^0$)

$n = 7$  $n = 0$

*Worked Example*  Find x if  (a) $16^x = 2$  (b) $(\frac{1}{3})^x = 81$  (c) $4^{-x} = 8$.

**Answer**  (a) $16^x = 2$  (b) $(\frac{1}{3})^x = 81$  (c) $4^{-x} = 8$

$(2^4)^x = 2^1$  $(3^{-1})^x = 3^4$  $(2^2)^{-x} = 2^3$

$2^{4x} = 2^1$  $3^{-x} = 3^4$  $2^{-2x} = 2^3$

$4x = 1$  $-x = 4$  $-2x = 3$

$x = \frac{1}{4}$  $x = -4$  $x = -\frac{3}{2}$

*Worked Example*  Solve the equations.  (a) $8^{x+1} = 2^x$  (b) $4^{\frac{n}{2}} = 128$

**Answer**  (a)  $8^{x+1} = 2^x$  (b) $4^{\frac{n}{2}} = 128$

$(2^3)^{x+1} = 2^x$  $(2^2)^{\frac{n}{2}} = 2^7$

$2^{3x+3} = 2^x$  $2^{2 \times \frac{n}{2}} = 2^7$

$3x + 3 = x$  $2^n = 2^7$

$2x = -3$  $n = 7$

$x = -\frac{3}{2}$

## EXERCISE 7:4

1. Find the value of x.
   - (a) $x^3 = 0.027$
   - (b) $x^4 = 0.1296$
   - (c) $x^5 = 0.00001$
   - (d) $x^4 = 2.0736$
   - (e) $x^6 = 0.015625$
   - (f) $x^3 = 3.375$

2. Find the value of n.
   - (a) $p^3 \times p^{-\frac{1}{2}} = p^n$
   - (b) $x^n = x^2 \times x^{1.5}$
   - (c) $a^4 \times \sqrt{a} = a^n$
   - (d) $n^{-1} = 4^{-1}$
   - (e) $n^{-1} = 2^{-4}$
   - (f) $n^{-2} = 3^{-4}$

3. Solve these equations.
   - (a) $2^x = 8$
   - (b) $3^n = 81$
   - (c) $5^y = 25$
   - (d) $7^x = 1$
   - (e) $3^y = 27$
   - (f) $6^n = 216$
   - (g) $10^x = 1$
   - (h) $10^x = 100\ 000$

4. Solve for x.
   - (a) $3^x = \frac{1}{9}$
   - (b) $(\frac{1}{16})^x = 4$
   - (c) $8^x = 2$
   - (d) $(\frac{1}{4})^x = 16$
   - (e) $4^x = 32$
   - (f) $9^x = 27$
   - (g) $(\frac{1}{4})^x = 8$
   - (h) $16^{-x} = \frac{1}{2}$
   - (i) $5^{-x} = \frac{1}{125}$
   - (j) $3^{-x} = 81$
   - (k) $2^{-x} = 32$

5. Find n if
   - (a) $2^{n+1} = 16$
   - (b) $9^{n-1} = 27$
   - (c) $2^{n+4} = 4^n$
   - (d) $4^n = 8^{n-3}$
   - (e) $3^{\frac{n}{2}} = 27$
   - (f) $2^{\frac{3n}{2}} = 8$
   - (g) $3 \times 9^n = 81$
   - (h) $8 \times 2^{\frac{n}{2}} = 4$
   - (i) $9^n = (\sqrt{3})^6$

6. The number, n, of yeast cells in a yeast culture after time, t, is given by $n = 4^t$. (t is in hours.)
   - (a) How many yeast cells are there after 8 hours?
   - (b) Solve the equation $64 = 4^t$ to find the time taken for 64 yeast cells to grow.
   - (c) How long does it take for 32 yeast cells to grow?
   - (d) How many yeast cells were in this culture when it was started?

**Review 1** Solve these equations.
   - (a) $x^5 = 0.00032$
   - (b) $2^x = 1$
   - (c) $2^n = 64$
   - (d) $5^y = 125$
   - (e) $16^x = 4$
   - (f) $(\frac{1}{3})^x = 9$
   - (g) $100^x = 10$
   - (h) $32^{-x} = \frac{1}{4}$
   - (i) $4^y = 8$
   - (j) $3^{-1} = n^{-2}$

**Review 2** For what value of n is $x^{-\frac{1}{2}} \times x^2 = x^n$?

**Review 3** Find the value of x.
   - (a) $3^{x+3} = 3$
   - (b) $2^{x+3} = 4$
   - (c) $2^{\frac{x}{2}} = 8$
   - (d) $3^{x+4} = 9^x$

**Review 4** The formula $N = 2^t$ gives the number, N, of wasps in a colony after t days.
   - (a) How many wasps were there after 2 days?
   - (b) Solve the equation $128 = 2^t$ to find how long it takes for the colony to grow to 128 wasps.
   - (c) After how many days are there 64 wasps?

Exponential equations may also be solved graphically.

*Worked Example* Draw the graph of $y = 2^x$ for values of x between –2 and 3.
Use this graph to find the value of x for which $2^x = 5$.
What line must be drawn on the graph of $y = 2^x$ to be able to solve the equation $2^{x+2} = 5$?

*Answer*

| x | –2 | –1 | 0 | 1 | 2 | 3 |
|---|----|----|---|---|---|---|
| y | 0·25 | 0·5 | 1 | 2 | 4 | 8 |

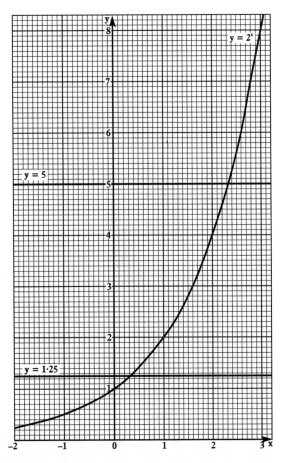

To solve $2^x = 5$ we find where the graphs $y = 2^x$ and $y = 5$ meet.
The curve $y = 2^x$ and the line $y = 5$ meet at about the point (2·3, 5).
Hence if $2^x = 5$ then $x = 2·3$ to 1 d.p.

The equation $2^{x+2} = 5$ may be solved as follows.
$$2^{x+2} = 5$$
$$2^x \times 2^2 = 5$$
$$2^x \times 4 = 5$$
$$2^x = \tfrac{5}{4}$$
$$2^x = 1·25$$

The curve $y = 2^x$ meets the line $y = 1·25$ at about the point (0·3, 1·25).
Hence the solution to $2^x = 1·25$ is $x = 0·3$ (1 d.p.). That is, the solution to $2^{x+2} = 5$ is $x = 0·3$ (1 d.p.).

## EXERCISE 7:5

1. Draw the graph of $y = 3^x$ for values of x between –2 and 2. Use this graph to find approximate solutions for the equations  (a) $3^x = 8$
   (b) $3^x = 4·5$.

2. Draw the graph of $y = 2^{-x}$ for values of x between –3 and 2. Use this graph to find approximate solutions for the equations
   (a) $2^{-x} = 6$
   (b) $\dfrac{1}{2^x} = 3·5$.

3.  What lines need to be drawn on the graph of $y = 3^x$ to be able to solve the equations
    (a) $3^x = x + 3$
    (b) $3^x - 2 + 2x = 0$?

4.  Use the graph of $y = 3^x$ drawn in **question 1** to find approximate solutions for the
    equations    (a) $3^{x+1} = 6$          (b) $3^{x-1} = 2$.

5.  Use the graph of $y = 2^{-x}$ drawn in **question 2** to explain why the equation $2^{-x} = -2$ has no
    solution.

6.  The formula $V = 5000 \times 0.8^t$ gives the value of a car after t years.
    (a) What is the new value of this car?
    (b) What is the value of this car after 2 years?
    (c) Draw the graph of V against t for t between 0 and 10 years.
    (d) Use the graph to find the approximate time it takes for this car to halve in value.

**Review** (i) Copy and complete this table of values for $y = 10^x$, rounding each y-value to 2 d.p.

| x | −1·0 | −0·8 | −0·6 | −0·4 | −0·2 | 0 | 0·2 | 0·4 | 0·6 | 0·8 | 1·0 |
|---|---|---|---|---|---|---|---|---|---|---|---|
| y | 0·1 | 0·16 | 0·25 | | | | | | | | 10 |

Draw the graph of $y = 10^x$ for values of x between −1 and 1.
(ii) Use the graph to solve the equations    (a) $10^x = 7.8$
                                             (b) $10^{x+2} = 450$
                                             (c) $10^{x-2} = \frac{3}{100}$.

## RESEARCH PROJECT 7:6

Logarithms

The equation $9^x = 27$ may be solved by firstly rewriting both 9 and 27 as powers of 3.
$$\text{That is,} \quad 9^x = 27$$
$$(3^2)^x = 3^3$$
$$3^{2x} = 3^3$$
$$2x = 3$$
$$x = 1.5.$$
The equation $9^x = 25$ cannot be solved in this way. This equation may be solved
graphically or by using logarithms.
Research logarithms.

# CHAPTER 7 REVIEW

1. To what power must $x^3$ be raised to give

   **(i)** $x^6$,

   **(ii)** $\dfrac{1}{x^3}$ ?  SEG

2. $$y = 2^{-x}$$

   **(a)** Calculate the value of $y$ when $x = 0$.

   **(b)** Calculate the value of $y$ when $x = 3$.  ULEAC

3. Simplify

   **(a)** $\dfrac{x^2}{x^5}$        **(b)** $(x^{\frac{5}{2}})^2$        **(c)** $x^3 \div \dfrac{x^0}{x^4}$  ULEAC

4. Evaluate:

   **(a)** $16^{\frac{1}{4}}$,        **(b)** $2^{-4}$,        **(c)** $27^{-\frac{1}{3}}$.  SEG

5. Find the values of $n, p$ and $q$ for which

   **(a)** $2^n = 128$      **(b)** $2^p = 1$      **(c)** $2^q = (\sqrt{2})^5$  NICCEA

6. **(a)** Simplify $x^4 \div x^{-3}$.

   **(b)** Find the value of $x$ for which $4^{\frac{x}{2}} = 32$.  ULEAC

7. Find the values of $p, q$ and $r$.

   **(a)** $64 = 4^p$      **(b)** $5^q = 1$      **(c)** $\frac{1}{4} = 2^r$  SEG

8. **(a)** Express $81^{\frac{1}{2}}$ as a fraction in the form $\frac{a}{b}$ where $a$ and $b$ are integers.

   **(b)** Simplify $a^6 \div a^{-2}$.

   **(c)** Find the value of $y$ for which $2 \times 4^y = 64$.  ULEAC

**9.** John places a cake in his freezer. The temperature, $T\,°C$, of the cake after $t$ minutes is given by the formula

$$T = 32\,(2^{-t}) - 18.$$

**(a)** Complete the table below.

| $t$ (minutes) | 0 | 1 | 2 | 3 | 4 |
|---|---|---|---|---|---|
| $T\,(°C)$ | | | | | |

**(b)** Draw the graph of $T$ against $t$.

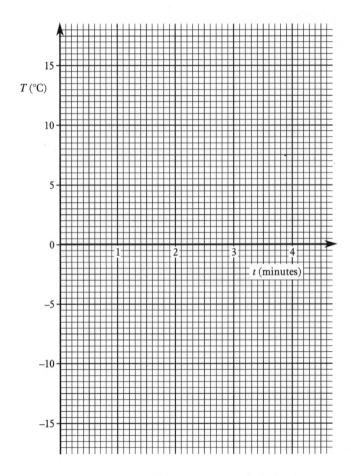

**(c)** John knows that the cake's temperature is 14°C when he places it in the freezer. He does not know the formula for its temperature after $t$ minutes.

He estimates that its temperature will fall by 10°C every minute.

On the grid, draw the graph showing how John thinks the temperature will vary during the first three minutes.

**(d)** Use your graph to find the time when the estimated temperature is the same as the true temperature of the cake.

**MEG**

**10.** On 1st September bacteria were introduced into a lake. The bacteria grew and spread so that after $t$ days the volume of water containing bacteria, $V$, was given by the formula
$$V = 2^t \text{ units.}$$
**(a)** Complete the table for the given values of $t$

| $t$ | 0 | 1 | 2 | 3 | 4 | 5 | 6 |
|-----|---|---|---|---|---|---|---|
| $V$ | | | | | | | |

**(b)** Draw the graph of $V = 2^t$ on graph paper.

At the same time on 1st September the lake was contaminated by a pollutant. The pollutant spread so that the volume of water containing pollutant, $P$, after $t$ days was given by the formula
$$P = 30 + 4t.$$

**(c)** On the same graph page draw the graph of $P = 30 + 4t$.

**(d)** After how many days was the volume containing bacteria equal to the volume containing pollutant? (Give your answer to one decimal place). **NICCEA**

**11.** The formula below is used to forecast the population, $P$ million people, of a small island at a time $t$ years after the 1st of January, 1993.

$$P = 1 \cdot 3 \, (1 \cdot 05)^t$$

**(a)** Complete the table below which shows the values of $P$ for values of $t$ from 0 to 18 in steps of 2.

| $t$ | 0 | 2 | 4 | 6 | 8 | 10 | 12 | 14 | 16 | 18 |
|-----|------|------|------|------|------|------|----|----|------|------|
| $P$ | 1·3 | 1·43 | 1·58 | 1·74 | 1·92 | 2·12 | | | 2·84 | 3·13 |

**(b)** On graph paper, plot a graph of the forecasted population figures for values of $t$ from 0 to 18.

**(c)** Use the graph to estimate the population of the island on the 1st of January, 1996.

**(d)** Use your graph to find out when the population will be double the population on the 1st of January, 1996. **WJEC**

**12.** The time, $T$ minutes, needed to cook a turkey and the weight, $W$ pounds, of the turkey are connected by the formula

$$T^3 W^{-2} = k, \text{ where } k \text{ is a constant.}$$

It takes 140 minutes to cook an 8 pound turkey.

**(a)** Calculate the value of $k$.

The formula can be rewritten as $T = aW^n$.

**(b)** Find the values of $a$ and $n$. **ULEAC**

# Expressing Laws in Symbolic Form

## LINEAR LAWS

When the relationship between two variables x and y, for which we have sets of data, is known to be of the form y = ax + b, we can proceed as follows to find this relationship.

*Step 1*  Plot the data.

*Step 2*  Draw the line of best fit.

*Step 3*  Find the gradient of this line and the point where the line crosses the y-axis. Use y = mx + c to write down the equation of this line.

This equation gives the approximate relationship between the two variables; that is, the law connecting the two variables.

*Example*  Agna conducted an experiment on the solubility of salt. She heated a quantity of water to 20°C, then added salt slowly until no more would dissolve at this temperature. Agna then raised the temperature of the water, adding more salt and noting the maximum amount that would dissolve at the higher temperature. Her results are shown on the table. T is the temperature of the water, A is the maximum amount of salt.

| T (°C)     | 20 | 30 | 40 | 45 | 50 | 55 | 60 |
|------------|----|----|----|----|----|----|----|
| A (grams)  | 29 | 32 | 36 | 38 | 40 | 41 | 43 |

This data is shown plotted on the following graph. The line of best fit is drawn.

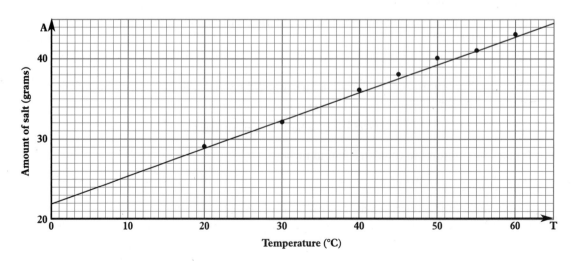

140

The line of best fit crosses the vertical axis at about 22. The gradient of this line is worked out as follows.

Choose two points on the line, say (3, 23) and (55, 41).

Vertical distance between these two points = 18

Horizontal distance between these two points = 52

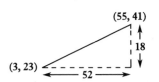

Gradient of line = $\frac{18}{52}$

$\qquad\qquad\quad = 0.35$ (2 d.p.)

Using $y = mx + c$, equation of line is $A = 0.35T + 22$.

That is, the law connecting A and T is $A = 0.35T + 22$.

---

### DISCUSSION EXERCISE 8:1

Suppose the data for the previous example was plotted as shown below.

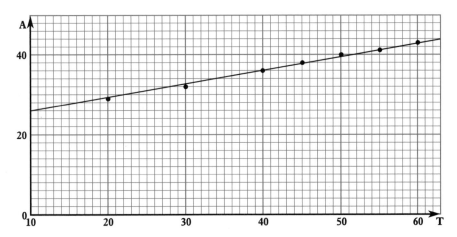

Can m still be worked out easily? Can c still be read from this graph? If not, how can you find the value of c? **Discuss**.

---

### EXERCISE 8:2

1.

| x | 1 | 2 | 5 | 8 | 10 |
|---|---|---|---|---|---|
| y | 1·3 | 3·8 | 11·2 | 18·7 | 24 |

In an experiment, these values were obtained for x and y. x and y are known to be connected by the law $y = ax + b$.

(a) Plot the graph of y against x. Draw the line of best fit.

(b) Use the line of best fit to find approximate values for b and a. Hence, write down the approximate law connecting x and y.

2.  The relationship between the resistance R, of a length of wire, and the temperature t is known to be R = at + b. Michelle conducted an experiment to find this relationship for a particular length of wire. Her results are shown in the table.

| t (°C) | 20 | 25 | 30 | 35 | 40 | 45 | 50 |
|---|---|---|---|---|---|---|---|
| R (ohms) | 5·40 | 5·49 | 5·61 | 5·68 | 5·79 | 5·90 | 5·99 |

(a) Plot the graph of R against t. Draw the line of best fit.
(b) Find approximate values for a and b. Hence find the approximate relationship between t and R for Michelle's length of wire.
(c) Use this relationship to estimate the resistance at 38°C.

3.  "Alpha Print" quotes for printing a book. The quotes for various numbers of this book are shown below.

| Number of books, n | 100 | 400 | 500 | 700 |
|---|---|---|---|---|
| Quote, q, in pounds | 350 | 800 | 950 | 1250 |

(a) Draw the graph of q against n.
(b) Use the graph to find the law connecting q and n.
(c) What will Alpha Print quote for printing 300 copies of this book?
(d) The data given in this example differs from that in the previous examples. In what way is this data different?

4.

| t (sec) | 4 | 5 | 10 | 20 | 25 |
|---|---|---|---|---|---|
| v (m/sec) | 11 | 13·5 | 22 | 30 | 53 |

The velocity v of a vehicle, moving with constant acceleration, is known to obey the law v = u + at. t is time, a is the constant acceleration and u is the initial velocity. The data in the table was collected. For this data:
(a) Plot a graph of v against t.
(b) One of the sets of data is inconsistent with the others. Which set is this?
(c) Draw the line of best fit for the data.
(d) Use the line of best fit to find the law connecting v and t.

Review Adam hung various masses m on the end of an uncoiled spring. For each mass, he measured the total length *l* of the spring. Adam's results are shown in the table.

| m (grams) | 10 | 20 | 30 | 40 | 50 | 60 | 70 | 80 |
|---|---|---|---|---|---|---|---|---|
| *l* (cm) | 4·3 | 5·5 | 6·6 | 7·3 | 8·3 | 9·5 | 10·7 | 11·4 |

Adam suspected that the law connecting m and *l* was *l* = am + b.
(a) Graph m against *l*.
(b) If the law *l* = am + b seems to be true, find approximate values for a and b. Write down the approximate relationship between m and *l*.
(c) Estimate the length of the spring when a mass of 25 grams is hung from it.

# NON-LINEAR LAWS

Consider the relationship $y = 2x^2 - 5$. We can plot the graph of $y = 2x^2 - 5$ by drawing up a table of values.

| x | −3 | −2 | −1 | 0 | 1 | 2 | 3 |
|---|----|----|----|---|---|---|---|
| y | 13 | 3 | −3 | −5 | −3 | 3 | 13 |

The parabola is drawn by plotting y against x.

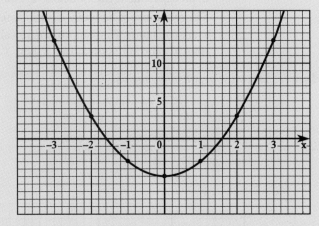

We can "transform" the parabola into a straight line by plotting y against $x^2$, instead of y against x.

| x | −3 | −2 | −1 | 0 | 1 | 2 | 3 |
|---|----|----|----|---|---|---|---|
| x² | 9 | 4 | 1 | 0 | 1 | 4 | 9 |
| y | 13 | 3 | −3 | −5 | −3 | 3 | 13 |

Where does this line cross the y-axis?
What is the gradient of this line?

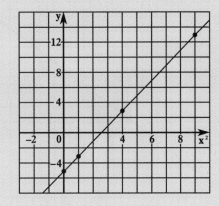

## DISCUSSION EXERCISE 8:3

- Suppose we are given sets of data and we know the relationship between the variables x and y is of the form $y = ax^2 + b$, where a and b are constants. How can we use the above to find the actual relationship? **Discuss.**
  What if the relationship was of the form $y = ax^3 + b$?
  What if the relationship was of the form $y = \dfrac{a}{x} + b$?

- Suppose we are given sets of data and we know the relationship is of the form $y = ax^n + b$ where a and b are constants. How could we find n? Do we have to find n before we find a and b? Could we use sketch graphs or do we have to plot accurate graphs? **Discuss.**

143

**Worked Example**

| x | 50 | 60 | 75 | 100 | 150 |
|---|----|----|----|-----|-----|
| y | 150 | 145 | 140 | 135 | 130 |

In an experiment the values of x and y, shown in the table, are measured. The relationship between x and y is known to be $y = \frac{a}{x} + b$ where a and b are constants. Find approximate values for a and b. Hence find an approximate law connecting x and y.

**Answer**  Draw the graph of y against $\frac{1}{x}$.

| x | 50 | 60 | 75 | 100 | 150 |
|---|----|----|----|-----|-----|
| $\frac{1}{x}$ | 0·02 | 0·017 | 0·013 | 0·01 | 0·007 |
| y | 150 | 145 | 140 | 135 | 130 |

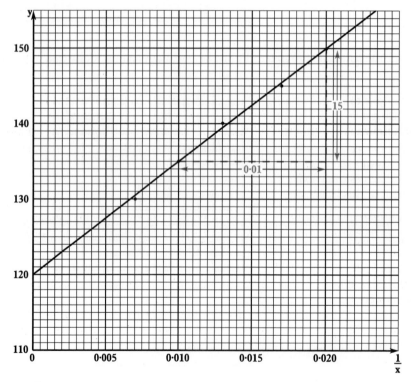

$y = \frac{a}{x} + b$ may be rewritten as $y = a(\frac{1}{x}) + b$ which is of the same form as $y = mx + c$.

Then b is where the line crosses the y-axis; a is the gradient of the line.
From the graph, b = 120.
Two points on the line are (0·01, 135), (0·02, 150). Gradient of the line = $\frac{15}{0·01} = 1500$.
That is, a = 1500.

Hence an approximate law connecting x and y is  $y = \frac{1500}{x} + 120$.

Note  Suppose we were not told the relationship between x and y was of the type
$y = \frac{a}{x} + b$ but we did know it was of the type $y = ax^n + b$ where n is an integer.
In this case, the first step is to draw the graph of y against x. This is shown below.

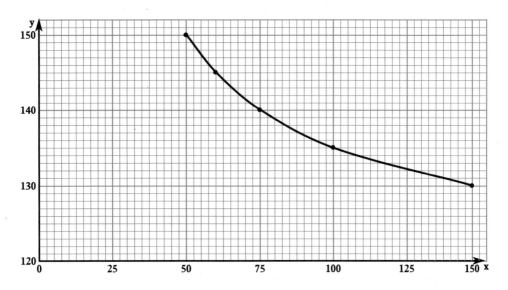

The next step is to decide whether the graph is part of a straight line (then n = 1) or a
parabola (then n = 2) or a cubic (then n = 3) or a hyperbola (then n = –1).
The graph drawn above is part of a hyperbola. Hence n = –1. That is, the relationship is
of the type $y = ax^{-1} + b$ or $y = \frac{a}{x} + b$. We then continue, as in the worked example, to
find a and b and hence find the approximate relationship.

## EXERCISE 8:4

1.  A vehicle starts from rest and accelerates for 10 sec. If the acceleration, a, is constant the
    formula connecting time, t, with distance, s, is $s = at^2$. For this vehicle, the following
    measurements were taken.

    | t | 0 | 2 | 3 | 4 | 5 | 6 | 10 |
    |---|---|---|---|---|---|---|----|
    | s | 0 | 18 | 40·5 | 72 | 112·5 | 162 | 450 |

    By plotting s against $t^2$ determine if the
    acceleration was constant. If so, find this
    acceleration.

2.  To test the theory that, at a constant
    temperature, the pressure P of a gas is
    inversely proportional to the volume V an

    | V | 2 | 2·5 | 3 | 4 | 5 | 6 | 9 | 10 |
    |---|---|-----|---|---|---|---|---|----|
    | P | 7·5 | 6·1 | 5·0 | 3·7 | 3·0 | 2·4 | 1·6 | 1·5 |

    experiment was conducted. The results are shown in the table.

    Plot P against $\frac{1}{V}$.

    Does this graph confirm that $P = \frac{k}{V}$ where k is a constant? If so, find an approximate
    formula connecting P and V for this gas.

3. The force, F, needed to keep a trolley moving at a steady speed, v, is thought to obey the law $F = av^2 + b$ where a and b are constants. For this trolley, Dianne took the measurements shown.

| v (m/s) | 1 | 1·5 | 2·5 | 5 | 7 | 10 |
|---------|---|-----|-----|---|---|-----|
| F (N) | 45 | 48 | 51 | 72 | 95 | 140 |

(a) Plot F against $v^2$.

(b) Draw a line of best fit. Use this line to find an approximate law connecting F and v.

4. It is thought that the formula $P = av^3 + b$ gives the relationship between the speed, v, of a ship and the power, P, developed. The data in the table gives some corresponding values of v and P for this ship.

| v | 2 | 2·5 | 3 | 3·5 | 4 | 4·5 | 5 |
|---|---|-----|---|-----|---|-----|---|
| P | 49 | 53 | 59 | 66 | 77 | 91 | 108 |

Plot P against $v^3$.

Does this graph verify that $P = av^3 + b$? If so, find the approximate relationship between v and P for this ship.

5. In the formula $R = \dfrac{E}{I} - R_B$, E is the e.m.f. of a battery of resistance $R_B$; I is the current and R is the resistance in a circuit of which the battery is part.

To find E and $R_B$, Cheung took various readings for I and R. His readings are shown in the table.

| I (amps) | 2 | 4 | 5 | 10 | 12 |
|----------|---|---|---|----|----|
| R (ohms) | 3·37 | 1·38 | 1·08 | 0·21 | 0·10 |

(a) Cheung plotted R against $\dfrac{1}{I}$. Explain how he could use this graph to find the e.m.f. and the resistance of the battery.

(b) Find an approximate formula connecting I and R.

6. Light from two sources is striking an object. One source is the background lighting of the laboratory and the other is a lamp shining directly onto the object. The total light intensity on the object obeys a law of the form $I = \dfrac{k}{d^2} + l$ where d is the distance of the lamp from the object and both k and l are constants.

The data in the table was gathered in order to find an approximate law connecting d and I.

| d | 0·4 | 0·5 | 1 | 2 | 2·5 |
|---|-----|-----|---|---|-----|
| I | 55 | 36 | 13 | 7 | 6·3 |

Plot I against $\dfrac{1}{d^2}$. Explain how this graph can be used to find an approximate law connecting d and I. Find this law.

7. The length, $l$, of a pendulum and the time, T, for one complete swing are known to be related by $T = k\sqrt{l}$ where k is a constant.

| $l$ (m) | 0·6 | 0·8 | 2·0 | 2·4 | 2·8 | 3·0 |
|---------|-----|-----|-----|-----|-----|-----|
| T (sec) | 1·6 | 1·8 | 2·8 | 3·1 | 3·4 | 3·5 |

Melissa measured T for various lengths $l$. She then plotted T against $\sqrt{l}$. How should Melissa continue to find the approximate relationship between $l$ and T? What is this relationship?

8. The data given in each of the following was collected in experiments. For each, it is known that the formula connecting x and y is of the form $y = ax^n + b$ where n is an integer and a and b are constants. For each, sketch a graph to find n. Confirm your value for n by plotting y against $x^n$. Use the graph of y against $x^n$ to find approximate values for a and b. Hence find an approximate formula connecting x and y.

(a)

| x | 2 | 3 | 4 | 5 | 6 |
|---|---|---|---|---|---|
| y | 1·5 | 6·3 | 13·5 | 22·1 | 33·6 |

(b)

| x | 2 | 3 | 5 | 8 | 10 |
|---|---|---|---|---|---|
| y | 5·3 | 6·5 | 9·9 | 14·0 | 17·1 |

(c)

| x | 2 | 3 | 5 | 8 | 10 |
|---|---|---|---|---|---|
| y | 5·8 | 5·5 | 5·2 | 5·05 | 5·0 |

(d)

| x | 2 | 3 | 5 | 8 | 10 |
|---|---|---|---|---|---|
| y | 1·5 | 5·0 | 8·0 | 13·0 | 17·5 |

(e)

| x | 2 | 3 | 5 | 8 | 10 |
|---|---|---|---|---|---|
| y | 2·5 | 4·7 | 10·8 | 26·6 | 40·8 |

(f)

| x | 2 | 3 | 5 | 8 | 10 |
|---|---|---|---|---|---|
| y | 4·8 | 3·3 | 2·2 | 1·6 | 1·3 |

(g)

| x | 2 | 3 | 4 | 5 | 6 |
|---|---|---|---|---|---|
| y | 0·2 | 4·0 | 11·5 | 23·5 | 41·5 |

Review 1  For a particular type of wire the diameter, d, of the wire and the current, I necessary to fuse the wire is thought to be related by the formula $I = ad^2 + b$ where a and b are constants.

In an experiment, these values of d and I were obtained.

| d (mm) | 1 | 2 | 4 | 5 | 7 |
|---|---|---|---|---|---|
| I (amps) | 5·06 | 5·21 | 5·80 | 6·22 | 7·45 |

(a) Plot I against $d^2$.
(b) Draw the line of best fit.
(c) Find approximate values for a and b. Hence find an approximate formula connecting I and d.

Review 2  In each of the following, x and y are related by a formula of the type $y = ax^n + b$. Find the approximate formula.

(a)

| x | 5 | 6 | 7 | 12 | 15 |
|---|---|---|---|---|---|
| y | 4·50 | 4·42 | 4·31 | 4·21 | 4·17 |

(b)

| x | 5 | 6 | 8 | 12 | 15 |
|---|---|---|---|---|---|
| y | 1 | 3 | 9 | 25 | 40 |

147

## DISCUSSION EXERCISE 8:5

- *"Simultaneous equations may be used to find the law connecting the variables in all the examples in Exercise 8:2."* Discuss this statement. As part of your discussion, use simultaneous equations to find some of the laws.
  Could simultaneous equations be used to find the laws connecting the variables in all the examples in Exercise 8:4? Discuss.

- *"Some of the laws connecting the variables in this chapter could be found by using proportion."* Discuss this statement. As part of your discussion, discuss which of the examples in the exercises could be answered by using direct or indirect proportion.

- Can you think of ways other than using graphs or simultaneous equations or proportion of finding the law connecting two variables? Discuss.

- Discuss the "best" way of finding the relationship between two variables.

## RESEARCH PROJECT 8:6

"Least Squares" calculations

The equation of a line is $y = mx + c$. To find the equation of the line of best fit for sets of data we can *calculate* m and c rather than find these values by drawing. We may use the method of least squares to calculate m and c.
Research this method of least squares.

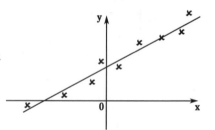

## RESEARCH PROJECT 8:7

Using logarithms to find relationships

| x | 1·2 | 2·0 | 3·8 | 5·1 | 8·9 | 9·2 | 9·5 | 12·3 | 19·4 |
|---|-----|-----|-----|-----|-----|-----|-----|------|------|
| y | 3·1 | 3·4 | 4·1 | 4·6 | 5·8 | 5·9 | 6·0 | 6·9 | 8·8 |

The relationship between these variables, x and y, is $y = 0.6x^{0.8} + 2.4$. This is of the type $y = ax^n + b$. Unlike the examples in this chapter, n is not an integer.
We can find the values of n, a and b by using logarithms. Research the use of logarithms in finding the relationship between two variables for which we are given sets of data.

# CHAPTER 8 REVIEW

1. In an experiment the following values of $x$ and $y$ were measured.

| $x$ | 0·12 | 0·24 | 0·36 | 0·48 | 0·60 | 0·72 |
|-----|------|------|------|------|------|------|
| $y$ | 0·45 | 0·54 | 0·64 | 0·73 | 0·83 | 0·93 |

(a) Plot these points on the graph paper.

(b) Explain why it would appear that $x$ and $y$ obey a relationship of the form $y = ax + b$.

(c) Use your graph to calculate the values of $a$ and $b$.

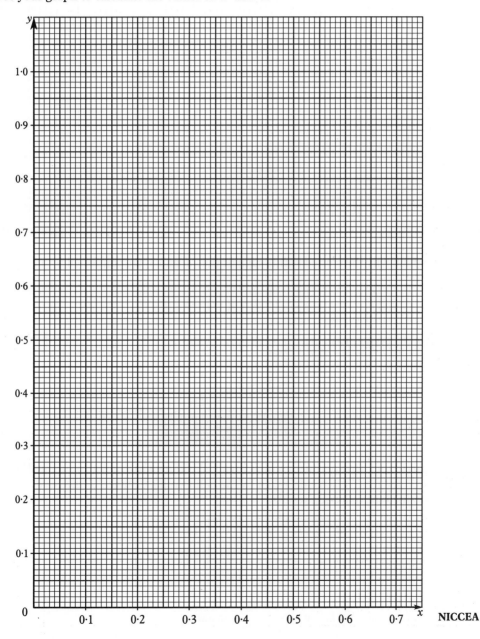

NICCEA

2. In an experiment, values of $d$ and $t$ were measured. Values of $d$ and $\frac{1}{t}$ were plotted as below.

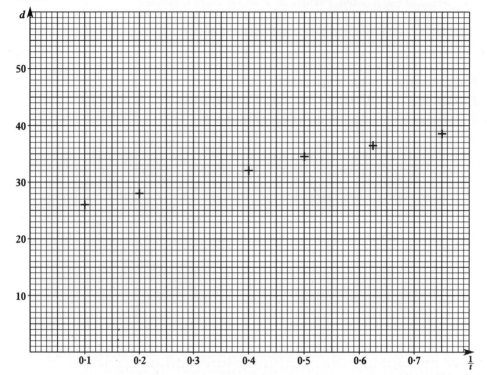

(a) Explain why the plotted points suggest that $d$ and $t$ are connected by an equation of the form

$$d = a\left(\frac{1}{t}\right) + b$$

(b) Use the graph to calculate the values of $a$ and $b$.    **NICCEA**

3.

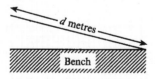

Julie carried out an experiment which involved rolling a ball down an inclined plane. She measured the time, $t$ seconds, taken by the ball to roll a distance $d$ metres down the plane. She obtained the following results.

| $d$ | 0·50 | 0·75 | 1·00 | 1·25 | 1·50 |
|-----|------|------|------|------|------|
| $t$ | 1·32 | 1·60 | 1·83 | 2·05 | 2·25 |
| $t^2$ | | | | | |

She was told that $d = kt^2$, where $k$ is a constant.

150

(a) (i) Fill in the values of $t^2$ in the table.

   (ii) On the grid, plot these values of $d$ against $t^2$.

(b) Explain why these points suggest that $d = kt^2$.

(c) Hence find the value of $k$.

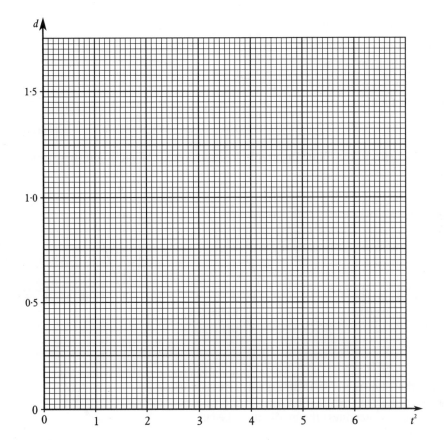

NEAB

## GRADIENT of a CURVE

### DISCUSSION EXERCISE 9:1

The gradient of this line is $\frac{2}{5}$. This may be interpreted as "the daily increase in height of this plant is $\frac{2}{5}$ cm" or as "$\frac{2}{5}$ cm per day is the rate of increase of the height of this plant".

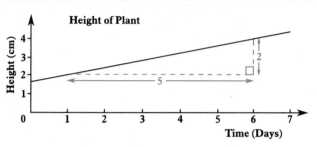

How could the gradients of the following graphs be interpreted? What might these graphs refer to? **Discuss**.

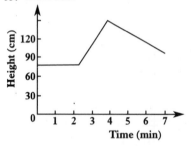

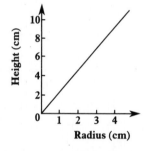

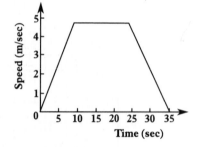

A curve, such as that shown, varies in steepness. The section between Q and R is steeper than that between P and Q. Since gradient is a measure of steepness the gradient of the curve changes throughout.

As we move along the curve from P to Q the gradient increases. If, at Q, we continue straight ahead (along the dotted line) the gradient stops increasing and has the same value as at Q. The gradient of the curve at Q is then the gradient of the dotted line.

The dotted line at Q may be extended backwards as shown in this diagram. (The dotted line is now shown as a solid line.) This line **touches** the curve at Q and is called the **tangent** at Q.

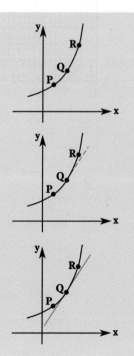

The gradient of a curve at a point is the gradient of the tangent to the curve at that point.

*Example* The gradient of this curve at the point P is found by drawing the tangent to the curve at P, then finding the gradient of this tangent.

Gradient at P = $\frac{2\cdot6}{18}$

$= 0\cdot14$ (2 d.p.)

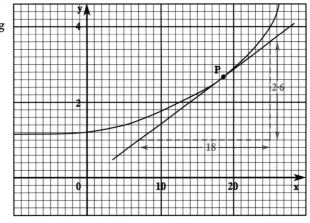

*Worked Example*

| Time, t (sec) | 0 | 10 | 20 | 30 | 40 | 50 | 60 | 70 | 80 |
|---|---|---|---|---|---|---|---|---|---|
| Depth, d (cm) | 0 | 2·8 | 5·8 | 9·0 | 12·2 | 15·7 | 20·8 | 26·5 | 33·9 |

As part of an experiment, Jamal poured liquid into this container at a steady rate. Jamal recorded the depth of water at 10 second intervals.
(a) Draw the graph of d against t. Draw the tangent to the curve at t = 50 sec.
    Find the gradient of this tangent.
(b) Explain what this gradient tells you.

*Answer* (a) The curve is drawn and the tangent constructed.
Gradient of this

tangent $= \frac{16}{40}$

$= 0\cdot4$

(b) When t = 50 sec the depth of water is increasing at the rate of 0·4cm per sec.

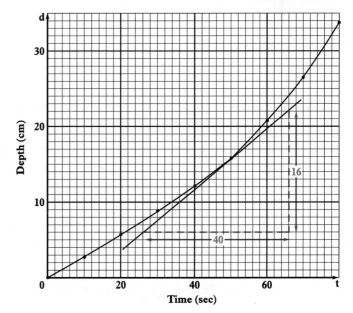

## EXERCISE 9:2

1.

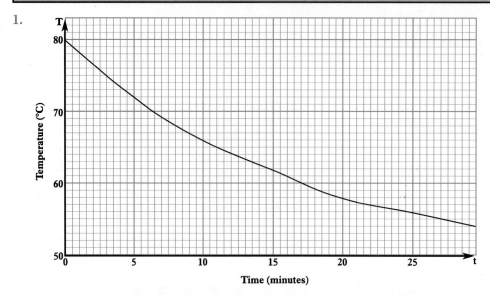

In an experiment Jon heated a liquid to 80°C then allowed it to cool. Jon drew the above graph for the first 30 minutes of cooling.

(a) Copy and complete this set of ordered pairs that Jon graphed:
   $(0, 80), (5, 72), (10, \ldots), (15, \ldots), (20, \ldots), (25, \ldots), (30, \ldots)$.

(b) Plot the ordered pairs in (a). Join these to draw the cooling curve.

(c) On *your* graph, draw the tangent at the point $(20, 58)$. Find the gradient of this tangent.

(d) Explain the meaning of this gradient.

2.

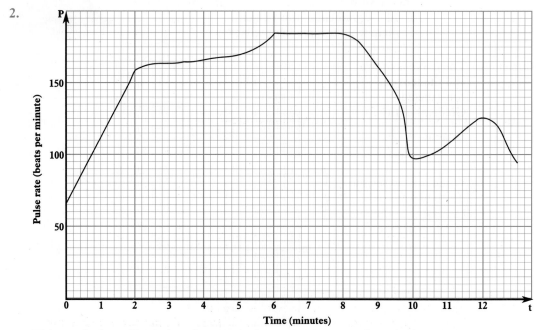

This graph shows Tracey's pulse rate during a 13-minute workout in the gym.

(i)  What are the missing numbers in the following?
Tracey's pulse rate increased during the following intervals of time:
    (a) 0 minutes and . . . minutes
    (b) . . . minutes and 12 minutes.

(ii)  At what time did Tracey's pulse rate increase most rapidly? Explain how you can answer this from the shape of the graph.

(iii)  For how long, during this workout, did Tracey's pulse rate neither increase nor decrease?
Explain how you can tell this from the gradient of the graph.

(iv)  Find the rate of increase of Tracey's pulse rate during the first minute of the workout.

(v)  At t = 9·5 minutes Tracey's pulse rate is decreasing at about 40 beats per minute. At what time during the last three minutes of the workout is Tracey's pulse rate decreasing again at this rate? Explain how you can answer this from the shape of the graph.

3.  As a tank of an unusual shape was being emptied the depth of the water was recorded.

| Time (minutes) | 0 | 0·5 | 1 | 1·5 | 2 | 2·5 | 3 | 3·5 | 4 | 4·5 | 5 | 5·5 |
|---|---|---|---|---|---|---|---|---|---|---|---|---|
| Depth (metres) | 3·00 | 2·95 | 2·90 | 2·80 | 2·70 | 2·60 | 2·45 | 2·25 | 1·95 | 1·50 | 0·90 | 0·00 |

(a) Plot the graph of depth against time.
(b) Draw the tangent to the curve at (3, 2·45) and find its gradient.
(c) Find the rate of decrease of the water level when the depth is 1·5 metres.

4.

| x | −3 | −2·5 | −2 | −1·5 | −1 | −0·5 | 0 | 0·5 | 1 | 1·5 | 2 | 2·5 | 3 | 3·5 | 4 |
|---|---|---|---|---|---|---|---|---|---|---|---|---|---|---|---|
| y | −10 | 3 | 10 | 15 | 19 | 22 | 25 | 27 | 28 | 27 | 25 | 22 | 19 | 15 | 10 |

Plot these points. Join to form a smooth curve.
(i)  Find the gradient of this curve at     (a) (3, 19)     (b) (−2, 10).
(ii)  For what value of x is the gradient equal to zero?

5.  (a) Copy and complete this table of values for $y = x^2 - 2x - 3$.

| x | −2·5 | −2·0 | −1·5 | −1·0 | −0·5 | 0 | 0·5 | 1·0 | 1·5 | 2·0 | 2·5 | 3·0 | 3·5 | 4 | 4·5 |
|---|---|---|---|---|---|---|---|---|---|---|---|---|---|---|---|
| y | 8·25 | 5 | | | | | | | | | | | | | |

(b) Draw the graph of $y = x^2 - 2x - 3$.
(c) Find the gradient of the graph at the point where x = 3.
(d) Give the coordinates of the point where y stops decreasing and begins increasing. Explain how you can answer this using the shape of the graph.

6.

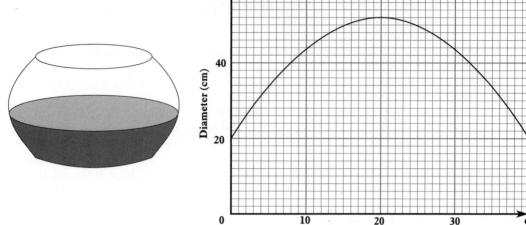

The goldfish bowl is being filled with water. The graph shows how the diameter of the surface of the water changes as the depth of the water increases.
Trace the graph.
Draw the tangent at the point where d = 10cm and find its gradient.
Explain what this gradient tells you.

**Review** In an experiment on sound Diane took the following measurements for the length of wire, $l$, and tension, T.

| Length, $l$ (cm) | 0 | 10 | 20 | 30 | 40 | 50 | 60 | 70 | 80 | 90 | 100 |
|---|---|---|---|---|---|---|---|---|---|---|---|
| Tension, T (N) | 0 | 27 | 38 | 46 | 54 | 60 | 66 | 71 | 76 | 81 | 85 |

Draw the graph of T against $l$.
Find the gradient of this curve at the point (50, 60).
Explain what this gradient tells you.

## INVESTIGATION 9:3

Parabola gradients

Either accurately draw the graph of $y = x^2$ for values of x between –5 and 5 or print this graph using a computer graphics package.
Construct tangents and calculate the gradient of the curve for various values of x.
**Investigate** to find the relationship between the x-value of a point on $y = x^2$ and the gradient of the curve at this point. Make and test statements as part of your investigation.
What if $y = 2x^2$?
What if $y = 3x^2$?
What if $y = 4x^2$?
What if . . .

# AREA UNDER a CURVE

## DISCUSSION EXERCISE 9:4

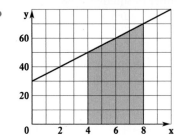 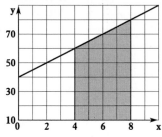 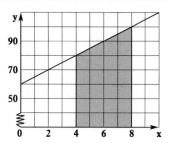

The areas of the shaded regions may be found by counting squares or by calculating the area of the trapeziums. Use both methods to find these areas. **Discuss** your answers.

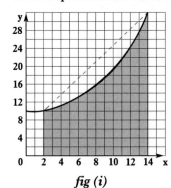 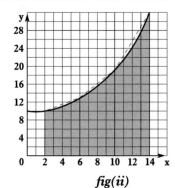

*fig (i)*                *fig(ii)*

An approximate value for the area of the shaded region may be found by counting squares. The area of the trapezium shown in red on *fig (i)* can be used as an estimate of the shaded region. *Fig (ii)* illustrates a way to get a better estimate. How many trapeziums do you think a region such as this should be divided into to find the area? How accurate is this method? **Discuss.**

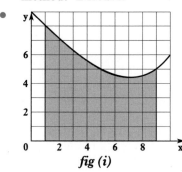 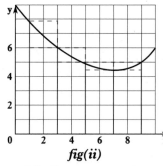 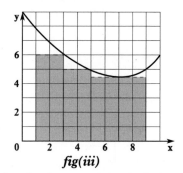

*fig (i)*                *fig(ii)*                *fig(iii)*

These diagrams show another way of finding an approximate value for the area of the shaded region.

*fig (i)*     shows the shaded region.

*fig (ii)*    shows two sets of rectangles drawn; a set in which the areas add to less than the shaded region and a set in which the areas add to more than the shaded region.

*fig (iii)*   shows the set of "lower rectangles".

How could we use these diagrams to find an approximate value for the area of the shaded region? **Discuss.**

*Example*

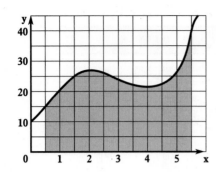

The area of the region between the curve and the x-axis from x = 0·5 to x = 5·5 may be estimated by counting squares as follows:
Estimated number of squares = 48
Area of each square = 0·5 × 5
$\qquad\qquad\qquad\quad$ = 2·5
Area of region = 48 × 2·5
$\qquad\qquad\qquad\quad$ = 120 square units

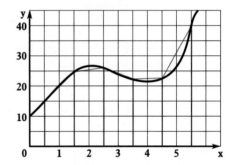

The area may also be estimated by dividing the region into 5 strips, each of width 1 as shown. Using $A = \frac{1}{2}(a + b) \times h$ and working from left to right, the sum of the areas of the trapeziums is:

$\frac{1}{2}(15 + 25) \times 1 + \frac{1}{2}(25 + 27) \times 1 + \frac{1}{2}(27 + 22) \times 1 + \frac{1}{2}(22 + 23) \times 1 + \frac{1}{2}(23 + 40) \times 1 = 124{\cdot}5$ square units.

**Note** An even better estimate of the area may be found by dividing the region into 10 strips, each of width 0·5.

## EXERCISE 9:5

**In this exercise use a method of your choice (other than counting squares) to find the areas. Briefly explain your method.**

1. Estimate the area of the region between the graph and the x-axis from x = 10 to x = 55.

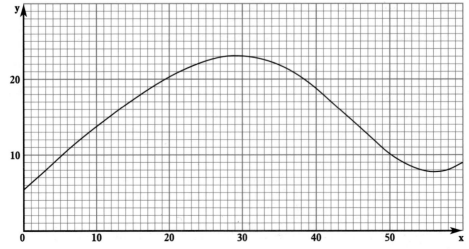

2. Find an approximate value for the area of the region bounded by the curve, the x-axis and the line x = 5.

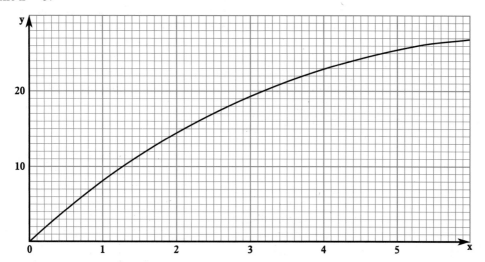

3.

Estimate the area bounded by the curve, the x-axis and the lines x = 1 and x = 5.

4. Sketch the graph of y = 2x + 3 for values of x between x = 0 and x = 10.
   Calculate the area of the region between the x-axis and the lines y = 2x + 3, x = 2 and x = 10.

5. (a) Copy and complete this table of values for $y = 12 + 4x - x^2$.

| x | –3 | –2 | –1 | 0 | 1 | 2 | 3 | 4 | 5 | 6 | 7 |
|---|----|----|----|---|---|---|---|---|---|---|---|
| y | –9 | 0 |   |   |   |   |   |   |   |   |   |

   (b) Draw the graph of $y = 12 + 4x - x^2$.
   (c) Find an approximate value for the area of the region between the graph and the x-axis from x = 0 to x = 6.

6.  (a) Draw the graph of $y = 4x - x^2$ for values of $x$ between $-1$ and $5$.
    (b) Estimate the area of the region bounded by the graph, the x-axis and the lines $x = 2$ and $x = 4$.
    (c) Use symmetry to estimate the area of the region between the graph and the x-axis.

7.

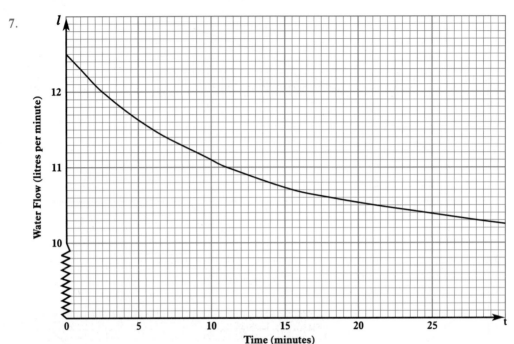

This graph shows the rate at which water is flowing from a pipe.
    (a) Estimate the area of the region between the graph and the t-axis from $t = 0$ to $t = 30$ minutes.
    (b) What meaning can be given to this area?

**Review 1**

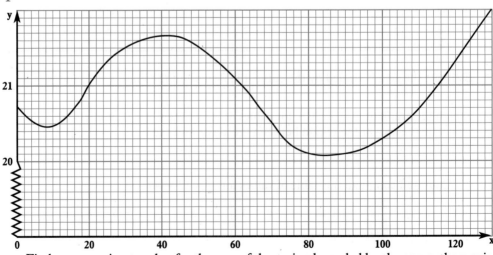

Find an approximate value for the area of the region bounded by the curve, the x-axis and the lines $x = 20$ and $x = 120$.

Review 2 (a) Copy and complete this table of values for $y = 7x - 6 - x^2$.

| x | 0 | 0·5 | 1 | 1·5 | 2 | 2·5 | 3 | 3·5 | 4 | 4·5 | 5 | 5·5 | 6 |
|---|---|-----|---|-----|---|-----|---|-----|---|-----|---|-----|---|
| y | −6 | | | | | | | | | | | | |

(b) Draw the graph. Use this graph to estimate the area of the region between the curve and the x-axis, between $x = 2$ and $x = 6$.

## DISCUSSION EXERCISE 9:6

It can be proven that the sum of the areas of the shaded trapeziums is

$$A = \tfrac{1}{2} h (y_0 + y_5 + 2y_1 + 2y_2 + 2y_3 + 2y_4).$$ **Discuss** how to prove this.

- **Discuss** how to extend the above to show that for a region divided into n strips of the same width h, the area is given by $A = \tfrac{1}{2} h (y_0 + y_n + 2y_1 + 2y_2 + 2y_3 + \ldots + 2y_{n-1})$.

**Discuss** how to use this result, which is known as **The Trapezium Rule**. As part of your discussion find the area between the curve $y = x^2$ and the x-axis from $x = 2$ to $x = 8$ firstly by dividing into strips of width 2 and then by reducing the width of the strips.

- The following program may be used to estimate the area between a curve and the x-axis between two values of x. N is the number of strips, A is the first value of x, B is the last value of x.

```
10   INPUT "N = "N : INPUT "A = "A : INPUT "B = "B
20   INPUT "EQUATION CURVE : Y = "FX$
30   H = (B – A) / N
40   FOR X = A TO B STEP H
50   Y = EVAL (FX$)
60   IF X = A OR X = B THEN GOTO 70 ELSE Y = Y * 2
70   SUM = SUM + Y
80   NEXT X
90   PRINT "AREA = "H/2 * SUM
100  END
```

Use this program to estimate some areas. **Discuss** the curves you chose, the values of x you chose and the results obtained.

## DISTANCE/TIME, VELOCITY/TIME GRAPHS

### DISCUSSION EXERCISE 9:7

- This graph represents the distance travelled by a walker.
  What distance is travelled during the first 20 seconds?
  Describe what is happening to the speed during this time.
  What is the gradient of this part of the graph?
  What does the gradient of a distance/time graph tell you? Discuss.

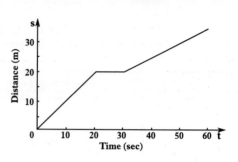

What meaning can be given to the gradient of the tangent at P? Discuss.

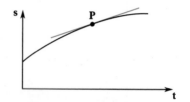

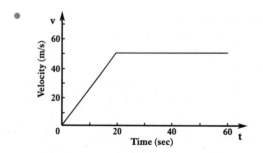

This graph represents the speed of a car during the first minute of a journey.
Acceleration is defined as:

$$\frac{\text{change in velocity}}{\text{change in time}}.$$ Describe the

acceleration of this car during the first 20 sec. and during the next 40 sec.
What does the gradient of a velocity/time graph tell you?
What units are used for acceleration?
Discuss.

During the first 20 seconds the average speed was 25m/s. Use $s = vt$ to find the distance travelled in this time. Discuss the relationship between the area under the graph and the distance travelled.

On a distance/time graph,

$$\text{gradient} = \frac{\text{change in distance } s}{\text{change in time } t}$$

$$= \text{velocity}$$

For instance, the velocity at $t = 5$ is given by the gradient of the curve at $t = 5$; that is, by the gradient of the tangent at $t = 5$.

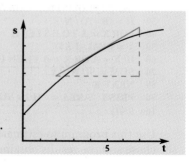

On a **velocity/time graph**,

$$\text{gradient} = \frac{\text{change in velocity v}}{\text{change in time t}}$$

$$= \text{acceleration}$$

For instance, the acceleration at $t = 8$ is given by the gradient of the curve at $t = 8$; that is, by the gradient of the tangent at $t = 8$.
The most commonly used unit for acceleration is $m/s^2$; also written as $ms^{-2}$.

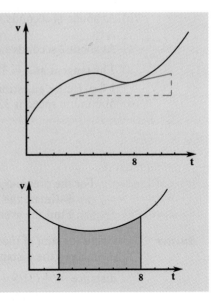

The area under a velocity/time graph gives the distance travelled.
For instance, the distance travelled between $t = 2$ and $t = 8$ is given by the shaded area.

*Worked Example* This table gives the velocity of a car at 5 second intervals.

| Time, t (sec) | 0 | 5 | 10 | 15 | 20 | 25 | 30 | 35 | 40 | 45 | 50 | 55 | 60 |
|---|---|---|---|---|---|---|---|---|---|---|---|---|---|
| Velocity, v (m/s) | 0 | 8·0 | 12·5 | 15·5 | 18·0 | 21·0 | 24·5 | 30·0 | 31·5 | 32·0 | 30·0 | 25·5 | 20·5 |

(a) Draw the velocity/time graph.
(b) At what instant was the acceleration zero? Explain.
(c) At what instant was the acceleration the greatest? Explain.
(d) Find the acceleration when $t = 35$ seconds.
(e) In km/h, what was the maximum speed?

*Answer*
(a)

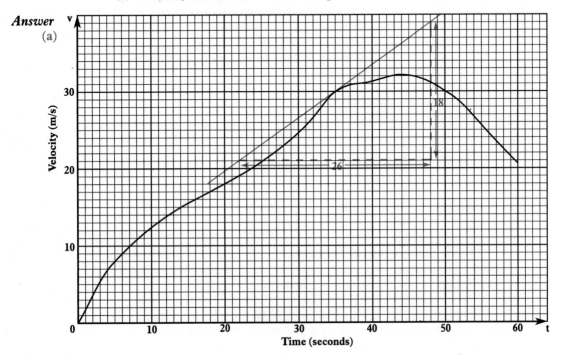

(b) At about 44 seconds since the gradient of the tangent to the curve at $t = 44$ is zero.

(c) At about 2 seconds since the curve is steepest here.

(d) The tangent at $t = 35$ is shown on the graph. Its gradient is about $\frac{18}{26} = 0\cdot7$ to 1 d.p. Hence an estimate of the acceleration at $t = 35$ sec is $0\cdot7$m/s².

(e) Maximum speed is 32m/s = $32 \times 60 \times 60$ m/hour

$$= \frac{32 \times 60 \times 60}{1000} \text{ km/hour}$$
$$= 115\cdot2 \text{ km/h}$$

*Worked Example*  For the previous worked example:

(a) Estimate the distance travelled between $t = 40$ and $t = 60$ seconds.

(b) Find the average speed between $t = 40$ and $t = 60$ seconds.

*Answer*  (a) Using the sum of the area of these trapeziums as an estimate of the distance we get:

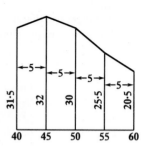

distance $= \frac{1}{2}(31\cdot5 + 32) \times 5 + \frac{1}{2}(32 + 30) \times 5$
$\qquad + \frac{1}{2}(30 + 25\cdot5) \times 5 + \frac{1}{2}(25\cdot5 + 20\cdot5) \times 5$
$\qquad = 567\cdot5$m

To 2 s.f. distance = 570m.

Note: The distance may also be found by using the trapezium rule – see Page 161.

(b) Using     average speed $= \dfrac{\text{distance travelled}}{\text{time taken}}$,

average speed $\approx \dfrac{567\cdot5}{20}$
$\qquad = 28$m/s (2 s.f.)

*Worked Example*  A train accelerates steadily from rest to 100m/s in 20 seconds, then travels at a constant speed for 2 minutes, then decelerates to rest in 40 seconds.

(a) Sketch the velocity/time graph.

(b) Use this graph to calculate the total distance travelled.

(c) How long did it take this train to travel 4km?

*Answer*  (a) The graph is sketched here.

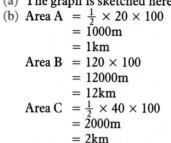

(b) Area A $= \frac{1}{2} \times 20 \times 100$
$\qquad = 1000$m
$\qquad = 1$km

Area B $= 120 \times 100$
$\qquad = 12000$m
$\qquad = 12$km

Area C $= \frac{1}{2} \times 40 \times 100$
$\qquad = 2000$m
$\qquad = 2$km

Hence distance travelled = 15km.

Note: The distance may also be found by using the formula for the area of a trapezium.

(c) Area A = 1km. Time to travel first km = 20 seconds.

To travel 4km the train needs to travel a further 3km or 3000m "into rectangle B."

Since the height of the rectangle is 100m the train needs to travel for a further 30 seconds. Hence the train takes 50 seconds to travel 4km.

## EXERCISE 9:8

1.

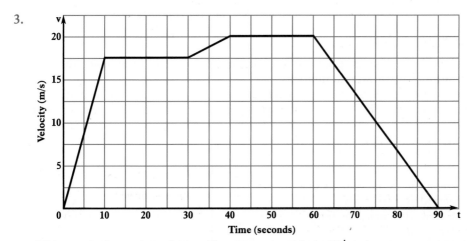

This graph shows the distance Ben cycles in 1 minute.
Trace this graph.
Draw the tangent to the curve at t = 20 seconds.
Find the gradient of this tangent.
Explain what the gradient of this tangent tells you about Ben's cycling.

2.

| Time (sec) | 0 | 1 | 2 | 3 | 4 | 5 | 6 | 7 | 8 | 9 | 10 | 11 | 12 |
|---|---|---|---|---|---|---|---|---|---|---|---|---|---|
| Distance (m) | 5 | 11 | 17 | 21 | 23 | 25 | 26 | 26 | 25 | 23 | 19 | 13 | 9 |

Plot these points. Join to form a smooth distance/time graph.
Explain how you can use the graph to find the velocity when t = 4 sec.
Find the velocity when t = 4 sec.

3.

This graph shows the velocity of a car over a period of $1\frac{1}{2}$ minutes.
(a) Describe what is happening to the car during this time.
(b) During which time interval is the acceleration the greatest? Find this acceleration.

4. For the previous question, calculate the distance travelled during the first minute. Give the answer in kilometres.

5. A motorbike accelerates steadily from rest to 70km/h in 5 seconds, then changes gear and accelerates steadily to 120km/h in a further 5 seconds.
   Draw a velocity/time graph to find the distance travelled before the motorbike reached 120km/h. Explain why m/s rather than km/h should be used as the unit for velocity on this graph.

6.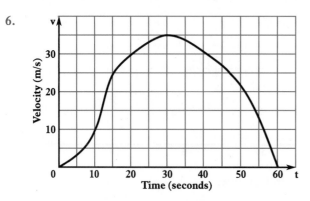

   This is the velocity/time graph for a vehicle.
   (a) What is the maximum speed?
   (b) At what time is the acceleration equal to zero?
   (c) At what instant is the acceleration the greatest? Explain your answer.

7. For the previous question:
   (a) Estimate a value for the area of the region between the graph and the t-axis. What does this value represent?
   (b) What is the average speed during these 60 seconds?

8.

| Time, t (sec) | 0 | 2 | 4 | 6 | 8 | 10 | 12 | 14 | 16 |
|---|---|---|---|---|---|---|---|---|---|
| Speedometer Reading, v (km/h) | 0 | 38 | 67 | 90 | 110 | 126 | 137 | 148 | 153 |

   Jason's friend accelerated his car from rest to 153km/h in 16 seconds. Jason noted the speedometer reading at two second intervals.
   Jason planned to draw a graph to find the acceleration, in ms$^{-2}$, when t = 10 seconds. Explain why Jason cannot find this by plotting the points in the table. What points should Jason plot?
   Find the acceleration when t = 10 seconds.

9. This sketch graph shows the velocity of a vehicle for a period of 60 seconds.
   (a) Using the graph, calculate the total distance travelled.
   (b) Find the time taken to travel the first *half* of this distance.

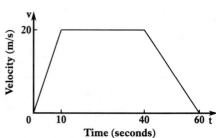

10. The formula $v = t^2 + 3t + 5$ gives the velocity, v metres per second, of an object at time t seconds.

    (a) Copy and complete:

| t | 0 | 1 | 2 | 3 | 4 | 5 |
|---|---|---|---|---|---|---|
| v | 5 | 9 | 15 | | | |

    (b) Plot v against t. Join with a smooth curve.
    (c) By finding an appropriate area on your graph, estimate the distance travelled between t = 1 and t = 3 seconds.

11.

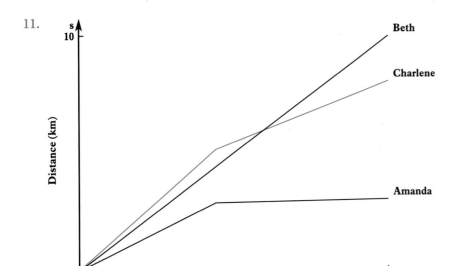

These are the distance/time graphs for three joggers. Sketch the velocity/time graphs.

**Review 1**

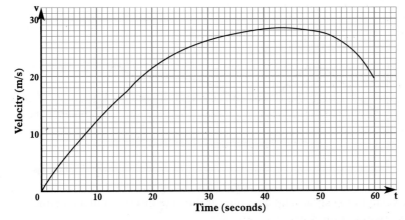

This graph shows the velocity of a car during the first minute of a journey.

(a) At about what time did the velocity stop increasing?
(b) At about what time did the car begin to decelerate?
(c) Use the graph to estimate the acceleration at t = 30 seconds.

**Review 2** For the previous question:

Use the graph to estimate the distance travelled during the first minute. Give your answer in kilometres. Describe the method you use.

**Review 3** A car accelerates steadily from rest to 60km/h in 10 seconds, then travels at 60km/h for 80 seconds, then decelerates to rest in 30 seconds.

(a) Copy and complete: 60km/h = ... m/s.

(b) Draw a velocity/time graph. Have time, in seconds, on the horizontal axis and velocity, in m/s, on the vertical axis.

(c) What was the acceleration during the first 5 seconds?

(d) Find the deceleration.

**Review 4** For the previous question:

(a) Find the total distance travelled during the two minutes. Give the answer in kilometres.

(b) At what time has the car travelled half of this distance?

(c) Find the average speed of this car during the two minutes. Give the answer in km/h.

## INVESTIGATION 9:9

**The Car Race**

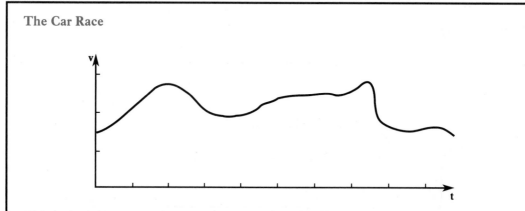

This is the velocity/time graph for a racing car during one circuit of a racetrack.

What units might be on the axes?

How long is the racetrack?

What shape might this racetrack be?

Investigate these and other questions.

## RESEARCH PROJECT 9:10

### Calculus

It can be proven that the gradient of the tangent at any point $(x, y)$ on the curve $y = ax^2$ is given by gradient $= 2ax$. In general, the gradient of the tangent at any point $(x, y)$ on the curve $y = ax^n$ is given by $nax^{n-1}$.

Calculus is a branch of mathematics that deals with this. We can also use calculus to find areas under curves.

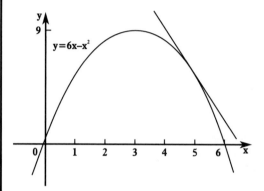

$y = 6x - x^2$

$\dfrac{dy}{dx} = 6 - 2x$

Gradient of tangent at the point where $x = 5$ is $6 - 2 \times 5 = -4$.

$$\text{Shaded area} = \int_1^4 (6x - x^2)\,dx$$

$$= \left[ \frac{6x^2}{2} - \frac{x^3}{3} \right]_1^4$$

$$= 6 \times \frac{4^2}{2} - \frac{4^3}{3} - \left( 6 \times \frac{1^2}{2} - \frac{1^3}{3} \right)$$

$$= 24$$

Research calculus.

## CHAPTER 9   REVIEW

1.  A water trough of height 80cm and length 200cm is filled up at a constant rate.

The graph on the next page shows how the depth of water in the trough changes with time.

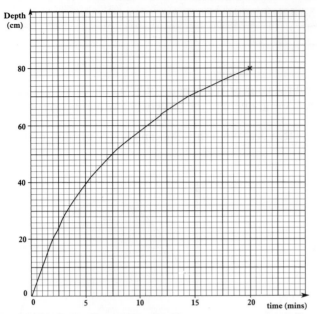

Use this graph to estimate the rate at which the water is rising after 10 minutes.　　　**NEAB**

**2.**

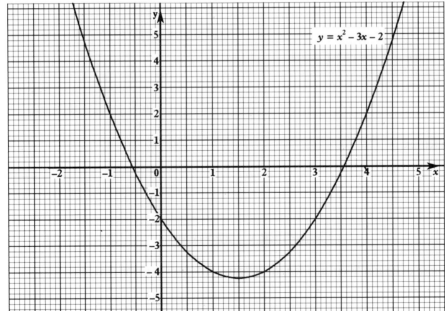

The graph of $y = x^2 - 3x - 2$ has been drawn on the grid.

**(a)** Draw the graph of $y = x - 2$ on the same grid.

**(b)** Use the graphs to solve the equation $x^2 - 3x - 2 = x - 2$

**(c)** Calculate an estimate of the gradient of the curve $y = x^2 - 3x - 2$ at the point where
$x = 2 \cdot 5$.　　　**ULEAC**

**3.** A marble is projected up a groove in a sloping plane. After $t$ seconds its distance, $s$ cm, from the starting point is given by $\qquad s = 24t - t^2$

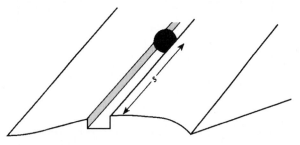

The graph of $s = 24t - t^2$ is drawn.

**(a) (i)** What is the value of $t$ when the marble reaches its highest point?
**(ii)** What is its speed at this point?

**(b)** Use the graph to work out the speed of the marble after 7 seconds. Show clearly how you obtained your answer.

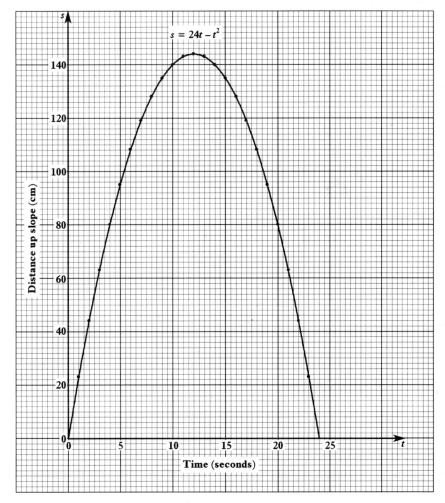

**NEAB**

**4.**

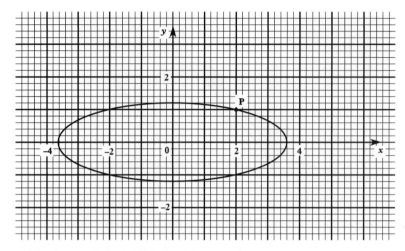

**(a)** Draw the tangent at P to the curve.

**(b)** Calculate the gradient of the tangent you have drawn.
Give your answer correct to 1 decimal place.                    **ULEAC**

**5.**

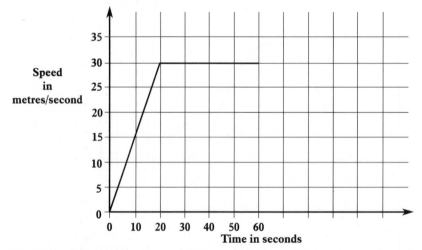

The diagram represents the speed-time graph for the first minute of a train journey from station A to station B.

**(a)** Calculate the distance travelled by the train in the first minute.

After 60 seconds, the train slowed down with constant deceleration until it came to rest at station B.

The total distance travelled by the train on its journey from A to B was 2·1 km.

**(b)** Calculate the time taken for the journey.                    **ULEAC**

**6.** The graph opposite is a velocity time graph of a skier as she skis down a mountain. The velocity, v, is measured in m/s at a time t minutes after the start of the motion.

**(a)** Calculate the acceleration of the skier, in m/s², at t = 2 minutes.

**(b)** Find the approximate distance travelled by the skier during the first three minutes of her journey down the mountain.

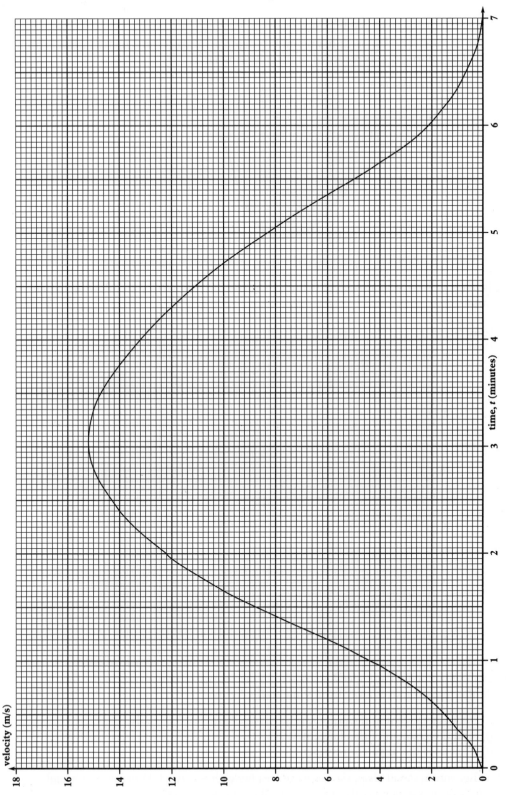

WJEC

7. The cross-section of a river bed is shown below.

The width of the river, $AB$, is 12 metres and its depth is measured at 2 metre intervals from point $A$. The information is recorded in the following table.

| Distance from $A$ | 0 | 2 | 4 | 6 | 8 | 10 | 12 |
|---|---|---|---|---|---|---|---|
| Depth | 0 | 1·8 | 4·0 | 6·0 | 6·6 | 4·6 | 0 |

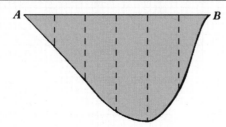

(a) Estimate the area of cross-section of the river to the nearest square metre.

(b) The river is flowing at a speed of 0·2m/s. Estimate the volume of water flowing in one second.  **SEG**

8.

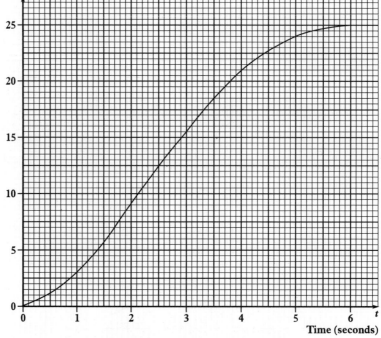

The graph shows how a car's speed, measured in metres per second, varies in the first 6 seconds after the car moves away from some traffic lights.

(a) (i) Draw the tangent at the point on the curve where $t = 5$ seconds.
   (ii) Find the gradient of this tangent.
   (iii) What does this gradient represent?

(b) Making your method clear, estimate the area beneath the graph between $t = 0$ and $t = 6$. Hence estimate the distance travelled by the car in the first 6 seconds.  **MEG**

174

**9.** A two-stage rocket was launched and its velocity recorded for the first 200 seconds.
The velocity time graph for the first 200 seconds is drawn on the axes.

**(a) (i)** Use the graph to find the gradient of the curve when $t = 160$.

  **(ii)** What does this gradient represent?

**(b) (i)** Calculate, by a suitable method of estimation, the area under the curve between 20 and 100 seconds.

  **(ii)** What does this area represent?

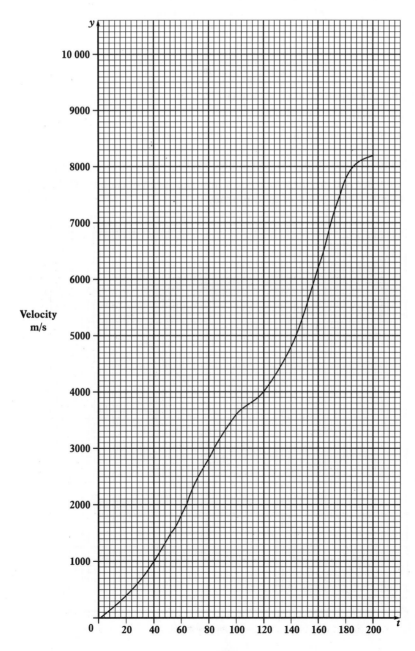

**SEG**

**10.** The graph shows the speed of a Grand Prix car over part of a racing circuit.

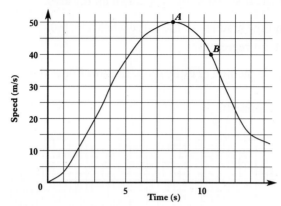

(a) Explain what is happening at (i) *A* and (ii) *B*.

(b) Find the acceleration at time 4 seconds.

(c) Find the distance travelled during the time from 0 to 10 s.

**MEG**

**11.** Two trains *A* and *B* start from rest on parallel tracks.

On the grid below are two graphs which show how the speed of each train varies with time over the first twenty five seconds of their journey.

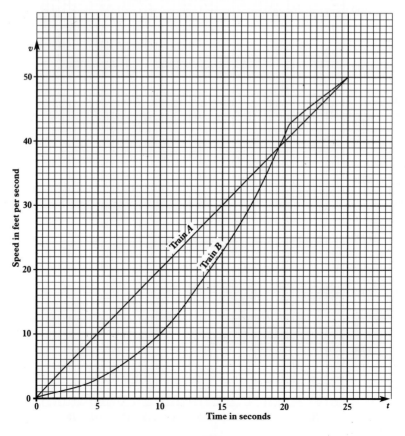

176

**(a)** What is the equation of the graph relating to train $A$?

**(b)** What is the value of $t$ when the trains are travelling at the same speed?

**(c)** **(i)** After how many seconds do the trains have the same acceleration?
**(ii)** Calculate the size of this acceleration.

**(d)** When the trains are travelling at the same speed,
**(i)** how far has train $A$ gone?
**(ii)** how far has train $B$ gone?                                          **NEAB**

### FACTORISING by GROUPING

Remember, an expression such as $pq + qr$ is factorised as $q(p + r)$. The $q$ which is common to both $pq$ and $qr$ is placed outside a bracket.
An expression such as $ab + ac + b^2 + bc$ can be factorised in a similar way.

---

### DISCUSSION EXERCISE 10:1

- Discuss each step of the factorising of the expressions $ab + ac + b^2 + bc$,
  $8by - 2bx + 2ax - 8ay$ shown below.

$$ab + ac + b^2 + bc = (ab + ac) + (b^2 + bc)$$
$$= a(b + c) + b(b + c)$$
$$= (b + c)(a + b)$$

$$8by - 2bx + 2ax - 8ay = 2b(4y - x) + 2a(x - 4y)$$
$$= 2b(4y - x) - 2a(4y - x)$$
$$= (4y - x)(2b - 2a)$$
$$= 2(4y - x)(b - a)$$

Could different steps be taken to factorise these expressions? Are different answers possible? **Discuss.**

- This rectangle may be used to help factorise
  $8by - 2bx + 2ax - 8ay$. How should we continue? **Discuss.**

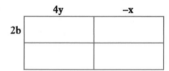

*Worked Example*   Factorise $ef - gd - ge + df$.

*Answer*  
$$ef - gd - ge + df = ef - ge - gd + df$$
$$= e(f - g) - d(g - f)$$
$$= e(f - g) + d(f - g)$$
$$= (f - g)(e + d)$$

---

### EXERCISE 10:2

Factorise the following expressions.

1. $ac + bc + ad + bd$
2. $xy + zy + xw + zw$
3. $cy + dy - cz - dz$
4. $pr - qr - ps + qs$
5. $pq + rq - pr - r^2$
6. $pq - zq + pz - z^2$
7. $ab + xy + xb + ay$
8. $ca - bd - ad + bc$
9. $xz + yw - yz - xw$
10. $wx - y^2 + xy - wy$
11. $ab - x^2 - ax + bx$
12. $ax - 3 + a - 3x$
13. $xy - 12ab + 3ay - 4xb$
14. $ab^2 - 1 + a - b^2$
15. $5yz - xz + ax - 5ay$

Review 1   $p^2 + ap + aq + pq$
Review 2     $ax + by - ay - bx$
Review 3   $px + 2 - p - 2x$

## FACTORISING QUADRATIC EXPRESSIONS

A **quadratic expression** such as $4x^2 + 3x$ has a common factor and may be factorised as $x(4x + 3)$. Quadratic expressions such as $4x^2 + 3x - 1$ or $4x^2 - 1$, which do not have common factors, may sometimes be factorised into two brackets. As discussed in the following exercise, $4x^2 + 3x - 1 = (4x - 1)(x + 1)$ and $4x^2 - 1 = (2x + 1)(2x - 1)$.

### DISCUSSION EXERCISE 10:3

- $(x - 4)(2x + 5)$ may be expanded to $2x^2 - 3x - 20$ using the "rectangle method".

  We may use the reverse of this method to factorise $2x^2 - 3x - 20$ as $(x - 4)(2x + 5)$. The first step is shown at the right. What other steps need to be taken? **Discuss**. As part of your discussion factorise $4x^2 + 5x + 1$, $x^2 - 7x + 12$, $2x^2 - x - 10$. Check your factorising by expanding.

- Simon's method of factorising a quadratic expression uses factorising by grouping. Simon explained his steps for factorising $2x^2 - 3x - 20$ as:
  - *Step 1*  Multiply the two outside numbers to get $-40$.
  - *Step 2*  Find two numbers which multiply to this product, i.e. to $-40$, and which add to the middle number, $-3$.
    These are $-8$ and $5$.
  - *Step 3*  Rewrite $2x^2 - 3x - 20$ as $2x^2 - 8x + 5x - 20$.
  - *Step 4*  Factorise $2x^2 - 8x + 5x - 20$ by grouping as follows.
    $$2x^2 - 8x + 5x - 20 = 2x(x - 4) + 5(x - 4)$$
    $$= (x - 4)(2x + 5)$$

  **Discuss** this method. As part of your discussion, factorise $4x^2 + 5x + 1$, $x^2 - 7x + 12$, $2x^2 - x - 10$.

  **Discuss** how this method relates to the method you already know for factorising expressions such as $x^2 + 5x + 6$, $x^2 - 5x + 4$, $x^2 + x - 12$ etc.

- Denise's working for the factorising of $2x^2 - 3x - 20$ is shown below.

  **Discuss** this method of factorising a quadratic expression. As part of your discussion, factorise $4x^2 + 5x + 1$, $x^2 - 7x + 12$, $2x^2 - x - 10$.

179

- Discuss the advantages and disadvantages of each of the previous methods. You may like to adapt one or more of these methods.

- Using the method of your choice, factorise $x^2 - 9$. Check your answer by expanding. **Discuss** how to quickly factorise $x^2 - 9$. Test your theory on the following: $x^2 - 4$, $4x^2 - 1$, $9x^2 - 16$. These particular quadratic expressions are sometimes called "the difference of two squares" or "$a^2 - b^2$ type". What are the factors of the expression $a^2 - b^2$? **Discuss.**

- The quadratic expression $4x^2 + 3x$ may be factorised by taking out the common factor of $x$; that is $4x^2 + 3x = x(4x + 3)$. Can $4x^2 + 3x$ be factorised by the "rectangle method" or by using Simon's or Denise's method? **Discuss.**

For factorising, quadratic expressions are sometimes divided into three categories.
1. Those, such as $4x^2 + 3x$, which have a common factor. $4x^2 + 3x = x(4x + 3)$.
2. Those, such as $4x^2 - 1$, which are the difference of two squares. $4x^2 - 1 = (2x + 1)(2x - 1)$.
3. Those, such as $4x^2 + 3x - 1$, which have three terms. That is, those which have an $x$ term and a number term as well as the $x^2$ term. $4x^2 + 3x - 1 = (4x - 1)(x + 1)$.

Some examples are given below, with brief explanatory notes.

*Examples*
   (a) $x^2 + 5x = x(x + 5)$               common factor of $x$
   (b) $2x^2 + 6 = 2(x^2 + 3)$          common factor of 2
   (c) $x^2 - 100 = (x + 10)(x - 10)$    difference of two squares
   (d) $2x^2 - 18 = 2(x^2 - 9)$         common factor of 2
              $= 2(x + 3)(x - 3)$       difference of two squares
   (e) $x^2 + 4x - 12 = (x + 6)(x - 2)$
   (f) $6x^2 - 15x + 9 = 3(2x^2 - 5x + 3)$      common factor of 3
               $= 3(2x - 3)(x - 1)$
   (g) $10x^2 - 6 + 11x = 10x^2 + 11x - 6$    rearrange before factorising
                $= (5x - 2)(2x + 3)$
   (h) $(2x + 3)^2 - (x - 1)^2 = [(2x + 3) + (x - 1)][(2x + 3) - (x - 1)]$ difference of two squares
                $= [2x + 3 + x - 1][2x + 3 - x + 1]$
                $= (3x + 2)(x + 4)$

## EXERCISE 10:4

1. Factorise the following.
   (a) $x^2 + 4x - 5$      (b) $x^2 + 5x + 6$      (c) $x^2 - x - 12$      (d) $x^2 - 3x - 28$
   (e) $a^2 - 10a + 9$     (f) $a^2 - 2a - 15$     (g) $a^2 + 2a - 35$     (h) $a^2 - 8a + 16$
   (i) $2x^2 + 7x + 3$      (j) $3x^2 + 5x + 2$      (k) $2x^2 + 5x - 3$      (l) $6x^2 + x - 2$
   (m) $4n^2 + 11n - 3$    (n) $12n^2 - 16n + 5$   (o) $6n^2 - 7n - 10$    (p) $10n^2 - 3n - 4$
   (q) $20y^2 - 7y - 6$    (r) $9y^2 + 12y + 4$    (s) $6y^2 - 17y - 10$   (t) $4y^2 + 5y - 6$
   (u) $8n^2 + 7n - 15$    (v) $12n^2 - 11n + 2$   (w) $n^2 - 9n - 36$     (x) $x^2 - 5x - 36$
   (y) $6y^2 - 13y + 6$    (z) $12a^2 + 13a - 4$

2. Factorise completely.
   (a) $3a^2 - 12$        (b) $n^2 - 16$        (c) $4x^2 - 10x + 4$     (d) $2x^2 + x - 10$
   (e) $2x^2 - 3 - x$     (f) $x^2 - 5x$        (g) $a^2 - 25$         (h) $2x^2 - 2$
   (i) $10 - 5x^2$       (j) $8n^2 - 2$        (k) $2y^2 - 6y + 4$     (l) $5a^2 + 15a - 20$

(m) $12n^2 + 39n + 9$    (n) $3n^2 + 9n$    (o) $50 - 2n^2$    (p) $100 - x^2$

(q) $5a^2 + 15$    (r) $3n^2 + n - 4$    (s) $2x^2 + 2 + 4x$    (t) $8x^2 + 2 - 8x$

(u) $2x^2 + 4x$    (v) $x^3 + 3x^2 - 4x$    (w) $(2n - 1)^2 - n^2$    (x) $(p + q)^2 - (p + r)^2$

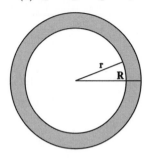

3. (a) Write down the formula for the area of a circle of radius n.

     (b) Show that the area of the shaded ring is given by
Area $= \pi(R + r)(R - r)$.

     (c) Use the result given in **(b)** to show that the area of the ring with internal diameter of 17mm and external diameter of 19mm is $18\pi$ square millimetres.

4. Use the result $x^2 - y^2 = (x + y)(x - y)$ to calculate the following.

     (a) $58^2 - 57^2$    (b) $20305^2 - 20304^2$    (c) $18 \cdot 6^2 - 8 \cdot 6^2$    (d) $5 \cdot 1^2 - 4 \cdot 9^2$

     (e) $(5\frac{3}{7})^2 - (4\frac{3}{7})^2$

5. Daniel made at least one mistake when he attempted to factorise $3 - 5x - 2x^2$.
$$3 - 5x - 2x^2 = -2x^2 - 5x - 3$$
$$= -(2x^2 - 5x - 3)$$
$$= -(2x + 1)(x - 3)$$
$$= (1 - 2x)(x - 3)$$
Find and correct Daniel's mistakes.

6. Consider the following factorising of the expression $x^4 + x^2 + 1$.
$$x^4 + x^2 + 1 = x^4 + x^2 + 1 + x^2 - x^2$$
$$= x^4 + x^2 + x^2 + 1 - x^2$$
$$= x^4 + 2x^2 + 1 - x^2$$
$$= (x^2 + 1)^2 - x^2$$
$$= (x^2 + 1 + x)(x^2 + 1 - x)$$
$$= (x^2 + x + 1)(x^2 - x + 1)$$
Use similar reasoning to show that $4x^4 + 1$ may be factorised as $(2x^2 + 2x + 1)(2x^2 - 2x + 1)$.

7. (a) The number 145 may be written as the product of two whole numbers in two different ways.
One way is $145 = 1 \times 145$. Write down the other way.

     (b) The number 145 may be written as the difference of two square numbers; i.e. $145 = x^2 - y^2$.
Use $x^2 - y^2 = (x + y)(x - y)$ and **(a)** to find the two ways in which this may be done.

8. (a) Factorise $5n^2 + 48n + 27$.

     (b) Use the result of **(a)** to write the number 54827 as a product of two prime numbers. Explain your reasoning.

     (c) The number 41309 is the product of two prime numbers. What expression could you factorise to help find these prime numbers? Find these prime numbers.

**Review**    Factorise the following completely.

     (a) $x^2 + 5x + 6$    (b) $6x^2 - 7x - 20$    (c) $4p^2 - 9$

     (d) $4n^2 - 34n + 42$    (e) $5a^2 - 3a$    (f) $15n^2 - 2mn - 8m^2$

     (g) $\pi x^2 - \pi y^2$    (h) $18 - 8x^2$    (i) $25y^2 - 20y + 4$

     (j) $11x - 6x^2 - 3$    (k) $(5n + 2)^2 - (n - 1)^2$

# EXPRESSIONS involving FRACTIONS

## DISCUSSION EXERCISE 10:5

- $\dfrac{24}{32} = \dfrac{8 \times 3}{8 \times 4}$ $\qquad \dfrac{2x+2}{x^2-1} = \dfrac{2(x+1)}{(x+1)(x-1)}$ $\qquad \dfrac{x^2+x-6}{x^2+3x} = \dfrac{(x+3)(x-2)}{x(x+3)}$

  $\qquad = \dfrac{3}{4}$ $\qquad\qquad\qquad = \dfrac{2}{x-1}$ $\qquad\qquad\qquad\qquad = \dfrac{x-2}{x}$

  Discuss each step in the above.
  Can the 4's be cancelled in $\dfrac{8+4}{2+4}$ ? Can the 12's be cancelled in $\dfrac{x^2+8x+12}{2x+12}$ ? Discuss.

- $\qquad \dfrac{2}{5} + \dfrac{3}{8} = \dfrac{16}{40} + \dfrac{15}{40}$ $\qquad\qquad\qquad \dfrac{a}{5} + \dfrac{b}{8} = \dfrac{8a}{40} + \dfrac{5b}{40}$

  $\qquad\qquad = \dfrac{31}{40}$ $\qquad\qquad\qquad\qquad\qquad = \dfrac{8a+5b}{40}$

  Discuss each step in the above.

- $$\dfrac{2x}{5} - \dfrac{3y}{10} = \dfrac{4x-3y}{10} \qquad \dfrac{3x}{4} - \dfrac{2x}{5} = \dfrac{7x}{20} \qquad \dfrac{2}{x} + \dfrac{3}{y} = \dfrac{2y+3x}{xy} \qquad \dfrac{3}{2x} - \dfrac{5}{x} = -\dfrac{7}{2x}$$

  Each expression on the left may be simplified to the expression on the right.
  Discuss the steps to be taken.

- The expression $\dfrac{2}{x-3} - \dfrac{3}{x+1}$ may be simplified to $\dfrac{11-x}{(x-3)(x+1)}$ . The steps below show how this may be done. Discuss.

  $$\dfrac{2}{x-3} - \dfrac{3}{x+1} = \dfrac{2}{(x-3)} \times \dfrac{(x+1)}{(x+1)} - \dfrac{3}{(x+1)} \times \dfrac{(x-3)}{(x-3)}$$
  $$= \dfrac{2(x+1)}{(x-3)(x+1)} - \dfrac{3(x-3)}{(x+1)(x-3)}$$
  $$= \dfrac{2(x+1) - 3(x-3)}{(x-3)(x+1)}$$
  $$= \dfrac{2x+2-3x+9}{(x-3)(x+1)}$$
  $$= \dfrac{11-x}{(x-3)(x+1)}$$

- $\dfrac{11-x}{(x-3)(x+1)}$ may be rewritten as $\dfrac{x-11}{(3-x)(x+1)}$ but not as $\dfrac{x-11}{(x-3)(1+x)}$ . Discuss.

- $\dfrac{1}{R} = \dfrac{1}{R_1} + \dfrac{1}{R_2}$ is a formula that occurs in physics. The following steps could be taken to make R the subject of the formula.

  $$\dfrac{1}{R} = \dfrac{1}{R_1} + \dfrac{1}{R_2}$$
  $$\dfrac{1}{R} = \dfrac{R_2}{R_1 R_2} + \dfrac{R_1}{R_1 R_2}$$
  $$\dfrac{1}{R} = \dfrac{R_2+R_1}{R_1 R_2}$$
  $$R = \dfrac{R_1 R_2}{R_1+R_2}$$

  Discuss the above steps. Discuss other ways in which R can be made the subject of the formula.

*Worked Example*   Simplify.   (a) $\dfrac{2x^2-18}{x^2+2x-3}$     (b) $\dfrac{4x^2+12}{x-3} \times \dfrac{x^2-9}{x^2+3}$

*Answer*  (a) $\dfrac{2x^2-18}{x^2+2x-3} = \dfrac{2(x^2-9)}{x^2+2x-3}$    (b) $\dfrac{4x^2+12}{x-3} \times \dfrac{x^2-9}{x^2+3} = \dfrac{4(x^2+3)}{x-3} \times \dfrac{(x+3)(x-3)}{x^2+3}$

$$= \dfrac{2(x+3)(x-3)}{(x+3)(x-1)} \qquad\qquad\qquad = 4(x+3)$$

$$= \dfrac{2(x-3)}{x-1}$$

*Worked Example*   Simplify.   (a) $\dfrac{3a}{5} - \dfrac{5a}{8}$       (b) $\dfrac{2}{3x} + \dfrac{5}{2y}$

(c) $\dfrac{2}{m-n} + \dfrac{3}{n-m}$     (d) $\dfrac{4}{x-2} - \dfrac{3}{2x+1}$

*Answer*  (a) $\dfrac{3a}{5} - \dfrac{5a}{8} = \dfrac{24a}{40} - \dfrac{25a}{40}$     (b) $\dfrac{2}{3x} + \dfrac{5}{2y} = \dfrac{4y}{6xy} + \dfrac{15x}{6xy}$

$$= \dfrac{24a-25a}{40} \qquad\qquad\qquad = \dfrac{4y+15x}{6xy}$$

$$= -\dfrac{a}{40}$$

(c) $\dfrac{2}{m-n} + \dfrac{3}{n-m} = \dfrac{2}{m-n} - \dfrac{3}{m-n}$

$$= -\dfrac{1}{m-n}$$

$$= \dfrac{1}{n-m}$$

(d) $\dfrac{4}{x-2} - \dfrac{3}{2x+1} = \dfrac{4(2x+1)}{(x-2)(2x+1)} - \dfrac{3(x-2)}{(2x+1)(x-2)}$

$$= \dfrac{4(2x+1)-3(x-2)}{(x-2)(2x+1)}$$

$$= \dfrac{8x+4-3x+6}{(x-2)(2x+1)}$$

$$= \dfrac{5x+10}{(x-2)(2x+1)}$$

$$= \dfrac{5(x+2)}{(x-2)(2x+1)}$$

## EXERCISE 10:6

1.   Simplify.   (a) $\dfrac{4x+8}{4}$     (b) $\dfrac{2x}{6x-2x^2}$     (c) $\dfrac{3a-6b}{12ab}$     (d) $\dfrac{6a^2-12a}{3ab-6b}$

(e) $\dfrac{x^2+2xy}{xy+2y^2}$     (f) $\dfrac{3y^2+15y}{10y+2y^2}$     (g) $\dfrac{5x^2+25}{x^2+5}$     (h) $\dfrac{x^2-25}{x+5}$

(i) $\dfrac{x+2}{x^2+5x+6}$     (j) $\dfrac{4x-4}{x^2+2x-3}$     (k) $\dfrac{x^2-4x+3}{2x-6}$     (l) $\dfrac{9x^2-1}{9x+3}$

(m) $\dfrac{9x^2-3x+12}{6x^2-2x+8}$     (n) $\dfrac{a^2-a-6}{a^2-8a+15}$     (o) $\dfrac{x^2+xy}{x^2-y^2}$     (p) $\dfrac{3a^2+3ab}{6ab+6b^2}$

(q) $\dfrac{3(a-b)}{b-a}$     (r) $\dfrac{2x-2y}{y-x}$     (s) $\dfrac{am-ax}{bx-bm}$     (t) $\dfrac{2x^2-2}{(1-x)^2}$

2. **Simplify.**

  (a) $\dfrac{3x^2+x-2}{2} \times \dfrac{8x+4}{6x^2-x-2}$     (b) $\dfrac{2a-2}{6a-3} \times \dfrac{2a-1}{a^2-1}$

  (c) $\dfrac{a}{a+1} \times \dfrac{a^2-1}{2a^2}$     (d) $\dfrac{4n^2-9}{3-2n} \div \dfrac{3+2n}{2n-3}$

  (e) $\dfrac{x+1}{2x} \div \dfrac{3x^2-3}{x^2}$     (f) $\dfrac{x^2-4x+3}{x^2+x-12} \div \dfrac{x^2-6x-7}{x^2-3x-28}$

  (g) $\dfrac{y^2-4y+4}{y^2-2y} \div \dfrac{y^2-4}{y-2}$

3. **Simplify.**

  (a) $\dfrac{x}{3}-\dfrac{x}{4}$     (b) $\dfrac{2a}{3}+\dfrac{a}{5}$     (c) $\dfrac{4}{5a}-\dfrac{1}{2a}$

  (d) $\dfrac{2}{n}+\dfrac{3}{2n}$     (e) $\dfrac{3x+y}{10}+\dfrac{x-3y}{15}$     (f) $\dfrac{a-5b}{5}-\dfrac{2a+b}{2}$

  (g) $\dfrac{3(2x+4)}{5}-\dfrac{2(3x-2)}{3}$     (h) $\dfrac{2}{x+1}+\dfrac{3}{x-1}$     (i) $\dfrac{4}{2a-1}-\dfrac{1}{a-2}$

  (j) $\dfrac{6}{n-3}-\dfrac{5}{n+2}$     (k) $\dfrac{3}{x-2}+\dfrac{2}{2-x}$     (l) $\dfrac{3}{x}-\dfrac{4}{x+3}$

  (m) $\dfrac{a}{m}-\dfrac{b}{n}$     (n) $\dfrac{2}{m-n}-\dfrac{3}{n-m}$     (o) $\dfrac{a}{a-b}+\dfrac{b}{b-a}$

  (p) $\dfrac{2}{a^2+a}+\dfrac{3}{a^2-a}$     (q) $\dfrac{x}{2x^2-2}-\dfrac{2}{x+1}$

4. Given that $a=\dfrac{x+1}{x-2}$ and $b=\dfrac{2x-1}{x+2}$ show that $a-b=\dfrac{x(8-x)}{x^2-4}$.

5. This diagram represents a rail tunnel with a semi-circular section.

   O is the centre of the circle.

   AB is the distance between the rails.

   OD is the maximum height of a train able to use this tunnel.

  (a) Find an expression for OD in terms of r and h.

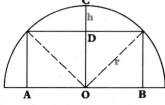

  (b) If AB = x, show that the relationship between x, h and r is $x^2+4h^2=8rh$. (*Hint:* use the Theorem of Pythagoras.)

6. The formula $\dfrac{1}{f}=\dfrac{1}{u}+\dfrac{1}{v}$ is used in a physics experiment. Make u the subject of this formula.

**Review** **Simplify.**

  (a) $\dfrac{3x+6}{x^2-4}$     (b) $\dfrac{5y-10x}{2x-y}$     (c) $\dfrac{a^2-2a-15}{2a^2-9a-5}$

  (d) $\dfrac{3a}{4}-\dfrac{a}{3}$     (e) $\dfrac{1}{m}+\dfrac{2}{n}$.     (f) $\dfrac{x+3}{x^2-3x+2} \times \dfrac{2x-4}{x^2-9}$

  (g) $\dfrac{4}{x-3}+\dfrac{2}{x+1}$     (h) $\dfrac{x-2y}{2}-\dfrac{2x-y}{3}$     (i) $\dfrac{y^2-xy}{y} \div \dfrac{x-y}{x}$

  (j) $\dfrac{2x}{x-y}+\dfrac{2y}{y-x}$

## The EXPRESSION $(x + a)^2 + b$

In the expression $3x^2 - 5x + 7$, 3 is the coefficient of $x^2$, $-5$ is the coefficient of x and 7 is the constant term.

### DISCUSSION EXERCISE 10:7

$x^2 - 8x + 16 = (x - 4)(x - 4)$
$\qquad\qquad\quad = (x - 4)^2$        We say that $x^2 - 8x + 16$ is a perfect square.
Which of the following expressions are perfect squares?

| | | | |
|---|---|---|---|
| $x^2 + 8x + 16$ | $x^2 - 4x + 4$ | $x^2 - 6x + 12$ | $x^2 - 6x + 9$ |
| $x^2 + 2x + 2$ | $x^2 - 2x + 1$ | $x^2 - 12x + 36$ | $x^2 - 10x - 25$ |

For those that are perfect squares, what is the relationship between the coefficient of x and the constant term? **Discuss.**

Notice that in the expressions given above, the coefficient of x is an even number. Write down some more perfect squares in which the coefficient of $x^2$ is 1 and the coefficient of x is an even number.
    **What if** the coefficient of x is an odd number?
    **What if** the coefficient of $x^2$ is not 1?

*Worked Example* What must be added to $x^2 - 14x$ to make the expression a perfect square?

***Answer***    $\left(\frac{-14}{2}\right)^2 = 49$.    Check: $x^2 - 14x + 49 = (x - 7)(x - 7)$

*Worked Example*   Write the following as the sum of a square and a constant.
           (a) $x^2 + 6x + 8$                 (b) $x^2 - 3x + 10$

***Answer***     (a) $x^2 + 6x + 8 = (x^2 + 6x) + 8$
$$= [x^2 + 6x + \left(\tfrac{6}{2}\right)^2] + 8 - \left(\tfrac{6}{2}\right)^2$$
$$= (x^2 + 6x + 9) + 8 - 9$$
$$= (x + 3)^2 - 1$$

       (b) $x^2 - 3x + 10 = (x^2 - 3x) + 10$
$$= [x^2 - 3x + \left(-\tfrac{3}{2}\right)^2] + 10 - \left(-\tfrac{3}{2}\right)^2$$
$$= (x^2 - 3x + \tfrac{9}{4}) + 10 - \tfrac{9}{4}$$
$$= (x - \tfrac{3}{2})^2 + 7\tfrac{3}{4}$$

### EXERCISE 10:8

1. Which of the following expressions are perfect squares?
     (a) $x^2 + 4x + 4$        (b) $x^2 + 6x + 12$        (c) $x^2 - 6x + 36$        (d) $x^2 + 2x + 1$
     (e) $x^2 - 10x + 25$     (f) $x^2 - 4x - 16$        (g) $x^2 + 3x + 9$        (h) $x^2 + 3x + \tfrac{9}{4}$
     (i) $x^2 - 5x + \tfrac{25}{4}$      (j) $x^2 + x - \tfrac{1}{4}$

2. Find the value of n if these are perfect squares.
   (a) $x^2 - 12x + n$      (b) $x^2 + 7x + n$      (c) $x^2 - x + n$      (d) $x^2 - nx + 1$
   (e) $x^2 + nx + 36$      (f) $x^2 - nx + 4$

3. What must be added to the following to make the expressions perfect squares?
   (a) $x^2 + 8x$      (b) $x^2 - 2x$      (c) $x^2 + 14x$      (d) $x^2 - 7x$
   (e) $x^2 + 5x$      (f) $x^2 - 9x$

4. Write the following in the form $(x + a)^2 + b$.
   (a) $x^2 + 2x + 3$      (b) $x^2 + 6x - 1$      (c) $x^2 - 2x + 2$      (d) $x^2 - 4x - 2$
   (e) $x^2 + x + 1$      (f) $x^2 + 3x - 2$      (g) $x^2 - x + 1$      (h) $x^2 - 5x$

5. (a) Show that $x^2 - 10x + 40$ may be written as $(x - 5)^2 + 15$.
   (b) What is the smallest possible value of $(x - 5)^2$?
   (c) What is the least value of the expression $x^2 - 10x + 40$?
   (d) For what value of x does this expression have this least value?
   (e) Does the expression $x^2 - 10x + 40$ have a maximum value?

6. Find the values of a, b and c if    (a) $4x^2 + 24x + 1 = a(x + b)^2 + c$
                              (b) $4x^2 + 24x + 1 = a[(x + b)^2 + c]$
                              (c) $4x^2 + 24x + 1 = (ax + b)^2 + c$

**Review 1** Write the following as the sum of a square and a constant.
         (a) $x^2 + 4x - 2$      (b) $x^2 - 2x + 6$      (c) $x^2 - 5x - 1$

**Review 2** Show that $x^2 + 6x + 2$ may be written as $(x + 3)^2 - 7$.
         Hence write down the minimum value of the expression $x^2 + 6x + 2$.

## QUADRATIC EQUATIONS: using factors

Some quadratic equations, such as $2x^2 - 11x + 5 = 0$, may be solved by factorising. We rewrite $2x^2 - 11x + 5$ as the product of two expressions, then use the fact that if the product of two expressions is zero then one of the expressions must be zero.

*Worked Example*   Solve    (a) $x(2x + 3) = 0$      (b) $2x^2 - 11x + 5 = 0$      (c) $x(x + 3) = 10$

*Answer*   (a) $x(2x + 3) = 0$
             Either $\underline{x = 0}$   or   $2x + 3 = 0$
                                      $2x = -3$
                                      $\underline{x = -1{\cdot}5}$

                                     (b) $2x^2 - 11x + 5 = 0$
                                      $(2x - 1)(x - 5) = 0$
                                      Either $2x - 1 = 0$   or   $x - 5 = 0$
                                                  $2x = 1$            $\underline{x = 5}$
                                                  $x = \frac{1}{2}$

(c)
$$x\,(x + 3) = 10$$
$$x^2 + 3x = 10$$
$$x^2 + 3x - 10 = 0$$
$$(x + 5)(x - 2) = 0$$
Either $x + 5 = 0$    or    $x - 2 = 0$
$$\underline{x = -5} \qquad\qquad \underline{x = 2}$$

---

**If an equation is formed to solve a problem, one of the solutions for the equation may not be an answer to the problem.**

---

*Worked Example*   The sum of the squares of two consecutive whole numbers is 145. Find the whole numbers.

*Answer*   Let one of the numbers be n.     Then the next number is $n + 1$.

The equation is
$$n^2 + (n + 1)^2 = 145$$
$$n^2 + n^2 + 2n + 1 = 145$$
$$2n^2 + 2n + 1 - 145 = 0$$
$$2n^2 + 2n - 144 = 0$$
$$n^2 + n - 72 = 0$$
$$(n + 9)(n - 8) = 0$$
Either $n + 9 = 0$   or   $n - 8 = 0$
$$n = -9 \qquad\qquad n = 8$$

If $n = –9$, the next number is –8.     If $n = 8$, the next number is 9.
Hence, there are two answers: –9 and –8 or 8 and 9.

---

*Worked Example*   The length of a rectangle is 7cm more than the width. Find the width of this rectangle if the diagonals are each 17cm.

*Answer*   Let the width be x cm. Then the length is $(x + 7)$ cm.

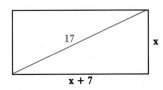

$$(x + 7)^2 + x^2 = 17^2 \quad \text{(Pythagoras' Theorem)}$$
$$x^2 + 14x + 49 + x^2 = 289$$
$$2x^2 + 14x + 49 = 289$$
$$2x^2 + 14x + 49 - 289 = 0$$
$$2x^2 + 14x - 240 = 0$$
$$x^2 + 7x - 120 = 0$$
$$(x + 15)(x - 8) = 0$$

Either $x + 15 = 0$     or     $x - 8 = 0$
$$x = -15 \qquad\qquad x = 8$$
Since the width cannot have a negative value, $x \neq -15$. Then the width = 8cm.

*Expressions and Equations*

*Worked Example* An open box is made by cutting 2cm squares from the corners of a square
sheet of cardboard and then folding.
If the length of the sheet of cardboard is xcm, show that an expression for the
volume of the box is $2x^2 - 16x + 32$.
Given that the volume of the box is 128cm³ find the value of x.

*Answer*

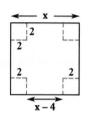 

Length of box = x – 4, width of box = x – 4, height of box = 2.
Volume of box $= (x - 4)(x - 4) \times 2$
$= 2(x^2 - 8x + 16)$
$= 2x^2 - 16x + 32$
Since volume = 128 then $2x^2 - 16x + 32 = 128$
$2x^2 - 16x - 96 = 0$
$x^2 - 8x - 48 = 0$
$(x - 12)(x + 4) = 0$
Either x – 12 = 0   or   x + 4 = 0
x = 12          x = – 4
Since x is the length of the sheet of cardboard, x cannot have a negative value.
Hence x = – 4 is not possible.
The required answer is x = 12.

## EXERCISE 10:9

1.  Solve these equations.
    (a) $(x - 2)(x - 5) = 0$        (b) $(x + 2)(x - 1) = 0$        (c) $(x + 4)(x + 5) = 0$
    (d) $x(x + 6) = 0$             (e) $(2x + 1)(x - 4) = 0$       (f) $(2x - 3)(2x - 1) = 0$
    (g) $(x + 2)(4x - 5) = 0$      (h) $(4x + 5)(2x + 3) = 0$      (i) $x(4x - 3) = 0$
    (j) $(2x + 5)(3x - 2) = 0$

2.  Find the possible values for **a**.
    (a) $a^2 + 3a + 2 = 0$          (b) $a^2 + a - 6 = 0$           (c) $a^2 - 2a + 1 = 0$
    (d) $a^2 - 2a - 8 = 0$          (e) $a^2 - 3a - 4 = 0$          (f) $a^2 + 4a - 5 = 0$
    (g) $a^2 - 2a - 15 = 0$         (h) $a^2 + 9a + 20 = 0$         (i) $2a^2 - 5a - 3 = 0$
    (j) $3a^2 + 4a + 1 = 0$         (k) $6a^2 - a - 1 = 0$          (l) $6a^2 - 5a - 4 = 0$
    (m) $3a^2 + 14a + 8 = 0$        (n) $8a^2 + 6a - 9 = 0$         (o) $12a^2 + 7a - 12 = 0$
    (p) $4a^2 - 20a + 25 = 0$       (q) $4a^2 - 19a + 12 = 0$       (r) $a^2 - 16 = 0$
    (s) $4a^2 - 9 = 0$              (t) $a^2 - 9a = 0$              (u) $4a^2 + a = 0$

3.  Solve these equations.
    (a) $x^2 + 5x = 6$              (b) $y^2 + 28 = 11y$            (c) $35 - 2a = a^2$
    (d) $11x - 6 = 4x^2$           (e) $x^2 = x$                  (f) $6y^2 - 11y = 7$
    (g) $a^2 + 4a + 5 = 2$         (h) $n^2 = 4$                  (i) $3a^2 + 5a = 2$

188

(j)  $12 = x + x^2$       (k)  $4x^2 = 25$           (l)  $y^2 - 3y = 10$
(m) $a^2 = 4a$            (n)  $n^2 - 3n + 3 = 1$     (o)  $n(n + 4) = 60$
(p)  $(x + 2)(x - 3) = 14$     (q)  $(3a + 1)(2a - 1) = 4$

4.

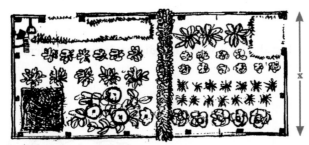

The length of the rectangular allotment is 3 metres more than the length of the square allotment. The width of each allotment is x.
(a)  Write an expression, in terms of x, for the total area of both allotments.
(b)  Given that the total area is 90m², write an equation for x.
(c)  Solve the equation.
(d)  What is the area of the rectangular allotment?

5.  The following is a famous problem written by the Arab mathematician Al-Khwarizmi over a thousand years ago.
*"A square has two rectangles, each of length 5 units, added to it. If the total area is then 39 square units, what is the length of the square?"*
This problem was written before quadratic equations were developed. It was solved by construction.
Write and solve a quadratic equation to find the answer to the problem.

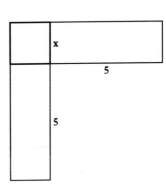

6.  The sum of the first  n  numbers in the sequence  1, 2, 3, 4, . . . is given by  Sum = $\frac{n}{2}(n + 1)$. How many numbers must be taken to give a sum of 55?

7.  Find two consecutive integers such that the sum of their squares is 113.

8.  The formula  $d = \frac{n}{2}(n - 3)$  gives the number of diagonals, d, of a polygon with  n  sides. A particular polygon has 275 diagonals. How many sides does this polygon have?

9.

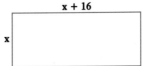

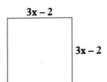

*Not drawn to scale*

The area of the rectangle exceeds that of the square by 16 square units.
Find the width of the rectangle.

10. Iona cycles  x  kilometres North, then 3 kilometres less than this to the East. She is then 15km from where she started.
How far north did Iona cycle?

11. A rectangle is 7cm longer than it is wide. The diagonals are each 13cm.
Find the width of this rectangle.

12.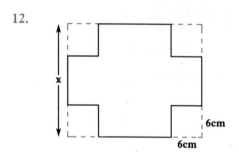

Jessie makes fruit containers by cutting 6cm squares from the corners of sheets of cardboard, then folding. These sheets of cardboard are 5cm longer than they are wide.
(i) If the width of a sheet of cardboard is x cm find expressions, in terms of x, for
 (a) the length of a sheet
 (b) the length of a container
 (c) the width of a container.
(ii) Show that an expression for the volume of a container is $6x^2 - 114x + 504$.
(iii) Find the width of a sheet of cardboard given that the volume of a container is 1800cm³.

13.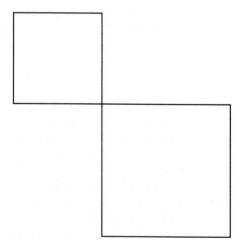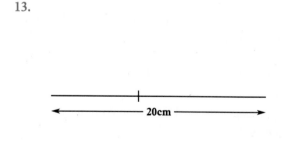

A line, 20cm long, is to be divided into two parts so that the sum of the squares on the two parts is 218cm². Where should the line be divided?

Review 1 Solve these equations.
(a) $(x - 7)(x + 4) = 0$
(b) $x(4x - 1) = 0$
(c) $x^2 - 2x - 15 = 0$
(d) $2n^2 + 9n - 5 = 0$
(e) $n^2 + 5n = 0$
(f) $8n^2 + 2n - 15 = 0$
(g) $a^2 = 25$
(h) $4a^2 + 18 = 27a$
(i) $a(a + 2) = 24$

Review 2

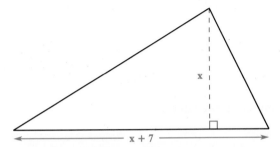

The area of this triangle is 22m².
(a) Show that x satisfies the equation $x^2 + 7x = 44$.
(b) Solve this equation.
(c) Write down the length of the base of this triangle.

Review 3 Two positive numbers differ by $\frac{1}{2}$.
Their product is 60.
(a) If the smaller of these numbers is n, show that n satisfies the equation
$2n^2 + n - 120 = 0$.
(b) Find the two numbers.

Review 4 Bruce's vegetable garden measures 12 metres by 10 metres. Bruce decides to make this garden larger by increasing both the length and the width by x metres.
(a) Show that an expression for the total area of the enlarged vegetable garden is
$x^2 + 22x + 120$.
(b) Write an expression, in terms of x, for the area of the extension.
(c) By how much does Bruce increase the length if he increases the area by 104 square metres?

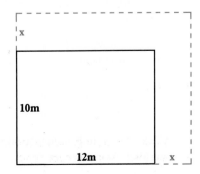

**Review 5**

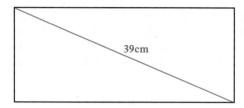

The perimeter of this rectangle is 102cm.
Each diagonal measures 39cm.
Write and solve a quadratic equation to find the length of this rectangle.

## QUADRATIC EQUATIONS: completing the square

### DISCUSSION EXERCISE 10:10

- **Discuss** the following solutions for the equations $x^2 = 4$ and $(x-3)^2 = 25$.

$$x^2 = 4 \qquad\qquad\qquad (x-3)^2 = 25$$
$$x = \pm 2 \qquad\qquad\qquad x - 3 = \pm 5$$

That is, $x = 2$ or $x = -2$     Either $x - 3 = 5$   or   $x - 3 = -5$
$$\qquad\qquad\qquad\qquad\qquad\qquad x = 8 \qquad\qquad x = -2$$

**What if** the equations were $x^2 = 3$ and $(x - 3)^2 = 8$?

- Consider the following solution for the equation $x^2 - 10x + 1 = 0$.

$$x^2 - 10x + 1 = 0$$
$$x^2 - 10x = -1$$
$$x^2 - 10x + 25 = -1 + 25$$
$$(x - 5)^2 = 24$$
$$x - 5 = \pm\sqrt{24}$$
$$x - 5 = \pm 4\!\cdot\!9 \,(1 \text{ d.p.})$$

Either $x - 5 = 4\!\cdot\!9$   or   $x - 5 = -4\!\cdot\!9$
$$x = 9\!\cdot\!9 \qquad\qquad x = 0\!\cdot\!1$$

The technique used above is often called "completing the square". Is this the same technique as rewriting an expression in the form $(x + a)^2 + b$? **Discuss.**

**Discuss** how to solve $x^2 + 3x - 2 = 0$ by "completing the square". Can this equation be solved using factors?

- 
$$2x^2 + 10x - 3 = 0$$
$$x^2 + 5x - \tfrac{3}{2} = 0$$

The first step to be taken to solve $2x^2 + 10x - 3 = 0$ by "completing the square" is shown. Is this step necessary? **Discuss.**

## EXERCISE 10:11

**Solve the following equations by "completing the square".** Give the answers correct to 1 decimal place.

1.  $x^2 + 4x - 6 = 0$
2.  $x^2 + 2x = 4$
3.  $x^2 - 2x - 2 = 0$
4.  $x^2 - 7x + 3 = 0$
5.  $x^2 + x - 4 = 0$
6.  $x^2 + 3x + 2 = 0$
7.  $2x^2 - 6x + 3 = 0$
8.  $2x^2 + 3x - 7 = 0$
9.  $5x^2 + x - 4 = 0$
10. $4x^2 - 7x + 2 = 0$

Review 1  $x^2 - 4x - 3 = 0$
Review 2  $x^2 + 5x = 1$
Review 3  $2x^2 + 4x - 5 = 0$

## QUADRATIC EQUATIONS: the common formula

## DISCUSSION EXERCISE 10:12

**Discuss** each step in making x the subject of the formula $ax^2 + bx + c = 0$.

$$ax^2 + bx + c = 0$$

$$x^2 + \frac{b}{a}x + \frac{c}{a} = 0$$

$$x^2 + \frac{b}{a}x = -\frac{c}{a}$$

$$x^2 + \frac{b}{a}x + \left(\frac{b}{2a}\right)^2 = -\frac{c}{a} + \left(\frac{b}{2a}\right)^2$$

$$\left(x + \frac{b}{2a}\right)^2 = -\frac{c}{a} + \frac{b^2}{4a^2}$$

$$\left(x + \frac{b}{2a}\right)^2 = -\frac{4ac}{4a^2} + \frac{b^2}{4a^2}$$

$$\left(x + \frac{b}{2a}\right)^2 = \frac{b^2 - 4ac}{4a^2}$$

$$x + \frac{b}{2a} = \pm\sqrt{\frac{b^2 - 4ac}{4a^2}}$$

$$x + \frac{b}{2a} = \frac{\pm\sqrt{b^2 - 4ac}}{2a}$$

$$x = -\frac{b}{2a} \pm \frac{\sqrt{b^2 - 4ac}}{2a}$$

$$x = \frac{-b \pm \sqrt{b^2 - 4ac}}{2a}$$

The quadratic equation $ax^2 + bx + c = 0$ may be solved by using the formula

$x = \dfrac{-b \pm \sqrt{b^2 - 4ac}}{2a}$. This formula is often called the **common formula.**

*Worked Example*  Solve  (a) $x^2 - 5x + 2 = 0$  (b) $5x^2 = 1 - 3x$ giving the answers correct to 1 decimal place.

*Answer*  (a) In $x^2 - 5x + 2 = 0$  $a = 1, b = -5, c = 2$

Using $x = \dfrac{-b \pm \sqrt{b^2 - 4ac}}{2a}$

$x = \dfrac{-(-5) \pm \sqrt{(-5)^2 - 4 \times 1 \times 2}}{2 \times 1}$

$= \dfrac{5 \pm 4 \cdot 12}{2}$  (2 d.p.)

$x = 4 \cdot 6$ or $0 \cdot 4$ (1 d.p.)

(b) Rearrange $5x^2 = 1 - 3x$ as $5x^2 + 3x - 1 = 0$; then $a = 5, b = 3, c = -1$.

Using $x = \dfrac{-b \pm \sqrt{b^2 - 4ac}}{2a}$

$x = \dfrac{-3 \pm \sqrt{3^2 - 4 \times 5 \times (-1)}}{2 \times 5}$

$= \dfrac{-3 \pm 5 \cdot 39}{10}$  (2 d.p.)

$x = -0 \cdot 8$ or $0 \cdot 2$ (1 d.p.)

## EXERCISE 10:13

1.  The formula $x = \dfrac{-b \pm \sqrt{b^2 - 4ac}}{2a}$ is to be used to solve the following equations. Write down the values of a, b and c.
    (a) $x^2 + 2x + 4 = 0$   (b) $x^2 + 3x - 1 = 0$   (c) $2x^2 - x - 7 = 0$   (d) $3x^2 = 5x - 2$
    (e) $x^2 = 1 - 4x$   (f) $5x^2 + 7x = 4$   (g) $6x^2 - 5 = 0$   (h) $2x^2 = 3x$

2.  Solve the following equations. Give the values of x correct to 2 decimal places.
    (a) $x^2 - 5x + 2 = 0$   (b) $2x^2 + 3x - 1 = 0$   (c) $5x^2 - 4x - 2 = 0$   (d) $3x^2 + x - 1 = 0$
    (e) $4x^2 - x = 2$   (f) $x^2 = 4x - 3$   (g) $2 - 3x - x^2 = 0$   (h) $5 + 4x = 2x^2$
    (i) $x(x + 2) = 5$   (j) $(x - 2)(x + 1) = 3$

3.

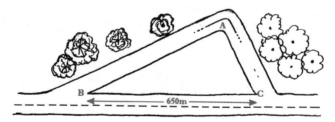

The new road shown in the diagram is built to cut off a dangerous right-angled bend. AB is 50 metres longer than AC. The length of AC is x metres.
(a) Use the Theorem of Pythagoras to write down an equation for x.
(b) Show that this equation may be simplified to $x^2 + 50x - 210000 = 0$.
(c) Solve this equation.
(d) How much shorter is the new road than the old road?

4.  A ball is thrown vertically upwards with a speed of 15m/sec. The height, h metres, of this ball after t seconds is given by the formula $h = 15t - 4 \cdot 9t^2$.
    Find the time taken for this ball to reach a height of 10 metres. Explain why both answers are correct.

5. Three cubes are placed as shown. The middle cube has edges which are 1cm longer than the top cube and 1cm shorter than the bottom cube.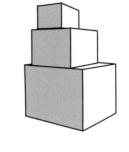
   (i) If the top cube has edges of length n write expressions, in terms of n, for
   (a) an edge of the middle cube
   (b) an edge of the bottom cube
   (c) the area of a face of the middle cube.
   (ii) Find an expression for the area of the shaded face of the shape. Show that this expression simplifies to $3n^2 + 6n + 5$.
   (iii) Given that the area of the shaded face is 38·75cm² find the length of an edge of the top cube.

6.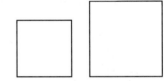

   The total area, A, of metal needed to make the tin shown is given by $A = 2\pi r(r + h)$.
   Find r if A = 395cm² and h = 12·5cm. (Take $\pi = 3\cdot14$.) Round your answer sensibly.

7.

   ←————————— 50cm —————————→

   A piece of wire, 50cm long, is cut into two parts. Each part is then bent to form a square. If the area of the large square is four times the area of the small square, find the length of a side of the small square.

**Review 1** Solve the following equations, giving the answers correct to 1 decimal place.
   (a) $x^2 + 9x + 12 = 0$    (b) $2x^2 - 5x - 8 = 0$    (c) $x^2 = 3x + 1$
   (d) $4 - 5x - x^2 = 0$

**Review 2** A 30cm × 30cm picture is mounted centrally on a square board. w is the width of the border.
   (a) Write an expression, in terms of w, for the area of the border.
   (b) Given that the picture takes up half the space on the board, write an equation for w.
   (c) Show that this equation simplifies to $w^2 + 30w - 225 = 0$.
   (d) Find the width of the border, to the nearest mm.

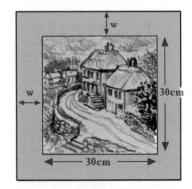

## QUADRATIC EQUATIONS: iteration

Iteration may be used to solve quadratic equations.

*Worked Example*    (a) Show that the equation $x^2 - 5x + 2 = 0$ may be rearranged as $x = \dfrac{2}{5-x}$.

      (b) Use the iteration $x_{n+1} = \dfrac{2}{5-x_n}$ with $x_1 = 1$ to find a solution for $x^2 - 5x + 2 = 0$, to 2 correct decimal places.

      (c) Show that the equation may also be rewritten as $x = \pm\sqrt{5x - 2}$.

      (d) Use the iteration $x_{n+1} = \sqrt{5x_n - 2}$, with starting value of 5, to find the other solution to 2 correct decimal places.

*Answer*    (a)    $x^2 - 5x + 2 = 0$

$$x^2 - 5x = -2 \qquad \text{(subtracting 2 from both sides)}$$
$$x(x-5) = -2 \qquad \text{(factorising)}$$
$$x = \frac{-2}{x-5} \qquad \text{(dividing both sides by } x-5)$$
$$x = \frac{2}{5-x} \qquad \text{(multiplying by } \tfrac{-1}{-1})$$

(b) Writing the first 4 figures of each calculator value we get

$$x_1 = 1$$
$$x_2 = 0.5$$
$$x_3 = 0.4444$$
$$x_4 = 0.4390$$
$$x_5 = 0.4385$$
$$x_6 = 0.4384$$

Hence, to 2 correct d.p. a solution is $x = 0.43$.

(c)    $x^2 - 5x + 2 = 0$

$$x^2 = 5x - 2$$
$$x = \pm\sqrt{5x - 2}$$

(d) Writing the first 5 figures of each calculator value we get

$$x_1 = 5$$
$$x_2 = 4.7958$$
$$x_3 = 4.6881$$
$$x_4 = 4.6304$$
$$x_5 = 4.5991$$
$$x_6 = 4.5821$$
$$x_7 = 4.5728$$
$$x_8 = 4.5677$$
$$x_9 = 4.5649$$
$$x_{10} = 4.5634$$
$$x_{11} = 4.5625$$
$$x_{12} = 4.5621$$

Hence, to 2 correct d.p. a solution is $4.56$.

**Note** Using a graphics calculator, the keying sequences for **(b)** and **(d)** are:

(b) 　1　EXE　2　÷　(　5　−　ANS　)　EXE　EXE　EXE　EXE ...

(d) 　5　EXE　√　(　5　ANS　−　2　)　EXE　EXE　EXE ...

---

## EXERCISE 10:14

**In this exercise give the solutions to two correct decimal places.**
**Use a graphics calculator if you have one available.**

1. (a) Show that the equation $x^2 + x - 3 = 0$ may be rewritten as $x = \dfrac{3}{1+x}$.
   (b) Use the iteration $x_{n+1} = \dfrac{3}{1+x_n}$, with $x_1 = 1$, to find one solution for the equation $x^2 + x - 3 = 0$.
   (c) Use the iteration $x_{n+1} = -\sqrt{3 - x_n}$, with $x_1 = -2$, to find the other solution.

2. (a) Show that $x = \dfrac{5}{x-1}$ is the same as $x^2 - x - 5 = 0$.
   (b) Use the iterative formula $x_{n+1} = \dfrac{5}{x_n - 1}$, with $x_1 = -2$, to find one solution for the equation $x^2 - x - 5 = 0$.
   (c) The other solution is about 3. What happens if we use 3 as the starting value in the iteration $x_{n+1} = \dfrac{5}{x_n - 1}$?
   (d) Show that $x = \dfrac{x^2 + 5}{2x - 1}$ is equivalent to $x^2 - x - 5 = 0$.
   (e) Use the iteration $x_{n+1} = \dfrac{x_n^2 + 5}{2x_n - 1}$ to find the other solution to $x^2 - x - 5 = 0$.

3. (a) Show that the equation $2x^2 + x - 5 = 0$ may be rewritten as $x = \pm\sqrt{\tfrac{1}{2}(5 - x)}$.
   (b) The positive solution of $2x^2 + x - 5 = 0$ is about 1. Use the iterative formula $x_{n+1} = \sqrt{\dfrac{5 - x_n}{2}}$ to find this solution.
   (c) The negative solution of $2x^2 + x - 5 = 0$ is about –2. Adapt the iterative formula used in **(b)** to find this solution.

4. (a) The iteration $x_{n+1} = \dfrac{4}{x_n - 1}$ is used to solve a quadratic equation. By replacing both $x_{n+1}$ and $x_n$ with x, show that the equation is $x^2 - x - 4 = 0$.
   (b) Use the iteration $x_{n+1} = \dfrac{4}{x_n - 1}$, with $x_1 = -1$, to find one solution for the equation $x^2 - x - 4 = 0$.
   (c) The iteration $x_{n+1} = -\sqrt{4 + x_n}$ may also be used to find the negative solution for $x^2 - x - 4 = 0$.

   For which iteration, $x_{n+1} = \dfrac{4}{x_n - 1}$ or $x_{n+1} = -\sqrt{4 + x_n}$, does the sequence $x_1, x_2, x_3, \ldots$ converge more quickly?

**Review** (a) Show that the equation $3x^2 - 8x + 2 = 0$ may be rewritten as $x = \dfrac{2}{8 - 3x}$.

(b) One solution of the equation $3x^2 - 8x + 2 = 0$ is about $x = 0$. Use the iteration $x_{n+1} = \dfrac{2}{8 - 3x_n}$ to find this solution.

(c) Show that the equation may be rearranged as $x = \pm\sqrt{\dfrac{8x - 2}{3}}$

(d) Use the iteration $x_{n+1} = \sqrt{\dfrac{8x_n - 2}{3}}$, with $x_1 = 2$, to find the other solution of the equation.

## QUADRATIC EQUATIONS: choosing an appropriate method

### DISCUSSION EXERCISE 10:15

- In this chapter we have used the following methods to solve quadratic equations:
  factors
  completing the square
  common formula
  iteration
  Think of examples where it would be appropriate to use each of these methods. **Discuss.**

- Suppose we wish to solve $x^2 - 3x - 8 = 0$. We could begin with the following "table of signs".

| x | −3 | −2 | −1 | 0 | 1 | 2 | 3 | 4 | 5 | 6 |
|---|---|---|---|---|---|---|---|---|---|---|
| $x^2 - 3x - 8$ | + | + | − | − | − | − | − | − | + | + |

What conclusions can we make about the solutions from this table? How could we continue to find the solutions? **Discuss.**

- **Discuss** the following statement.
  "A quadratic equation may be solved graphically in more than one way."

- **Discuss** the advantages and disadvantages of each method of solving quadratic equations.

### EXERCISE 10:16

**Solve the quadratic equations in this exercise by the most appropriate method. Where rounding is necessary, give the answers to 2 s.f.**

1. (a) $x^2 + x - 12 = 0$    (b) $x^2 - 5x + 3 = 0$    (c) $x^2 = 15$    (d) $6x^2 + 11x - 10 = 0$
   (e) $2x^2 + 11x = 6$    (f) $x^2 - 3x + 1.6 = 0$    (g) $x^2 + 2x = 10$    (h) $5x^2 - 2 = x$

2. The sum of the square of a number and the number itself is 20.
   Write and solve a quadratic equation to find the two possible values of the number.

3. A ball bearing is dropped into a glass of water. The formula $s = t^2 + 3t$ gives the distance, s cm, travelled by the ball bearing in t seconds.
   How long does it take the ball bearing to reach the bottom of the glass if the water is 10cm deep?

4.  The length of a diagonal of this rectangle is 44m.
    Given that the shorter sides are 15m shorter than the longer sides,
    find the area of the rectangle.

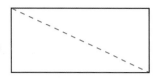

5.  The number of terms, n, of the sequence 3, 7, 11, 15, . . . which must be added to reach a
    total of S is given by the formula $S = 2n^2 + n$.
    How many terms must we add to get a total of 171?

6.  A computer uses the iteration $x_{n+1} = \dfrac{2}{3 + x_n}$ to find one solution for a quadratic equation.

    (a) What quadratic equation is being solved?
    (b) Find the positive solution of this equation.

7.

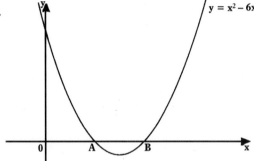
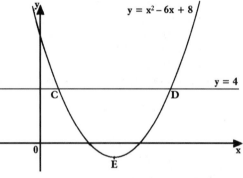

    (a) Find where the parabola $y = x^2 - 6x + 8$ meets the x-axis (the line $y = 0$) by solving the
        quadratic equation $0 = x^2 - 6x + 8$. Hence write down the coordinates of A and B.
    (b) Write down the quadratic equation which gives the x-values of the points of intersection
        of the parabola $y = x^2 - 6x + 8$ with the line $y = 4$. Solve this equation. Hence find the
        coordinates of C and D.
    (c) Write $x^2 - 6x + 8$ in the form $(x + a)^2 + b$.
        Hence find the coordinates of E, the lowest point on the graph of $y = x^2 - 6x + 8$.

    (d) Solve the equation $x^2 - 6x + 8 = 8x - x^2$.
        What is the connection between the solution
        of this equation and the sketch shown here?

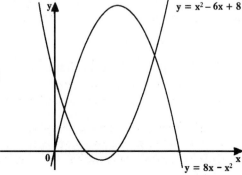

**Review 1** Solve. (a) $2x^2 = 3x + 4$  (b) $2x^2 + x - 3 = 0$  (c) $x^2 = 5x$

**Review 2**

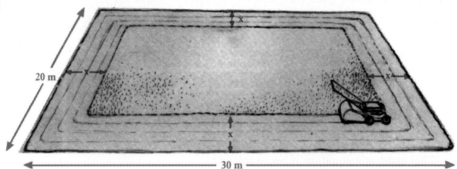

Sarah and Jamie shared the mowing of their rectangular lawn. Sarah began by mowing a strip around the outside. She stopped when she estimated she had done half the lawn.

(a) If Sarah's estimate was correct, write down an expression, in terms of x, for the area of lawn Sarah had mowed.

(b) Write an equation for x.
Show that this equation simplifies to $x^2 - 25x + 75 = 0$.

(c) Solve this equation to find the width of the strip Sarah had mowed.

---

## INVESTIGATION 10:17

Relationships between a, b and c when $ax^2 + bx + c = 0$

Can the following quadratic equations be solved? If so, how many solutions do they have?
$x^2 - 2x - 5 = 0$    $x^2 - 2x + 3 = 0$    $x^2 - 2x + 1 = 0$

There are relationships between a, b and c which indicate the number of solutions of the equation $ax^2 + bx + c = 0$. **Investigate** to find these relationships.

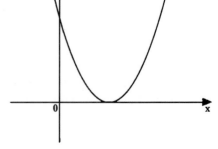

This is the graph of the quadratic equation for which $a > 0$ and $b^2 = 4ac$.

**Investigate** to find relationships between a, b, c and the position of the graph on the axes.

# EQUATIONS involving FRACTIONS

$$3x + 3\tfrac{1}{2} = \frac{2x}{5}$$

$$3x + \frac{7}{2} = \frac{2x}{5}$$

$$10 \times 3x + {}^{5}\!\cancel{10} \times \frac{7}{\cancel{2}_1} = {}^{2}\cancel{10} \times \frac{2x}{\cancel{5}_1}$$

$$30x + 35 = 4x$$

$$26x = -35$$

$$x = -\frac{35}{26}$$

$$x = -1\tfrac{9}{26}$$

$$\frac{4}{3y} + \frac{2}{y} = 1$$

$$\cancel{3y} \times \frac{4}{\cancel{3y}} + 3\cancel{y} \times \frac{2}{\cancel{y}} = 3y \times 1$$

$$4 + 6 = 3y$$

$$10 = 3y$$

$$y = \frac{10}{3}$$

$$y = 3\tfrac{1}{3}$$

**Discuss** each step of the solutions. Are there alternative ways of solving these equations?
**Discuss**.
**Discuss** how the calculator can be used to check the solutions.

$$\frac{3}{a-2} - \frac{4}{a+1} = 5$$

$$(a-2)(a+1) \times \frac{3}{a-2} - (a-2)(a+1) \times \frac{4}{a+1} = (a-2)(a+1) \times 5$$

$$3(a+1) - 4(a-2) = 5(a^2 - a - 2)$$

Possible first steps in solving the equation $\frac{3}{a-2} - \frac{4}{a+1} = 5$ are given above.
**Discuss** these steps. **Discuss** how we could continue to solve the equation. Solve the
equation. Check the solutions in the original equation.

- "In solving equations involving fractions, the most important step is eliminating the denominators." **Discuss** this statement.

- The following equation has solution $a = 2$.

$$\frac{2}{a-4} + \frac{3}{a+3} = \frac{4}{a^2 - a - 12}$$

$$\frac{2}{a-4} + \frac{3}{a+3} = \frac{4}{(a-4)(a+3)}$$

$$(a-4)(a+3) \times \frac{2}{a-4} + (a-4)(a+3) \times \frac{3}{a+3} = (a-4)(a+3) \times \frac{4}{(a-4)(a+3)}$$

$$2(a+3) + 3(a-4) = 4$$

$$2a + 6 + 3a - 12 = 4$$

$$5a - 6 = 4$$

$$5a = 10$$

$$a = 2$$

Checking: $\frac{2}{2-4} + \frac{3}{2+3} = -\frac{2}{5}$; $\frac{4}{4-2-12} = -\frac{2}{5}$; Solution is $a = 2$.

The next equation seems to have solution $a = 4$. In fact, the equation has no solution.

$$\frac{2}{a-4} + \frac{3}{a+3} = \frac{14}{a^2 - a - 12}$$

$$\frac{2}{a-4} + \frac{3}{a+3} = \frac{14}{(a-4)(a+3)}$$

$$(a-4)(a+3) \times \frac{2}{a-4} + (a-4)(a+3) \times \frac{3}{a+3} = (a-4)(a+3) \times \frac{14}{(a-4)(a+3)}$$

$$2(a+3) + 3(a-4) = 14$$

$$2a + 6 + 3a - 12 = 14$$

$$5a - 6 = 14$$

$$5a = 20$$

$$a = 4$$

What happens when you check $a = 4$ in the original equation? What has gone wrong? Discuss.

*Worked Example*  Solve  (a) $\frac{x+2}{6} + 3 = \frac{4x}{5}$   (b) $\frac{3}{x} - \frac{2}{x+2} = 4$

*Answer*  (a) $\frac{x+2}{6} + 3 = \frac{4x}{5}$

$$\overset{5}{30} \times (\frac{x+2}{6_1}) + 30 \times 3 = \overset{6}{30} \times \frac{4x}{5_1}$$

$$5(x+2) + 90 = 6 \times 4x$$

$$5x + 10 + 90 = 24x$$

$$100 = 19x$$

$$x = \frac{100}{19}$$

$$x = 5\frac{5}{19}$$

(b) $\frac{3}{x} - \frac{2}{x+2} = 4$

$$x(x+2) \times \frac{3}{x} - x(x+2) \times (\frac{2}{x+2}) = x(x+2) \times 4$$

$$3(x+2) - 2x = 4x(x+2)$$

$$3x + 6 - 2x = 4x^2 + 8x$$

$$0 = 4x^2 + 7x - 6$$

$$x = \frac{-7 \pm \sqrt{7^2 - 4 \times 4 \times (-6)}}{2 \times 4}, \text{ using}$$

the formula for the solution of a quadratic equation. Hence, to 2 d.p., $x = -2 \cdot 38$ or $0 \cdot 63$.

*Worked Example*  Ann and Belinda take the same time to travel to work in the mornings. Ann travels 20km while Belinda travels 15km. If Ann's average speed is 25km/h faster than Belinda's find the average speed of each girl.

*Answer*  Let $x$ be Belinda's average speed. Then Ann's average speed is $x + 25$.

Rearranging the formula $v = \frac{s}{t}$ to $t = \frac{s}{v}$, Belinda's time for 15km is $t = \frac{15}{x}$;

Ann's time for 20km is $t = \frac{20}{x+25}$.

Since these times are the same, $\frac{20}{x+25} = \frac{15}{x}$

$$20x = 15(x+25) \text{ [multiplying both sides by}$$
$$x(x+25)]$$

$$20x = 15x + 375$$

$$5x = 375$$

$$x = 75$$

Hence Belinda's average speed is 75km/h; Ann's average speed is 100km/h.

*Worked Example*  (a) Show that $x = 1, y = -7$ satisfy the equation $y = 2x - \frac{9}{x}$.

(b) There are two points on the graph of $y = 2x - \frac{9}{x}$ for which $y = -7$. One of these points has x-coordinate of 1. The x-coordinate of the other point can be found by writing and solving the quadratic equation, in x, formed when y is replaced by $-7$.
Find the x-coordinate of this other point.

*Answer*  (a)  Replacing x by 1, $y = 2 \times 1 - \frac{9}{1}$
$$= -7$$
That is, if $x = 1$ then $y = -7$.

(b)   $-7 = 2x - \frac{9}{x}$
$$-7x = 2x^2 - 9 \quad \text{(multiplying by x)}$$
$$0 = 2x^2 + 7x - 9$$
$$0 = (2x + 9)(x - 1)$$
Either $2x + 9 = 0$     or     $x - 1 = 0$
$$2x = -9 \qquad\qquad x = 1$$
$$x = -4\tfrac{1}{2}$$
Hence the required x-coordinate is $-4\tfrac{1}{2}$.

## EXERCISE 10:19

1.  Solve the following equations.

(a) $2a - \frac{a}{5} = \frac{2}{3}$

(b) $\frac{3(a+4)}{5} + 1 = \frac{a}{2}$

(c) $\frac{4x-1}{3} + 2(x+6) = 1\tfrac{1}{2}$

(d) $\frac{2}{x} - \frac{3}{4x} = 2$

(e) $3n - \frac{5}{n} = 14$

(f) $\frac{3}{x} + \frac{2}{x+2} = 1$

(g) $\frac{2}{n+2} + \frac{3}{n-1} = 5$

(h) $\frac{2}{a+1} - \frac{3}{2a+3} = \frac{1}{2}$

(i) $\frac{3}{2x-1} - \frac{2}{1-3x} = 0$

(j) $\frac{1}{y} + \frac{2}{y-1} = 3$

(k) $\frac{1}{a+8} + \frac{2}{3a-1} = \frac{1}{2}$

2.  The coordinates of the points of intersection of the hyperbola $y = \frac{2}{x}$ and the line $y = x - 1$ may be found by drawing the graphs or by solving the equation $\frac{2}{x} = x - 1$.

(a) Show that $\frac{2}{x} = x - 1$ may be written as the quadratic equation $x^2 - x - 2 = 0$.

(b) Solve the equation $x^2 - x - 2 = 0$.

(c) Using the answer to **(b)** find the coordinates of the points where the line $y = x - 1$ meets the hyperbola $y = \frac{2}{x}$.

3.  The numerator of a fraction is 3 less than the denominator. If the numerator and denominator are each increased by 1 the value of the new fraction formed is $\frac{10}{11}$.
Find the original fraction.

4.  Most Saturdays Jenny travels from Cardiff to Newcastle, a distance of about 500km. Jenny usually travels at an average speed of x km/h.

(a) In terms of x, write an expression for Jenny's usual travelling time.

(b) If Jenny increases her average speed by 10km/h, find her travelling time in terms of x.

(c) If Jenny's travelling time is 30 minutes less at the faster average speed show that
$$\frac{500}{x} - \frac{500}{x+10} = \frac{1}{2}.$$

(d) Find Jenny's usual average speed, rounding the answer sensibly.

5. A class of 36 students can be divided into $n$ equally sized groups or $(n-1)$ equally sized groups.

   (a) Show that the difference between the sizes of these groups is given by the expression
   $$\frac{36}{n(n-1)}.$$

   (b) Write an equation for $n$ if this difference is 3. Solve this equation to find the value of n.

6. In the formula $\frac{1}{f} = \frac{1}{u} + \frac{1}{v}$, $f$ is the focal length of a spherical mirror, $u$ is the distance of an object from the mirror and $v$ is the distance of the image from the mirror.

   Given that an object is 15cm nearer a mirror than the image and that the focal length of the mirror is 20cm, find the distance of the object from the mirror. Give the answer to the nearest centimetre.

7. Lampposts are to be erected at equal spacings along a 1200 metre length of straight road.

   (a) If the lampposts are $x$ metres apart, find an expression, in terms of $x$, for the number needed.

   (b) Find an expression for the number needed if they are $(x + 2)$ metres apart.

   (c) In terms of $x$, find how many more are needed if they are to be erected $x$ metres apart rather than $(x + 2)$ metres.

   (d) Given that one more lamppost is needed for the smaller spacing, calculate the value of $x$.

8. On Christine's birthday, some of her friends took her to a restaurant. The total bill was £112. Each of Christine's friends paid an equal share of this bill. Each paid £2 more than they would have if Christine had paid for herself.

   How many of Christine's friends took her to the restaurant?

**Review 1** Solve the following equations.

   (a) $\frac{3x}{4} + \frac{2}{3} = x$     (b) $\frac{3}{x-1} - \frac{1}{2x} = 4$     (c) $\frac{3a+2}{2} - \frac{a-1}{5} = 3$

   (d) $\frac{5}{2a-5} - \frac{3}{a+1} = \frac{1}{2}$     (e) $\frac{3}{n-5} + \frac{4}{n+2} = 3$

**Review 2** The aero club plane that Nessa is learning to fly can travel at a speed of 200mph in still air. Yesterday, it took Nessa the same time to fly 50 miles with the wind as it did to fly 40 miles against the wind.

   (a) Write an expression in terms of $w$, the wind speed, for the time Nessa flew with the wind.

   (b) Write an expression, in terms of $w$, for the time Nessa flew against the wind.

   (c) Write and solve an equation to find $w$. Give the answer to 2 significant figures.

**Review 3** Adam plays cricket for his school. So far this season he has made 184 runs. If he makes 41 runs in his next match Adam will increase his average by 2.

   (a) Write down an equation for $n$, the number of matches it took for Adam to make 184 runs.

   (b) Solve this equation to find $n$.

## PROVING RELATIONSHIPS

*Worked Example*   For the sequence $1, \frac{1}{2}, \frac{1}{3}, \frac{1}{4}, \ldots$ prove that $t_n - t_{n+1} = \dfrac{1}{n(n+1)}$.

*Answer*   $1, \frac{1}{2}, \frac{1}{3}, \frac{1}{4}, \ldots$

$t_1 = 1, t_2 = \frac{1}{2}, t_3 = \frac{1}{3}, t_4 = \frac{1}{4}, \ldots$ From this pattern we see that $t_n = \dfrac{1}{n}$.

Replacing n by n + 1 we get $t_{n+1} = \dfrac{1}{n+1}$.

Then $t_n - t_{n+1} = \dfrac{1}{n} - \dfrac{1}{n+1}$

$$= \frac{n+1-n}{n(n+1)}$$

$$= \frac{1}{n(n+1)} \text{ as required.}$$

*Worked Example*   $1^2 + 2^2 = 5$,  $2^2 + 3^2 = 13$,  $3^2 + 4^2 = 25$,  $4^2 + 5^2 = 41$.
It seems that the sum of the squares of any two consecutive integers is an odd number. Prove that this is so.

*Answer*   Let the consecutive integers be n and n + 1.
$$n^2 + (n + 1)^2 = n^2 + n^2 + 2n + 1$$
$$= 2n^2 + 2n + 1$$
$$= 2(n^2 + n) + 1$$
Since $2(n^2 + n)$ is divisible by 2, $2(n^2 + n)$ is an even number. Then $2(n^2 + n) + 1$ is an odd number.
Hence the sum of the squares of any two consecutive integers is an odd number.

*Worked Example*   $53^2 - 35^2 = 1584$          $47^2 - 74^2 = -3267$
$$= 99 \times 16 \qquad\qquad = -99 \times 33$$
These numbers, $53^2 - 35^2$ and $47^2 - 74^2$ have a common factor of 99.
Prove that the difference between the squares of any 2-digit number and the number written in reverse order has a common factor of 99.

*Answer*   Let the 2-digit number be xy. This is the same as 10x + y.
Written in reverse order the number is yx. This is the same as 10y + x.
The difference of the squares is
$$(10x + y)^2 - (10y + x)^2 = 100x^2 + 20xy + y^2 - (100y^2 + 20xy + x^2)$$
$$= 100x^2 + 20xy + y^2 - 100y^2 - 20xy - x^2$$
$$= 99x^2 - 99y^2$$
$$= 99(x^2 - y^2) \text{ which has a factor of 99.}$$

## EXERCISE 10:20

1.  For the sequence of odd numbers $1, 3, 5, 7, \ldots$ prove that $t_n + t_{n+1} = 4n$.

2.  $n, n + 1, n + 2$ are three consecutive whole numbers. Prove that the sum of any three consecutive whole numbers is divisible by 3.

3.  (i) Consider the sequence $2, 6, 12, 20, 30, \ldots$ The first three terms may be rewritten as $1 \times 2$, $2 \times 3$, $3 \times 4$.
    (a) Rewrite the 4th and 5th terms in a similar way. Hence find an expression for the *n*th term.
    (b) Prove that $t_{n+1} - t_n = 2(n + 1)$.

    (ii) Consider the sequence $\frac{1}{2}, \frac{1}{6}, \frac{1}{12}, \frac{1}{20}, \frac{1}{30}, \ldots$

    Prove that $t_n - t_{n+1} = \dfrac{2}{n(n+1)(n+2)}$.

4.  The numbers $341341$, $587587$, $611611$, $229229$ are all divisible by $1001$.
    Prove that any 6-digit number which is formed by writing down three digits then repeating these digits is always divisible by $1001$.

5.  The following proves that $2 = 1$. Find the mistake.
    $$a^2 - b^2 = (a + b)(a - b)$$
    Let $a = b$. Then replacing $b^2$ with $ab$ we have
    $$a^2 - ab = (a + b)(a - b)$$
    $$a(a - b) = (a + b)(a - b)$$
    $$a = a + b \quad \text{(dividing by } a - b)$$
    $$a = a + a \quad \text{(since } b = a)$$
    $$a = 2a$$
    $$1 = 2 \quad \text{(dividing by a)}$$

**Review 1** (a) $5, 6, 7, 8, 9$ are five consecutive integers. Show that the sum of the squares of these five numbers is divisible by 5.
(b) Prove that the sum of the squares of any five consecutive integers is divisible by 5.

**Review 2** (a) For the sequence $1, 4, 9, 16, \ldots$ prove that $t_{n+1} - t_n = 2n + 1$.
(b) Use **(a)** to prove that the first differences in the sequence of square numbers generates the odd numbers.

## INVESTIGATION 10:21

### Birthdate

Younger students can have fun with the following without knowing why it always works:

*"Ask a friend to key the following, pressing* ▣ *after each number is entered:*

*Key the number of the month in which you were born.*
*Multiply by 5.*
*Add 7.*
*Multiply by 4.*
*Subtract 20.*
*Multiply by 5.*
*Add the day of the month on which you were born.*
*Subtract 40.*
*Now look at your friend's calculator and tell your friend his or her birthdate."*

If  x  is the month and  y  is the day of birth prove that the above instructions always result in the number  $100x + y$.
What is the connection between the number  $100x + y$  and the result on the calculator screen?

Investigate  ways to adapt these instructions. As part of your investigation include different instructions for reading the month and day of birth and also instructions for reading a birthdate such as 12/6/77.

## RESEARCH PROJECT 10:22

### Partial Fractions

We know how to add the fractions  $\frac{2}{x-3}$  and  $\frac{3}{x+1}$  to get  $\frac{5x-7}{(x-3)(x+1)}$.
That is,  $\frac{2}{x-3} + \frac{3}{x+1} = \frac{5x-7}{(x-3)(x+1)}$.

Suppose we were given the expression  $\frac{5x-7}{(x-3)(x+1)}$  and asked to rewrite this as the sum of two fractions, one with denominator  $x-3$  and the other with denominator  $x+1$.

Writing  $\frac{5x-7}{(x-3)(x+1)}$  as  $\frac{2}{x-3} + \frac{3}{x+1}$  is called writing  $\frac{5x-7}{(x-3)(x+1)}$  in partial fractions.

Research partial fractions. As part of your research find how to write expressions such as
$\frac{3}{(x+4)(x+5)}$,  $\frac{5-x}{(2x+3)(x-2)}$,  $\frac{3x}{(x+2)^2}$,  $\frac{2x-3}{(x+4)(2x+1)^2}$,  $\frac{4}{x^2-11x+24}$,  $\frac{6x-5}{(3x-1)(x^2+1)}$  as the sum of two or more fractions.

| RESEARCH PROJECT 10:23 |
|---|

---

**Remainder Theorem**

Consider the following.   $f(x) = x^2 - 5x + 6$
$f(0) = 0 - 0 + 6 = 6$
$f(1) = 1 - 5 + 6 = 2$
$f(2) = 4 - 10 + 6 = 0$
$f(3) = 9 - 15 + 6 = 0$
Hence $x^2 - 5x + 6 = (x - 2)(x - 3)$

In the above, the Remainder Theorem has been used to factorise $x^2 - 5x + 6$.
Research the Remainder Theorem and its uses.

---

## CHAPTER 10   REVIEW

1.  Factorise
    **(a)** $3d + 6e$ **(b)** $4x^2 + 8xy$ **(c)** $x^2 - 11x + 30$ **(d)** $25x^2 - 1$ **NICCEA**

2.  **(a)** By writing the quadratic expression
    $$x^2 - 4x + 2$$
    in the form $(x + a)^2 + b$, find $a$ and $b$ and **hence** find the minimum value of the expression.

    **(b)** Solve the equation
    $$x^2 - 4x + 2 = 0$$
    giving your answers correct to 2 decimal places. **SEG**

3.  One night, a boy was cycling downhill without lights when he passed a police car in a layby. The car gave chase and quickly caught him up.

    The distance $d$ metres the boy has travelled past the layby is given by the formula
    $$d = 10t$$
    where $t$ is the time in seconds.

    The distance travelled by the police car is given by the formula
    $$d = 2t^2$$

    **(a)** When did the police car catch up with the cyclist?

    **(b)** How far had they both travelled in this time? **NEAB**

4.  Simplify $\frac{1}{x+3} + \frac{1}{x-5}$. **ULEAC**

208

5.  A farmer wants to build a fence to make a rectangular pen.
    He is using his barn as one side of the pen, as shown.

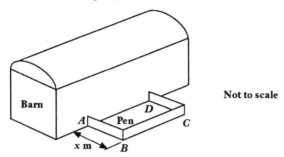

Not to scale

He has 60 metres of fencing and he wants the area of the pen to be 300m².
The length of *AB* is *x* metres.

(a) Show that if the area is 300m², *x* must satisfy the equation
$$x^2 - 30x + 150 = 0$$

(b) Solve the equation in (a) to find the two values of *x* that give the pen an area of 300m².

**SEG**

6.  (a) Simplify $(3x + y)(x - y) + 2y(x + y)$.
    (b) Factorise $a^2 - b^2$.

**NICCEA**

7.  The diagram represents a greenhouse.
    The volume of the greenhouse is given by the formula
    $$V = \tfrac{1}{2}LW(E + R).$$

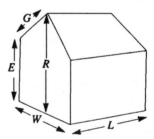

(a) Make *L* the subject of the formula, giving your answer as simply as possible.

The surface area *A*, of the greenhouse is given by the formula
$$A = 2GL + 2EL + W(E + R).$$

$V = 500$, $A = 300$, $E = 6$ and $G = 4$.

(b) By substituting these values into the equations for *V* and *A* show that *L* satisfies the equation.
$$L^2 - 15L + 50 = 0.$$

Make the steps in your working clear.

(c) Solve the equation $L^2 - 15L + 50 = 0$.

**ULEAC**

**8.** The equation $x^2 - x - 7 = 0$ can be rearranged to give $x = \sqrt{x + 7}$.
This information can be used to obtain the iterative formula
$$x_{n+1} = \sqrt{x_n + 7}.$$

**(a)** Starting with $x_1 = 4$ calculate the values of $x_2$, $x_3$ and $x_4$, giving all the figures on your calculator display.

**(b)** Find one solution of $x^2 - x - 7 = 0$ correct to 3 decimal places.            **SEG**

**9.** Alison is given £20 for her birthday.
She uses the £20 to start saving for her holiday.
Then each week she adds £4 to her savings.
She does not spend any of her savings.

**(a)** After $n$ weeks, Alison will have saved £$S$.
Write down a formula connecting $S$ and $n$.

**(b)** Wesley is also saving for his holiday.
He starts saving at the same time as Alison.
Wesley's total savings are given by the formula

$$T = 20 + \frac{n^2}{10}$$

where $T$ is his total savings in pounds after $n$ weeks.

Work out the number of weeks after which Wesley's total savings will be the same as Alison's total savings.

**(c)** Write down an expression for the difference between Alison's total savings after $n$ weeks and Wesley's total savings after $n$ weeks.

Comment on the value of the difference between Alison's total savings and Wesley's total savings as $n$ increases.            **ULEAC**

**10.** A possible points system for the HIGH JUMP event in athletics is given by
$$P = a(M - b)^2.$$

$M$ is the height jumped in cm, $P$ is the number of points awarded and $a$ and $b$ are positive constants.

**(a)** Zero points are scored for a height jumped of 75cm.
What is the value of the constant $b$?

**(b)** The constant $a = 0 \cdot 1$. What height will need to be jumped to obtain a points score of 1000?

**(c)** Express $M$ in terms of $P$, $a$ and $b$.            **SEG**

11. A firework is launched vertically upwards at time $t = 0$. Its vertical height, $h$, in metres from its point of launch is given by $h = 20t - 5t^2$ where $t$ is in seconds.

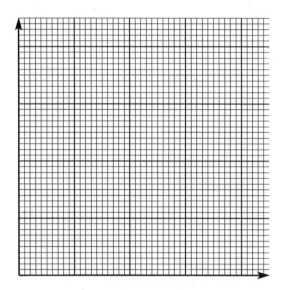

(a) Use a graphical method to estimate,

   (i) the first time at which the firework reaches a height of 12 metres;

   (ii) the maximum height reached by the firework.

(b) Use your graph to estimate the speed of the firework when it first reaches a height of 12 metres.

(c) Solve an appropriate quadratic equation to calculate the second time that the firework reaches a height of 12 metres. Give your answer correct to two decimal places.　　**SEG**

12. Fred cycled from home to his friend's house and back again.

   The distance from Fred's home to his friend's house is 20km.

   On his way from home to his friend's house, Fred cycled at $x$ km per hour.

   On the way back, Fred's speed had decreased by 2km per hour.

   It took Fred 4 hours altogether to cycle to his friend's house and back.

(a) Write down an equation for $x$.

(b) Show that the equation can be written as
$$x^2 - 12x + 10 = 0.$$

(c) Solve the equation in part (b).

   Give your answers correct to 1 decimal place.

   Only one of the answers in part (c) can be Fred's speed.

(d) Explain why.　　　　　　　　　　　　　　　　　**ULEAC**

**13.** Some students are planning a coach trip.

They ask sixty friends how much they will pay for a ticket to come on the trip.

Here is a graph of their results.

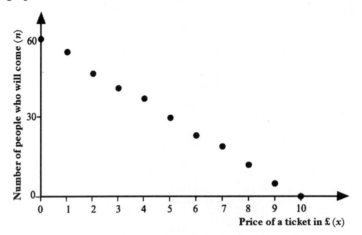

$x$ = the price of a ticket in £s
$n$ = the number of people who will come

**(a)** Explain how you can tell that a good approximation for $n$ is given by the formula $n = 60 - 6x$.

**(b)** It will cost £120 to hire the coach.

The students want to make a profit of £12.

They know that:

> Profit made = (ticket price) × (number who come) – (cost of coach hire)

Use this to help you explain why    $x^2 - 10x + 22 = 0$.

**(c)** Solve $x^2 - 10x + 22 = 0$ to find the ticket prices which give £12 profit. Give your answers to the nearest 10p.

**(d)** Find how many people need to come on the trip if these prices are used.    **NEAB**

**14.**

Surface Area of Cone $= \pi r^2 + \pi r l$

A cone of base radius $r$ cm and slant height 20cm has surface area 314cm². Taking $\pi = 3{\cdot}14$ calculate the value of $r$.    **NICCEA**

**15.** Factorise fully the expression $x^3 - 4x$.                              **SEG**

**16. (a) (i)** Show that

$$x = 1 + \frac{11}{x - 3}$$

is a rearrangement of the equation $x^2 - 4x - 8 = 0$.

**(ii)** Use the iterative formula

$$x_{n+1} = 1 + \frac{11}{x_n - 3}$$

together with a starting value of $x_1 = -2$ to obtain a root of the equation $x^2 - 4x - 8 = 0$ accurate to 1 decimal place.

**(b) (i)** Use the quadratic equation formula to solve the equation
$$x^2 - 4x - 8 = 0.$$

**(ii)** Comment on how the answer to part **(b) (i)** compares with your answer to part **(a) (ii)**.                              **MEG**

**17. (a)** Factorise $m^2 - n^2$.

**(b)** Rewrite 9991 as the difference of two squares. Hence find the prime factors of 9991.

                              **ULEAC**

**18. (a) (i)** Verify that the formula for the $n$th triangle number is

$$\frac{n(n+1)}{2}.$$

**(ii) Prove** that 171 is a triangle number.

**(b)** 'The sum of two consecutive triangle numbers is equal to a square number.'

**(i)** Investigate this statement.

**(ii)** Prove that the statement is true.                              **MEG**

# 11 — Graphs of Related Functions — 11

## INTRODUCTION

### DISCUSSION EXERCISE 11:1

**Use a graphics calculator or a computer graphics package throughout this exercise.**

- The graph of $y = x^2 + 3$ is congruent with the graph of $y = x^2$. The graph of $y = x^2 + 3$ may be found by translating the graph of $y = x^2$ three units in the positive y-direction.
  On the same set of axes draw $y = x^2$ and $y = x^2 - 3$. Compare the graphs.
  How can the graphs of $y = x^2 + 2$ and $y = x^2 - 2$ be obtained from the graph of $y = x^2$?
  What is the relationship between the graphs of $y = x^2$, $y = x^2 - a$, $y = x^2 + a$? **Discuss.**

- On the same set of axes draw $y = x^2$ and $y = (x + 3)^2$. Compare the graphs.
  What if $y = (x + 3)^2$ is replaced with $y = (x - 3)^2$ or $y = (x + 2)^2$ or $y = (x - 2)^2$?

  What is the relationship between the graphs of $y = x^2$, $y = (x - a)^2$, $y = (x + a)^2$? **Discuss.**

- What is the relationship between the graphs of $y = x^2$ and $y = (x + 3)^2 + 2$? Where is the vertex (the turning point) of the graph of $y = (x + 3)^2 + 2$? What is the equation of the axis of symmetry? **Discuss.**
  How can we find the equation of the axis of symmetry and the coordinates of the vertex of the graph of $y = x^2 - 4x + 3$? **Discuss.**
  Simone discovered that by rewriting $y = (x - 1)^2 - 3$ as $y + 3 = (x - 1)^2$ she could easily tell where the graph lay in relation to the graph of $y = x^2$. Why do you think Simone rewrote the equation in this way? **Discuss.**

- What is the relationship between the graphs of $y = x^2$ and $y = -x^2$? Does this same relationship exist between the graphs of $y = x^3$ and $y = -x^3$? **Discuss.**
  What if the graphs were $y = x^2 + 3x$ and $y = -x^2 - 3x$?
  What if the graphs were $y = x^3 + 2x - 1$ and $y = -x^3 - 2x + 1$?

- On one set of axes draw the graphs of $y = x^2 - 4x + 3$ and $y = x^2 + 4x + 3$; on another draw $y = x^3$ and $y = -x^3$. The same relationship exists between $y = x^2 - 4x + 3$ and $y = x^2 + 4x + 3$ as $y = x^3$ and $y = -x^3$. What is this relationship? Does the same relationship exist between the following pairs of graphs? $y = x^2 + 3x$ and $y = x^2 - 3x$; $y = x^3 + 4$ and $y = -x^3 + 4$? **Discuss.**

- The graph of $y = x^2 + 2x$ is shown here. What is the relationship between this graph and the graphs of the following: $y = x^2 + 2x + 3$, $y = (x + 1)^2 + 2(x + 1)$, $y = (x + 1)^2 + 2(x + 1) + 3$, $y = -(x^2 + 2x)$, $y = x^2 - 2x$? **Discuss.**

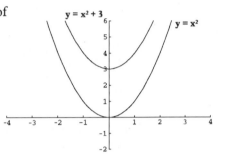

- Suppose the graph of $y = x^3$ is given. How could this graph be used to sketch the graphs of $y = x^3 + 3$, $y = x^3 - 1$, $y = (x + 2)^3$, $y = (x - 2)^3 + 1$, $y = -x^3$?

  Suppose the graph of $y = \dfrac{1}{x}$ is given. How can this graph be used to sketch the graphs of $y = \dfrac{1}{x} + 2$, $y = \dfrac{1}{x+3}$, $y = \dfrac{-1}{x}$, $y - 2 = \dfrac{1}{x+3}$? **Discuss.**

- If $x$ is replaced with $2x$, the equation $y = x^2 - 6x + 8$ becomes $y = (2x)^2 - 6(2x) + 8$ or $y = 4x^2 - 12x + 8$. Draw the graphs $y = x^2 - 6x + 8$ and $y = 4x^2 - 12x + 8$ on the same set of axes. What is the relationship between these graphs? **Discuss.**
  What if $x$ is replaced with $3x$ instead of $2x$?
  What if $x$ is replaced with $\frac{1}{2}x$? What if $x$ is replaced with $\frac{1}{3}x$?

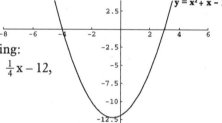

The graph of $y = x^2 + x - 12$ is shown.
**Discuss** how to use this graph to sketch the following:
$y = 4x^2 + 2x - 12$, $y = 16x^2 + 4x - 12$, $y = \frac{1}{16}x^2 + \frac{1}{4}x - 12$,
$y = \frac{1}{4}x^2 + \frac{1}{2}x - 12$.

- $2(x^2 - 6x + 8) = 2x^2 - 12x + 16$; $3(x^2 - 6x + 8) = 3x^2 - 18x + 24$.
  On the same set of axes, draw the graphs of $y = x^2 - 6x + 8$, $y = 2x^2 - 12x + 16$, $y = 3x^2 - 18x + 24$. How could the graphs of $y = 2x^2 - 12x + 16$ and $y = 3x^2 - 18x + 24$ be obtained from the graph of $y = x^2 - 6x + 8$? **Discuss.**

  How could the graphs of $y = \frac{1}{2}x^2 - 3x + 4$ and $y = \frac{1}{3}x^2 - 2x + \frac{8}{3}$ be obtained from the graph of $y = x^2 - 6x + 8$? **Discuss.**

## GRAPHS of FUNCTIONS RELATED by translation, reflection, enlargement

Remember: $f(x)$ means a function of $x$. This notation is often used when we are considering related functions.

For instance:   if $f(x) = x^2$, then $f(x) + 3 = x^2 + 3$
$$f(x + 3) = (x + 3)^2$$
$$= x^2 + 6x + 9$$
$$f(3x) = (3x)^2$$
$$= 9x^2$$
$$3f(x) = 3 \times x^2$$
$$= 3x^2$$
$$f(-x) = (-x)^2$$
$$= x^2$$

If we are given the graph of $y = f(x)$, the graphs of some related functions may be obtained as follows.

$y = f(x) + a$      translate $y = f(x)$ by the vector $\begin{pmatrix} 0 \\ a \end{pmatrix}$

$y = f(x - a)$      translate $y = f(x)$ by the vector $\begin{pmatrix} a \\ 0 \end{pmatrix}$

$y = -f(x)$      reflect $y = f(x)$ in the x-axis
$y = f(-x)$      reflect $y = f(x)$ in the y-axis
$y = af(x)$      enlarge $y = f(x)$ by a factor of $a$ in the y-direction
$y = f(ax)$      enlarge $y = f(x)$ by a factor of $\frac{1}{a}$ in the x-direction

$y - b = f(x - c)$      translate $y = f(x)$ by the vector $\begin{pmatrix} c \\ b \end{pmatrix}$

*Worked Example* The graph of $y = f(x)$, where
$f(x) = x^2 + 6x$, is sketched.
  (i) Explain how this graph could be used to sketch graphs of the following.

    (a) $y = -f(x)$        (b) $y = f(x) + 9$
    (c) $y = f(x + 2)$     (d) $y = f(x - 4)$
    (e) $y + 2 = f(x)$     (f) $y = f(x + 2) - 3$
    (g) $y = f(-x)$       (h) $y = f(3x)$
    (i) $y = f(\frac{1}{3}x)$     (j) $y = 2f(x)$
    (k) $y = \frac{1}{2}f(x)$
  (ii) Draw separate sketches of each of the graphs in **(i)**.

*Answer*  (i)  (a) The graph of $y = -f(x)$ is obtained by reflecting $y = f(x)$ in the x-axis.
    (b) The graph of $y = f(x) + 9$ is obtained by translating $y = f(x)$ by 9 units in the positive y-direction.
    (c) The graph of $y = f(x + 2)$ is obtained by translating $y = f(x)$ by 2 units in the negative x-direction.
    (d) The graph of $y = f(x - 4)$ is obtained by translating $y = f(x)$ by 4 units in the positive x-direction.
    (e) The graph of $y + 2 = f(x)$ is obtained by translating $y = f(x)$ by 2 units in the negative y-direction.
    (f) The graph of $y = f(x + 2) - 3$ is obtained by translating $y = f(x)$ by the vector $\begin{pmatrix} -2 \\ -3 \end{pmatrix}$.
    (g) The graph of $y = f(-x)$ is obtained by reflecting $y = f(x)$ in the y-axis.
    (h) The graph of $y = f(3x)$ may be obtained from the graph of $y = f(x)$ as follows: Choose some points on $y = f(x)$; leave the y-coordinates the same and multiply the x-coordinates by $\frac{1}{3}$ to get the corresponding points on $y = f(3x)$.
    (i) Proceed as in **(h)** but multiply the x-coordinates by 3.
    (j) The graph of $y = 2f(x)$ may be obtained from the graph of $y = f(x)$ as follows: Choose some points on $y = f(x)$, leave the x-coordinates the same and multiply the y-coordinates by 2 to get the corresponding points on $y = 2f(x)$.
    (k) Proceed as in **(j)** but multiply the y-coordinates by $\frac{1}{2}$.

(ii) (a)

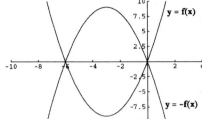

(b)

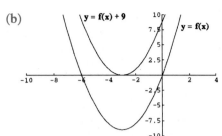

(c)

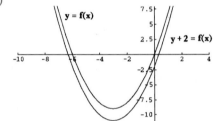

(d)

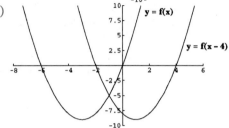

(e)

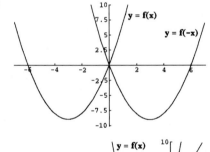

(f)

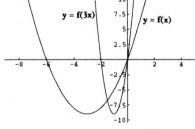

(g)

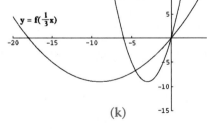

(h)

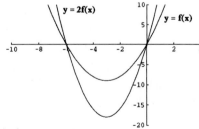

(i)

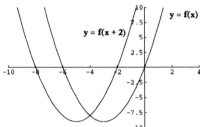

(j)

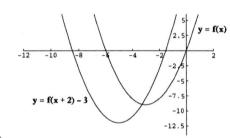

(k)

217

***Worked Example*** (a) Rewrite $x^2 - 6x + 7$ as $(x + a)^2 + b$. Hence find the coordinates of the vertex of the graph of $y = x^2 - 6x + 7$.
(b) Sketch the graph of $y = x^2$.
Use (a) to sketch the graph of $y = x^2 - 6x + 7$ on the same set of axes.

***Answer*** (a) $\quad x^2 - 6x + 7 = [x^2 - 6x] + 7$
$$= [(x - 3)^2 - 9] + 7$$
$$= (x - 3)^2 - 2$$
Hence $y = x^2 - 6x + 7$ may be rewritten as $y = (x - 3)^2 - 2$. The graph of $y = x^2 - 6x + 7$ is the same as the graph of $y = x^2$ translated by the vector $\binom{3}{-2}$. Hence the vertex is the point $(3, -2)$.

(b)

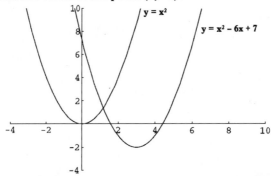

---

## EXERCISE 11:2

1. Draw the graph of $y = x^2$.
   Explain how the following graphs may be obtained from the graph of $y = x^2$. Sketch each graph on the same grid as $y = x^2$.
   (a) $y = x^2 + 3$      (b) $y = x^2 - 1$      (c) $y = (x - 1)^2$      (d) $y = (x + 2)^2$
   (e) $y = (x - 1)^2 + 3$      (f) $y + 2 = (x + 3)^2$

2. The graph of $y = x^3$ is drawn.
   Use this graph to sketch    (a) $y = (x - 3)^3$
                           (b) $y = x^3 + 3$
                           (c) $y = (x + 2)^3 - 4$

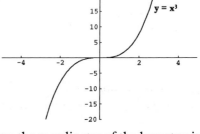

3. $f(x) = x^2 - 4$. Make sketches of the following, indicating the coordinates of the lowest point on each graph.
   (a) $y = f(x)$      (b) $y = f(x + 2)$      (c) $y = f(x) + 2$      (d) $y = f(2x)$      (e) $y = 2f(x)$

4.

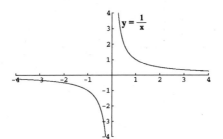

Use this graph to make sketches of
   (a) $y = \dfrac{1}{x} + 2$      (b) $y = \dfrac{1}{x + 2}$

5.

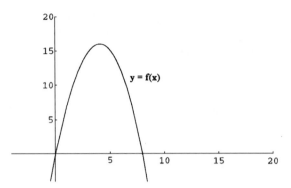

f(x) = 8x – x². The graph of y = f(x) is drawn.

Use this graph to sketch      (a) $y = \frac{1}{2} f(x)$

                                (b) $y = f(\frac{1}{2} x)$

indicating clearly where these graphs cross the x-axis and the coordinates of the highest points.

6. f(x) = x² + 4x + 3.
  (i) Find the values of a and b if f(x) = (x + a)² + b.
  (ii) What are the coordinates of the vertex of the graph of y = f(x)?
  (iii) Sketch      (a) y = f(x)      (b) y = f(x – 2)      (c) y = f(x) – 2      (d) y = f(–x)
                (e) y = –f(x).

7. Two functions are defined as f(x) = x², g(x) = x² + 4x – 1.
  (a) g(x) may be rewritten as f(x + a) + b. Find the values of a and b.
  (b) Use the result of **(a)** to explain how the graph of y = g(x) is related to the graph of y = f(x).

8. In each of the following, explain how the graph of y = g(x) may be sketched from the graph of y = f(x). Hence write the expression g(x) in terms of f(x).

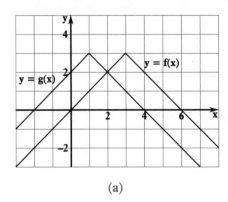

(a)

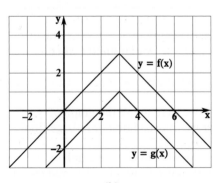

(b)

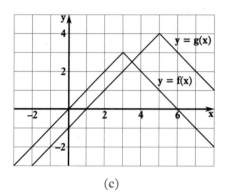

(c)

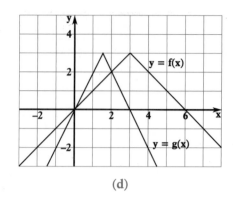

(d)

**Review 1**  $f(x) = x^2 - 4x$. The graph of $y = f(x)$ is shown.
Explain how the following graphs may be obtained from the graph of $y = f(x)$.
Hence sketch each graph, giving the coordinates of the highest or lowest point.

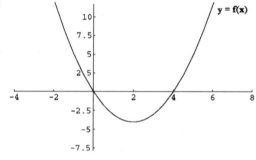

(a) $y = f(x + 2)$    (b) $y = f(x) + 2$

(c) $y = \frac{1}{2}f(x)$    (d) $y = f(\frac{1}{2}x)$

(e) $y = f(-x)$    (f) $y = -f(x)$

**Review 2**  Rewrite $x^2 - 6x - 1$ as $(x + a)^2 + b$. Hence sketch the graph of $y = x^2 - 6x - 1$, indicating the coordinates of the vertex.

---

## DISCUSSION EXERCISE 11:3

Suppose the graph of $y = f(x)$ is drawn and we are to use this to sketch the graph of $y = f(x - 2) - 4$. Does it matter whether we first translate in the x-direction or y-direction? Discuss.
As part of your discussion choose various functions $f(x)$.

**What if** we were to use the graph of $y = f(x)$ to sketch the graph of $3f(x - 2)$? Does it matter whether we translate first or enlarge first?

**What if** we were to use the graph of $y = f(x)$ to sketch the graph of $3f(x - 2) + 5$?
As part of your discussion, write and test guidelines for the order in which transformations should be dealt with.

## INVESTIGATION 11:4

Positioning the parabola

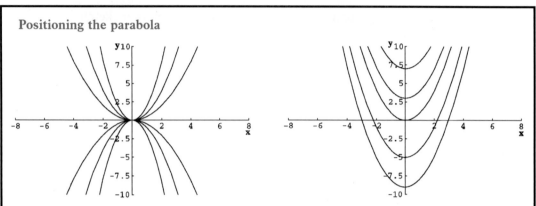

Investigate the shape and position on the axes of the graph $y = ax^2 + bx + c$ for various values of the coefficients a, b and c.

## GRAPHS of RECIPROCAL FUNCTIONS

The graph of $y = \dfrac{1}{x^2}$ may be obtained from the graph of $y = x^2$ by finding the reciprocal of each y-coordinate.

*fig* (i)  shows the graph of $y = x^2$.

*fig* (ii)  shows some points on $y = \dfrac{1}{x^2}$ obtained by finding the reciprocal of the y-coordinates of $y = x^2$.

*fig* (iii)  shows the graphs of $y = x^2$ and $y = \dfrac{1}{x^2}$.

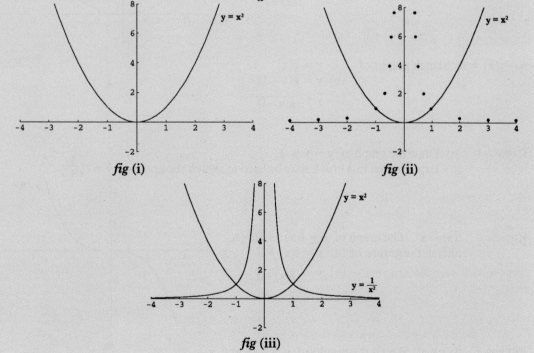

*fig* (i)

*fig* (ii)

*fig* (iii)

## EXERCISE 11:5

**Use a graphics calculator or a computer graphics package to check your sketches.**

1. Draw the graph of $y = x$.
   By finding the reciprocal of the y-coordinate of each point, sketch the graph of $y = \frac{1}{x}$.

2. $f(x) = x^3$. Draw the graph of $y = f(x)$. Use this graph to sketch the graph of $y = \frac{1}{f(x)}$.

3. Draw the graph of $y = 2x - 1$. Use this graph to sketch the graph of $y = \frac{1}{2x - 1}$.

4. (a) Sketch the graph of $y = x^2 + 1$.
   (b) What are the coordinates of the lowest point of $y = x^2 + 1$?
   (c) Use the graph of $y = x^2 + 1$ to sketch the graph of $y = \frac{1}{x^2 + 1}$.
   (d) What are the coordinates of the highest point of $y = \frac{1}{x^2 + 1}$?

5. $f(x) = x^2$. The graph of $y = x^2$ is shown.
   (i) Explain how this graph can be used to sketch the graphs of   (a) $y = f(x) + 2$
       (b) $y = \frac{1}{f(x) + 2}$.
   (ii) Sketch the graphs of   (a) $y = f(x) + 2$
       (b) $y = \frac{1}{f(x) + 2}$.

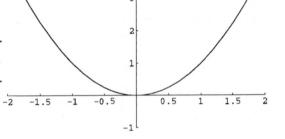

6. $g(x) = x^3$. Sketch graphs of   (a) $y = g(x)$
       (b) $y = g(x - 1)$
       (c) $y = \frac{1}{g(x - 1)}$.

**Review 1**   (a) Draw the graph of $y = x + 3$.
    (b) Explain how this graph may be used to sketch the graph of $y = \frac{1}{x + 3}$.

**Review 2**   $f(x) = x^3$. The graph of $y = f(x)$ is drawn.
    Sketch the graphs of (a) $y = f(x) + 2$
    (b) $y = \frac{1}{f(x) + 2}$.

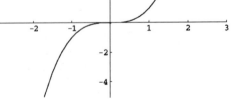

**Review 3**   $f(x) = x^2$. Sketch the graphs of $y = f(x)$ and $y = \frac{1}{f(x - 1)}$.

## INVESTIGATION 11:6

The Graph of $y = \dfrac{1}{x^n}$

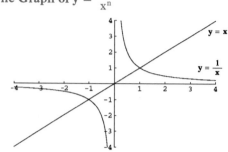 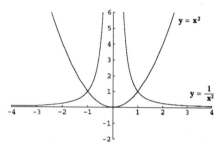

The graphs of $y = \dfrac{1}{x}$ and $y = \dfrac{1}{x^2}$ are shown sketched from the graphs of $y = x$ and $y = x^2$. **Investigate** the shape of the graphs of $y = \dfrac{1}{x^n}$ for various values of n.

## GRAPHS of TWO RELATED FUNCTIONS

We can use the graphs of $y = f(x)$ and $y = g(x)$ to find the graph of
$$y = f(x) + g(x)$$
$$y = f(x) - g(x)$$
$$y = f(x) \times g(x)$$
$$y = f(x) \div g(x).$$

For instance, if we are given the graphs of $y = x^3$ and $y = x^2 + 2$ we can use these to draw the graphs of $y = x^3 + x^2 + 2$, $y = x^3 - x^2 - 2$, $y = x^2 + 2 - x^3$, $y = x^5 + 2x^3$, $y = \dfrac{x^3}{x^2 + 2}$, $y = \dfrac{x^2 + 2}{x^3}$.

The graph of $y = f(x) + g(x)$ is obtained by adding the y-coordinates on the graphs of $y = f(x)$ and $y = g(x)$. How are the graphs of $y = f(x) - g(x)$, $y = f(x) \times g(x)$ and $y = f(x) \div g(x)$ obtained?

*Example*   **fig (i)**    shows the graphs of $y = x^3$ and $y = -x^2 + 10$
            **fig (ii)**   shows some points on $y = x^3 - x^2 + 10$ obtained by adding the y-coordinates
                       on $y = x^3$ and $y = -x^2 + 10$.
            **fig (iii)**  shows the points joined to give the graph of $y = x^3 - x^2 + 10$.

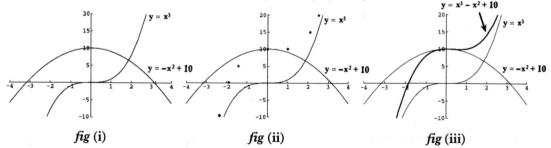

**fig (i)**                         **fig (ii)**                      **fig (iii)**

## EXERCISE 11:7

1. On the same set of axes, sketch $y = x^3$ and $y = x^2$.
   Use these graphs to sketch  (a) $y = x^3 + x^2$
                                (b) $y = x^3 - x^2$

2. Explain how you could use the graphs of $y = x^3$ and $y = x^2$ to draw the graph of $y = x^3 + 2x^2$.

3. What two graphs could be drawn to sketch the graph of $y = x^2 - 2x + 6$? Is there more than one answer?

4. Explain how the graphs shown could be used to sketch the graphs of $y = x^3$ and $y = \frac{1}{x}$.
   Sketch $y = x^3$ and $y = \frac{1}{x}$ in this way.

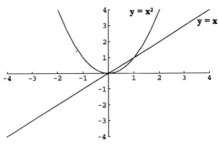

**Review 1**  Sketch the graphs of $y = x^3$ and $y = x + 2$.
            Use these graphs to sketch  (a) $y = x^3 + x + 2$
                                        (b) $y = x^3 - x - 2$

**Review 2**  Explain how the graph of $y = x^2 - 4x$ may be sketched from the graphs of $y = x$ and $y = x - 4$.

## CHAPTER 11   REVIEW

1.

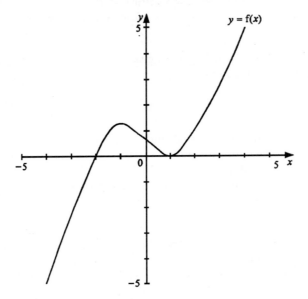

The graph of $y = f(x)$ has been drawn on the grid.
On the diagram above, sketch the graph of $y = f(x - 2)$.

**ULEAC**

2.  On each of the grids below, the graph of $y = f(x)$ for $-4 \leq x \leq 4$ is drawn.

    (a) On grid A, sketch the graph of $y = 2f(x)$.

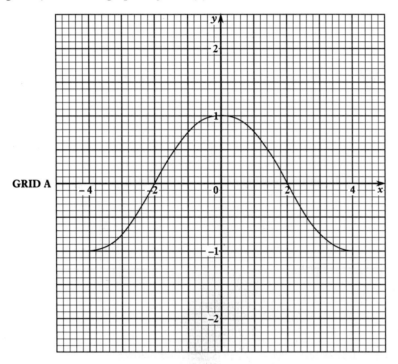

GRID A

(b) On grid B, sketch the graph of $y = f(x - 1)$.

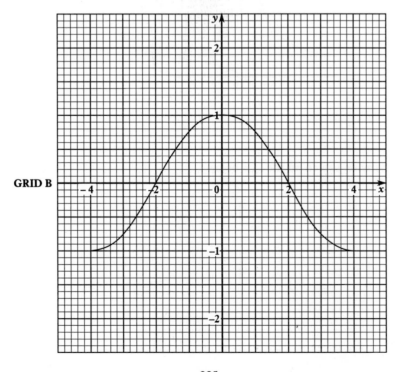

GRID B

**MEG**

3. The function $y = f(x)$ is defined for $0 \leq x \leq 2$.
   The function is sketched below.

   (a) Sketch $y = f(x) + 1$ on the axes below.

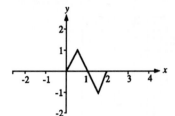

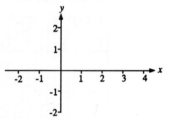

(b) Sketch $y = f(x - 1)$ on the axes below.

(c) Sketch $y = f(\frac{x}{2})$ on the axes below.

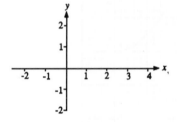

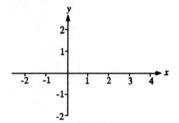

4. The graph of $y = f(x)$ where $f(x) = \frac{x}{x+1}$ is sketched below.

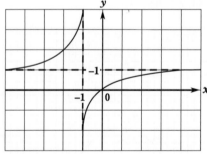

Hence, or otherwise, sketch on the axis below

(a) $y = f(x - 1)$

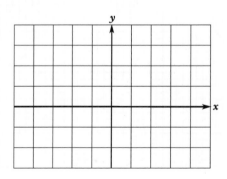

**(b)** $y = f(2x)$

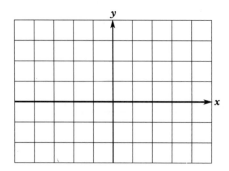

5.  The graph of $y = x^3 + x$ is sketched below.

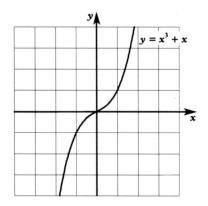

On the same axes sketch and label the graphs of
(a) $y = x^3 + x + 2$,
(b) $y = -x^3 - x$.

6.  **(a)** Use the quadratic equation formula to solve the equation
$$x^2 + 6x - 11 = 0,$$
giving your answers correct to two decimal places.

**(b)** Find the values of $p$ and $q$ such that
$$x^2 + 6x - 11 = (x + p)^2 + q.$$

**(c)** Here is a sketch of $y = x^2$.

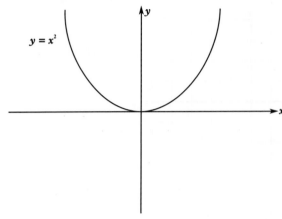

On the axes below, use your values of $p$ and $q$ to sketch the graphs of
**(i)** $y = (x + p)^2$, **(ii)** $y = x^2 + 6x - 11$.

**(i)** $y = (x + p)^2$

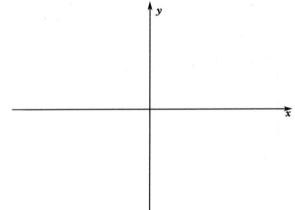

**(ii)** $y = x^2 + 6x - 11$

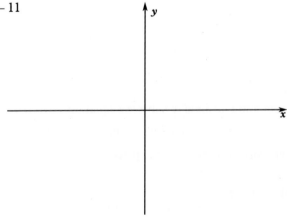

**WJEC**

7. A sketch of the graph of $y = x^2$ is drawn below.

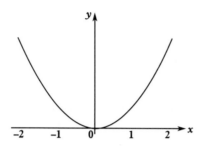

(a) On the graph above, sketch a graph of $y = (x + 1)^2$.

The two graphs intersect at one point.
(b) Calculate the $x$ coordinate of the point of intersection.

Two points on the graph of $y = (x + 1)^2$ are at a distance of 9 units from the $x$-axis.
(c) Calculate the $x$ coordinates of these two points.

ULEAC

8. The graphs of $y = \pi h^2$ and $y = \frac{4}{h}$ are shown below.

Use these graphs to sketch, on the same axes, the graph of

$$y = \pi h^2 + \frac{4}{h}$$

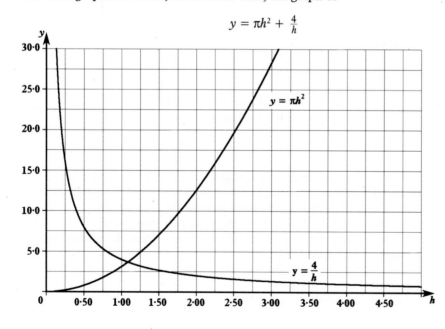

NEAB

**WRITING and GRAPHING INEQUALITIES**

To indicate a region of a plane we may either shade the region we want or shade the unwanted region. For instance, the region R in which $x \le 3$, $y > 1$, $y \le 3$, and $y \le x + 1$ may be shown in either of the two ways below.

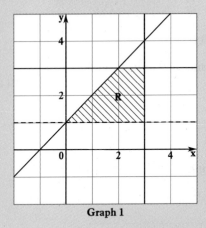

Graph 1

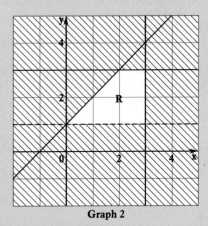

Graph 2

On graph 1, the wanted region is shaded.
On graph 2, the unwanted region is shaded.

*Worked Example*  Scouts from Hampshire and East Anglia are going to a Scout jamboree in Scotland. From these counties there are to be at least 14 but fewer than 20 Scouts. Fewer than 10 are to be from Hampshire. The number from East Anglia must not exceed those from Hampshire by more than 4.
  (a) Write inequalities for x, the number of Scouts from Hampshire and y, the number from East Anglia.
  (b) Draw a graph to show the possible numbers of Scouts from each of these counties.
  (c) List all the possible combinations.

*Answer*  (a) The inequalities are: $x + y \ge 14$, $x + y < 20$, $x < 10$, $y - x \le 4$.
  (b) The unwanted regions are shaded on the following graph. Points in the region with no shading give all the possible combinations of numbers of Scouts from the two counties.

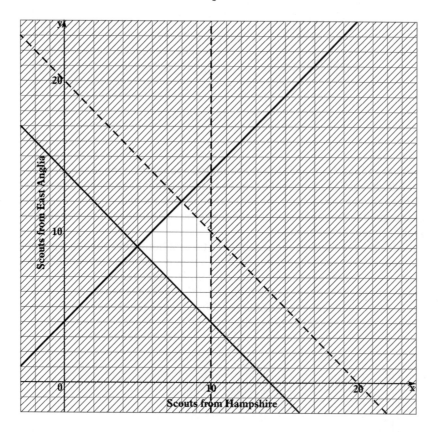

(c) The points in the region which is not shaded give all the possible combinations. These are $(7, 11)$, $(8, 11)$, $(6, 10)$, $(7, 10)$, $(8, 10)$, $(9, 10)$, $(5, 9)$, $(6, 9)$, $(7, 9)$, $(8, 9)$, $(9, 9)$, $(6, 8)$, $(7, 8)$, $(8, 8)$, $(9, 8)$, $(7, 7)$, $(8, 7)$, $(9, 7)$, $(8, 6)$, $(9, 6)$, $(9, 5)$ where the first number gives the number of Scouts from Hampshire and the second number gives the number of Scouts from East Anglia.

## EXERCISE 12:1

**For some of the questions in this exercise, shade the wanted region and for others shade the unwanted region. State clearly which region you have shaded.**

1. A factory which makes lounge suites makes both 2 and 3-seat couches.
   (a) A maximum of 12 couches can be made each month. To meet the demand, between four and eight should be 2-seat and at least two should be 3-seat.
   Write four inequalities for this information. Let $x$ be the number of 3-seat couches and $y$ the number of 2-seat couches.
   (b) Show these inequalities on a graph.
   (c) Use the graph to write down all the possible numbers of each type of couch that could be made in one month.

2. The cabin area on a cruise ship is 2160m². 1st class cabins which each need 12m² and 2nd class cabins which each need 9m² are to be built.
   (a) If x 1st class cabins and y 2nd class cabins are built show that $y \leq -\frac{4}{3}x + 240$.
   (b) There must be at least 50 1st class cabins and at least 70 2nd class cabins. The number of 2nd class cabins must not exceed the number of 1st class cabins by more than 40. Write three inequalities for this information.
   (c) Draw a graph to show all the possible values of x and y.

3. A manufacturer of bicycles makes both mountain bikes and racing bikes.
   (a) Each week, at least 22 mountain bikes and more than 6 racing bikes are made. At least three times as many mountain bikes as racing bikes are made.
      Write inequalities for these constraints. Let x be the number of mountain bikes and y the number of racing bikes made.
   (b) The finishing work on each mountain bike takes 2 hours and that on each racing bike takes 5 hours. Each week a maximum of 90 hours is spent on this finishing work.
      Show that $y \leq -0{\cdot}4x + 18$ is an inequality for this constraint.
   (c) Draw a graph to show the region which satisfies all of the constraints.
      Use your graph to list all the possible combinations of numbers of mountain and racing bikes which can be made in one week.

4.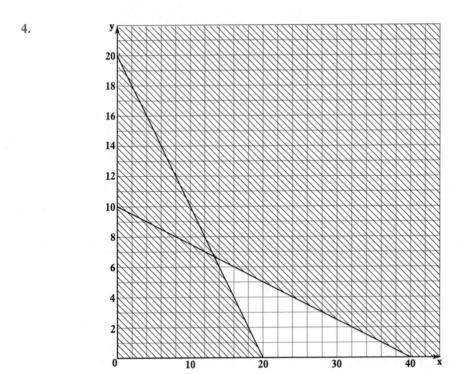

Make up a problem for which all the values of x and y in the unshaded region are possible solutions.

**Review** Seats to a show are £20 and £25. The theatre can hold a maximum of 400 people. No more than 140 of the seats must be at the dearer price. Fewer than 75% must be at the cheaper price.
   (a) If x is the number of £20 seats and y is the number of £25 seats, one inequality is $y \geq 0$. Write down three more inequalities from the given information.
   (b) To make a profit, at least £5000 must be taken in ticket sales. Write an inequality for this.
   (c) On a graph, show the region which contains all possible values for x and y.

## LINEAR PROGRAMMING

*Worked Example*

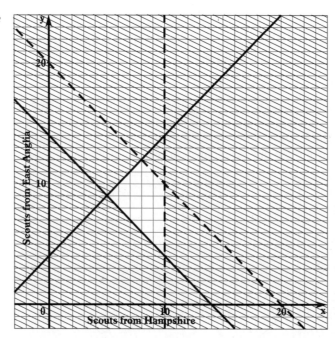

This is the graph from the Worked Example on Page 231. The points in the unshaded region give all possible combinations of Scouts from Hampshire and East Anglia.
If it costs £50 to send a Scout from Hampshire and £100 to send a Scout from East Anglia find the cost of each possible combination. How many Scouts should be sent from these counties for the cost to be a minimum? What is this minimum cost?

*Answer* The possible combinations are $(7, 11)$, $(8, 11)$, $(6, 10)$, $(7, 10)$, $(8, 10)$, $(9, 10)$, $(5, 9)$, $(6, 9)$, $(7, 9)$, $(8, 9)$, $(9, 9)$, $(6, 8)$, $(7, 8)$, $(8, 8)$, $(9, 8)$, $(7, 7)$, $(8, 7)$, $(9, 7)$, $(8, 6)$, $(9, 6)$, $(9, 5)$.
   The costs are as follows.
   For $(7, 11)$, Cost is $7 \times 50 + 11 \times 100 = £1450$.
   For $(8, 11)$, Cost is $8 \times 50 + 11 \times 100 = £1500$.
   For $(6, 10)$, Cost is $6 \times 50 + 10 \times 100 = £1300$.
   For $(7, 10)$, Cost is $7 \times 50 + 10 \times 100 = £1350$.
   For $(8, 10)$, Cost is $8 \times 50 + 10 \times 100 = £1400$.
   For $(9, 10)$, Cost is $9 \times 50 + 10 \times 100 = £1450$.

For $(5, 9)$, Cost is $5 \times 50 + 9 \times 100 = £1150$.
For $(6, 9)$, Cost is $6 \times 50 + 9 \times 100 = £1200$.
For $(7, 9)$, Cost is $7 \times 50 + 9 \times 100 = £1250$.
For $(8, 9)$, Cost is $8 \times 50 + 9 \times 100 = £1300$.
For $(9, 9)$, Cost is $9 \times 50 + 9 \times 100 = £1350$.
For $(6, 8)$, Cost is $6 \times 50 + 8 \times 100 = £1100$.
For $(7, 8)$, Cost is $7 \times 50 + 8 \times 100 = £1150$.
For $(8, 8)$, Cost is $8 \times 50 + 8 \times 100 = £1200$.
For $(9, 8)$, Cost is $9 \times 50 + 8 \times 100 = £1250$.
For $(7, 7)$, Cost is $7 \times 50 + 7 \times 100 = £1050$.
For $(8, 7)$, Cost is $8 \times 50 + 7 \times 100 = £1100$.
For $(9, 7)$, Cost is $9 \times 50 + 7 \times 100 = £1150$.
For $(8, 6)$, Cost is $8 \times 50 + 6 \times 100 = £1000$.
For $(9, 6)$, Cost is $9 \times 50 + 6 \times 100 = £1050$.
For $(9, 5)$, Cost is $9 \times 50 + 5 \times 100 = £950$.

If the cost is to be a minimum, 9 Scouts from Hampshire and 5 from East Anglia should be sent. The minimum cost is £950.

For the previous worked example, an equation for the cost, c, is $50x + 100y = c$. To find the values of x and y for which c is a minimum we can proceed as follows.

*Step 1*  Draw the lines $50x + 100y = c$ for various values of c. The gradient of these lines is $-0.5$. Five of these lines are shown, in red, on the graph.

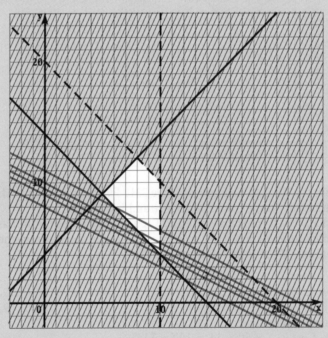

*Step 2*  Find the coordinates of the lowest point in the unshaded region that is on one of these lines. This is the point $(9, 5)$.

*Step 3*  Substitute these values of x and y into the equation $50x + 100y = c$ to find the minimum value of c.

Putting $x = 9$ and $y = 5$ gives $c = 50 \times 9 + 100 \times 5$, i.e. $c = £950$.

## DISCUSSION EXERCISE 12:2

- Vicky claims that the minimum cost, in the previous example, can be found by finding where the lowest line $50x + 100y = c$, that passes through a point in the unshaded region, meets the y-axis. What reasoning might Vicky have used? **Discuss.**

- Simon claims that the point which gives the minimum cost is the point which is closest to the lowest vertex of the unshaded region. Is Simon's claim correct? **Discuss.**
  **What if** the cost of sending a Scout from Hampshire was £75 and a Scout from East Anglia was £100?
  **What if** the costs were £40 and £60?
  **What if** ...

- The maximum cost, in the previous worked example, is £1500. This is the cost of sending 8 Scouts from Hampshire and 11 from East Anglia. **Discuss** ways of finding this maximum cost other than from the list given in the answer to the example.
  **What if** the cost of sending a Scout from Hampshire was £100 and a Scout from East Anglia was £50?
  **What if** ...

In **linear programming** we find the maximum or minimum value of a linear function which is subject to a number of constraints.
The previous worked example was an example of linear programming. We found the minimum cost, c, which was given by $c = 50x + 100y$ with the constraints $x + y \geq 14, x + y < 20$, $x < 10, y - x \leq 4$.

## EXERCISE 12:3

1.  The region for which $y \geq 2, x \geq 3$, $2y \leq x + 8$ and $x + y \leq 13$ is shown unshaded.
    (i)  Write down the coordinates of the vertices of this region.
    (ii) For whole number values of x and y within this region find the
       (a) maximum value of k if $x + 2y = k$
       (b) minimum value of k if $x + 2y = k$
       (c) greatest value of c if $y + 2x = c$
       (d) least value of c if $2x + y = c$
       (e) minimum value of m if $y - x = m$
       (f) maximum value of m if $y - x = m$.

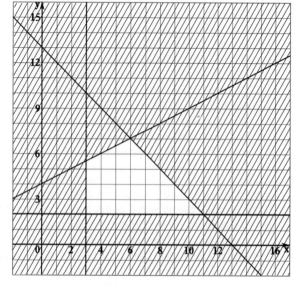

2.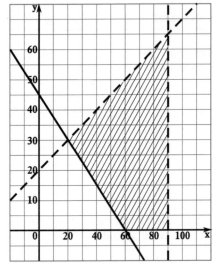

All of the points (x, y) in the shaded region satisfy the four inequalities y ≥ 0, x < 90, 2y < x + 40, 3x + 4y ≥ 180.

(a) Find the integer values of x and y within the shaded region which give the greatest value for 10x + 10y. What is this greatest value?

(b) Find the integer values of x and y which give the minimum value of 2x + 10y subject to the constraints y ≥ 0, x < 90, 2y < x + 40, 3x + 4y ≥ 180. What is this minimum value?

3. Northend Rental Cars have two types of rental cars, a medium sized Toyota and a large Ford. Each day they hire no more than 8 Toyotas, between 5 and 10 Fords and never more than 15 cars altogether.

(a) If x is the number of Fords hired on one day, two inequalities for x are x ≥ 5 and x ≤ 10.
If y is the number of Toyotas hired write two inequalities for y.

(b) An inequality for x and y can be written from the given information. Write this inequality.

(c) Draw a graph which shows all the possible values of x and y which satisfy the 5 inequalities.

(d) Northend Rental Cars charge £50 to hire a Ford for one day and £40 for a Toyota. R is the total amount received on one day from the hire of the cars. Write an equation for x, y and R. Find the greatest amount this firm receives on one day.

4. Robbie and Deborah both operate knitting machines in a factory. In a week Robbie can make 50 jerseys on his machine while Deborah can make 25 on hers. At least 400 jerseys are to be made on these machines within 12 weeks. If x is the number of weeks Robbie works on these jerseys and y is the number of weeks Deborah works then one inequality is 50x + 25y ≥ 400.

(a) Write down another inequality for x and y.

(b) Draw a graph to show the region which contains all possible values for x and y.

(c) The operating costs for Robbie's machine are £300 per week and those for Deborah's machine are £100 per week.
Write an equation for the total operating costs, C, to make the 400 jerseys.

(d) For how many weeks should each machine operate to make these jerseys for the least cost? What is this minimum cost?

5. Andrew has two after-school jobs, mowing lawns and trimming hedges. He can spend a maximum of 15 hours a week on these jobs. For his regular clients he must spend 6 hours a week mowing lawns and 3 hours a week trimming hedges.

(a) Write down three inequalities for the given information. Let x be the time (in hours) spent mowing lawns and y the time spent trimming hedges.

(b) Andrew must not spend more than twice as much time mowing lawns as he does trimming hedges. Write an inequality for this.

(c) Draw a graph to show all the possible values for x and y.

(d) Andrew is paid £2 an hour for mowing lawns and £3 an hour for trimming hedges. Find the maximum amount he can earn in a week.

6. Lisa is making coffee and chocolate cakes for a cake stall. Each coffee cake needs 3 eggs and 150 grams of margarine. Each chocolate cake needs 2 eggs and 250 grams of margarine. Lisa has three dozen eggs and 3kg of margarine.

(a) If Lisa makes x coffee cakes and y chocolate cakes two inequalities are x ≥ 0, y ≥ 0. Write down two inequalities which involve both x and y.

(b) Draw a graph to show all the possible values of x and y.

(c) Lisa wants to make as many cakes as possible. That is, she wants to find values of x and y which make x + y a maximum. How many of each type of cake should Lisa make?

**Review 1**

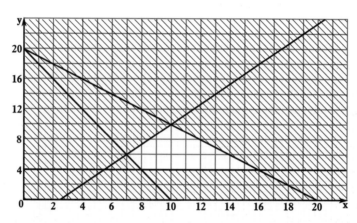

The region for which y ≥ 4, 3y ≤ 4x – 10, y + 2x ≥ 20 and x + y ≤ 20 is shown unshaded.

(a) Write down the coordinates of the vertices of this region.

(b) What values of x and y give the least value of y – x subject to the constraints y ≥ 4, 3y ≤ 4x – 10, y + 2x ≥ 20, y ≤ 20 – x? What is this least value?

(c) Subject to the constraints given in (b) find the maximum value of k if 2y + 5x = k.

**Review 2** Gareth is making sweets for his niece's birthday party. He is making between 500g and 1kg of chocolates and between 200g and 400g of toffees. Altogether Gareth is making at most 1kg of sweets.

(a) Let x be the quantity (in grams) of chocolates and y be the quantity (in grams) of toffees. One inequality for x is x ≥ 500. Write four more inequalities involving x and/or y.

(b) Draw a graph to show all the possible values of x and y.

(c) For each 100g, the chocolates cost 40p and the toffees cost 10p. If T is the total cost for the sweets Gareth made, show that an equation connecting x, y and T is
y = –4x + 10T.

(d) Find the maximum cost of Gareth's sweets.

## CHAPTER 12   REVIEW

1. The school hall seats a maximum audience of 200 people for performances.
   Tickets for the Christmas concert cost £2 or £3 each.
   The school needs to raise at least £450 from this concert.
   It is decided that the number of £3 tickets must not be greater than twice the number of £2 tickets.

   There are $x$ tickets at £2 each and $y$ tickets at £3 each.
   (a) Explain why:   (i) $x + y \le 200$   (ii) $2x + 3y \ge 450$   (iii) $y \le 2x$

   The graphs of $x + y = 200$, $2x + 3y = 450$ and $y = 2x$ are drawn on the grid below.
   (b) Leave **unshaded** the region of the grid which satisfies all three inequalities in (a).

   (c) Hence find the number of £2 and £3 tickets which should be sold to obtain the maximum profit.

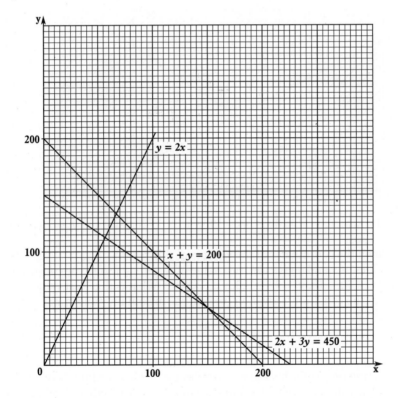

**NEAB**

2. Jack was made redundant and because he could not find another full-time job, he took two part-time jobs.

   One was an early morning job in a newsagent's for which he was paid £3·60 per hour. The other was an evening job in a filling station for which he was paid £4·50 per hour.

   Each week, Jack works $x$ hours in the newsagent's and $y$ hours in the filling station. Both $x$ and $y$ are whole numbers.

**(a)** Jack did not want to work more than 40 hours in a week.
Express this information as an inequality.

**(b)** It is known that
$$x \geq 12 \text{ and } y \geq 15$$
Write down a sentence to explain the first of these inequalities.

**(c)** Jack needs to earn at least £126 per week.
Show that $4x + 5y \geq 140$

**(d)** Illustrate the above four inequalities by a suitable diagram on the graph paper.
Identify the region containing the set of points $(x, y)$ satisfying all four inequalities.

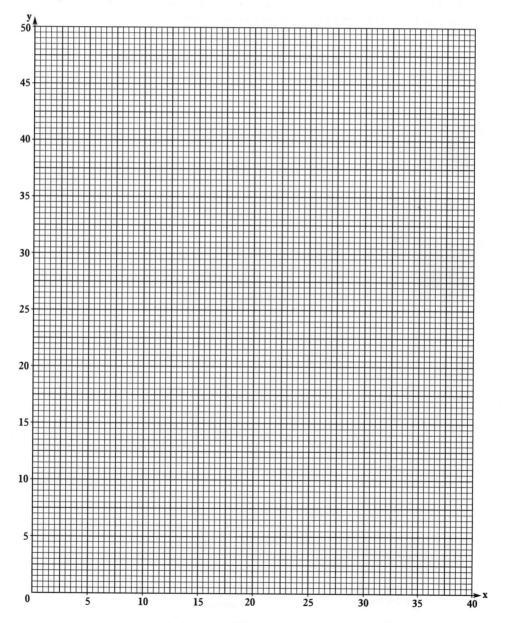

**(e)** From your solution set find,
  **(i)** the maximum amount Jack could earn in a week in which he works the same number of hours in each job.
  **(ii)** the minimum number of hours Jack must work in a week to earn at least £126.
  **(iii)** the minimum amount Jack could earn in a week in which he works 40 hours.
  **(iv)** the number of hours Jack works in a week in which he earns the same amount in each job.                                                                    **NICCEA**

3.  At each performance of a school play the number of people in the audience must satisfy the following conditions.
  **(i)** The number of children in the audience must be less than 250.
  **(ii)** The maximum size of the audience must be 300.
  **(iii)** There must be at least twice as many children as adults in the audience.

On any one evening there are $x$ children and $y$ adults in the audience.
**(a)** Write down the three inequalities that $x$ and $y$ must satisfy other than $x \geq 0$ and $y \geq 0$.

**(b)**

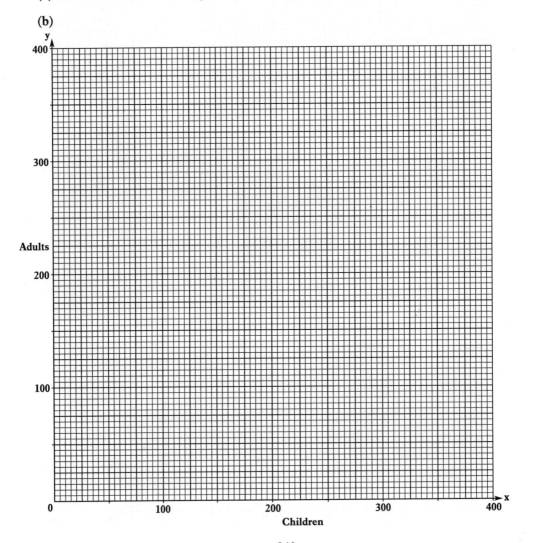

240

By drawing straight lines and shading, indicate the region within which $x$ and $y$ must lie to satisfy all the inequalities.

Tickets for each performance cost £3 for a child and £4 for an adult.

**(c)** Use your diagram to find the maximum possible income from ticket sales for one performance.

To make a profit, the income from ticket sales must be at least £600.

**(d)** Use your diagram to find the least number of children's tickets which must be sold for a performance to make a profit. **ULEAC**

4. The 3rd Guide Company are going to knit squares to make a blanket.
   They have some thick wool and some thin wool.
   One blanket requires at least 100 squares.
   There must be at least as many squares made from thin wool as from thick wool.

   Each square takes $\frac{1}{2}$ hour to knit in thick wool and $1\frac{1}{2}$ hours to knit in thin wool.
   Their time is limited.

   The graph shows these constraints with $x$ standing for the number of thick wool squares and $y$ for the number of thin wool squares.

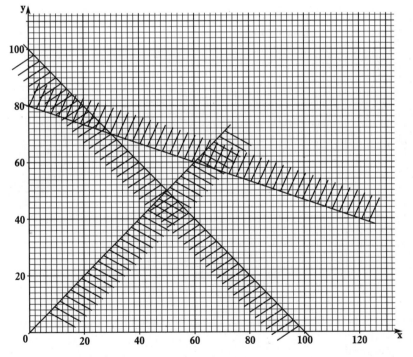

**(a)** How many hours do they have to finish the knitting?

**(b)** The wool was a bargain!
   The thick wool costs 50p for each square and the thin wool costs 20p for each square.
   **(i)** Write down an expression for the cost of $x$ thick wool squares and $y$ thin wool squares.
   **(ii)** Find the cost of the cheapest blanket, making your method clear. **MEG**

1. The graph of $y = x^3 - 6x^2 + 8x + 7$ is drawn.
   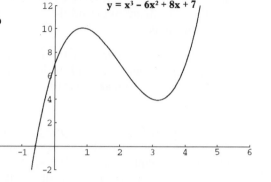
   **(i)** What lines would you draw on this graph to solve the following equations?
   (a) $x^3 - 6x^2 + 8x + 5 = 0$
   (b) $x^3 - 6x^2 + 8x - 1 = 0$
   (c) $x^3 - 6x^2 + 6x + 7 = 0$
   (d) $x^3 - 6x^2 + 9x + 4 = 0$
   (e) $x^3 - 6x^2 + 8x + 7 = 0$
   **(ii)** How many solutions do the equations in **(i)** have?

2. **(i)** Simplify (a) $\dfrac{n^2}{n}$ (b) $(n^{\frac{3}{4}})^8$ (c) $(2n^{-2})^3$ (d) $\dfrac{n^{-1} \times n^3}{n^{-2}}$ (e) $\dfrac{8m^{-1}n}{2mn^{-2}}$
   **(ii)** Find the value of n for which (a) $4^n = 2$ (b) $4^{-n} = 32$ (c) $4^n = 1$ (d) $4^{1-n} = 2$.
   **(iii)** Explain how to find the value of $9^{-\frac{1}{2}}$ without using the calculator.
   **(iv)** Use the calculator to find the value of $\sqrt[4]{66}$.

3. 
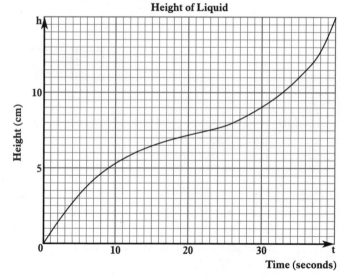

**Height of Liquid**

The container is being filled with liquid. The graph shows how the height of the liquid is increasing with time.
   **(a)** Trace this graph.
   Draw the tangent at the point (30, 9).
   **(b)** Calculate the gradient of the tangent. Hence find the rate at which the height is increasing when t = 30 sec.
   **(c)** Find the rate at which the height is increasing when t = 10 sec.
   **(d)** Explain how you can use the graph to write down the approximate time when the height is increasing most slowly. What time is this?

4. A system of pulleys is used to lift a load. E is the effort required to lift a load W. The relationship between E and W, is believed to be of the form $E = aW + b$.
   To determine this relationship, the following measurements of E and W were taken.

   | Load, W | 5 | 10 | 20 | 35 | 60 | 75 |
   |---|---|---|---|---|---|---|
   | Effort, E | 4·3 | 6·7 | 11·9 | 19·3 | 31·6 | 39·4 |

   (a) Plot a graph of E against W.
   (b) Use this graph to estimate values of a and b. Hence write down an approximate relationship between E and W.

5. (i) Copy and complete this table for $y = 3^{-x}$, rounding each y-value to 1 d.p.

   | x | −3·0 | −2·5 | −2·0 | −1·5 | −1·0 | −0·5 | 0 | 0·5 | 1·0 | 1·5 | 2·0 |
   |---|---|---|---|---|---|---|---|---|---|---|---|
   | y | 27 | 15·6 | | | | | | | | | |

   (ii) Draw the graph of $y = 3^{-x}$ for values of x between −3 and 2.
   (iii) Use the graph to solve these equations. (a) $3^{-x} = 6$ (b) $\frac{1}{3^x} = 10$ (c) $3^{2-x} = 180$

6.

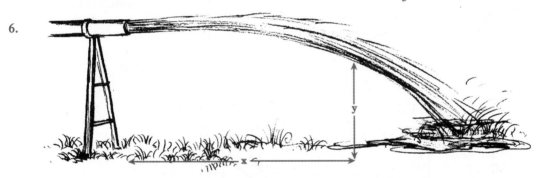

Water is squirted horizontally from a pipe, as shown in the drawing. At a distance of x metres from the pipe, the height of the water is y metres.
The following measurements of x and y were taken.

| x (metres) | 0 | 1 | 3 | 4 | 7 | 8 |
|---|---|---|---|---|---|---|
| y (metres) | 9·18 | 9·10 | 8·29 | 7·61 | 4·32 | 2·80 |

It is believed that a relationship of the type $y = ax^2 + b$ exists between x and y.
(a) Explain how you could use a graph to find approximate values for a and b.
(b) Find an approximate relationship between x and y.
(c) What is the maximum distance the water is squirted?

7. (a) Copy and complete this table of values for $y = (2 - x)(4 + x)$.

   | x | −6 | −5 | −4 | −3 | −2 | −1 | 0 | 1 | 2 | 3 | 4 |
   |---|---|---|---|---|---|---|---|---|---|---|---|
   | y | −16 | | | | | | | | | | |

   (b) Draw the graph of $y = (2 - x)(4 + x)$.
   Use your graph to find the approximate solutions for the equation $(2 - x)(4 + x) = 6$.
   (c) Could you use the graph to solve the equation $x^2 = 7$? Explain.

8.

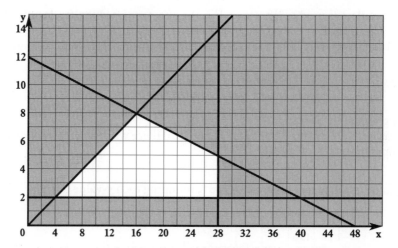

The region for which $y \geq 2, x \leq 28, 2y \leq x$ and $x + 4y \leq 48$ is shown unshaded.

(a) Write down the coordinates of the vertices of this region.

(b) Find the values of x and y which give the greatest value of $x + y$ subject to the constraints $y \geq 2, x \leq 28, 2y \leq x$ and $x + 4y \leq 48$. What is this greatest value?

(c) $4y - x = k$. Find the least value of k subject to the constraints given by (b).

9.

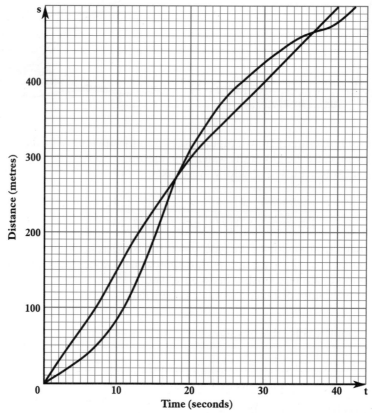

Time (seconds)

This is the distance/time graph for two animals running a distance of 500 metres. At what times are these animals running at the same speed? Explain your answer.

10.

**A.**

| x | 1 | 2 | 4 | 5 | 10 |
|---|---|---|---|---|---|
| y | 2 | 7 | 17 | 22 | 47 |

**B.**

| x | 1 | 2 | 4 | 5 | 10 |
|---|---|---|---|---|---|
| y | 1 | 0 | $-0.5$ | $-0.6$ | $-0.8$ |

**C.**

| x | 1 | 2 | 4 | 5 | 8 |
|---|---|---|---|---|---|
| y | 2.51 | 2.58 | 3.14 | 3.75 | 7.62 |

**D.**

| x | 1 | 2 | 4 | 5 | 8 |
|---|---|---|---|---|---|
| y | 3.5 | 5 | 11 | 15.5 | 35 |

The relationship between x and y, for these sets of data, is known to be of the form
$y = ax^n + b$ where n is an integer.

(a) Sketch a graph for each set of data to find n.
Explain what the graph of y plotted against $x^n$ will look like if the correct value has been chosen for n.

(b) Find the approximate relationship between x and y for each set of data.

11.

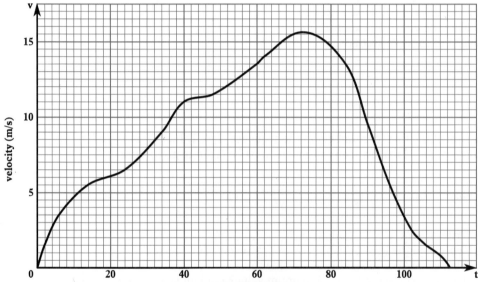

This is the velocity/time graph for Hari's ride on a "big dipper" at a fair.

(a) Find the gradient of the tangent at the point (14, 5·5). What meaning can be given to this value?

(b) At approximately what time is the acceleration equal to zero?

(c) During which 10-second interval is the acceleration the greatest?

(d) Write a brief description of Hari's ride on this "big dipper".

12. Factorise     (a) $n^2 - 4n$    (b) $n^2 - 4n - 12$    (c) $n^2 - 4$    (d) $n^2 - (n - 4)^2$
           (e) $n^2 - 10m - 5n + 2mn$

13. The cost of food is expected to rise by 5% each year for the next 10 years.
(a) Which of the following iterations describes this?
     **A.** $c_{n+1} = 0.9c_n$      **B.** $c_{n+1} = 1.1c_n$      **C.** $c_{n+1} = 0.95c_n$      **D.** $c_{n+1} = 1.05c_n$
(b) This year, a "basket of food" costs £66. Use the iteration from **(a)** to write down the sequence which gives the expected cost each year for this year and the following five years.

14. The following shows that $2 = 4$. Find the mistake in this "proof".

   Let $x = 2$
   Then $x^2 = 4$
   Also $6x - 8 = 4$
   Hence $x^2 = 6x - 8$
   $$x^2 = 2x + 4x - 8$$
   $$x^2 - 2x = 4x - 8$$
   $$x(x - 2) = 4(x - 2)$$
   Hence $x = 4$

15. This is the velocity/time graph for the last 15 seconds of Annelise's ski-run. Calculate the distance Annelise travelled in these 15 seconds.

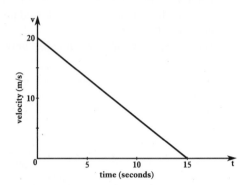

16. The sum of the first $n$ numbers in the sequence $1, 4, 7, 10, \ldots$ is given by Sum $= \frac{n}{2}(3n - 1)$. How many numbers must be taken to give a sum of 425?

17. Simplify
   (a) $\dfrac{x^2 + x - 2}{x^2 - x - 6}$
   (b) $\dfrac{xy - x^2}{x^2 - y^2}$
   (c) $\dfrac{x - 1}{x} \div \dfrac{x^2 - 1}{x^2}$
   (d) $\dfrac{2}{x - 2} - \dfrac{1}{x - 3}$

18. (a) Write $x^2 - 2x + 5$ as $(x + a)^2 + b$.
   (b) Hence find the least possible value of the expression $x^2 - 2x + 5$.
   (c) What value of $x$ gives this least value?
   (d) Does the expression have a maximum value? Explain your answer.

19. (i) Write down the first 5 terms of the sequences defined iteratively as

   (a) $t_{n+1} = \frac{1}{t_n} + 1;\ t_1 = 2$

   (b) $t_{n+1} = \frac{1}{1 + t_n};\ t_1 = 2$

   (ii) Describe the following sequences as either convergent or divergent.

   (a) $\frac{1}{2}, -\frac{2}{3}, \frac{3}{4}, -\frac{4}{5}, \ldots$

   (b) $\frac{1}{2}, -\frac{1}{3}, \frac{1}{4}, -\frac{1}{5}, \frac{1}{6}, \ldots$

   (c) $\frac{1}{2}, \left(\frac{1}{2}\right)^2, \left(\frac{1}{2}\right)^3, \ldots$

   (d) $t_{n+1} = \frac{3}{t_n} + 1;\ t_1 = 2$

   (e) $t_{n+1} = \frac{t_n}{3};\ t_1 = 2$

   (f) $t_{n+1} = \frac{1}{t_n} + 1;\ t_1 = 2$

   (iii) Write down the number to which each of the convergent sequences in (ii) converges.

20. The quadratic expression $n^2 - 79n + 1601$ gives some of the prime numbers.
   (a) What prime number is given if $n = 40$?
   (b) Find the two values of $n$ which give the prime number 61.

21.    $f(x) = x^2 - 2x + 2$
   (a) Write $x^2 - 2x + 2$ in the form $(x + a)^2 + b$.
   (b) Sketch the graph of $y = x^2$.
       On the same set of axes sketch the graph of $y = f(x)$, indicating clearly the coordinates of the turning point.
   (c) Use the graph of $y = f(x)$ to sketch the graph of $y = \frac{1}{f(x)}$.

22. The iteration $x_{n+1} = \frac{10}{1+x_n}$ is used to find the positive solution for a quadratic equation.
   (a) By replacing both $x_{n+1}$ and $x_n$ with $x$ show that this equation is $x^2 + x - 10 = 0$.
   (b) Use 3 as the starting value in the iteration $x_{n+1} = \frac{10}{1+x_n}$ to find the positive solution to 2 correct decimal places.
   (c) The negative solution of the equation is about $-4$. What happens if $-4$ is used as the starting value in $x_{n+1} = \frac{10}{1+x_n}$?
   (d) $x_{n+1} = \sqrt{10 - x_n}$ is another iteration which may be used to find the positive solution for the equation $x^2 + x - 10 = 0$. Is there an advantage in using this iteration rather than $x_{n+1} = \frac{10}{1+x_n}$? Explain.
   (e) $x_{n+1} = \sqrt{10 - x_n}$ may be adapted to find the negative solution of the equation. How should this iteration be adapted?
       Find the negative solution to 2 correct decimal places.

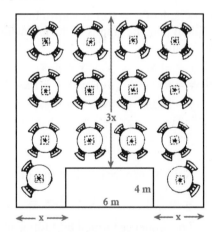

23. The 130 square metre extension to a restaurant consists of an area for 14 extra tables and a dance floor area as shown in the diagram.
   (a) Write a quadratic equation for $x$.
   (b) Show that this equation can be simplified to $3x^2 + 13x - 53 = 0$.
   (c) Find the dimensions of the extension.

24. $v = t^2 - t + 4$ gives the velocity, $v$ metres per second, of an object at time $t$ seconds.
   Draw the graph of $v$ against $t$ for values of $t$ between 0 and 4 seconds.
   Estimate the distance travelled during the first four seconds. Explain your method clearly.

25. (a) On the same set of axes draw the graphs of $y = x^3$ and $y = 3 - x^2$ for values of $x$ between $-2$ and 2.
   (b) Use the graph to estimate, to the nearest integer, the solution of the equation $x^3 + x^2 - 3 = 0$.
   (c) Show that $x = \sqrt{\frac{3}{x+1}}$ may be rewritten as $x^3 + x^2 - 3 = 0$.
   (d) Use the iterative formula $x_{n+1} = \sqrt{\frac{3}{x_n+1}}$ to find the solution for the equation $x^3 + x^2 - 3 = 0$ to 3 correct decimal places.

26. Jon makes two types of fruit drink. To make 10 litres of Fruit Cup, 1kg of sugar and 2kg of fruit is needed. To make 10 litres of Tropical Delight, 1·5kg of sugar and 1·5kg of fruit is needed. Jon has 12kg of sugar and 18kg of fruit.

    Let $x$ be the number of 10 litre quantities of Fruit Cup and $y$ be the number of 10 litre quantities of Tropical Delight that Jon makes.

    (a) One inequality for the given information is $2x + 1\cdot5y \leq 18$. Write another inequality from the given information.

    (b) Draw a graph to show the possible values for x and y.

    (c) Jon wishes to make as many 10 litre quantities as possible. Use your graph to find the values of $x$ and $y$ which give this maximum quantity.

27. Lorna and Kathy were competitors in a 50km cycle event. Lorna's average speed was 2km/h faster than Kathy's. Kathy took 20 minutes more than Lorna for the event.

    (a) Write down an equation for $x$, Lorna's average speed.

    (b) Show that this equation can be rewritten as $x^2 - 2x - 300 = 0$.

    (c) Find Lorna's average speed, giving the answer to 3 significant figures.

28. $f(x) = 4 - x^2$

    The graph of $y = f(x)$ is shown here.

    Explain how the graphs of the following are related to this graph.

    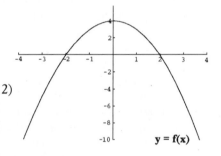

    (a) $y = -f(x)$     (b) $y = f(-x)$     (c) $y = f(x + 2)$

    (d) $y = f(x) + 4$   (e) $y + 1 = f(x - 2)$   (f) $y = f(2x)$

    (g) $y = 2f(x)$     (h) $y = f(\frac{1}{2}x)$     (i) $y = \frac{1}{2}f(x)$

    $y = f(x)$

29. (a) Write an expression, in terms of n, for the $n$th term of the sequence $\frac{1}{2}, \frac{2}{3}, \frac{3}{4}, \frac{4}{5}, \ldots$

    (b) $\frac{1}{2} + \frac{2}{3} = \frac{7}{6}$    $\frac{2}{3} + \frac{3}{4} = \frac{17}{12}$    $\frac{3}{4} + \frac{4}{5} = \frac{31}{20}$    $\frac{4}{5} + \frac{5}{6} = \frac{49}{30}$

    The sequence formed by adding adjacent terms is $\frac{7}{6}, \frac{17}{12}, \frac{31}{20}, \frac{49}{30}, \ldots$

    Prove that, for this sequence, $t_n = \frac{2n^2 + 4n + 1}{(n+1)(n+2)}$.

    (c) Find the positive solution of the equation $\frac{2n^2 + 4n + 1}{(n+1)(n+2)} = \frac{161}{90}$.

    What is the relationship between this solution and the sequence $\frac{1}{2}, \frac{2}{3}, \frac{3}{4}, \frac{4}{5}, \ldots$?

    You could have deduced this by just considering the fraction $\frac{161}{90}$. Explain.

30. (a) Factorise $p^2 - q^2$.

    (b) Rewrite 91 as the difference of two squares. Hence or otherwise find the prime factors of 91.

**31.** A graph of $y = f(x)$ has been drawn on the grid below.
   **(a)** Sketch the graph of $y = f(x) - 4$ on the grid.

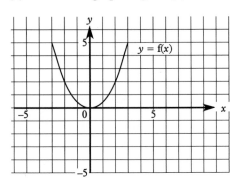

The grid below shows a second graph of $y = f(x)$.
**(b)** Sketch a graph of $y = f(x - 4)$ on the grid.

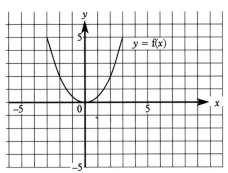

**ULEAC**

**32.**

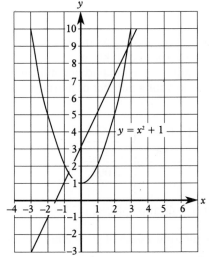

**(a)** The equation of the straight line shown in the diagram above is
$$x = \frac{y - 3}{2}.$$
   This equation can be written in the form $y = mx + c$.
   Find the values of $m$ and $c$.

**(b)** Find, by drawing tangents to the curve $y = x^2 + 1$,
   **(i)** the gradient when $x = 1$;
   **(ii)** the gradient when $x = 0$.

**(c)** Use the graph to find approximate solutions of
$$x^2 - 2x - 2 = 0.$$

**SEG**

249

**33. (a)** Expand and simplify $(2x + 3)(x - 4)$.

   **(b)** Factorise completely $10x^2 - 5x$

   **(c)** Calculate the value of $y$, when $x^{\frac{1}{2}} \times x^{-3} = x^y$                    **ULEAC**

**34. (a)** Factorise these two expressions

   **(i)** $x^2 + 3x + 2$,
   **(ii)** $2x^2 - x - 10$.

   **(b)** Simplify the expression $\dfrac{6}{2x+1} - \dfrac{3}{x+1}$.                    **SEG**

**35. (a)** Show how to find the value of $8^{\frac{1}{3}}$ without using a calculator.

   **(b)** Find the value of $(8 \times 10^{-3})^{\frac{1}{3}}$, without using a calculator.
   You **must** show all your working.                    **SEG**

**36.** A hovercraft operates as a cross-channel ferry. It always leaves and enters the ferry ports at the same low speed. On the open sea it travels at a constant speed of $V$ km/h.
On different journeys the value of $V$ will be chosen to suit weather and other conditions.
The table shows the time $T$ hours (from port to port) taken for a number of journeys with different values of $V$.

| $T$ hours | 1·70 | 1·38 | 1·00 | 0·84 | 0·63 |
|-----------|------|------|------|------|------|
| $V$ km/h | 36 | 45 | 67 | 83 | 120 |
| $\frac{1}{V}$ | 0·028 | | | | 0·008 |

   **(a)** Complete the table by giving values of $\frac{1}{V}$ correct to 3 decimal places.

   **(b)** On the opposite page draw the graph obtained by plotting values of $T$ against values of $\frac{1}{V}$.

   **(c)** Explain why $T$ and $V$ are connected by a law of the form
   $$T = a\left(\tfrac{1}{V}\right) + b.$$

   **(d)** Use information from your graph to find the values of $a$ and $b$, each correct to 2 significant figures.

   **(e)** From your graph, or otherwise, find
   **(i)** the time taken for a journey on which $V$ was 55km/h,
   **(ii)** the speed which will cut 12 minutes off this time.

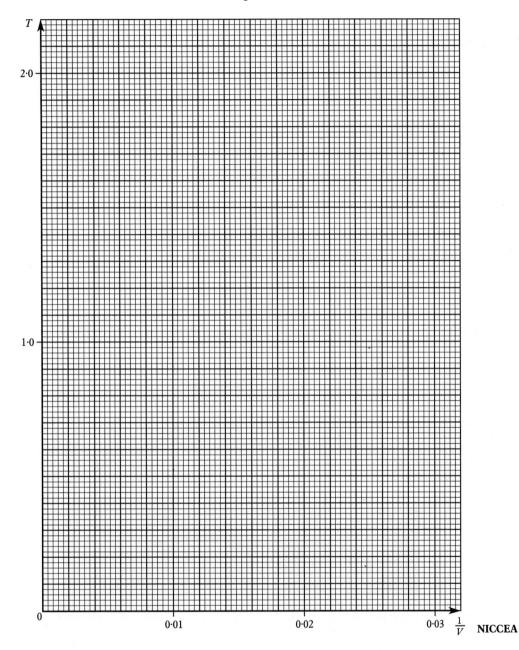

**37.** It is known that

$$3^2 + 4^2 = 5^2$$
$$3^3 + 4^3 + 5^3 = 6^3$$

(a) (i) What do you think the next line of the pattern should read?

(ii) Showing your working, check whether your answer to part (a) (i) is correct.

(b) (i) Without using a calculator, explain why $3^5$ is an odd number.

(ii) By considering powers of odd and even numbers, explain, without using a calculator, why

$$3^5 + 4^5 + 5^5 + 6^5 + 7^5 \text{ cannot equal } 8^5.$$

**MEG**

**38.**

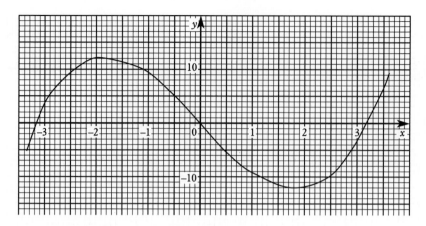

The graph of $y = x^3 - 10x$ has been drawn on the grid above.

(a) On the same grid, draw the graph of $y = 2x^2$.

(b) Use the graphs to find two solutions to the equation
$$x^3 - 2x^2 - 10x = 0.$$

The third solution to the equation $x^3 - 2x^2 - 10x = 0$ may be found by using the iteration
$$x_{n+1} = \sqrt{(2x_n + 10)}\ .$$

(c) (i) Starting with $x_1 = 4$, calculate $x_2$.

Write down all the figures on your calculator display.

(ii) Continue this iteration until there is no change in the second decimal place.

Write down all the figures shown on your calculator for each value of $x_n$.

**ULEAC**

**39.**

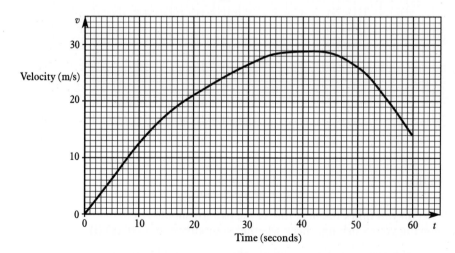

The first minute of a car's journey is represented by the velocity time graph.

Use the graph to calculate an estimate for the acceleration of the car at time $t = 30$ seconds.

**ULEAC**

**40.** Peter is planning a meal of baked beans and sausages.
He wants his meal to contain no more than 3 grams of salt and no more than 640 calories.

Each spoonful of beans contains 0·4 grams of salt and 60 calories.
Each sausage contains 0·6 grams of salt and 160 calories.

Peter eats $x$ spoonfuls of baked beans and $y$ sausages.

(a) An inequality which expresses the restriction on salt content is
$$0{\cdot}4x + 0{\cdot}6y \leq 3.$$
Write a second inequality in $x$ and $y$ which expresses the restriction on calorie content.

(b) The line $0{\cdot}4x + 0{\cdot}6y = 3$ is drawn on the given axes.
Illustrate the two inequalities in (a) by drawing a second line and shading the excluded regions.

(c) Peter wants his meal to contain the maximum amount of protein.
Each spoonful of beans contains 8 grams of protein and each sausage contains 16 grams of protein.

If Peter may eat fractions of a spoonful of beans but must choose a whole number of sausages, find the values of $x$ and $y$ which make the protein content of the meal greatest and write down this maximum amount of protein.

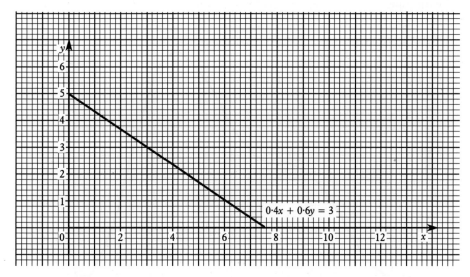

**MEG**

**41.** A sequence is given by

$$x_{n+1} = \frac{12}{x_n + 4}$$

(a) (i) The first term of the sequence is $x_1 = 3$. Find the next three terms.

(ii) What do you think is the value of $x_n$ as $n$ becomes larger? Write down this value.

(b) (i) Show that the quadratic equation which the sequence above is intended to solve is
$$x^2 + 4x - 12 = 0.$$

(ii) Solve this quadratic equation.                    **SEG**

**42.**

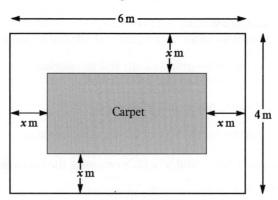

A rectangular carpet is placed centrally on the floor of a room 6 metres by 4 metres.
The distance from the edges of the carpet to the walls is $x$ metres.
The carpet covers half the area of the floor.

**(a)** Show that $x^2 - 5x + 3 = 0$

**(b)** Solve the equation in **(a)** to find $x$, correct to 3 significant figures.     **ULEAC**

**43.** The graph shows how the rate, in centimetres per hour, at which rain fell during a storm varied with time.

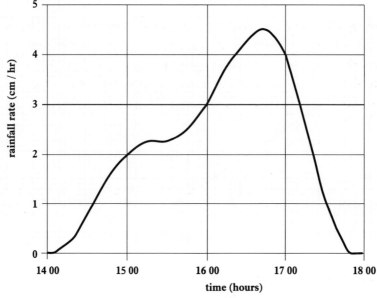

**(a)** Estimate the area under the graph. Show clearly the method you use.

**(b)** Indicate briefly what this area represents.     **MEG**

**44. (a)** Evaluate
  **(i)** $7^0$          **(ii)** $27^{\frac{2}{3}}$

**(b)** Find the values of $n$ for which
  **(i)** $n^{-1} = 2^{-2}$,       **(ii)** $4^n = (\sqrt{2})^4$.     **NICCEA**

**45.** The graph of $n = \dfrac{80}{t^{1.5}}$ is given.

(a) On the grid draw a graph so that the equation $\dfrac{80}{t^{1.5}} = 2t^2$ can be solved.

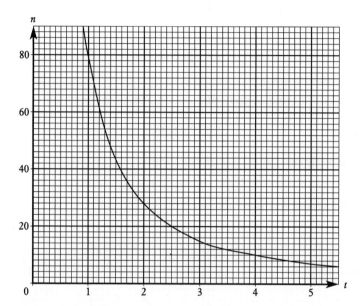

(b) (i) Use your graph to find the value of $t$ at the point of intersection of the two curves.

   (ii) Write the equation $\dfrac{80}{t^{1.5}} = 2t^2$ in the form $40 = \dots\dots\dots\dots$

   Simplify the right hand side as far as possible.

(c) For the equation $n = \dfrac{80}{t^{1.5}}$ estimate the rate of decrease of $n$ when $t = 2$.

(d) Estimate, by drawing, the gradient of the tangent at the point when $t = 4$, on the graph you have drawn.  **SEG**

**46. Prove** that when 2 is subtracted from the sum of the squares of three consecutive integers, the answer is always 3 times a square number.  **ULEAC**

**47.** A formula used to measure population density is
$$p = p_0(1 + k)^{-r}.$$
Here $r$ is the radial distance from the centre, $p_0$ is the inner city density, corresponding to $r = 0$.

(a) When $k = \frac{1}{2}$ and $r = 4$, find the ratio of the population density, $p$, to the inner city density, $p_0$.

(b) In another city, at radial distance 4 from the centre, the ratio of the population density, $p$, to its inner city density, $p_0$, is 0·4096.

   Find the value of $k$ for this city.  **SEG**

**48.** A sequence approaches the number $f$ given by the equation

$$f = \tfrac{1}{f} + 1$$

**(a)** The graph of $y = f$ has been plotted below.
On the same axes, plot the graph of

$$y = \tfrac{1}{f} + 1$$

for values of $f$ from 1 to 4.
Use the graph lines to find an approximate solution to the equation

$$f = \tfrac{1}{f} + 1$$

**(b)** Rearrange the equation $f = \tfrac{1}{f} + 1$ in the form

$$af^2 + bf + c = 0.$$

Solve it to find a more accurate value for $f$.

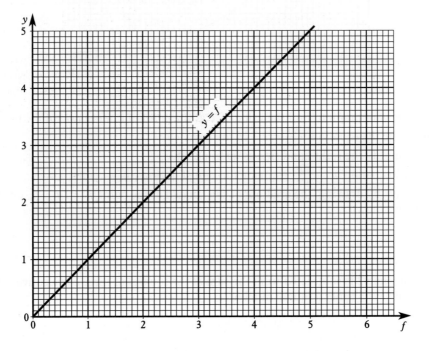

**NEAB**

# SHAPE, SPACE AND MEASURES

## REVISION

### Congruence. Symmetry

**Congruent** shapes are shapes of the same size and the same shape. Corresponding lengths are equal; corresponding angles are equal.

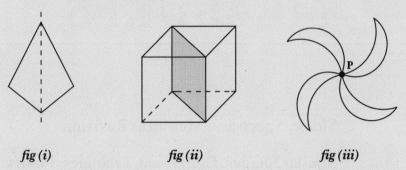

|        fig (i)         |        fig (ii)        |        fig (iii)        |

A **line of symmetry (axis of symmetry)** divides a 2–D shape into two congruent shapes – see **fig (i)**.

A **plane of symmetry** divides a 3–D shape into two congruent shapes – see **fig (ii)**.

A shape has **reflective symmetry** if it has a line or a plane of symmetry – both **fig (i)** and **fig (ii)** have reflective symmetry.

A shape has **rotational symmetry** if it coincides with itself more than once when it is rotated a complete turn about some point. The point about which it is rotated is called the **centre of rotational symmetry.** The number of times the shape coincides with itself during one complete turn is called the **order of rotational symmetry.** For instance, **fig (iii)** has rotational symmetry of order 4. P is the centre of rotational symmetry for **fig (iii)**.

### Quadrilaterals

Some of the properties of special quadrilaterals are shown in the following table.

|  | Square | Rhombus | Rectangle | Parallelogram | Kite | Trapezium |
|---|---|---|---|---|---|---|
| **one pair of opposite sides parallel** | √ | √ | √ | √ |  | √ |
| **two pairs of opposite sides parallel** | √ | √ | √ | √ |  |  |
| **all sides equal** | √ | √ |  |  |  |  |
| **opposite sides equal** | √ | √ | √ | √ |  |  |
| **all angles equal** | √ |  | √ |  |  |  |
| **opposite angles equal** | √ | √ | √ | √ |  |  |
| **diagonals equal** | √ |  | √ |  |  |  |
| **diagonals bisect each other** | √ | √ | √ | √ |  |  |
| **diagonals perpendicular** | √ | √ |  |  | √ |  |
| **diagonals bisect the angles** | √ | √ |  |  |  |  |

*continued . . .*

. . . *from previous page*

## Polygons

A  regular polygon  has all its sides equal and all its angles equal.

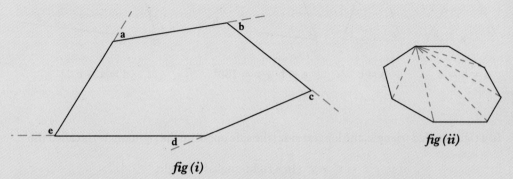

*fig (i)*

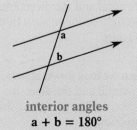

*fig (ii)*

The sum of the  exterior angles  of any polygon is equal to 360°. Hence in *fig (i)*
$a + b + c + d + e = 360°$.
The sum of the  interior angles  of any polygon may be found as follows.

> *Step 1*   From one vertex, draw all the diagonals to divide the polygon into triangles –
> see *fig (ii)*.

> *Step 2*   Find the sum of the angles in all of these triangles.

For instance, *fig (ii)* can be divided into 6 triangles. Hence the sum of the interior angles of
this 8-sided polygon is $6 \times 180° = 1080°$.

## Angles made with Intersecting Lines

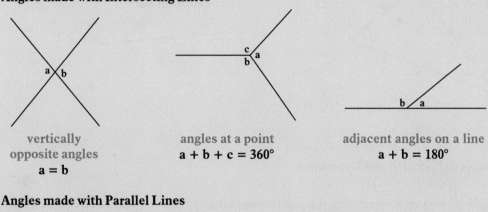

vertically
opposite angles
$a = b$

angles at a point
$a + b + c = 360°$

adjacent angles on a line
$a + b = 180°$

## Angles made with Parallel Lines

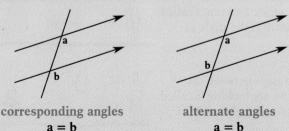

corresponding angles
$a = b$

alternate angles
$a = b$

interior angles
$a + b = 180°$

*continued . . .*

*. . . from previous page*

## Triangles

  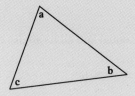 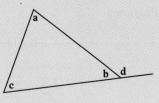

| equilateral | isosceles | interior angles | exterior angle |
|:-:|:-:|:-:|:-:|
| **a = b = c** | **b = c** | **a + b + c = 180°** | **d = a + c** |

In a right-angled triangle, the longest side (the side opposite the right-angle) is called the hypotenuse.
Pythagoras' Theorem: $r^2 = x^2 + y^2$ (In a right-angled triangle, the square on the hypotenuse equals the sum of the squares on the other two sides.)

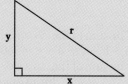

## Trigonometry

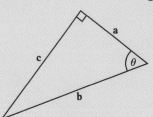

For the angle $\theta$,　　b is the hypotenuse
c is the opposite side
a is the adjacent side

$$\sin\theta = \frac{c}{b}, \quad \cos\theta = \frac{a}{b}, \quad \tan\theta = \frac{c}{a}$$

## Angles of Elevation and Depression

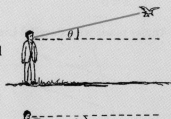

When we look **up** at something, the angle between the horizontal and the direction in which we are looking is called the angle of elevation. In this diagram, $\theta$ is the angle of elevation.

When we look **down** at something, the angle between the horizontal and the direction in which we are looking is called the angle of depression. In this diagram, $\theta$ is the angle of depression.

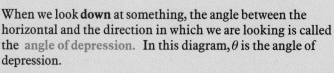

*continued . . .*

. . . *from previous page*

## Metric Measures

| length | km | hm | Dm | m | dm | cm | mm |
|---|---|---|---|---|---|---|---|
| capacity | k*l* | h*l* | D*l* | *l* | d*l* | c*l* | m*l* |
| mass | kg | hg | Dg | g | dg | cg | mg |

Each unit on the table is 10 times as large as the unit immediately to its right. The relationships between the metric units in common use are as follows.

**Length**
1km = 1000m
1m = 1000mm
1m = 100cm
1cm = 10mm

**Capacity**
1*l* = 1000m*l*
1m*l* = 1cm³ (1c.c.)

**Mass**
1kg = 1000g
1g = 1000mg
1 tonne = 1000kg

## Imperial Measure and Metric Measure

Some imperial units still in common use and the relationships between these units are as follows.

**Length**
1 mile = 1760 yards
1 yard = 3 feet
1 foot = 12 inches

**Capacity**
1 gallon = 8 pints

**Mass**
1 ton = 160 stone
1 stone = 14 lb
1 lb = 16 oz

Rough approximations between imperial and metric units are:

1kg is about $2\frac{1}{4}$ lb, 1 litre is about $1\frac{3}{4}$ pints, 1 inch is about $2\frac{1}{2}$ cm, 5 miles is about 8km, 1m is a little longer than 3 feet.

## Area, Perimeter, Volume

The formulae for the area of some common shapes are given below.

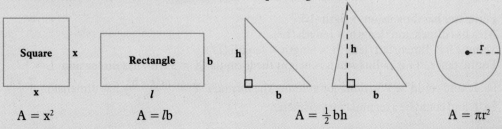

$A = x^2$ $\qquad$ $A = lb$ $\qquad$ $A = \frac{1}{2}bh$ $\qquad$ $A = \pi r^2$

*continued . . .*

*. . . from previous page*

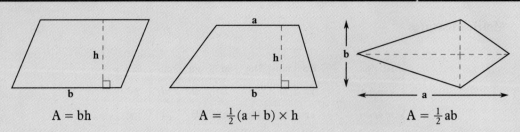

$$A = bh \qquad A = \tfrac{1}{2}(a + b) \times h \qquad A = \tfrac{1}{2}ab$$

Common metric units for land area are the hectare (ha) and square kilometre ($km^2$). The hectare is derived from the unit of land measure, the are.

Some small land areas, such as building plots, are measured in $m^2$.

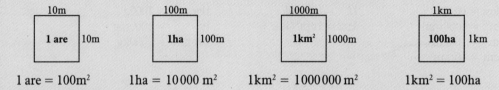

$$1 \text{ are} = 100m^2 \qquad 1ha = 10\,000\ m^2 \qquad 1km^2 = 1\,000\,000\ m^2 \qquad 1km^2 = 100ha$$

The acre is an imperial unit used for land areas. The approximate relationship between acres and hectares is 1ha = 2·5 acres.

The perimeter is the distance right around the outside. The perimeter of a circle is called the circumference. The formula for the circumference of a circle is $C = 2\pi r$ or $C = \pi d$; r is the radius and d is the diameter of the circle, the value of $\pi$ to 3 d.p. is 3·142.

The formulae for the volume of some common shapes are given below.

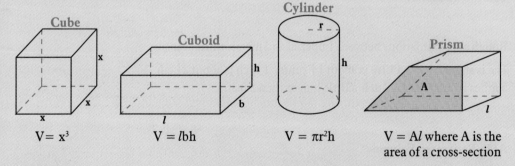

$$V = x^3 \qquad V = lbh \qquad V = \pi r^2 h \qquad V = Al \text{ where A is the area of a cross-section}$$

## Dimensions

Perimeter has dimension length (L).
Area has dimension length × length ($L^2$).
Volume has dimension length × length × length ($L^3$).
For instance, if r is radius and h is height the formula $X = 3\pi rh^2$ has dimension $L \times L^2$
i.e. $L^3$ and could be a formula for volume; the formula $Y = \dfrac{\pi r(r + h)}{4h}$ has dimension $\dfrac{L \times L}{L}$
i.e. L and could be a formula for perimeter.

*continued . . .*

. . . *from previous page*

## Compound Measures

$$\text{average speed} = \frac{\text{distance travelled}}{\text{time taken}} \quad (v = \tfrac{s}{t}) \quad \text{Units for speed are km/h, m/s, mph.}$$

$$\text{density} = \frac{\text{mass}}{\text{volume}} \quad (d = \tfrac{m}{v}) \quad \text{Units for density are g/cm}^3, \text{kg/m}^3.$$

## Possible Error in a Measurement

The maximum possible error in a measurement is half a unit. That is, a measurement given to the nearest mm has a possible error of 0·5mm, a measurement given to the nearest tenth of a second has a possible error of half of one-tenth of a second i.e. 0·05sec.
For instance, a distance given as 289km could be between 288·5km and 289·5km.

## Bearings from North

Bearings from North are always given as 3 digits.
To find the bearing of A from B proceed as follows.

*Step 1*   Join AB.
*Step 2*   Draw a North line from B.
*Step 3*   Measure the angle (in a *clockwise* direction) between this North line and the line AB.

In this diagram, the bearing of A from B is 342°.

## Movements – Reflection, Translation, Rotation. Tessellations

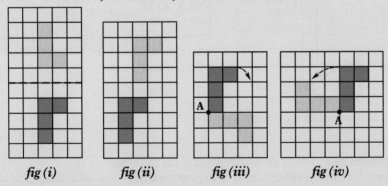

| *fig (i)* | *fig (ii)* | *fig (iii)* | *fig (iv)* |

*fig (i)* illustrates a reflection (or **flip movement**). The red shape has been reflected in the dotted line to the shaded shape. The dotted line is called the mirror line. A point and its image are the same distance from the mirror line.

*fig (ii)* illustrates a translation (or **straight movement**). The vector $\left(\begin{smallmatrix}1\\4\end{smallmatrix}\right)$ translates the red shape onto the shaded shape.

*fig (iii)* and *fig (iv)* illustrate rotation (or **turning movement**). In *fig (iii)* the red shape has been rotated clockwise about A, through 90°.

In *fig (iv)* the red shape has been rotated anticlockwise about A, through 90°.

*continued* . . .

A shape is tessellated if, when it is translated and/or reflected and/or rotated, it completely fills a space leaving no gaps.

### Enlargement

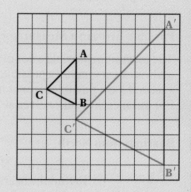

The scale factor of an enlargement can be found by taking the ratio of the length of a side on the image shape to the length of the corresponding side on the original shape.

For instance, in the diagram, ABC has been enlarged to A′B′C′. Scale factor $= \dfrac{\text{length of A}'\text{B}'}{\text{length of AB}}$

$\qquad\qquad\qquad = \dfrac{9}{3}$

$\qquad\qquad\qquad = 3.$

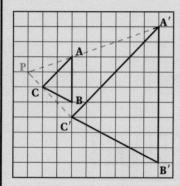

This diagram shows how the centre of enlargement can be found. The steps needed to find the centre of enlargement in this case are:

*Step 1*  Join A′ and A.
*Step 2*  Join C′ and C.
*Step 3*  Extend the lines A′A and C′C. The point P, where these lines meet, is the centre of enlargement.

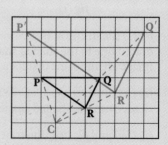

This diagram shows how to draw an enlargement of the triangle PQR, scale factor 2, centre of enlargement C. Beginning with just the point C and the triangle PQR we proceed as follows:

*Step 1*  Join C to P, C to Q and C to R.
*Step 2*  Extend the line CP to P′ so that the length of CP′ is twice the length of CP.
*Step 3*  Extend the line CQ to Q′ so that the length of CQ′ is twice the length of CQ.
*Step 4*  Extend the line CR to R′ so that the length of CR′ is twice the length of CR.
*Step 5*  Join P′, Q′ and R′ to form the image triangle P′Q′R′.

*continued . . .*

*... from previous page*

If the scale factor is greater than 1, the image is larger than the original.
If the scale factor is between 0 and 1, the image is smaller than the original — see the
diagram below where ABC has been enlarged, centre P, scale factor $\frac{1}{2}$.

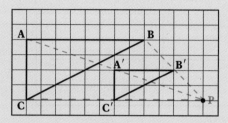

### Similar Shapes

Similar figures are the same shape but different sizes. Any enlargement of a given shape gives
a **similar shape.** On similar shapes, corresponding angles are equal and corresponding
lengths are in the same ratio.
For instance, if we are given $\angle A = \angle P$, $\angle B = \angle Q$, $\angle C = \angle R$ and $\angle D = \angle S$ then the
quadrilaterals shown below are similar.

If we are given that $\dfrac{AB}{PQ} = \dfrac{4}{3}$ then each of the ratios $\dfrac{BC}{QR}$, $\dfrac{CD}{RS}$ and $\dfrac{AD}{PS}$ is also equal to $\dfrac{4}{3}$.

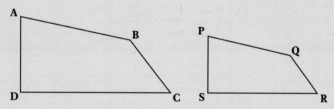

We can say that **two triangles are similar** if we are given one of the following sets of
information.

1. The corresponding angles are equal. (The triangles are equiangular).

or 2. The corresponding sides are in the same ratio.

or 3. Two pairs of corresponding sides are in the same ratio and the angles between these
sides are equal.

*continued ...*

. . . *from previous page*

## Compass Constructions

The following diagrams show  the construction of the bisector of the line BC.

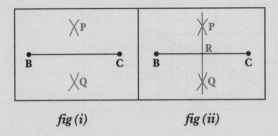

*fig (i)*          *fig (ii)*

*Step 1*   Open out the compass so the length on the compass is a little more than half the length of the line BC. Keep this length on the compass throughout.

*Step 2*   With compass point firstly on B and then on C, draw arcs to meet at P and Q – see *fig (i)*.

*Step 3*   Draw the line through P and Q – see *fig (ii)*. This line is the required bisector of the line BC.

*Note*   The point R, where PQ meets BC, is the **mid-point** of the line BC.

The following diagrams show  the construction of the line through A that is perpendicular to the line BC.

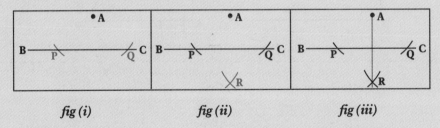

*fig (i)*               *fig (ii)*               *fig (iii)*

*Step 1*   Open out the compass to any reasonable length. This length should be such that when the compass point is placed at A two arcs can be drawn that will cross BC. Keep this length on the compass throughout.

*Step 2*   With compass point on A, draw two arcs to meet BC at P and Q – see *fig (i)*.

*Step 3*   With compass point firstly on P, then on Q, draw two arcs to meet at R – see *fig (ii)*.

*Step 4*   Join AR – see *fig (iii)*. AR is the required line.

*continued* . . .

. . . *from previous page*

The following diagrams show **the construction of the line through A that is parallel to the line BC.**

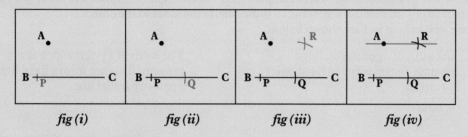

| *fig (i)* | *fig (ii)* | *fig (iii)* | *fig (iv)* |

*Step 1*  Mark any point P on BC – see *fig (i)*.

*Step 2*  Open out the compass to the length AP. Keep this length on the compass throughout.

*Step 3*  With compass point on P, draw an arc to meet BC at Q – see *fig (ii)*.

*Step 4*  With compass point firstly on Q and then on A, draw two arcs to meet at R – see *fig (iii)*.

*Step 5*  Draw the line through A and R – see *fig (iv)*. This is the required line.

The following diagrams show **the construction of the bisector of the angle P.**

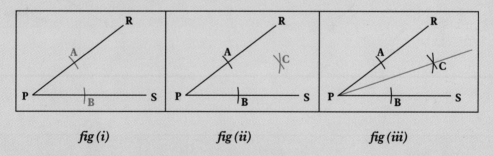

| *fig (i)* | *fig (ii)* | *fig (iii)* |

*Step 1*  Open out the compass to any reasonable length. This length should be less than the length of either arm (PR or PS) of the angle P. Keep this length on the compass throughout.

*Step 2*  With compass point on P, draw arcs to meet PR and PS at A and B – see *fig (i)*.

*Step 3*  With compass point firstly on A and then on B, draw two arcs to meet at C – see *fig (ii)*.

*Step 4*  Draw the line from P through C – see *fig (iii)*. This line is the required bisector of the angle P.

*continued . . .*

. . . *from previous page*

## Locus

The **locus** of an object is the set of all possible positions that this object can occupy. The path of an object, moving according to some rule, is the locus of the object.
Some well known loci are shown below.

1.  The locus of a point which is a constant distance from a fixed point is a circle.

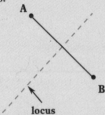

2.  The locus of a point which is a constant distance from a fixed line is a pair of parallel lines.

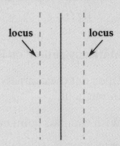

3.  The locus of a point which is equidistant from two fixed points is the mediator (perpendicular bisector) of the line joining the fixed points.

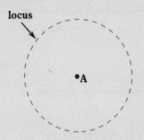

4.  The locus of a point which is equidistant from two intersecting lines is the pair of lines which bisect the angles between the fixed lines.

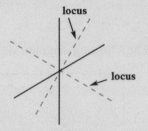

## REVISION EXERCISE

1.  (a) Find the size of the angles marked as a, b, c, d and e.
    (b) Explain why triangle ABC is isosceles.

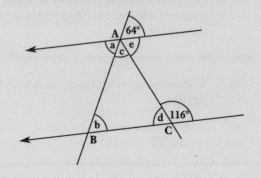

2. Sean cut 45cm off a plank measuring 3·15m. What fraction of the plank was left?

3.

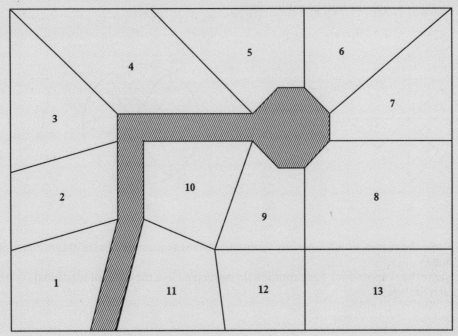

Scale: 1cm represents 10m

Brookfield Builders are to build houses on the housing estate shown in this diagram.

(i)   Which plots are  (a)  trapeziums
                       (b)  kites
                       (c)  pentagons?
(ii)  Find the length of the diagonals of plot 1. Hence calculate the area of this plot, in square metres.
(iii) Calculate the area of plot 3, in square metres.
(iv)  Find, in hectares, the total area of this housing estate. Include the area taken for the road.

4.

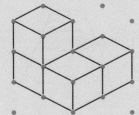

This shape consists of four cubes, three of which are on the base. Use isometric dot paper to draw shapes which consist of five cubes, two of which are on the base.

5. **Parallelogram      Kite      Rhombus      Trapezium**
From this list name the shapes which have     (a)  diagonals perpendicular
                                              (b)  just one axis of symmetry
                                              (c)  opposite angles equal
                                              (d)  just one pair of parallel sides
                                              (e)  equal diagonals.

269

6. Nathan designed a logo for his school. To the nearest mm, he measured the width of the logo as 12·3cm. Find  (a) the greatest possible width
   (b) the least possible width.

7.

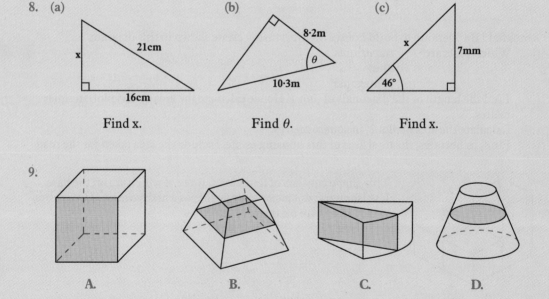

| A. | B. | C. | D. |

(a) Name the shapes which have line symmetry. Give the number of axes of symmetry of these shapes.
(b) Name the shapes which have rotational symmetry. Give the order of rotational symmetry of each of these.

8. (a)  ...  Find x.  (b) ... Find θ.  (c) ... Find x.

9.

A. is a cuboid.  B. is part of a square-based pyramid.  C. is part of a cylinder.  D. is part of a cone.

(a) For which of these is the shaded plane a plane of symmetry?
(b) Which of these has exactly four planes of symmetry?
(c) Which of these has exactly two planes of symmetry?
(d) Which of these has an infinite number of planes of symmetry?
(e) How many congruent faces do each of these shapes have?

10.

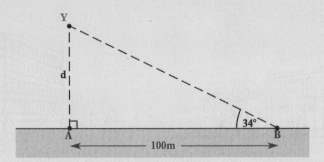

A yacht is anchored at Y, d metres from shore. To calculate this distance, Tony walks along the beach for 100m from A then measures the angle ABY.
What calculation should Tony now do? What answer should he get?

11. (a) The Earth is about $1{\cdot}496 \times 10^8$km from the sun. Write this distance in decimal form.
    (b) The velocity of light is about $3{\cdot}0 \times 10^5$km/sec. How long does light take to travel from the sun to the Earth? Round your answer sensibly.

12.

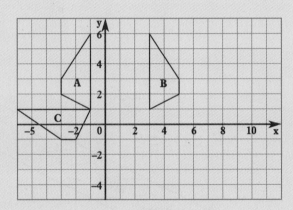

(a) A has been reflected onto B. Describe this reflection.
(b) A has been rotated onto C. Give the angle of this rotation and the coordinates of the centre of rotation.
(c) B is translated onto D. The vector of the translation is $\binom{-2}{1}$. Give the coordinates of the vertices of D.

13. (a) Victoria wrote down the formula $A = \frac{4}{3}\pi r^3$ for the surface area of a sphere.
    Use dimensions to explain why this formula cannot be correct.
    (b) Which of the following expressions could be for perimeter? (d is diameter, h is height, $l$ is length.)

    A. $3\pi l$       B. $\pi d l^2$       C. $\pi(l + d)$       D. $\dfrac{(l\mathrm{d})^2}{\pi\mathrm{h}}$

    E. $\dfrac{\pi \mathrm{d}^2}{l}$    F. $\dfrac{4(\mathrm{h}+l)\times\mathrm{d}}{\pi l}$    G. $\dfrac{4(\mathrm{h}+l)}{\pi\mathrm{d}}$    H. $\dfrac{4\mathrm{d}l(\mathrm{h}+l)}{\pi}$

    (c) Which of the expressions given in (b) could be for volume?

14.

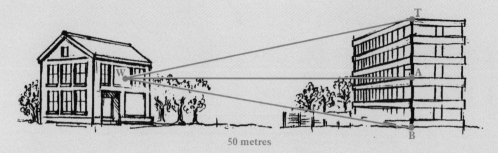

50 metres

New flats have been built 50 metres from Lee's school. From a window, W, in the school Lee measured the angle of elevation of the top of the flats to be 9° and the angle of depression of the base of the flats to be 6°. In the diagram WA is perpendicular to TB.

(a) Which angle in the diagram is 9°; which is 6°?

(b) Explain how Lee could calculate the height of the flats. Find this height.

15.

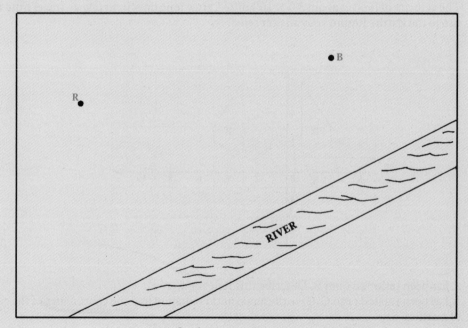

Scale: 1cm represents 5m

Caroline and Anne took their nephews, Robin and Ben, on a hiking trip. They each carried their own tent.

The diagram represents one of their camp sites. Ben and Robin have erected their tents at B and R.

(a) Trace the diagram.

(b) Use your compass to construct the set of points which are equidistant from B and R.

(c) Caroline erects her tent so that it is 15 metres from the river and the same distance from Ben's tent as it is from Robin's. Find the position of Caroline's tent.

(d) Anne erects her tent so that it is as close as possible to Ben's but no more than 10 metres from the river. Use your compass to draw construction lines to find the position of Anne's tent.

(e) How far is Caroline's tent from Anne's?

272

16.

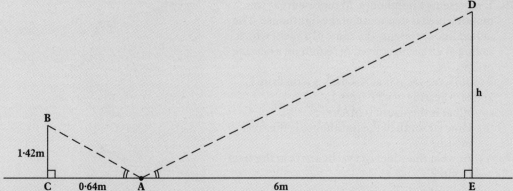

This diagram shows the method Sarah used to find the height of a tree.

DE represents the tree, A represents a mirror lying flat on the ground, B represents the height of Sarah's eyes.

Sarah places the mirror on the ground, 6 metres from the foot of the tree. She then moves back until she can see the top of the tree in the mirror. The top comes into view when she has moved back 64cm. From Sarah's work in Physics she knows that $\angle BAC = \angle DAE$.

(a) Explain why $\triangle$s ABC and ADE are similar.

(b) What is the missing length in the ratio $\dfrac{DE}{BC} = \dfrac{AE}{\ldots}$ ?

(c) Find the height of the tree, giving the answer to the nearest cm.

17.

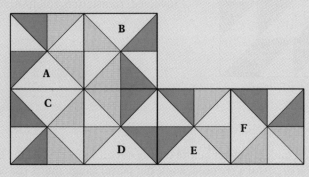

Margo is tiling a wall in her bathroom. She places the first 6 tiles as shown in the diagram.

(a) Tile A maps onto tile B under a rotation. What is the angle of this rotation?

(b) Which other tile is a rotation of tile A?

(c) Which tile (or tiles) shows a translation of tile A?

(d) Which tile (or tiles) shows a reflection of tile A?

18. Melanie was making designs based on the square. One of her shapes consisted of a square of side 12cm with two corners cut away as shown. The curved portions are arcs of circles with centre, the centre of the square.

(a) Calculate the area of this shape.

(b) Calculate the perimeter of this shape.

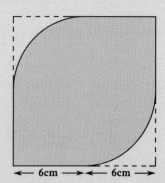

19. L represents a lighthouse. M represents a river mouth which is due south of the lighthouse. The dotted line represents the route of a yacht which is sailing at an average speed of 6km/h on a bearing of 228°.

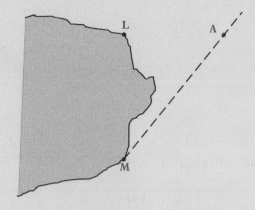

At 13:05, the yacht is at A which is 8km from L and on a bearing of 090° from L.
   (a) What is the size of Ð MAL?
   (b) How far south of the lighthouse is the river mouth?
   (c) At what time does the yacht arrive at the river mouth?

20.

A shape has been tessellated to make this pattern, then the pattern coloured.
   (a) Which shape has been tessellated?
   (b) Which of the following movements have been involved: translation, rotation, reflection?

21. (a) Julia filled up the tank of her car before setting out on a journey. At the end of the journey she finds that 24*l* of petrol were used, while her petrol gauge shows the tank is still − full. How many litres does the tank of Julia's car hold?
   (b) Julia and a friend will be touring Holland in the holidays in a rental car. They will be away for 10 days and will travel a distance of about 800km. The rental car does 32 miles to the gallon. In Holland petrol costs 1·23 guilders per litre. How much should Julia budget for petrol if the exchange rate is £1 = 2·96 guilders?

22.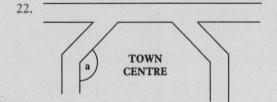

The planners of a new town centre decide to make it the shape of a regular octagon. Part of the sketch plan is shown.
   (a) Find the size of an exterior angle of a regular octagon.
   (b) Find the size of the angle marked as **a**.

23.

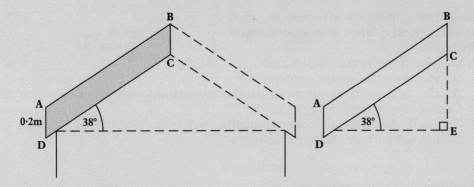

ABCD represents a bargeboard on the end of a roof of a barn. The pitch of the roof is 38°.
(a) What shape is ABCD?
(b) Calculate, with reasons, the size of ∠DCE, ∠DCB and ∠ADC.

The bargeboard is cut from a 4·5m plank of timber.
(c) Sketch △ADX. On this triangle, write the lengths and angles you know.
(d) Use trigonometry to find AX. Hence find the length, AB, of the bargeboard.
(e) Use Pythagoras' Theorem to find XD. Hence calculate the area of ABCD.

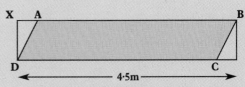

24.

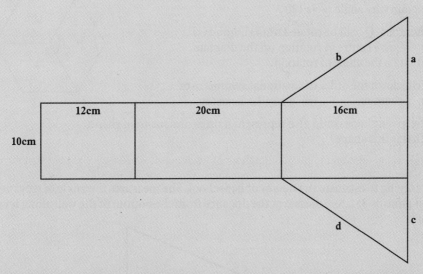

Some of Adam's class made sweets for the school fête. Others made cardboard containers for the sweets. The net for a container that Adam made is sketched.
(a) How long did Adam make the edges, a, b, c and d?
(b) How many vertices does this container have?
(c) Name the shape of this container.
(d) Calculate the capacity of the container. Give the answer in litres.
(e) Calculate the total surface area of this container.

275

Wendy made cylinders for the sweets. She made three of these, all different sizes. One of these is sketched.

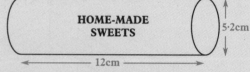

(f) Calculate the volume of the sketched cylinder, giving the answer correct to 2 s.f.

(g) Another cylinder was the same length as that sketched and had a volume of 320cm³, to 2 s.f. Calculate the radius of this cylinder.

(h) The third cylinder Wendy made was a similar shape to that sketched. This cylinder was 18cm long. Find the radius of this cylinder.

25. This diagram represents the cross-section of a swimming pool. The pool is being filled. Using similar shapes, or otherwise, find how far the surface of the water is from the top of the pool when the length of the surface of the water is 10 metres.

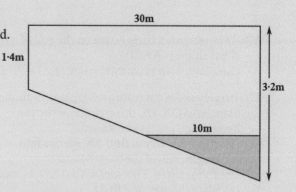

26. The diagram shows three identical rhombuses *P*, *Q* and *T*.

(a) Explain why angle *x* is 120°.

(b) Rhombus *Q* can be rotated onto rhombus *T*.
   (i) Mark a centre of rotation on the diagram.
   (ii) State the angle of rotation.

(c) Write down the order of rotational symmetry of
   (i) a rhombus,   (ii) a regular hexagon.

(d) The given shape could also represent a three dimensional shape. What is this shape?

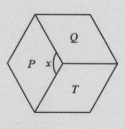

**NEAB**

27. Sally is trying to estimate the height of her school. She measures the angle of elevation of the highest point as 35°. She measures the distance from the bottom of the wall along level ground as 12·6m.

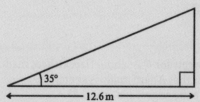

(a) Calculate the height of the school.

(b) To what degree of accuracy should Sally give her answer? Give a reason for your answer.

**NEAB**

**28.** The diagram below is the net of a small open box, with no top face.

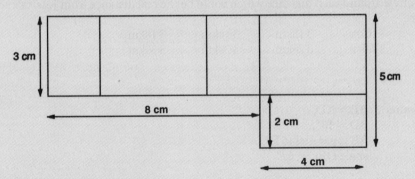

(a) Find the perimeter of the net.

(b) Calculate the area of the net.

(c) Add one more rectangle in a suitable position to change the diagram above to the net of a closed box.

(d) Write down the length, width and height of the box (in any order).

(e) Calculate the volume of the box.

(f) Draw an isometric view of the closed box on the grid below.

MEG

**29.** A school badge is made in two sizes.

Not to scale

The width of the small size is 3cm.

The large size is an enlargement of the small size in the ratio 2 : 3.

Calculate the width of the large size badge.

SEG

**30.** The distance from Jessica's home to school is 3·2km correct to one decimal place.
Draw a circle around each distance which could be the real distance from Jessica's school to her home.

3·00km     3·10km     3·15km     3·16km     3·18km

3·20km     3·24km     3·25km     3·28km     3·30km        **ULEAC**

**31.** In the figure,    AB = AD,
                     BD = BC,
                     AB is parallel to DC,
                     angle DBC = 62°.

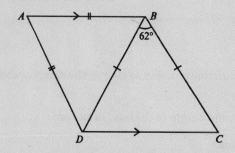

**(a)** Calculate the sizes of the other angles in the diagram.
Hence decide whether each of the following statements is true or false.
     **(i)**     BD bisects angle ABC.
     **(ii)**    BD bisects angle ADC.
     **(iii)**   Angle DAB is equal to angle DBC.

**(b)** Explain why BC is not parallel to AD.            **NEAB**

**32.**

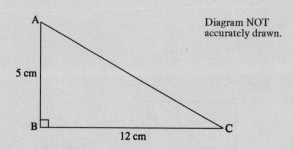

Diagram NOT accurately drawn.

Triangle ABC has angle B = 90°, AB = 5cm and BC = 12cm.

**(a)** Calculate the **smallest** angle in the triangle ABC. Give your answer to the nearest tenth of a degree.

All the sides of the triangle are doubled in length.

**(b)** State, without further calculation, the size of the smallest angle in the new triangle.

                                                 **ULEAC**

**33.**

One lap of a race track is 5km. A car covers this distance in 2 minutes. What is the average speed of the car in kilometres per hour for this lap?          **NICCEA**

**34.**

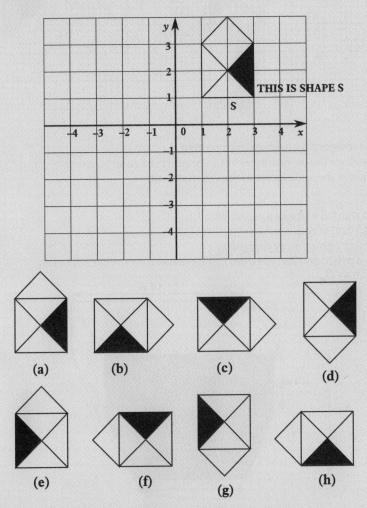

**(a)** Which of the shapes a, b, c, d, e, f, g, h would be the same as the image of shape S under the transformation

  **(i)** a reflection in the *x* axis,       **(ii)** a reflection in the *y* axis,

  **(iii)** a rotation of 180° about the origin,   **(iv)** a rotation of 90° clockwise about the origin,

  **(v)** a translation,            **(vi)** a reflection in the line $y = x$,

  **(vii)** a reflection in the line $y = -x$?

279

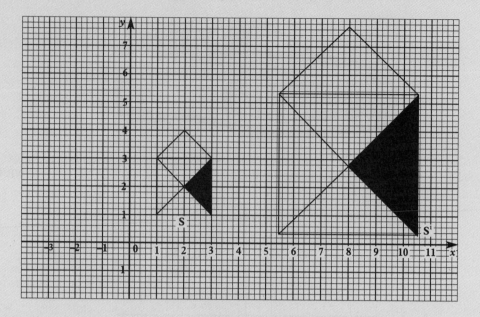

(b) S¹ is the image of S under an enlargement.
   (i)   What are the co-ordinates of C, the centre of enlargement?
   (ii)  What is the scale factor of the enlargement?

**NICCEA**

35. Mr Maragh wanted to make a garden pond.
    He dug out $5.2 \text{m}^3$ of soil.
    He hired a skip to take away the soil.
    The skip is a prism and has the dimensions marked on the sketch below.

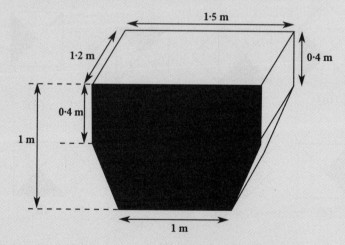

(a) Calculate
   (i)   the area of the cross-section of the skip (the shaded part),
   (ii)  the volume of the skip.
(b) How many skips are needed to remove all the soil?
    (They can only be filled up level with the top.)

**MEG**

**36.** A fishing boat sails from a harbour $H$ to a point $F$.
$F$ is due east of a lighthouse $L$.
Angle $FLH$ is $75°$ and angle $LFH$ is $35°$.

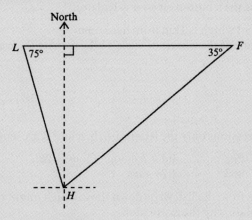

(a) Calculate the bearing of $F$ from $H$.
(b) Calculate the bearing of $L$ from $H$.
(c) Calculate the bearing of $H$ from $F$.                    **NEAB**

**37.** Two ships $A$ and $B$ both hear a distress signal from a fishing boat.
The positions of $A$ and $B$ are shown on the map below.
The map is drawn using a scale of 1cm to represent 1km.
The fishing boat is less than 4km from ship $A$ and is less than 4·5km from ship $B$.
A helicopter pilot sees that the fishing boat is nearer to ship $A$ than to ship $B$.
Use accurate construction to show the region which contains the fishing boat. Shade this region.

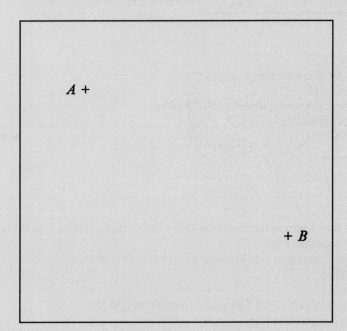

Scale   1cm = 1km

**NEAB**

**38.** Susie has a new bike.
The radius of its wheels is 30cm.
**(a)** Work out the circumference of one of the wheels.
(Take $\pi$ to be $3\cdot14$ or use the $\pi$ button on your calculator.)

Susie rides her bike to school which is 1km from her home.
**(b)** How many times will one of the wheels of Susie's bike turn on the way to school?   **ULEAC**

**39.** In the following list of expressions only the letters a, b, h, r, and R are lengths.

$$\pi(R^2 - r^2), \qquad abh, \qquad 4(a + b + h), \qquad b^2 - 2a^2,$$
$$a^2b, \qquad 3\pi r^2, \qquad 2(2b + a)$$

**(a)** Using only expressions from the list, write down those which might represent volume.
**(b)** Use dimensions to explain why the expression
$$2\pi(R - r)$$
could not represent area.   **SEG**

**40. (a)** The model of the cross-section of a roof is illustrated below.

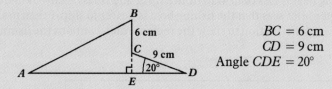

$BC = 6$ cm
$CD = 9$ cm
Angle $CDE = 20°$

    **(i)**    Calculate the length of $CE$.
    **(ii)**   Triangles $ABE$ and $DCE$ are similar triangles.
        Calculate the length of $AB$.
**(b)** When the roof is constructed, the actual length of $BC$ is $4\cdot5$m.
    **(i)**    Calculate the actual length of $CD$.
    **(ii)**   Calculate the angle $DCE$.   **SEG**

**41.** A helicopter leaves base B and flies 13km in the direction 270° to an oilrig C. It then flies 19km to a second oilrig D which is due south of B.
**(a)** Make a scale drawing of the course B to C to D, using a scale of 1cm to 2km.
**(b)** Using your scale drawing, find
    **(i)**    the distance from B to D;
    **(ii)**   the direction in which the helicopter flies while going from C to D.
        Give your answer as a 3-figure bearing.

The helicopter now flies 16km in the direction 075° to a third oilrig E.
  (c) (i)  Add the course D to E to your scale drawing.
     (ii) Hence find, as a 3-figure bearing, what course the helicopter follows as it flies directly
          back from E to B.                                                    **NICCEA**

**42.** The quadrilateral $ABCD$ is a kite.
  $DO = OB$, $DC = 104$cm, $CO = 96$cm and $AC = 126$cm.

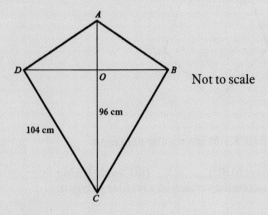

Not to scale

  (a) Calculate the length of
     (i)  $DB$,
     (ii) $AD$.
  (b) Work out the area of the kite.
  (c) Calculate the size of angle $CBO$.                                       **SEG**

**43.** Triangle $ABC$ is right-angled at $B$. The lengths of $AB$ and $BC$ are 21·4cm and 16·3cm
respectively, correct to the nearest mm.

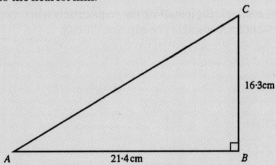

  (a) Calculate the largest possible value of the area of triangle $ABC$, correct to the nearest tenth
      of a cm².
  (b) Use Pythagoras' Theorem to calculate the range of possible values of the length of $AC$,
      correct to the nearest mm.
  (c) Calculate the largest possible value of angle $A$.                        **WJEC**

**44.**

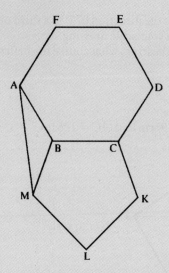

ABCDEF is a regular hexagon, and BCKLM is a regular pentagon.
**(a)** Calculate the size of
    **(i)** angle ABC;     **(ii)** angle MBC;        **(iii)** angle BAM.
**(b)** Prove that D, C, K *cannot* be successive vertices of a regular polygon.     **NICCEA**

**45.** A company is setting up a mobile phone network in a city and needs to install transmitters so that every point in the city is within the range of at least one transmitter.
Each transmitter serves a circular area of radius 250 metres, centred on the transmitter.

The size of the city means that a large number of transmitters will be required, but the company does not want to waste money by installing more transmitters than necessary.

The company's engineer suggests installing the transmitters at the vertices of a square grid. Is this the best arrangement?

Assume that sites are available for installing the transmitters wherever they are required and that you can ignore what happens near the edges of the city.     **MEG**

# Similar Shapes.
# Congruent Triangles. Proofs

## SIMILAR SHAPES

### INVESTIGATION 14:1

**Area and Volume of Similar Shapes**

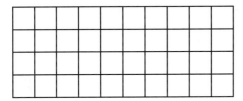

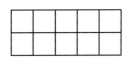

Rectangle A        Rectangle B

The rectangles A and B are similar. A is an enlargement of B, scale factor 2. That is, the ratio of corresponding lengths is 2.
What is the relationship between the area of A and the area of B?

    What if    A is an enlargement of B, scale factor 3?
    What if    A is an enlargement of B, scale factor $\frac{1}{2}$ ?
    What if    B is a triangle?
    What if    B is a circle?
    What if    . . .

Make and test a statement about the relationship between the surface areas of similar shapes.

Shape P

Shape Q

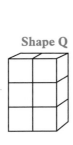

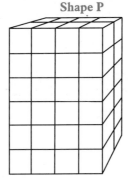

These shapes are similar. P is an enlargement of Q, scale factor 2.
What is the volume of Q? What is the volume of P? What is the relationship between the volume of P and the volume of Q?

    What if    P is an enlargement of Q, scale factor 3?
    What if    P is an enlargement of Q, scale factor 4?
    What if    Q is a triangular prism?
    What if    Q is a cylinder?
    What if    . . .

Make and test a statement about the relationship between the volumes of similar shapes.

If k is the ratio of corresponding lengths on two similar shapes then $k^2$ is the **ratio of the areas** and $k^3$ is the **ratio of the volumes.**

For instance, since the ratio of corresponding lengths on these prisms is 2, the area of each surface on B is $2^2$ or 4 times as large as the corresponding surface on A. Also, the volume of B is $2^3$ or 8 times that of A.

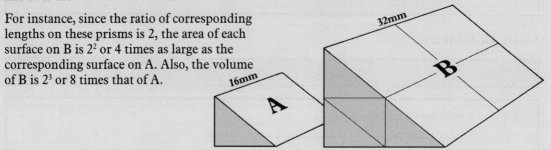

*Worked Example* A′ is an enlargement of A.
The area of A is 40cm².
Find the area of A′.

*Answer* Since ratio of corresponding lengths is $\frac{6}{4}$ or $\frac{3}{2}$, then ratio of the areas is $\left(\frac{3}{2}\right)^2$ or $\frac{9}{4}$.
Hence area of A′ $= \frac{9}{4} \times$ area of A
$$= \frac{9}{4} \times 40$$
$$= 90\text{cm}^2.$$

*Worked Example* These cylinders are similar.
Find the capacity of the smaller cylinder.

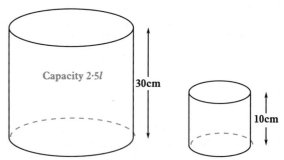

*Answer* Since the ratio of corresponding lengths is $\frac{10}{30}$ or $\frac{1}{3}$, the ratio of the capacities is $\left(\frac{1}{3}\right)^3$ or $\frac{1}{27}$.
Hence capacity of smaller cylinder $= \frac{1}{27} \times$ capacity of larger
$$= \frac{1}{27} \times 2 \cdot 5l$$
$$= 93\text{m}l \text{ (2 s.f.)}$$

*Worked Example*

These pottles of cream cheese are similar in shape. Find the diameter of the circular top of the smaller pottle.

*Answer*  Since both pottles contain the same cheese the ratio of the masses will be the same as the ratio of the volumes.

Since ratio of volumes $= \frac{300}{425}$  then  $\left(\frac{d}{10}\right)^3 = \frac{300}{425}$

$$\frac{d^3}{1000} = \frac{300}{425}$$

$$d^3 = \frac{1000 \times 300}{425}$$

$$d = \sqrt[3]{\frac{1000 \times 300}{425}}$$

$$= 8.9\text{cm (to the nearest mm).}$$

## EXERCISE 14:2

**The diagrams are *not* drawn to scale.**

1.

These similar shapes are used by a manufacturer of pet food in advertising its products.
The smaller shape covers an area of 20cm². How much space does the large shape cover?

2.

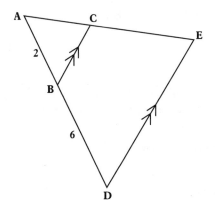

(a) Explain why △ ABC is similar to △ ADE.
(b) Find the area of △ ABC given that the area of △ ADE is 7·2 square units.

3. The side-front pattern pieces for a size 10 and a size 14 dress are similar in shape. The width of the size 14 pattern is 12cm and its area is 360cm². The width of the size 10 pattern is 10cm. Find its area.

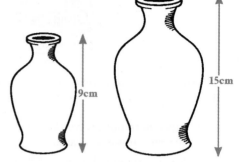

4. These flower vases are similar. To fill the small vase with water takes 0·8*l*.
   How much water is needed to fill the large vase?

5. Cottage Craft Cooperative make hand-knotted rugs in a variety of sizes. All of the different sizes are mathematically similar. All sell for the same price per square metre. The 2m × 1·5m rug sells for £72. How much does a 1·5m long rug sell for?

6. Two jam jars are of similar shape. When full, the larger holds 500g of jam. Find the maximum amount of jam in the smaller jar given that the heights of the jars are 8cm and 9cm.

7. 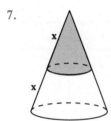 A cone is divided into two shapes by a cut parallel to the base and halfway between the base and the top.
   What is the ratio of the volume of the large shape formed to the small shape?

8. (i) This shape, which is built from four cubes, is enlarged by a scale factor of 2.
   (a) Draw the new shape. Hence find the number of cubes in the new shape.
   (b) Explain how the number of cubes in the new shape can be found by calculation.

   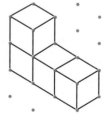

   (c) If each cube measures 2cm × 2cm × 2cm find the total surface area of the shape built from four cubes.
   (d) Find the total surface area of the enlarged shape.

   (ii) 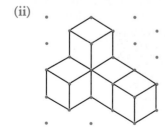 Find the number of cubes needed if this shape is enlarged by a scale factor of (a) 2   (b) 3   (c) 4   (d) 6.

9.

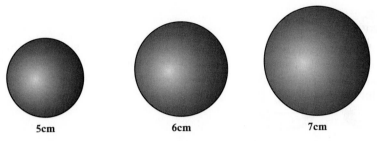

5cm          6cm          7cm

A toy company makes these three sizes of solid rubber balls. The 6cm diameter ball is priced at £2·50. To the nearest 5p, what should be the price of the 5cm and 7cm diameter balls? (Assume the balls are the same price per cubic centimetre.)

10. Two troughs on Michael's farm are mathematically similar. The larger is 1·6m long and can hold 150 litres of water. The smaller is 1m long. What is the maximum amount of water it can hold?

11.

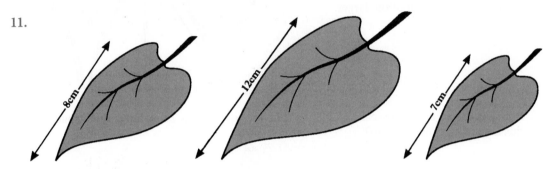

These leaves are similar. By placing a transparent grid over the smallest leaf, Adrian estimated its surface area to be 20cm².
Estimate the area of    (a) the leaf on the left
                        (b) the leaf in the middle.

12. (a) *"All cubes are mathematically similar"*. Is this statement correct?
    (b) *"All cuboids are mathematically similar"*. Is this statement correct?
    (c) Two cubes have edges of 2cm and 5cm. What is the ratio of the total surface areas of these cubes?

13. Two spheres, one of radius 2cm and the other of radius 4cm are dipped in gold. How many times as much gold is needed for the larger sphere?

14. A paving tile is the shape shown. Another paving tile is eight times heavier than this one. If the tiles are mathematically similar find the dimensions of the heavier tile.

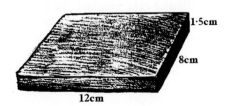

1·5cm

8cm

12cm

15.

These two bottles are similar in shape. The smaller bottle has a base diameter of 38mm. Find the base diameter of the larger bottle.

16. Simone has two maps of The New Forest. On one map the forest covers an area of 176cm² and on the other it covers an area of 215cm². Simone measures the length of a road on the larger map as 84mm. How long is this road on the smaller map?

17. These funnels are mathematically similar.
Find the diameter of the smaller funnel and the height of the larger.

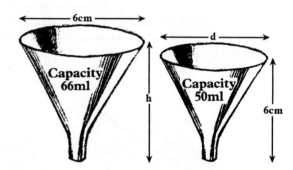

18. A map is drawn using the scale 1 : 50000. The area of a lake is 25ha. How much space does this lake take up on the map?

Review 1  Box A has been enlarged to Box B.
    (a) What is the scale factor of the enlargement?
    (b) What is the scale factor for area?
    (c) If the area of the top face of Box A is 5cm²,
        what is the area of the top face of Box B?
    (d) What is the scale factor for volume?
    (e) If the volume of Box B is 114cm³, what is the
        volume of Box A?

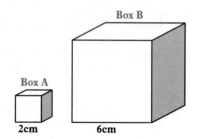

Review 2  Joanne made a 3-tier wedding cake for her brother's wedding. The 3 tiers were mathematically similar.
If the middle-tier cake weighed 2kg find the weight of the whole wedding cake.
Give the answer to the nearest kg.

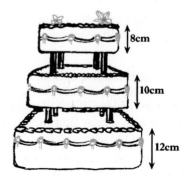

**Review 3**

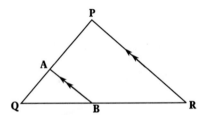

(a) Explain why △ ABQ is similar to △ PQR.
(b) AB : PR = 2 : 5 and area △ PQR = 40cm².
Find the area of △ AQB.

**Review 4** The shape shown is built from 8 cubes. This shape is to be enlarged by a scale factor of 3.
(a) How many cubes will be needed to build the new shape?
(b) If each cube has sides of 1cm, find the total surface area of the shape shown. Hence calculate the surface area of the new shape.

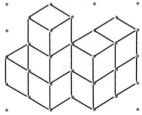

**Review 5** Robert uses the scale *5cm represents 2m* to make a scale drawing of his bedroom. If the area of Robert's scale drawing is 125cm² what is the area of his bedroom?

**Review 6**

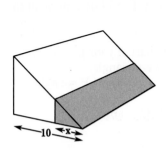

These soup tins are similar. The label for the large tin is 4 times the size of the label for the small tin. How tall is the large tin?

## DISCUSSION EXERCISE 14:3

- A small prism, cone and cylinder are cut from a large prism, cone and cylinder. Are any of these small shapes similar to the large shapes? Discuss.

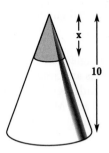

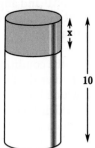

For which of these is the statement $\frac{\text{Volume of small shape}}{\text{Volume of large shape}} = \left(\frac{x}{10}\right)^3$ true?

For one of these the statement $\frac{\text{Area of small shape}}{\text{Area of large shape}} = \left(\frac{x}{10}\right)^2$ is true. Which one? Discuss. As part of your discussion prove that this statement is true.

- Megan claimed that if a 3-D shape was "enlarged in 2 dimensions only" then the ratio of the volumes was equal to the square of the ratio of corresponding lengths. Discuss Megan's claim.

## CONGRUENT TRIANGLES

Since these two triangles are identical they are  congruent.

We write Δs $^{ABC}_{QRP}$  are congruent. That is, we write the equal angles underneath one another. When the triangles are written in this way the equal sides are also underneath one another. For instance, since QR is written underneath AB then QR is equal to AB.

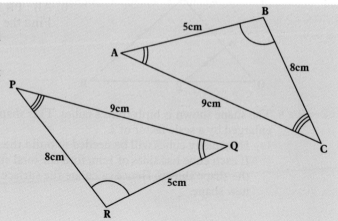

---

## INVESTIGATION 14:4

**Congruence Conditions**

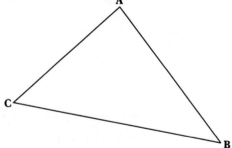

Measure AC, AB and angle A.
Draw Δ PQR in which PQ = AC, PR = AB and angle P = angle A. Is Δ PQR congruent to the given triangle?

Investigate the conditions for two triangles to be congruent. As part of your investigation consider whether the following triangles are congruent to the given triangle.
Δ DEF in which DE = AC, DF = AB and angle E = angle C.  What if angle F = angle B?
Δ LMN in which LM = AC, LN = AB and MN = CB.
Δ STU in which angle S = angle A, angle T = angle B and angle U = angle C.

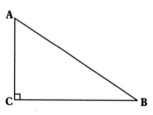

What if the given triangle is a right-angled triangle?

Two triangles are congruent if one of the following sets of conditions is true. The abbreviation for each of these is shown in brackets. In these abbreviations S stands for side, A for angle, R for right angle and H for hypotenuse.

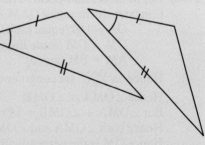

1.  Two sides of one triangle are equal to two sides of the other and the angle between these sides is equal. (SAS).

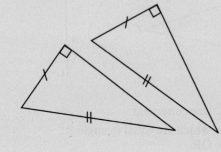

The three sides of one triangle are equal to the three sides of the other triangle. (SSS).

3.  Two angles and a side of one triangle are equal to two angles and the corresponding side of the other. (AAS).

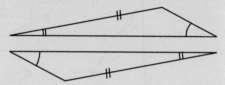

4.  Each triangle contains a right angle. The hypotenuses and another pair of sides are equal. (RHS).

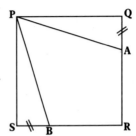

*Worked Example*

PQRS is a square.
A and B are points on QR and SR such that QA = SB.
Use congruent triangles to prove that ∠PAQ = ∠PBS.

*Proof*  Consider the triangles PQA and PSB.
PQ = PS (sides of square)
QA = SB (given)
∠Q = ∠S (right angles)
Hence Δs $^{PQA}_{PSB}$ are congruent. (RHS)
Hence ∠PAQ = ∠PBS.

*Worked Example*  Prove that the line drawn from the centre of a circle through the mid-point of a chord is the perpendicular bisector of the chord.

*Proof*  Let M be the mid-point of the chord AB. Let O be the centre of the circle.

Consider the triangles OAM, OBM.

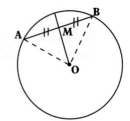

OA = OB (equal radii)
OM = OM (same line)
AM = BM (given)

Hence Δs $^{OAM}_{OBM}$ are congruent. (SSS)
Hence ∠OMA = ∠OMB.
But ∠OMA + ∠OMB = 180° (adjacent angles on straight line)
Hence both ∠OMA and ∠OMB are equal to 90°.
Hence OM is the perpendicular bisector of the chord AB.

## EXERCISE 14:5

**The diagrams are *not* drawn to scale.**

1.

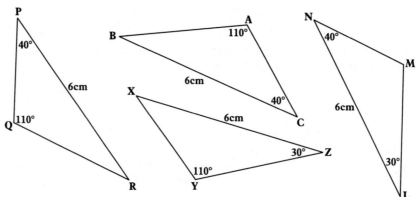

These four triangles are congruent.

(a) Copy and complete: Δs $^{PQR}_{C.....}$, Δs $^{PQR}_{..Y..}$, Δs $^{PQR}_{.....L}$ are congruent.

(b) Use your answers to **(a)** to write down the angles which are equal to angle R.

(c) Use your answers to **(a)** to find the sides equal to QR.

2.

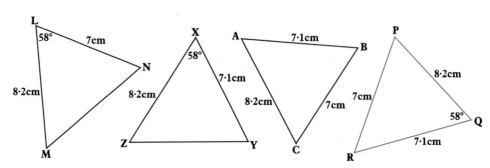

Which of the black triangles are congruent to the red triangle? Give reasons for your answer.

3. Three of these triangles are congruent. Which three?

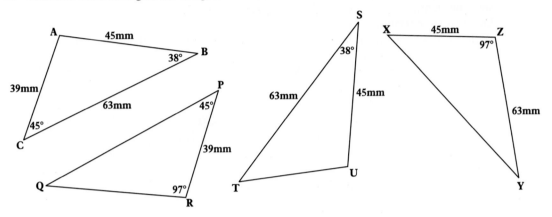

4. Which of the following pairs of triangles, A and B, are congruent? For those that are, state whether the reason is SSS or SAA or SAS or RHS.

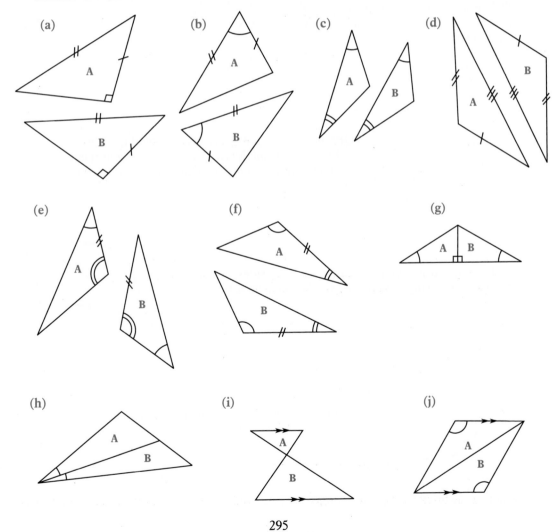

5. (a) Both △ ABC and △ PQR have angles of 80° and 60° and a side of 5cm. These triangles are *not* congruent.
Draw possible triangles ABC and PQR.
(b) Both △ LMN and △ XYZ have sides of 5cm and 8cm and an angle of 50°. These triangles are *not* congruent.
Draw possible triangles LMN and XYZ.

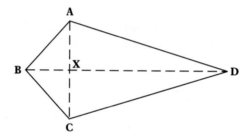

6. AC is a horizontal line; BD is a vertical line. Use congruent triangles to prove that AB = BD.

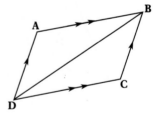

7. ABCD is a kite. The diagonals meet at X. Name all the pairs of congruent triangles in this diagram.

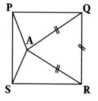

8.

PQRS is a square. △ AQR is an equilateral triangle.
(a) Prove that triangles APQ and ASR are congruent.
(b) Hence, or otherwise, show that △ PAS is isosceles.

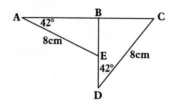

9. ABCD is a quadrilateral in which the opposite sides are parallel. Use congruent triangles to prove that the opposite sides are equal.

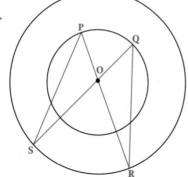

10.

O is the centre of both circles. Prove that ∠PSQ = ∠QRP.

296

11. This diagram represents a cuboid of length 4, width 4 and height 3 units.
    Is △ ABF congruent to △ CDB? Give reasons for your answer.

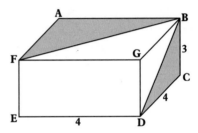

12.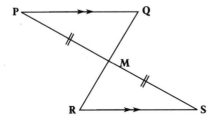

    PQ is parallel to RS. M is the mid-point of PS.
    Prove that QM = MR.

13. PQR is an equilateral triangle.
    X, Y, Z are points on the sides PQ, QR, RP such that PX = QY = RZ.
    Prove that △ XYZ is an equilateral triangle. (Hint: Prove that triangles PXZ, QYX, RZY are congruent).

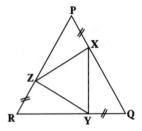

14.

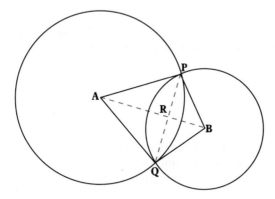

P and Q are the points where these two circles meet. A and B are the centres of the circles.
(a) Use congruent triangles to prove that ∠PAB = ∠QAB.
(b) Prove that △ PAR and △ QAR are congruent.
(c) Hence find the relationship between the line joining the centres and the chord that is common to both circles.

15. Prove that the bisector of the angle between the equal sides of an isosceles triangle bisects the third side.

16. The diagonals of a quadrilateral PQRS bisect each other at right angles. Prove that PQRS is a rhombus.

17.

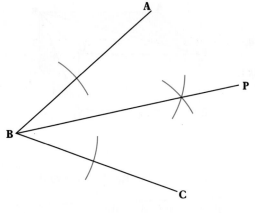

This diagram shows a construction for the bisector of the angle ABC.
Use congruent triangles to **prove** that the line BP bisects the angle ABC.

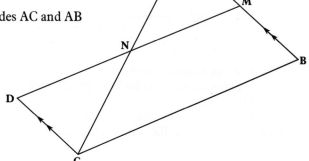

18. N and M are the mid-points of the sides AC and AB of the △ ABC. CD is parallel to BA.
   (a) Use congruent triangles to prove that CD = AM.
   (b) Hence prove that NM is parallel to CB.

**Review 1** Is it possible to draw two non-congruent triangles given that these triangles have a pair of equal angles and two pairs of equal sides? Explain your answer.

**Review 2** ABC is an isosceles triangle. M and N are the mid-points of the equal sides AB and AC. Use congruent triangles to prove that MC = NB.

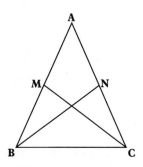

**Review 3**

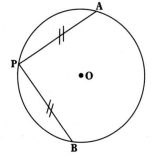

PA and PB are equal chords of the circle, centre O. Use congruent triangles to prove that OP bisects ∠BPA.

# FURTHER GEOMETRIC PROOFS

Facts other than congruence may be used to prove geometric results. (Geometry is the name given to the branch of mathematics concerned with points, lines, planes etc. That is, geometry is concerned with shape and space).

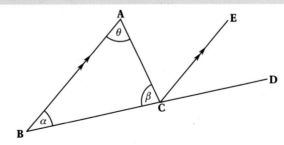

*Worked Example*  Using this diagram, prove that the sum of the angles in a triangle is 180°.

*Proof*  $\angle$ACE = $\theta$ (alternate angles, parallel lines)
$\angle$DCE = $\alpha$  (corresponding angles, parallel lines)
$\beta + \angle$ACE $+ \angle$DCE $= 180°$ (adjacent angles on straight line)
That is, $\beta + \theta + \alpha = 180°$.
Hence the sum of the angles in a triangle is 180°.

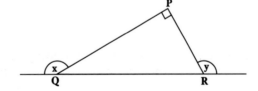

*Worked Example*  Prove that $x + y = 270°$.

*Proof*  $\angle$PQR $+ 90° = y$ (exterior angle of triangle)
$\angle$PQR $= 180° - x$  (adjacent angles on straight line)
Hence   $180° - x + 90° = y$
$270° - x = y$
$270° = x + y$

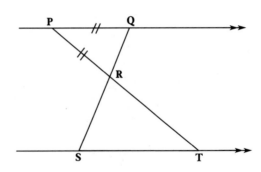

*Worked Example*  Prove that $\triangle$ SRT is an isosceles triangle.

***Proof***    Consider triangles PQR and TSR.

$$\angle PQR = \angle TSR \text{ (alternate angles, parallel lines)}$$
$$\angle QPR = \angle STR \text{ (alternate angles, parallel lines)}$$
$$\angle PRQ = \angle TRS \text{ (vertically opposite angles)}$$

Hence $\Delta$s $\frac{PQR}{TSR}$ are similar (equiangular).

Hence $\frac{PQ}{PR} = \frac{TS}{TR}$.

Since $\frac{PQ}{PR} = 1$, then $\frac{TS}{TR} = 1$. Hence TS = TR.

Hence $\Delta$ SRT is isosceles.

---

## EXERCISE 14:6

1. Use this diagram to prove that the exterior angle of a triangle is equal to the sum of the interior opposite angles.

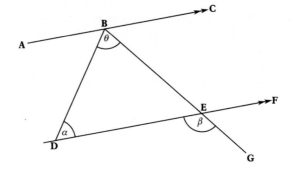

2.

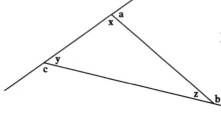

Prove that $a + b + c = 2(x + y + z)$.

3. Prove that $\Delta$s $\frac{XYZ}{NYM}$ are similar.

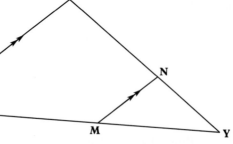

4.

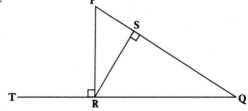

Prove that $\angle RPQ = \angle SRQ$.

5. Prove that $\beta = \alpha + \theta$.

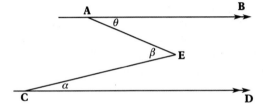

6. Read the following proof. Explain what the result of this proof is.
   What reason should be given for each numbered statement?

   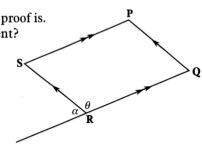

   | | |
   |---|---|
   | Angle S $= \alpha$ | ...(1) |
   | Angle Q $= \alpha$ | ...(2) |
   | Angle P $= 180° -$ Angle Q | ...(3) |
   | $= 180° - \alpha$ | |

   $$\angle P + \angle Q + \angle R + \angle S = 180° - \alpha + \alpha + \theta + \alpha$$
   $$= 180° + \alpha + \theta$$
   $$= 180° + 180° \qquad ...(4)$$
   $$= 360°$$

7.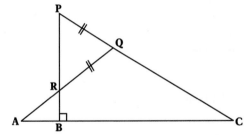

   Given that PQ = QR and $\angle$PBC = 90°
   prove that $\triangle$ QAC is isosceles.

**Review 1** Use this diagram to prove that the exterior angle of a triangle is equal to the sum of the interior opposite angles.

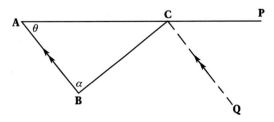

**Review 2**

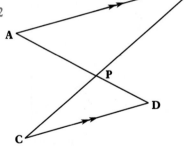

Prove that $\triangle$s $\frac{ABP}{DCP}$ are similar.

Review 3 Given that CF = FD and both ∠BAC and ∠BED are right angles, prove that ∠ABD = ∠EBD.

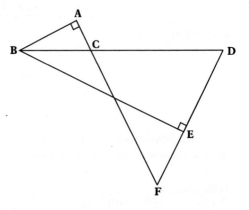

---

## RESEARCH PROJECT 14:7

**Euclid's Methods**

In this chapter we have used formal setting out when proving a geometric result. This setting out is based on the methods used by the Greek mathematician Euclid who lived in the 3rd century B.C. Research some of Euclid's work.

---

### CHAPTER 14   REVIEW

1.  The pattern on a certain wallpaper is made using two **similar** kite shapes as shown.

Not to scale

In the larger kite *ABCD*, *AD* = 9cm and *CD* = 16cm.
In the smaller kite *PQRS*, *PQ* = 12cm.

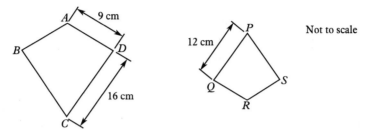

(a) Calculate the length of *QR*.
(b) What is the connection between angles *ADC* and *PQR*?

The area of the small kite, *PQRS* is 81cm².
(c) Calculate the area of the large kite, *ABCD*.          **SEG**

2. Two tins of pet food are similar in shape.
   The small size has height 12cm and volume 150cm³.
   The large size has height 16cm.

Calculate the volume of the large size.          **SEG**

3. A sign manufacturer makes solid plastic letters for shop names. He made a scale model of the
   letter F from a rectangular block of wood measuring 15cm high, 7·5cm wide and 1cm thick.

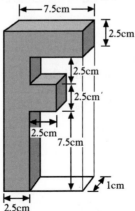

(a) Calculate the volume of the wooden letter F.
(b) The height of the actual letter is to be 60cm. What is the ratio of the height of the actual
    letter to that of the scale model? Give your answer in its simplest form.
(c) What volume of plastic would be used in the actual letter F?          **NICCEA**

**4.** $AD = 4$cm, $BC = 6$cm, angle $BCD = 35°$.
$BD$ is perpendicular to $AC$.

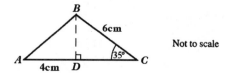

Not to scale

(a) Calculate $BD$.

(b) Calculate angle $BAC$.

(c) Triangle $A'B'C'$ is similar to triangle $ABC$.
The area of triangle $A'B'C'$ is nine times the area of triangle $ABC$.
  (i) What is the size of angle $A'B'C'$?
  (ii) Work out the length of $B'C'$.

**SEG**

**5.**

Cheesecake Recipe

Base  6 oz. Crushed digestive biscuits     Filling   12 oz. Soft cheese
      2 oz. Butter                                   2 oz. Sugar
      2 oz. Chopped nuts                             2 Teaspoons of cornflour

Grease a 7½ inch diameter cake tin. Cover the base of the tin with the chopped nuts. Melt the butter and mix with the crushed biscuits. Spoon the mixture ...

The recipe continues to explain how to make the cheesecake.
A 15 inch diameter cheesecake is to be made for a party. It is not simply a matter of doubling the quantities of ingredients.

Find the quantity of chopped nuts needed to make the cheesecake for the party.
You **must** show your working.

**WJEC**

**6.** Two wine bottles have similar shapes.
The standard bottle has a height of 30cm and the small bottle has a height of 23·5cm.

(a) Calculate the ratio of the areas of the bases of the two bottles.
    Give your answer in the form $n : 1$.

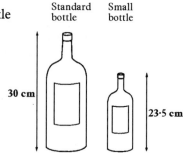

(b) What is the ratio of the volumes of the two bottles?
    Give your answer in the form $n : 1$.

(c) Is it a fair description to call the small bottle a 'half bottle'? Give a reason for your answer.

**MEG**

304

**7.**

These two tins are mathematically similar.
One holds 400ml and the other holds 800ml. The height of the smaller tin is 8cm.
Calculate the height of the larger tin. Give your answer to the nearest millimetre.    **ULEAC**

**8.**

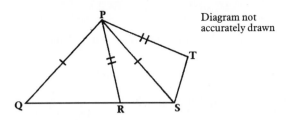

Diagram not accurately drawn

In the diagram, PQ = PS and PR = PT. Angle RPT = angle SPQ.
**(a)** Show that triangles PRQ and PTS are congruent.
**(b)** Hence, show that PS bisects angle QST.    **ULEAC**

**9.**

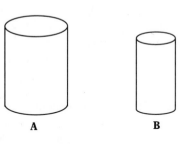

Diagram NOT accurately drawn

The two containers A and B are similar.
The surface area of container A is 1000cm².
The surface area of container B is 62·5cm².
The volume of container A is 2500cm³.
Calculate the volume of container B.    **ULEAC**

### ARC LENGTH. AREA of SECTOR and SEGMENT

Part of the circumference of a circle is
called an arc. A sector of a circle is
bounded by two radii and an arc.
A segment of a circle is bounded by
an arc and a chord.

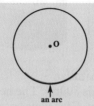
an arc

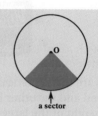
a sector

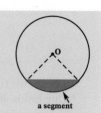
a segment

## DISCUSSION EXERCISE 15:1

- What fraction of a complete circle is the shaded section? What is the area of
  the shaded section?

  What if the shaded section is a quarter-circle?

  Discuss how to find the area of the sectors shown below.

- What information do you need, to find the area of the shaded segment?
  Discuss.

- Which arc is the arc AB? Discuss.

  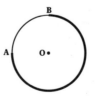 

  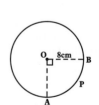

  What fraction of the circumference is the arc APB? What is the length
  of the arc APB?

  Discuss how to find the length of the arcs APB shown below.

$$\frac{\text{Length of arc APB}}{\text{Length of circumference}} = \frac{\theta}{360}$$

$$\frac{\text{Length of arc APB}}{2\pi r} = \frac{\theta}{360}$$

$$\text{Length of arc APB} = \frac{\theta}{360} \times 2\pi r$$

$$\frac{\text{Area of sector OAPB}}{\text{Area of circle}} = \frac{\theta}{360}$$

$$\frac{\text{Area of sector OAPB}}{\pi r^2} = \frac{\theta}{360}$$

$$\text{Area of sector OAPB} = \frac{\theta}{360} \times \pi r^2$$

*Worked Example*   Find the area and perimeter of a sector of a circle of radius 16cm if the angle at the centre is 7.6°.

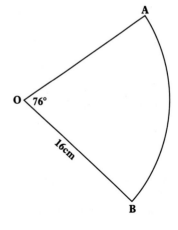

*Answer*

$$\frac{\text{Area of sector}}{\text{Area of circle}} = \frac{76}{360}$$

$$\frac{\text{Area of sector}}{\pi \times 16^2} = \frac{76}{360}$$

$$\text{Area of sector} = \pi \times 16^2 \times \frac{76}{360}$$
$$= 170\text{cm}^2 \text{ (3 s.f.)}$$

$$\frac{\text{Length of arc AB}}{\text{Circumference of circle}} = \frac{76}{360}$$

$$\frac{\text{Length of arc AB}}{2\pi \times 16} = \frac{76}{360}$$

$$\text{Length of arc AB} = 2\pi \times 16 \times \frac{76}{360}$$
$$= 21\cdot2\text{cm (3 s.f.)}$$

$$\text{Perimeter of sector} = 21\cdot2 + 16 + 16$$
$$= 53\cdot2\text{cm (3 s.f.)}$$

*Worked Example*   John made a clown's hat for his brother. The diagram represents the pattern he used. Find r if the area of the pattern is 700cm².

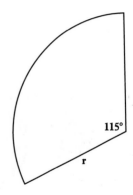

**Answer**    $\dfrac{\text{Area of sector}}{\text{Area of circle}} = \dfrac{115}{360}$

$$\dfrac{700}{\pi r^2} = \dfrac{115}{360}$$

$$700 \times 360 = 115\pi r^2$$

$$\dfrac{700 \times 360}{115\pi} = r^2$$

$$r = \sqrt{\dfrac{700 \times 360}{115\pi}}$$

$$= 26\text{cm (2 s.f.)}$$

## EXERCISE 15:2

**Use the calculator value for π or use π = 3·14.**

1. Find the area of the sectors OPR.

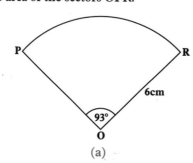

(a)

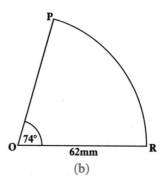

(b)

2. Find the length of the curved edge of each of the shapes in **question 1**.

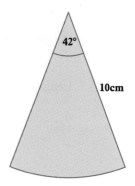

3. Christmas decorations are made from the pattern shown.
   (a) What area is this pattern?
   (b) Braid is sewn right around the outside of each decoration. How much braid is needed for 15 decorations.

4.

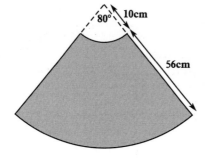

Karen is making a ballroom dancing skirt. Each panel of this skirt is the shape shown shaded in the diagram. How much material is used for each panel? Give the answer in square metres.

5.  (a) If the area of this shape is 100mm²
        and CB = 8mm, find the size of
        angle ACB.
    (b) If the area of this shape is 82·5cm²
        and ∠ACB = 110°, find the length
        of the radius AC.

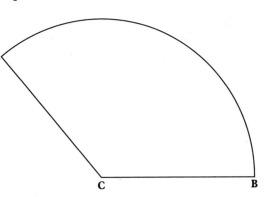

6.

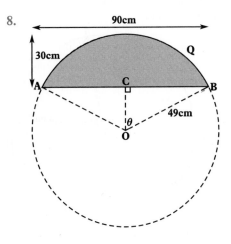

A portion of cheesecake is shown. The area of the shaded
surface is 50cm².
Find r, giving the answer to 2 significant figures.

7.  A group of security lights can be
    adjusted to light up an area close to the
    lights (shown shaded) or a much larger
    area. This larger area has a radius of
    80m as shown.
    (a) Find the size of the angle marked
        as θ.
    (b) Find the area of the shaded
        section.

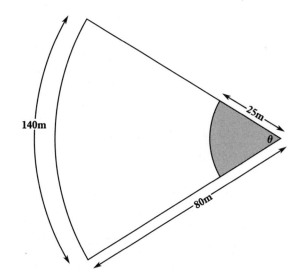

8.

The shaded segment represents the template for
the back of a plastic outdoor chair.
(a) Find the lengths of CB and OC.
(b) Find the area of triangle OCB. Hence find the
    area of triangle OAB.
(c) Use trigonometry to find θ. Hence find the
    size of ∠AOB.
(d) Find the area of the sector OAQB.
(e) Find the surface area of the back of the chair.

9. An archway consists of a straight base AB and two arcs, AC and CB. Arc CB has centre A and arc AC has centre B.
   (a) Explain why triangle ACB is an equilateral triangle.
   (b) Show that the area of triangle ACB is $4\sqrt{3}$ square metres.
   (c) Show that the area under the archway is $\frac{16}{3}\pi - 4\sqrt{3}$ square metres.

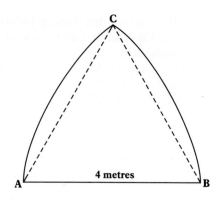

**Review 1**

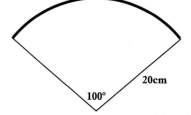

A fan is the shape of a sector of a circle.
(a) Find the area of this fan.
(b) Find the length of the perimeter of this fan.

**Review 2**

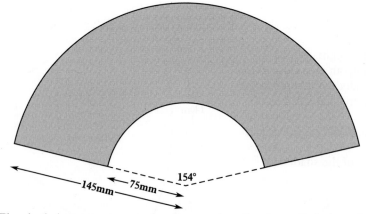

The shaded area represents the pattern piece for the neck facing of a jacket.
(a) How much material is used for this facing? Give your answer in cm².
(b) Find the perimeter of this facing. Give your answers in cm.

**Review 3** (a) Use trigonometry to find the radius, OB, of the circle.
Hence find the area of the sector OAXB.
(b) Find the length of OP.
Hence find the area of triangle OAB.
(c) Find the area of the shaded segment.

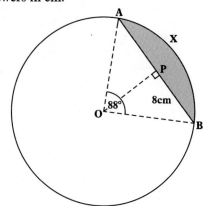

**Review 4**

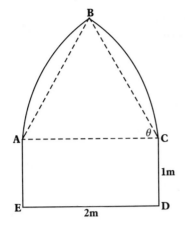

ABCDE represents a stained glass window. Arc BC has centre A; arc AB has centre C.
(a) Explain why the angle marked as $\theta$ is 60°.
(b) Show that the perimeter of this window is $(\frac{4}{3}\pi + 4)$ metres.

## SURFACE AREA of CYLINDER, CONE, SPHERE

### DISCUSSION EXERCISE 15:3

● Which of the nets below fold to give this hollow cylinder? (Each circle has radius r.) Discuss.

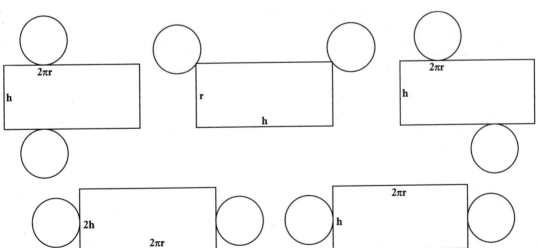

Can those nets which do not fold to give the cylinder be adjusted to do so? Discuss.

● Discuss how the net of a cylinder may be used to find formulae for the curved surface area and for the total surface area.

Adrian claimed that a formula for the total surface area of a cylinder with base radius r and height h is $A = 2\pi r (r + h)$. Is Adrian correct? Discuss.

## INVESTIGATION and DISCUSSION EXERCISE 15:4

### Curved Surface Area of a Cone

Show that the area of the shaded sector is 40πcm² and the
length of the arc ABC is 8πcm.
If the sector OABC is cut out and folded so that the edges
OA and OC are joined, a cone is formed – see the diagram
below.

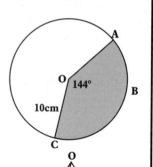

Karla stated that for this cone, the area of the curved surface = $\pi rl$
where r is the radius of the base and $l$ is the slant height (the
length OA or OB). Karla began her argument in support of her
statement as follows.

Since length of arc = $8\pi$ then length of circumference of cone = $8\pi$.
Using $C = 2\pi r$, $8\pi = 2\pi r$

$$\frac{8\pi}{2\pi} = r$$

$$r = 4\text{cm}$$

Since area of sector = $40\pi$ then area of curved surface of cone = $40\pi$.

How might Karla have continued her argument? **Discuss.**

Find the areas of cones formed from sectors of other sizes.
Is the formula  Curved Surface Area = $\pi rl$  true for these cones? **Discuss.**
**Discuss** how to **prove** that the expression $\pi rl$ gives the curved surface area of a cone.
*Hint:* Begin with a sector of a circle of radius $l$ and angle $\theta$ at the centre.

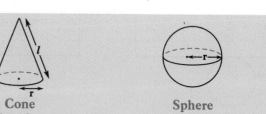

| Cylinder | Cone | Sphere |
|---|---|---|
| Curved surface area = $2\pi rh$ | Curved surface area = $\pi rl$, | Surface area = $4\pi r^2$ |
| Total surface area = $2\pi rh + 2\pi r^2$ | where $l$ is the slant height. | |

*Worked Example*  The radius of the base of a cone is 15mm.  The height is 20mm. Find the
curved surface area.

*Answer*  $l^2 = 20^2 + 15^2$ (Pythagoras' Theorem)
$l = 25$mm
Curved surface area $= \pi rl$
$= \pi \times 15 \times 25$
$= 1180$mm³ (3 s.f.)

*Worked Example*   A chimney is 4m high and has a diameter of 60cm.
Find its surface area.

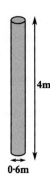

*Answer*   A chimney is an open cylinder, with no top or bottom.
The surface area is the curved surface area.
Curved surface area = 2πrh
$$= 2\pi \times 0.3 \times 4$$
$$= 7.5m^2 \text{ (2 s.f.)}$$

*Worked Example*   Find the total surface area of this
hemisphere, both base area and
curved surface area.

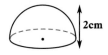

*Answer*   Curved surface area of sphere = $4\pi r^2$.
Curved surface area of hemisphere = $2\pi r^2$
$$= 2\pi \times 2^2$$
$$= 25cm^2 \text{ (2 s.f.)}$$

Base area = $\pi r^2$
$$= \pi \times 2^2$$
$$= 13cm^2 \text{ (2 s.f.)}$$
Total surface area = $38cm^2$ (2 s.f.)

*Worked Example*   The curved surface area of a cylinder is 272cm². Find the height of this
cylinder if the diameter is 20cm.

*Answer*   Curved surface area = 2πrh
$$272 = 2\pi \times 10 \times h$$
$$\frac{272}{2\pi \times 10} = h$$
$$h = 4.3cm \text{ (2 s.f.)}$$

## EXERCISE 15:5

**Use the calculator value for π or use π = 3·14.**

1.  A cylindrical tin has radius 3cm and height 10cm. How much metal is used to manufacture this tin?

2.  Alan is going to cover a hot-water cylinder with insulating cloth. Alan measured the diameter of the cylinder as 52cm and the height as 1·2m. Alan then calculated the curved surface area. What answer should he get?

3.  A concrete tank has diameter 2·7m and stands 3m high. What is the total surface area of this tank?

4.  Find the surface area of a tennis ball which has a diameter of 6·4cm.

5.  A label is to cover the curved surface of a Baked Beans tin. This tin has a diameter of 74mm and a height of 115mm. What are the dimensions of the label if it is to have an overlap of 5mm?

6. Find the curved surface area of these cones.
   (a) diameter 10cm, slant height 6cm
   (b) radius 5mm, height 8mm

7. A spherical balloon had radius 110mm. Find the surface area.

8. A funnel is an "upside-down" cone with base diameter 12cm and slant height 8·3cm. Find the surface area of this funnel.

9. The cardboard centre of a toilet roll is 10cm long and has diameter of 3·8cm. How much cardboard is used for one of these centres?

10. Which tin needs the most sheet metal?

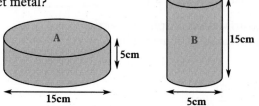

11. The shapes below consist of cones, spheres or hemispheres and cylinders. Find the curved surface area of each. (a)    (b)    (c)

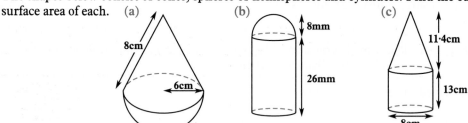

12. A 5·2m tall cylindrical lamppost is covered with ivy. The circumference of the lamppost is measured as 45cm.
    List the steps which need to be taken to find the area covered with ivy.
    Find this area.

13. (a) Find the height of the cylinder which has a curved surface area of 340cm² and radius of 18cm.
    (b) Find the diameter of the cylinder which has a curved surface area of 8m² and height of 1·4m.
    (c) The diameter of a cylinder is the same as the height. Find the diameter if the curved surface area is 560cm².
    (d) Find the radius of a sphere which has surface area of 40cm².

14. The height and radius of a cone are equal. The curved surface area is 14cm². Calculate the height of this cone.

15. (a) Make h the subject of the formula $A = 2\pi rh + 2\pi r^2$.
    (b) Hence, or otherwise, find the height of the cylinder which has a total surface area of 20m² and a diameter of 2·8m.

16. (a) The total surface area of a 4m high tank is 40m². If $\pi$ is taken as 3·1 show that the radius of this tank can be found by solving the quadratic equation $6·2r^2 + 24·8r - 40 = 0$.
    (b) Solve the equation to find the radius.

Review 1 (a) An ice-cream cone has base radius 32mm and slant height 9·5cm. Find its surface area.

(b) A paper weight is a hemispherical shape with diameter 7cm. Find the total surface area of this paper weight.

Review 2  Find the minimum area of paper required for the label on the outside of this tin, if the height is 3·1cm and the diameter of the circular base is 12cm.

Review 3 Find the amount of metal needed to make 100 of the tins shown in **Review 2**. Give the answer in square metres.

Review 4 The curved surface area of a cylinder is 6·2m². If the height of this cylinder is 1·6m, find the radius.

Review 5 Ann is making fancy dress hats for herself and Floyd. She is making herself a conical "witches" hat and Floyd a cylindrical hat. Both are to be 40cm tall. Ann measures her head circumference as 55cm and Floyd's as 56cm. Which hat will have the greater surface area and by how much?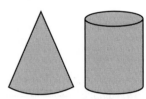

## INVESTIGATION 15:6

### Container Size

A manufacturer wishes to make a cylindrical metal can which has a volume of 400cm³. He wants this can to be as cheap as possible to produce, which means he must use as little metal as possible. Find the dimensions of the can that will cost the least. Comment on your findings.

## VOLUME of CONE and SPHERE

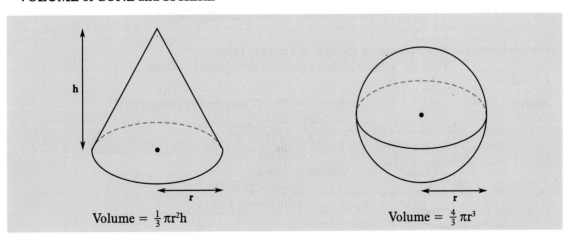

Volume = $\frac{1}{3}\pi r^2 h$          Volume = $\frac{4}{3}\pi r^3$

*Worked Example*  Find the volume of  (a) a sphere of diameter 14cm
(b) a cone of height 2m and base radius 60cm.

***Answer***  (a)

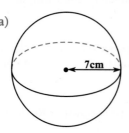

(b)

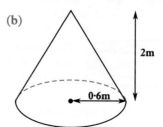

$V = \frac{4}{3}\pi r^3$

$= \frac{4}{3}\pi \times 7^3$

$= 1440 \text{cm}^3$ (3 s.f.)

$V = \frac{1}{3}\pi r^2 h$

$= \frac{1}{3}\pi \times 0{\cdot}6^2 \times 2$

$= 0{\cdot}75 \text{m}^3$ (2 s.f.)

*Worked Example*  Both a cone and a hemisphere have base diameter of 18cm. If the height of the cone is 10cm show that the ratio of the volume of the cone to the volume of the hemisphere is 5 : 9.

***Answer***

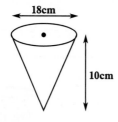

$V = \frac{1}{3}\pi r^2 h$

$= \frac{1}{3}\pi \times 9^2 \times 10$

$V = \frac{1}{2} \times \frac{4}{3}\pi r^3$

$= \frac{1}{2} \times \frac{4}{3}\pi \times 9^3$

$$\frac{\text{Volume of cone}}{\text{Volume of hemisphere}} = \frac{\frac{1}{3}\pi \times 9^2 \times 10}{\frac{2}{3}\pi \times 9^3}$$

$$= \frac{10}{18}$$

$$= \frac{5}{9}$$

That is,  Volume of cone : Volume of hemisphere = 5 : 9

*Worked Example*  The diameter of the base of a cone is 14cm.
Find the volume of the cone if the slant height is 25cm.

***Answer***

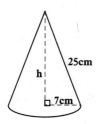

$h^2 + 7^2 = 25^2$  (Theorem of Pythagoras)

$h^2 = 25^2 - 7^2$

$h = \sqrt{25^2 - 7^2}$

$= 24 \text{cm}$

$\text{Volume} = \frac{1}{3}\pi r^2 h$

$= \frac{1}{3}\pi \times 7^2 \times 24$

$= 1230 \text{cm}^3$ (3 s.f.)

## EXERCISE 15:7

**Throughout this exercise use the calculator value for π or π = 3·14.**

1. Find the volume of these. Round your answers sensibly.

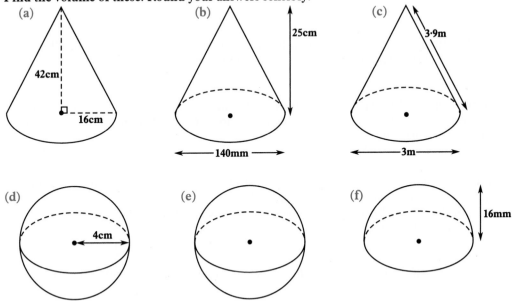

(a) 42cm, 16cm

(b) 25cm, 140mm

(c) 3·9m, 3m

(d) 4cm

(e) 1·2m

(f) 16mm

2. Find the volume of the following cones.   (a) Base diameter 34cm, height 150mm.
   (b) Base radius 1·5m, slant height 2·5m.

3. A table tennis ball has diameter 35mm. What is its volume?

4. This sketch is of a spherical bowl. The top half is a lid. Its diameter is 16cm. The lid is removed and the bottom of the bowl is filled to the top with jelly. How many litres of jelly are there in the bowl?

5. The shapes below consist of cones, spheres or hemispheres and cylinders. Find the volumes.

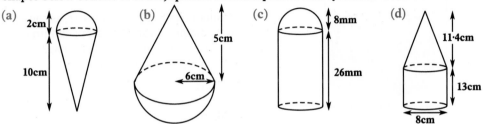

(a) 2cm, 10cm

(b) 5cm, 6cm

(c) 8mm, 26mm

(d) 11·4cm, 13cm, 8cm

6. Tennis balls are packed into rectangular boxes 325mm × 260mm × 195mm. Each tennis ball is 65mm in diameter. Estimate the maximum number of balls in a box. Calculate this maximum number.

7. 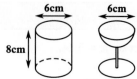 The tumbler is cylindrical in shape. The wine glass is hemispherical. The wine glass is filled with wine then this wine is poured into the tumbler. How far up the tumbler does the wine reach?

8. A ball of string fits snugly inside a cardboard box which is a cube of side 8cm. What percentage of the space inside the box is not taken up with the string?

9. Joanne bought a 2-litre pack of ice-cream for her nephews's birthday party. She scooped the ice-cream into spherical balls using a scoop of diameter 6cm. How many ice-cream balls could Joanne make from this pack?

10. A tree in Deborah's garden is a perfect conical shape. Deborah measures the circumference of the base as 5·42m and the slant height as 4·84m.
    (a) List the steps to be taken to calculate the volume of this tree.
    (b) Calculate this volume.

11. Which is worth more, three gold spheres each of radius 2mm or one gold sphere of radius 3mm?

12. A boiler consists of a cylindrical section with a hemispherical section on each end.
    Find the maximum weight of water this boiler can hold. (1 litre of water weighs 1kg.)

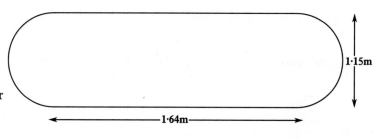

13. 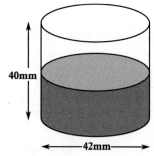 This cylinder is half filled with water, as shown. A sphere of diameter 15mm is dropped into the water and sinks. How much does the water rise?

14. A hollow fibreglass ball has inside diameter 17cm and outside diameter 17·5cm. How many litres of molten fibreglass are needed for one of these balls? (Give the answer to the nearest tenth of a litre.)

15.

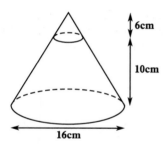 

The top part of a cone is sliced off, forming the shaded shapes.
(a) Use similar triangles to find the radius r of the red shaded cone.
(b) Find the volume of the red cone. (Leave π in your answer.)
(c) What is the ratio   volume of original cone : volume of red cone?

16. The sphere fits snugly into the cylinder. Find the following ratios
(a) volume of sphere : volume of cylinder
(b) volume of sphere : volume not occupied by sphere.

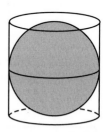

17. A sphere has volume of 82cm³. Find the diameter of this sphere.

18.

The shaded sector is folded to make a cone. Show that
(a) the radius of the base is 6cm
(b) the volume is 96πcm³.

**Review 1**   Find the volume of
(a) a cone of height 13cm and base diameter 9cm
(b) a sphere of radius 1·2m
(c)                                                             (d)

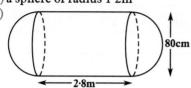 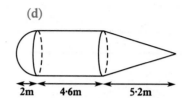

**Review 2**  A metal bar, shaped as
shown, is melted down and
reformed into spherical balls
of diameter 6mm. What is the
maximum number of such
balls that can be made from this bar?

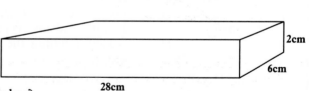

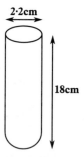

**Review 3** This test-tube consists of a cylindrical part and a hemispherical part. What is the maximum weight of water that can be held in this test-tube? (1 m*l* of water weighs 1 gram.)

**Review 4**

Four tennis balls, each of diameter 64mm, fit snugly into one of these tubes. Find the ratio of the space occupied by the tennis balls to the space not occupied.

---

## DISCUSSION EXERCISE 15:8

Volume of cylinder = πr²h
Volume of cone = $\frac{1}{3}$πr²h

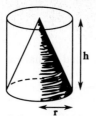

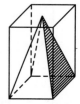

Is it also true that the volume of the pyramid is one-third the volume of the prism? Discuss.

---

## RESEARCH PROJECT 15:9

**Radians**

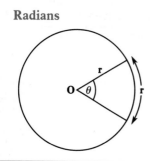

Angles may be measured in **radians** rather than degrees. In this diagram $\theta = 1$ radian.
Research radians. As part of your research include the use of radians in finding the length of an arc and the area of a sector.

## CHAPTER 15   REVIEW

1. There is an infra-red sensor in a security system.
   The sensor can detect movement inside a sector of a circle.
   The radius of the circle is 15m.
   The sector angle is 110°.

   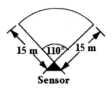

   Calculate the area of the sector.                                        **ULEAC**

2. A cylindrical pencil holder is shown.
   The height is 15cm and the diameter 6cm.
   **(a)** What is the capacity of the pencil holder?
   **(b)** The outer curved surface area is covered with coloured paper.
   What is the area of the paper?

   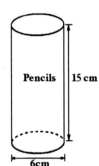

                                                                            **NEAB**

3.

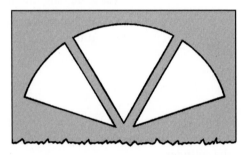

   The diagram shows glass sectors in a wooden door. The angles of the sectors are 40°, 60°, 40°
   and the radius of each sector is 24cm.
   **(a)** Calculate the total area of glass used in the sectors. You may take $\pi = 3 \cdot 14$.
   **(b)** Thin strips of wooden framing (which can be curved) are to be placed along the
   perimeter of each sector.

   Calculate the total length of framing required, giving the answer in metres correct to
   1 decimal place.                                                         **NICCEA**

4. A spinning top which consists of a cone of base radius 5cm, height 9cm and a hemisphere of
   radius 5cm is illustrated below.

   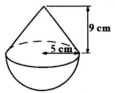

   **(a)** Calculate the volume of the spinning top.
   **(b)** Calculate the total surface area of the spinning top.            **SEG**

5. The diagram represents the landing area for a shot put competition. OACB is a sector of a circle, centre O, radius 10m. Angle AOB equals 80°.

   (a) Calculate the length of the straight line AB.

   (b) Calculate the length of the arc ACB.

   (c) Calculate the area of the sector OACB.

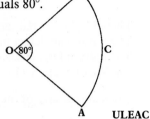

**ULEAC**

6.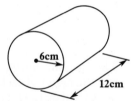

NOT TO SCALE

The diagram shows the cross-section of a tunnel which has a maximum height of 4m above its horizontal base AB. The roof of the tunnel is part of a circle, centre O and radius 14·5m.

The mid point of AB is X.

   (a) (i) Write down the length of OX.
      (ii) Calculate the length of AB.

   (b) Calculate the size of angle BOX.

   (c) Calculate the area of cross-section of the tunnel. **MEG**

7. (a) This diagram shows a cylinder of radius 6cm and length 12cm. Calculate the volume of the cylinder.

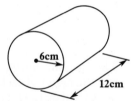

   (b) This diagram shows the same cylinder fitting tightly inside a box. The box is a cube. Calculate the volume of the space around the cylinder inside the cube.

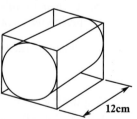

   (c) This diagram shows a sphere of radius 6cm fitting tightly inside a box. The box is a cube. Calculate the volume of the space around the sphere, inside the cube.

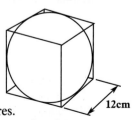

   (d) The **same** sized cube is tightly filled with 216 **identical** smaller spheres. What is the ratio of the radius of a small sphere to the radius of the large sphere? **SEG**

**8.** Paul is painting a wall. He can reach an area *ABCDE* as shown.
The area consists of three parts:
a sector *BDE* of a circle of radius 2·5m and angle 70° and two right angled congruent
triangles *EAB* and *DCB*.

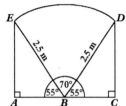

(a) Calculate the distance *AB*.
(b) Calculate the area of the sector *BDE*.
　　Take π to be 3.14 or use the π key on your calculator.
(c) Calculate the area *ABCDE* Paul can reach.
(d) Calculate the perimeter of the shape *ABCDE*.

**SEG**

**9.**

  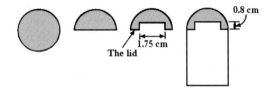

A shampoo company makes a small container. The lid is made from a solid sphere, cut in
half. A cylindrical shape is removed so that the lid pushes onto a cylindrical shape at the top
of the container.
The diameter of the sphere is 3·5cm.

(a) Calculate the volume of the sphere.
　　Volume of sphere $\frac{4}{3}\pi r^3$. (You may take π = 3·14.)

　　The cylindrical shape has diameter 1·75cm and height 0·8cm.
(b) Calculate the volume of the cylindrical shape.
(c) Calculate the volume of the lid.
(d) The company also makes a larger container and lid with all dimensions double the sizes
　　above. Calculate the volume of the lid of the larger container.　　**NICCEA**

**10.**

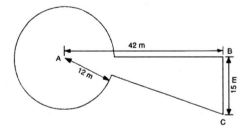

The diagram shows a plan of a water-hazard on a new golf course. The hazard is bounded by
the arc of a circle centre A and part of a right-angled triangle ABC. The radius of the circle is
12 metres, AB = 42m, BC = 15m.
Calculate the surface area of the water.　　**MEG**

# Angle and Tangent Properties of Circles

## INTRODUCTION

Angle Relationships

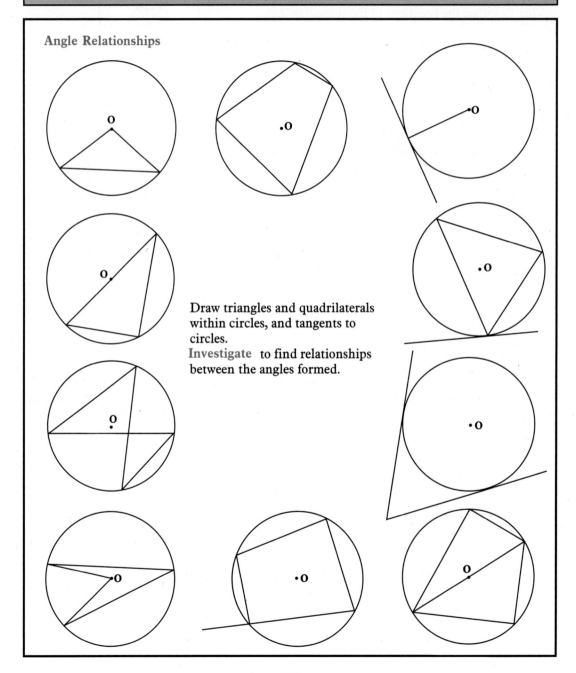

Draw triangles and quadrilaterals within circles, and tangents to circles.
Investigate to find relationships between the angles formed.

# ANGLES in CIRCLES

Some relationships between angles in circles are illustrated in the following diagrams.

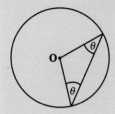

Equal angles are at the base of the isosceles triangle formed by two radii and a chord.

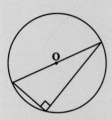

The angle at the circumference, standing on a diameter, is a right angle. This relationship is usually known as "angle in a semicircle".

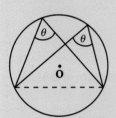

Angles at the circumference, which stand on the same arc, are equal. This relationship is usually known as "angles in the same segment".

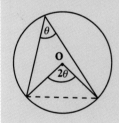

If an angle at the centre and an angle at the circumference stand on the same arc then the angle at the centre is double the angle at the circumference. This relationship is usually known as "angle at centre".

*Worked Example* Find the size of α. Give reasons.

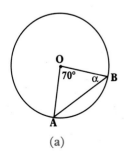

(a)

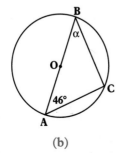

(b)

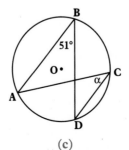

(c)

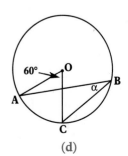

(d)

***Answer***    (a)   ∠OAB = α   (isosceles triangle formed with equal radii)
            $70° + α + α = 180°$   (angle sum of triangle)
                     $2α = 110°$
                     $α = 55°$
       (b)   ∠ACB = 90°   (angle in semicircle)
            $α + 46° + 90° = 180°$   (angle sum of triangle)
                    $α = 44°$
       (c)   $α = 51°$   (angles in same segment)
       (d)   $60° = 2α$   (angle at centre)
              $α = 30°$

*Worked Example*

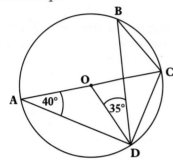

Find the size of   (a)   angle ADO
                      (b)   angle ACD
                      (c)   angle CBD
                      (d)   angle COD
                      (e)   angle BDC.

***Answer***    (a)   ∠ADO = 40°   (ΔAOD is isosceles)
       (b)   Since ∠ADC = 90° (angle in semicircle) then   ∠ACD = 50° (angle sum of ΔACD).
       (c)   ∠CBD = 40° (∠CBD = ∠CAD, angles in same segment)
       (d)   ∠COD = 80° (angle at centre)
       (e)   Since ∠BDC + 35° + ∠ADO = 90° (angle in semicircle) then   ∠BDC = 15°.

*Worked Example*

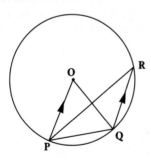

If OP = PQ, prove that RQ = PQ.

***Proof***    Since OP = OQ (equal radii) and OP = PQ (given) then OP = OQ = PQ.
         Hence ΔOPQ is an equilateral triangle.
         Hence angle POQ = 60°.
         Since ∠POQ = 2 ∠PRQ (angle at centre) then ∠PRQ = 30°.
         Since ∠OPR = ∠PRQ (alternate angles, parallel lines) then ∠OPR = 30°.
         Then ∠RPQ = 30° (∠RPQ = ∠OPQ – ∠OPR).
         Since ∠PRQ = ∠RPQ then ΔPRQ is isosceles. Hence RQ = PQ.

## EXERCISE 16:2

1.

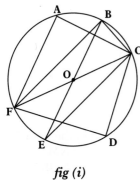

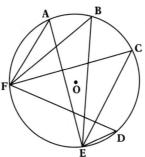

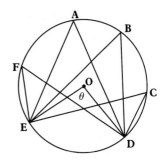

fig (i)                    fig (ii)                    fig (iii)

(a) Name all the right angles in *fig (i)*.
(b) In *fig (ii)*, name all the angles which are equal to ∠FBE.
(c) In *fig (iii)*, name all the angles which are equal to $\frac{1}{2}\theta$.
(d) In *fig (iii)*, name an angle which is equal to ∠ADC.

2. Find the size of $\theta$. Give a reason for your answer.

(a)              (b)              (c)              (d)

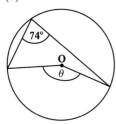

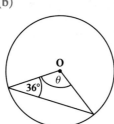

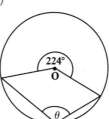

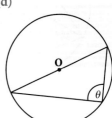

3. Find, with reasons, the size of the angles marked as $\alpha$, $\beta$ and $\theta$.

(a)                    (b)                    (c)

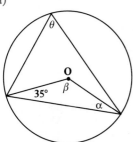

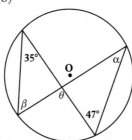

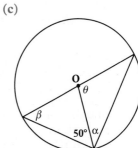

4. (i)

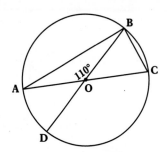

(ii)

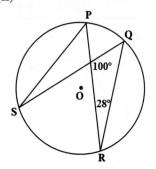

(iii)

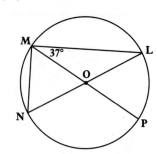

Find the size of
(a) angle BOC
(b) angle CBD
(c) angle ABO
(d) angle AOD.

Find the size of
(a) ∠PSQ
(b) ∠SPR.

Find the size of
(a) ∠NML
(b) ∠NOP.

5. Find the size of the angles marked as p, q and r.

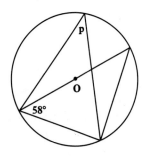

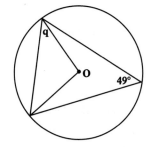

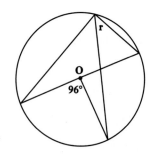

6. (i)

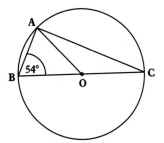

(ii)

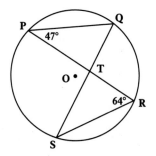

(iii)

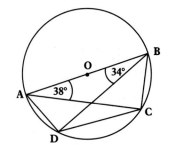

Find the size of
(a) ∠AOC
(b) ∠BAO.

Find the size
of ∠PTQ.

Find the size of
(a) ∠ADC
(b) ∠BCD.

7. (i)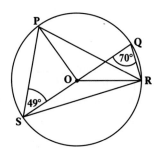

(ii)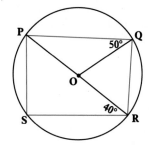

Find the size of
(a) angle QRP
(b) angle SRP
(c) angle ROS
(d) angle ORP.

Find the size of ∠PQR.

8. Is the quadrilateral PQRS a rectangle? Explain your answer.

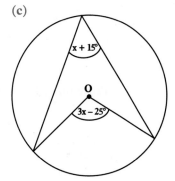

9.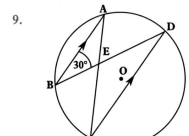

The chords AB and CD are parallel.
Prove that both the triangles ABE and DEC are isosceles.

10. Calculate the value of x.

(a)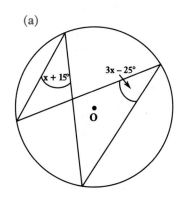

(b)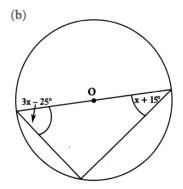

(c)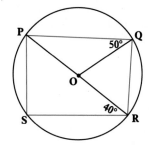

11.

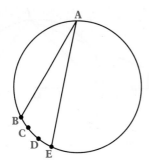

Screw holes are equally spaced around the edge of a disc. Some of these holes are shown. Angle BAE = 15°.
How many screw holes are there on the disc? Show your working.

12. Dancers in a musical are arranged in a circle. The lead dancers, Amy and Jon, are directly opposite each other. Amy dances to Naomi and then to Jon. What angle does Amy dance through? Does this angle depend on where Naomi is? Explain your answer.

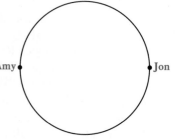

13.

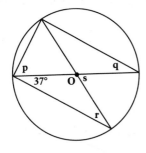

O is the centre of the circle.
(a) Use congruent triangles to prove that PR = SQ.
(b) Explain why PRQS is a rectangle.

**Review 1** Find the size of the named angles. Give brief reasons.

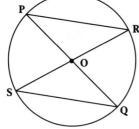

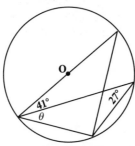

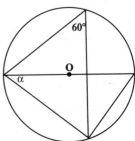

**Review 2** Prove that triangle PQR is an isosceles triangle.

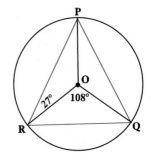

## DISCUSSION EXERCISE 16:3

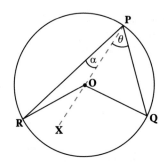

In terms of $\alpha$ and/or $\theta$, find the size of $\angle$PRO, $\angle$PQO, $\angle$ROX, $\angle$QOX.
**Discuss** how to continue to prove that $\angle$ROQ = 2 $\angle$RPQ.
What is this result usually known as?

• **Discuss** how to prove that $\angle$SPR = $\angle$SQR.
What is this result usually known as?

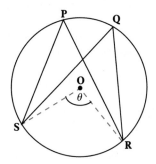

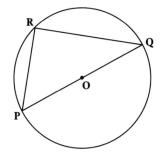

What is the size of $\angle$POQ?
Which arc does angle POQ stand on? Which arc does angle PRQ stand on?
**Discuss** how to continue to prove that angle PRQ is a right angle.
What is this result usually known as?

• In one of the following diagrams a circle can be drawn through the points A, B, C and D. Which diagram? **Discuss.**

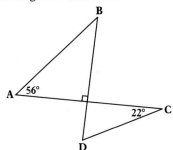

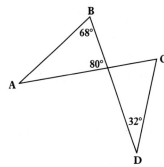

## CYCLIC QUADRILATERALS

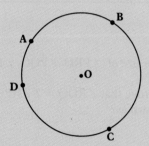 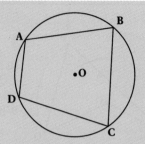

The points A, B, C, D lie on a circle. They are known as **concyclic points**.

The vertices A, B, C, D of the quadrilateral ABCD lie on a circle. This quadrilateral is called a **cyclic quadrilateral**.

Two of the relationships between the angles of a cyclic quadrilateral follow.

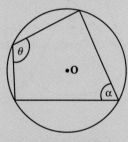

$$\theta + \alpha = 180°$$

In words, this relationship is "the opposite angles of a cyclic quadrilateral add to 180°." This result is known as **"opposite angles of cyclic quadrilateral."**

$$\beta = \theta$$

In words, this relationship is "an exterior angle of a cyclic quadrilateral equals the opposite interior angle." This result is known as **"exterior angle of cyclic quadrilateral."**

*Worked Example* Find the size of the angle marked as **a**.

(a)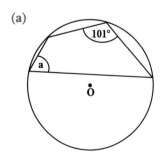

(b)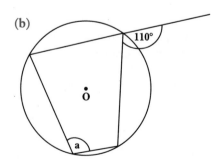

***Answer*** (a) a + 101° = 180° (opposite angles of cyclic quadrilateral)

   a = 79°

(b) a = 110° (exterior angle of cyclic quadrilateral)

*Worked Example* Find the size of ∠AED.

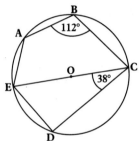

**Answer** Since ∠AEC and ∠ABC are opposite angles of cyclic quadrilateral ABCE then ∠AEC = 68°.
Since ∠EDC = 90° (angle in semicircle) then ∠CED = 52° (angle sum of Δ).
Hence ∠AED = 68° + 52°
= 120°

## EXERCISE 16:4

1. Which of p, q, r or s is the opposite interior angle to m?

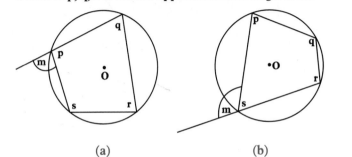

(a)          (b)          (c)

2. Find the size of θ.

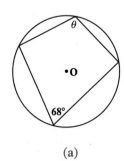

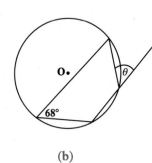

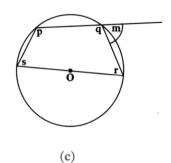

(a)          (b)          (c)

3. Find the size of a, b, c, d, and e. Give reasons.

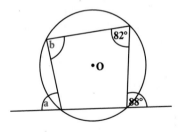

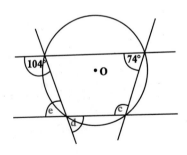

4. Find the size of $\theta$, $\alpha$ and $\beta$. State your reasons and show your working.

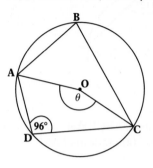 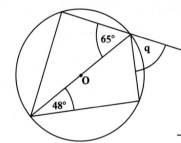

5. Find the size of p, q and r. Show your working.

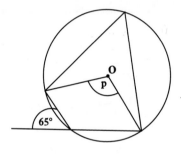 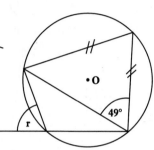

6. Find   (a) $\angle$SPQ
       (b) $\angle$PSO
       (c) $\angle$QRS.

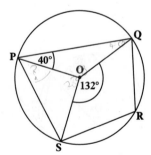

7.

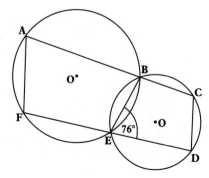

(i) Find the size of (a) angle BCD
                   (b) angle BEF
                   (c) angle FAB.

(ii) What can you say about the lines AF and CD? Give a reason.

8. Find the value of x. (a) 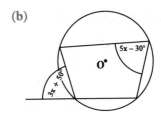 (b)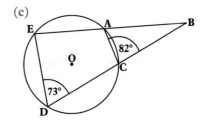

9.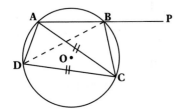

If AC = CD prove that CB bisects angle DBP.

Review 1  Find the size of ∠ABC.

(a) 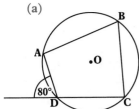 (b) 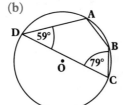 (c)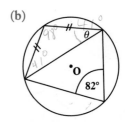

Review 2  Find the size of the angle θ.

(a) 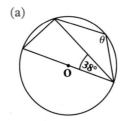 (b)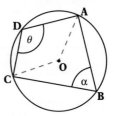

## DISCUSSION EXERCISE 16:5

- In terms of θ and/or α, find the size of the obtuse angle and the reflex angle at O.
  **Discuss** how to continue to prove that the opposite angles of a cyclic quadrilateral add to 180°.

-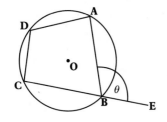

In terms of θ, what is the size of angle ∠ABC?
**Discuss** how to continue to prove that an exterior angle of a cyclic quadrilateral is equal to the opposite interior angle.

## ANGLES formed with TANGENTS

A **tangent** is a line which touches a circle. That is, a tangent meets a circle at just one point. This tangent, AB, touches the circle at P.

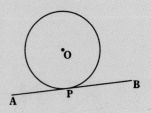

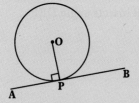

The radius, OP, is perpendicular to the tangent at P.

Two tangents may be drawn from any point outside the circle. For instance, this diagram shows the two tangents TP and TQ drawn from the point T.
The triangles TPO and TQO are congruent.

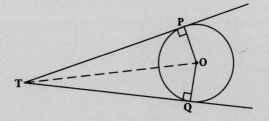

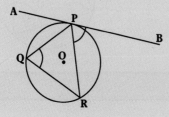

The angle between a tangent and a chord is equal to an angle at the circumference standing on that chord.
For instance, ∠BPR = ∠PQR.
This result is known as "angle in alternate segment."

---

## DISCUSSION EXERCISE 16:6

- TP and TQ are tangents to the circle.
  Prove that △s TPO and TQO are congruent.

  The fact that these triangles are congruent leads to the result "the line joining the centre of a circle to the point where two tangents meet, bisects the angle between the tangents." What other results can you deduce from the fact that these triangles are congruent? Discuss.

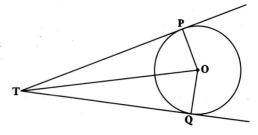

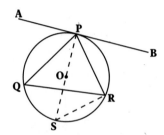

If ∠BPR = 60°, find the size of ∠RPS, ∠PSR, ∠PQR.
What if ∠BPR = 54°?
Discuss how to prove the result known as "angle in alternate segment."

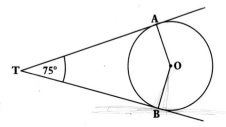

- TA and TB are tangents to the circle.
  Anita claims that a circle can be drawn through the four points A, T, B and O. Is Anita correct?
  Discuss.

*Worked Example* Find the value of **a** and **b** giving reasons.

(a)

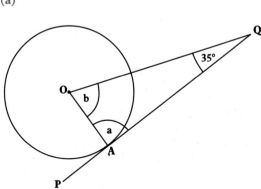

The tangent PQ meets
the circle at A.

(b)

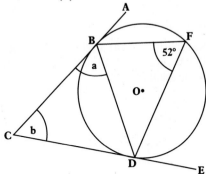

The tangents AC and EC meet
the circle at B and D.

*Answer*  (a)  a = 90° (radius perpendicular to tangent)
           b = 55° (angle sum of triangle)

(b)  a = 52° (angle in alternate segment)
     Since CB = CD (equal tangents from C) then △BCD is isosceles.
     Hence b + 52° + 52° = 180° (angle sum of triangle)
                 b = 76°

*Angle and Tangent Properties of Circles*

**Worked Example** Find the size of θ giving reasons.

(a)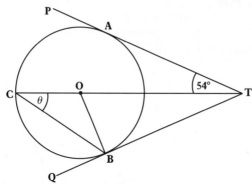

(b)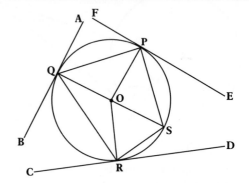

The tangents PT and QT meet the circle at A and B.

The tangent ED meets the circle at C.

**Answer** (a) ∠QTO = 54° (OT bisects ∠QTP)
∠OBT = 90° (radius perpendicular to tangent)
∠TOB = 36° (angle sum of triangle)
θ = 18° (angle at centre)

(b) ∠CBA = 70° (angle in alternate segment)
∠COA = 140° (angle at centre)
θ = 20° (isosceles triangle)

---

## EXERCISE 16:7

1. Name all the right angles in this diagram.
   The tangents AB, FE and CD meet the circle at Q, P and R.

2. Which of a, b or c is equal to p?

(a)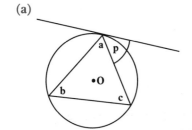

(b)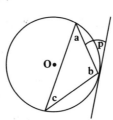

(c)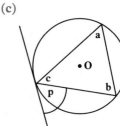

3. (a)

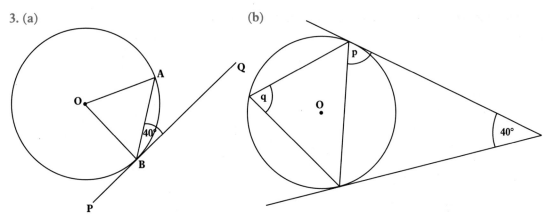

(b)

Find the size of ∠AOB.

Find the size of the angles marked as p and q.

4. Find the size of the angle θ.

(a)

(b)

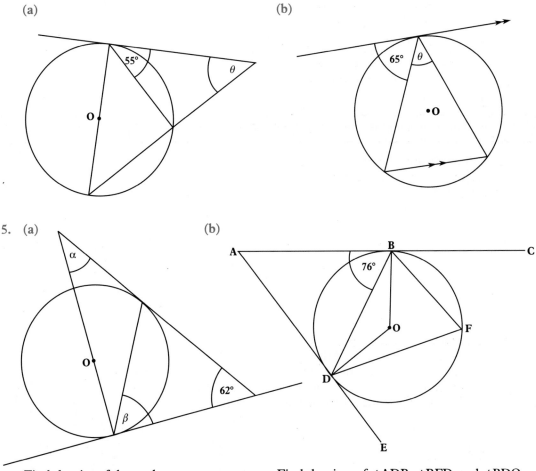

5. (a)

(b)

Find the size of the angles α and β, giving reasons.

Find the sizes of ∠ADB, ∠BFD, and ∠BDO giving reasons.

6. Find the size of a, b, c, d, e, f, g, h, i, j, k and m giving reasons and showing your working.

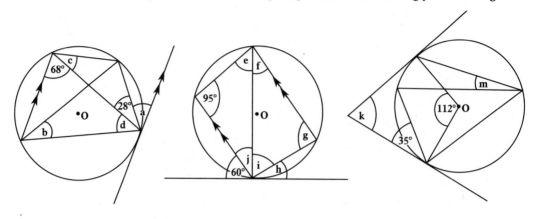

7. This diagram represents part of the mechanism of an antique treadle sewing machine. A continuous belt PQRSTUVW goes around two wheels, centres A and B.
   (i) To find QS, one of the straight sections of the belt, the line AC is drawn parallel to QS.
      (a) Explain why ∠ACB is a right angle.
      (b) The diameter of the large wheel is 40cm, the diameter of the small wheel is 18cm and the distance between the centres of the wheels is 80cm.
         Use Pythagoras' Theorem to find the length of AC. Hence find the length of QS.

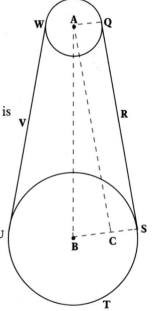

   (ii) (a) Use trigonometry to find the size of ∠ABC. Hence find the size of angle $\theta$, to the nearest degree.
      (b) Use your answer to (a) to find the length of the arc STU.
      (c) Find the total length of the belt on this sewing machine.

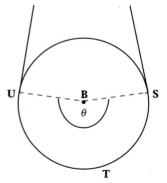

**Review 1** **(a)**                                                      **(b)**

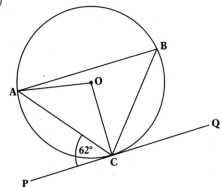

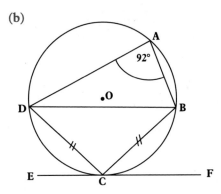

Find the size of ∠ABC and ∠OCA.

DC = CB.
Find the size of ∠DCB, ∠BDC
and ∠BCF.

**Review 2**  Find the size of the angles marked as a, b, c, and d. Give reasons.

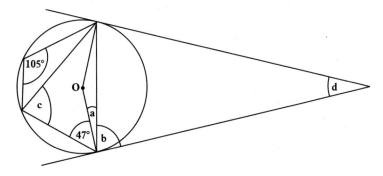

**Review 3**

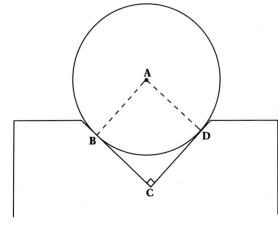

This diagram represents a cross-section of a
cylinder, placed in a "90° Vee block" of wood.
Explain why ABCD is a square.

## DISCUSSION and PRACTICAL EXERCISE 16:8

● One way of constructing the tangents from P to a circle, centre O, is shown below.

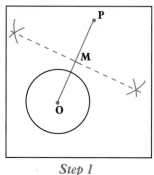 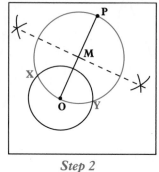 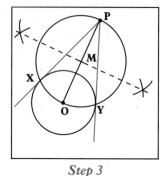

|        |        |        |
|:------:|:------:|:------:|
| *Step 1* | *Step 2* | *Step 3* |

*Step 1:* Join OP. Bisect OP to find M, the mid-point.
*Step 2:* Draw the circle with M as centre and OP as diameter.
  Label as X and Y the points where this circle meets the original circle.
*Step 3:* Join PX and PY.

Why are PX and PY tangents from P to the original circle? **Discuss**.

●

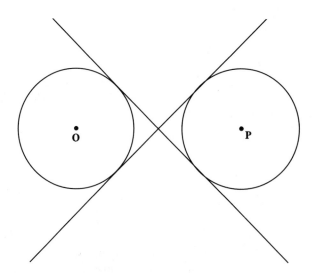

These two tangents are common to both circles. **Discuss** how these tangents can be accurately constructed.

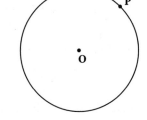

● **Discuss** possible ways of constructing the tangent at the point P. As part of your discussion, do the construction.

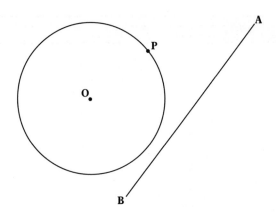

A circle is to be constructed which touches the given circle at P and touches the given line AB.

The following instructions give one way of doing this.

*Construct the tangent at P. Let this tangent meet AB at C. Bisect ∠PCA. Let this bisector meet OP produced at D. With centre D and radius DP, draw the required circle.*

**Note:** OP produced means the same as OP extended.

**Discuss** why the above instructions give the circle which touches the given circle at P and touches the given line.

There are other ways of constructing the required circle. **Discuss** other ways.

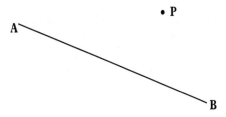

• The line AB is a tangent to a circle which passes through the point P. How can this circle be constructed? Is there more than one possible circle? **Discuss.**

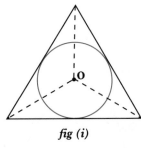

**Discuss** how to construct the circle which touches BC at D and touches AB.

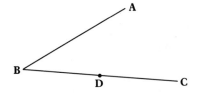

fig (i)

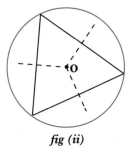

fig (ii)

*fig (i)* shows a circle drawn inside a triangle so that the circle touches the sides. This circle is called an **incircle**. The sides of the triangle are tangents to the incircle.

*fig (ii)* shows a circle drawn around a triangle so that each vertex of the triangle is on the circle. This circle is called a **circumcircle**. The sides of the triangle are chords of the circumcircle.

**Discuss** the steps to be taken to construct an incircle and a circumcircle to a triangle.

## RESEARCH PROJECT 16:9

"Rectangle" Properties of Chords

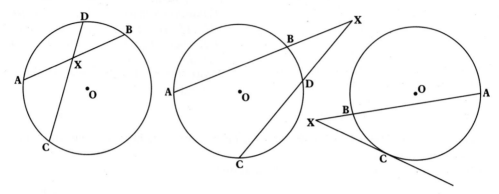

There are relationships between the lengths AX, BX, CX, DX in the above diagrams.
These relationships are sometimes known as the "rectangle" properties.
Research these relationships.

## CHAPTER 16   REVIEW

1. The diagram shows a circle with its centre at O.
   A, B and C are points on the circumference of the circle.
   At C, a tangent to the circle has been drawn.
   D is a point on this tangent.
   Angle OCB = 24°.

   **(a)** Find the size of angle BCD.
   Give a reason for your answer.
   **(b)** Find the size of angle CAB.
   Give a reason for your answer.

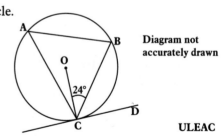

Diagram not
accurately drawn

ULEAC

2. *O* is the centre of a circle. *ABC* is a tangent to the circle at *B*.

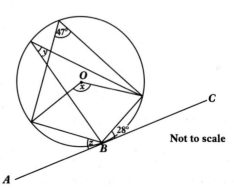

Not to scale

Work out the size of angles *x*, *y* and *z*.

SEG

344

**3.**

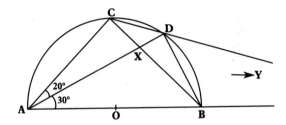

AB is a diameter of a circle whose centre is O. D and C are chosen so that angle
BAD = 30° and angle DAC = 20°.
Calculate the size of:
**(i)** angle CBD       **(ii)** angle ACD

If CD and AB are both produced, a triangle CYA will (eventually) be formed.
Calculate the size of:
**(iii)** angle CYA.                                             **NICCEA**

**4.**

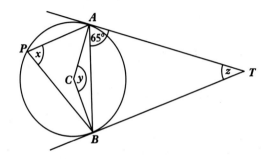

*AT* and *BT* are tangents to the circle, centre *C*.
*P* is a point on the circumference as shown.
Angle *BAT* = 65°.
Calculate the size of x, y and z.                               **NEAB**

**5. (a)**

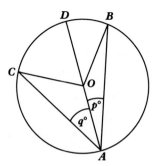

In the diagram, *O* is the centre of the circle and *AD* is a diameter.
Angle *BAO* is $p°$ and angle *CAO* is $q°$.
**(i)** Using angle properties of triangles only, find the size of angle *BOC* in terms of $p$ and $q$.
Give a reason for each step in your working.
**(ii)** What is the relationship between angle *BAC* and angle *BOC*?

**(b)**

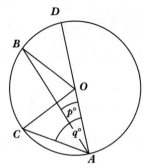

In this diagram, $O$ remains the centre of the circle and $AD$ is a diameter.
Angle $BAO$ is again $p°$ and angle $CAO$ is $q°$.
Show that the relationship between angle $BAC$ and angle $BOC$ is still true.     **MEG**

**6.** $P, Q, R$ and $S$ are four points on the circumference of a circle centre $O$. $TSV$ is a tangent
which touches the circle at $S$. $R\widehat{P}S = 54°$ and $P\widehat{S}R = 68°$.

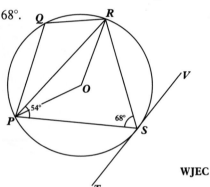

   **(a)** Find the values of

      **(i)** $P\widehat{Q}R$.

      **(ii)** $P\widehat{O}R$ (obtuse).

   **(b)** Explain clearly why $T\widehat{S}P = 58°$.

   **(c)** Find the value of $O\widehat{R}S$.

                                                **WJEC**

**7.**

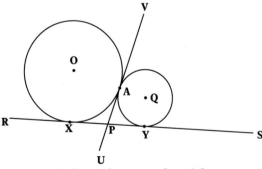

The diagram shows two circles with centres O and Q.
The circles touch at the point A. The line UV is a tangent touching both circles at A.
The line RS is also a tangent to both circles.
RS touches the circle, centre O, at X.
RS also touches the circle, centre Q, at Y.
The lines UV and RS meet at P.

   **(a)** Show that the line UV bisects the line XY.
   **(b)** Show that angle XAY = 90°.     **ULEAC**

8. In the diagram below, the line $AB$ is 8cm long.
   (a) Draw the locus of points, $P$, which lie above the line $AB$ such that the area of triangle $ABP$ is 12cm².
   (b) On the same diagram construct the locus of points, $Q$, which lie above the line $AB$ such that angle $AQB$ is 90°.
   (c) Hence draw all triangles $ABC$ which have $C$ above $AB$, an area of 12cm² and an angle of 90°.

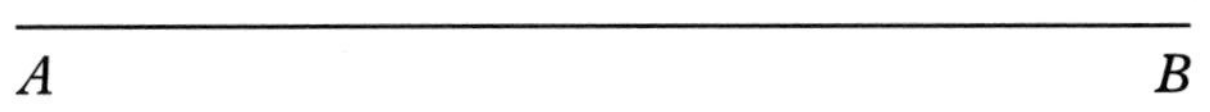

_____

$A$                                              $B$                    **MEG**

# Trigonometrical Ratios and Graphs

## ANGLES of ANY SIZE

Trig. Ratios

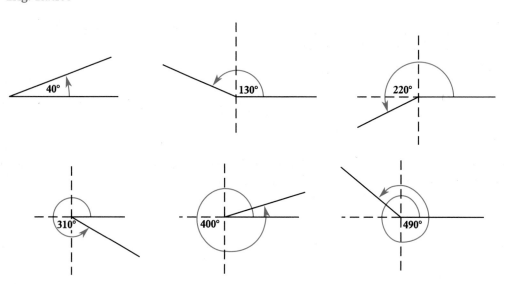

Choose an acute angle such as 40°. Add multiples of 90° to form the angles shown in the diagram. Use your calculator to **investigate** the sequence sin 40°, sin 130°, sin 220°, sin 310°, sin 400°, sin 490°, . . .

What if the acute angle was 55°?
What if the acute angle was 70°?
What if . . .
What if sine was replaced with cosine?
What if sine was replaced with tangent?

Make and test statements as part of your investigation.

The sequence sin 70°, sin 110°, sin 250°, sin 290°, sin 430°, sin 470°, . . . is the same as the sequence sin 70°, sin (180° – 70°), sin (180° + 70°), sin (2 × 180° – 70°), sin (2 × 180° + 70°), sin (3 × 180° – 70°), . . . Use your calculator to **investigate** sequences formed in this way from an acute angle.

What if sine was replaced with cosine?
What if sine was replaced with tangent?

The ratios sin $\theta$ and cos $\theta$ may be defined in relation to the lengths of the sides of a right-angled triangle.

sin $\theta$ is defined as $\dfrac{\text{length of opposite side}}{\text{length of hypotenuse}}$ ,

cos $\theta$ is defined as $\dfrac{\text{length of adjacent side}}{\text{length of hypotenuse}}$ .

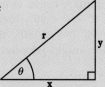

Since $\theta < 90$, sin $\theta$ and cos $\theta$ defined in this way only have meaning for angles less than 90°.

$$\sin \theta = \frac{y}{r} \qquad \cos \theta = \frac{x}{r}$$
$$y = r \sin \theta \qquad x = r \cos \theta$$

We will now look at an alternative definition for sin $\theta$ and cos $\theta$ which has meaning for angles of any size. In this diagram, the coordinates of P are (x, y).

Since $\frac{x}{1} = \cos \theta$, then x = cos $\theta$. Since $\frac{y}{1} = \sin \theta$, then y = sin $\theta$.

Hence the coordinates of P are (cos $\theta$, sin $\theta$). This gives the following alternative definition for the ratios cos $\theta$ and sin $\theta$.

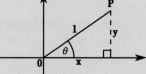

**The ratios cos $\theta$ and sin $\theta$ may be defined as the coordinates of a point P where OP makes an angle of $\theta$ with the positive x-axis and is of length 1. Defined in this way, the ratios cos $\theta$ and sin $\theta$ have meaning for angles of any size.**

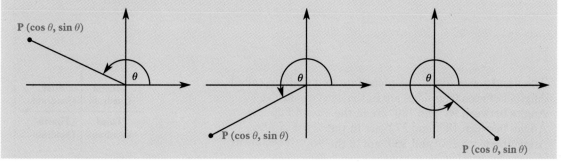

## DISCUSSION EXERCISE 17:2

- **Discuss** the following method for writing sin 164° and cos 164° in terms of an acute angle.

In this diagram P is the point (cos 164°, sin 164°).
From the right-angled triangle OPR, the x-coordinate of
P is – cos 16° and the y-coordinate is sin 16°.
Hence sin 164° = sin 16° and cos 164° = – cos 16°.

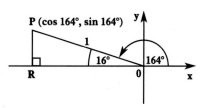

- **Discuss** how to use diagrams to show that sin 202° = – sin 22°, cos 202° = – cos 22° and sin 290° = – sin 70°, cos 290° = cos 70°.

- Jake made a summary of the signs of sin $\theta$ and cos $\theta$ for angles between 0° and 360°. His summary began as follows.
  If $0° < \theta < 90°$, then sin $\theta$ is positive and cos $\theta$ is positive.
  If $90° < \theta < 180°$, then sin $\theta$ is positive and cos $\theta$ is negative.
  How might Jake have completed this summary? **Discuss.**

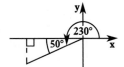

- Jenny proved that $\tan \theta = \dfrac{\sin \theta}{\cos \theta}$. She began her proof as follows: $\sin \theta = \dfrac{AC}{AB}$
  How might Jenny have continued? **Discuss.**

  Jenny then summarised the signs of sin $\theta$, cos $\theta$ and tan $\theta$ in this table. **Discuss** Jenny's summary.

- David's method for writing cos 950° in terms of an acute angle is shown.
  **Discuss** David's method.

  $$950° = 360° + 360° + 230°$$
  $$\cos 950° = \cos 230°$$
  $$\cos 230° = -\cos 50°$$

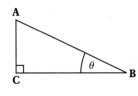

---

The x and y axes divide the plane into four regions, called **quadrants.**
Angles between 0° and 90° are in the **first quadrant.**
Angles between 90° and 180° are in the **second quadrant.**
Angles between 180° and 270° are in the **third quadrant.**
Angles between 270° and 360° are in the **fourth quadrant.**

| | |
|---|---|
| Second Quadrant | First Quadrant |
| Third Quadrant | Fourth Quadrant |

This diagram shows where the ratios sine, cosine , tangent are positive.
All of them are positive for first quadrant angles, just the sine is positive for second quadrant angles, just the tangent is positive for third quadrant angles and just the cosine is positive for fourth quadrant angles.

| sine **S** | all **A** |
|---|---|
| tangent **T** | cosine **C** |

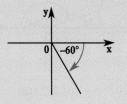

We move anticlockwise (↺) for a positive angle.
We move clockwise for a **negative angle.** For instance, the angle –60° is shown in this diagram.

*Worked Example* Write the following in terms of an acute angle.

          (a)  sin 240°         (b)  cos 320°         (c)  tan 120°

*Answer*  (a)  Since 240° is in the third quadrant, sin 240° is negative.
            From the diagram, sin 240° = – sin 60°.

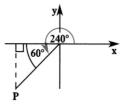

        (b)  Since 320° is in the fourth quadrant, cos 320° is positive.
            From the diagram, cos 320° = cos 40°.

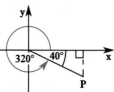

        (c)  Since 120° is in the second quadrant, tan 120° is negative.
            From the diagram, tan 120° = – tan 60°.

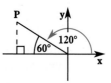

*Worked Example* Given that sin 40° = 0·64 (2 d.p.) and sin 50° = 0·77 (2 d.p.) find the values of
          (a)  sin 130°         (b)  sin 310°         (c)  sin (–140°).

*Answer*  (a)                      (b)                     (c)

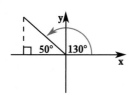    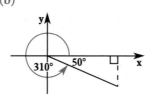    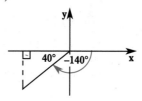

      sin 130° = sin 50°        sin 310° = – sin 50°       sin (–140°) = – sin 40°
              = 0·77 (2 d.p.)             = – 0·77 (2 d.p.)          = – 0·64 (2 d.p.)

## EXERCISE 17:3

1.  A mnemonic for remembering the quadrants in which sin, cos and tan are positive is **A**ll
    **S**cience **T**eachers **C**are. Invent another mnemonic for this.

2.  (a)  Is the cosine of an obtuse angle positive or negative?
    (b)  Is the sine of an obtuse angle positive or negative?

3. Are the following statements true or false?
   (a) If $90° < \alpha < 180°$, $\tan \alpha$ is negative.
   (b) If $270° < \alpha < 360°$, $\cos \alpha$ is positive.
   (c) If $180° < \alpha < 270°$, $\sin \alpha$ is negative.

4. If $\tan \theta = 0.54$ to 2 d.p. which of the following statements is correct?
   A. $\theta$ is in the 1st or 2nd quadrant.
   B. $\theta$ is in the 2nd or 3rd quadrant.
   C. $\theta$ is in the 1st or 3rd quadrant.
   D. $\theta$ is in the 2nd or 4th quadrant.

5. If $\cos \theta = -0.8$ to 1 d.p. which of the following statements is *incorrect*?
   A. $\theta$ could be in the 2nd quadrant.
   B. $\theta$ could be in the 3rd quadrant.
   C. $\theta$ could be in the 4th quadrant.

6. (a) $\cos 150° =$    A. $\cos 30°$    B. $-\cos 30°$    C. $\cos(-30°)$    D. $\cos 60°$
   (b) $\sin 100° =$    A. $\sin 80°$    B. $-\sin 80°$    C. $\sin(-80°)$    D. $\sin 10°$
   (c) $\tan 280° =$    A. $\tan 10°$    B. $\tan 80°$    C. $-\tan 10°$    D. $-\tan 80°$
   (d) $\sin 200° =$    A. $\sin 20°$    B. $\sin 70°$    C. $-\sin 70°$    D. $-\sin 20°$
   (e) $\cos 300° =$    A. $\cos 30°$    B. $\cos 60°$    C. $-\cos 60°$    D. $-\cos 30°$
   (f) $\tan(-50°) =$    A. $\tan 50°$    B. $\tan(-40°)$    C. $-\tan 40°$    D. $-\tan 50°$
   (g) $\cos(-100°) =$    A. $-\cos 10°$    B. $-\cos 80°$    C. $\cos 10°$    D. $\cos 80°$
   (h) $\sin 440° =$    A. $-\sin 40°$    B. $\sin 40°$    C. $\sin 80°$    D. $-\sin 80°$
   (i) $\tan 800° =$    A. $-\tan 80°$    B. $\tan 10°$    C. $\tan(-80°)$    D. $\tan 80°$

7. Given that $\sin 30° = 0.5$ find the values of:
   (a) $\sin 150°$
   (b) $\sin(-30°)$
   (c) $\sin 330°$
   (d) $\sin 210°$.

8. Given that $\tan 10° = 0.18$ (2 s.f.) and $\tan 80° = 5.7$ (2 s.f.) find the values of:
   (a) $\tan 100°$
   (b) $\tan 280°$
   (c) $\tan 190°$
   (d) $\tan(-170°)$.

9. Express the following in terms of an acute angle.
   (a) $\sin 220°$    (b) $\cos 120°$    (c) $\tan 320°$    (d) $\tan 170°$    (e) $\sin 370°$
   (f) $\tan 140°$    (g) $\cos 95°$    (h) $\sin 140°$    (i) $\tan 210°$    (j) $\sin(-30°)$
   (k) $\tan 390°$    (l) $\tan(-120°)$    (m) $\sin 95°$    (n) $\cos 290°$    (o) $\cos 420°$
   (p) $\cos(-200°)$    (q) $\sin 920°$

10. Write down all the angles between $-360°$ and $720°$ with the same (a) cosine as $20°$
    (b) tangent as $80°$
    (c) sine as $50°$.

Review 1  If $\beta = 210°$, which statement is correct?
    A.  Both tan $\beta$ and cos $\beta$ are negative.
    B.  Both sin $\beta$ and tan $\beta$ are negative.
    C.  Both cos $\beta$ and sin $\beta$ are negative.
    D.  All of sin $\beta$, cos $\beta$, tan $\beta$ are negative.

Review 2  If $\sin \theta = 0{\cdot}6$, which of the following statements is correct?
    A.  $\theta$ is in the 1st or 4th quadrant.
    B.  $\theta$ is in the 2nd or 4th quadrant.
    C.  $\theta$ is in the 2nd or 3rd quadrant.
    D.  $\theta$ is in the 1st or 3rd quadrant.
    E.  $\theta$ is in the 1st or 2nd quadrant.
    F.  $\theta$ is in the 3rd or 4th quadrant.

Review 3  (a)  tan 140° =  A.  tan 40°  B.  – tan 40°  C.  tan 50°  D.  – tan 50°
      (b)  sin 240° =  A.  sin 40°  B.  sin 60°  C.  – sin 30°  D.  – sin 60°
      (c)  cos (– 40°) =  A.  cos 40°  B.  cos 50°  C.  – cos 40°  D.  – cos 50°
      (d)  cos 140° =  A.  cos 40°  B.  – cos 40°  C.  cos 50°  D.  – cos 50°
      (e)  tan (–140°) =  A.  – tan 40°  B.  tan 40°  C.  tan 50°  D.  – tan 50°

Review 4  (a)  Write tan 125° in terms of an acute angle.
      (b)  Express sin (–200°) in terms of an acute angle.

## DISCUSSION EXERCISE 17:4

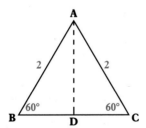

ABC is an equilateral triangle of side 2 units. AD is an axis of symmetry.

We can use this triangle to show that  $\sin 60° = \frac{\sqrt{3}}{2}$, $\cos 60° = \frac{1}{2}$, $\tan 60° = \sqrt{3}$.

How can this be shown? Discuss.

Use the triangle to find values for the ratios sin 30°, cos 30°, tan 30°. Leave irrational numbers in your answers.

We can use a triangle to show that  $\sin 45° = \frac{1}{\sqrt{2}}$, $\cos 45° = \frac{1}{\sqrt{2}}$, $\tan 45° = 1$.

What triangle should we use? Discuss.

## GRAPHS of TRIG. FUNCTIONS

---

### DISCUSSION EXERCISE 17:5

---

- | x | 0° | 30° | 60° | 90° |
  |---|----|-----|-----|-----|
  | cos x | 1 | 0·87 | 0·5 | 0 |

  Between 0° and 90°, cos x decreases from 1 to 0.

  Use the calculator to find other values of cos x. Include values of x as small as −360° and as large as 720°. **Discuss** the way cos x varies. Sketch graphs as part of your discussion.

- **Discuss** the way in which sin x varies for various values of x. Sketch graphs as part of your discussion.

- | x | 0° | 30° | 60° | 80° |
  |---|----|-----|-----|-----|
  | tan x | 0 | 0·58 | | |

  Use your calculator to complete this table of values for tan x.

  What happens if you attempt to find the value of tan 90°? Find values of tan x if x is close to 90°. Include values of x such as 89°, 89·5°, 89·99°, 90·01°, 90·1°. **Discuss.**

  Charles used $\tan \theta = \dfrac{\sin \theta}{\cos \theta}$ to show that tan 90° has no value. What steps might Charles have taken? **Discuss.**

  Which of the following could be part of the graph of y = tan x? **Discuss.**

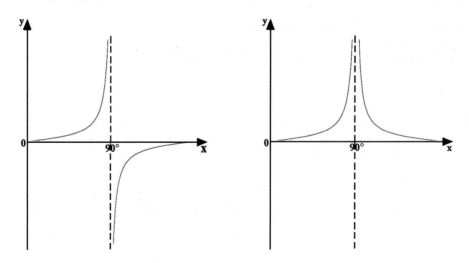

  Use the calculator to find various values of tan x. Include values as small as −720° and as large as 1080°. **Discuss** the way tan x varies. As part of your discussion, sketch graphs.

*Worked Example* (a) On the same set of axes draw the graphs of $y = 5 \cos x°$ and $y = \frac{x}{20} - 2$ for values of x between –90 and 270.

(b) Explain why the x-value of the point of intersection of these graphs gives the solution of the equation $100 \cos x° + 40 = x$.

(c) Write down an approximate solution to this equation.

*Answer* (a)

| x | –90 | – 60 | –30 | 0 | 30 | 60 | 90 | 120 | 150 | 180 | 210 | 240 | 270 |
|---|---|---|---|---|---|---|---|---|---|---|---|---|---|
| 5 cos x° | 0 | 2·5 | 4·3 | 5 | 4·3 | 2·5 | 0 | –2·5 | – 4·3 | –5 | – 4·3 | –2·5 | 0 |
| $\frac{x}{20} - 2$ | – 6·5 | –5 | –3·5 | –2 | –0·5 | 1 | 2·5 | 4 | 5·5 | 7 | 8·5 | 10 | 11·5 |

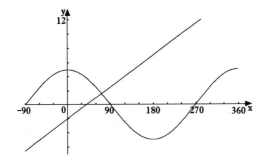

(b) Since $y = 5 \cos x°$ and $y = \frac{x}{20} - 2$ then $5 \cos x° = \frac{x}{20} - 2$

$$100 \cos x° = x - 40$$
$$100 \cos x° + 40 = x$$

(c) The x-coordinate of the point of intersection is about 70. Hence an approximate solution of the equation $100 \cos x° + 40° = x$ is about x = 70.

## EXERCISE 17:6

1. Graphs for $y = \sin x$, $y = \cos x$ and $y = \tan x$ follow.
   (a) Which graph has which equation?
   (b) Write down the coordinates of the points A, B, C, . . . R.

**Graph 1**

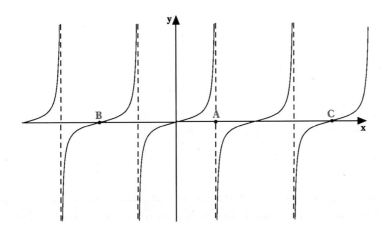

**Graph 2**

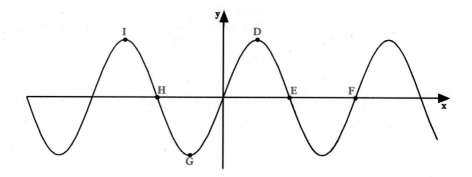

**Graph 3**

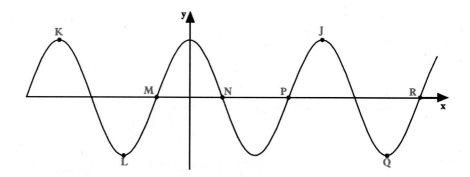

2. Which of the graphs below could be part of the graph of   (a) $y = \sin x$     (b) $y = \cos x$?

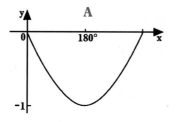

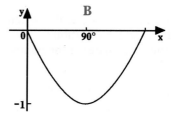

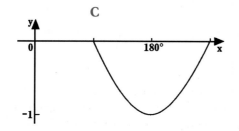

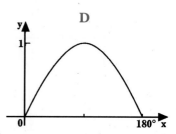

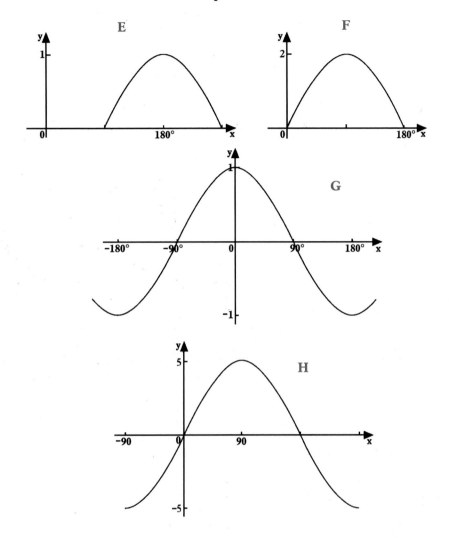

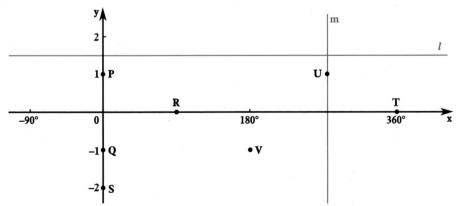

 3.

(i)  Which of the graphs  y = sin x,  y = cos x,  y = tan x  goes through the point
(a) P        (b) Q        (c) R        (d) S        (e) T        (f) U        (g) V?
(ii) Which of the graphs  y = sin x,  y = cos x,  y = tan x  crosses the line   (a) *l*        (b) m?

4. **Use a graphics calculator or a graphics package on the computer for this question.**

(i) (a) Draw the graph of $y = \sin 2x$ for values of x between 0° and 360°.
   (b) Use **(a)** to sketch the graph of $y = \sin 2x$ for values of x between –720° and 720°.
   (c) Explain the relationship between the graph of $y = \sin 2x$ and the graph of $y = \sin x$.

(ii) (a) Draw the graph of $y = \sin \frac{1}{2} x$.

   (b) What is the relationship between the graphs of $y = \sin \frac{1}{2} x$ and $y = \sin x$?

(iii)(a) On the same set of axes, draw the graphs of $y = \sin x$, $y = 2 \sin x$ and $y = \sin \frac{1}{2} x$.
   (b) Explain the relationship between these graphs.

(iv) (a) On the same set of axes, draw the graphs of $y = \sin x$, $y = \sin x + 2$ and $y = \sin x - 2$.
   (b) Explain the relationship between these graphs.

(v) (a) What do you think the relationship between the graphs of $y = -\sin x$ and $y = \sin x$ might be? Draw these graphs to test your hypothesis.
   (b) What do you think the relationship between the graphs of $y = \sin (-x)$ and $y = \sin x$ might be? Draw these graphs to test your hypothesis.

(vi) The equation of this graph is $y = a \sin bx$.
What is a?
What is b?

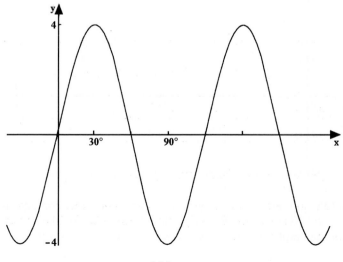

5. **Use a graphics calculator or a graphics package on the computer for this question.**

   (a) On the same set of axes, draw the graphs of $y = \cos x$, $y = 3 \cos x$, $y = \cos(-x)$.

   (b) Draw the graphs of $y = \cos x$, $y = \frac{1}{3} \cos x$, and $y = \cos x - 3$ on the same set of axes.

   (c) What is the relationship between the graphs of $y = -\cos x$ and $y = \cos x$?

   (d)

   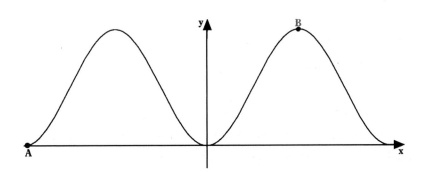

   The equation of this graph is $y = 1 - \cos x$.
   What are the coordinates of A and B?

6. The expression $3 + 2 \sin(30t)°$ gives the approximate depth (in metres) of water at the end of a jetty, t hours after midnight. Find the depth of water at   (a) midnight
     (b) 3a.m.
     (c) 6a.m.

7. t hours after midday the approximate height, h metres, of water above the floor of a boatshed is given by $h = 2.5 + 3 \cos(30t)°$.
   Find the height of the water at 5p.m. Explain your answer.

8. t hours after midnight the approximate depth, d metres, of water at a wharf is given by $d = 9 + 4 \sin(30t)°$.
   (a) Copy and complete the following table, giving d to the nearest cm.

   | t (hours after midnight) | 0 | 1 | 2 | 3 | 4 | 5 | 6 | 7 | 8 | 9 | 10 |
   |---|---|---|---|---|---|---|---|---|---|---|---|
   | d (metres) | 9 | 11 | 12·46 | | | | | | | | |

   (b) At what time, during this 10-hour time span, is low tide? How deep is the water then?
   (c) Draw the graph of d against t.
   (d) To berth, a ship needs a minimum of 11·5 metres of water. For how long between midnight and 10a.m. could this ship berth at this wharf? (Give the answer to the nearest half an hour).

9. This diagram represents a Big Wheel at a fairground. The
bottom of the wheel is 2m from the ground; the diameter of
the wheel is 20m.

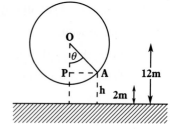

(a) Find, in terms of $\theta$, the distance OP.
(b) Show that $h = 12 - 10 \cos \theta$ gives the height, above the
ground, of the chair at A.
(c) Copy and complete this table of values.

| $\theta$ | −180° | −135° | −90° | −45° | 0° | 45° | 90° | 135° | 180° | 225° | 270° | 315° | 360° |
|---|---|---|---|---|---|---|---|---|---|---|---|---|---|
| h | 22 | 19·1 | | | | | | | | | | | |

(d) Draw a graph to show how the height of a chair varies with the angle $\theta$.
(e) A chair is 15 metres above the ground when $\theta$ is about 107°. What is the value of $\theta$ when
the chair is next 15 metres above the ground? (The wheel is moving anticlockwise).
(f) Another Big Wheel has radius of 5m. Its centre is 6m above the ground. This wheel
rotates steadily anticlockwise and takes 12 seconds to make one complete revolution.
*fig (i)* shows the position P, of a chair, at t = 0. At what time is this chair next in the
positions shown in the other diagrams? How far above the ground is the chair in each of
these diagrams?

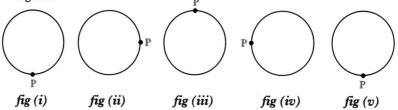

*fig (i)*       *fig (ii)*       *fig (iii)*       *fig (iv)*       *fig (v)*

On axes similar to those shown,
sketch a graph showing how the
height of a chair varies with time.

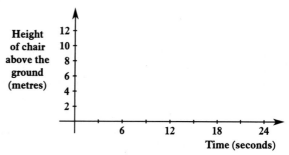

10. (a) Copy and complete this table of values.

| x | −180 | −150 | −120 | −90 | −60 | −30 | 0 | 30 | 60 | 90 | 120 | 150 | 180 |
|---|---|---|---|---|---|---|---|---|---|---|---|---|---|
| cos x° | | | | | | 0·87 | 1 | 0·87 | | | | | |
| $\frac{x}{100}$ | −1·8 | | | | | | | | | | | 1·5 | 1·8 |

(b) Draw the graphs of $y = \cos x°$ and $y = \frac{x}{100}$.
(c) Use these graphs to find an approximate solution for the equation $x = 100 \cos x°$.
(d) What line do you need to draw on the graph to be able to solve the equation $\cos x° = 0·6$?
How many solutions are there for this equation in the range $−180 < x < 180$?
(e) Explain why there are many solutions for $\cos x° = 0·6$ but only one solution for
$x = 100 \cos x°$.

360

11. (a) Accurately draw the graphs of $y = 20 \cos (\frac{1}{2} x°)$ and $50y = x$ for values of x between 0 and 360.

(b) Show that these graphs can be used to find a solution to the equation $1000 \cos (\frac{1}{2} x°) = x$. Use the graphs to find an approximate solution for this equation.

(c) What line do you need to draw on the graph to solve the equation $10 \cos (\frac{1}{2} x°) = 8$?

12. (a) Accurately draw the graph $y = 15 \sin x°$ for values of x between 0 and 360. On the same set of axes, draw the graph of $x - 20y = 100$.

(b) Show that these graphs can be used to find solutions to the equation $300 \sin x° = x - 100$.

(c) Use the graphs to find one solution for this equation.

**Review 1** (a) On a set of axes, similar to that shown, sketch the graph of $y = \cos x$.

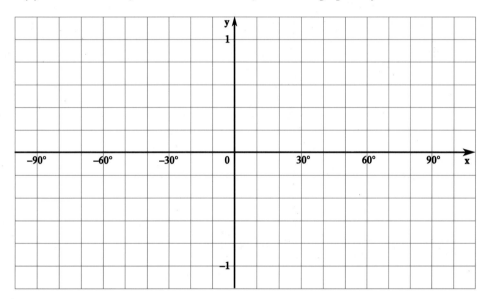

(b) Extend the axes from $-360°$ to $360°$. Sketch the graph of $y = \sin x$ on these axes.

(c) The graph of $y = \cos x$ can be translated to give the graph of $y = \sin x$. Describe this translation.

**Review 2** The depth, d metres, of water at a river mouth is given by the formula $d = 6 + 2 \cos (30t)°$ where t is the number of hours after high tide.

(a) Copy and complete the following table, giving d to the nearest cm.

| t | 0 | 1 | 2 | 3 | 4 | 5 | 6 | 7 | 8 | 9 | 10 |
|---|---|---|---|---|---|---|---|---|---|---|----|
| d | 8 | 7·73 | | | | | | | | | |

(b) Draw the graph of d against t for $t = 0$ to 10.

(c) If high tide is at 4 p.m. at what time is low tide?

(d) How soon after low tide can a ship, which needs a depth of at least 5·5 metres of water, enter the river?

**Review 3** (a) For values of x between 0 and 360, accurately draw the graph of y = tan x °.
(Number the y-axis from –16 to 16.)
(b) On the same set of axes draw the graph of 20y = x – 300.
(c) Explain why these graphs may be used to solve the equation x = 300 + 20 tan x°.
(d) Find an approximate solution to this equation.

## INVESTIGATION 17:7

**Gradient of Trig. Graphs**

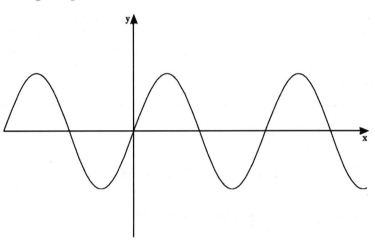

Find the gradient at various points on the graph of y = sin x. Look for relationships.

What if the graph was y = 2 sin x?
What if the graph was y = sin 2x?
What if . . .

**Investigate** to find the gradient at various points on cosine graphs.

## DISCUSSION EXERCISE 17:8

A wave with the shape of a cosine or sine curve is called a sine wave. Light waves and waves in the ocean are two examples. Another example is the wave movement set up in the string of a musical instrument when it is plucked.
What other examples of sine waves can you think of? **Discuss.**

## RESEARCH PROJECTS 17:9

**The Six Trig. Ratios**

There are 6 trig. ratios. Three of these are sine, cosine, tangent. The other three are secant, cosecant, cotangent.
Research secant, cosecant, cotangent.

**Compound Angles**

$\sin (30° + 40°) \neq \sin 30° + \sin 40°$. In fact $\sin (30° + 40°) = \sin 30° \cos 40° + \cos 30° \sin 40°$.
There are formulae which give $\sin (A + B)$, $\sin (A - B)$, $\cos (A + B)$, $\cos (A - B)$,
$\tan (A + B)$, $\tan (A - B)$ in terms of sin A, cos A, tan A, sin B, cos B, tan B. These formulae
are called compound angle formulae.
Research compound angle formulae.

## CHAPTER 17   REVIEW

**1. (a)** **(i)** Sketch the graph of $y = \sin x$, for $x = 0°$ to $360°$.

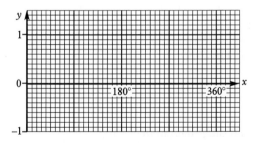

**(ii)** Sketch the graph of $y = \frac{1}{2} \sin x$ for $x = 0°$ to $360°$.

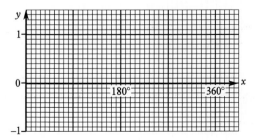

**(iii)** Sketch the graph of $y = \sin(x - 45°)$ for $x = 0°$ to $360°$.

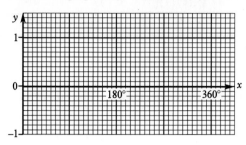

**(b)** Angle $p$ satisfies the equation
$$\sin p = \sin 190°.$$
Angle $p$ is not equal to $190°$.
Find the value of $p$. **SEG**

2. **(a)** The diagram shows part of the graph of $y = \cos x$.

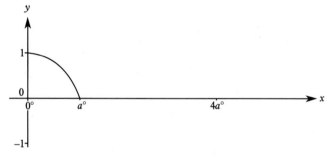

**(i)** Write down the value of $a$.
**(ii)** On the diagram, sketch the rest of the graph of $y = \cos x$ as far as $x = 4a$.
**(b)** The angle $y$ is between $0°$ and $360°$.
Work out accurately the two solutions of the equation
$$\cos y = -0·5.$$ **SEG**

3. Use your calculator to find
   **(a)** the two values of $\theta$ between 0 and 360 such that $\sin \theta° = 0·7$,
   **(b)** the two values of $\theta$ between 0 and 360 such that $\tan \theta° = -1$. **MEG**

4.

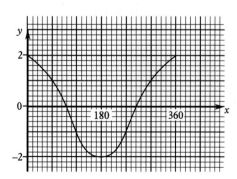

The equation of the curve is of the form $y = a \cos bx°$, where $a$ and $b$ are constants.
(a) Write down the values of $a$ and $b$.
(b) Use the graph to find two values of $x$ which are solutions to the equation $a \cos bx° = 1$, for these values of $a$ and $b$.                                                  **ULEAC**

5.  The graph of $y = \sin x$ for $0° \le x \le 360°$ is drawn below.

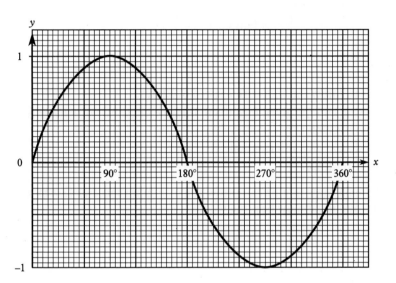

(a) Angle $p$ satisfies the equation
$$\sin p = \sin 210°.$$
Angle $p$ is not equal to $210°$.
What is the value of $p$?

(b) On the same axes as $y = \sin x$, draw the graph of $y = \frac{1}{2}\cos x$ for $0° \le x \le 360°$.
(c) Use the graphs to solve the equation $\sin x = \frac{1}{2}\cos x$ for the range of $x$ that the graphs allow.                                                                          **SEG**

6.  (a) Complete the table for $y = \sin x°$.

| $x$ | 0 | 30 | 60 | 90 | 120 | 150 | 180 | 210 | 240 | 270 | 300 | 330 | 360 |
|---|---|---|---|---|---|---|---|---|---|---|---|---|---|
| $y = \sin x°$ | 0 | 0·5 | 0·866 | | | | | | | | | | |

(b) Plot the points and draw the graph of $y = \sin x°$.
(c) Using the same axes draw the line $y + \frac{x}{400} = 0$.
(d) Use your graph to solve the equation $\sin x° + \frac{x}{400} = 0$ for positive values of $x$.   **NICCEA**

7.  $\sin x° = \cos 300°$.
Find the two values for $x$, given that $0 \le x \le 360$.                                **ULEAC**

365

8.  **You must use graph paper for part (a) (ii) of this question.**

    The school shot put record is 15 metres.
    Looking in an 'A' level text book, Stefan finds a diagram and a formula connecting the speed, $V$ metres per second, and the angle, $x°$, of the throw and the range achieved, $R$ metres.

    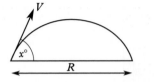

    $$R = \frac{V^2}{5} \times (\sin x°) \times (\cos x°)$$

    **(a)** Stefan knows that he can throw the shot with a speed of 12 m/s.

       **(i)**   Use this information and the given formula to find the range he can achieve for different values of the angle $x°$.

      **(ii)**   Draw a graph to display this information.

     **(iii)**  Comment on your findings.

    **(b)** After some training Stefan finds that he can throw at a maximum speed of 13·2 m/s. Investigate different ways he can now beat the record.     **MEG**

## INTRODUCTION

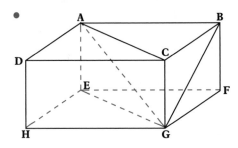

• There are many right-angled triangles in this cuboid. One of them is ∆AEG which is redrawn at the right.
In this drawing ∠AEG is drawn as a true right angle.

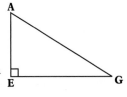

What other right-angled triangles can you find? **Discuss.** As part of your discussion draw each triangle with its right angle a true right angle.

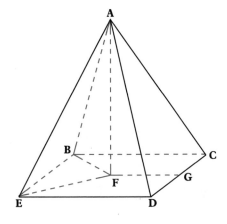

• The base of this pyramid is a square. F is directly below A. G is the mid-point of CD.
Which triangles are right-angled triangles? **Discuss.**

**What if** the base is a rectangle rather than a square?

• The end faces of this prism are right-angled triangles. Each of the other faces is rectangular.
Is ∆ADF a right-angled triangle? Draw all the right-angled triangles showing their right angles as true right angles.
**What if** the face ABFE is a square?

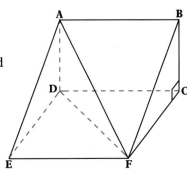

## USING PYTHAGORAS' THEOREM

**Remember:** In the right-angled triangle shown $r^2 = x^2 + y^2$.

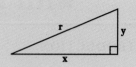

**Worked Example**  Find the length of  (a)  HF
(b)  HB.

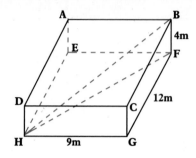

**Answer**  (a)

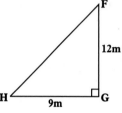

$HF^2 = 12^2 + 9^2$ (Pythagoras' Theorem)
$HF = 15m$

(b)

$HB^2 = 15^2 + 4^2$ (Pythagoras' Theorem)
$HB = 15 \cdot 5m$ (1 d.p.)

**Worked Example**  (a)  Calculate the length of DX.
(b)  Find the height of this pyramid.

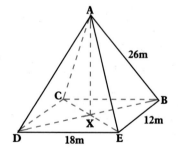

**Answer**  (a)

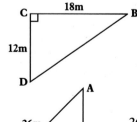

$DB^2 = 18^2 + 12^2$ (Pythagoras' Theorem)
$DB = 21 \cdot 6m$ (1 d.p.)

$DX = \dfrac{DB}{2}$
$= 10 \cdot 8m$ (1 d.p.)

(b)

$26^2 = AX^2 + 10 \cdot 8^2$ (Pythagoras' Theorem)
$26^2 - 10 \cdot 8^2 = AX^2$
$AX = 23 \cdot 7m$ (1 d.p.)

*Worked Example*   A cupboard is 1·6m high, 40cm wide and 50cm deep. What is the length of
the longest fishing rod which can be placed in this cupboard?

*Answer*

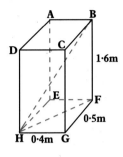

The length HB will give the fishing rod of greatest length.

From $\triangle$HFG, $HF^2 = 0\cdot4^2 + 0\cdot5^2$

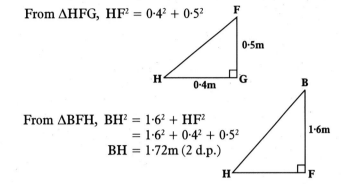

From $\triangle$BFH, $BH^2 = 1\cdot6^2 + HF^2$
$= 1\cdot6^2 + 0\cdot4^2 + 0\cdot5^2$
$BH = 1\cdot72m$ (2 d.p.)

That is, to the nearest centimetre, the length of the longest fishing rod is 1·72m.

## EXERCISE 18:2

1. (a)

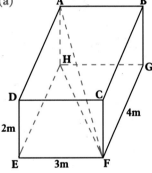

Use $\triangle$EHF to find HF.
Use $\triangle$AHF to find AF.

(b)

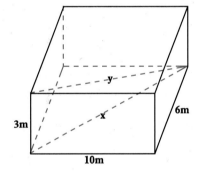

Find the length of x and y.

2.

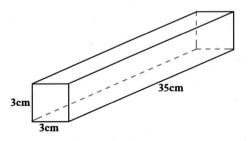

Find the length of the longest knitting needle
which can be placed in this container.

3. Pencils are stored in a cuboid container with dimensions 6cm × 3cm × 16cm. What is the
length of the longest pencil which can be placed in this container?

4.  (a)

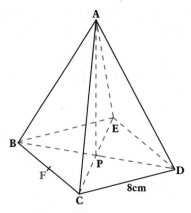

This diagram represents a square-based pyramid of height 12cm. F is the mid-point of BC.
Find the lengths of FP and AF.

(b)

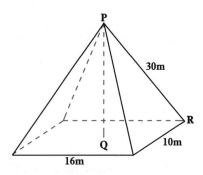

Calculate the length of QR. Hence find the height of this pyramid.

5.

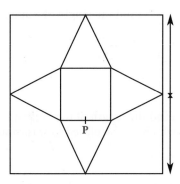 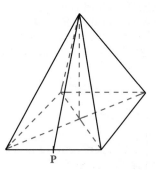

The diagram on the left shows the net of a pyramid drawn on a square piece of cardboard. The net is folded into the pyramid shown at the right. The edges of the base of this pyramid are each 5cm; the height is 6cm. P is the mid-point of one of the edges of the base. Calculate the length shown as x.

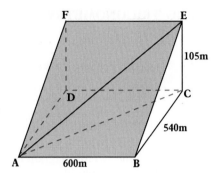

6.  The shaded face on this prism represents a hill. The rectangle ABCD is horizontal, the line EC is vertical. Tony cycles diagonally up this hill, from A to E at an average speed of 8m/sec. How long does it take Tony to go from A to E?

7.

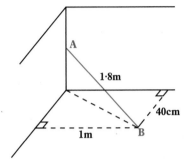

This diagram represents a plank of wood, AB, leaning against a wall. The end A rests on the wall; the end B rests on the floor.
How far up the wall is A?

**Review 1**

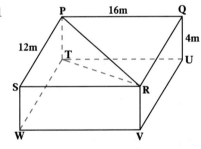

Calculate the length of  (a) PR
(b) TR.

**Review 2**   The luggage compartment of a Ford station wagon is 1·6m long, 1·3m wide and 80cm high. What is the length of the longest thin stick which can be carried if the doors are kept shut?

**Review 3**   This diagram represents a tent. The floor is a square of area 9m². Calculate the height, AB, of the centre pole.

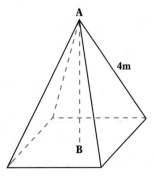

## USING TRIGONOMETRY

**Remember:** $\sin\theta = \dfrac{y}{r}$, $\quad \cos\theta = \dfrac{x}{r}$, $\quad \tan\theta = \dfrac{y}{x}$

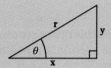

*Worked Example*  This diagram represents a cuboid.

Calculate　(a) QU
　　　　　　　(b) WU
　　　　　　　(c) WQ
　　　　　　　(d) ∠QWU.

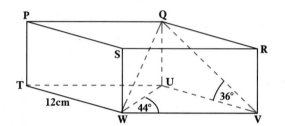

*Answer* (a)

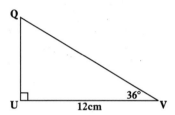

$$\frac{QU}{12} = \tan 36°$$
$$QU = 12\tan 36°$$
$$= 8{\cdot}7\text{cm (1 d.p.)}$$

(b)

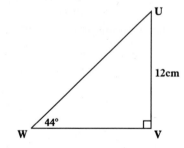

$$\frac{12}{WU} = \sin 44°$$
$$\frac{12}{\sin 44°} = WU$$
$$WU = 17{\cdot}3\text{cm (1 d.p.)}$$

(c)

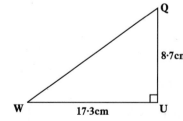

$$WQ^2 = 8{\cdot}7^2 + 17{\cdot}3^2 \text{ (Pythagoras' Theorem)}$$
$$WQ = 19{\cdot}4\text{cm (1 d.p.)}$$

(d) From the above diagram, $\tan QWU = \dfrac{8{\cdot}7}{17{\cdot}3}$
$$\angle QWU = 27° \text{ (to the nearest degree)}$$

## EXERCISE 18:3

1.

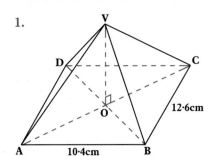

The height, VO, of this pyramid is 6·2cm.
(a) Use Pythagoras' Theorem to calculate the length of AC.
(b) Use trigonometry to calculate the size of ∠VCO.

2. This diagram represents a rectangular box.
Calculate  (a) the height of the box
 (b) ∠BGF
 (c) the length of EG.

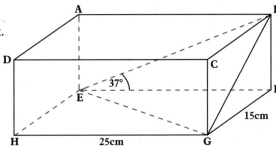

3.

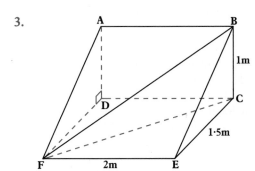

This diagram represents a ski jump.
Calculate  (a) the length of CF
 (b) the length of BF
 (c) ∠CFE
 (d) ∠BFC.

4. The slant height PQ of this cone is 12·5cm. O is the centre of the base.
If PQ makes an angle of 40° with OQ, find the diameter of the base.

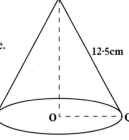

5.

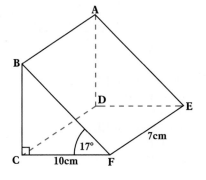

A door wedge is shaped as a triangular prism.
(a) Use trigonometry to find the length of BC.
(b) Calculate the volume of this door wedge.

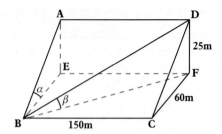

6. (a) Calculate the size of the angle marked as $\alpha$.
   (b) List the steps needed to calculate the size of
       the angle marked as $\beta$.
       Find the size of this angle.

7.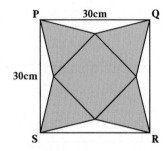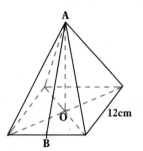

The shaded net, on the left, is folded to make the square-based pyramid at the right.
(a) Calculate the length of QS.
    Hence show that the length of AB is 15·2cm, correct to 1 d.p.
(b) Calculate the size of ∠ABO.

8.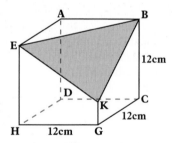

One corner of a block of wood is sawn off along the
shaded plane. GK = 3cm.
(a) Explain why △EBK is isosceles.
(b) Calculate the lengths of the sides of △EBK.
(c) Calculate the size of the angles of △EBK.

**Review 1** This diagram represents a square-based pyramid.
M is the mid-point of one of the edges of the base.
(a) Calculate the height of this pyramid.
(b) List the steps needed to find the length of the edge TQ.
    Find the length of this edge.

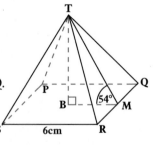

**Review 2**

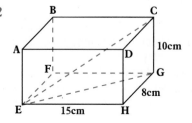

Calculate (a) the length of EG
          (b) ∠GEH
          (c) ∠CEG
          (d) the length of CE
          (e) ∠BGF.

## ANGLE between a LINE and a PLANE. ANGLE between TWO PLANES.

In this diagram, $\theta$ is the angle between the line MN and the shaded plane. This angle is found as follows.

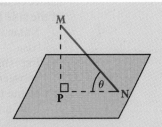

*Step 1*  From M, drop a perpendicular to the plane to meet the plane at P.

*Step 2*  Join PN.
The angle $\theta$ between MN and PN is the angle between the line MN and the plane.

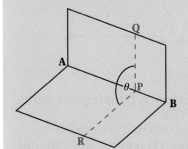 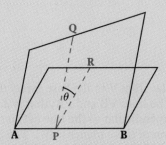 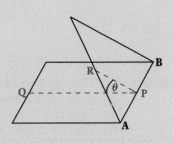

In these diagrams, $\theta$ is the angle between the two planes. This angle is found as follows:

*Step 1*  Take any point P on AB, the line of intersection of the planes.

*Step 2*  From P, draw PQ on one plane and PR on the other so that PQ and PR are both perpendicular to AB.
The angle $\theta$ between PQ and PR is the angle between the planes.

*Worked Example*  In this cuboid, the faces ABCD and EFGH are horizontal.
  (a) Name the angle between AG and the plane EFGH.
  (b) Name the angle between BF and the plane ABCD.
  (c) Name the angle which gives the inclination of BG to the horizontal.
  (d) Name the angle between the planes AEG and ADHE.

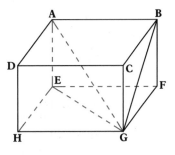

*Answer*  (a) Since the perpendicular from A to the plane EFGH meets the plane at E, the required angle is the angle between AG and EG; that is, $\angle$AGE.
  (b) Since BF is perpendicular to the plane ABCD, the required angle is either $\angle$FBA or $\angle$FBC.
  (c) We need the angle between BG and the plane EFGH. Since the perpendicular from B to the plane EFGH meets the plane at F, the required angle is the angle between BG and GF; that is, $\angle$BGF.
  (d) The line of intersection of these planes is EA. The line EH is on the plane ADHE and is perpendicular to AE. The line EG is on the plane AEG and is perpendicular to AE. The required angle is the angle between EH and EG; that is, $\angle$HEG.

*Worked Example* In this pyramid, V is directly above the centre of the base, P. M is the mid-point of the side BC.
(a) Name the angle between VB and the base.
(b) Explain why ∠VBA is *not* the angle between the faces VBC and ABCD.
(c) Name the angle between the faces VBC and ABCD.

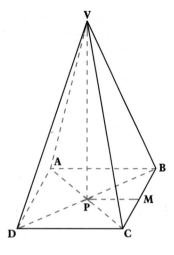

*Answer* (a) Since the perpendicular from V to the base meets the base at P, the required angle is the angle between the lines VB and PB; that is ∠VBP.
(b) Because VB is not perpendicular to the line of intersection, BC, of the faces.
(c) The line of intersection of these planes is BC. The line VM is on the face VBC; the line PM is on the face ABCD. Both VM and PM are perpendicular to the line BC. Hence the required angle is the angle between VM and PM; that is, ∠VMP.

## EXERCISE 18:4

1.  This diagram represents a cuboid. Name the angle between
    (a) EG and the face AEHD
    (b) EG and the face CDHG
    (c) ED and the face CDHG
    (d) ED and the face EFGH
    (e) the faces EFGH and AEHD
    (f) the faces EFGH and CDHG.

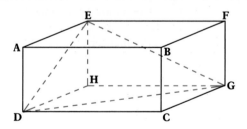

2.

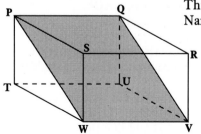

This diagram represents a rectangular box.
Name the angle between
(a) QV and the plane PQUT
(b) QV and the plane TUVW
(c) QW and the plane PSWT
(d) the planes PQVW and TUVW
(e) the front face and the base.

3. This diagram represents a pyramid on a rectangular base PQRS. V is directly above B. M is the mid-point of SR, N is the mid-point of PS.

Name the angle between   (a) the line VS and the plane PQRS
                     (b) the line VP and the base
                     (c) the planes VPS and PQRS
                     (d) the triangular face VSR and the base.

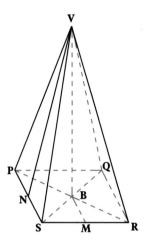

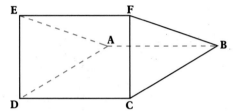

4. In this prism, the face ABCD is horizontal and the face CDEF is vertical. Both ABCD and CDEF are rectangular.
(a) Name the angle the edge FB makes with the face ABCD.
(b) Name the angle between the faces ABFE and CDEF.
(c) The angle EAD is the angle between two faces. Which faces?

5. This diagram represents a green-house. The rectangular base ABCD is horizontal, as is PQ. The end faces APD and BQC are congruent triangles with PA = PD = QB = QC. These faces are vertical.
(a) Name the angle which gives the inclination of the line DQ to the horizontal.
(b) Name the angle between the planes ABQP and ABCD.

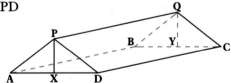

**Review 1**

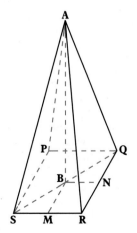

This diagram represents a square-based pyramid. M and N are the mid-points of SR and RQ.
Name the angle   (a) between the edge AQ and the base
             (b) the line AN makes with the plane PQRS
             (c) between the faces ASR and PQRS.

**Review 2**

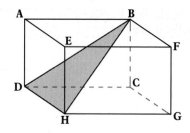

This diagram represents a cuboid.
(a) Name the angle between the line BH and the base.
(b) Name the angle between the edge AB and the face AEHD.
(c) Explain why ∠BHC is not an angle between the planes BDH and DCGH.
(d) Name the angle between the planes DBH and DCGH.

*Worked Example*  The top and bottom faces of this cuboid are horizontal.
(a) Calculate the length of FH.
(b) Find the size of ∠ACD.
(c) Calculate the angle the line FD makes with the face EHGF.
(d) Find the angle of inclination of the plane ADGF to the vertical.

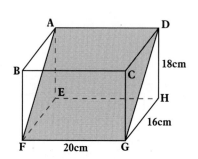

*Answer*  (a)

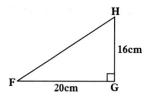

FH² = 20² + 16² (Pythagoras' Theorem)
FH = 25·6cm (1 d.p.)

(b)

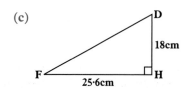

$$\tan ACD = \frac{20}{16}$$
∠ACD = 51° (to the nearest degree)

(c)

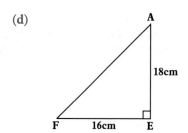

Since the perpendicular from D meets the face EHGF at H, the required angle is ∠DFH.
$$\tan DFH = \frac{18}{25.6}$$
∠DFH = 35° (to the nearest degree)

(d)

The line of intersection of the planes ADGF and ADHE is AD. Since the lines AF and AE are both perpendicular to AD, the required angle is the angle between AF and AE; that is ∠FAE.
$$\tan FAE = \frac{16}{18}$$
∠FAE = 42° (to the nearest degree)

378

## EXERCISE 18:5

1.  (a) Use Pythagoras' Theorem to calculate FH.
    (b) Use trigonometry to calculate ∠FBG.
    (c) Name the angle between the line AG and the
        plane EFGH. Calculate this angle.

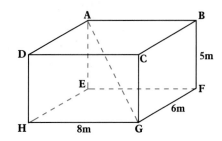

2.

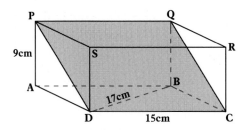

In this cuboid, the planes PQRS and ABCD
are horizontal. The length of DB is 17cm.
(a) Calculate the length of the edge AD.
(b) Calculate angle AQB.
(c) Calculate the angle the shaded plane
    makes with the horizontal.

3.  The roof of a newly designed disco is shown.
    The roof has a horizontal face, BCD, which is right-angled
    at D. The face ABC is vertical and right-angled at B.
    Calculate  (a) the length of BD
               (b) the length of AC
               (c) the length of AD
               (d) ∠CBD
               (e) the angle AD makes with the horizontal.

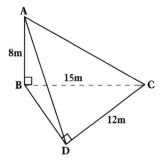

4.

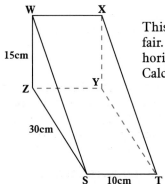

This diagram represents a large block of cheese on display at a food
fair. WXYZ is a rectangular vertical face; STYZ is a rectangular
horizontal face.
Calculate  (a) the length of TW
           (b) the angle between the line WS and the plane WXYZ
           (c) the angle between the planes STYZ and STXW.

5.  This diagram represents a pyramid on a square base of length 15cm. O is directly below P. M is the mid-point of BC. The sloping edges are each 20cm.
    (a) Calculate the length of DB.
    (b) Calculate the height, PO.
    (c) Name the angle the edge DP makes with the base. Calculate this angle.
    (d) Calculate the angle the triangular face PBC makes with the base.

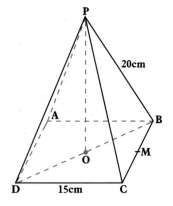

6.

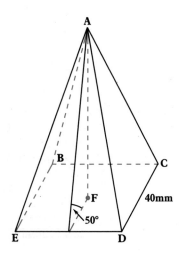

This diagram represents a large wooden die with edges of 5cm.
(a) Calculate the length of HF.
(b) Calculate the angle between the line AG and the plane EFGH.

7.  A paperweight is shaped as a square-based pyramid. A is directly above F, the mid-point of the base. The face AED is inclined at an angle of 50° to the base.
    (a) Calculate the height, AF.
    (b) Calculate the length of the sloping edge AE.

8.

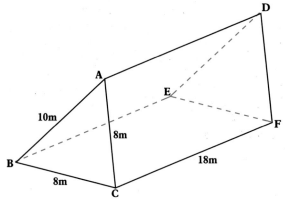

This diagram represents a triangular prism.
(a) Use the fact that ∆ABC is isosceles to calculate ∠ABC. Give your answer to the nearest degree.
(b) Use your answer to (a) to calculate the height of A above the face BCFE. Give your answer to the nearest centimetre.
(c) Calculate the angle the line FA makes with the face BCFE.

9.  This diagram represents a rubbish bin. The top and bottom horizontal faces are square.
Calculate  (a) angle AEF
            (b) the vertical height of the rubbish bin.

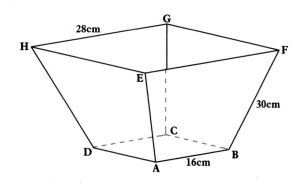

10.

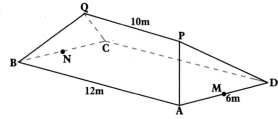

This diagram represents the roof of a shed. The rectangular base ABCD is horizontal as is the ridge PQ. PQ is 2 metres above ABCD. The end faces PAD and QBC are congruent isosceles triangles with AP = PD = BQ = QC. M and N are the mid-points of AD and BC. Name the angle the triangular end face PAD makes with the base ABCD. Calculate this angle.

Review 1   The top and bottom faces of this cuboid are horizontal. Calculate
(a) the length of DG
(b) the length of AG
(c) ∠BFC
(d) the angle the line EG makes with the shaded plane
(e) the inclination of the shaded plane to the horizontal.

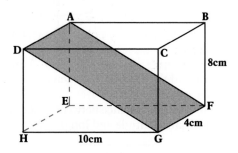

381

**Review 2**

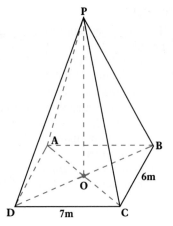

This diagram represents a pyramid on a rectangular base. The height, OP, is 9 metres.
(a) Calculate the lengths of BD, OB and PB.
(b) Calculate the angle between the triangular face PDC and the base.
(c) Explain why the angle between the planes PDC and ABCD is *not* the same as the angle between the planes PCB and ABCD.

**Review 3** This diagram represents a triangular prism used in a science laboratory.
In this prism the faces PQR and SUT are right-angled isosceles triangles. N and M are the mid-points of ST and PR.
(a) Calculate the length of SN.
(b) Name the angle the line SR makes with the face SUT. Calculate this angle.
(c) Calculate the angle between the planes SQT and SUT.

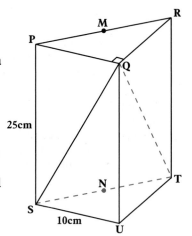

**RESEARCH PROJECT 18:6**

Latitude and Longitude

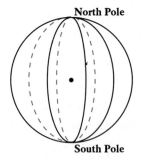

Parallels of latitude          Meridians of longitude

To find the distance between places which have the same longitude we find the length of an arc of a circle.
To find the distance between places which have the same latitude we use trigonometry.
Research latitude and longitude.

## CHAPTER 18  REVIEW

1.  The diagram shows a glass paperweight in the form of a pyramid, having vertex *A* and a square base, *BCDE*. The edges *AB*, *AC*, *AD* and *AE* are each 58mm long. The edges, *BC*, *CD*, *DE* and *EB* are each 52mm long. The diagonals of *BCDE* intersect at *F*.

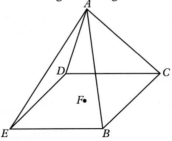

(a)   Calculate
   (i)   the length of *BF*,
   (ii)  the angle between the edge *AB* and the base of the paperweight,
   (iii) the height of the paperweight.

(b)   *X* is the mid-point of *BC*. Calculate the angle between *AX* and the base of the pyramid.

   **WJEC**

2.  *ABCDEF* is a triangular prism, 16cm long, as shown.

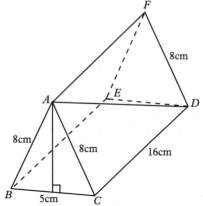

Calculate the size of the angle between *AD* and the base *BCDE*.

   **NEAB**

3.  Students are designing a wheelchair ramp to put alongside some steep steps.
   (i)   The diagram below shows a side view of the ramp.
      The line *CB* is horizontal and *AC* is vertical.

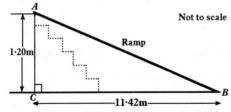

*AC* = 1·20m and *CB* = 11·42m
Use trigonometry to find angle $\widehat{ABC}$.

**(ii)** The ramp is made from plywood fixed to a metal frame.
The frame is 2·00m wide.

The frame consists of a sloping rectangle *ABED* and a horizontal rectangle *CBEF* with four
equally spaced vertical supports on each side, as shown.

There are also 2 diagonal bars *CW* and *AW* to keep the frame rigid.

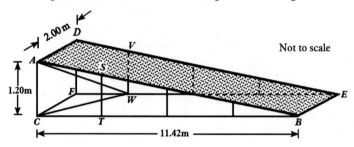

**(a)** Use similarity to explain why *ST* is 0·90m long.
**(b)** Calculate the length of the diagonal bar *CW*.
**(c)** Calculate the length of the diagonal bar *AW*.

**NEAB**

**4.**

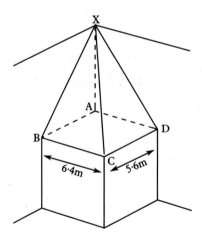

The diagram shows part of the roof of a new out-of-town superstore. The point X is vertically
above A, and ABCD is a horizontal rectangle in which CD = 5·6m, BC = 6·4m. The line XB
is inclined at 70° to the horizontal. Calculate the angle that the ridge XC makes with the
horizontal.

**MEG**

## VECTOR and SCALAR QUANTITIES

Quantities which have both size and direction are called vector quantities.
Quantities which have just size are called scalar quantities.

## VECTOR NOTATION

Vector quantities may be represented by a line.
The length of the line represents the size of the vector. An arrow is placed on the line to show the direction of the vector.

For instance, the vector **a** represents a velocity of 5km/h in a North-East direction.

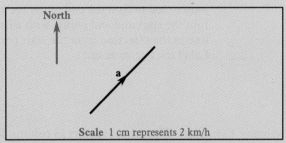

Scale  1 cm represents 2 km/h

Vectors are sometimes labelled with a single lower-case letter such as **a**. In hand-written material we place a wavy line underneath the letter. That is, a̰ , b̰ , d̰ , m̰ etc. are used to label vectors. In typed material, the lower-case letters are usually written in bold typeface and the wavy line is omitted. That is, **a, b, d, m** etc. are used to label vectors.

Vectors are sometimes labelled with two upper case letters such as AB. A is the point where the vector begins; B is the point where the vector ends. We place an arrow over the AB to

indicate the vector. That is, $\overrightarrow{AB}$ represents the vector which begins at A and finishes at B.

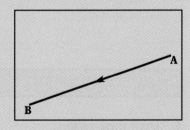

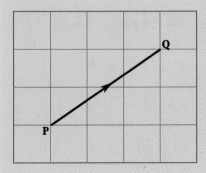

Vectors drawn on a grid can be described by giving the position of the end point in relation to the start point.
Since Q is 3 squares in the x-direction and 2 squares in the y-direction from P, the vector $\overrightarrow{PQ}$ can be described by $\overrightarrow{PQ} = \left(\begin{smallmatrix} 3 \\ 2 \end{smallmatrix}\right)$. When a vector is written like this it is said to be written as a column vector.
**Note** We cannot write $\overrightarrow{PQ} = (3, 2)$ since $(3, 2)$ refers to a point.

***Worked Example*** Draw the vectors (a) $\overrightarrow{EF} = \begin{pmatrix} 4 \\ -1 \end{pmatrix}$ (b) $\mathbf{m} = \begin{pmatrix} -3 \\ 4 \end{pmatrix}$

***Answer*** (a) These diagrams show the steps to take.

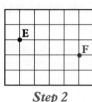

*Step 1* Start at any point E.

*Step 2* From E, move 4 in the x-direction, then −1 in the y-direction to find the point F.

*Step 1*    *Step 2*    *Step 3*

*Step 3* Join E and F with a line. Place an arrow on this line in the direction from E to F.

(b) Start at any point, move −3 in the x-direction then 4 in the y-direction to find the end of the vector.
Join the start and end points with a line. Place an arrow on the line in the direction from the start point to the end point.
Label the vector as **m**.

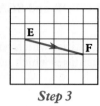

***Worked Example*** Write these vectors in column form.

***Answer*** $\overrightarrow{AB} = \begin{pmatrix} -4 \\ -1 \end{pmatrix}$    $\mathbf{p} = \begin{pmatrix} 2 \\ 4 \end{pmatrix}$    $\overrightarrow{ML} = \begin{pmatrix} 0 \\ 4 \end{pmatrix}$

$\mathbf{q} = \begin{pmatrix} 2 \\ -5 \end{pmatrix}$    $\mathbf{b} = \begin{pmatrix} -4 \\ 0 \end{pmatrix}$

## EXERCISE 19:1

1. Draw these vectors.

$\overrightarrow{AB} = \begin{pmatrix} 2 \\ 1 \end{pmatrix}$    $\overrightarrow{CD} = \begin{pmatrix} 3 \\ 2 \end{pmatrix}$    $\overrightarrow{EF} = \begin{pmatrix} 1 \\ 3 \end{pmatrix}$    $\overrightarrow{GH} = \begin{pmatrix} 1 \\ 2 \end{pmatrix}$    $\overrightarrow{KL} = \begin{pmatrix} -2 \\ 3 \end{pmatrix}$

$\overrightarrow{MN} = \begin{pmatrix} 3 \\ -2 \end{pmatrix}$    $\overrightarrow{PQ} = \begin{pmatrix} -2 \\ -3 \end{pmatrix}$    $\overrightarrow{RS} = \begin{pmatrix} -1 \\ -2 \end{pmatrix}$    $\mathbf{a} = \begin{pmatrix} 3 \\ 1 \end{pmatrix}$    $\mathbf{b} = \begin{pmatrix} -3 \\ -1 \end{pmatrix}$

$\mathbf{c} = \begin{pmatrix} 1 \\ -3 \end{pmatrix}$    $\mathbf{d} = \begin{pmatrix} 2 \\ -3 \end{pmatrix}$    $\mathbf{p} = \begin{pmatrix} -3 \\ 2 \end{pmatrix}$    $\mathbf{o} = \begin{pmatrix} -3 \\ -2 \end{pmatrix}$    $\mathbf{u} = \begin{pmatrix} 3 \\ 3 \end{pmatrix}$

$\mathbf{v} = \begin{pmatrix} -2 \\ -2 \end{pmatrix}$    $\mathbf{e} = \begin{pmatrix} 2 \\ 0 \end{pmatrix}$    $\mathbf{s} = \begin{pmatrix} 0 \\ 2 \end{pmatrix}$    $\mathbf{f} = \begin{pmatrix} -3 \\ 0 \end{pmatrix}$    $\mathbf{r} = \begin{pmatrix} 0 \\ -3 \end{pmatrix}$

2. Write these vectors as column vectors.

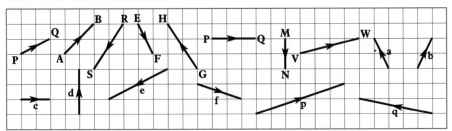

3. P shows the starting position of a car on a racing track. The car moves around this track, from P to A to B to C . . . to L, as described by the following vectors.

$$P \text{ to A: } \begin{pmatrix} 3 \\ 1 \end{pmatrix} \qquad A \text{ to B: } \begin{pmatrix} 3 \\ -1 \end{pmatrix} \qquad B \text{ to C: } \begin{pmatrix} 4 \\ -4 \end{pmatrix} \qquad C \text{ to D: } \begin{pmatrix} 1 \\ -2 \end{pmatrix}$$

$$D \text{ to E: } \begin{pmatrix} -1 \\ -1 \end{pmatrix} \qquad E \text{ to F: } \begin{pmatrix} -1 \\ -1 \end{pmatrix} \qquad F \text{ to G: } \begin{pmatrix} -7 \\ 0 \end{pmatrix} \qquad G \text{ to H: } \begin{pmatrix} -2 \\ -1 \end{pmatrix}$$

$$H \text{ to I: } \begin{pmatrix} -3 \\ 2 \end{pmatrix} \qquad I \text{ to J: } \begin{pmatrix} -1 \\ 1 \end{pmatrix} \qquad J \text{ to K: } \begin{pmatrix} 1 \\ 3 \end{pmatrix} \qquad K \text{ to L: } \begin{pmatrix} 3 \\ 3 \end{pmatrix}$$

(a) How many times did the car go off the track?
(b) Describe, using vectors, a possible route around the track in which the car does not go off the track at any stage.

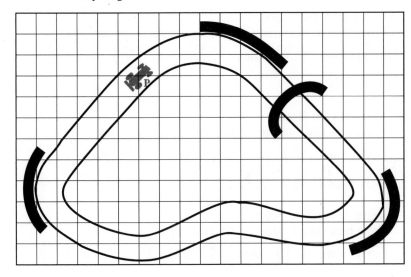

4. Draw a pair of axes. Number both the x and y-axes from –5 to 5.
Plot points to answer this question.

The coordinates of two points, P and Q are given. Write the vector $\overrightarrow{PQ}$ as a column vector.

(a) P(3, 1)  Q(4, 3)
(d) P(–3, 0)  Q(–1, –3)

(b) P(–2, 0)  Q(4, 1)
(e) P(2, 4)  Q(0, 0)

(c) P(1, 4)  Q(–2, 4)

Review

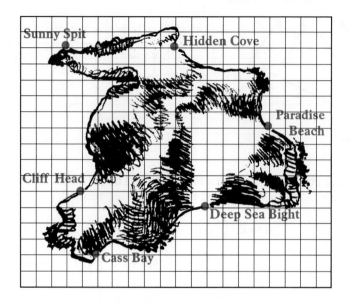

(i) Groups of people travelled by boat to this island. Each group was dropped off at a different place. These groups then made the journeys described below.
Which group, or groups, finished their journeys where they began?

**Ann's group**   Began at Hidden Cove.
From here their journey is described by these vectors:
$\begin{pmatrix} 0 \\ -4 \end{pmatrix}$ then $\begin{pmatrix} 6 \\ -1 \end{pmatrix}$ then $\begin{pmatrix} -4 \\ -5 \end{pmatrix}$ then $\begin{pmatrix} -5 \\ 0 \end{pmatrix}$ then $\begin{pmatrix} 2 \\ 6 \end{pmatrix}$
then $\begin{pmatrix} -5 \\ -5 \end{pmatrix}$.

**Simon's group**   Began at Cliff Head.
From here their journey is described by these vectors:
$\begin{pmatrix} 2 \\ -2 \end{pmatrix}$ then $\begin{pmatrix} 3 \\ 4 \end{pmatrix}$ then $\begin{pmatrix} -2 \\ 4 \end{pmatrix}$ then $\begin{pmatrix} 3 \\ 2 \end{pmatrix}$ then $\begin{pmatrix} 6 \\ -4 \end{pmatrix}$
then $\begin{pmatrix} -4 \\ -5 \end{pmatrix}$ then $\begin{pmatrix} -8 \\ 1 \end{pmatrix}$.

**Bik's group**   Began at Paradise Beach.
From here their journey is described by these vectors:
$\begin{pmatrix} -4 \\ -5 \end{pmatrix}$ then $\begin{pmatrix} -8 \\ 1 \end{pmatrix}$ then $\begin{pmatrix} 6 \\ 9 \end{pmatrix}$ then $\begin{pmatrix} -1 \\ -2 \end{pmatrix}$ then $\begin{pmatrix} 7 \\ -3 \end{pmatrix}$.

(ii) Write one column vector to describe each of these journeys.
　(a) From Cliff Head to Deep Sea Bight.
　(b) From Cass Bay to Hidden Cove.
　(c) From Paradise Beach to Deep Sea Bight.
　(d) From Hidden Cove to Paradise Beach.
　(e) From Paradise Beach to Hidden Cove.

# RELATIONSHIPS BETWEEN VECTORS

## DISCUSSION EXERCISE 19:2

- P is the point (2, 3). Q is the point (5, 1).

  The vector $\overrightarrow{PQ} = \left(\begin{smallmatrix} 3 \\ -2 \end{smallmatrix}\right)$.

  Write the vector $\overrightarrow{AB}$ as a column vector. What do you notice about the column vectors for $\overrightarrow{PQ}$ and $\overrightarrow{AB}$? What do you notice about the vectors $\overrightarrow{PQ}$ and $\overrightarrow{AB}$ on the diagram? Discuss.

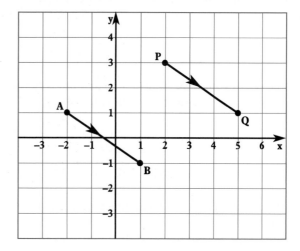

- In the above diagram the vector $\overrightarrow{PQ} = \left(\begin{smallmatrix} 3 \\ -2 \end{smallmatrix}\right)$.

  Write the vector $\overrightarrow{QP}$ as a column vector. What do you notice?

  **What if** the points P and Q were P(0, 1), Q(4, 3) or P(–1, 5), Q(–2, 2)? **Discuss.**

- $\mathbf{a} = \left(\begin{smallmatrix} 4 \\ 2 \end{smallmatrix}\right)$, $\mathbf{b} = \left(\begin{smallmatrix} 8 \\ 4 \end{smallmatrix}\right)$. What do you notice about $\mathbf{a}$ and $\mathbf{b}$ on the diagram?

  $\mathbf{a} = \left(\begin{smallmatrix} 4 \\ 2 \end{smallmatrix}\right)$, $\mathbf{c} = \left(\begin{smallmatrix} 2 \\ 1 \end{smallmatrix}\right)$. What do you notice about $\mathbf{a}$ and $\mathbf{c}$ on the diagram?

  Could we write $\mathbf{b}$ as $2\mathbf{a}$? Could we write $\mathbf{c}$ as $\frac{1}{2}\mathbf{a}$? What would the vector $3\mathbf{a}$ look like? What would the vector $-2\mathbf{a}$ look like? Discuss.

  As part of your discussion, make and test a statement which begins "If a vector $\mathbf{a}$ is multiplied by a number then . . .".

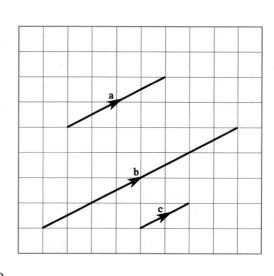

Vectors are **equal** if they have the same length and are in the same direction.
The vectors shown on this diagram are all equal.

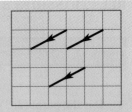

The vector **–a** has the same length as **a** but is in the opposite direction.
The vectors **a** and **–a** are shown on this diagram.

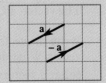

The vector 2**a** is in the same direction as **a** but twice as long as **a**.
The vector 3**a** is in the same direction as **a** but three times as long as **a**.

The vector $\frac{1}{2}$**a** is in the same direction as **a** but half the length of **a**.

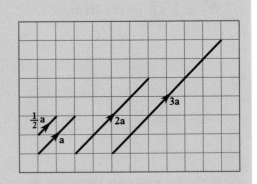

## EXERCISE 19:3

1.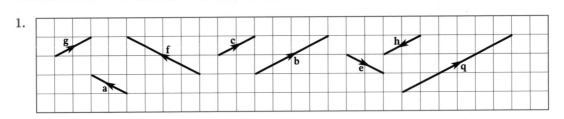

Name the vector equal to   (a) **g**    (b) **–c**    (c) 2**a**    (d) 2**g**    (e) 3**c**

                 (f) **–a**    (g) **–2h**    (h) $\frac{1}{2}$**f**    (i) $-\frac{1}{3}$**q**

2. $\mathbf{p} = \begin{pmatrix} -3 \\ 3 \end{pmatrix}$,      $\mathbf{q} = \begin{pmatrix} -4 \\ -1 \end{pmatrix}$,      $\mathbf{r} = \begin{pmatrix} 6 \\ 2 \end{pmatrix}$

Draw the vectors 2**p**, –**p**, 3**q**, $\frac{1}{2}$**r**, $-\frac{1}{3}$**p**.

3. $\overrightarrow{PQ} = \begin{pmatrix} 5 \\ 2 \end{pmatrix}$ as shown on the diagram.

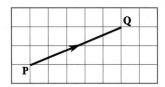

   (a) Write the vector $\overrightarrow{QP}$ as a column vector.

   (b) Copy and complete: $\overrightarrow{QP} = \ldots \overrightarrow{PQ}$.

4.

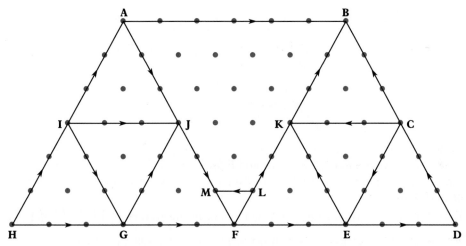

Copy and complete the following.

   (a) $\overrightarrow{CK} = \ldots \overrightarrow{KC}$     (b) $\overrightarrow{AB} = \ldots \overrightarrow{ED}$     (c) $\overrightarrow{AF} = \ldots \overrightarrow{IG}$     (d) $\overrightarrow{AB} = \ldots \overrightarrow{CK}$

   (e) $\overrightarrow{LM} = \ldots \overrightarrow{CK}$     (f) $\overrightarrow{DC} = \ldots \overrightarrow{AF}$     (g) $\overrightarrow{LM} = \ldots \overrightarrow{ED}$

## Review 1

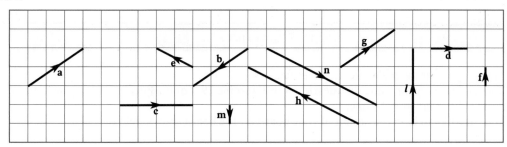

Name a vector equal to    (a) **a**     (b) **−a**     (c) **2d**     (d) $\frac{1}{2}$**c**     (e) **3e**

                         (f) $\frac{1}{4}$*l*     (g) **−m**     (h) **−3e**

**Review 2**    $\mathbf{a} = \begin{pmatrix} 1 \\ 2 \end{pmatrix}$    $\mathbf{m} = \begin{pmatrix} 3 \\ -2 \end{pmatrix}$    $\mathbf{p} = \begin{pmatrix} -8 \\ 4 \end{pmatrix}$

         Draw the vectors $2\mathbf{m}$, $-\mathbf{m}$, $\frac{1}{4}\mathbf{p}$, $3\mathbf{a}$, $-\frac{1}{2}\mathbf{p}$.

## PUZZLE 19:4

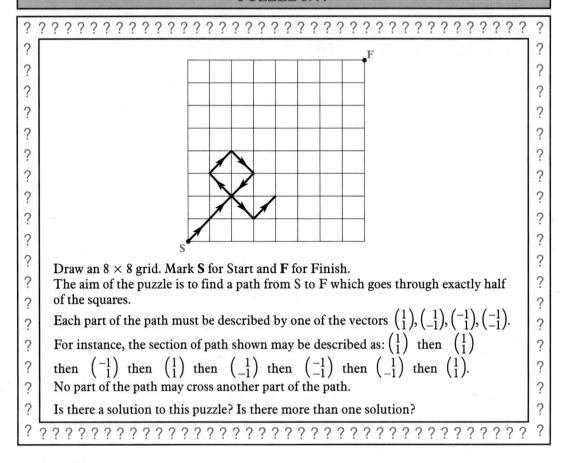

Draw an 8 × 8 grid. Mark **S** for Start and **F** for Finish.
The aim of the puzzle is to find a path from S to F which goes through exactly half of the squares.

Each part of the path must be described by one of the vectors $\binom{1}{1}, \binom{1}{-1}, \binom{-1}{1}, \binom{-1}{-1}$.

For instance, the section of path shown may be described as: $\binom{1}{1}$ then $\binom{1}{1}$

then $\binom{-1}{1}$ then $\binom{1}{1}$ then $\binom{1}{-1}$ then $\binom{-1}{-1}$ then $\binom{1}{-1}$ then $\binom{1}{1}$.

No part of the path may cross another part of the path.

Is there a solution to this puzzle? Is there more than one solution?

## PRACTICAL EXERCISE 19:5

Make up a board game which involves vectors.
You could base your game on **question 3** in **Exercise 19:1** or on **Puzzle 19:4** or you could design quite a different sort of game.
You may like to base the design of your board on the board shown below.

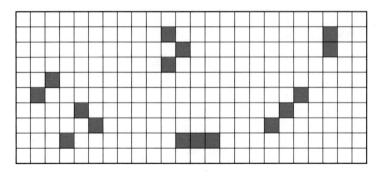

## ADDING and SUBTRACTING VECTORS

A movement from A to B is a translation of 3 squares in the x-direction and 4 squares in the y-direction. This translation may be described by the vector $\overrightarrow{AB} = \begin{pmatrix} 3 \\ 4 \end{pmatrix}$.

A movement from B to C is a translation of 2 squares in the x-direction and 3 squares in the negative y-direction. This translation may be described by the vector $\overrightarrow{BC} = \begin{pmatrix} 2 \\ -3 \end{pmatrix}$.

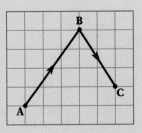

A movement from A directly to C is a translation of 5 squares in the x-direction and 1 square in the y-direction. This translation may be described by the vector $\overrightarrow{AC} = \begin{pmatrix} 5 \\ 1 \end{pmatrix}$.

A translation from A to B followed by a translation from B to C has the same start and end points as a translation directly from A to C.

Hence $\overrightarrow{AB} + \overrightarrow{BC} = \overrightarrow{AC}$.

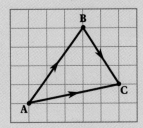

### DISCUSSION EXERCISE 19:6

- In the previous example, $\overrightarrow{AB} = \begin{pmatrix} 3 \\ 4 \end{pmatrix}$, $\overrightarrow{BC} = \begin{pmatrix} 2 \\ -3 \end{pmatrix}$ and $\overrightarrow{AC} = \begin{pmatrix} 5 \\ 1 \end{pmatrix}$. $\overrightarrow{AB} + \overrightarrow{BC} = \overrightarrow{AC}$ may be rewritten as $\begin{pmatrix} 3 \\ 4 \end{pmatrix} + \begin{pmatrix} 2 \\ -3 \end{pmatrix} = \begin{pmatrix} 5 \\ 1 \end{pmatrix}$. What is the relationship between the x-components 3, 2 and 5? What is the relationship between the y-components 4, –3 and 1? **Discuss.**
 What if $\overrightarrow{AB} = \begin{pmatrix} 0 \\ 3 \end{pmatrix}$ and $\overrightarrow{BC} = \begin{pmatrix} -2 \\ 1 \end{pmatrix}$? What if $\overrightarrow{AB} = \begin{pmatrix} -1 \\ -2 \end{pmatrix}$ and $\overrightarrow{BC} = \begin{pmatrix} 3 \\ 5 \end{pmatrix}$? What if . . .

- 
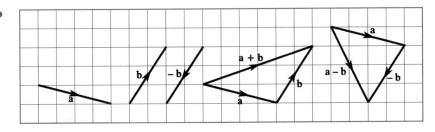

These diagrams show how to draw the vectors **a + b** and **a – b**. **Discuss** these diagrams. As part of your discussion write brief instructions on how to draw diagrams to show the vectors **a + b** and **a – b**.

From the diagrams, we see that $\mathbf{a} = \begin{pmatrix} 4 \\ -1 \end{pmatrix}$, $\mathbf{b} = \begin{pmatrix} 2 \\ 3 \end{pmatrix}$, $\mathbf{a + b} = \begin{pmatrix} 6 \\ 2 \end{pmatrix}$ and $\mathbf{a - b} = \begin{pmatrix} 2 \\ -4 \end{pmatrix}$. **Discuss** how to write **a + b** and **a – b** as column vectors *without* drawing diagrams.

To **add** the vectors **a** and **b** take the following steps.

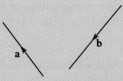

*Step 1* Draw **a**.
*Step 2* From the end of **a**, draw **b**.
*Step 3* Draw the vector from the beginning of **a** to the end of **b**. This is the vector **a + b**.

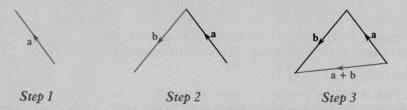

*Step 1*                    *Step 2*                    *Step 3*

To **subtract** the vector **b** from **a** (i.e. to draw **a − b**) add the vectors **a** and **−b**.

If the vectors are given as column vectors they may be added (or subtracted) by adding (or subtracting) the x-components and adding (or subtracting) the y-components.

*Worked Example*   Draw diagrams to represent
(a) **p + q**   (b) **q − p**   (c) **p − 2q**.

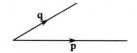

*Answer*   (a)                                    (b)

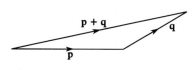      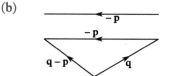

(c)

*Worked Example*  $\mathbf{a} = \begin{pmatrix} -2 \\ 6 \end{pmatrix}$, $\mathbf{b} = \begin{pmatrix} 1 \\ -1 \end{pmatrix}$, $\mathbf{c} = \begin{pmatrix} 0 \\ 3 \end{pmatrix}$.

As a column vector, find   (a) $\mathbf{c} + \mathbf{a}$   (b) $\mathbf{b} - \mathbf{a}$   (c) $2\mathbf{b}$   (d) $\frac{1}{2}\mathbf{a} - 2\mathbf{c}$.

*Answer*  (a) $\mathbf{c} + \mathbf{a} = \begin{pmatrix} 0 \\ 3 \end{pmatrix} + \begin{pmatrix} -2 \\ 6 \end{pmatrix}$   (b) $\mathbf{b} - \mathbf{a} = \begin{pmatrix} 1 \\ -1 \end{pmatrix} - \begin{pmatrix} -2 \\ 6 \end{pmatrix}$   (c) $2\mathbf{b} = 2\begin{pmatrix} 1 \\ -1 \end{pmatrix}$

$\qquad\qquad = \begin{pmatrix} -2 \\ 9 \end{pmatrix} \qquad\qquad\qquad\qquad = \begin{pmatrix} 3 \\ -7 \end{pmatrix} \qquad\qquad\qquad = \begin{pmatrix} 2 \\ -2 \end{pmatrix}$

(d) $\frac{1}{2}\mathbf{a} - 2\mathbf{c} = \frac{1}{2}\begin{pmatrix} -2 \\ 6 \end{pmatrix} - 2\begin{pmatrix} 0 \\ 3 \end{pmatrix}$

$\qquad\qquad\quad = \begin{pmatrix} -1 \\ 3 \end{pmatrix} - \begin{pmatrix} 0 \\ 6 \end{pmatrix}$

$\qquad\qquad\quad = \begin{pmatrix} -1 \\ -3 \end{pmatrix}$

## EXERCISE 19:7

1.  $\mathbf{p} = \begin{pmatrix} 3 \\ 2 \end{pmatrix}$   $\mathbf{q} = \begin{pmatrix} 2 \\ -1 \end{pmatrix}$   $\mathbf{r} = \begin{pmatrix} -1 \\ -3 \end{pmatrix}$   $\mathbf{s} = \begin{pmatrix} 4 \\ 0 \end{pmatrix}$     Write the following as column vectors.

| | | | | |
|---|---|---|---|---|
| (a) $\mathbf{p} + \mathbf{q}$ | (b) $\mathbf{p} + \mathbf{r}$ | (c) $\mathbf{s} + \mathbf{q}$ | (d) $\mathbf{p} + \mathbf{q} + \mathbf{r}$ | (e) $\mathbf{s} + \mathbf{r} + \mathbf{p}$ |
| (f) $\mathbf{p} - \mathbf{q}$ | (g) $\mathbf{q} - \mathbf{p}$ | (h) $\mathbf{s} - \mathbf{r}$ | (i) $3\mathbf{q}$ | (j) $\frac{1}{2}\mathbf{s}$ |
| (k) $\mathbf{p} + 3\mathbf{q}$ | (l) $\mathbf{r} - \frac{1}{2}\mathbf{s}$ | (m) $2\mathbf{q} - 3\mathbf{r}$ | | |

2.  Draw the vectors named underneath each diagram.

(a)   (b)   (c)   (d)

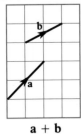    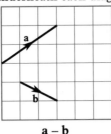    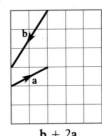    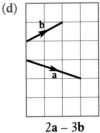

$\quad\quad \mathbf{a} + \mathbf{b} \qquad\qquad \mathbf{a} - \mathbf{b} \qquad\qquad \mathbf{b} + 2\mathbf{a} \qquad\qquad 2\mathbf{a} - 3\mathbf{b}$

3.

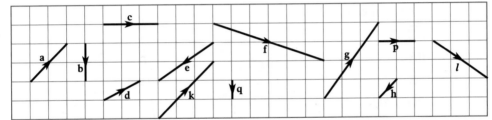

Which of these vectors is equal to  (a) $\mathbf{a} + \mathbf{b}$   (b) $\mathbf{b} - \mathbf{c}$   (c) $\mathbf{d} + \mathbf{e}$   (d) $\mathbf{c} + \mathbf{e}$   (e) $\mathbf{f} - \mathbf{c}$
(f) $\mathbf{d} - \mathbf{a}$   (g) $\mathbf{a} - \mathbf{h}$?

4. PQRS is a parallelogram. If $\overrightarrow{PQ} = \begin{pmatrix} 4 \\ 2 \end{pmatrix}$ and $\overrightarrow{SP} = \begin{pmatrix} -1 \\ 3 \end{pmatrix}$ write the following in the form $\begin{pmatrix} x \\ y \end{pmatrix}$.

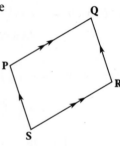

    (a) $\overrightarrow{SR}$    (b) $\overrightarrow{RS}$    (c) $\overrightarrow{RQ}$    (d) $\overrightarrow{SQ}$    (e) $\overrightarrow{PR}$

5.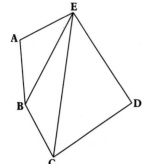

Which vector is equal to

    (a) $\overrightarrow{AC} + \overrightarrow{CB}$

    (b) $\overrightarrow{CE} + \overrightarrow{ED}$

    (c) $\overrightarrow{CB} + \overrightarrow{BE}$

    (d) $\overrightarrow{CD} + \overrightarrow{DE} + \overrightarrow{EB}$

    (e) $\overrightarrow{CE} - \overrightarrow{DE}$

    (f) $\overrightarrow{AC} - \overrightarrow{BC}$?

**Review 1**    $\mathbf{a} = \begin{pmatrix} 2 \\ -3 \end{pmatrix}$  $\mathbf{b} = \begin{pmatrix} -4 \\ 0 \end{pmatrix}$  $\mathbf{c} = \begin{pmatrix} 4 \\ 2 \end{pmatrix}$  $\mathbf{d} = \begin{pmatrix} -4 \\ -1 \end{pmatrix}$    Write the following in the form $\begin{pmatrix} x \\ y \end{pmatrix}$.

    (a) $\mathbf{a} + \mathbf{b}$    (b) $\mathbf{a} - \mathbf{d}$    (c) $2\mathbf{a} + \mathbf{c}$    (d) $3\mathbf{b} - \mathbf{d}$    (e) $\frac{1}{2}\mathbf{c} + \mathbf{a}$.

**Review 2**    Draw the vectors named underneath each diagram.

    (a)        (b)        (c)

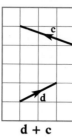    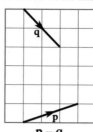    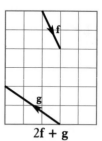

        **d + c**            **p − q**           **2f + g**

**Review 3**    Name a vector equal to

    (a) $\overrightarrow{AD}$

    (b) $\overrightarrow{BA}$

    (c) $\overrightarrow{BE}$

    (d) $\overrightarrow{CD} + \overrightarrow{DA}$

    (e) $\overrightarrow{BC} + \overrightarrow{CE}$

    (f) $\overrightarrow{AB} - \overrightarrow{EB}$.

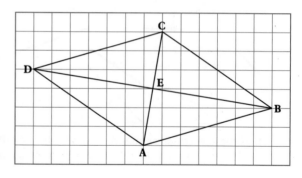

# USING VECTORS in GEOMETRY

The vector **2a** is parallel to the vector **a** and twice the length of **a**. Similarly, the vector 2 (**a** + **b**) is parallel to the vector **a** + **b** and twice the length of **a** + **b**.

*Worked Example*   ABC is a triangle. M is the mid-point of AB, N is the mid-point of AC. $\overrightarrow{NP} = \frac{2}{3}\overrightarrow{BC}$.

If $\overrightarrow{AC} = \mathbf{c}$ and $\overrightarrow{AB} = \mathbf{b}$

(a) express $\overrightarrow{BC}$ and $\overrightarrow{MN}$ in terms of **b** and **c**

(b) show that $\overrightarrow{NP} = \frac{2}{3}(\mathbf{c} - \mathbf{b})$

(c) explain why M, N and P lie on a straight line.

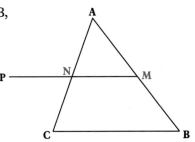

*Answer*   (a) $\overrightarrow{BC} = \overrightarrow{BA} + \overrightarrow{AC}$

$= -\mathbf{b} + \mathbf{c}$

$= \mathbf{c} - \mathbf{b}$

$\overrightarrow{MN} = \overrightarrow{MA} + \overrightarrow{AN}$

$= -\frac{1}{2}\mathbf{b} + \frac{1}{2}\mathbf{c}$

$= \frac{1}{2}(\mathbf{c} - \mathbf{b})$

(b) Since $\overrightarrow{NP} = \frac{2}{3}\overrightarrow{BC}$ then $\overrightarrow{NP} = \frac{2}{3}(\mathbf{c} - \mathbf{b})$.

(c) The vector $\overrightarrow{MN}$ is a multiple of the vector $\mathbf{c} - \mathbf{b}$ as is the vector $\overrightarrow{NP}$. Hence $\overrightarrow{MN}$ is parallel to $\overrightarrow{NP}$. Since these vectors have a common point, N, the points M, N and P must be on the same straight line.

*Worked Example*   ABCD is a quadrilateral. E, F, G and H are the mid-points of the sides AB, BC, CD and DA, as shown.
Prove that EFGH is a parallelogram.

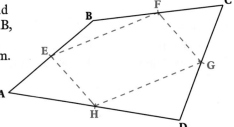

*Proof*   $\overrightarrow{EF} = \overrightarrow{EB} + \overrightarrow{BF}$

$= \frac{1}{2}\overrightarrow{AB} + \frac{1}{2}\overrightarrow{BC}$

$= \frac{1}{2}(\overrightarrow{AB} + \overrightarrow{BC})$

$= \frac{1}{2}\overrightarrow{AC}$

$\overrightarrow{HG} = \overrightarrow{HD} + \overrightarrow{DG}$

$= \frac{1}{2}\overrightarrow{AD} + \frac{1}{2}\overrightarrow{DC}$

$= \frac{1}{2}(\overrightarrow{AD} + \overrightarrow{DC})$

$= \frac{1}{2}\overrightarrow{AC}$

Since $\overrightarrow{EF} = \overrightarrow{HG}$, then the sides EF and HG of the quadrilateral EFGH are parallel and equal in length. Hence EFGH is a parallelogram.

## EXERCISE 19:8

1. (a) Write $\overrightarrow{PR}$ in terms of **a** and **b**.
   (b) Write $\overrightarrow{QT}$ in terms of **a** and **c**.
   (c) Show that $\overrightarrow{TR} = \mathbf{a} + \mathbf{b} - \mathbf{c}$.

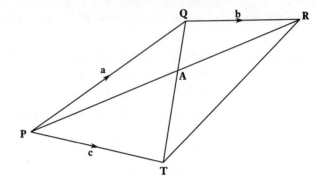

2. ABCD is a quadrilateral. $\overrightarrow{AB} = \mathbf{p}$, $\overrightarrow{BC} = \mathbf{q}$, $\overrightarrow{DA} = \mathbf{r}$. Write the following vectors in terms of **p, q** and **r**.
   (a) $\overrightarrow{DB}$      (b) $\overrightarrow{DC}$      (c) $\overrightarrow{CA}$

3.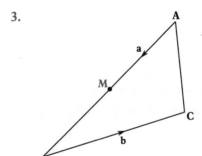

   M is the mid-point of the side AB of the triangle ABC. $\overrightarrow{AM} = \mathbf{a}$, $\overrightarrow{BC} = \mathbf{b}$.
   (a) Find $\overrightarrow{BM}$ and $\overrightarrow{MC}$ in terms of **a** and **b**.
   (b) Show that $\overrightarrow{AC} = 2\mathbf{a} + \mathbf{b}$.

4. $\overrightarrow{QT} = \frac{1}{4}\overrightarrow{QP}$, $\overrightarrow{RS} = 3\overrightarrow{QR}$.
   (a) Express $\overrightarrow{TR}$ and $\overrightarrow{PS}$ in terms of $\overrightarrow{QR}$ and $\overrightarrow{QT}$.
   (b) Explain why TRSP is a trapezium.

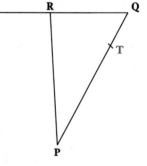

5.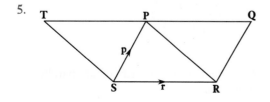

   PQRS is a parallelogram. $\overrightarrow{ST} = \overrightarrow{RP}$.
   If $\overrightarrow{SP} = \mathbf{p}$ and $\overrightarrow{SR} = \mathbf{r}$
   (a) express $\overrightarrow{QP}$, $\overrightarrow{RP}$ and $\overrightarrow{PT}$ in terms of **p** and **r**
   (b) prove that P is the mid-point of QT.

6. P and Q are points such that $\overrightarrow{BP} = 2\overrightarrow{PC}$
   and $\overrightarrow{AQ} = 2\overrightarrow{QC}$.
   Prove that the line joining P and Q is parallel
   to the side BA and one-third the length of BA.

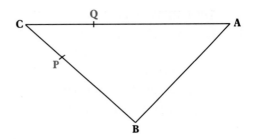

7.

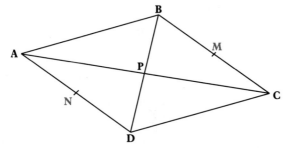

The diagonals of the parallelogram
ABCD meet at P. M and N are the
mid-points of the sides BC and AD.

(a) Write the vectors $\overrightarrow{AB}$, $\overrightarrow{DP}$, $\overrightarrow{MP}$
   and $\overrightarrow{PN}$ in terms of $\overrightarrow{DA}$ and $\overrightarrow{DC}$.

(b) What can you say about the points
   M, P and N? Explain your answer.

8. M is the mid-point of UV. Write the
   following in terms of **a, b** and **c**.

   (a) $\overrightarrow{VT}$
   (b) $\overrightarrow{VU}$
   (c) $\overrightarrow{VM}$
   (d) $\overrightarrow{MT}$

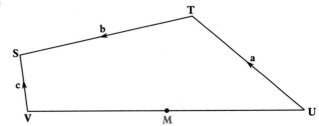

9.

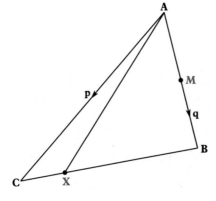

$\overrightarrow{AC} = \mathbf{p}$, $\overrightarrow{AB} = \mathbf{q}$. M is the mid-point of AB.
The point X divides the line CB in the ratio 1 : 4.

(a) Write $\overrightarrow{CB}$, $\overrightarrow{CX}$ and $\overrightarrow{AX}$ in terms of **p** and **q**.

(b) Show that $\overrightarrow{MX} = \frac{1}{10}(8\mathbf{p} - 3\mathbf{q})$.

10. ABCDEF is a regular hexagon.

$\overrightarrow{BC} = \mathbf{p}$, $\overrightarrow{BA} = \mathbf{q}$, $\overrightarrow{AF} = \mathbf{r}$.

(i) (a) Express $\overrightarrow{CD}$, $\overrightarrow{BF}$, $\overrightarrow{BD}$ and $\overrightarrow{CA}$ in terms of $\mathbf{p}$, $\mathbf{q}$ and $\mathbf{r}$.

(b) Write the vector $\overrightarrow{DF}$ in terms of $\overrightarrow{BF}$ and $\overrightarrow{BD}$. Hence show that the diagonals CA and DF are equal and parallel.

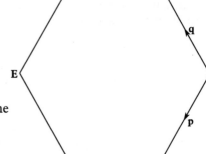

(ii) E is the point $(0, 0)$, F is the point $(1, \sqrt{3})$, D is the point $(1, -\sqrt{3})$.

(a) Show that the length of the side EF is 2 units.

(b) Find the coordinates of B and A.

(c) Show that the area of the hexagon is $6\sqrt{3}$ square units.

**Review 1**

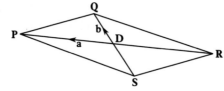

The diagonals of the parallelogram PQRS meet at D. $\overrightarrow{DP} = \mathbf{a}$, $\overrightarrow{DQ} = \mathbf{b}$.

Write $\overrightarrow{PQ}$, $\overrightarrow{RD}$ and $\overrightarrow{SP}$ in terms of $\mathbf{a}$ and $\mathbf{b}$.

**Review 2**  M is the mid-point of QR; N is the mid-point of PR. $\overrightarrow{PQ} = \mathbf{b}$, $\overrightarrow{PR} = \mathbf{a}$.

(a) Write $\overrightarrow{QR}$, $\overrightarrow{QM}$, $\overrightarrow{PM}$ and $\overrightarrow{QN}$ in terms of $\mathbf{a}$ and $\mathbf{b}$.

(b) G is the point on the line PM such that $\overrightarrow{PG} = 2\overrightarrow{GM}$.

Show that $\overrightarrow{NG} = \frac{1}{6}(2\mathbf{b} - \mathbf{a})$.

(c) Prove that N, G and Q are on the same straight line.

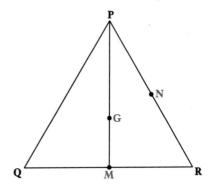

## VELOCITIES, FORCES

If we are told a yacht is moving through the water at a speed of 20km/h we do not know anything about the direction in which this yacht is travelling. If we are told both the speed and the direction of the yacht we then know the velocity of the yacht.

**Velocity** is a vector quantity which has both size and direction. **Speed** is a scalar quantity which has no direction.

**Force** is also a vector quantity since a force acting on an object pushes or pulls it in a particular direction.

## DISCUSSION EXERCISE 19:9

- A bird is flying due north at a speed of 40km/h. An easterly wind (a wind blowing from the east) begins to blow and the bird is blown off course. In which direction is the bird blown if the wind is 40km/h? **Discuss.**
    What if the wind speed is 20km/h?
    What if the wind speed is 10km/h?
    What if the wind speed is 60km/h?

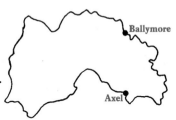

- Axel and Ballymore are two villages on the side of a lake. Ballymore is due north of Axel. Jane wishes to row her boat directly from Axel to Ballymore. Jane rows at a speed of 6km/h. There is an easterly current of 4km/h in the lake. In which direction should Jane point her boat? **Discuss.**

We use vector addition to find the resultant velocity of an object subject to two velocities or to find the resultant force on an object that is acted on by two forces.
We take the following steps to solve problems concerning vectors:
    *Step 1* Sketch the given vectors individually.
    *Step 2* Combine these vectors on a vector diagram.
**Note** To distinguish the resultant, it is a good idea to place two arrows on it, rather than one.

*Worked Example*  In still water, Tom's motorboat can travel at a maximum speed of 10km/h. Tom points his boat directly across a river in which there is a current of 2km/h. What is the maximum resultant velocity of Tom's boat?

*Answer*

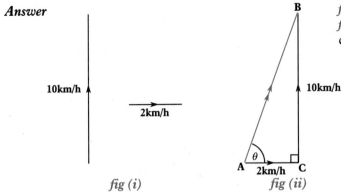

fig (i)  shows the given vectors.
fig (ii) shows the given vectors combined and the resultant drawn.

To find the maximum resultant velocity we need to find the length and direction of the vector $\overrightarrow{AB}$.

$AB^2 = 10^2 + 2^2$ (Theorem of Pythagoras)      $\tan \theta = \frac{10}{2}$
    $= 10 \cdot 2$ (1 d.p.)                      $\theta = 79°$ (2 s.f.)

Hence the resultant velocity is 10·2km/h at an angle of 79° to the direction of the current.

*Worked Example*   The bearing of B from A is 315°. An aircraft, whose speed relative to the air is 250km/h, flies from A to B. There is a SW wind of 60km/h blowing.
(a) In what direction must the pilot face the nose of the plane?
(b) Show that the resultant speed of the plane is about 243km/h.

*Answer*

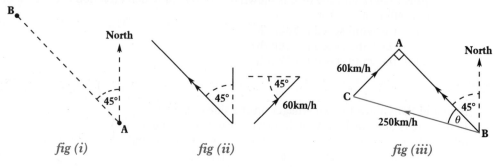

*fig (i)*          *fig (ii)*                    *fig (iii)*

*fig (i)*    shows the direction in which the plane flies.
*fig (ii)*   shows a sketch of the given vectors. We know the direction of the resultant but not the magnitude (size).
*fig (iii)*  shows the given vectors combined. The magnitude of the vector $\overrightarrow{BC}$ is 250km/h since the speed relative to the air is 250km/h.

(a) $\sin \theta = \frac{60}{250}$
      $\theta = 14°$ (to the nearest degree)
      The required direction is a bearing of $360° - 45° - 14° = 301°$.
(b) $AB^2 + 60^2 = 250^2$ (Theorem of Pythagoras)
        $AB^2 = 250^2 - 60^2$
        $AB = 243$ (3 s.f.)
      Hence the resultant speed is about 243km/h.

*Worked Example*   An object is subject to two forces acting at right angles. One force has magnitude of 170N, the other has magnitude of 205N.
(a) Find the angle the resultant force makes with the 170N force.
(b) Find the magnitude of the resultant force.

*Answer*

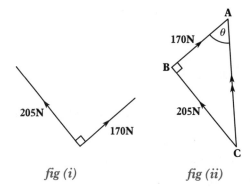

*fig (i)* shows possible vectors for the two forces.
*fig (ii)* shows the two forces combined and the resultant drawn.

*fig (i)*          *fig (ii)*

(a) $\tan \theta = \frac{205}{170}$
$\quad\quad \theta = 50°$ (2 s.f.)

Hence the resultant force makes an angle of 50° (2 s.f.) with the 170N force.

(b) $AC^2 = AB^2 + BC^2$  (Theorem of Pythagoras)
$\quad\quad = 170^2 + 205^2$
$AC = 266$ (3 s.f.)  Hence the magnitude of the resultant force is 266N (3 s.f.).

Scale drawing, rather than calculation, may be used to solve vector problems on velocities and forces. If scale drawing is used, sketches should be made before the accurate drawing is done.

For instance, the answer to the previous worked example may be found as follows.

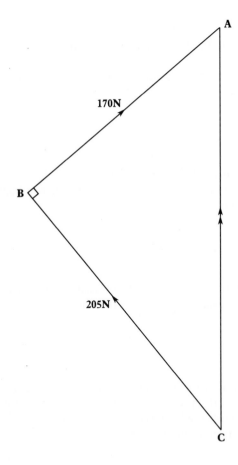

This vector diagram is drawn to scale using *1cm represents 25N*. The angle A is measured, using a protractor, as 50° to the nearest degree.

The length of AC is measured as 10·65cm.

Hence the answers are  (a) 50° (to the nearest degree)
$\quad\quad\quad\quad\quad\quad\quad\quad\quad$ (b) 10·65 × 25N = 266N.

## EXERCISE 19:10

**Solve some of these vector problems by calculation and some by scale drawing.**

1. Andrew canoes across a river. In still water, the canoe travels at 6m/s. The current, of 4m/s, carries the canoe down the river.

   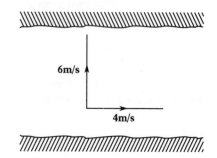

   (a) Sketch a vector diagram to show the direction in which the canoe moves.
   (b) Find the resultant speed of the canoe.
   (c) Find the angle between the direction of the canoe and the current.

2. Kay swims at a speed of 2km/h. She attempts to swim directly across a river in which the current is 1km/h.
   (a) At what angle to the bank of the river does Kay actually move?
   (b) What is Kay's resultant speed?

3. A pilot faces a plane due north. A westerly wind of 80km/h is blowing. If the plane's speed in still air is 300km/h find the resultant speed and direction of the plane.

   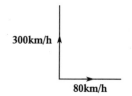

4. A small plane flies at 150km/h in still air. It heads east but is blown off course by a southerly wind of 50km/h. Find the resultant velocity of the plane.

5. A boat is to travel directly across a lake in which the cross current is 3km/h. If the boat travels at 10km/h in still water find the direction in which the driver must steer the boat. Give this direction as the angle made with the direction of the current.

   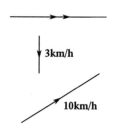

6. A helicopter, whose speed in still air is 124km/h, flies in an easterly wind of 42km/h. In which direction should the pilot steer the helicopter for the resultant velocity to be due south? What is the resultant speed?

7. Each of the following diagrams shows two forces acting on an object. For each, find the resultant force, giving the angle this resultant makes with the smaller of the two forces.

(a)

8N

5N

(b)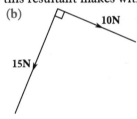

10N

15N

(c)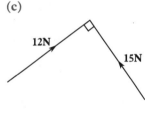

12N

15N

8. A ship is subject to velocities of 30 knots in a southerly direction and 8 knots in an easterly direction. Find the resultant velocity of this ship.

9.

14·7N

32N

This diagram shows the resultant of two forces and one of the forces.
(a) Find the magnitude of the second force.
(b) Find the angle this force makes with the resultant.

10. An object is acted on by two forces at right angles. One force is 16N and the other is 12N.
(a) Find the magnitude of the resultant force.
(b) Find the angle the resultant force makes with the 12N force.

11. A canoeist, whose canoe travels at 8ms⁻¹ in still water, steers directly across a river which is 40 metres wide. The current is 3ms⁻¹. How far downstream has the canoe travelled by the time it reaches the opposite bank?

12. Tina is able to swim at a maximum speed of 0·5m/s. She swims in a harbour which has a current of 0·2m/s from the west. Tina swims into the current so that her resultant velocity is towards the north.
(a) Find Tina's resultant speed.
(b) On what bearing does Tina head?
(c) How long does it take Tina to swim 100 metres?

13. A sculpture S is hung from a ceiling with two wires. These wires make angles of 50° and 40° with the ceiling. The tensions in the wires are $T_1$ and $T_2$ newtons. These tensions are equivalent to a single force of 60N acting vertically.
Find the tensions in the wires.

40°    50°

$T_2$    $T_1$

S

*Vectors*

**Review 1**  An aeroplane, which can travel at 400km/h in still air, is on an East-West flight path. There is a southerly wind of 100km/h.
    **(a)** In which direction must the pilot face the nose of the plane in order to stay on the flight path?
    **(b)** How far does this plane travel in 2 hours?

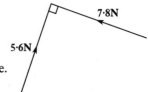

**Review 2**  These two forces act on an object.
    Find  **(a)**  the magnitude of the resultant force
           **(b)**  the angle the resultant makes with the 7·8N force.

**Review 3**  Jayne steers her motorboat on a bearing of 135°. The boat's speed, relative to the water, is 15ms⁻¹. The water is flowing north-east at a speed of 6ms⁻¹.
    **(a)** What is the resultant speed of Jayne's motorboat?
    **(b)** In what direction does Jayne's boat travel?

---

## DISCUSSION EXERCISE 19:11

All of the vector problems in **Exercise 19:10** could be solved by either calculation or scale drawing. Some vector problems are more easily solved by using scale drawing. Make up some problems that are like this. **Discuss** your problems.

---

## RESEARCH PROJECT 19:12

---

**Position Vectors. The vectors i and j.**

The vectors **i** and **j** are shown on this diagram. These vectors are fixed in position. Both begin at the origin. Research position vectors. Research the use of the vectors **i** and **j**.

## CHAPTER 19 REVIEW

1. $\overrightarrow{PQ} = \begin{pmatrix} 2 \\ 3 \end{pmatrix}$, $\overrightarrow{QR} = \begin{pmatrix} 4 \\ 5 \end{pmatrix}$, $\overrightarrow{TS} = \begin{pmatrix} 3 \\ 4 \end{pmatrix}$.

   **(a)** Show that PR is parallel to TS.
   **(b)** Write down the ratio of the length of PR to the length of TS.

   ULEAC

2. Sarah can swim at 0·4m/s in still water.
   She tries to swim across a stream at right angles to the current.
   The speed of the current is 0·5m/s.

   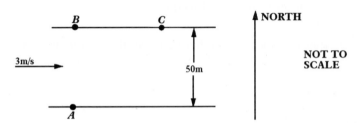

   Find Sarah's actual swimming speed in the stream.

   SEG

3.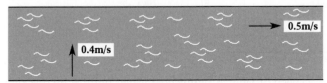

   A river with parallel banks 50m apart flows at a speed of 3m/s from West to East. A girl can swim in still water with a speed of 1·6m/s. She starts from *A* and intends to swim to *B*, which is due North of *A* and on the opposite bank. She heads North all the time but lands at *C*, further down stream.

   Calculate the distance *BC*.

   MEG

4. *ABCDEF* is a regular hexagon

   $$\overrightarrow{OA} = \mathbf{a}, \ \overrightarrow{OB} = \mathbf{b}$$

   **(a)** Write down, in terms of **a** and **b**, the vectors
      **(i)** $\overrightarrow{AB}$
      **(ii)** $\overrightarrow{FC}$

   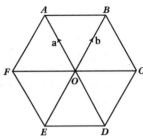

   **(b)** Write down one geometrical fact about *AB* and *FC* which could be deduced from your answers to part **(a)**.

   ULEAC

5. A ship, whose speed in still water is 20km per hour, sets course due West.
   The ship is driven off course by a current flowing due South-West at 5km per hour.

   **(a)** Draw an accurate vector diagram to show the resultant speed and direction of the ship.
   [Use a scale of 1cm to represent 2km per hour.]

**(b) (i)** What is the resultant speed of the ship? Give your answer to the nearest 0·1 km per hour.

    **(ii)** What is the resultant direction of the ship? Give your answer as a 3 figure bearing correct to the nearest degree.        **ULEAC**

**6.**

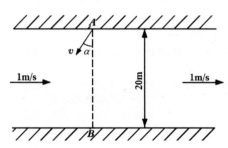

A river is flowing steadily at a speed of 1m/s. A motor boat leaves point $A$ on one side of the river. The boat has a constant speed, $v = 2$m/s.

**(a)** What is the resultant speed of the boat in the direction:
    **(i)** $AB;$     **(ii)** downstream?

**(b)** The boatman wishes to travel to a point $B$ on the other side of the river, directly opposite to $A$. Calculate the angle $\alpha$ (as shown on the diagram) at which the boat should be steered.        **SEG**

**7.** $OABC$ is a parallelogram.
$\overrightarrow{OA} = 3\mathbf{p} - 2\mathbf{q}$
$\overrightarrow{OC} = 5\mathbf{p} + 6\mathbf{q}$

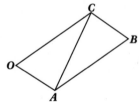

**(a)** Find $\overrightarrow{AC}$. Express your answer as simply as possible in terms of $\mathbf{p}$ and $\mathbf{q}$.

**(b)** $D$ is the point where $\overrightarrow{BD} = -2\mathbf{p} + 6\mathbf{q}$.
Using vector methods, show that $D$ lies on the line $AC$ produced.        **MEG**

**8.** A man can row a boat at 3mph in still water.

He wishes to cross a river from $A$ to $B$ at right angles to the river bank. The current is flowing at 2mph.

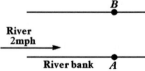

**(a) (i)** Draw a vector diagram to help you calculate the angle between the river bank and the direction in which he must row.
    **(ii)** Calculate the size of this angle.
**(b)** The river is 50 yards wide.
How many seconds will it take the man to row across the river?
(1 mile = 1760 yards)        **NEAB**

# Calculations with Non Right-Angled Triangles

**The SINE RULE**

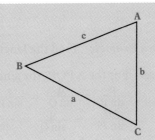

Upper case letters are used to label the angles of a triangle.
Lower case letters are used to label the sides of a triangle.
For instance, in the triangle shown, the side opposite angle A
is a, the side opposite angle B is b and the side opposite
angle C is c.

---

### DISCUSSION EXERCISE 20:1

- Since △ ABC is a right-angled triangle, we can
  use $\frac{b}{4 \cdot 6}$ = tan 35° to find the length of AC.
  Can we use one of the ratios sin, cos or tan to
  find the length of the side PQ in the isosceles
  triangle PQR? **Discuss.**

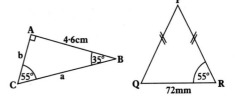

-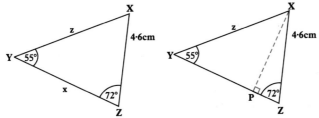

Since △ XYZ is not a right-angled triangle, we cannot use one of the ratios sin, cos or tan to
find the length of XY.
The second diagram shows the same △ XYZ divided into two right-angled triangles. To find
the length of XY we could begin as follows.

  Consider △ XYP. Since $\frac{XP}{z}$ = sin 55° then XP = z sin 55°.

  Consider △ XZP. Since $\frac{XP}{4 \cdot 6}$ = sin 72° then XP = 4·6 sin 72°.

How could we continue? **Discuss.**

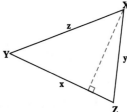

- Use reasoning similar to the above to show that $\frac{y}{\sin Y} = \frac{z}{\sin Z}$.
  It is also true that $\frac{x}{\sin X} = \frac{y}{\sin Y}$. **Discuss** how to show this.

For the $\triangle$ ABC, the **Sine Rule** is $\dfrac{a}{\sin A} = \dfrac{b}{\sin B} = \dfrac{c}{\sin C}$.

This may be rearranged as $\dfrac{\sin A}{a} = \dfrac{\sin B}{b} = \dfrac{\sin C}{c}$.

We use the first form of this when finding a side and the second form when finding an angle.

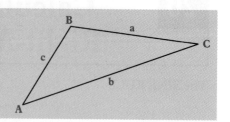

*Worked Example*   Find the length of the side PQ.

*Answer*   For the $\triangle$ PQR, the sine rule is

$\dfrac{p}{\sin P} = \dfrac{q}{\sin Q} = \dfrac{r}{\sin R}$ ; that is,

$\dfrac{48}{\sin 29°} = \dfrac{q}{\sin Q} = \dfrac{r}{\sin 110°}$.

We can find r by using $\dfrac{r}{\sin 110°} = \dfrac{48}{\sin 29°}$

$$r = \dfrac{48 \sin 110°}{\sin 29°} \text{ (multiplying both sides by sin 110°)}$$

$$r = 93\text{mm (to the nearest mm)}$$

(Keying   48 × 110 sin ÷ 29 sin = )

*Worked Example*   Find the length of the side AN.

*Answer*     For the $\triangle$ MAN, $\dfrac{m}{\sin M} = \dfrac{a}{\sin A} = \dfrac{n}{\sin N}$ ;

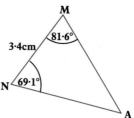

that is, $\dfrac{m}{\sin 81·6°} = \dfrac{3·4}{\sin A} = \dfrac{n}{\sin 69·1°}$

To find AN, we need $\dfrac{m}{\sin 81·6°}$ as part of our equation. Since there is an unknown in both $\dfrac{3·4}{\sin A}$

and $\dfrac{n}{\sin 69·1°}$ we cannot use either of these as they are. Since the angles of a triangle add to 180°

we can calculate angle A to be 29·3°. Then we can use $\dfrac{m}{\sin 81·6°} = \dfrac{3·4}{\sin 29·3°}$

$$m = \dfrac{3·4 \sin 81·6°}{\sin 29·3°}$$

$$m = 6·9 \text{ (1 d.p.)}$$
Hence the length of AN $= 6·9\text{cm (1 d.p.)}$

*Worked Example*   Find the size of $\angle$ABC.

*Answer*   Since $\dfrac{\sin A}{a} = \dfrac{\sin B}{b} = \dfrac{\sin C}{c}$

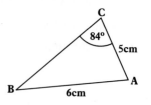

then $\dfrac{\sin A}{a} = \dfrac{\sin B}{5} = \dfrac{\sin 84°}{6}$.

Using $\dfrac{\sin B}{5} = \dfrac{\sin 84°}{6}$, $\sin B = \dfrac{5 \sin 84°}{6}$

angle B $= 56°$ (to the nearest degree)

(Keying   5 × 84 sin ÷ 6 = SHIFT sin⁻¹ )

## EXERCISE 20:2

1. Which statement is true?

(a)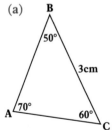

A. $b = \dfrac{3 \sin 70°}{\sin 50°}$

B. $b = \dfrac{3 \sin 60°}{\sin 50°}$

C. $b = \dfrac{3 \sin 60°}{\sin 70°}$

D. $b = \dfrac{3 \sin 50°}{\sin 70°}$

(b)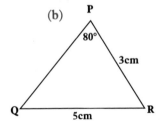

A. $\sin Q = \dfrac{5 \sin 80°}{3}$

B. $\sin Q = \dfrac{5}{3 \sin 80°}$

C. $\sin Q = \dfrac{3 \sin 80°}{5}$

D. $\sin Q = \dfrac{3}{5 \sin 80°}$

(c)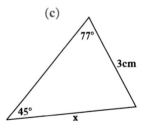

A. $x = \dfrac{3 \sin 45°}{\sin 77°}$

B. $x = \dfrac{3 \sin 77°}{\sin 45°}$

C. $x = \dfrac{\sin 45°}{3 \sin 77°}$

D. $x = \dfrac{\sin 77°}{3 \sin 45°}$

(e)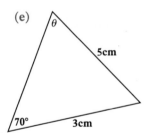

A. $\sin q = \dfrac{3 \sin 70°}{5}$

B. $\sin q = \dfrac{5 \sin 70°}{3}$

C. $\sin q = \dfrac{3}{5 \sin 70°}$

D. $\sin q = \dfrac{5}{3 \sin 70°}$

(f)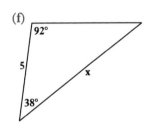

A. $x = \dfrac{5 \sin 92°}{\sin 38°}$

B. $x = \dfrac{5 \sin 38°}{\sin 92°}$

C. $x = \dfrac{5 \sin 92°}{\sin 50°}$

D. $x = \dfrac{5 \sin 50°}{\sin 92°}$

2.  (a)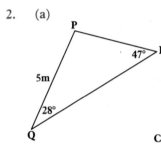

Find the length of PR.

(b)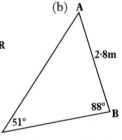

Find b.

(c)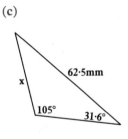

Find x.

(d)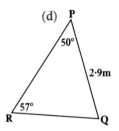

Find q.

(e)

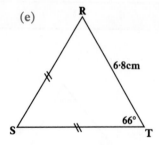

Find the length of ST.

3.

(a)

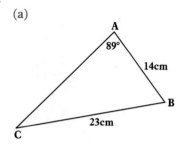

Find angle ACB.

(b)

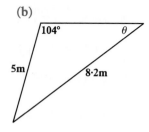

Find the angle $\theta$.

(c)

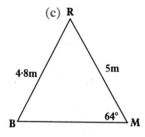

Find ∠BRM.

(d)

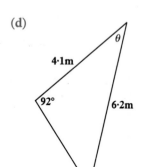

Find the angle $\theta$.

Review  In this triangle, find the size of the other two
angles and the third side.

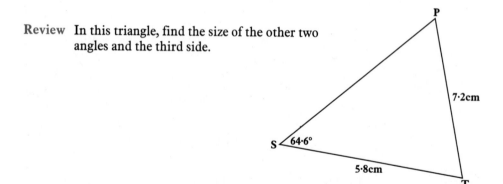

## The COSINE RULE

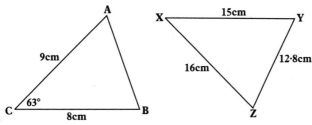

Colin claims that there is not enough information given in the triangles above to be able to find the other sides and angles using the sine rule. Is Colin correct? **Discuss.**

- Latifa found a way of finding the length of the side AB. She began by dividing the triangle into two right-angled triangles as shown. Her working is shown below. **Discuss** this working.

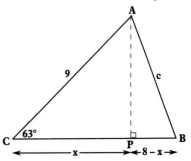

$AP^2 = 9^2 - x^2$
$AP^2 = c^2 - (8 - x)^2$
Hence $c^2 - (8 - x)^2 = 9^2 - x^2$
$$c^2 = 9^2 - x^2 + (8 - x)^2$$
$$= 9^2 - x^2 + 8^2 - 16x + x^2$$
$$= 9^2 + 8^2 - 16x$$
$$= 9^2 + 8^2 - 16 \times 9 \cos 63°$$

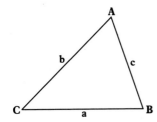

Reasoning, similar to Latifa's, can be used to show that for this triangle $c^2 = a^2 + b^2 - 2ab \cos C$. **Discuss** this reasoning.

For the △ ABC, the **Cosine Rule** is

$$a^2 = b^2 + c^2 - 2bc \cos A$$
$$\text{or } b^2 = a^2 + c^2 - 2ac \cos B$$
$$\text{or } c^2 = a^2 + b^2 - 2ab \cos C.$$

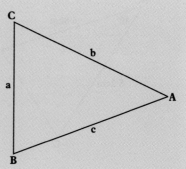

To find a we use the first formula, to find b we use the second and to find c we use the last.

We can rearrange these formulae as

$$\cos A = \frac{b^2 + c^2 - a^2}{2bc}, \quad \cos B = \frac{a^2 + c^2 - b^2}{2ac}, \quad \cos C = \frac{a^2 + b^2 - c^2}{2ab}.$$

These rearrangements can be used to find an angle.

***Worked Example*** (a)

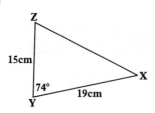

Find the length of XZ.

(b)

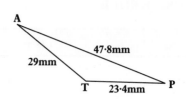

Find the size of ∠PTA.

***Answer*** (a) We need to find y.

$$y^2 = x^2 + z^2 - 2xz \cos Y$$
$$= 15^2 + 19^2 - 2 \times 15 \times 19 \times \cos 74°$$
$$y = 20{\cdot}7 \text{cm (1 d.p.)}$$

**Keying** $\boxed{15}$ $\boxed{\text{SHIFT}}$ $\boxed{x^2}$ $\boxed{+}$ $\boxed{19}$ $\boxed{\text{SHIFT}}$ $\boxed{x^2}$ $\boxed{-}$ $\boxed{2}$ $\boxed{\times}$ $\boxed{15}$ $\boxed{\times}$ $\boxed{19}$ $\boxed{\times}$ $\boxed{74}$ $\boxed{\cos}$ $\boxed{=}$ $\boxed{\sqrt{\phantom{x}}}$

(b) We need to find angle T.

$$\cos T = \frac{a^2 + p^2 - t^2}{2ap}$$
$$= \frac{23{\cdot}4^2 + 29^2 - 47{\cdot}8^2}{2 \times 23{\cdot}4 \times 29}$$
$$T = 131° \text{ (to the nearest degree)}$$

**Keying** $\boxed{(}$ $\boxed{23{\cdot}4}$ $\boxed{\text{SHIFT}}$ $\boxed{x^2}$ $\boxed{+}$ $\boxed{29}$ $\boxed{\text{SHIFT}}$ $\boxed{x^2}$ $\boxed{-}$ $\boxed{47{\cdot}8}$ $\boxed{\text{SHIFT}}$ $\boxed{x^2}$ $\boxed{)}$ $\boxed{\div}$ $\boxed{(}$ $\boxed{2}$ $\boxed{\times}$ $\boxed{23{\cdot}4}$ $\boxed{\times}$ $\boxed{29}$ $\boxed{)}$ $\boxed{=}$ $\boxed{\text{SHIFT}}$ $\boxed{\cos^{-1}}$

**Note** Other keying sequences may be used, including using the memory function.

## EXERCISE 20:4

1.

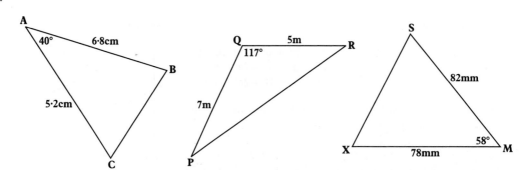

Find the length of     (a) BC          (b) q          (c) SX.

2.

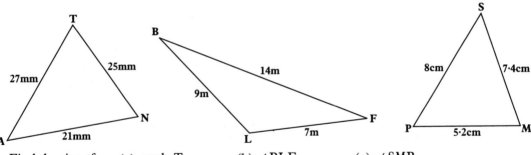

Find the size of    (a) angle T    (b) ∠BLF    (c) ∠SMP.

3. Use the cosine rule to find the size of angle P.
   Comment on your answer.

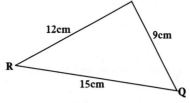

4. (a)

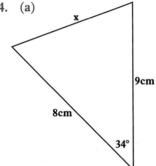

(b)

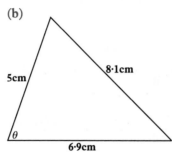

(c)

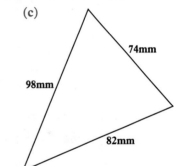

Find the length of the
side marked as x.

Find the size of
angle θ.

Use the cosine rule to find
the size of each of the angles
of this triangle. Give the
answers to the nearest
degree. Comment on the
answers.

5.

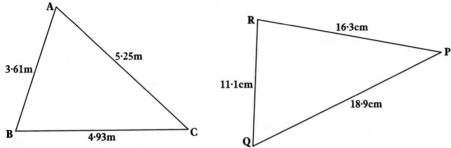

(a) Is it true that the largest angle of a triangle is opposite the largest side?
(b) What statement can you make about the smallest angle?
(c) Find the smallest angle of the triangle ABC.
(d) Find the largest angle of the triangle PQR.

## Review

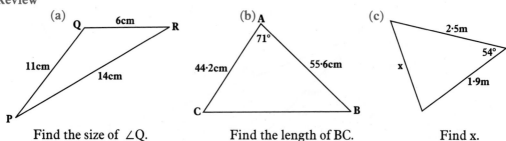

(a) Find the size of ∠Q.

(b) Find the length of BC.

(c) Find x.

## USING the SINE and COSINE RULES

We use the cosine rule if we are given either 3 sides or 2 sides and the angle between these sides. That is, if we are given the information on either of these diagrams we use the cosine rule.
For all other sets of information we use the sine rule.

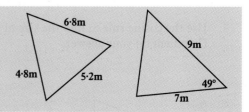

*Worked Example*  Find (a) the length of AB
(b) angle A
(c) angle B.

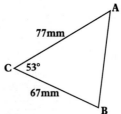

*Answer*  (a) Using $c^2 = a^2 + b^2 - 2ab \cos C$
$$c^2 = 67^2 + 77^2 - 2 \times 67 \times 77 \times \cos 53°$$
$$c = 64.9 \text{mm (3 s.f.)}$$

(b) Using $\dfrac{\sin A}{a} = \dfrac{\sin C}{c}$, $\dfrac{\sin A}{67} = \dfrac{\sin 53°}{64.9}$
$$\sin A = \frac{67 \sin 53°}{64.9}$$
$$A = 56° \text{ (to the nearest degree)}$$

(c) angle B $= 180° - 53° - 56°$
$$= 71°$$

*Worked Example*  A helicopter base is 20km due west of a hospital H. From B, a helicopter flies 8·4km on a bearing of 072° to pick up an injured person.
How far is this injured person from the hospital?

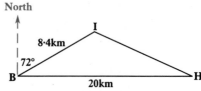

*Answer*  Let I be the position of the injured person.
$$∠IBH = 90° - 72°$$
$$= 18°$$
Using the cosine rule, $IH^2 = BI^2 + BH^2 - 2 \times BI \times BH \times \cos ∠IBH$
$$= 8.4^2 + 20^2 - 2 \times 8.4 \times 20 \times \cos 18°$$
$$IH = 12.3 \text{km (1 d.p.)}$$

*Worked Example*

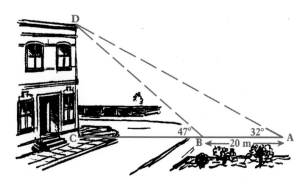

At A, Tim measures the angle of elevation of the top of a building as 32°. At B, 20 metres nearer the building than A, Tim measures this angle to be 47°.
(a) Calculate the distance BD.
(b) From B, Tim walks directly to C at an average speed of 1·5 metres per second. How long does it take Tim to walk from B to C?

*Answer* (a) $\angle BDA = 47° - 32°$ (exterior angle of triangle)
$$= 15°$$

Using the sine rule in $\triangle$ BDA, $\dfrac{BD}{\sin 32°} = \dfrac{20}{\sin 15°}$
$$BD = \dfrac{20 \sin 32°}{\sin 15°}$$
$$BD = 41m \text{ (2 s.f.)}$$

(b) In $\triangle$ DCB, $\dfrac{CB}{DB} = \cos 47°$
$$\dfrac{CB}{41} = \cos 47°$$
$$CB = 41 \cos 47°$$
$$= 28m \text{ (2 s.f.)}$$

Using average speed $= \dfrac{\text{distance}}{\text{time}}$, $1·5 = \dfrac{28}{t}$
$$t = \dfrac{28}{1·5}$$
$$= 19 \text{ seconds (2 s.f.)}$$

*Worked Example*

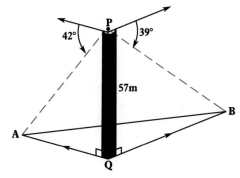

PQ represents a vertical tower, 57m high. A and B are two points at ground level. The angles of depression from P to A and B are 42° and 39°, as shown in the diagram.
(a) Use $\triangle$ PQA to calculate PA.
(b) Use $\triangle$ PBQ to calculate BP.
(c) A person at P, when looking from A to B looks through an angle of 77°. Which angle in the diagram is this?
(d) Use the cosine rule in $\triangle$ PAB to calculate the distance from B to A.

**Answer**  (a) Since $\frac{57}{PA} = \cos 48°$ then $PA = \frac{57}{\cos 48°}$

$= 85\cdot2$m (3 s.f.)

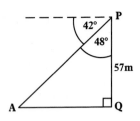

(b)

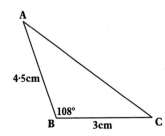

Since $\frac{57}{PB} = \cos 51°$ then $PB = \frac{57}{\cos 51°}$

$= 90\cdot6$m (3 s.f.)

(c) $\angle APB$

(d) $p^2 = a^2 + b^2 - 2ab \cos P$

$\quad = 90\cdot6^2 + 85\cdot2^2 - 2 \times 90\cdot6 \times 85\cdot2 \times \cos 77°$

$\quad p = 110$m (to the nearest metre)

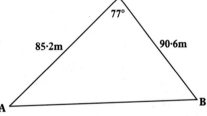

## EXERCISE 20:5

1.  (a) Use the cosine rule to find $\angle QPR$.
    (b) Use the sine rule to find $\angle PQR$.
    (c) Find the size of $\angle QRP$.

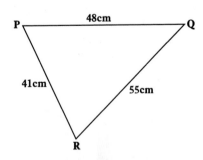

2.

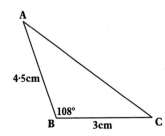

(a) Use the cosine rule to find the length of AC.
(b) Use the sine rule to find angle A.
(c) Find the size of angle C.

3. X and Y are two points on a jetty. B is a buoy.
   Mandy measures the distance XY and the angles BXY and BYX. She then calculates the distance BX.
   What answer should Mandy get?

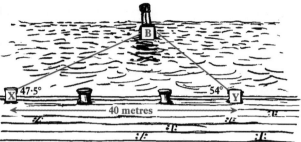

4. A tree T is observed from two points P and Q which are 50 metres apart. ∠TPQ is measured as 105° and ∠TQP as 43°. How far is the tree from P?

5.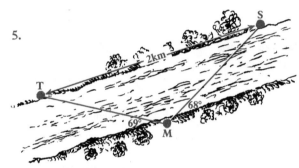

   Megan knows that two markers, T and S, on one side of a river, are 2km apart.
   At M, on the other side of the river, Megan measures the angles shown.
   Which marker, T or S, is nearer to M?
   Calculate the distance between M and this marker.
   Assume the banks of the river are parallel.

6. This diagram represents a crane working on a wharf. PQ is vertical.
   (a) Find the size of ∠PQR.
   (b) List the steps needed to find the height of R above the wharf.
       Calculate this height, giving the answer to the nearest half of a metre.

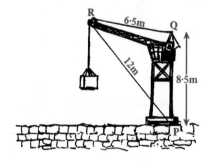

7.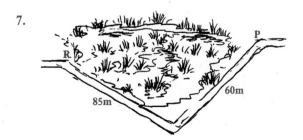

   A surveyor, Murray, is walking due west when he comes to a marsh. To avoid the marsh Murray turns at P and walks for 60m on a bearing of 215° and then for 85m on a bearing of 290°.
   Murray then calculates the distance PR.
   What answer should he get?

8. A and B represent two forest lookout towers. A is 4·27km from B and on a bearing of 206° from B.
   A forest fire is sighted at F, on a bearing of 032° from A and 164° from B.
   A fire-fighting helicopter leaves A for F. What distance does this helicopter travel to reach the fire?

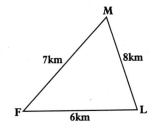

9. Broughton is 34km due east of Campbell Town and 56km north-east of Hampden. A plane flies directly from Hampden to Campbell Town.
   (a) Calculate the distance the plane flies.
   (b) Calculate the bearing on which the plane flies.

10. On a hike, Melissa and her friends walk 6km due East from the Fernley car park, F, to L where they have lunch. After lunch they walk 8km to M, as shown in the diagram. From M they walk back to the Fernley car park, a distance of 7km.
    (a) Calculate the angle MLF.
    (b) What is the bearing of M from L?

11. 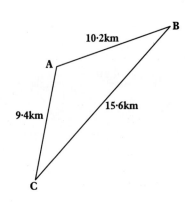 Two canoes, which are in line with the base of a vertical cliff, are 120 metres apart. The angles of depression from the top of the cliff to the canoes are 44° and 29°, as shown in the diagram.
    (a) Calculate the distance TQ.
    (b) Calculate the height, TB, of the cliff.

12. Two ships leave Liverpool at the same time. One of them travels north-west at an average speed of 10·5km/h while the other travels at an average speed of 14km/h on a bearing of 280°. How far apart are these ships after 2 hours?

13. The roads between three villages A, B and C are straight Roman roads as shown in the diagram. B is north-east of C.
    Find the bearing of A from C.

14. A is on a bearing of 080° from B.
    An aircraft, which can fly at 250km/h in still air, flies from A to B. There is a southerly wind of 45km/h.
    (a) Sketch a vector diagram which shows the velocities of 250km/h and 45km/h and the resultant velocity of the aircraft.
    (b) Calculate the bearing on which the pilot should face the aircraft.

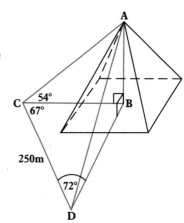

15. Angela takes measurements from two points, C and D, at ground level to find the height AB of the pyramid. At C, she measures the angle of elevation of the top of the pyramid as 54°. She measures the distance between C and D as 250 metres and the angles BCD and BDC as 67° and 72° respectively.
    (a) Use the sine rule in △ CBD to calculate the length of CB.
    (b) Use the right-angled triangle CAB to calculate the height of the pyramid, giving the answer to the nearest 10m.

16.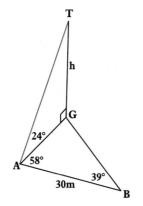

TG represents a vertical flagpole. A and B are two points on the ground which are 30 metres apart. From A, William measured the angle of elevation of the top of the flagpole to be 24°. He measured ∠GAB as 58° and ∠GBA as 39°.
William used the sine rule in △ GAB to calculate the distance of A from G. He then used △ TAG to calculate h, the height of the flagpole. What answers should William get for his calculations?

17. AB represents a vertical cliff, 90 metres high. X and Y represent two yachts at sea. From the top of the cliff the angles of depression to these yachts are 31° and 16°, as shown in the diagram.
    (a) Write down the sizes of ∠YAB and ∠XAB.
    (b) Explain why angles ABY and ABX are right angles.
    (c) Use △ ABX to find the distance from X to B.
    (d) Use △ ABY to find the distance from Y to B.
    (e) Y is due west of B and the bearing of X from B is 234°. Find the size of ∠YBX. Hence calculate the distance between the two yachts.

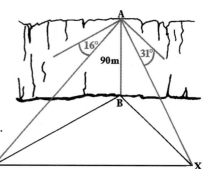

18.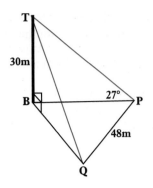

From a point P, due east of the bottom of a 30m high vertical cliff TB, the angle of elevation of the top of the cliff is 27°. The point Q is on a bearing of 200° from P, in the same plane as P and 48m from P.
   (a) Name the angle in the diagram which gives the angle of elevation of T from Q.
   (b) State the size of ∠BPQ.
   (c) Show that $BP = \dfrac{30}{\tan 27°}$
   (d) Calculate the angle of elevation of T from Q.

19. Two adjacent sides of a parallelogram are 8cm and 7·5cm. If the shorter diagonal is 9cm, find the length of the other diagonal.

20. Jayne and Mandy leave Bramwell market to cycle to their homes. Jayne cycles due south for 10km while Mandy cycles due east at a speed of 15km/h for 20 minutes and then on a bearing of 100° for 6km.
   As the crow flies, how far is it from Jayne's home to Mandy's?

21. The lighthouses at Gavin Point (G) and Beach End (B) are 20km apart. The bearing of G from B is 240°. A yacht takes bearings on these lighthouses. The bearing of B from the Yacht is 105° and the bearing of G from the yacht is 214°.
   (a) Calculate the distance of the yacht from the lighthouse at Gavin Point.
   (b) If the bearings given are correct but the 20km distance is only accurate to one significant figure find the least possible distance of the yacht from the lighthouse at Gavin Point.

**Review 1**   Two of the sides of a triangle are 8·7cm and 5·2cm. The angle between these sides is 66°. Calculate the perimeter of this triangle.

**Review 2**

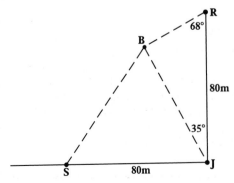

Janine and Robert organised a "cricket ball throw" competition. Each student throws the ball from S. Janine is at J and Robert is at R. The line SJ is at right angles to RJ.
When Dipak throws the ball it lands at B. Janine measures angle BJR as 35° and Robert measures angle BRJ as 68°.
   (a) Calculate the length of BJ.
   (b) Calculate the distance Dipak threw the ball.

**Review 3**

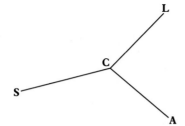

Amy and Louise cycle together from their school S to the church C. At the church, Amy cycles towards her home at A at an average speed of 15km/h while Louise cycles towards her home at L at an average speed of 18km/h. The bearing of L from C is 030° and that of A from C is 134°. How far apart are Amy and Louise, 20 minutes after passing the church?

**Review 4** XY represents a vertical tower. M and N are two points at ground level.
(a) Use the sine rule in △ XMN to calculate the distance MX.
(b) Explain why ∠XYM is a right angle.
(c) Calculate the height of the tower.
(d) Name the angle that gives the angle of elevation of the top of the tower from M. Calculate this angle.

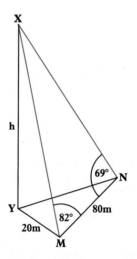

## INVESTIGATION 20:6

**Ambiguous Case**

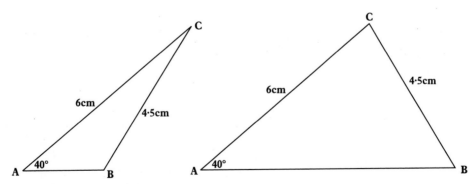

If we are given two angles and a side of a triangle, or two sides and an angle not between these sides, we can use the sine rule to find the other sides and angles. Sometimes the given information can give two sets of solutions. For instance, if we are given ∠A = 40°, a = 4·5cm, b = 6cm we could get either of the triangles drawn above.
**Investigate** to find the relationship between a, b, and angle A which gives two sets of solutions; that is, gives the ambiguous case.

## AREA of a TRIANGLE

The area of a triangle can be found using the formula Area = $\frac{1}{2}$bh where b is the base and h is the height.

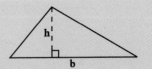

The area of a triangle can also be found using the formula **Area = $\frac{1}{2}$ ab sin C** where a and b are the lengths of two of the sides and C is the angle between these sides.

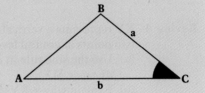

DISCUSSION EXERCISE 20:7

In this triangle, BP is the perpendicular from B to the side AC.

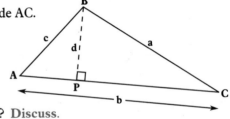

Using Area = $\frac{1}{2}$ base × height, area of $\triangle$ ABC = $\frac{1}{2}$ bd.
We can use the right-angled triangle BPC to find d in terms of a and angle C.

What expression do we get for d?

How could we continue to show that Area = $\frac{1}{2}$ ab sin C? **Discuss**.

*Worked Example*  Find the area of this triangle.

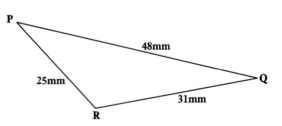

*Answer*  A formula for the area is Area = $\frac{1}{2}$ qr sin P. We must find the size of angle P.

$$\text{Using } \cos P = \frac{q^2 + r^2 - p^2}{2qr}, \quad \cos P = \frac{25^2 + 48^2 - 31^2}{2 \times 25 \times 48}$$
$$P = 34 \cdot 9° \text{ (3 s.f.)}$$

$$\text{Using Area} = \tfrac{1}{2} qr \sin P, \quad \text{Area} = \tfrac{1}{2} \times 25 \times 48 \times \sin 34 \cdot 9°$$
$$= 340\text{mm}^2 \text{ (2 s.f.)}$$

## EXERCISE 20:8

1. Calculate the area of these triangles.

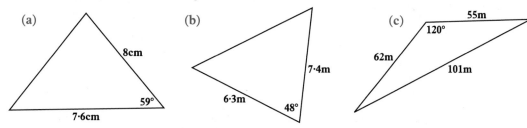

(a)    (b)    (c)

2. Find the area of these triangles. Give the answers to 2 s.f.

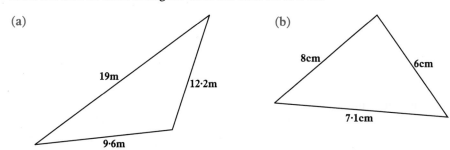

(a)    (b)

3. (a) Use the sine rule to find the size of angle B.
   (b) Find the size of angle C.
   Hence find the area of this triangle.

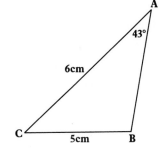

4. This sketch represents two
   adjacent fields, A and B.
   (a) Find the area of field B.
   (b) Find the area of field A.

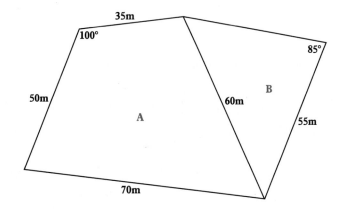

**5.**

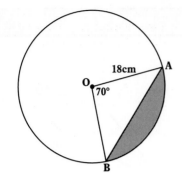

(a) Use Area $= \frac{1}{2}ab \sin C$ to calculate the area of $\triangle$ OAB.
(b) Calculate the area of the sector OAB.
Hence find the area of the shaded segment.

**6.** The dimensions of a triangular prism are shown.
Calculate the volume of this prism.

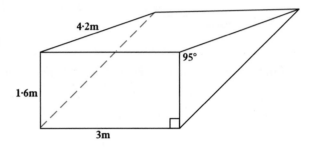

**7.** Mike runs around the boundaries of a triangular park. He runs 250m on a bearing of 300°. From there he runs on a bearing of 050° and then on a bearing of 190° back to the start. Calculate the area of this park to the nearest 10 square metres.

**8.**

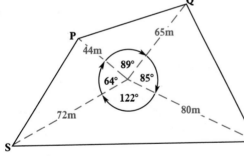

PQRS represents a field. From a point within the field a surveyor took bearings on the points P, Q, R and S and measured the distance to each of these points. The surveyor then drew this sketch.
Calculate the area of this field. (Do your working to 4 s.f. Give the answer to 3 s.f.)

**9.** PABQ and QCDR are squares drawn on two of the sides of $\triangle$ PQR.
(a) Express $\angle$BQC in terms of $\theta$.
(b) Explain why the triangles PQR and BQC are the same area.

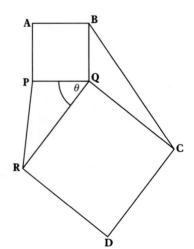

10.

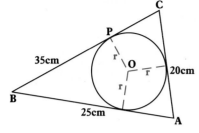

This diagram shows a triangle and its incircle. The sides of the triangle are 35cm, 25cm and 20cm.
(a) Calculate ∠B.
(b) Calculate the area of the triangle.
(c) Explain why ∠OPC = 90°.
(d) Show that the area of the triangle is equal to $\frac{1}{2}$r (35 + 25 + 20).
Hence find the radius of the incircle.

11. Garth proved that the area of a quadrilateral is equal to half the product of its diagonals and the sine of either angle between the diagonals. The first and last lines of Garth's proof are given below. What might Garth have written on the other lines?

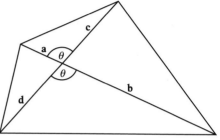

Area = $\frac{1}{2}$ac sin θ + $\frac{1}{2}$cb sin (180° − θ) + $\frac{1}{2}$bd sin θ + $\frac{1}{2}$ad sin (180° − θ)

.
.
.

= $\frac{1}{2}$sin θ (c + d)(a + b)

**Review 1** Find the area of these triangles.

(a)

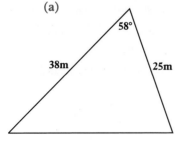

(b)

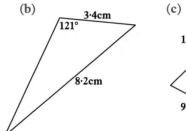

(c)

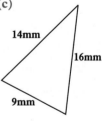

**Review 2**

This sketch represents a supermarket car park.
Calculate its area.

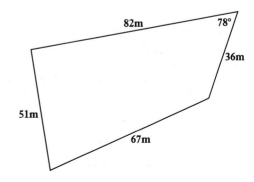

## DISCUSSION EXERCISE 20:9

- We can use the formulae for area of a triangle to prove the sine rule. We can begin as follows. Since Area of $\Delta = \frac{1}{2}ab \sin C$ and Area of $\Delta = \frac{1}{2}bc \sin A$ and Area of $\Delta = \frac{1}{2}ac \sin B$ then $\frac{1}{2}ab \sin C = \frac{1}{2}bc \sin A = \frac{1}{2}ac \sin B$.

  **Discuss** how we could continue get $\frac{\sin C}{c} = \frac{\sin A}{a} = \frac{\sin B}{b}$.

- We can also prove the sine rule by relating each of the ratios $\frac{\sin A}{a}$, $\frac{\sin B}{b}$, $\frac{\sin C}{c}$ to the radius of the circumcircle of the triangle. We can begin as follows.

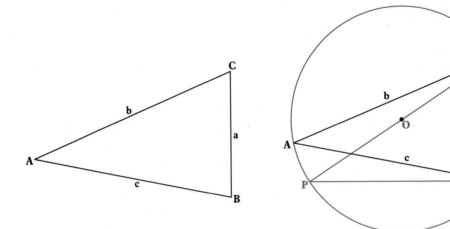

The circumcircle is drawn around the triangle. The diameter from C is drawn to meet the circle again at P. P and B are joined. In this diagram, $\angle CBP = 90°$ and $\angle CAB = \angle CPB$. Why?

In $\Delta$ CPB, $\frac{CB}{CP} = \sin P$. This statement may be rewritten in terms of a, sin A and R where R is the radius of the circumcircle. What is the rewritten statement?

By drawing different lines on the diagram it may be shown that $\frac{b}{\sin B} = 2R$ and $\frac{c}{\sin C} = 2R$. **Discuss**.

## CHAPTER 20   REVIEW

1. K

   Diagram NOT
   accurately drawn

   14cm

   81°

   N

   21cm

   B

   (a) Calculate the length KB.
   (b) Calculate the size of the angle NKB.

   ULEAC

428

2. A gardener pegs out a rope, 19 metres long, to form a flower bed.

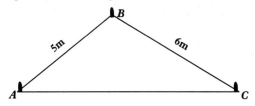

Calculate
(a) the size of the angle BAC;
(b) the area of the triangular flower bed.

**NEAB**

3.

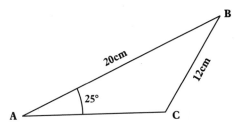

In the diagram AB = 20cm, BC = 12cm and angle BAC = 25°.
Given that the angle ACB is an obtuse angle, use the sine rule to find angle ACB.

**MEG**

4. A flag pole stands on the side of a hill supported by two cables.

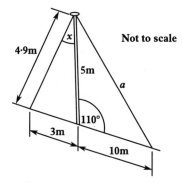

(a) Calculate the length of the lower cable $a$.
(b) Calculate the angle $x$ between the upper cable and the flagpole.

**SEG**

5.

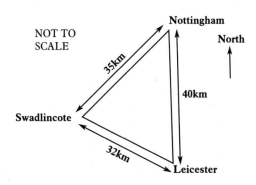

Nottingham is 40km due North of Leicester. Swadlincote is 32km from Leicester and 35km from Nottingham. Calculate the bearing of Swadlincote from Leicester.

**MEG**

6. A and C are two lighthouses. A is 15 miles due West of C.
   The bearing of a boat, B, from A is 030° and the distance from B to A is 10 miles.
   **Calculate** the distance of B from C. Give your answer in miles, correct to 3 significant
   figures.
   
   ULEAC

7. The diagram represents a concrete ramp for wheelchairs.

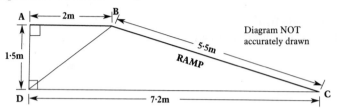

   BD has a length of 2·5m.
   **(a)** Calculate the size of angle ABD.
   **(b)** Calculate the size of angle DBC.

   The length of DC has been measured correct to one decimal place.
   **(c)** Write down the upper and lower bound of the length DC.

   All lengths in the diagram have been rounded to 0·1 of a metre.
   **(d)** State how the length of AB should have been written.
   
   ULEAC

8. Two ships, A and B, leave Dover Docks at the same time.
   Ship A travels at 25km/h on a bearing of 120°.
   Ship B travels at 30km/h on a bearing of 130°.
   Calculate how far apart the two ships are after 1 hour.
   
   SEG

9.

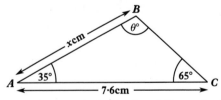

   In triangle $ABC$, $AC = 7\cdot6$cm, angle $BAC = 35°$, angle $ACB = 65°$.
   The length of $AB$ is $x$ cm. The size of angle $ABC$ is $\theta°$.
   **(a) (i)** Write down the value of $\theta$.
      **(ii)** Hence calculate the value of $x$.

   Alison constructs this triangle by first drawing the side $AC$.
   She then uses a protractor to draw the angles at $A$ nad $C$.
   In constructing the triangle, the length of $AC$ is measured correct to the nearest mm.
   The angles at $A$ and $C$ are measured correct to the nearest degree.
   **(b) (i)** Write down the minimum value $\theta$ can take.
      **(ii)** Hence calculate the maximum and minimum values $x$ can take.
   
   NEAB

**10.** A surveyor wishes to measure the height of a church.
Measuring the angle of elevation, she finds that the angle increases from 30° to 35° after walking 20 metres towards the church.

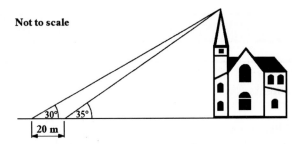

**Not to scale**

What is the height of the church?                                                    **SEG**

**11.**

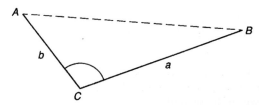

A surveyor is asked to find the area of this plot of ground, the triangle *ACB*.
As she has no accurate instruments with her, she decides to estimate the area.
She measures the lengths of *AC* and *BC* by pacing and the angle *ACB* with a simple compass.
These are the results and errors:

$AC = b = 34$ metres $(\pm 2\%)$
$BC = a = 87$ metres $(\pm 2\%)$
Angle $ACB = C = 130° \, (\pm 5°)$

**(a)** Use the formula

$$\text{Area} = \tfrac{1}{2}ab \sin C$$

to find the largest the area could be.

**(b)** Use the cosine rule to find the longest possible length of *AB*.                **MEG**

## ENLARGEMENTS with NEGATIVE SCALE FACTOR

### INVESTIGATION 21:1

"Upside-Down" Enlargements

To enlarge this triangle ABC by a scale factor of 2 with P as the centre of enlargement we proceed as follows:

*Step 1*   Join P to A, P to B, P to C.

*Step 2*   Extend PA, PB, PC so that
$$PA' = 2PA, \quad PB' = 2PB, \quad PC' = 2PC.$$

What if we had drawn PA′, PB′, PC′ in the opposite direction to PA, PB, PC? That is, we began as shown in the second diagram. **Investigate.**

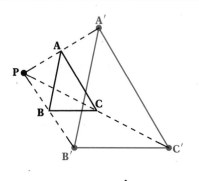

If the **scale factor of an enlargement is negative,** the image and the original are on opposite sides of the centre of enlargement.

*Worked Example*    A (13, 7)    B (16, 7)    C (16, 10)    D (13, 9)
                   Draw the quadrilateral ABCD. Enlarge this, scale factor –3, centre of enlargement P (11,8).

*Answer*

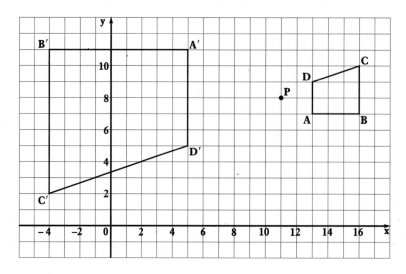

**Note** To find A′ we can join P to A, then find A′ so that PA′ = 3PA and A′ and A are on opposite sides of P.

On squared paper, we can find A′ by counting squares. To go from P to A we move 2 squares to the right and 1 square down. To find A′ we begin at P and move 6 squares to the left and 3 squares up.

We find B′, C′ and D′ in a similar way.

---

## EXERCISE 21:2

1. A (0, 2), B (2, 2), C (2, 0). Draw △ABC. Enlarge this triangle, centre P (3, 1), scale factor −2. Write down the coordinates of A′, B′, C′.

2. P (0, −1), Q (4, −1), R (4, 1). Draw △PQR. Enlarge this triangle, centre P (0, −1), scale factor −$\frac{1}{2}$. Give the coordinates of P′, Q′, R′.

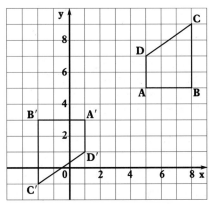

3. The trapezium A′B′C′D′ is an enlargement of ABCD. What are the coordinates of the centre of enlargement? What is the scale factor?

4. P (3, 0), Q (3, 2), R (7, 2), S (7, 0). Draw the rectangle PQRS. Give the coordinates of P′, Q′, R′, S′ for these enlargements.
   (a) scale factor −2, centre of enlargement (2, −1)
   (b) scale factor −3, centre of enlargement S
   (c) scale factor −1, centre of enlargement R
   (d) scale factor −$\frac{1}{2}$, centre of enlargement (−1, 4)
   (e) scale factor −2, centre of enlargement (5, 2)
   (f) scale factor −3, centre of enlargement (4, 1)
   (g) scale factor −$\frac{1}{2}$, centre of enlargement (7, 2)

**Review** Draw △ABC. Give the coordinates of A′, B′, C′ for these enlargements.
   (a) scale factor −2, centre of enlargement (5, 2)
   (b) scale factor −2, centre of enlargement C
   (c) scale factor −1, centre of enlargement (1, −1)
   (d) scale factor −$\frac{1}{2}$, centre of enlargement B

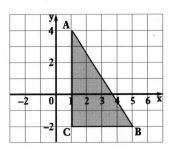

## Finding **MIRROR LINES** by **CONSTRUCTION**

**Remember:** For a reflection, a point and its image are the same distance from the mirror line.

*Example*  ΔABC is reflected onto  ΔA′B′C′.
To **construct the mirror line,** take these steps.

  *Step 1*  Join B and B′.

  *Step 2*  Construct the perpendicular bisector
of BB′.
This is the mirror line.

*Step 1*                                              *Step 2*

mirror line ⟶

---

## DISCUSSION and PRACTICAL EXERCISE 21:3

- This shape is reflected so the image of P is P′.
  What steps do you need to take to draw the image shape?
  **Discuss.**
  As part of your discussion, draw the image shape.

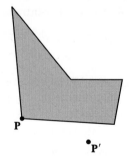

- Draw another shape. Mark an image of one of the points on your shape. Draw the image shape.

## ROTATION THROUGH ANY ANGLE

If △ABC is to be rotated anticlockwise through 90°, about P, we can find the new positions of A, B and C by tracing △ABC onto tracing paper, then rotating the tracing paper about P.

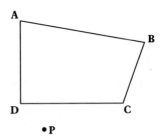

If we wish to rotate △ABC about P, through an angle such as 60° or 45° or 125° or 58° or . . . we should proceed as shown in the example given below. That is, for rotation through an angle other than a multiple of 90° we must use our protractors.

*Example*  ABCD ⟶ A′B′C′D′ under rotation, centre P, clockwise through 60°.
To draw the image A′B′C′D′ take these steps.

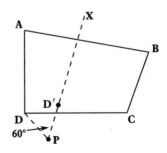

*Step 1*  Join P to D.
Use your protractor to draw
∠DPX = 60°.
Mark the point D′ on the line
PX so that PD′ = PD.

*Step 2*  Join P to each of A, B and C.
Locate A′, B′ and C′ in a similar way to point D′.
Join A′, B′, C′ and D′ to form the image A′B′C′D′.

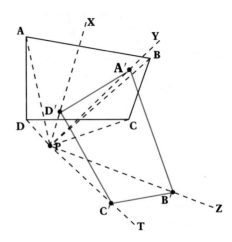

435

## PRACTICAL EXERCISE 21:4

1.  Choose a shape. You could choose a triangle or rectangle or any other shape.
    Mark a centre of rotation. This could be inside the shape or outside the shape or at a vertex of the shape or on an edge of the shape.
    Decide on an angle of rotation, either anticlockwise or clockwise.
    Draw the image shape after rotation about your chosen centre and through your chosen angle.

2.  Choose another shape.
    Rotate this shape about different centres of rotation and/or different angles of rotation to make a pattern of shapes.

**Finding the CENTRE of ROTATION by CONSTRUCTION. Finding the ANGLE of ROTATION.**

*Example*  ABCDE has been rotated to A′B′C′D′E′. To find the **centre of rotation** take these steps.

    *Step 1*  Join B and B′. Construct the perpendicular bisector of BB′.

    *Step 2*  Join E and E′. Construct the perpendicular bisector of EE′.

The point where these perpendicular bisectors meet is the centre of rotation, P.

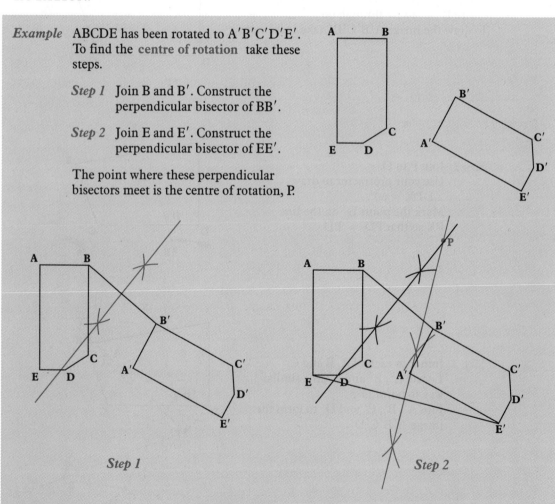

    *Step 1*                      *Step 2*

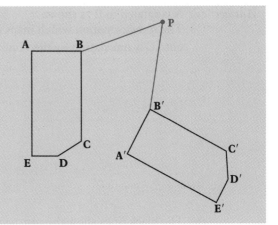

To find the **angle of rotation,** join P to a point on the original and a corresponding point on the image. For instance, join P to B and P to B′ as shown here.

The angle of rotation is the angle between these two lines.
In this diagram ∠BPB′ = 60°. Hence the angle of rotation is 60°.

## PRACTICAL EXERCISE 21:5

Draw some shapes.
Choose centres of rotation.
Draw the images after rotation about these centres.

Swap with your neighbour.
Find the centres of rotation and angles of rotation for your neighbour's rotations.

## COMBINATIONS of TRANSFORMATIONS

*Worked Example*    Triangle A is rotated anticlockwise through 90° about (0, 1) to triangle B.

(a) Describe the transformation that maps triangle B onto triangle C.

(b) Describe the single rotation that maps triangle A onto triangle C.

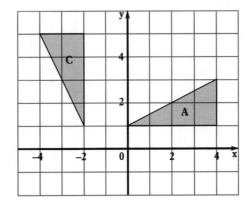

***Answer*** (a) A is rotated to B as shown.
The transformation which maps B
onto C is translation by the vector $\binom{-2}{0}$.

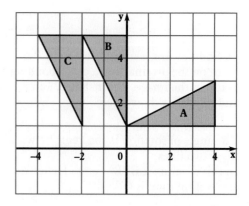

(b) The black lines show the construction to
find the centre of rotation. This is at
$(-1, 0)$. The red dotted lines show the
construction to find the angle of rotation.
This is 90° anticlockwise. The single
rotation which maps A onto C is rotation
anticlockwise about $(-1, 0)$ through 90°.

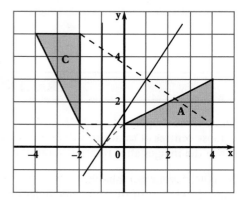

## EXERCISE 21:6

1. (a) P maps onto Q after rotation through 180°
about $(-1, 2)$.
This transformation may also be described
as an enlargement. Fully describe this
enlargement.

(b) P maps onto R after rotation through 180°
about $(3, 3)$.
What single transformation will map Q
onto R?

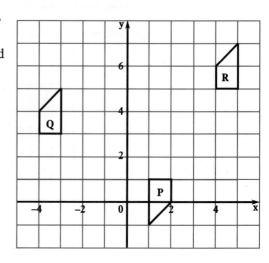

2.  (a) $\triangle XYZ \longrightarrow \triangle X'Y'Z'$ under an anticlockwise
    rotation of 90° about (–1, 2). Draw $\triangle X'Y'Z'$.
    Write down the coordinates of $X'$, $Y'$ and $Z'$.

    (b) $\triangle X'Y'Z' \longrightarrow \triangle X''Y''Z''$ under reflection in
    the line $x = -1$. Draw $X''Y''Z''$.
    Write down the coordinates of $X''$, $Y''$ and $Z''$.

    (c) What single transformation maps $\triangle XYZ$ onto
    $\triangle X''Y''Z''$?

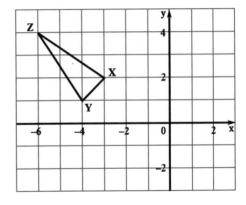

3.  (a) Fully describe the single transformation
    which maps the red shape onto the grey
    shape.

    (b) Fully describe the two transformations
    which map the pink shape onto the grey
    shape.

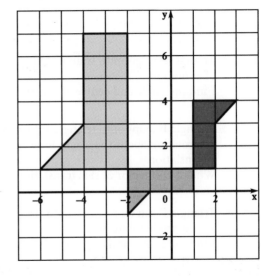

4.  (a) Enlarge ABCD, centre P, scale factor –1.
    Write down the coordinates of the vertices of the
    image shape $A'B'C'D'$.

    (b) Describe the transformation which maps
    $A'B'C'D'$ onto $A''B''C''D''$.

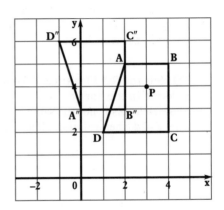

439

5. Triangle A can be transformed onto triangle B by a combination of two transformations. Fully describe these two transformations.

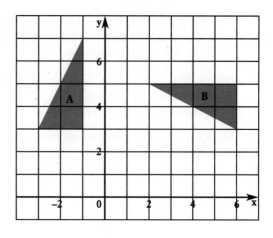

6. (a) Triangle P maps onto triangle Q by means of a rotation.
   Find the angle and centre of this rotation.

   (b) Triangle P maps onto triangle R by means of a rotation about the origin followed by a translation.
   What is the vector of this translation?

   (c) Triangle P can be mapped onto triangle R after a single rotation.
   Find the centre and angle of this rotation.

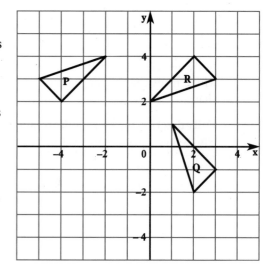

7. PQRS is rotated 90° anticlockwise about A then reflected in the line y = x.
   Show that this is not the same as reflection in the line y = x then rotation 90°anticlockwise about A.

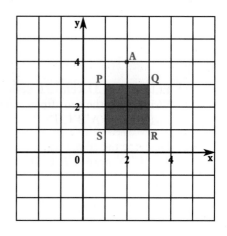

8. Triangle ABC has vertices at A (– 6, –1), B (– 4, –1), C (– 6, –3). Triangle A′B′C′ is an enlargement of triangle ABC. This enlargement has centre (–3, 0) and scale factor –3. Triangle A′B′C′ $\longrightarrow$ Triangle A″B″C″ after an enlargement with scale factor $\frac{1}{3}$, centre A′. Describe the enlargement which maps triangle ABC directly onto triangle A″B″C″.

9. (a) $S_2$ is the image of $S_1$ after a translation given by the vector $\binom{0}{-4}$. Draw $S_2$.
   $S_3$ is the image of $S_2$ after a translation given by the vector $\binom{-2}{3}$. Draw $S_3$.
   What single transformation will map $S_1$ onto $S_3$?

   (b) $S_4$ is the image of $S_1$ after reflection in the line x = 1. Draw $S_4$.
   $S_5$ is the image of $S_4$ after reflection in the x-axis. Draw $S_5$.
   What single transformation will map $S_1$ onto $S_5$?

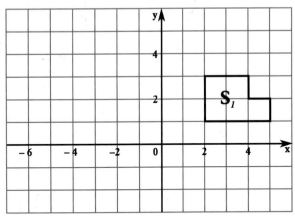

10. The pink shape has been translated then enlarged with centre (–3, 1). What is the vector of the translation?

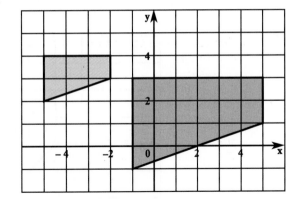

Review 1 Tim described the transformation of $S_1$ onto $S_2$ as reflection in the line y = 1 followed by translation by the vector $\binom{3}{3}$. Maree described the transformation in a different way. How might she have described it?

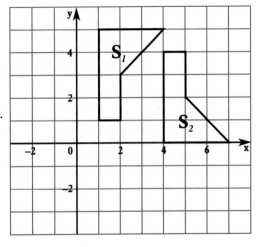

**Review 2**

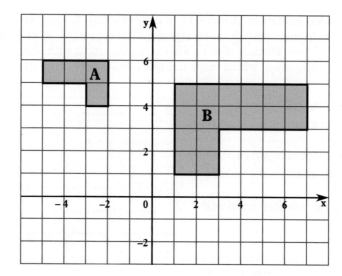

Shape A maps onto shape B under two successive transformations.
Describe these fully.

## CHAPTER 21   REVIEW

**1.**

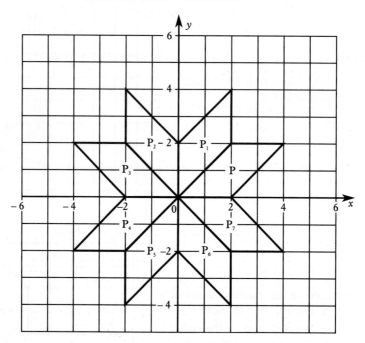

The star shape is formed by transformations of the parallelogram marked P onto the parallelograms marked $P_1, P_2, P_3 \ldots P_7$.

**(a)** Describe fully a single transformation which would map
    **(i)** P onto $P_3$     **(ii)** P onto $P_1$     **(iii)** P onto $P_6$

**(b)** Describe fully two *different* transformations which would map P onto $P_4$.

**(c)** Describe fully a pair of *successive* transformations which would map P onto $P_5$.

442

**(d)** **(i)** On the grid draw the enlargement of the star shape, scale factor $\frac{3}{2}$, centre $(0, 2)$.

**(ii)** State the ratio of the area of the enlarged star shape to the area of the original star shape. **NICCEA**

**2.**

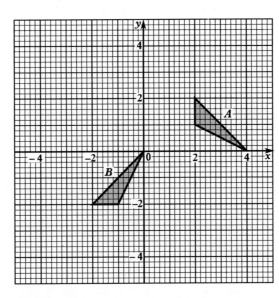

**(a)** Triangle $A$ is mapped onto triangle $B$ by means of an **anticlockwise** rotation centre the origin, followed by a translation.
  **(i)** Write down the angle of rotation.
  **(ii)** Find the column vector of the translation.

**(b)** Triangle $A$ may be mapped onto triangle $B$ by means of a single rotation. Find the coordinates of the centre of rotation.

**(c)** Triangle $B$ is reflected in the line $y = -2$ to form triangle $C$. Describe the single transformation which would map triangle $A$ onto triangle $C$. **MEG**

**3.**

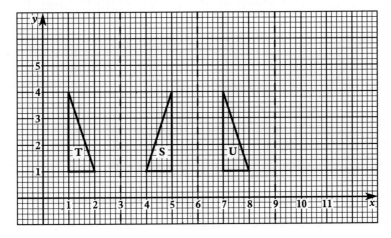

The diagram shows triangles **T**, **S** and **U**.
**S** is the image of **T** under a reflection in the line $x = 3$. **U** is the image of **S** under reflection in the line $x = 6$.
A reflection in the line $x = 3n$ where $n$ is an integer, is denoted by $R_n$.
So **S** is the image of **T** under $R_1$ and **U** is the image of **T** under $R_1$ followed by $R_2$.
**V** is the image of **T** under the successive transformations $R_1$ followed by $R_2$ followed by $R_3$.

**(a)** Draw **V** on the diagram.

**(b)** Describe fully the single transformation that will map **T** to **V**.

**W** is the image of **T** under the successive transformations $R_1$ followed by $R_2$, followed by $R_3$ and so on to $R_n$.

**(c)** Describe fully the single transformation that will map **T** to **W**
     **(i)** when $n$ is even,          **(ii)** when $n$ is odd.          **ULEAC**

**4.**

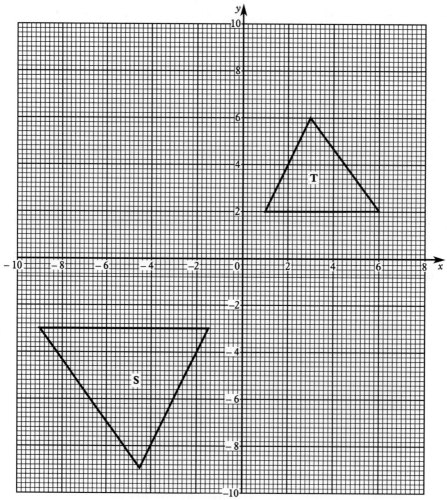

Triangle **T** can be transformed onto triangle **S** by a combination of two transformations.

Write down the two transformations, describing them fully.          **SEG**

Use the calculator value of $\pi$ or $\pi = 3\cdot142$.

1.

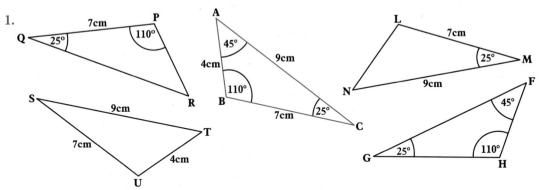

From the information given on these triangles we can tell that three of the black triangles are congruent to the red triangle. Which three? Explain your answer.

2.     $\mathbf{p} = \begin{pmatrix} 1 \\ 2 \end{pmatrix}$    $\mathbf{q} = \begin{pmatrix} -2 \\ 3 \end{pmatrix}$    $\mathbf{r} = \begin{pmatrix} 4 \\ -6 \end{pmatrix}$    $\mathbf{s} = \begin{pmatrix} 0 \\ -1 \end{pmatrix}$.

Write the following as column vectors.

(a) $\mathbf{p} + \mathbf{r}$    (b) $\mathbf{q} - \mathbf{p}$    (c) $3\mathbf{s}$    (d) $2\mathbf{p} + 5\mathbf{r}$

3.  AB and CB represent the two ropes from a fishing boat, at B, which are attached to a net AC. Each rope is 180 metres long. The angle between the ropes is 35°.
The ropes and net make the shape of a sector of a circle.
Find the length of the net AC, rounding your answer sensibly.

4.  A rectangular box has dimensions 45cm × 21cm × 9cm. Find the length of the longest thin rod that will fit into this box.

5.

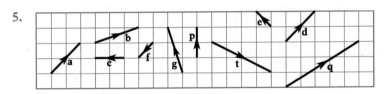

Name the vector equal to    (a) $\mathbf{a} + \mathbf{b}$    (b) $\mathbf{a} + \mathbf{c}$    (c) $\mathbf{p} + \mathbf{f}$    (d) $\mathbf{a} - \mathbf{b}$
(e) $\mathbf{b} - \mathbf{g}$    (f) $\mathbf{q} - \mathbf{b}$

6. ΔABC and ΔXYZ each have an angle of 66°. ΔABC has two sides of length 54mm and 49mm, as does ΔXYZ. Must these two triangles be congruent? Explain your answer.

7. (a) sin 200° =     A. sin 70°     B. − sin 70°     C. − sin 20°     D. sin 20°
   (b) cos 120° =     A. cos 60°     B. − cos 60°     C. cos 30°      D. − cos 30°
   (c) tan 320° =     A. tan 50°     B. − tan 50°     C. tan 40°      D. − tan 40°
   (d) sin 120° =     A. sin 60°     B. − sin 60°     C. sin 30°      D. − sin 30°
   (e) tan 220° =     A. tan 70°     B. − tan 70°     C. tan 40°      D. − tan 40°
   (f) sin (−120°) =  A. sin 60°     B. − sin 60°     C. sin 30°      D. − sin 30°

8.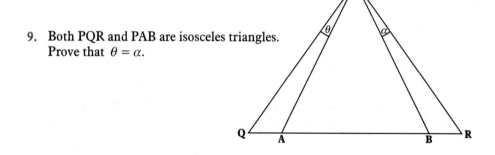

   This diagram represents a ramp. The rectangular plane ABFE is horizontal; the rectangular plane CDEF is vertical.
   Calculate   (a) AB   (give answer to 3 s.f.)
               (b) CB   (give answer to 3 s.f.)
               (c) ∠BCA.

9. Both PQR and PAB are isosceles triangles. Prove that $\theta = \alpha$.

10. (a)

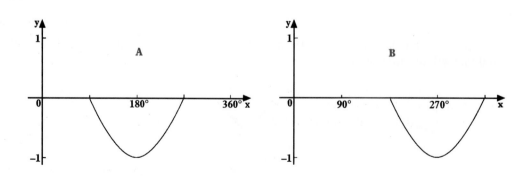

One of the graphs is part of the graph of y = sin x and the other is part of the graph of y = cos x. Which is which?

(b)

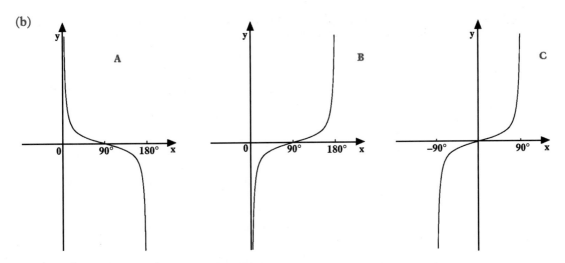

One of these graphs is part of the graph of $y = \tan x$. Which one?

11. In a laboratory all the measuring cylinders are of similar shape. One which is 10cm tall can hold a maximum of $1.5l$ of liquid. What is the maximum capacity of one of these cylinders which is 18cm tall?

12. ABCD is a parallelogram. $\overrightarrow{AB} = \begin{pmatrix} 3 \\ 4 \end{pmatrix}$, $\overrightarrow{AC} = \begin{pmatrix} 4 \\ 3 \end{pmatrix}$.

(a) Write $\overrightarrow{BD}, \overrightarrow{DC}, \overrightarrow{CB}, \overrightarrow{DA}$ in the form $\begin{pmatrix} x \\ y \end{pmatrix}$.

(b) Find the lengths of the diagonals of ABCD.

13.

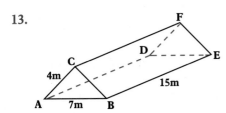

This diagram represents the loft of a barn. The faces BCFE and ACFD are rectangular. They each measure 15m by 4m.
The pitch of the roof is given by the size of ∠CAB. Calculate this pitch.

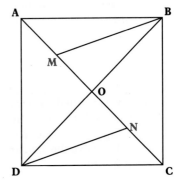

14. ABCD is a square. The diagonals meet at O. M is the mid-point of AO; N is the mid-point of CO.
Use congruent triangles to prove that BM = DN.

15. An albatross flying due north is blown off course by an easterly wind of 30km/h. If the albatross flies at a speed of 90km/h relative to the air, find its resultant velocity.

16. The legs of this chair are made from tubular steel.
Each is 2·2cm in diameter and 0·44m high.
Calculate the curved surface area of each leg.

17.

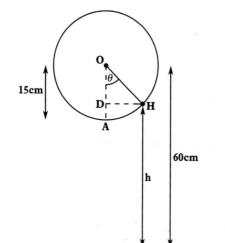

This diagram represents the steering wheel of a boat. The radius of the wheel is 15cm. The centre of the wheel is 60cm above the deck. The wheel is in a vertical plane; the deck is in a horizontal plane.

(a) In the diagram, the handle of the wheel is at H. By writing the distance OD in terms of $\theta$ show that the height, h, of the handle above the deck is given by h = 60 – 15 cos $\theta$.

(b) How high is the handle, above the deck, when it has been turned through an angle of 30° from A?

(c) Copy and complete this table, giving h to the nearest half of a centimetre.

| $\theta$ | 0° | 30° | 60° | 90° | 120° | 150° | 180° | 210° | 240° | 270° | 300° | 330° | 360° |
|---|---|---|---|---|---|---|---|---|---|---|---|---|---|
| h | | | 52·5 | | | 73 | | | | | | | |

(d) Draw a graph to show how the height of the handle above the deck varies during a complete turn from A back to A again.
Number the vertical axis from 40m to 75m. Number the horizontal axis from 0° to 360°.

(e) Use the graph to find the angle (or angles) through which the handle is turned from A if it is 70cm above the deck. Give your answers to the nearest 5°.

18. The cone is filled with water which is then poured into the cylinder.
How high is the water level in the cylinder? Give the answer to the nearest mm.

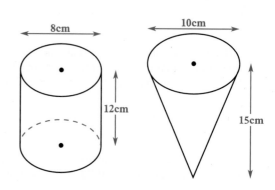

19.

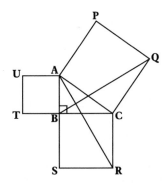

This diagram shows the three squares drawn on the sides of a right-angled triangle.
(a) Explain why ∠BCQ = ∠ACR.
(b) Prove that △ACR is congruent to △QCB.

20. Two forces act on a trolley. The 200N force is at right angles to the other force. If the magnitude of the resultant force is 250N find
(a) the angle the resultant force makes with the 200N force
(b) the magnitude of the second force acting on the trolley.

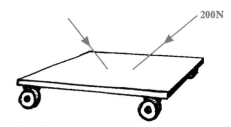

21.

Beth made these two boxes by constructing nets on heavy paper and folding. Beth made each length on the net for the small box two-thirds of the corresponding length on the net for the large box. The net for the large box took 900cm² of paper.
How much paper does the net for the small box take?

22. A river is 20 metres wide. Zeke wishes to row directly across this river. He rows at 5km/h. The current is 3km/h.
(a) In which direction should Zeke point his boat?
(b) How long does it take Zeke to cross this river?

23. In the triangle PQR, N is the mid-point of PQ and M is the mid-point of PR.

(a) Express $\overrightarrow{MN}$ in terms of $\overrightarrow{MP}$ and $\overrightarrow{PN}$.
(b) Prove that MN is parallel to RQ and half the length of RQ.

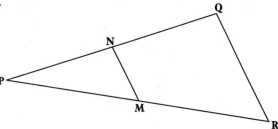

24. The curved surface area of a closed cylinder is 6·8m². The height is 1·9m. Show that the total surface area of this cylinder is given by $A = 6·8 + \frac{2}{\pi}\left(\frac{6·8}{3·8}\right)^2$.

25.

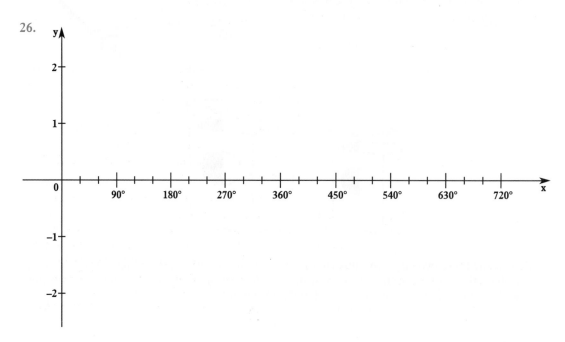

In this cuboid, the faces ABCD and EFGH are horizontal.
   (a) Name and calculate the angle between the line AB and the shaded plane.
   (b) Calculate the inclination of the shaded plane to the vertical.
   (c) Name and calculate the angle BH makes with the horizontal plane.

26.

(a) On a set of axes, similar to that shown, accurately draw the graph of $y = \sin x$.
(b) On the same set of axes, *sketch* the graphs of $y = \sin x - 1$, $y = -\sin x$ and $y = \sin 2x$.

27.

ABCD is a parallelogram. The points P and Q divide the diagonal AC into thirds. $\overrightarrow{DA} = \mathbf{a}$, $\overrightarrow{DC} = \mathbf{c}$.
   (a) Express $\overrightarrow{BC}$, $\overrightarrow{CA}$ and $\overrightarrow{CQ}$ in terms of $\mathbf{a}$ and $\mathbf{c}$.
   (b) Show that $\overrightarrow{BQ} = -\frac{1}{3}(\mathbf{c} + 2\mathbf{a})$.
   (c) Express $\overrightarrow{PD}$ in terms of $\mathbf{a}$ and $\mathbf{c}$.
   (d) Explain why BQDP is a parallelogram.

450

28. (a) For values of x between 0 and 360, accurately draw the graph of $y = 5 \cos x°$.
    On the same set of axes, draw the graph of $50y + x = 200$.
    (b) Show that these graphs can be used to solve the equation $250 \cos x° = 200 - x$.
    Use the graphs to find two approximate solutions to this equation.

29.

These two paint tins are mathematically similar. How tall is the 1 litre tin? Give the answer to the nearest millimetre.

30.

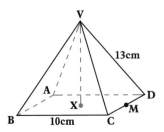

The base of this pyramid is a square of side 10cm. M is the mid-point of CD. To the nearest cm, each of the slant edges is 13cm.
(a) Calculate the height, VX.
(b) Name and calculate the angle the edge VC makes with the base.
(c) Name and calculate the angle the face VCD makes with the base.

A sketch of the net from which the pyramid is made is shown shaded.

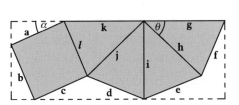

(d) Name the lengths on the net which are 10cm.
(e) Name the lengths on the net which are 13cm.
(f) Explain why the angle marked as $\theta$ is 45°.
(g) Show that the angle marked as $\alpha$ is 22·5°.
(h) Find the dimensions of the smallest rectangular piece of card needed to make this net.

31. This diagram represents the illustration of an ice-cream on an advertising placard. O is the centre of the circle of which QRS is a segment. The radius of this circle is 0·5m. T is the centre of QS. QP = 1·2m. ∠QOS = 80°.
    (a) Calculate the lengths of QT and PT.
    (b) Calculate the area of triangle PQS.
    (c) Calculate the area of the segment QRS. Hence show that the total area covered by this illustration is about 1·1m².

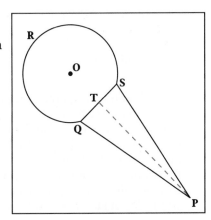

32.

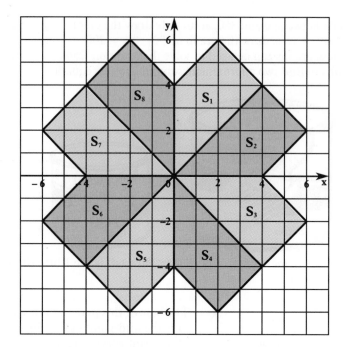

(a) $S_1 \longrightarrow S_7$ under an anticlockwise rotation of 90° about the origin. Use the diagram to find two successive reflections which are equivalent to this rotation.

(b) $S_1$ is enlarged, centre the origin, scale factor –1. Name the image of $S_1$ after this transformation.

(c) Use the diagram to find a single enlargement which is equivalent to reflection in the line $y = -x$ followed by reflection in the line $y = x$.

33.

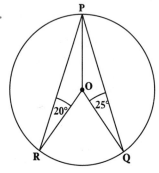

Find ∠ROQ

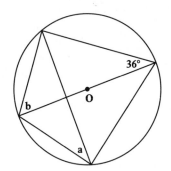

Find a and b.

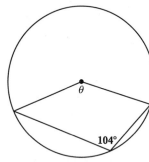

Find θ.

34. T and R represent two trees on a river bank. P is a tree on the other river bank.

Dianne measures the distance between T and R. She also measures ∠PTR and ∠PRT. Her measurements are shown on the diagram.

To find the width w of this river Dianne firstly calculates the distance PR. What answer should she get for PR? What answer should she get for w?

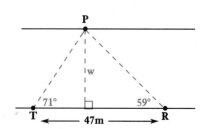

452

35.

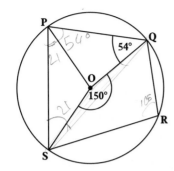

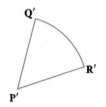

Find the size of ∠QPO, ∠SPO and ∠SRQ.

Find the size of ∠ABE.

36.

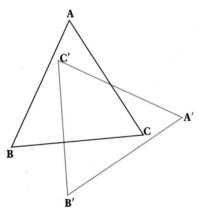

(a) △ABC is reflected to △A′B′C′.
    Trace the diagram and construct the mirror line.
(b) PQR is rotated onto P′Q′R′.
    Trace the diagram. Find the centre of rotation. Measure the angle of rotation.

37. This shape has a horizontal face, BCD, which is
    right-angled at D. The faces ABC and ABD are vertical
    and right-angled at B.
    Calculate  (a) BD
               (b) AC
               (c) AD
               (d) ∠CBD
               (e) the angle AD makes with the horizontal plane
               (f) ∠DAC

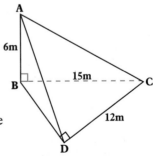

38.

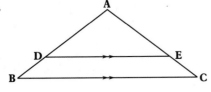

△ABC is an isosceles triangle with AB = AC.
DE is parallel to BC.
Prove that DECB is a cyclic quadrilateral.

39.

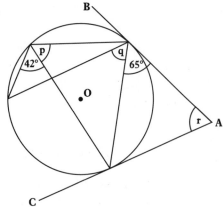

AB and AC are tangents.
Find p, q and r, giving reasons for your answers.

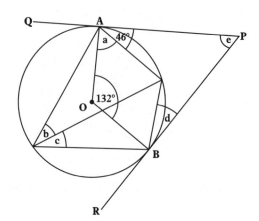

PAQ and PBR are tangents.
Find a, b, c, d and e, giving reasons for your answers.

40. (a) P ⟶ Q under an enlargement.
Fully describe this enlargement.

(b) Q is translated by the vector $\begin{pmatrix} -5 \\ -4 \end{pmatrix}$ to R then rotated clockwise through 90° about the point (2, 4) to S.
Write down the coordinates of the vertices of S.

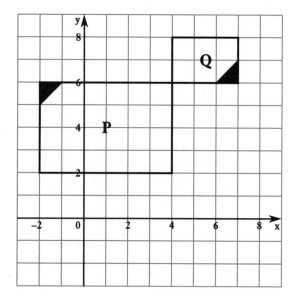

41. The diagonal BD of the cyclic quadrilateral ABCD is a diameter of the circle. This diameter bisects the angle ADC as shown.
Show that the diameter BD also bisects the angle ABC.

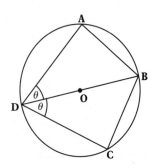

42.

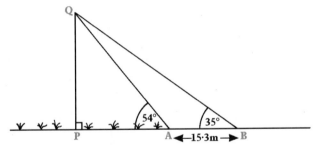

PQ represents a tree growing in a swamp. A is at the edge of the swamp, B is 15·3m from A. P, A and B lie on a straight line.

Alice uses the following method to find the height of the tree. She measures the angles of elevation of the top of the tree from A and B. Her measurements are shown on the diagram. Alice then uses ∆QAB to calculate the length of QA. Finally she uses ∆QAP to calculate PQ. What answer should Alice get for   (a)  QA

                                        (b)  PQ?

43.

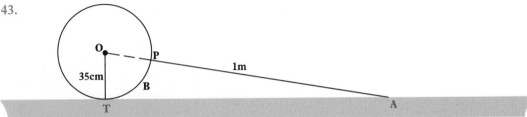

This diagram represents the cross-section of a garden roller. The centre is O and the radius 35cm. PA is 1 metre long.

(a) Explain why angle OTA is a right angle.

(b) Calculate the size of angle TOA.

(c) Calculate the length of the arc TBP.

44.

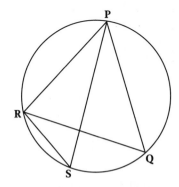

Triangle PQR is an equilateral triangle. The line PS bisects the angle RPQ.

(a) Find the size of ∠QRP, ∠RPS, ∠RSP and ∠SRQ.

(b) Explain why the line PS must be a diameter of the circle.

45. Two spheres of radius 6cm and 4cm and centres A and B sit snugly on the bottom of a box of width d – see the diagram on the next page.

(a) Explain why ∠APQ is a right angle.

(b) Find the width of the box, giving your answer correct to the nearest millimetre.

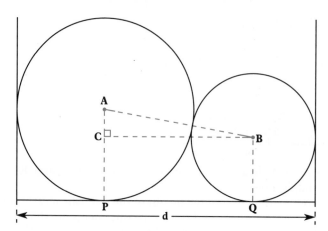

**46.**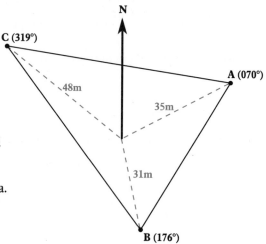

CDE is a tangent to the circle, meeting the circle at D.
(a) Explain why ∠DAB = ∠BDC.
(b) Explain why Δs ACD and DCB are similar.
(c) Copy and complete:
$$\frac{AC}{DC} = \frac{\ldots}{BC}.$$
(d) If AB = 10cm and CB = 8cm, calculate the length of CD.

**47.** A, B and C are the vertices of a triangular shaped park.
From a point within the park, a surveyor measures the distance to A, B and C as 35m, 31m and 48m respectively. From this point the bearings of A, B and C are 070°, 176° and 319° respectively.
From these measurements, the surveyor calculated the area of the park. Find this area.

**48.** (a) Two yachts sail from Hastings at the same time. One travels at a constant speed of 20km/h on a bearing of 099° while the other travels at a constant speed of 16km/h on a course of 236°.
How far apart are these yachts after 30 minutes?
(b) If, for the yachts in (a), the bearings of 099° and 236° are given to the nearest degree find the least value of the angle between the directions in which the yachts travel.

**49.** In the diagram, the circle through
A, B, C, D and E has centre O,
which lies on AC. AT is the tangent
to the circle at A.

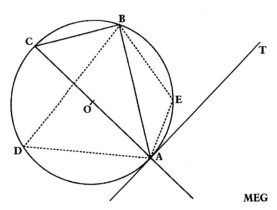

(a) Explain why angles TAC and ABC
are right angles.

(b) If angle TAB = 58°, find the following
angles, in each case giving a reason for
your answer:

    **(i)** BAC;     **(ii)** ACB;

    **(iii)** ADB;     **(iv)** AEB.

**MEG**

**50.**

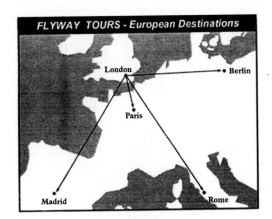

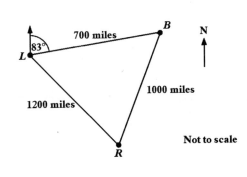

**Not to scale**

To fly direct from London to Berlin, the aircraft flies on a bearing of 083°.
Calculate the size of angle *BLR* and hence find the bearing of London from Rome.     **SEG**

**51.** In the diagram below, *X* and *Y* are the mid-points of *AO* and *BO*.

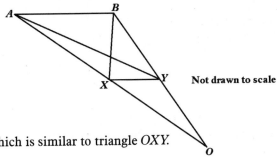

Not drawn to scale

    **(i)** Write down a triangle which is similar to triangle *OXY*.

    **(ii)** Explain why $\frac{XY}{AB} = \frac{1}{2}$

    **(iii)** Calculate $\dfrac{\text{area triangle } OXY}{\text{area triangle } OAB}$     **NEAB**

**52.** Two rectangles are joined to form the shape denoted by L on the grid.
   **(a) (i)**   Draw the image of L after a reflection in the $y$ axis. Label this image $L_1$.
       **(ii)**   Draw the image of L after a rotation of 90° clockwise about the origin. Label this image $L_2$.
      **(iii)**   Describe fully a single transformation which maps $L_2$ onto $L_1$.

   **(b) (i)**   Draw the image of L after a reflection in the line $y = 2$, followed by a rotation of 180° about the origin. Label this image $L_3$.
      **(ii)**   Describe fully a single transformation which maps $L_3$ onto $L_1$.

   **(c) (i)**   Draw the image of L after a reflection in the line $y = x$. Label this image $L_4$.
      **(ii)**   Describe fully a pair of successive transformations which maps $L_4$ onto $L_3$.

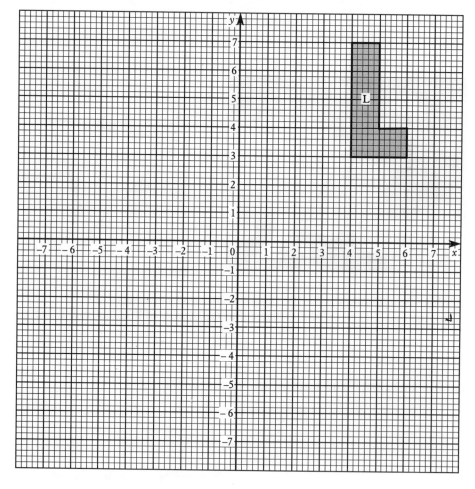

**NICCEA**

**53.** Triangle P is mapped to triangle Q by an enlargement of scale factor $-0.5$.
If AB is of length 6·4cm, how long is FD?

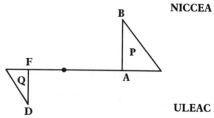

**ULEAC**

458

**54. (a)** Complete the table below to show the values of $y = 4\sin x$ for values of $x$ from $0°$ to $180°$ in steps of $30°$.

| $x$ | $y = 4\sin x$ |
|---|---|
| $0°$ | |
| $30°$ | |
| $60°$ | |
| $90°$ | |
| $120°$ | |
| $150°$ | |
| $180°$ | |

**(b)** On graph paper, draw the graph of $y = 4\sin x$ for values of $x$ from $0°$ to $180°$.

Use your graph to find all the solutions of the equation $4\sin x = 1·5$ between $x = 0°$ and $x = 180°$, showing how you have arrived at your solutions.

**WJEC**

**55.**

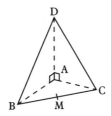

Diagram NOT accurately drawn

The diagram represents a pyramid ABCD.
ABC is an isosceles triangle with AB = AC = 7cm and BC = 10cm.
BCD is an isosceles triangle with BD = CD = 9cm.
D is vertically above A and angle BAD = angle CAD = $90°$.
M is the mid point of BC.

**(a)** Calculate the length of AM.
**(b)** Calculate the size of angle BCD.
**(c)** Calculate the size of angle DMA.

**ULEAC**

**56.** Silver pendants are made in the shape of a sector of a circle with radius $r$ cm and angle $\theta$.

**(a)** Calculate the **total** perimeter of the pendant when $r = 3$, and $\theta = 30°$.

**(b)** Another pendant has the same perimeter **but** $r = 2·5$ cm.

Calculate, to the nearest degree, the angle $\theta$ required for this pendant.

**SEG**

**57.** Fred is going to paddle his canoe across this river, which is 50m wide.
The water is flowing at 1·5m/s and Fred can paddle through the water at 2m/s.

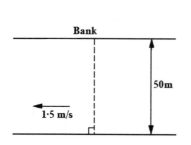

(a) He steers straight across the river. How far along the opposite bank will he land?

   Instead he decides to steer the canoe so that he does land directly across the river.

(b) At what angle (θ) across the river should he steer?

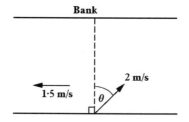

**MEG**

**58.** Two bottles of perfume are similar to each other.
The heights of the bottles are 4cm and 6cm.
The smaller bottle has a volume of 24cm³.

(a) Calculate the volume of the larger bottle.

(b) Two bottles of aftershave are similar to each other.
The areas of the bases of these bottles are 4·8cm² and 10·8cm².
The height of the smaller bottle is 3cm.
Calculate the height of the larger bottle.

**NEAB**

**59.** (a) This is a sketch of the front face of a tent.
The size of angle $x$ can be found from the formula $20\sin x = 19$.
What are the possible sizes of angle $x$?

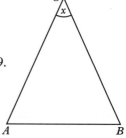

**(b)** Here is an enlarged sketch of the curved end of the floor of another tent.
The curve *FE* is an arc of a circle centre *O*.
The straight line *FE* = 90cm.

Calculate the area of the shaded segment of the circle formed by this arc.

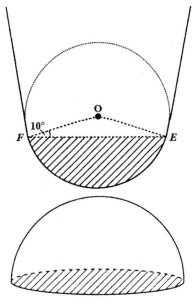

**(c)** A dome tent is a half sphere.
The volume of a dome tent is 3m³. Calculate its floor area. Show your working.

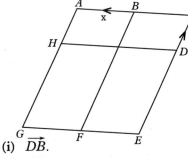

**NEAB**

60. The diagram shows two sets of parallel lines.

$\overrightarrow{BA} = \mathbf{x}$ and $\overrightarrow{DC} = \mathbf{y}$.

$\overrightarrow{AH} = \frac{1}{3}\overrightarrow{AG}$ and $\overrightarrow{AB} = \frac{1}{2}\overrightarrow{AC}$.

**(a)** Write each of these vectors in terms of **x** and **y**.

**(i)** $\overrightarrow{AG}$.         **(ii)** $\overrightarrow{BH}$.         **(iii)** $\overrightarrow{CG}$.

**(b)** Write each of these vectors in terms of **x** and **y**.         **(i)** $\overrightarrow{DB}$.

**(ii)** $\overrightarrow{EH}$.

**(iii)** Using your answers to (b) (i) and (ii) write down two statements about line segments *EH* and *DB*.         **SEG**

61. The banks of a river are straight and parallel.

To find the width of the river, two points, *A* and *B*, are chosen 50m apart.

The angles made with a tree at *C* on the opposite bank are measured as angle *CAB* = 56°, *CBA* = 40°.

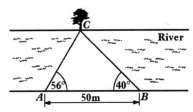

Calculate the width of the river.         **SEG**

**62.** This question is about angles between 0° and 360°.

(a) Find the **two** solutions of the equation
$$\cos x = 0 \cdot 5.$$

(b) Angle $p$ satisfies the equation
$$\sin p = \sin 210°.$$

Angle $p$ is not equal to 210°.
Find the value of $p$.

(c) Sketch the graph of $y = 5 \sin x$.

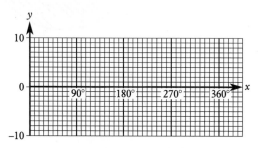

(d) Angle $q$ is shown in the diagram.

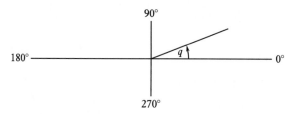

Angles $q$ and $r$ are connected by the equation
$$\tan q = \tan r.$$

Angles $q$ and $r$ are not equal.
Mark clearly angle $r$ on the diagram.

**SEG**

**63.** The glass test tube shown is cylindrical with a hemispherical base.
The internal diameter is 2·6cm.
It is filled with water to a depth of 11·3cm.

(a) Calculate

   (i) the volume of water in the test tube,
   (ii) the area of glass in contact with the water.

(b) A stone sinks into the water in the test tube, causing the water level
to rise by 24mm. Calculate the volume of the stone.

Volume of sphere, radius $r$, $= \frac{4}{3}\pi r^3$.

Surface area of sphere, radius $r$, $= 4\pi r^2$.
(You may take $\pi = 3 \cdot 14$)

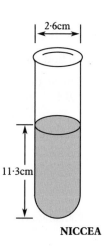

**NICCEA**

**64.** An aeroplane's velocity in still air is 400km per hour on a bearing of 045°. The wind is blowing at 100km per hour on a bearing of 070°.

Draw an accurate vector diagram to show the actual velocity of the aeroplane. (Use a scale of 1cm to represent 50km per hour)                                                         **ULEAC**

**65.**

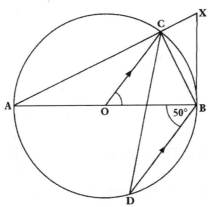

**(a)** O is the centre of the circle, AB is a diameter and BX is a tangent. The lines OC and DB are parallel. (This diagram is not drawn to scale.)

Angle ABD = 50°

Find the sizes of:

(i) angle COB,

(ii) angle OBC,

(iii) angle CBX,

(iv) angle BXC,

(v) angle CAB.

**(b)** Prove that OC bisects angle ACD. State your reasons clearly.           **NICCEA**

**66.**

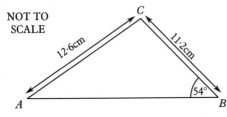

NOT TO SCALE

In triangle $ABC$, $AC = 12\cdot6$cm, $BC = 11\cdot2$cm and angle $B = 54°$. The lengths $AC$ and $BC$ are correct to the nearest millimetre and angle $B$ is correct to the nearest degree.

Use the Sine Rule

$$\frac{\sin A}{a} = \frac{\sin B}{b}$$

to calculate the smallest possible value of angle $A$.                          **MEG**

463

# HANDLING DATA

# Handling Data Revision

## Types of Data

Discrete data can take only particular values, usually whole numbers.
Continuous data can take any value within a given range.
For instance, size of shoes is discrete data; length of shoes is continuous data.

## Tables. Charts. Graphs.

27   29   28   28   30   29   27   27   29   28   29   27   30   29   28   27   28   29   29   27
This data, which gives the number of biscuits in each of 20 packets, is summarized on the
tally chart below and graphed on a bar-line graph. Since the tally chart includes a
column for frequency, it is a combined tally chart and frequency table.

### Biscuits Tally Chart

| Number | Tally | Frequency |
|--------|-------|-----------|
| 27     | ﬀﬀﬀ I | 6         |
| 28     | ﬀﬀﬀ   | 5         |
| 29     | ﬀﬀﬀ II | 7        |
| 30     | II    | 2         |

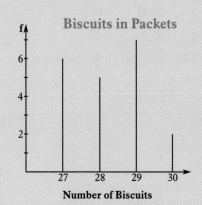

A bar graph may be drawn for the biscuits data.
The bar graph is similar to the bar-line graph with
the lines becoming bars.
On a bar graph the bars are not joined.

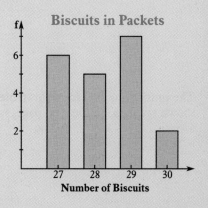

continued . . .

. . . *from previous page*

The following figures give the number of times the letter e appears in each sentence on the last page of "The Clan of the Cave Bear".

1 2 2 1 6 10 2 8 3 3 5 5 3 1 6 7 3 9 3 4 5 2 4 9 11 15 0 8

This discrete data has been grouped into 6 categories on the combined tally chart and frequency table, shown below.

Notice that each category is the same width. The first column on the table (Number of e's) could also be labelled "class interval". When we group data, we should have between 6 and 15 class intervals.

The information on the tally chart is graphed as a frequency diagram. On a frequency diagram the bars are joined.

### e's Frequency Table

| Number of e's | Tally | Frequency |
|---|---|---|
| 0–2 | 卌 ||| | 8 |
| 3–5 | 卌 卌 | 10 |
| 6–8 | 卌 | 5 |
| 9–11 | |||| | 4 |
| 12–14 | | 0 |
| 15–17 | | | 1 |

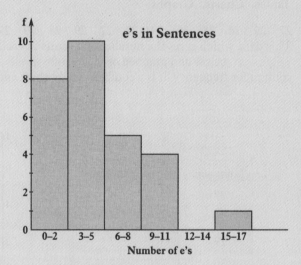

Pie Charts are circle graphs.
The circle is divided into sections.
The number of degrees in the angle at the centre of each section represents the frequency.

**Hockey Matches**

| Won | 3 |
| Lost | 15 |
| Drawn | 6 |

The continuous data from this table is shown graphed, on the next page, as a frequency diagram and as a frequency polygon.

### Handspan of Students

| Class interval (mm) | Frequency |
|---|---|
| $170 \leq l < 180$ | 2 |
| $180 \leq l < 190$ | 3 |
| $190 \leq l < 200$ | 5 |
| $200 \leq l < 210$ | 4 |
| $210 \leq l < 220$ | 4 |

*continued . . .*

*. . . from previous page*

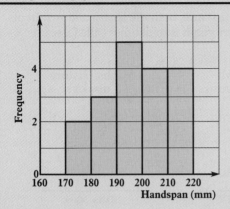

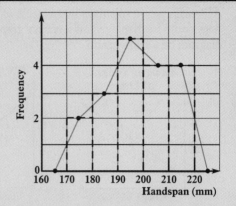

To find **cumulative frequencies** we add up the frequencies as we go. The following table shows the cumulative frequencies for the handspans in the previous table.

The **cumulative frequency graph** is drawn by plotting each cumulative frequency against the upper boundary of each class interval. We always begin the cumulative frequency graph on the horizontal axis.

| Handspan of Students | |
|---|---|
| **Handspan** | **Cumulative Frequency** |
| less than 180mm | 2 |
| less than 190mm | 5 |
| less than 200mm | 10 |
| less than 210mm | 14 |
| less than 220mm | 18 |

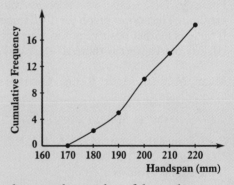

For **continuous data** the cumulative frequency values are the number of data values which are **less than** the upper boundaries of each class interval. For **grouped discrete data,** the cumulative frequency values are the number of data values which are **less than or equal to** the upper boundaries of each class interval as shown below.

| Test Mark | Frequency |
|---|---|
| 1–5 | 2 |
| 6–10 | 7 |

| Test Mark | Cumulative Frequency |
|---|---|
| ≤ 5 | 2 |
| ≤ 10 | 9 |

During Jane's first 12 hours in hospital her temperature was taken at 4-hourly intervals.

This **line graph** shows these temperatures. It was drawn by plotting the temperatures at 8a.m., Noon, 4p.m., 8p.m. and joining the points with straight lines.

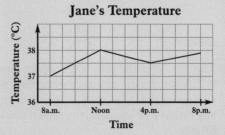

Jane's Temperature

*continued . . .*

*. . . from previous page*

A scatter graph displays two aspects of data. For instance, both the length and weight of dogs could be displayed on a scatter graph. A scatter graph is sometimes called a scatter diagram or a scattergram.

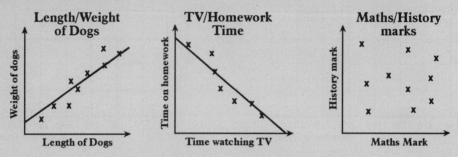

The word correlation is used to describe the relationship between the variables on a scatter graph. If the data shows some correlation, we can draw a line of best fit.

For positive correlation the points must be clustered around a line that has positive gradient. The scatter graph for Length/Weight of dogs shows positive correlation.

For negative correlation the points must be clustered around a line that has negative gradient. The scatter graph for TV/Homework time shows negative correlation.
If there is neither positive nor negative correlation, as in the scatter graph for Maths/History marks, we say there is no correlation.

### Mean, Median, Mode, Range, Quartiles, Interquartile range

$$\text{Mean} = \frac{\text{Sum of all data values}}{\text{No. of items of data}} \quad \text{i.e. mean} = \frac{\Sigma x}{n}$$

For instance the mean of 3, 2, 6, 2, 2, 3, 7 is $\dfrac{3+2+6+2+2+3+7}{7} = 3{\cdot}6$ to 1 d.p.

If the data is given as a frequency distribution, mean $= \dfrac{\Sigma(fx)}{\Sigma f}$

For instance,

| x | 3 | 4 | 5 | 6 |
|---|---|---|---|---|
| f | 2 | 3 | 0 | 5 |

; mean $= \dfrac{2\times3+3\times4+0\times5+5\times6}{2+3+0+5} = 4{\cdot}8$.

If the data is grouped, we can find an approximate value for the mean by assuming that all the items of data in a given class interval have the value of the mid-point of that interval. For instance,

| Test mark | 1 – 20 | 21 – 40 | 41 – 60 | 61 – 80 | 81 – 100 |
|---|---|---|---|---|---|
| Mid-point | 10·5 | 30·5 | 50·5 | 70·5 | 90·5 |
| Frequency | 2 | 5 | 7 | 10 | 1 |

mean $= \dfrac{2\times10{\cdot}5+5\times30{\cdot}5+7\times50{\cdot}5+10\times70{\cdot}5+1\times90{\cdot}5}{2+5+7+10+1} = 52{\cdot}9$.

The mode is the value that occurs most often. For instance, the mode of 3, 2, 6, 2, 2, 3, 7 is 2. A set of data may have more than one mode or no mode. If the data is grouped we may talk about the modal class which is the class interval that contains more data values than any other. For instance, the modal class for the Test Marks shown above is the interval 61–80.

*continued . . .*

*. . . from previous page*

The median is the middle value of a set of data which is arranged in order. For instance, arranged in order 3, 2, 6, 2, 2, 3, 7 is 2, 2, 2, 3, 3, 6, 7. The median is the 4th value which is 3. If there is an even number of values, the median is the mean of the middle two values. If the data is grouped we can talk about the class interval which contains the median. For instance, for the previous Test Marks, the class interval which contains the median is 41–60 since the middle value (the 13th value) lies in this interval. We can calculate an approximate value for the median. For instance, for the test marks on the previous page, the median is the 13th value. An approximate value is $41 + \frac{6}{7} \times 19 = 57 \cdot 3$ to 1 d.p.

The range of a set of data is the difference between the largest and smallest data values. For instance, the range of 3, 2, 6, 2, 2, 3, 7 is $7 - 2 = 5$.

For a set of data arranged in order, the median is the middle value, the lower quartile is the middle value of the lower half of the data and the upper quartile is the middle value of the upper half of the data.
The interquartile range is the difference between the upper and lower quartiles.

That is,

> **interquartile range = upper quartile – lower quartile**

*Example*

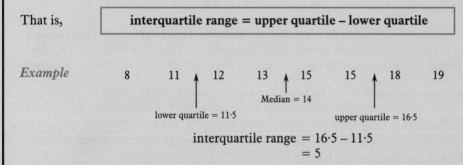

$$\text{interquartile range} = 16 \cdot 5 - 11 \cdot 5$$
$$= 5$$

The median, the lower quartile and the upper quartile may be read from a cumulative frequency graph. For instance, in the cumulative frequency graph below there are 26 data values. Since $\frac{1}{4}$ of $26 = 6 \cdot 5$, $\frac{1}{2}$ of $26 = 13$ and $\frac{3}{4}$ of $26 = 19 \cdot 5$ then the lower quartile is 47 seconds, the median is 58·5 seconds and the upper quartile is 68 seconds.

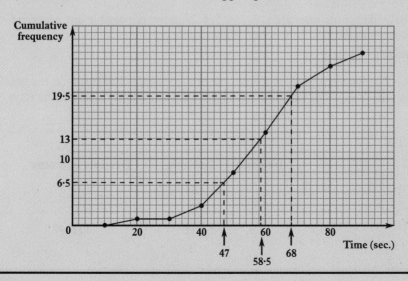

*continued . . .*

469

. . . *from previous page*

**Probability**
The probability of an event that is certain to happen is 1.
The probability of an event that will never happen is 0.
The probability of any other event is between 0 and 1.

Probability may be estimated from experiments. The frequency of an event is the number of times that event occurs in a number of trials. The relative frequency of an event compares the frequency with the number of trials. It is the proportion of times the event occurs in a number of trials.

$$\text{Relative frequency of an event} = \frac{\text{Number of times the event occurs}}{\text{Number of trials}}$$

If an experiment is repeated a great number of times, the relative frequency of an event occurring can be used as an estimate of the probability of that event occurring. The more often the experiment is repeated, the better the estimate will be. For instance, if in 1000 tosses of an unfair die, a "six" came up 620 times, we can estimate the probability of getting a "six" the next time we toss this die as $\frac{620}{1000}$ or $0.62$.

The expected number of times an event will occur is equal to the product of the number of trials and the probability of the event occurring in any one trial. For instance, if we toss the unfair die mentioned above 200 times we expect to get a "six" $0.62 \times 200$ or 124 times.

Choosing at random means every item has the same chance of being chosen. Equally likely outcomes are outcomes which have the same probability of occurring. For instance, when a coin is tossed the outcomes "a head", "a tail" are equally likely; each of these outcomes has probability of $\frac{1}{2}$. The probability of an event may be calculated if all the possible outcomes are equally likely.

For equally likely outcomes
$$\text{P(an event occurring)} = \frac{\text{Number of favourable outcomes}}{\text{Number of possible outcomes}}$$

For instance, the probability of getting a prime number when a die is tossed is calculated as follows.
Possible equally likely outcomes are 1, 2, 3, 4, 5, 6. Number of possible outcomes = 6.
Favourable outcomes are 2, 3, 5. Number of favourable outcomes = 3.
P(prime number) $= \frac{3}{6}$ or $\frac{1}{2}$.

Outcomes may be given as a list, in a table or in a diagram. For instance, the possible equally likely outcomes when two coins are tossed could be shown in any of the ways below.

HH  HT  TH  TT

| 1st coin \ 2nd coin | H | T |
|---|---|---|
| H | HH | HT |
| T | TH | TT |

| 1st coin | 2nd coin | Possible outcome |
|---|---|---|
| H | H | HH |
|  | T | HT |
| T | H | TH |
|  | T | TT |

*continued . . .*

. . . *from previous page*

A tree diagram is another diagram used to show possible outcomes. The probability of each possible outcome may be written on the tree diagram.

A tree diagram for showing the possible outcomes when a coin is tossed twice is shown below.

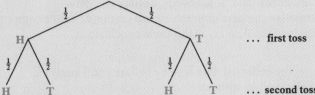

The probability of an event not happening is equal to $1 - P(A)$, where $P(A)$ is the probability of the event happening. For instance, when a card is chosen at random from a pack, the probability of getting the Jack of spades $= \frac{1}{52}$; the probability of not getting the Jack of spades $= \frac{51}{52}$.

Exhaustive events account for all possible outcomes. If events are exhaustive, it is certain that one of them will happen. For instance, when a die is thrown the events "an odd number", "an even number" are exhaustive events.

Events which cannot happen at the same time are called mutually exclusive events. For instance, if a die is tossed the events "a four", "a prime number" are mutually exclusive since both of these events cannot happen together.

The addition principle for probability is: If events A and B are mutually exclusive, then $P(A \text{ or } B) = P(A) + P(B)$. For instance, when a die is tossed

$$P(\text{four or prime no.}) = P(\text{four}) + P(\text{prime no.})$$
$$= \frac{1}{6} + \frac{3}{6}$$
$$= \frac{2}{3}$$

Event A and event B are independent if event A happening (or not happening) has no influence on whether event B happens. The probability of event B happening will be the same regardless of whether or not event A has happened. For instance, if a coin is tossed twice the events "a head on the first toss", "a tail on the second toss" are independent.

The multiplication principle for probability is: If events A and B are independent then $P(A \text{ and } B) = P(A) \times P(B)$.

For instance, when a coin is tossed twice $P(\text{Head and Head}) = P(\text{Head}) \times P(\text{Head})$
$$= \frac{1}{2} \times \frac{1}{2}$$
$$= \frac{1}{4}$$

If we need to calculate the probability of two or more events happening a tree diagram may be useful. Take the following steps.

*Step 1* Draw a tree diagram for the situation.

*Step 2* Write the given probabilities on the branches.

*Step 3* Work out the other probabilities and write these on.

*Step 4* Decide which branches answer the question.

*Step 5* Do the calculation. We do this as follows:

To find the probability of the outcome given by any branch, we multiply the probabilities written on that branch.

To find the probabilities of the outcomes given by more than one branch, we calculate the probabilities on each of the branches and then add these together.

*continued* . . .

. . . *from previous page*

**Surveys**

The steps taken to conduct a survey are:

*Step 1* **Decide** on the purpose of the survey.

*Step 2* **Design** an observation sheet or a questionnaire.

*Step 3* **Collect** the data. If necessary, **collate** the data.

*Step 4* **Organise** the data onto tables and graphs or into a computer database.

*Step 5* **Analyse** the data i.e. make some conclusions.

Some guidelines for designing a questionnaire are:

- Decide how the collected data is to be collated and analysed.
- Allow for *all* possible answers.
- Give clear instructions on how the questions are to be answered.
- Do not ask for information that is not needed.
- Avoid questions which people may not be willing to answer.
- Make the questions clear and concise.
- If your questions are asking for opinions, word them so that *your* opinion is not evident.
- Keep the questionnaire as short as possible.

Responses must be consistent with the wording of a question and should be balanced with an equal number of positive and negative responses.

Some useful responses to questions are:

Yes    No

Agree    Neither Agree nor Disagree    Disagree

Always    Usually    Sometimes    Seldom    Never

One way of analysing a list of items which have been ranked in order of preference is by adding the products of the rank and the number of times the item was given this rank.

For instance, the order of colour preference of 100 students shown on the table below can be analysed as follows:

$$\text{Blue:} \quad 1 \times 14 + 2 \times 28 + 3 \times 21 + 4 \times 19 + 5 \times 18 = 299$$
$$\text{Green:} \quad 1 \times 18 + 2 \times 10 + 3 \times 2 + 4 \times 32 + 5 \times 38 = 362$$
$$\text{Red:} \quad 1 \times 23 + 2 \times 19 + 3 \times 21 + 4 \times 23 + 5 \times 14 = 286$$
$$\text{White:} \quad 1 \times 11 + 2 \times 28 + 3 \times 17 + 4 \times 20 + 5 \times 24 = 318$$
$$\text{Black:} \quad 1 \times 34 + 2 \times 15 + 3 \times 39 + 4 \times 6 + 5 \times 6 = 235$$

Since Black has the lowest total, Black is the most popular.

| Rank \ Colour | Blue | Green | Red | White | Black |
|---|---|---|---|---|---|
| 1 | 14 | 18 | 23 | 11 | 34 |
| 2 | 28 | 10 | 19 | 28 | 15 |
| 3 | 21 | 2 | 21 | 17 | 39 |
| 4 | 19 | 32 | 23 | 20 | 6 |
| 5 | 18 | 38 | 14 | 24 | 6 |

An hypothesis is a statement of one person's opinion about an issue. For instance, the statement "most students do not eat breakfast" is an hypothesis. A survey could be conducted to test this hypothesis; that is, to find whether the hypothesis is true or false. There are usually four steps in making and testing an hypothesis.

*Step 1* State the hypothesis.

*Step 2* Collect data related to this hypothesis.

*Step 3* Collate and analyse the data.

*Step 4* Use the analysis to test the hypothesis.

*continued . . .*

. . . *from previous page*

**Experiments** which involve several variables should be carefully planned. With the exception of the variable being changed, all other conditions should remain the same throughout the experiment.

Planning should consist of:     Deciding which conditions to vary.
                                  Deciding what data to collect.
                                    Deciding how and when the data will be collected.
                                    Deciding how the data will be collated and displayed.
                                    Deciding how the data will be analysed.

## REVISION EXERCISE

1. The ages of those entered in the four sections of the Young Craftsman of the Year Competition at the 1993 South of England Show are given below.

   **Section A: Wood**   18, 20, 16, 19, 18, 20, 16, 16, 20, 16, 20, 20, 17, 16, 16, 16, 16, 18, 16, 16, 20, 15, 16, 16, 16, 19, 17

   **Section B: Metal**   20, 18, 16

   **Section C: Ceramics**   17, 15, 18, 16, 15, 15, 14, 15, 17, 19, 15, 18, 15, 14, 15, 15, 16, 18, 18, 17, 17, 18, 18, 18, 14, 18, 18, 14, 19, 15, 17, 16, 14, 15, 16, 18, 16, 18, 18, 17

   **Section D: Design & Technology**   18, 18, 20, 20, 20, 15, 16, 17, 16, 19, 19, 19, 18, 15, 18, 15, 14, 18, 18, 17, 15, 16, 18, 18

   (a) Find the mean age of those entered in section A.
   (b) Which section has the highest median age?
   (c) Find the upper and lower quartiles of section C.
   (d) Compare the interquartile ranges of sections C and D.
   (e) Compare the ranges of sections C and D.
   (f) A bar graph and a pie graph for the ages of those entered in the Design and Technology section are given below.

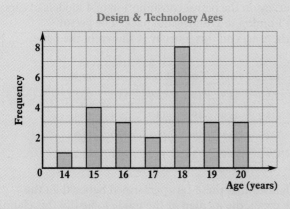

Design & Technology Ages

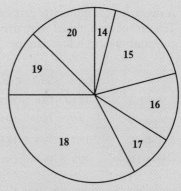

Design & Technology Ages

Draw a bar graph and a pie graph to represent the ages of those entered in section C.

   (g) List one advantage of using the pie graphs to compare the data.
   (h) List one advantage of using the bar graphs to compare the data.

473

2. Richard's group were writing a questionnaire to survey the opinions of the Year 9 students who had been on an outdoor education weekend. Some of the questions suggested are given below. The responses to these questions were all changed. Suggest more suitable responses for each question.

   *How old are you?*     *13* ☐     *14* ☐

   *I enjoyed the evening activities.*     *All of them* ☐     *Most of them* ☐     *Some of them* ☐

   *Did you prefer the evening or the daytime activities?*  *Yes* ☐     *No* ☐

3. For homework, the students in a Year 9 class were asked to toss a die 20 times and record whether the result was an even number (E) or an odd number (O). Of three students, one used an unbiased die, one used a biased die and the other just made up the results. The results are given below.
   Christine:  E O E E E O O E O E O O O E E O E O E E
   Lucinda:  E O E O E O E O E O E O E O E O E O E O
   Nicholas:  E E E E E O E E E E O O E E O E E O E E

   (i) Which student used the unbiased die, which used the biased die, which made up the results? Explain your answer.
   (ii) The student who had the biased die, tossed it 100 times. The results are given in this frequency table.

   | Result | 1 | 2 | 3 | 4 | 5 | 6 |
   |---|---|---|---|---|---|---|
   | Frequency | 8 | 15 | 7 | 20 | 15 | 35 |

   (a) Estimate the probability of getting a "5" the next time this die is tossed.
   (b) Estimate the probability of getting a "1" or a "3".
   (iii) The biased die is tossed twice. Estimate the probability of getting
   (a) a "2" followed by a "4"
   (b) a "2" and a "6" in either order
   (c) a total of more than 10.

4. A magazine for motorists carried out a survey on the petrol consumption of 4 models of cars. Ten cars of each model were driven from London to Dundee and back. The petrol consumption, in kilometres per litre, of these cars on this journey is shown in the table.

   |  | Car 1 | Car 2 | Car 3 | Car 4 | Car 5 | Car 6 | Car 7 | Car 8 | Car 9 | Car 10 |
   |---|---|---|---|---|---|---|---|---|---|---|
   | **Model A** | 18·1 | 19·0 | 18·3 | 19·2 | 19·5 | 18·3 | 18·6 | 18·9 | 18·3 | 20·1 |
   | **Model B** | 18·0 | 18·7 | 19·2 | 19·1 | 18·2 | 18·4 | 19·1 | 18·9 | 20·4 | 18·4 |
   | **Model C** | 19·2 | 18·4 | 18·8 | 18·0 | 19·3 | 18·1 | 19·1 | 18·1 | 19·0 | 18·9 |
   | **Model D** | 19·3 | 19·1 | 18·1 | 18·2 | 18·2 | 19·7 | 18·8 | 18·2 | 20·1 | 18·1 |

   The manufacturer of the Model C cars claimed that these cars performed better than the other cars. Did this manufacturer use the mean, the median or the mode to justify this claim?

5. (a) Two coins are tossed. Explain why the following events are not mutually exclusive.
   Event A:  Two heads.          Event B:  At least one head.

(b) A die is tossed twice. Are the following events independent? Explain your answer.
   Event A:   An even number on the first toss.
   Event B:   A prime number on the second toss.

(c) A coin and a die are tossed together.
   List all the possible outcomes. Hence find the probability of getting a head or an even number.

(d)

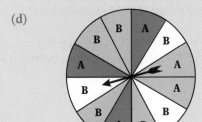

The arrow on this disc is spun. Are the events "the arrow stopping in a red section", "the arrow stopping in a section marked B" exhaustive? Explain your answer.

(e) The arrow on the disc, shown above, is spun. David calculated the probability of the arrow stopping in a grey section or a section marked B as follows:

Since $P(Grey) = \frac{6}{12}$,   $P(B) = \frac{7}{12}$    then $P(Grey \text{ or } B) = \frac{6}{12} + \frac{7}{12}$
$$= \frac{13}{12}$$

What is wrong with David's working?

6. Would you expect positive correlation or negative correlation or no correlation between the following?
   (a) ability to estimate 1 minute of time accurately and ability to estimate a distance of 10 metres accurately
   (b) time to swim 50 metres and time to swim 100 metres
   (c) average number of words on the pages of a book and number of pages in the books
   (d) number of days students are absent from school and test results
   (e) time spent on homework and marks in tests
   (f) time spent on hobbies and time spent watching TV

7. Each time Paul and Michelle played a computer game they kept a record of their scores. Paul drew a frequency polygon for his scores.

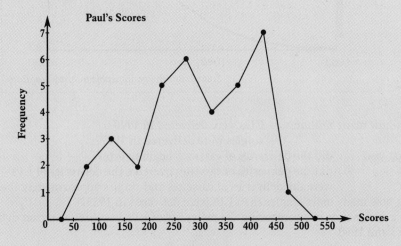

Michelle's scores are shown on the frequency table.

| Score | 50–99 | 100–149 | 150–199 | 200–249 | 250–299 | 300–349 | 350–399 | 400–449 |
|---|---|---|---|---|---|---|---|---|
| Frequency | 3 | 5 | 5 | 6 | 4 | 3 | 4 | 5 |

(a) Michelle drew a frequency polygon to illustrate her scores. The first three points she plotted were (24·5, 0), (74·5, 3), (124·5, 5). What other points should Michelle plot?

(b) Plot a frequency polygon for Michelle's scores.

(c) The frequency polygon for Paul's scores is shown on the previous page. Copy this frequency polygon onto the same set of axes as Michelle's. Use the frequency polygons to compare Paul and Michelle's scores.

8.    **Trade deliveries of LPs, cassettes, compact discs and singles**
*United Kingdom*

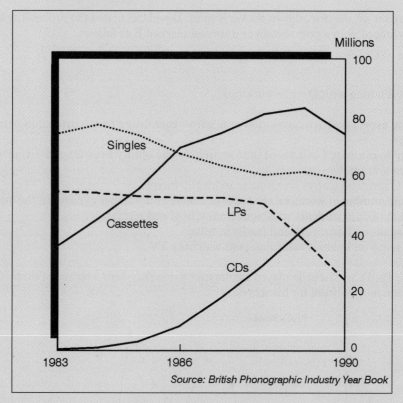

Source: British Phonographic Industry Year Book

(i) About how many million (a) CDs were delivered in 1990
        (b) singles were delivered in 1987?

(ii) In what year (a) did the deliveries of cassettes begin to drop
        (b) did the deliveries of cassettes overtake the deliveries of LPs
        (c) were the deliveries of cassettes and singles approximately the same?

(iii) About how many more singles than LPs were delivered in 1983?

(iv) Write a sentence or two comparing the deliveries of LPs, cassettes, compact discs and singles in 1983 and 1990.

476

9. Mrs Porreca's class estimated the length of the corridor outside their maths. classroom. The difference between these estimates and the actual length is shown in the frequency table.

| Difference (metres) | $0 \le d < 1$ | $1 \le d < 2$ | $2 \le d < 3$ | $3 \le d < 4$ | $4 \le d < 5$ | $5 \le d < 6$ |
|---|---|---|---|---|---|---|
| Frequency | 4 | 10 | 7 | 4 | 2 | 1 |

(a) Draw a frequency diagram for this data.
(b) The cumulative frequency graph is drawn below. Use this graph to find the median, the upper quartile, the lower quartile and the interquartile range.

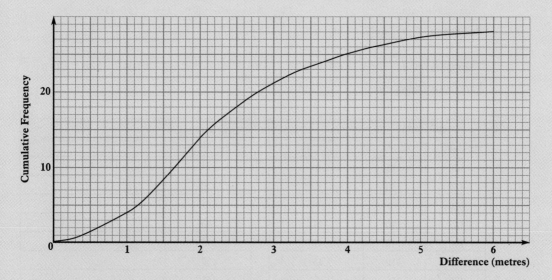

10. Fleur is on the committee which is organising a school dance. She is doing a survey about this dance. Three of the questions on Fleur's questionnaire are:

*What is your year group?*     *Year 7* ☐     *Year 8* ☐     *Year 9* ☐     *Year 10* ☐     *Year 11* ☐

*How will you travel to the dance?*     *Bus* ☐     *Train* ☐     *Taxi* ☐     *Walk* ☐     *Cycle* ☐     *Car* ☐

*What time do you think the dance should begin?*     *7p.m.* ☐     *7.30p.m.* ☐     *8p.m.* ☐

Write at least three more questions that Fleur could have on this questionnaire. Include suitable responses for each question.

11. Which of the following probabilities can be found by using equally likely outcomes; which can be estimated using relative frequency?
   A. The probability that an accountant, chosen at random, is left-handed.
   B. The probability that the batteries in a calculator, chosen at random, will last less than 100 hours.
   C. The probability that Jill's raffle ticket wins first prize.
   D. The probability that all people in the world will have enough to eat by the year 2025.
   E. The probability that the next news programme on BBC1 will begin late.

12. The picture cards are removed from a pack of cards. The remaining cards are shuffled, then a card chosen and its number noted. This is done many times. The results are shown.

| Number on card | 2 | 3 | 4 | 5 | 6 | 7 | 8 | 9 | 10 |
|---|---|---|---|---|---|---|---|---|---|
| Frequency | 15 | 21 | 16 | 11 | 14 | 10 | 12 | 16 | 9 |

(a) Calculate the mean of this data.

(b) What is the mode of this data?

13. (i) Copy and complete the cumulative frequency tables.

(a)

| Time taken (min.) | 5·0– | 6·0– | 7·0– | 8·0– | 9·0– | 10·0– | 11·0– | 12·0–13·0 |
|---|---|---|---|---|---|---|---|---|
| Frequency | 1 | 3 | 5 | 6 | 9 | 13 | 4 | 2 |

| Time taken (min) | < 6·0 | < 7·0 | < 8·0 | < 9·0 | < 10·0 | < 11·0 | < 12·0 | < 13·0 |
|---|---|---|---|---|---|---|---|---|
| Cumulative Frequency | 1 | 4 | 9 | | | | | |

(b)

| Length (mm) at least | below | Frequency | Length (mm) less than | Cumulative Frequency |
|---|---|---|---|---|
| 120 | 125 | 3 | 125 | 3 |
| 125 | 130 | 6 | 130 | |
| 130 | 135 | 7 | 135 | |
| 135 | 140 | 11 | 140 | |
| 140 | 145 | 13 | 145 | |
| 145 | 150 | 15 | 150 | |
| 150 | 155 | 5 | 155 | |
| 155 | 160 | 2 | 160 | |

(ii) Cumulative frequency graphs are drawn for the data in (i).

(a) Three of the points plotted for (a) are (5·0, 0), (6·0, 1), (7·0, 4). What other points should be plotted?

(b) What points should be plotted for the data in (b)?

(iii)

| Score | 31–40 | 41–50 | 51–60 | 61–70 | 71–80 | 81–90 | 91–100 |
|---|---|---|---|---|---|---|---|
| Frequency | 2 | 5 | 13 | 11 | 9 | 6 | 4 |

(a) Copy and complete the following cumulative frequency table for these scores.

| Score | ≤ 40 | ≤ 50 | ≤ 60 | ≤ 70 | ≤ 80 | ≤ 90 | ≤ 100 |
|---|---|---|---|---|---|---|---|
| Cumulative Frequency | 2 | | | | | | |

(b) What points should be plotted on the cumulative frequency graph for this data?

(iv) (a) Plot the cumulative frequency graph for the lengths given in (b) of (i).

(b) Use the cumulative frequency graph to estimate the median length, the upper quartile, the lower quartile and the interquartile range.

14. In a trampolining competition, points out of 10 were given for a compulsory routine and points, out of 20, were given for a routine of each competitor's choice.
The table shows the points given, in each of these categories, to 19 competitors.

| Competitor Initials | A.M. | N.P. | A.Z. | C.E. | E.A. | V.D. | K.V. | S.M. | S.H. | R.G. | B.G. | F.N. | N.M. | A.B. | B.D. | J.M. | J.B. | S.T. | J.N. |
|---|---|---|---|---|---|---|---|---|---|---|---|---|---|---|---|---|---|---|---|
| Routine of own choice | 4 | 15 | 7 | 10 | 19 | 8 | 2 | 12 | 15 | 9 | 13 | 4 | 12 | 18 | 6 | 16 | 20 | 6 | 12 |
| Compulsory routine | 4 | 9 | 6 | 7 | 10 | 6 | 3 | 8 | 10 | 5 | 7 | 3 | 7 | 9 | 4 | 7 | 9 | 5 | 6 |

(a) Draw a scatter diagram for this data. Have the routine of own choice on the horizontal axis.

(b) Draw the line of best fit.

(c) Does this data have positive or negative correlation? Explain your answer.

(d) Another competitor, Davina, scored 14 in the routine of her choice. Estimate Davina's score for the compulsory routine.

(e) Marita scored 9 for the compulsory routine. Estimate Marita's score for the routine of her choice.

15. Of the 8 maths. teachers in a school, 5 are women. Of the 3 P.E. teachers, 1 is a woman. Amanda uses a tree diagram to find the probability that her maths. and P.E. teachers next year will be men.

(i) Copy and complete this tree diagram.

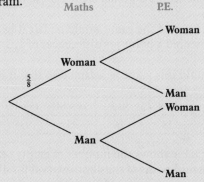

(ii) Find the probability that   (a) both Amanda's maths. and P.E. teachers are men
                                        (b) at least one of these teachers is a man.

16. The Shorefield Community Association have rented a hall in which they plan to run activities for the local teenagers. They surveyed a group of these teenagers. The results of a question in which those surveyed were asked to rank 5 activities in order of preference are shown.

| Activity \ Preference | 1st Preference | 2nd Preference | 3rd Preference | 4th Preference | 5th Preference |
|---|---|---|---|---|---|
| Aerobics | 24 | 21 | 18 | 5 | 22 |
| Badminton | 6 | 10 | 31 | 23 | 20 |
| Pool/Snooker | 25 | 19 | 12 | 22 | 12 |
| Table Tennis | 18 | 24 | 4 | 37 | 7 |
| Weight training | 17 | 16 | 25 | 3 | 29 |

After analysing these results, the community association decided to run three of these activities. Which three should they run? Justify your answer.

17. Matthew and Julia design and play a game with dice. They each toss one die at the same time. If the difference in the numbers obtained is 0, 1 or 2 Matthew scores a point. If the difference is 3, 4, or 5 Julia scores a point. The winner is the person with the most points after 10 tosses.

    (a) Copy and complete this table for the possible differences.

| M's die \ J's die | 1 | 2 | 3 | 4 | 5 | 6 |
|---|---|---|---|---|---|---|
| **1** | 0 | 1 | 2 | 3 | 4 | 5 |
| **2** | 1 |  |  |  |  |  |
| **3** | 2 |  |  |  |  |  |
| **4** | 3 |  |  |  |  |  |
| **5** | 4 |  |  |  |  |  |
| **6** | 5 |  |  |  |  |  |

    (b) Find the probability that Matthew scores a point when the two dice are tossed.
    (c) Explain why this game isn't fair.
    (d) Julia suggested the game would be fair if Matthew scored 1 point if the difference was 0, 1 or 2 while she scored 2 points if the difference was 3, 4 or 5. Comment on Julia's suggestion.
    (e) Matthew suggested the game would be fair if he scored a point for differences of 0, 2 and 4 and Julia scored a point for differences of 1, 3 and 5. Comment on Matthew's suggestion.
    (f) How else could this game be adapted so that it is fair?

18.

| Empty seats | 0 – 4 | 5 – 9 | 10 – 14 | 15 – 19 | 20 – 24 | 25 – 29 | 30 – 34 | 35 – 39 |
|---|---|---|---|---|---|---|---|---|
| Frequency | 18 | 26 | 25 | 13 | 8 | 5 | 3 | 2 |

This frequency table shows the number of empty seats on 100 flights made by FastAir planes.
    (a) What is the mid-point of the class interval 0 – 4?
    (b) Calculate an approximate value for the mean number of empty seats on these flights.
    (c) In which class interval does the median of the data occur?
    (d) What is the modal class interval?
    (e) Illustrate this data on a frequency diagram.

19. (i) A bag contains 8 red balls, 7 black balls and 5 white balls.
    (a) One ball is chosen at random. What is the probability that this ball is black?
    (b) The ball is replaced in the bag and another one chosen at random. What is the probability that this ball is either black or red?
    (c) Copy and complete this tree diagram.

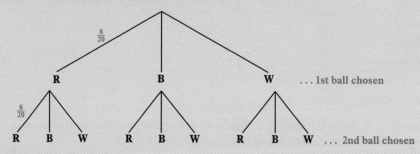

(ii) Another bag contains yellow, green and blue balls. Two balls are chosen at random from this bag with the first being replaced before the second is chosen. The probability that both balls are the same colour is $\frac{77}{200}$. What is the probability that the two balls are different colours?

20. Tina decided to survey students to test the hypothesis "People with small hands also have small feet".
Plan a survey to test this hypothesis. Include the way in which you will collect the data, the graphs you plan to use and the way in which you propose to analyse the data.

21. **(a)** What is the probability of throwing a five with a fair dice?
This frequency diagram shows the results of throwing a fair dice 60 times.

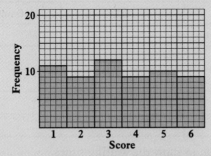

Joan throws another dice 60 times. Her results are shown below.

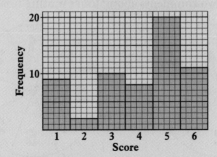

**(b)** Use Joan's results to give a reason why her dice might not be fair.

**(c)** Estimate the probability of throwing a five with Joan's dice. **SEG**

22. In a survey of community life on a new housing estate the following question is suggested.

(A) "What do you most like about living here?"

An alternative is proposed.

(B) "Tick the box which describes why you most like living here."

Design of houses ☐

Friendliness of neighbours ☐

More open space ☐

Give one advantage of each form of question. **SEG**

**23.** Tom gets a lift to work with his friend Jill. He waits for her at the corner of his street.

Tom always arrives at exactly 0800 hours (8 am) each week-day but Jill is often late.

Her arrival times, over a period of four weeks, are given below.

| 0833 | 0835 | 0825 | 0847 | 0815 | 0828 | 0828 | 0813 | 0848 | 0844 |
| 0825 | 0825 | 0801 | 0831 | 0841 | 0818 | 0820 | 0825 | 0811 | 0834 |

So, for example, 0833 means that Tom had to wait for 33 minutes and 0815 means that he had to wait for 15 minutes.

**(a)** Complete the grouped frequency table below, using 5 equal class intervals.

| Waiting time | Tally | Frequency |
|---|---|---|
| 0 and less than 10 | | |
| | | |
| | | |
| | | |
| 40 and less than 50 | | |

**(b)** Draw a frequency diagram to show the waiting times.

**(c)** Use the graph to make **two** comments about Tom's waiting time.     **SEG**

**24.**

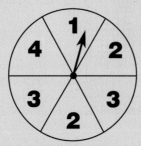

The diagrams show two fair spinners. Both spinners are spun and the scores are added together. What is the probability that the sum of the scores is at least 5?     **NEAB**

**25.** The marks given to two gymnasts for eight successive vaults are shown in the table below.

| | Score out of 20 | | | | | | | |
|---|---|---|---|---|---|---|---|---|
| Gymnast *A* | 11 | 6 | 6 | 3 | 15 | 9 | 18 | 4 |
| Gymnast *B* | 9 | 3 | 8 | 8 | 9 | 8 | 9 | 18 |

**(a)** Show that the range of marks in each case is exactly the same.

**(b)** Calculate the mean mark awarded in each case.

**(c)** What do you think is the main difference in the performances of the two competitors?     **NEAB**

**26.** The jockeys riding at a race meeting have these probabilities of wearing certain colours:

| Colour | Red & White | Blue & Pink | Red & Blue | Green | Yellow |
|---|---|---|---|---|---|
| Probability | 0.24 | 0.12 | 0.36 | 0.16 | 0.12 |

What is the probability that the first jockey you see is wearing some red in his colours?

**MEG**

**27.** A letter has a first-class stamp on it.
The probability that it will be delivered on the next working day is 0·86.

Sam posts 2 letters with first-class stamps.

**(a)** Complete the tree diagram.
Write all the missing probabilities on the appropriate branches.

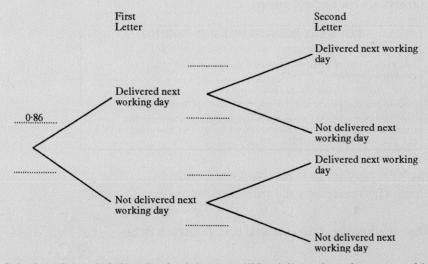

**(b)** Calculate the probability that both letters will be delivered on the next working day.

**ULEAC**

**28.** In September, a travel company asked customers about their holidays.
Eight customers were asked to give a score to their holiday.
They were asked to rate the holiday on a scale of 1 to 10.
(1 = very bad, 10 = perfect).
The table shows their replies and the cost of each holiday.

| Rating | 2 | 5 | 6 | 7 | 7 | 8 | 8 | 9 |
|---|---|---|---|---|---|---|---|---|
| Cost (£) | 210 | 250 | 265 | 270 | 300 | 290 | 315 | 329 |

**(a) (i)** Plot a scatter graph for these data.
**(ii)** What does this graph tell you about the connection between the rating and the cost?

**(b)** On the graph, draw the line of best fit.

Another customer gave a score of 4 for her holiday.
**(c) (i)** Use your scatter graph to estimate the cost of her holiday.
**(ii)** Give one reason why your answer may not be a very good estimate.

**SEG**

**29.** The spinner shown is biased.

The probabilities of getting a particular colour are shown in the table below.

**(a)** Complete the table to show the probability of getting GREEN.

| Colour | RED | YELLOW | BLUE | GREEN |
|---|---|---|---|---|
| Probability | 0.4 | 0.1 | 0.3 | |

**(b)** The spinner is spun once.

What is the probability of getting either RED or BLUE?

**(c)** The spinner is spun 50 times.

Approximately how many times would you expect to get RED?     **NEAB**

**30.** This report appeared in a school magazine.

> ### BOYS SAY 'NEIGHBOURS' IS BORING
> *Your ace investigator, Nick Bates reports*
>
> Last Friday I phoned 100 homes to find out what people think of the TV programme 'Neighbours'.
>
> An amazing 60% of adults said they never watch it.
>
> Half the girls said it was brilliant but only 48% of the boys thought the same.
>
> This means that in tens of thousands of homes throughout the country there is an argument between brothers and sisters when the 'Neighbours' tune comes on TV – and what about mums and dads?

Nick Bates states conclusions in his report and its title.

Choose three of his conclusions and criticise each one.     **NEAB**

**31.** A four sided dice has one of the letters A, B, C, D on each face.

Kathy throws the dice repeatedly. She keeps count of the number of times it lands with **A** on the bottom. Her first few results are shown in the table.

| Throw Number | 1 | 2 | 3 | 4 | 5 | 6 | 7 | 8 | 9 | 10 | 11 | 12 |
|---|---|---|---|---|---|---|---|---|---|---|---|---|
| Letter on bottom | B | A | B | C | D | A | B | A | B | C | D | A |
| Number of A's so far | 0 | 1 | 1 | 1 | 1 | 2 | 2 | 3 | 3 | | | |
| Proportion of A's so far | 0 | $\frac{1}{2}$ | $\frac{1}{3}$ | $\frac{1}{4}$ | $\frac{1}{5}$ | $\frac{2}{6}$ | $\frac{2}{7}$ | $\frac{3}{8}$ | | | | |

**(a)** Complete the table.

**(b)** Use the results to give the best possible estimate of the probability of throwing an **A** with this dice.

**(c)** Assuming the dice is fair, what will happen to the proportion of **A**'s as Kathy throws the dice more and more times?     **SEG**

**32.** One hundred boys, selected at random, were weighed.
The results were put into this frequency table.

| Weight (kg) | Mid value | Frequency | |
|---|---|---|---|
| 50 – | | 7 | |
| 60 – | | 49 | |
| 70 – | | 29 | |
| 80 – 90 | | 15 | |
| | Total | 100 | |

(a) Calculate an estimate of the mean.

(b) What is the modal class?

The **maximum** number of pupils allowed in the school lift is 10.

(c) Which of the averages, mean, median or mode, would you choose to calculate the maximum weight limit?

Give a reason for your answer. **SEG**

**33.** (a) What does it mean when we say that a coin is 'fair'?

(b) The following list of random numbers has been generated on a computer. Simulate 20 coin tosses by letting the even digits (0, 2, 4, 6, 8) correspond to 'heads' and the odd digits (1, 3, 5, 7, 9) correspond to 'tails'. List these 20 outcomes as H or T in the boxes below.

| 4 | 7 | 1 | 8 | 1 | 3 | 6 | 6 | 4 | 3 | 0 | 2 | 5 | 9 | 2 | 7 | 8 | 4 | 6 | 3 |
|---|---|---|---|---|---|---|---|---|---|---|---|---|---|---|---|---|---|---|---|
| | | | | | | | | | | | | | | | | | | | |

(c) **Use your simulation** to estimate the probability of tossing a head.

(d) What would you expect to happen to the proportion of heads obtained as the number of simulated throws is increased? **SEG**

**34.** When I answer the telephone the call is never for me.
Half the calls are for my daughter Janette.
One-third of them are for my son Glen.
The rest are for my wife Barbara.

(a) I answer the telephone twice this evening.

Calculate the probability that

(i) the first call will be for Barbara,

(ii) both calls will be for Barbara.

(b) The probability that both these two telephone calls are for Janette is $\frac{1}{4}$.
The probability that they are both for Glen is $\frac{1}{9}$.
Calculate the probability that either they are both for Janette or both for Glen. **NEAB**

**35.** Some Year 10 students are doing a survey about breakfast cereals.

They want to find out which cereals people prefer.

They make a list of 6 popular breakfast cereals:

| | |
|---|---|
| **Rice Crisps** | **Muesli** |
| **Sugar Pops** | **Cornflakes** |
| **Wheatabix** | **Bran Flakes** |

One person interviews 40 people to find out their first, second and third choices of breakfast cereals from the list.

**(i)** Design a table for the interviewer to use to collect all the data.
It must be easy to fill in and to analyse.

**(ii)** These are the results of the survey of the 40 people.

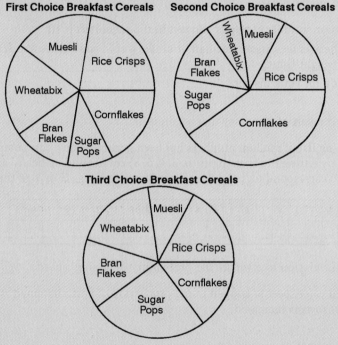

**(a)** Estimate the number of people who gave Sugar Pops as their third choice.

**(b)** Estimate the number of people who gave Muesli as their second choice.

**(c)** Which breakfast cereal was least popular?
Explain why you think so.

**(d)** Which breakfast cereal was most popular?
Explain why you think so.

**(iii)** The scattergraph compares the prices of supermarket and brand name packets of breakfast cereal. All of them are 250g packets.

Each cross represents a different type of cereal.

For example, the cross labelled '*A*' shows the prices of supermarket cornflakes and brand name cornflakes.

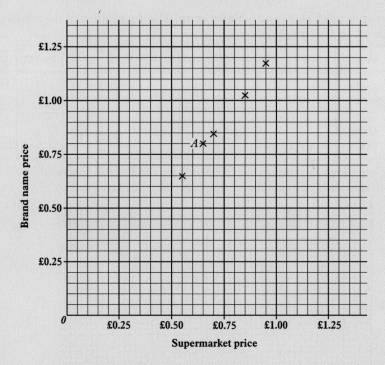

Which of the following statements about 250g packets of cereals are correct?

**A.** Supermarket cereals are about 20% cheaper than brand name cereals.

**B.** Supermarket cereals are about 40% cheaper than brand name cereals.

**C.** Supermarket cereals are about 20% more expensive than brand name cereals.

**D.** Supermarket cereals are about 40% more expensive than brand name cereals.

**E.** There is a strong correlation between the prices of supermarket cereals and brand name cereals.

**F.** There is no correlation between the prices of supermarket cereals and brand name cereals.

**(iv)**

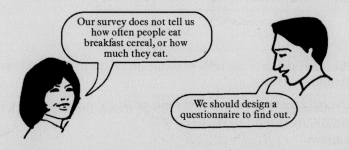

Design a suitable short questionnaire.                                    **NEAB**

**36. (a)** 50 pupils take an English exam and a Maths exam. The distribution of the marks they obtained is shown in the table below.

| | Mark | 21–30 | 31–40 | 41–50 | 51–60 | 61–70 | 71–80 | 81–90 | 91–100 |
|---|---|---|---|---|---|---|---|---|---|
| Number of pupils | English exam | 0 | 1 | 4 | 20 | 14 | 8 | 2 | 1 |
| | Maths exam | 2 | 3 | 6 | 10 | 12 | 10 | 4 | 3 |

The graph below shows the cumulative frequency for the English marks.
**(i)** On the graph, show the cumulative frequency for the Maths marks.

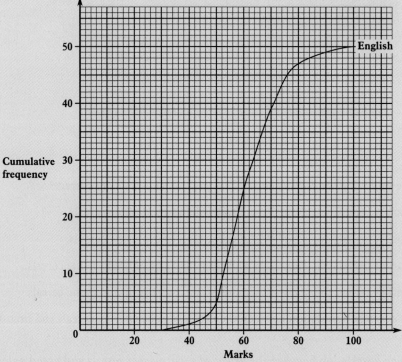

**(ii)** Complete the table.

| | English | Maths |
|---|---|---|
| Median | 60 | |
| Inter-quartile Range | 14 | |

**(iii)** Use the information in the table to comment on the differences between the two distributions of marks. **MEG**

**37.** Arrows are fired at a target. Each arrow either hits or misses the target. Each time Andy fires an arrow, the probability that it hits the target is $\frac{3}{5}$.
Andy fires two arrows.
**(a)** Calculate the probability that both shots hit the target.
**(b)** Calculate the probability that Andy hits the target exactly once with his two shots. **SEG**

**38.** A bag contains a total of 20 beads.

There are 6 red beads, 9 blue beads and 5 white beads.

**(a)** A bead is taken at random from the bag.
The probability that it is red is 0·3.

    **(i)** What is the probability that it is white?

    **(ii)** What is the probability that it is **not** white?

All the beads are taken from the bag, numbered 1, 2, 3 or 4 and then replaced.
When a bead is taken from the bag at random the probability of each number is

| Number on bead | Probability |
|:---:|:---:|
| 1 | 0.3 |
| 2 | 0.4 |
| 3 | 0.2 |
| 4 | 0.1 |

The red beads are numbered.

**(b)** A bead is taken at random from the bag.

    **(i)** What is the probability that it is red or numbered 4?

    **(ii)** Explain why the probability of getting a red bead or a bead numbered 2 is **not**
    0·3 + 0·4.
                                                                                     **SEG**

**39.** The height, to the nearest inch, of 500 adult females is given in the following table.

| Height | 58 | 59 | 60 | 61 | 62 | 63 | 64 | 65 | 66 | 67 | 68 | 69 | 70 | 71 | 72 |
|---|---|---|---|---|---|---|---|---|---|---|---|---|---|---|---|
| Frequency | 1 | 0 | 4 | 3 | 9 | 32 | 67 | 84 | 102 | 135 | 41 | 18 | 3 | 0 | 1 |

**(a)** Complete the grouped frequency table.

| Height (inches) | Class mid-point | Frequency |
|:---:|:---:|:---:|
| 54.5–59.5 | 57 | 1 |
| 59.5–64.5 | | |
| 64.5–69.5 | | |
| 69.5–74.5 | 72 | |

**(b)** Use your grouped frequency distribution from **(a)** to calculate an estimate of the mean
height of the 500 females.

**(c)** The frequency polygon showing the distribution for the height of 500 adult males is shown. On the same axes, draw the frequency polygon for the grouped distribution of the female height.

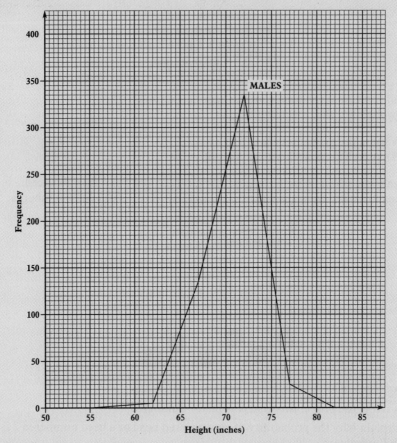

**(d)** Use the frequency polygons to compare the means and dispersions of the two distributions.

SEG

**40. You may use graph paper for this question.**

The table shows the Department of Transport statistics for road casualties in Great Britain for the years 1989–1990.

$Q_1$ represents the months January, February, March.

$Q_2$ represents the months April, May, June.

$Q_3$ represents the months July, August, September.

$Q_4$ represents the months October, November, December.

Prepare an analysis, with appropriate diagrams, suitable for a newspaper article highlighting the differences between the road casualty figures for children and adults at various times of the year.

| Road casualties in Great Britain | | |
|---|---|---|
| | *Total casualties* | |
| | *All ages* | *Under 15 years* |
| 1989 Q₁ | 77 828 | 9 364 |
| Q₂ | 83 305 | 11 865 |
| Q₃ | 87 747 | 12 209 |
| Q₄ | 92 712 | 9 603 |
| 1990 Q₁ | 81 015 | 9 700 |
| Q₂ | 84 522 | 12 341 |
| Q₃ | 87 051 | 12 537 |
| Q₄ | 88 553 | 9 275 |

*Sources: Department of Transport; Scottish Development Department; Welsh Office*

*(from Monthly Digest of Statistics, September 1992)*

MEG

490

**HISTOGRAMS**

Often we have class intervals of different widths as in the data given in the table below, which shows the test marks of 23 students grouped into various categories.

| Test marks | |
|---|---|
| Class interval | Frequency |
| 20–39 | 4 |
| 40–49 | 3 |
| 50–59 | 6 |
| 60–69 | 7 |
| 70–100 | 3 |

Jon graphed the data on this graph.

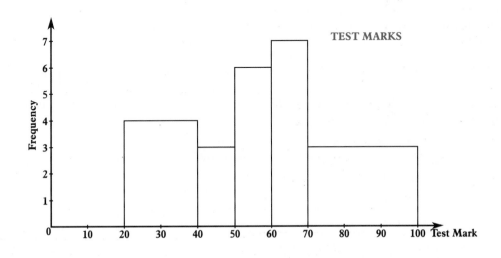

Why is Jon's graph misleading? **Discuss.**
How might the data be graphed so that the graph is not misleading? **Discuss.**

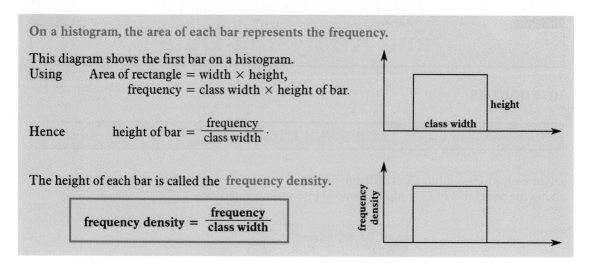

On a histogram, the area of each bar represents the frequency.

This diagram shows the first bar on a histogram.
Using     Area of rectangle = width × height,
            frequency = class width × height of bar.

Hence        height of bar = $\dfrac{\text{frequency}}{\text{class width}}$ .

The height of each bar is called the frequency density.

$$\text{frequency density} = \frac{\text{frequency}}{\text{class width}}$$

*Example*

| Distance (km) | Frequency |
|---|---|
| $0 \le d < 2$ | 7 |
| $2 \le d < 3$ | 3 |
| $3 \le d < 4$ | 4 |
| $4 \le d < 5$ | 2 |
| $5 \le d < 10$ | 8 |

This table shows the distance the workers at Jayes Joinery travel to work.
This data has unequal class widths. To graph this data on a histogram we need to find the frequency density for each class interval.
The width of the class interval $0 \le d < 2$ is 2. The frequency density for this class interval is $7 \div 2 = 3 \cdot 5$.
The width of the class interval $2 \le d < 3$ is 1. The frequency density for this class interval is $3 \div 1 = 3$.
The frequency densities for the other class intervals are found in a similar way. All the frequency densities are listed in the table below.

| Distance (km) | Frequency | Frequency Density |
|---|---|---|
| $0 \le d < 2$ | 7 | 3·5 |
| $2 \le d < 3$ | 3 | 3 |
| $3 \le d < 4$ | 4 | 4 |
| $4 \le d < 5$ | 2 | 2 |
| $5 \le d < 10$ | 8 | 1·6 |

The histogram for this data is shown on the next page.

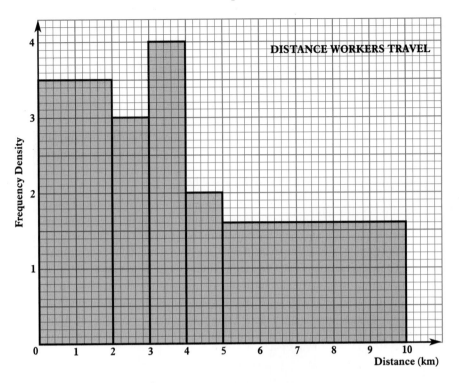

**DISTANCE WORKERS TRAVEL**

*Worked Example* Suppose the histogram in the previous example was given. Explain how you could use this histogram to find the number of workers. Use the histogram to find this number.

*Answer* The area of the histogram gives the frequency i.e. the total number of workers. Reading from left to right, the area of each bar is $2 \times 3·5$, $1 \times 3$, $1 \times 4$, $1 \times 2$, $5 \times 1·6$.

Total area $= 2 \times 3·5 + 1 \times 3 + 1 \times 4 + 1 \times 2 + 5 \times 1·6$
$= 24$

Hence there are 24 workers.

## EXERCISE 23:2

1. The students from Highcliff School took part in a "fun-run" for charity. The table shows the time these students took.

| Time, in minutes | $40 \leq t < 60$ | $60 \leq t < 70$ | $70 \leq t < 80$ | $80 \leq t < 90$ | $90 \leq t < 100$ | $100 \leq t < 120$ |
|---|---|---|---|---|---|---|
| Number of students | 28 | 43 | 58 | 40 | 34 | 18 |
| Frequency density | 1·4 | | | | | |

(a) Copy the table. Complete the frequency densities.
(b) Draw a histogram to illustrate this data.

2. This table shows the weekly earnings of a sample of Year 11 students who have regular part-time jobs.

| Pay (£) | 0·00–4·99 | 5·00–9·99 | 10·00–11·99 | 12·00–13·99 | 14·00–15·99 | 16·00–19·99 | 20·00–24·99 |
|---|---|---|---|---|---|---|---|
| Frequency | 6 | 8 | 8 | 7 | 6 | 4 | 3 |

Draw a histogram to illustrate this data.

3. Gillian estimated the speed of the cars which passed her farm between 10a.m. and 11a.m. last Saturday. She recorded the results on this table.
Illustrate this data on a histogram.

| Speed (mph) | Number of cars |
|---|---|
| 30 – | 2 |
| 40 – | 6 |
| 50 – | 5 |
| 55 – | 7 |
| 60 – 70 | 4 |

4.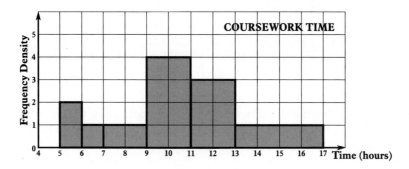

This histogram shows the distribution of the number of hours the students in Jenny's class spent on a coursework task.
How many students are there in Jenny's class?

5. This table gives the distribution of the ages of the staff of Torberry High School.

| Age | 21 – 24 | 25 – 27 | 28 – 30 | 31 – 35 | 36 – 40 | 41 – 45 | 46 – 50 | 51 – 60 | 61 – 64 |
|---|---|---|---|---|---|---|---|---|---|
| Number of Teachers | 6 | 6 | 3 | 5 | 7 | 12 | 8 | 5 | 4 |

(a) Explain why the upper bound of the 25 – 27 class interval is 28 and the lower bound is 25.
(b) What is the width of the class interval 25 – 27?
(c) Illustrate this data on a histogram.

6. One of the questions on Jake's questionnaire asked for the ages of the people who lived in the houses he surveyed. Jake collated the responses to this question on the following frequency table.

| Age | 0 – 4 | 5 – 9 | 10 – 15 | 16 – 18 | 19 – 21 | 22 – 29 | 30 – 39 | 40 – 49 | 50 – 59 | 60 – 84 |
|---|---|---|---|---|---|---|---|---|---|---|
| Number | 14 | 17 | 21 | 16 | 14 | 28 | 36 | 20 | 24 | 8 |

Jake then drew a histogram to illustrate these results. On his histogram, the height of the bar for the 40 – 49 class interval was 2cm. How high should the bars be for each of the other class intervals?

7. On Saturdays, Kevin cooks lunch for his family. For 22 Saturdays Kevin kept a record of how long this took. Kevin's data is shown in the table.

| Time, to the nearest minute | 18 – 23 | 24 – 26 | 27 – 29 | 30 – 31 | 32 – 33 |
|---|---|---|---|---|---|
| Number of occasions | 6 | 6 | 4 | 2 | 4 |

   (a) Explain why the upper bound of the first class interval is 23·5 minutes.
   (b) What is the lower bound for the second class interval?
   (c) What is the lower bound for the first class interval?
   (d) Draw a histogram for this data.

8. The data below gives the history exam. marks of 96 students.

   | 24 | 65 | 72 | 58 | 41 | 63 | 72 | 49 | 9 | 38 | 61 | 54 | 47 | 29 | 64 | 40 |
   |---|---|---|---|---|---|---|---|---|---|---|---|---|---|---|---|
   | 53 | 64 | 82 | 65 | 49 | 48 | 64 | 64 | 59 | 63 | 72 | 37 | 48 | 55 | 60 | 48 |
   | 74 | 91 | 36 | 52 | 45 | 61 | 95 | 69 | 43 | 58 | 39 | 57 | 82 | 69 | 42 | 81 |
   | 72 | 48 | 50 | 57 | 78 | 23 | 42 | 73 | 64 | 54 | 55 | 58 | 15 | 64 | 67 | 66 |
   | 96 | 54 | 57 | 65 | 71 | 63 | 49 | 54 | 45 | 63 | 68 | 70 | 64 | 57 | 51 | 46 |
   | 14 | 63 | 54 | 61 | 63 | 59 | 60 | 65 | 44 | 54 | 67 | 39 | 50 | 72 | 53 | 69 |

   (a) Group this data using the class intervals 1–10, 11–20, 21–30, . . . 91–100.
   (b) Regroup the data into 5 class intervals, none of which has fewer than 10 students.
   (c) Draw a histogram for the regrouped data.

9. (i) Karen was doing a project on netball. This frequency table shows the distribution of the number of goals scored in games played in Plymouth.

| Goals Scored | 0 – 19 | 20 – 39 | 40 – 49 | 50 – 59 | 60 – 69 | 70 – 99 |
|---|---|---|---|---|---|---|
| Frequency | 16 | 32 | 68 | 72 | 43 | 27 |

   (a) How many games are represented in the frequency table?
   (b) Draw a histogram to illustrate this data.

   (ii) This histogram shows the number of goals scored in the games played in Bristol.

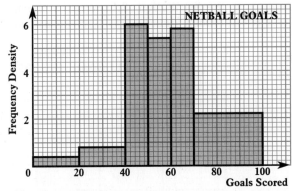

   By comparing the histograms we can see that a greater proportion of the Bristol games scored between 70 and 99 goals.
   Use the histograms to describe other differences (or similarities) between the distributions for the goals scored in Plymouth and Bristol.

**Review 1** This frequency table shows the number of runs John Best made in the cricket games he played for his county.

| Runs made | 0 – 19 | 20 – 29 | 30 – 39 | 40 – 44 | 45 – 49 | 50 – 69 | 70 – 99 |
|---|---|---|---|---|---|---|---|
| Number of games | 8 | 11 | 9 | 6 | 7 | 4 | 4 |
| Frequency density | | | | 1·2 | | | |

(a) Copy the table. Complete the frequency densities.
(b) Draw a histogram to illustrate the data.

**Review 2** In the Medbury High School grounds there is an unusual sort of pine tree. Donna gathered some pine needles from beneath this tree. Her data for the lengths of the needles is shown in the table.

| Length (cm) | 0 – | 1 – | 2 – | 3 – | 4 – | 5 – | 6 – | 7 – | 8 – | 9 – | 10 – | 11 – 12 |
|---|---|---|---|---|---|---|---|---|---|---|---|---|
| Frequency | 1 | 1 | 2 | 4 | 8 | 9 | 4 | 3 | ·6 | 3 | 1 | 2 |

(a) Regroup this data into 6 class intervals so that no group has a frequency of less than 5.
(b) Draw a histogram for this regrouped data.

**Review 3** (a) This frequency table shows the distribution of the weight of the luggage of the passengers on an early morning flight from Glasgow to Gatwick.

| Weight (kg) | $0 \leq w < 5$ | $5 \leq w < 7$ | $7 \leq w < 9$ | $9 \leq w < 10$ | $10 \leq w < 11$ | $11 \leq w < 12$ | $12 \leq w < 15$ | $15 \leq w < 20$ |
|---|---|---|---|---|---|---|---|---|
| Frequency | 20 | 7 | 18 | 10 | 9 | 8 | 15 | 10 |

Draw a histogram for this data.

(b) This histogram shows the distribution of the weight of the luggage of the passengers on a late afternoon flight from Glasgow to Gatwick.

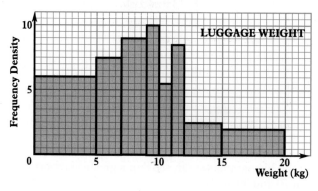

Use the histograms to compare the distribution of the weight of the luggage on the early morning and late afternoon flights.

# PRESENTATION of DATA

Data given in table form or in lists is often more readily understood if it is presented on a graph or diagram. This is particularly so if the data is complex.

The histograms we used in the previous section can be helpful in presenting complex data in a simplified form. Many other graphs or diagrams may also be used. A list of those we are familiar with follows.

| | | | |
|---|---|---|---|
| Bar Charts | Pie Charts | Pictograms | Scatter Diagrams |
| Line Graphs | Histograms | Frequency Polygons | |

Computer statistical packages and many spreadsheets produce a variety of graphs. Some examples of published graphs follow. These are all from **Key Data**.

**Road and rail passenger transport use**

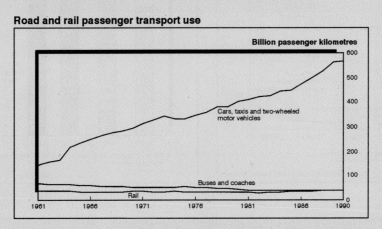

**Purchasing power of the pound in the European Community[1], 1981 and 1991**

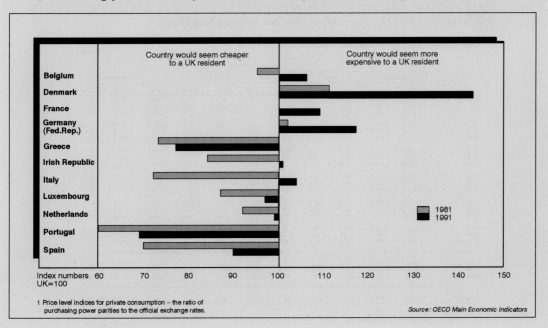

1 Price level indices for private consumption – the ratio of purchasing power parities to the official exchange rates.

*Source: OECD Main Economic Indicators*

## Noise - complaints received by Environmental Health Officers: by source[1]

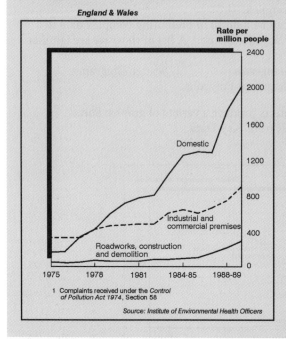

England & Wales

Rate per million people

Domestic

Industrial and commercial premises

Roadworks, construction and demolition

1975    1978    1981    1984-85    1988-89

1 Complaints received under the *Control of Pollution Act 1974*, Section 58

Source: *Institute of Environmental Health Officers*

## Personal customers cash withdrawals: by type of withdrawal

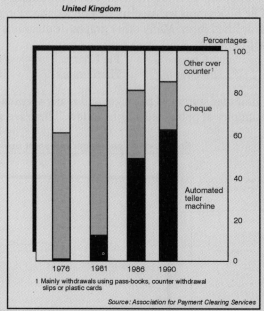

United Kingdom

Percentages

Other over counter[1]

Cheque

Automated teller machine

1976    1981    1986    1990

1 Mainly withdrawals using pass-books, counter withdrawal slips or plastic cards

Source: *Association for Payment Clearing Services*

## DISCUSSION EXERCISE 23:3

Which sorts of graphs or diagrams would be appropriate for presenting data in simplified form from the following tables? Discuss. All of the data is from **Key Data.**

**Age distribution of estimated resident population at 30 June 1989**

Thousands

| | England and Wales | | Wales | | Scotland | | Northern Ireland[1] | | United Kingdom | | |
|---|---|---|---|---|---|---|---|---|---|---|---|
| | Males | Females | Males | Females | Males | Females | Males | Females | Males | Females | Persons |
| 0-4 | 1 713.8 | 1 632.4 | 97.2 | 92.5 | 166.7 | 158.6 | 69.5 | 65.7 | 1 950.7 | 1 857.0 | 3 807.7 |
| 5-9 | 1 629.4 | 1 548.4 | 93.8 | 89.0 | 164.7 | 157.1 | 68.2 | 65.2 | 1 862.0 | 1 770.7 | 3 632.7 |
| 10-14 | 1 517.1 | 1 434.1 | 88.6 | 83.3 | 158.1 | 149.7 | 64.8 | 62.4 | 1 739.3 | 1 645.2 | 3 384.5 |
| 15-19 | 1 830.1 | 1 739.0 | 105.1 | 100.6 | 190.1 | 183.5 | 70.0 | 63.5 | 2 091.2 | 1 987.8 | 4 079.0 |
| 20-24 | 2 077.5 | 2 010.1 | 113.0 | 110.6 | 217.8 | 208.4 | 71.8 | 63.8 | 2 367.9 | 2 282.8 | 4 650.7 |
| 25-29 | 2 058.9 | 2 023.2 | 113.1 | 114.2 | 210.8 | 201.8 | 64.8 | 60.6 | 2 333.5 | 2 285.1 | 4 618.7 |
| 30-34 | 1 761.4 | 1 737.0 | 93.4 | 91.2 | 184.2 | 182.1 | 54.3 | 55.3 | 1 998.2 | 1 972.9 | 3 971.1 |
| 35-39 | 1 682.9 | 1 681.4 | 92.2 | 92.6 | 167.8 | 168.1 | 47.5 | 48.7 | 1 898.1 | 1 897.4 | 3 795.6 |
| 40-44 | 1 821.8 | 1 812.7 | 98.8 | 99.6 | 172.6 | 172.8 | 47.0 | 47.9 | 2 041.1 | 2 033.4 | 4 074.5 |
| 45-49 | 1 466.6 | 1 454.9 | 83.0 | 82.8 | 144.0 · | 149.1 | 43.1 | 44.6 | 1 652.6 | 1 647.2 | 3 299.9 |
| 50-54 | 1 367.3 | 1 367.4 | 77.1 | 77.6 | 136.9 | 145.7 | 37.7 | 39.4 | 1 541.5 | 1 552.2 | 3 093.7 |
| 55-59 | 1 293.7 | 1 323.7 | 74.1 | 77.3 | 131.2 | 144.3 | 34.0 | 37.2 | 1 458.8 | 1 505.4 | 2 964.2 |
| 60-64 | 1 245.2 | 1 333.3 | 74.2 | 81.5 | 123.1 | 141.1 | 31.3 | 36.5 | 1 399.7 | 1 510.8 | 2 910.4 |
| 65-69 | 1 215.0 | 1 422.9 | 73.3 | 86.2 | 113.2 | 142.0 | 28.0 | 35.1 | 1 356.6 | 1 600.6 | 2 957.1 |
| 70-74 | 784.9 | 1 050.7 | 48.3 | 65.4 | 73.2 | 106.3 | 20.6 | 29.2 | 878.4 | 1 185.9 | 2 064.2 |
| 75-79 | 648.3 | 1 022.9 | 37.1 | 60.2 | 59.1 | 99.6 | 15.5 | 25.4 | 723.1 | 1 147.8 | 1 870.9 |
| 80-84 | 365.7 | 734.1 | 20.5 | 43.0 | 31.9 | 70.1 | 8.5 | 17.3 | 405.9 | 820.9 | 1 226.8 |
| 85 and over | 189.3 | 565.2 | 10.6 | 31.9 | 15.0 | 50.3 | 3.8 | 11.3 | 208.1 | 626.6 | 834.7 |
| 0-14 | 4 860.4 | 4 614.8 | 279.6 | 264.7 | 489.5 | 465.3 | 202.5 | 193.3 | 5 552.0 | 5 272.9 | 10 824.9 |
| 15-64 | 16 605.4 | 16 482.8 | 924.1 | 928.1 | 1 678.4 | 1 696.8 | 501.5 | 497.4 | 18 782.6 | 18 675.0 | 37 457.6 |
| 65 and over | 3 203.3 | 4 795.8 | 189.8 | 286.7 | 292.4 | 468.2 | 76.4 | 118.3 | 3 572.0 | 5 381.8 | 8 953.8 |
| All ages | 24 669.1 | 25 893.4 | 1 393.5 | 1 479.6 | 2 460.4 | 2 630.3 | 780.4 | 809.0 | 27 906.5 | 29 329.7 | 57 236.2 |

Figures may not add due to rounding.
1 For Northern Ireland: population at June 1990

From: *Monthly Digest of Statistics, June 1992,*
*Tables 2.1 and 2.2*

498

## Landings of fish of British taking:  landed weight and value

*United Kingdom*

| | Landed weight (Thousand tonnes) | | | | | | Value (£ thousand) | | | | | | |
|---|---|---|---|---|---|---|---|---|---|---|---|---|---|
| | 1984 | 1985 | 1986 | 1987 | 1988 | 1989 | 1990 | 1984 | 1985 | 1986 | 1987 | 1988 | 1989 | 1990 |
| **Total all fish** | 733.7 | 762.1 | 716.9 | 790.4 | 742.0 | 671 763 | 621.5 | 297 863 | 323 825 | 361 680 | 435 162 | 402 893 | 394 346 | 430 503 |
| **Total wet fish** | 661.0 | 687.2 | 629.3 | 679.3 | 645.5 | 580 430 | 528.4 | 240 587 | 258 904 | 284 161 | 339 223 | 310 412 | 299 354 | 329 491 |
| Demersal: | | | | | | | | | | | | | | |
| Catfish | 1.3 | 1.4 | 1.5 | 1.6 | 1.6 | 1 758 | 1.7 | 589 | 755 | 1 035 | 1 318 | 1 223 | 1 557 | 1 816 |
| Cod | 90.9 | 90.0 | 76.5 | 93.4 | 77.7 | 68 184 | 60.4 | 65 258 | 69 945 | 69 140 | 86 312 | 74 849 | 69 568 | 76 759 |
| Dogfish | 12.3 | 13.8 | 11.6 | 13.6 | 13.0 | 11 297 | 110.8 | 3 547 | 4 550 | 6 376 | 7 201 | 7 066 | 7 762 | 8 944 |
| Haddock | 107.5 | 132.2 | 131.0 | 102.4 | 97.6 | 71 882 | 490.8 | 64 204 | 67 757 | 79 019 | 78 079 | 68 708 | 61 918 | 59 369 |
| Hake | 2.5 | 2.7 | 3.0 | 3.3 | 3.6 | 4 024 | 4.59 | 2 794 | 3 851 | 4 549 | 5 540 | 6 389 | 7 699 | 11 610 |
| Halibut | 0.1 | 0.1 | 0.1 | 0.1 | 0.1 | 117 | 0.1 | 319 | 365 | 372 | 446 | 482 | 442 | 1 171 |
| Lemon sole | 5.7 | 5.7 | 5.0 | 5.3 | 5.4 | 5 036 | 5.7 | 5 972 | 7 137 | 8 265 | 9 018 | 8 788 | 8 945 | 10 887 |
| Plaice | 21.5 | 20.4 | 21.3 | 25.7 | 27.3 | 26 173 | 25.3 | 14 097 | 13 821 | 16 048 | 22 541 | 22 348 | 20 400 | 23 815 |
| Redfish | 0.4 | 0.2 | 0.1 | 0.2 | 0.2 | 193 | 0.3 | 98 | 75 | 56 | 62 | 71 | 101 | 189 |
| Saithe (Coalfish) | 12.1 | 14.4 | 17.7 | 15.2 | 14.4 | 11 761 | 12.2 | 2 759 | 3 874 | 6 361 | 7 077 | 5 657 | 4 868 | 5 834 |
| Skate and ray | 6.8 | 7.0 | 6.9 | 8.6 | 8.4 | 7 405 | 7.3 | 2 792 | 2 992 | 3 908 | 4 742 | 4 796 | 4 596 | 5 326 |
| Sole | 2.4 | 2.7 | 3.2 | 3.1 | 3.0 | 2 880 | 3.1 | 6 717 | 9 093 | 14 500 | 16 991 | 14 067 | 14 370 | 14 274 |
| Turbot | 0.5 | 0.5 | 0.6 | 0.7 | 0.7 | 530 | 0.6 | 1 660 | 1 976 | 2 607 | 3 612 | 3 690 | 3 014 | 3 481 |
| Whiting | 60.7 | 50.2 | 41.1 | 51.9 | 45.6 | 38 419 | 38.3 | 23 006 | 18 997 | 18 460 | 25 198 | 21 143 | 20 834 | 26 085 |
| Livers[1] | .. | .. | .. | .. | .. | .. | 0 | .. | 1 | 1 | .. | .. | .. | 0 |
| Roes | 0.6 | 0.5 | 0.5 | 0.5 | 0.5 | 433 | 0.4 | 321 | 390 | 348 | 499 | 473 | 457 | 446 |
| Other demersal | 69.7 | 60.5 | 63.1 | 55.0 | 66.9 | 62 981 | 54.2 | 17 580 | 21 596 | 25 660 | 35 690 | 37 198 | 41 861 | 48 193 |
| Total | 395.0 | 402.3 | 383.2 | 381.3 | 366.0 | 313 073 | 274.3 | 211 713 | 227 175 | 256 705 | 304 326 | 276 948 | 268 392 | 298 649 |
| Pelagic: | | | | | | | | | | | | | | |
| Herring | 71.5 | 95.4 | 106.1 | 100.3 | 93.2 | 99 430 | 98.8 | 9 076 | 11 493 | 11 881 | 12 213 | 11 244 | 11 257 | 11 705 |
| Mackerel[2] | 186.3 | 174.2 | 132.1 | 189.4 | 176.1 | 157 927 | 146.6 | 18 768 | 18 694 | 14 766 | 21 484 | 20 791 | 18 702 | 18 043 |
| Other pelagic | 8.2 | 15.4 | 7.9 | 8.3 | 10.2 | 10 000 | 8.7 | 1 030 | 1 543 | 809 | 1 200 | 1 429 | 1 003 | 1 094 |
| Total | 266.0 | 285.0 | 246.1 | 298.0 | 279.5 | 267 357 | 254 | 28 874 | 31 730 | 27 456 | 34 897 | 33 464 | 30 962 | 30 842 |
| **Total shell fish** | 72.6 | 74.8 | 87.6 | 111.1 | 96.5 | 91 333 | 93.1 | 57 274 | 64 920 | 77 519 | 95 939 | 92 481 | 94 992 | 101 012 |
| Cockles | 5.4 | 7.8 | 19.4 | 39.0 | 24.6 | 14 775 | 19.6 | 311 | 476 | 1 165 | 4 285 | 3 276 | 1 274 | 1 663 |
| Crab | 14.0 | 13.5 | 12.6 | 13.5 | 15.2 | 14 135 | 16 | 8 422 | 8 557 | 9 599 | 11 400 | 13 908 | 14 143 | 15 064 |
| Lobster | 1.2 | 1.1 | 1.0 | 1.1 | 1.3 | 1 280 | 1.3 | 7 696 | 8 030 | 7 680 | 9 346 | 10 163 | 10 650 | 11 115 |
| Mussels | 4.3 | 5.8 | 6.3 | 4.9 | 6.9 | 9 034 | 6.6 | 314 | 467 | 541 | 543 | 906 | 1 190 | 923 |
| Nephrop (Norway lobster) | 22.2 | 24.8 | 25.4 | 24.2 | 27.4 | 27 008 | 25.4 | 24 545 | 31 548 | 39 119 | 43 007 | 44 585 | 42 122 | 49 659 |
| Oysters[3] | 0.4 | 0.5 | 0.6 | 0.1 | 0.1 | 51 | 0.2 | 770 | 734 | 845 | 241 | 225 | 179 | 4 367 |
| Shrimps[4] | 0.7 | 0.8 | 1.4 | 3.3 | 1.7 | 1 821 | 1.2 | 566 | 711 | 1 254 | 2 346 | 1 785 | 2 627 | 1 959 |
| Whelks | 2.2 | 1.6 | 2.0 | 2.7 | 2.0 | 1 184 | 0.8 | 456 | 355 | 418 | 665 | 473 | 251 | 175 |
| Other shell fish | 22.2 | 18.9 | 18.9 | 22.3 | 17.3 | 22 045 | 22 | 14 194 | 14 042 | 16 898 | 24 106 | 17 165 | 22 556 | 16 087 |

1  Including the raw equivalent of any liver oils landed.
2  Includes transhipments of mackerel or herring ie caught by British vessels but not actually landed at British ports. These quantities are transhipped to foreign vessels and are later recorded as exports.

3  The weight of oysters is calculated on the basis of one tonne being equal to 15 748 oysters in England and Wales.
4  From 1986, data for prawn is also included.

*Sources   Ministry of Agriculture, Fisheries and Food; Department of Agriculture and Fisheries for Scotland*

## Family practitioner and dental services

*United Kingdom*

| | General medical and pharmaceutical services | | | | | | General dental services | |
|---|---|---|---|---|---|---|---|---|
| | Number of doctors[1] in practice (thousands) | Average number of patients per doctor[1] (thousands) | Prescriptions dispensed[2] (millions) | Average total cost per prescription (£) | Average number of prescriptions per person | Average prescription cost[3] per person (£) | Number of dentists[4] in practice (thousands) | Average number of persons per dentist (thousands) |
| 1961 | 23.6 | 2.25 | 233.2 | 0.41 | 4.7 | 1.9 | 11.9 | 4.4 |
| 1971 | 24.0 | 2.39 | 304.5 | 0.77 | 5.6 | 4.3 | 12.5 | 4.5 |
| 1981 | 27.5 | 2.15 | 370.0 | 3.46 | 6.6 | 23.0 | 15.2 | 3.7 |
| 1985 | 29.7 | 2.01 | 393.1 | 4.77 | 7.0 | 33.4 | 17.0 | 3.3 |
| 1986 | 30.2 | 1.99 | 397.5 | 5.11 | 7.0 | 36.0 | 17.3 | 3.3 |
| 1987 | 30.7 | 1.97 | 413.6 | 5.47 | 7.3 | 40.0 | 17.6 | 3.2 |
| 1988 | 31.2 | 1.94 | 427.7 | 5.91 | 7.5 | 44.1 | 18.0 | 3.2 |
| 1989 | 31.5 | 1.91 | 435.8 | 6.26 | 7.5 | 47.2 | 18.4 | 3.1 |
| 1990 | 31.6 | 1.89 | 446.6 | 6.68 | 7.8 | 52.1 | 18.6 | 3.2 |

1  Unrestricted principals only.  See Appendix, Part 7:  Unrestricted principals.
2  Prescriptions dispensed by general practitioners are excluded. The number of such prescriptions in the United Kingdom is not known precisely, but in England during 1990 totalled some 27 million.

3  Total cost including dispensing fees and cost.
4  Principals plus assistants.

*Source:  Department of Health*

## UK airlines[1]: aircraft kilometres flown, passengers and cargo uplifted
## Tonne-kilometres and seat kilometres used

| | All services | | | Domestic services | | | International services | | |
|---|---|---|---|---|---|---|---|---|---|
| | Aircraft kilometres flown (000's) | Passengers uplifted (000's) | Cargo uplifted (tonnes)[2] | Aircraft kilometres flown (000's) | Passengers uplifted (000's) | Cargo uplifted (tonnes)[2] | Aircraft kilometres flown (000's) | Passengers uplifted | Cargo uplifted (tonnes)[2] |
| | BMIA | BMIB | BMIC | BMID | BMIE | BMIF | BMIG | BMIH | BMII |
| 1985 | 30 955 | 2 068.7 | 30 003 | 5 772 | 747.7 | 3 842 | 25 183 | 1 321.0 | 26 161 |
| 1986 | 32 067 | 2 083.1 | 31 330 | 5 932 | 756.8 | 3 962 | 26 136 | 1 326.3 | 27 368 |
| 1987 | 33 802 | 2 374.7 | 33 780 | 6 127 | 837.4 | 4 235 | 27 675 | 1 537.3 | 29 546 |
| 1988 | 36 562 | 2 603.7 | 35 669 | 6 446 | 933.2 | 4 064 | 30 117 | 1 670.5 | 31 606 |
| 1989 | 40 472 | 2 931.0 | 37 786 | 7 100 | 1 019.2 | 3 888 | 33 372 | 1 911.8 | 33 898 |
| 1990 | 43 653 | 3 196.0 | 40 461 | 7 207 | 1 057.5 | 3 818 | 36 446 | 2 138.5 | 36 643 |
| 1991 | 41 475 | 2 882.7 | 38 885 | 7 169 | 970.8 | 3 145 | 34 306 | 1 911.9 | 35 740 |
| 1990 Jan | 41 256 | 2 641.3 | 36 017 | 6 882 | 875.8 | 3 551 | 34 286 | 1 765.5 | 32 466 |
| Feb | 37 538 | 2 556.9 | 36 871 | 6 220 | 848.7 | 3 514 | 31 318 | 1 708.2 | 33 357 |
| Mar | 42 615 | 3 076.2 | 43 163 | 7 154 | 1 030.3 | 4 015 | 35 461 | 2 045.9 | 39 149 |
| Apr | 43 576 | 3 278.0 | 38 874 | 7 423 | 1 104.0 | 3 520 | 36 153 | 2 174.0 | 35 355 |
| May | 45 837 | 3 382.0 | 40 061 | 7 643 | 1 080.1 | 3 993 | 38 194 | 2 237.0 | 36 070 |
| Jun | 45 199 | 3 510.2 | 40 534 | 7 506 | 1 147.7 | 4 914 | 37 694 | 2 362.5 | 35 621 |
| Jul | 47 397 | 3 774.2 | 41 697 | 7 895 | 1 213.5 | 3 783 | 39 502 | 2 560.7 | 37 914 |
| Aug | 47 425 | 3 729.5 | 39 534 | 8 106 | 1 215.4 | 3 793 | 39 319 | 2 512.0 | 35 742 |
| Sep | 48 200 | 3 679.2 | 41 657 | 7 556 | 1 211.5 | 3 884 | 38 644 | 2 467.7 | 37 773 |
| Oct | 46 599 | 3 497.5 | 44 427 | 7 518 | 1 134.7 | 4 053 | 39 081 | 2 362.8 | 40 374 |
| Nov | 40 671 | 2 759.4 | 42 159 | 6 579 | 959.5 | 3 460 | 34 092 | 1 799.9 | 38 699 |
| Dec | 39 826 | 2 615.9 | 41 256 | 6 005 | 854.8 | 3 451 | 33 281 | 1 761.1 | 37 805 |
| 1991 Jan | 40 328 | 2 289.3 | 35 205 | 6 442 | 763.0 | 3 006 | 33 886 | 1 526.3 | 32 199 |
| Feb | 30 364 | 1 852.8 | 32 868 | 5 182 | 688.6 | 2 592 | 25 182 | 1 164.2 | 30 276 |
| Mar | 36 996 | 2 655.3 | 38 592 | 6 118 | 913.9 | 3 145 | 30 878 | 1 741.4 | 35 447 |
| Apr | 40 662 | 2 791.7 | 37 267 | 7 282 | 969.6 | 3 214 | 33 380 | 1 822.1 | 34 053 |
| May | 42 950 | 3 061.2 | 38 646 | 7 758 | 1 075.9 | 3 190 | 35 192 | 1 985.3 | 35 456 |
| Jun | 43 224 | 3 162.9 | 40 322 | 7 550 | 1 067.1 | 3 000 | 35 674 | 2 095.8 | 37 322 |
| Jul | 45 433 | 3 347.2 | 38 639 | 7 994 | 1 102.5 | 3 034 | 37 439 | 2 244.7 | 35 605 |
| Aug | 45 000 | 3 402.4 | 37 440 | 8 013 | 1 136.4 | 3 088 | 36 987 | 2 266.0 | 34 352 |
| Sep | 44 440 | 3 384.3 | 39 529 | 7 847 | 1 137.4 | 3 126 | 36 593 | 2 246.9 | 36 403 |
| Oct | 45 076 | 3 256.8 | 42 735 | 7 945 | 1 063.1 | 3 345 | 37 131 | 2 193.7 | 39 390 |
| Nov | 42 090 | 2 728.0 | 43 252 | 7 150 | 896.1 | 3 114 | 34 940 | 1 831.9 | 40 138 |
| Dec | 40 979 | 2 655.0 | 41 550 | 6 587 | 831.0 | 3 300 | 34 392 | 1 824.0 | 38 250 |
| 1992 Jan | 42 938 | 2 606.7 | 36 975 | 7 052 | 803.1 | 2 880 | 35 886 | 1 803.6 | 34 095 |

1 Scheduled services only. All kilometre statistics are based on standard (Great Circle) distance.
2 Including weight of freight mail, excess baggage and diplomatic bags, but excluding passengers' and crews' permitted baggage.

*Source: Civil Aviation Authority*

---

## PRACTICAL EXERCISE 23:4

1. Become familiar with the sorts of graphs you can produce on your school computer. You could produce appropriate graphs for some of the data given in the previous discussion exercise.

2. Collect some sets of data. Some suggestions follow. Present these on appropriate graphs or diagrams. Your graphs could be either hand drawn or computer drawn.

   Suggestions: Responses to a questionnaire on pollution control.

   The marks in the exams. of two or more subjects or in the exams. of one subject in two or more years. Use your graphs or diagrams to compare the marks.

   The ages of people in your village or your suburb or your area. Compare the distribution of these ages with the distribution of ages over the whole country.

3. Collect some published data. Some suggestions follow. Use graphs or diagrams to present this data in a simplified form. Use your graphs or diagrams to analyse the data.

   Suggestions: A government report on unemployment.

   The published results of an opinion poll.

   Data from the Education Year Book or Social Trends or some other statistical publication.

4. Use published data to examine relationships. Some suggestions follow. Use graphs or diagrams as part of your analysis.

      Suggestions: The relationship between the educational standard of the population and good nutrition in various countries.

                The relationship between air pollution and the wealth of a country.

                The relative importance of the occupation of the parents and the age of the teachers on student's GCSE results.

## CHAPTER 23   REVIEW

1. The histogram shows the distribution of the lengths of telephone calls made by a firm on one day.
   (a) In which interval were there most telephone calls?
   (b) How many telephone calls were made that day?
   (c) The mean length of a call was approximately 6 minutes.
   Estimate the percentage of calls which lasted longer than the mean length of call.

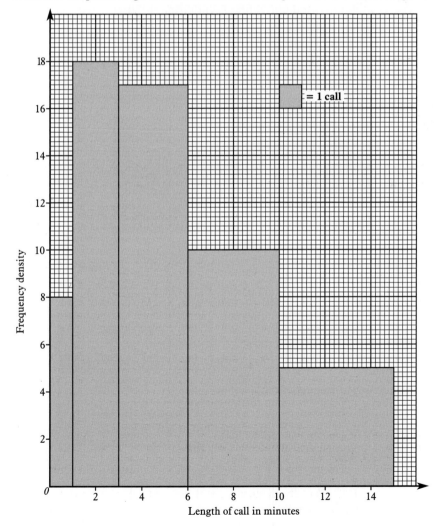

Length of call in minutes

**NEAB**

**2.** In a survey the children in a form were asked how far they travelled to school that morning. Their answers in miles are recorded below.

| 1·3 | 1·8 | 2·1 | 0·4 | 0·9 | 0·3 | 2·1 | 0·7 | 0·1 | 0·9 | 1·7 | 2·1 |
| 0·75 | 0·63 | 1·72 | 1·54 | 0·52 | 0·48 | 1·1 | 2·3 | 3·4 | 4·2 | 4·1 | 0·7 |

These answers were recorded in the frequency table below.

| Distance in miles | Tally marks | Frequency |
|---|---|---|
| 0 – | IIII | 4 |
| 0·5 – | JHT II | 7 |
| 1– | JHT I | 6 |
| 2– | IIII | 4 |
| 3 – 5 | III | 3 |

On the axes given, draw a histogram to display the data as grouped in the table.

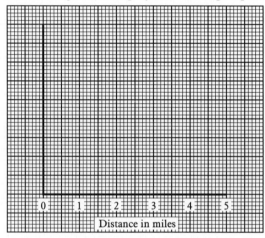

**3.** The following list shows the maximum daily temperature, in °F, throughout the month of April.

| 56·1 | 49·4 | 63·7 | 56·7 | 55·3 | 53·5 | 52·4 | 57·6 | 59·8 | 52·1 |
| 45·8 | 55·1 | 42·6 | 61·0 | 61·9 | 60·2 | 57·1 | 48·9 | 63·2 | 68·4 |
| 55·5 | 65·2 | 47·3 | 59·1 | 53·6 | 52·3 | 46·9 | 51·3 | 56·7 | 64·3 |

**(a)** Complete the grouped frequency table below.

| Temperature, T | | Frequency |
|---|---|---|
| $40 < T \le 50$ | | |
| $50 < T \le 54$ | | |
| $54 < T \le 58$ | | |
| $58 < T \le 62$ | | |
| $62 < T \le 70$ | | |

(b) Use your table of values in part (a) to calculate an estimate of the mean of this distribution. You **must** show your working clearly.

(c) On the grid below draw a histogram to represent your distribution in part (a).

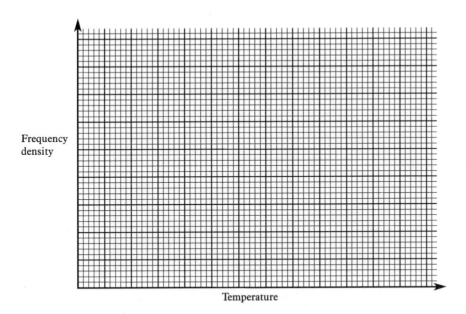

Frequency density

Temperature

**MEG**

4. The age of each person in a coach party is illustrated in the histogram below.

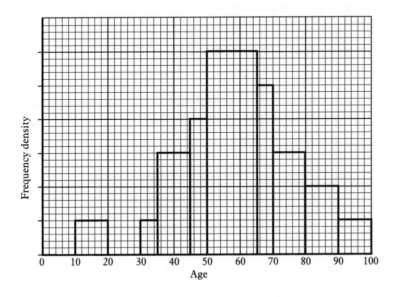

There are 6 people in the 70–80 age range.

(a) How many people are there in the 45–50 age range?

(b) How many people are there in the 50–70 age range?

**SEG**

5. The waiting times for patients to be seen by a doctor after arriving at the accident department of a hospital during a weekend period were recorded. The histogram shows the results.

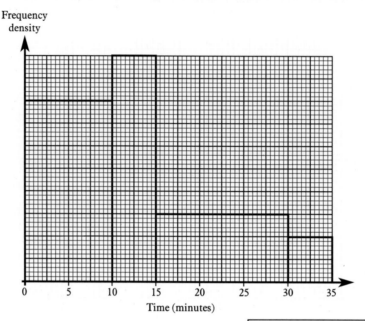

There were **exactly** 20 patients who were seen by a doctor in a time which was greater than or equal to 10 minutes and less than 15 minutes.

No patient had to wait 35 minutes or longer before being seen by a doctor.

Use the information in the histogram to complete the frequency table.

| Waiting time in minutes (t) | Frequency |
|---|---|
| $0 \leq t < 10$ | |
| $10 \leq t < 15$ | 20 |
| $15 \leq t < 30$ | |
| $30 \leq t < 35$ | |
| $35 \leq t$ | 0 |

**ULEAC**

6. The frequency table below is taken from the St Catherine's House database and shows the age at death of 100 people who died in the years 1880–1885.

   (a) (i) Complete the table below.

| Age | Frequency | Class width | Frequency density |
|---|---|---|---|
| 0 | 23 | 1 | 23 |
| 1 – 5 | 13 | 5 | 2·6 |
| 6 – 10 | 2 | | |
| 11 – 30 | 14 | | |
| 31 – 50 | 15 | | |
| 51 – 60 | 14 | | |
| 61 – 70 | 1 | | |
| 71 – 80 | 12 | | |
| 81 – 90 | 6 | | |

(ii) Use the table to complete the histogram, to illustrate the ages at death, excluding age 0.

**(b)** Why was it not appropriate to include the 'Age = 0' class on the histogram?

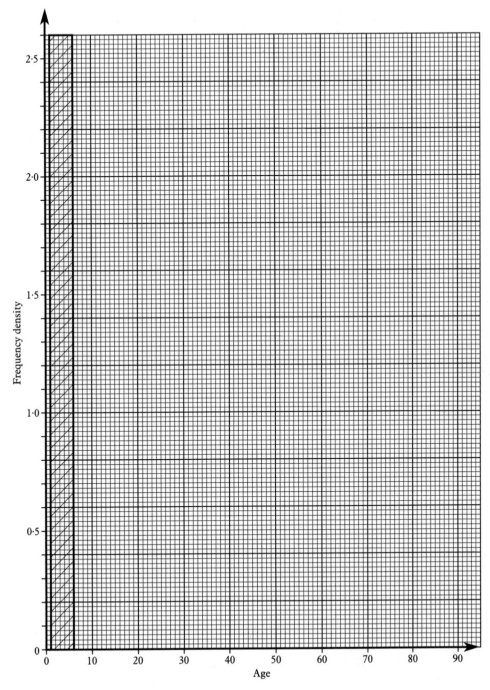

**SEG**

## RANDOM NUMBERS

A digit is chosen at random from the digits 0 to 9 inclusive. Another digit is then chosen, then another, then another, . . .

The sequence of digits formed is called a Random Number Sequence. The numbers obtained in such a sequence are often placed in a table, such as the one below. The table is called a Random Number Table. In the table below, there is a space between every 5 digits. This has no significance. A space has been placed after every 5 digits to make the table easier to read. The sequence of numbers which was put into the table below could have been

    5177274640423312904446621628989358204186240323491 . . .

or   524306102950285145 . . . Where do these numbers appear in the table?

| | | | | | | | |
|---|---|---|---|---|---|---|---|
| 51772 | 74640 | 42331 | 29044 | 46621 | 62898 | 93582 | 04186 |
| 24033 | 23491 | 83587 | 06568 | 21960 | 21387 | 76105 | 10863 |
| 45939 | 60173 | 52078 | 25424 | 11645 | 55870 | 56974 | 37428 |
| 30586 | 02133 | 75797 | 45406 | 31041 | 86707 | 12973 | 17169 |
| 03585 | 79353 | 81938 | 82322 | 96799 | 85659 | 36081 | 50883 |
| 64937 | 03355 | 95863 | 20790 | 65304 | 00745 | 00745 | 65253 |
| 15630 | 64759 | 51135 | 98527 | 62586 | 25439 | 25439 | 88036 |
| 09448 | 56301 | 57683 | 30277 | 94623 | 68829 | 68829 | 06652 |
| 21631 | 91157 | 73311 | 60710 | 52290 | 48653 | 48653 | 71590 |
| 91097 | 17480 | 29414 | 06829 | 87843 | 27279 | 27279 | 47152 |
| 50532 | 25496 | 95652 | 42457 | 73547 | 50020 | 50020 | 24819 |
| 07136 | 40876 | 79971 | 54195 | 25708 | 36732 | 36732 | 72484 |
| 27989 | 64728 | 10744 | 08396 | 56242 | 28868 | 28868 | 99431 |
| 85184 | 73949 | 36601 | 46253 | 00477 | 09908 | 09908 | 36574 |
| 54398 | 21154 | 97810 | 36764 | 32869 | 55261 | 55261 | 59009 |

A sequence of random numbers has the following properties:
1. Each digit has the same probability of being selected for any position.
2. Each digit is selected independently.

Some ways of generating random numbers follow.

Drawing numbers from a hat:
Write the digits 0 to 9 on ten counters. Place the counters in a container.
Choose a counter at random, note its number then replace it in the container.
Repeat this procedure.

Using a calculator:
Press the $\pi$ key. Alternately multiply and divide by any of the digits 1 to 9. To decide which of these digits, "draw from a hat" using nine counters numbered from 1 to 9.

For example, pressing $\boxed{\pi}$ then $\boxed{\times}\ \boxed{5}\ \boxed{=}$ gives 15707963, then pressing $\boxed{\div}\ \boxed{8}\ \boxed{=}$ gives 19634954.

**Using a computer:**
Use a program similar to that given below. The program given will print out 500 random
numbers between 0 and 9.

```
10    FOR I = 1 TO 500
20    PRINT RND(9)
30    NEXT I
```

**Using the Random Number key on a calculator:**
Most scientific calculators generate random numbers. Often these are 3 digit decimal numbers.

Key:  [ SHIFT ] [ RAN# ] [ SHIFT ] [ RAN# ] [ SHIFT ] [ RAN# ]  . . .

## INVESTIGATION 24:1

Random Numbers

Use the computer to generate a sequence of random numbers. Investigate patterns in
these numbers. You might like to investigate runs of three consecutive numbers, lengths
of sequences of odd numbers, identical adjacent numbers etc.

Generate random numbers using the calculator method given on the previous page. How
random are these numbers? Investigate.

Investigate ways of generating random numbers, other than the ways given above.

## SAMPLES and POPULATIONS

In statistics, the word population has a broader meaning than just a large group of people. We
take population to mean a group of anything, perhaps the students in a school, perhaps the
students in a class, perhaps the jeans manufactured by a factory in one day, perhaps the deck
chairs on Brighton beach.
A sample is part of the population we are considering. For instance, if our population is the
jeans manufactured by a factory in one day, a sample could be every 20th pair of jeans made. If
our population was the students in a school, a sample could be the students in a particular class
or the students taught by a particular teacher or 10% of the students in a school or the students
whose names begin with M.

## DISCUSSION EXERCISE 24:2

• Suppose we want to find the average height of the 15-year-old girls in England. Instead of
finding the height of all 15-year-old girls we could choose a representative sample, find the
average height of the girls in this sample and use this as an estimate of the average height of
all 15-year-old girls. One reason for using a sample rather than the population would be that
less time would be needed. What other reasons might there be? Discuss.

In choosing a representative sample two questions we could consider are "Are city girls taller
than country girls?" "Are Asian girls shorter than West Indian girls?" What other questions
should we consider? How might we get a representative sample? Discuss.

- Some populations and possible samples from these populations are given below. Will any of these samples represent the population well? If not, why not? How could we choose more representative samples for each of the given populations? Discuss.

| Population | Sample |
|---|---|
| Married men | Married men aged under 40 |
| Welsh football players | Football players from Cardiff |
| Cream packaged in a dairy | Cream packaged between 7a.m. and 8a.m. |
| Questions on a maths. exam. paper | Questions on algebra |

If each sample is to represent fairly the population from which it was taken, how large should each sample be? Discuss.

- To find whether a person has glandular fever we do not test all of their blood (the population), rather we test a small amount of blood (a sample)! Think of other situations, in which, even if time, money etc. was available to test the whole population it would not be sensible to do this. Discuss.

## CHOOSING REPRESENTATIVE SAMPLES

When we want to make statements about a population we often survey a sample of that population. For the results of the survey to apply to the population, the sample we choose to survey must be a representative sample.
We must consider both the nature of the population and the size of the population.
For instance, if we wish to find the average length of the leaves on a plant which has about twice as many large as small leaves our sample should contain about twice as many large as small leaves. A sample which is too small, say less than 5% of the population, is not likely to give valid results about the whole population of leaves.
A sample which is not a representative sample is sometimes called a biased sample.

## DISCUSSION EXERCISE 24:3

- Hamish's group are about to carry out a survey to estimate the average time, each week, that people in their village spend watching sport on TV. They decided to survey a sample of 8% of the village population. They discussed ways of choosing a representative sample. All of the ways below were discussed and rejected. What reasons might Hamish's group have given for rejecting these? Discuss.
    Interviewing people outside the supermarket.
    Interviewing school pupils and staff.
    Interviewing by phone during the day.
    Interviewing people at the railway station.
  Discuss ways in which Hamish's group could get a representative sample.

- Emily's group are about to do a survey on the publication date of the books in the school library. They considered and rejected each of the ways given below for taking a sample of books. Discuss reasons for rejecting these.
    Choosing the books closest to the library door.
    Choosing the novels whose authors names begin with R.
    Choosing the books on the bottom shelves.
  Discuss ways in which Emily's group could get a representative sample.

- Mustafa's group decided to ask a sample of students how they felt about school uniform being compulsory. They considered and rejected the following ways of choosing a sample. Discuss reasons for rejecting these.

    Asking the first 20 students who enter the school grounds.

    Asking their class.

    Asking the members of the drama club.

  Discuss ways in which Mustafa's group could choose an unbiased sample.

## SIMPLE RANDOM SAMPLING

In simple random sampling every member of the population has the same chance of being chosen. We could draw names from a hat or numbered marbles from a container or use random numbers. The use of a random number table is shown in the following example.

*Example*   Riffet decided to ask 50 students their opinion about a proposal to change the dates of the school holidays. Riffet chose her sample using the school roll, which listed students in alphabetical order, and the random number table on Page 506. She took the following steps.

  *Step 1*   Riffet numbered each student on the roll from 1 to 872. (There were 872 students on the roll.)

  *Step 2*   Riffet grouped the numbers from the random number table in groups of 3 as shown below. (Riffet read the numbers in rows, beginning at the start of the first row.)     517/727/464/042/331/290/444/662/162/898/935/820/418/...

  *Step 3*   Riffet then matched the numbers to students. That is, the first 10 students chosen were those that were numbered 517, 727, 464, 42, 331, 290, 444, 662, 162, 820 on the roll.

  *Note*   Numbers greater than 872 were ignored. Numbers that were repeats of earlier numbers would also be ignored.

### DISCUSSION EXERCISE 24:4

Richard claimed that Riffet should not have begun listing the random numbers with the first number in the first row. He claimed she should have chosen her starting point at random. Discuss.

Amy suggested that instead of using a random number table, Riffet could have adapted the program on Page 507 to print out 50 random numbers between 1 and 872. How could this program be adapted in this way? Discuss.

Debbie suggested that a counter could be drawn from each of 3 bags to find 50 random numbers between 1 and 872. Debbie gave a good argument. What might Debbie's argument have been? Discuss. How else might Riffet have made a simple random sample? Discuss.

### PRACTICAL EXERCISE 24:5

1.   Use random numbers to choose a simple random sample from the students in your school or your year group or your class.

2.   Use a method other than random numbers to select a simple random sample of the books in the school library or seats in the school hall.

3. Use random numbers to select a simple random sample of names from a telephone directory or words from a dictionary. You should select the pages first, then the name (or word) from the chosen pages.

## OTHER SAMPLING TECHNIQUES

In stratified sampling the population is divided into groups which have something in common, then simple random samples are taken from each group. The numbers in each of these samples is proportional to the size of the group.

*Example*  As part of a survey on attitudes to homework, a stratified sample of size 30 is to be taken from 194 Year 9, 152 Year 10 and 175 Year 11 students.
There is a total of 521 students in these year groups. Three separate simple random samples should be taken.

Since $\frac{194}{521} \times 30 \approx 11$, the size of the Year 9 sample should be 11.

Since $\frac{152}{521} \times 30 \approx 9$, the size of the Year 10 sample should be 9.

Since $\frac{175}{521} \times 30 \approx 10$, the size of the Year 11 sample should be 10.

In systematic sampling every 10th or every 20th or every 25th etc. item is chosen.

*Example*  A manufacturer makes 420 tins of baked beans every day. As part of quality control a sample of 5% of tins is weighed. The tins to be weighed are chosen as follows.
5% is 5 in 100 or 1 in 20. For weighing, the manufacturer selects the 3rd tin, the 23rd tin, the 43rd tin and so on.

In cluster sampling a group is chosen at random from the population, then a simple random sample is taken from this group.

*Example*  Ten students from every secondary school are to be given a thorough dental examination. Fairfield High School chose its 10 students by firstly selecting a tutor group at random then selecting, at random, 10 students from this tutor group.

---

## DISCUSSION and PRACTICAL EXERCISE 24:6

● To estimate the average height of the students in a school we could take a sample of students and find the average height of this sample.
What size sample do you think we need to take so that the average height of the sample can be used as a reliable estimate of the average height of all the students in your school? Would the sample size depend on whether we use simple random sampling or stratified sampling or systematic sampling or cluster sampling? Discuss.
Use each of these sampling techniques to select a sample to estimate the average height of students in your school. Compare the results.

- "Interviewing a sample of students chosen by cluster sampling takes less time than using a sample chosen by stratified sampling." Discuss this statement.
  Discuss the advantages and disadvantages of using cluster or systematic or stratified or simple random sampling in selecting a sample of students to be asked their opinion on the sporting activities organised by a school.
- "Systematic sampling is the best sampling technique to use in quality control in a manufacturing industry". Discuss this statement.
  Can you think of situations where one sampling technique is more appropriate than the others? Discuss.

## EXERCISE 24:7

1. Which of the following samples are likely to be representative samples? For those that are not representative, give a reason (or reasons) why they are not.
   (a) Survey task: to survey opinion about building a new library.
       Sample: chosen by interviewing people in the street.
   (b) Survey task: the publisher of a monthly magazine wishes to survey opinion about publishing the magazine weekly.
       Sample: chosen by selecting 5 readers of the magazine from each city.
   (c) Survey task: to survey opinion about proposed changes to the Network SouthEast timetable.
       Sample: chosen by giving a questionnaire to every 100th person who buys a rail ticket for this network.
   (d) Survey task: to test the effectiveness of a new drug for migraines.
       Sample: chosen by giving the drug to all the patients, of one doctor, who suffer from migraines.
   (e) Survey task: to check that a packaging machine for crisps is giving the correct weight in each packet.
       Sample: chosen by weighing the first 50 packets of crisps each day.
   (f) Survey task: to survey opinion about a supermarket baking fresh bread.
       Sample: chosen by interviewing every 20th shopper at the supermarket checkout on a Saturday.
   (g) Survey task: to survey opinion about the bus service to a city centre.
       Sample: chosen by selecting, at random, 5% of the population from the city's telephone directory.
   (h) Survey task: to check the standard of the maths. coursework being done by the students at a secondary school.
       Sample: chosen by selecting, at random, 25% of the students taught by a particular maths. teacher.
   (i) Survey task: to survey a TV channel's viewers about the programmes shown in the past week.
       Sample: chosen by asking viewers to write in for a questionnaire.
   (j) Survey task: to check the quality of the apples an orchard is selling direct to the public.
       Sample: chosen by having 50 people, chosen at random, buy a box of apples from the orchard at intervals throughout one week.

2. Briefly describe how you might select an unbiased sample of
   (a) the students in your class
   (b) the students in your school
   (c) the houses in your street
   (d) the trees in an orchard
   (e) the potatoes sold by one grower

   (f) the cars made by a manufacturer in one month
   (g) the shoppers at a bookshop during a one-day sale
   (h) the readers of a magazine
   (i) a shipment of bananas
   (j) the people in your town or city or district.

3. Which of the following is likely to give 100 random digits?
   (a) Choosing the last digit of the first 100 telephone numbers in a directory.
   (b) Choosing the first digit of 100 consecutive telephone numbers listed in a directory.
   (c) Taking the last number of the day of the month on which the first 100 students, on the school roll, were born.
   (d) Choosing the last number on the number plates of the next 100 cars to pass the school.
   (e) Asking 100 people to select a digit between 0 and 9.
   (f) Choosing 100 consecutive digits from a random number table.
   (g) Asking a student to call out 100 single-digit numbers.

4. This list shows the number of pupils in each year group at Barncroft Primary School.
Hanna takes a stratified sample of 100 pupils from this school.
How many pupils from each year group should be in Hanna's sample?

| Year 1 | 124 |
|---|---|
| Year 2 | 160 |
| Year 3 | 105 |
| Year 4 | 182 |
| Year 5 | 215 |
| Year 6 | 230 |

5. A mail order catalogue firm decides to survey its customers about the quality of service they receive. For their sample, they chose every customer whose name began with R.
   (a) This sampling method is:   **A.** simple random sampling
                                     **B.** stratified sampling
                                     **C.** systematic sampling
                                     **D.** cluster sampling
   (b) Is this sample likely to be representative?

6. In Year 11 at Starmead School there are 5 maths. classes. The exam. marks of the students in these classes are given in the table.

| Teacher | Marks | | | | | | | | | | | | | | |
|---|---|---|---|---|---|---|---|---|---|---|---|---|---|---|---|
| Mrs Kemp | 72 65 72 68 80 77 76 66 72 74 81 67 62 79 82 69 83 68 69 72 74 77 70 81 66 80 74 76 79 64 | | | | | | | | | | | | | | |
| Mr Habib | 55 58 59 62 63 48 47 50 55 42 61 63 64 68 59 57 59 60 66 44 | | | | | | | | | | | | | | |
| Miss Kennelly | 64 66 59 70 69 71 64 66 61 70 64 62 58 68 72 69 72 68 64 62 70 65 67 | | | | | | | | | | | | | | |
| Mr Ogilvie | 83 84 91 78 76 82 80 80 93 96 97 77 80 84 94 88 77 90 79 75 85 95 86 86 89 76 79 90 92 | | | | | | | | | | | | | | |
| Mrs McGill | 35 44 51 40 44 39 29 58 53 45 47 61 32 45 50 56 32 43 | | | | | | | | | | | | | | |

   (a) Take a stratified sample of size 12 from these classes. Calculate the mean mark of the students in your sample.

(b) Take a systematic sample of size 12 from these classes. Calculate the mean mark of the students in your sample.

(c) Explain how you could take a simple random sample of size 12 from these classes. Take a sample of this sort. Calculate the mean mark of the students in your sample.

(d) Explain how you could take a cluster sample of size 12 from these classes. Take a cluster sample of size 12. Calculate the mean mark of the 12 students in your sample.

(e) Calculate the mean mark of all the students in these classes.

(f) Write a sentence or two comparing the results of the samples with the actual mean mark.

7. A district council is conducting a survey about its child-care facilities. The council chose 5 suburbs at random, then chose 5 streets at random from each of these suburbs, then chose 5 houses at random from each of these streets. Once these 125 houses had been chosen, the council mailed a questionnaire to be completed by the "head of the household".
Are the results of this survey likely to be valid? If not, why not?

8. The manufacturer of Goliath golf balls claims that 95% of the golfers who try these will continue to use them. A survey was taken to investigate this claim. This survey found that of the 500 golfers known to have tried Goliath golf balls, 45 did not continue to use them.
The 5 groups involved are listed below.
   A. All golfers.
   B. All golfers who had tried Goliath golf balls.
   C. 95% of the golfers that the manufacturer claims will continue to use Goliath golf balls.
   D. The 500 golfers known to have tried Goliath golf balls.
   E. The 45 golfers who did not continue to use Goliath golf balls.
(a) Which group is the population for the survey?
(b) Which group is the sample for the survey?

Review 1 Which of the following methods of selecting adults is likely to give a representative sample?
   (a) choosing adults, at random, in the street
   (b) choosing every 20th adult at a concert
   (c) choosing names, at random, from a telephone directory
   (d) choosing names, at random, from an electoral register
   (e) choosing a street, at random, then choosing all the adults who live on that street.

Review 2 You are about to select a sample of students from your school and ask these students their opinions about proposed changes to the timetable. You want to choose a sample so that the results represent fairly the opinions of all the students in your school. Explain how you will select the sample. What size will your sample be?

Review 3 This list gives the number of students in the schools in one town.
Explain how a stratified sample of size 50 can be taken.
How many students should be taken from each school?

| School | Roll |
| --- | --- |
| A | 594 |
| B | 782 |
| C | 1034 |
| D | 985 |
| E | 649 |

**SURVEYS**

| PRACTICAL EXERCISE 24:8 |
| --- |

1. Conduct a survey on some issue that is of interest to you and other students in your school. Some suggestions follow.
   As part of your survey, write and trial a questionnaire, choose a representative sample of students to complete the final questionnaire, conduct your survey and analyse the results. As part of your analysis include appropriate graphs and tables. Also make some conclusions about the population from which you took the sample.
   *Suggestions*    Sports and/or hobbies
   School uniform
   Holiday preferences
   Attitudes to homework
   TV or video viewing habits
   Music preferences
   Subjects offered at school
   An environmental issue
   A local issue

2. Conduct a survey where a sample is taken from a population other than people. Your survey could be about one of the following.
   Books
   Bicycles
   The school shop
   Exam. or test marks
   Plants

3. Design and carry out a statistical investigation. Some suggestions follow. Choose a representative sample for your investigation. Analyse your results.
   *Suggestions*    Investigate whether estimation of distances is improved with practice.
   Investigate whether there is a relationship between being left-handed and accuracy at mental arithmetic.
   Investigate whether reaction time can be reduced with practice.
   Investigate whether there is a relationship between memory for numbers and memory for names.

### CHAPTER 24   REVIEW

1. Ioshi works for a company that employs about 100 people at each of 10 factories. She is designing a questionnaire to survey the employees on the number of working days lost through stress related illness.

   **(a)** One of the questions that she thought of is as follows.

   **How many days did you take off last year?**

   **Less than 10** [    ]          **10 to 20** [    ]          **Over 20** [    ]

   Suggest **two** improvements to this question.

   **(b)** Describe a method that could be used to select a representative sample for the survey.   **SEG**

2. Kay is doing a survey to find out what people think about the amount of sport on television. She designs two questions.

A

Most people think there is far too much sport on television.
Do you agree?

☐      ☐
Yes     No

B

What do you think about the amount of sport on television?

☐     ☐     ☐
Too little   About right   Too much

(a) Which is the better one for her to use? Give a reason for your answer.

(b) Write down, with a reason, **one** other question that she could ask in her survey.

(c) She asks people shopping on a Saturday afternoon. Why is this likely to result in a biased survey? **WJEC**

3. The CANTOR company has been employed by a newspaper to conduct an opinion poll just before a General Election. They decide to pick a sample of 1200 people.

Two methods are suggested for choosing the sample

(i) CANTOR has a Computer tape, listing the Electoral Register for the whole country. From this, the computer will select 1200 names at random, who will then be interviewed by CANTOR's staff.

(ii) Interviewers will be sent to a factory in Leeds, a Building Society Office in Edinburgh, a housing estate in London and a village in Devon, and 300 people will be interviewed in each.

(a) Explain briefly **one** advantage and **one** disadvantage of each method.

(b) Suggest a method for selecting the sample which is better than either (i) or (ii). **MEG**

4. For a survey, Lorraine investigates the spending habits of students at her school. The number of students in each year group is shown.

| Year group | 9 | 10 | 11 | 12 | 13 |
|---|---|---|---|---|---|
| Number of students | 200 | 200 | 200 | 120 | 80 |

Total 800

Explain, with calculations, how Lorraine obtains a stratified random sample of 100 students for her survey. **SEG**

5. Paul wants to find out how popular different flavours of ice cream are likely to be at the school fete.

(a) He intends to ask people this question:
"What ice cream flavour do you like best?"
Give two reasons why this question is unsatisfactory.

(b) This is Paul's sampling method.
"I will ask everyone in my class about their ice cream preferences. That will give me 27 people to ask. Our teacher will make sure they all answer – so there'll be no problem about people saying they don't want to answer my questions."

Describe two ways in which Paul could improve his sampling method.
Explain why each way is an improvement. **NEAB**

**6.** Sam was making a survey of pupils in his school.

He wanted to find out their opinions on noise pollution by motor bikes.

The size of each year group in the school is shown.

Sam took a sample of 80 pupils.

**(a)** Explain whether or not he should have sampled equal numbers of boys and girls in year 8.

**(b)** Calculate the number of pupils he should have sampled in year 8.

| Year Group | Boys | Girls | Total |
|---|---|---|---|
| 8 | 85 | 65 | 150 |
| 9 | 72 | 75 | 147 |
| 10 | 74 | 78 | 152 |
| 11 | 77 | 72 | 149 |
| 6th Form | 93 | 107 | 200 |
| | | | 798 |

**ULEAC**

## DISPERSION. STANDARD DEVIATION

To summarize a set of data we often give a measure of the average and a measure of the spread.
Three measures for average are the mean, the median and the mode.
There are also three commonly used measures of spread. Two of these are the range and the
interquartile range. The third is the standard deviation. The standard deviation of the set of
data 2, 3, 4, 5, 7, 9 may be found as follows.

*Step 1*  Find the mean. Mean $= \dfrac{2+3+4+5+7+9}{6}$
$= 5$

*Step 2*  Find the difference between each data value and the mean. These are $2 - 5 = -3$,
$3 - 5 = -2$, $4 - 5 = -1$, $5 - 5 = 0$, $7 - 5 = 2$, $9 - 5 = 4$. These differences are called
the deviations from the mean.

*Step 3*  Square the deviations from the mean and add.
This gives $(-3)^2 + (-2)^2 + (-1)^2 + 0^2 + 2^2 + 4^2 = 34$. The sum of the squares of the
deviations from the mean is then 34.

*Step 4*  Divide 34 by the number of data values. This is $34 \div 6 = 5 \cdot 67$ to 2 d.p. The average
of the squares of the deviations from the mean is then $5 \cdot 67$ to 2 d.p.

*Step 5*  Find the square root of $5 \cdot 67$. This is $\sqrt{5 \cdot 67} = 2 \cdot 4$ to 1 d.p. The square root of the
average of the squares of the deviations from the mean is then $2 \cdot 4$. This is the
standard deviation.

A formula for standard deviation is s.d. $= \sqrt{\dfrac{\Sigma(x - \bar{x})^2}{n}}$ where $\bar{x}$ is the mean.

## DISCUSSION EXERCISE 25:1

• **Discuss** how the formula s.d. $= \sqrt{\dfrac{\Sigma(x - \bar{x})^2}{n}}$ can be written from the steps shown above.

• Akbar suggested that the working for the standard deviation could be set out in a table. To
find the standard deviation of 2, 3, 4, 5, 7, 9 he suggested the following table. **Discuss** this
setting out.

| x | $x - \bar{x}$ | $(x - \bar{x})^2$ |
|---|---|---|
| 2 | $-3$ | 9 |
| 3 | $-2$ | 4 |
| 4 | $-1$ | 1 |
| 5 | 0 | 0 |
| 7 | 2 | 4 |
| 9 | 4 | 16 |
| $\Sigma x = 30$ | | $\Sigma(x - \bar{x})^2 = 34$ |
| $\bar{x} = 5$ | | |

- Sally thought that as taking the square root "undoes" squaring, the standard deviation could be found by just taking the average of the deviations from the mean. That is, Sally proposed that the standard deviation could be found by doing Step 1 and Step 2 shown on the previous page, then finding the average of the numbers found in Step 2. Tim explained why this wouldn't work. What might Tim's explanation have been? **Discuss.**

Instead of talking about the spread of a set of data we sometimes talk about the dispersion or the variability. In statistics, the words spread, dispersion and variability mean the same.

The mean is the most frequently used measure of the average of a set of data; the standard deviation is the most frequently used measure of dispersion.

## EXERCISE 25:2

Find the mean and standard deviation of each of these sets of data.
1. 1, 1, 2, 3, 3, 4, 4, 4, 5
2. 1, 1, 1, 2, 2, 3, 3, 3, 11
3. 5, 3, 14, 4, 5, 4, 2, 6, 2
4. 7, 4, 3, 1, 3, 7, 5, 3, 6, 1
5. 101, 101, 102, 103, 104, 101
6. 502, 504, 505, 505, 507, 508, 504
7. 1, 3, 4, 4, 5, 6, 6, 7
8. 12, 19, 8, 9, 7, 11, 8, 10

Review  345, 512, 308, 204, 240, 614

## DISCUSSION EXERCISE 25:3

- Is the standard deviation a better measure for dispersion than the range? **Discuss.** As part of your discussion consider the following sets of data and their "graphs". (Notice that the mean of each set of data is 8.)

A: 7, 8, 8, 9 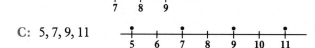   B: 8, 8, 8, 8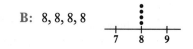

C: 5, 7, 9, 11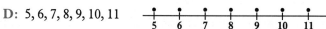

D: 5, 6, 7, 8, 9, 10, 11

E: 4, 5, 11, 12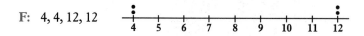

F: 4, 4, 12, 12

- What does a large standard deviation tell you about a set of data? What does a small standard deviation tell you? **Discuss.** You could include the sets of data given above in your discussion.

If the mean is not a whole number, the formula s.d. $= \sqrt{\frac{\Sigma(x - \bar{x})^2}{n}}$ can be quite cumbersome to use.

In this case it is preferable to use the alternative formula s.d. $= \sqrt{\frac{\Sigma x^2}{n} - \left(\frac{\Sigma x}{n}\right)^2}$ Since the mean

$\bar{x} = \frac{\Sigma x}{n}$, this formula may also be written as s.d. $= \sqrt{\frac{\Sigma x^2}{n} - (\bar{x})^2}$

*Worked Example* Find the standard deviation of 3, 5, 6, 6, 7, 8.

**Answer** $\Sigma x = 3 + 5 + 6 + 6 + 7 + 8$    $\Sigma x^2 = 3^2 + 5^2 + 6^2 + 6^2 + 7^2 + 8^2$
$= 35$    $= 219$

$$\text{Using s.d.} = \sqrt{\frac{\Sigma x^2}{n} - \left(\frac{\Sigma x}{n}\right)^2}$$

$$= \sqrt{\frac{219}{6} - \left(\frac{35}{6}\right)^2}$$

$$= 1{\cdot}6 \text{ to 1 d.p.}$$

## EXERCISE 25:4

Use the formula s.d. $= \sqrt{\frac{\Sigma x^2}{n} - \left(\frac{\Sigma x}{n}\right)^2}$ to find the standard deviation of the sets of data given in Exercise 25:2.

The standard deviation may be found using the statistical functions on the calculator. The keying sequence is similar to that used to find the mean.

*Example* To find the standard deviation of 2, 3, 4, 5, 7, 9 key as follows.

MODE · 2 x 3 x 4 x 5 x 7 x 9 x SHIFT $\sigma_n$ to get answer of 2·4 to 1 d.p.

**Notes**
- Pressing MODE followed by · gets the calculator ready to calculate statistical functions. (SD will appear on the screen.)

- Pressing x stores each value input in the memory.

- Pressing SHIFT $\sigma_n$ tells the calculator to calculate the standard deviation of the values it has stored in the memory.

- If another standard deviation calculation is to be done the memory must be cleared. This is done by pressing SHIFT followed by SAC .

- Pressing SHIFT n at any stage, gives the number of values stored in the memory. This can be used at the end to check that all values have been keyed in.

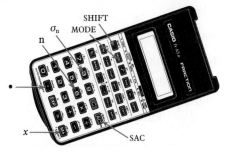

If the data is given as a frequency distribution, the x value is keyed, then the $\boxed{\times}$, then the frequency of the x value, then the $\boxed{x}$.

*Example*

| x | 2 | 3 | 8 | 11 | 20 | 25 |
|---|---|---|---|----|----|----|
| f | 5 | 2 | 4 | 3  | 2  | 6  |

To find the standard deviation of this data, key as follows.

$\boxed{\text{MODE}}$ $\boxed{\cdot}$ $\boxed{2}$ $\boxed{\times}$ $\boxed{5}$ $\boxed{x}$ $\boxed{3}$ $\boxed{\times}$ $\boxed{2}$ $\boxed{x}$ $\boxed{8}$ $\boxed{\times}$ $\boxed{4}$ $\boxed{x}$ $\boxed{11}$ $\boxed{\times}$ $\boxed{3}$ $\boxed{x}$ $\boxed{20}$ $\boxed{\times}$ $\boxed{2}$ $\boxed{x}$ $\boxed{25}$ $\boxed{\times}$ $\boxed{6}$ $\boxed{x}$ $\boxed{\text{SHIFT}}$ $\boxed{\sigma_n}$ to get answer of 9·2 to 1 d.p.

If the data is grouped, or is continuous, an approximate value for the standard deviation is found by assuming every value in a particular class interval has the value of the mid-point of the class interval.

*Worked Example*

| x | 1–30 | 31–40 | 41–50 | 51–60 | 61–70 | 71–80 | 81–90 | 91–100 |
|---|------|-------|-------|-------|-------|-------|-------|--------|
| f | 2    | 3     | 1     | 3     | 5     | 6     | 4     | 2      |

This table shows the maths. exam. results of the students in Ms Langham's class. Find the mean and standard deviation of these marks.

*Answer*  The mid-point of each class interval is shown on the following table.

| x | 1–30 | 31–40 | 41–50 | 51–60 | 61–70 | 71–80 | 81–90 | 91–100 |
|---|------|-------|-------|-------|-------|-------|-------|--------|
| mid-point of class interval | 15·5 | 35·5 | 45·5 | 55·5 | 65·5 | 75·5 | 85·5 | 95·5 |
| f | 2 | 3 | 1 | 3 | 5 | 6 | 4 | 2 |

Keying $\boxed{\text{MODE}}$ $\boxed{\cdot}$ $\boxed{15\cdot5}$ $\boxed{\times}$ $\boxed{2}$ $\boxed{x}$ $\boxed{35\cdot5}$ $\boxed{\times}$ $\boxed{3}$ $\boxed{x}$ $\boxed{45\cdot5}$ $\boxed{x}$ $\boxed{55\cdot5}$ $\boxed{\times}$ $\boxed{3}$ $\boxed{x}$ $\boxed{65\cdot5}$ $\boxed{\times}$ $\boxed{5}$ $\boxed{x}$ $\boxed{75\cdot5}$ $\boxed{\times}$ $\boxed{6}$ $\boxed{x}$ $\boxed{85\cdot5}$ $\boxed{\times}$ $\boxed{4}$ $\boxed{x}$ $\boxed{95\cdot5}$ $\boxed{\times}$ $\boxed{2}$ $\boxed{x}$

$\boxed{\text{SHIFT}}$ $\boxed{\overline{x}}$ gives 64·0 to 1 d.p. as an approximate value for the mean. Now Keying

$\boxed{\text{SHIFT}}$ $\boxed{\sigma_n}$ gives 21·8 to 1 d.p. as an approximate value for the standard deviation.

## INVESTIGATION 25:5

**Standard Deviation Formulae**

Two formulae for the standard deviation of ungrouped discrete data are s.d. $= \sqrt{\dfrac{\Sigma(x - \overline{x})^2}{n}}$ and s.d. $= \sqrt{\dfrac{\Sigma x^2}{n} - \left(\dfrac{\Sigma x}{n}\right)^2}$ . How could these formulae be adapted to find the standard deviation of grouped or continuous data? **Investigate.**

As part of your investigation use your proposed formulae to find the standard deviation of some grouped discrete data and/or continuous data. Check your results using the statistical functions on your calculator.

## EXERCISE 25:6

1. Find the mean and standard deviation of these frequency distributions.

(a)

| x | 2 | 3 | 6 | 8 | 9 | 11 | 15 |
|---|---|---|---|---|---|----|----|
| f | 3 | 4 | 6 | 4 | 3 | 2 | 4 |

(b)

| x | 12 | 15 | 20 | 24 | 32 | 38 |
|---|----|----|----|----|----|----|
| f | 6 | 8 | 14 | 10 | 9 | 4 |

2. The 5 judges in a gymnastics competition gave Karl scores of 8·9, 9·1, 8·7, 8·7, 9·2 for his routine on the parallel bars. Find the mean score and the standard deviation.

3. For 4 weeks, Jeremy kept a record of the time he spent on homework each evening. These times (in minutes) are given in the list. 24, 35, 23, 58, 23, 0, 0, 34, 27, 42, 19, 0, 25, 0, 53, 30, 28, 19, 0, 36, 10, 25, 64, 45, 27, 30, 0, 0
Find the mean time and the standard deviation.

4. The students in Katherine's class conducted an experiment to calculate the value of g, the acceleration due to gravity. Their results (in m/s$^2$) are given below.

$$9·804 \quad 9·807 \quad 9·810 \quad 9·808 \quad 9·807 \quad 9·809 \quad 9·812$$
$$9·813 \quad 9·805 \quad 9·806 \quad 9·810 \quad 9·811 \quad 9·806 \quad 9·814$$

Calculate the mean and standard deviation of these results.

5. Jamal tossed two dice together, 200 times. The distribution of the sum of the numbers obtained on each toss is shown in the table.

| Sum | 2 | 3 | 4 | 5 | 6 | 7 | 8 | 9 | 10 | 11 | 12 |
|-----|---|---|---|---|---|---|---|---|----|----|----|
| Number of times | 5 | 14 | 17 | 24 | 29 | 37 | 26 | 18 | 14 | 9 | 7 |

Calculate the mean sum. Calculate the standard deviation of this sum.

6. The Nixon family grow trees to sell for firewood. At the beginning of this year they measured the girth of their trees.

| Girth (to nearest cm) | 40 – | 50 – | 60 – | 70 – | 80 – | 90 – | 100 – | 110 –130 |
|-----------------------|------|------|------|------|------|------|-------|----------|
| Mid-point of class interval | 45 | | | | | | | |
| Frequency | 3 | 5 | 19 | 11 | 24 | 23 | 14 | 2 |

(a) Copy the table. Complete the row for the mid-points of the class intervals.
(b) Calculate the mean girth of the Nixon's trees and the standard deviation. Explain why these are approximate values.

7. The following frequency table shows the distribution of the fares collected by one taxi driver during one day.

| Fare (£) | 1·00 –1·99 | 2·00 –2·99 | 3·00 –3·99 | 4·00 – 4·99 | 5·00 – 9·99 | 10·00 –19·99 | 20·00 – 49·99 |
|----------|-----------|-----------|-----------|-------------|-------------|--------------|---------------|
| Frequency | 2 | 9 | 12 | 18 | 25 | 8 | 3 |

(a) Show that the mid-point of the first class interval is £1·495 and the mid-point of the last class interval is £34·995.
(b) Calculate the mean fare and the standard deviation. Round your answers sensibly.

8.  Julian collected data on the distance students, in his year group, travelled to school. He collated the results onto the table.

| Distance (km) | $0 \leq d < 1$ | $1 \leq d < 2$ | $2 \leq d < 3$ | $3 \leq d < 4$ | $4 \leq d < 5$ | $5 \leq d < 10$ |
|---|---|---|---|---|---|---|
| Number of students | 24 | 62 | 45 | 34 | 19 | 12 |
| Mid-point of class interval | | | | | | |

(a) Copy and complete the table.
(b) Find the mean distance travelled to school and the standard deviation.

9.  During one week of the school holidays, 30 students were given intensive training in throwing the javelin. At the beginning and end of the training, a record was made of each student's greatest throw. The improvements are shown in this table.

| Improvement (metres) | 0 – | 2 – | 4 – | 6 – | 8 – | 10 – | 12 – | 15–20 |
|---|---|---|---|---|---|---|---|---|
| Number of students | 1 | 3 | 4 | 6 | 5 | 2 | 5 | 4 |

Calculate approximate values for the mean improvement and the standard deviation.

Review 1  Kim asked each of her friends to calculate the area of the kitchen in their homes. The results (in m²) are given in the list.

10·6   9·8   12·4   14·1   11·5   10·6   12·3   10·8   9·6   9·2   12·1   14·4

Find the mean area of these kitchens and the standard deviation.

Review 2  The secretarial "temps", who worked for an agency, were given a typing test. The number of mistakes made is given in the table.

| Number of mistakes | 0 | 1 | 2 | 3 | 4 | 5 | 6 | 7 | 8 | 9 | 10 | 11 | 12 |
|---|---|---|---|---|---|---|---|---|---|---|---|---|---|
| Frequency | 4 | 7 | 11 | 14 | 15 | 16 | 18 | 20 | 13 | 9 | 9 | 5 | 3 |

(a) How many secretarial "temps" worked for this agency?
(b) Find the mean number of mistakes made and the standard deviation.

Review 3  The label on the outside of a muesli bar states *weight: 50g.* Andrew weighed 20 of these. His results are shown.

| Weight (g) | $46 \leq w < 47$ | $47 \leq w < 48$ | $48 \leq w < 49$ | $49 \leq w < 50$ | $50 \leq w < 51$ | $51 \leq w < 52$ | $52 \leq w < 53$ |
|---|---|---|---|---|---|---|---|
| Frequency | 2 | 2 | 3 | 7 | 2 | 3 | 1 |

Calculate an approximate value for the mean weight of the muesli bars that Andrew weighed. Calculate an approximate value for the standard deviation of these weights.

## PRACTICAL EXERCISE 25:7

1.  Toss a die 100 times. Use a tally chart to record the results.
Calculate the mean and standard deviation.

2. Toss 4 coins together a great number of times. Record the number of tails obtained on each toss. Calculate the mean number of tails and the standard deviation.

3. Use a random number table or a computer or calculator random number generator to select 200 random two-digit numbers. Find the mean and standard deviation of these numbers.

4. Gather data about a sports team. You could consider ages, heights etc. Calculate approximate values for the mean and standard deviation of each set of data.

5. Choose a sample of 20 students. Ask each student to try to open a book at the middle page. Record the difference between the page number of the middle page and the page number at which each student opened the book. Calculate the mean and standard deviation of these differences.

6. Design and carry out a statistical investigation. Calculate the mean and standard deviation of the data collected.

## COMPARING SETS OF DATA

The mean and standard deviation may be used to **compare two sets of data.** The greater the mean, the greater the average data value. The greater the standard deviation, the greater the dispersion of the data, that is, the greater the spread of the data.

*Worked Example*  Margaret and Robin each bought 15 packets of smarties. They counted the number of black smarties in each packet. Margaret's data was: 6, 9, 8, 10, 7, 8, 9, 11, 7, 9, 10, 9, 7, 8, 12. Robin's data was: 8, 7, 7, 4, 8, 9, 10, 3, 8, 8, 7, 6, 5, 7, 10. Use the means and standard deviations to compare the number of black smarties in Margaret's packets with the number in Robin's packets.

*Answer*  For Margaret's data: mean = 8·7 (1 d.p.), s.d. = 1·6 (1 d.p.).
For Robin's data: mean = 7·1 (1 d.p.), s.d. = 1·9 (1 d.p.)
Hence, on average there were more black smarties in Margaret's packets but there was greater variability of the number of black smarties in Robin's packets.

*Worked Example*  Which of the distributions graphed on these frequency diagrams has the greater standard deviation?

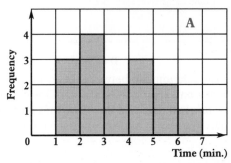 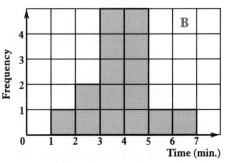

*Answer*  Distribution A has more low data values and more high data values than distribution B. That is, distribution A has the greater spread of data values. Hence distribution A has the greater standard deviation.

## DISCUSSION EXERCISE 25:8

- Consider the set of data A : 1, 4, 6, 7, 9, 13, 15, 15, 20. The mean is 10 and the standard deviation is 5·8 to 1 d.p.
  The set of data B is formed by adding 5 to each data value of A. That is, B: 6, 9, 11, 12, 14, 18, 20, 20, 25. How do you think the mean and standard deviation of B is related to the mean and standard deviation of A? **Discuss.**
  > What if B was formed by adding 3 to each data value of A?
  > What if B was formed by subtracting 2 from each data value of A?
  > What if . . .

- Consider the sets of data   A : 1, 4, 6, 7, 9, 13, 15, 15, 20
                              B : 5, 20, 30, 35, 45, 65, 75, 75, 100.
  How do you think the mean and standard deviation of B is related to the mean and standard deviation of A? **Discuss.**
  > What if B was formed by multiplying each data value of A by 2?
  > What if B was formed by dividing each data value of A by 10?
  > What if . . .

- The list of data 8, 27, 11, 25, 7, 20, 6, 24, 5, 39, 12, 26, 17, 23, 18, 32, 24, 14, 35, 19, 21, 18, 13, 28, 21, 19, 13, 21, 17, 25 is shown grouped on the table and graphed on the histogram.

| Data value | 5–9 | 10–14 | 15–19 | 20–24 | 25–29 | 30–39 |
|---|---|---|---|---|---|---|
| Frequency | 4 | 5 | 6 | 7 | 5 | 3 |

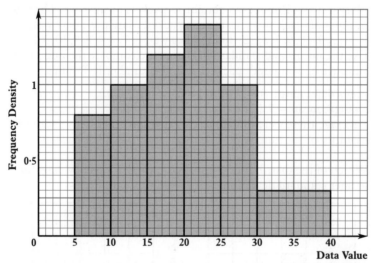

Suppose each data value is increased by 5. What is the relationship between the mean and standard deviation of this new set of data and the mean and standard deviation of the original data? Suppose you were given the histogram for the original data and the histogram for the new data. How could you use these histograms to compare the means and standard deviations? **Discuss.**
  > What if each data value is increased by 20?
  > What if each data value is decreased by 5?
  > What if each data value is doubled?
  > What if . . .

# EXERCISE 25:9

1. (a) The height (in metres) of the students in one class are given in the list.

    | 1·63 | 1·65 | 1·67 | 1·63 | 1·59 | 1·70 | 1·69 | 1·72 | 1·71 | 1·68 | 1·69 |
    |------|------|------|------|------|------|------|------|------|------|------|
    | 1·58 | 1·72 | 1·59 | 1·71 | 1·62 | 1·64 | 1·59 | 1·60 | 1·72 | 1·64 | 1·68 |

    Calculate the standard deviation of these heights.

   (b) The standard deviation of the heights of the students in another class is 0·071m. What difference between the two classes is shown by the two standard deviations?

2. Which of the following sets of data shows the greatest dispersion? Justify your answer.

   A: 6, 7, 7, 8, 18, 21, 17, 14, 9, 11, 13, 15, 24, 5, 8
   B: 23, 20, 18, 17, 24, 29, 14, 22, 19, 27, 24, 20, 23, 19, 18
   C: 123, 120, 118, 117, 124, 129, 114, 122, 119, 127, 124, 120, 123, 119, 118

3. Mrs Bryant and Mrs Bell gave their classes the same algebra test. Mrs Bryant told her class the test was easy; Mrs Bell told her class the test was difficult. The results of this test are shown.

   **Mrs Bryant's class**

   | Mark      | 0 | 1 | 2 | 3 | 4 | 5 | 6 | 7 | 8 | 9 | 10 |
   |-----------|---|---|---|---|---|---|---|---|---|---|----|
   | Frequency | 1 | 0 | 4 | 3 | 1 | 2 | 4 | 6 | 4 | 2 | 3  |

   **Mrs Bell's class**

   | Mark      | 0 | 1 | 2 | 3 | 4 | 5 | 6 | 7 | 8 | 9 | 10 |
   |-----------|---|---|---|---|---|---|---|---|---|---|----|
   | Frequency | 2 | 1 | 2 | 1 | 3 | 4 | 8 | 2 | 3 | 1 | 0  |

   (a) Calculate the mean and standard deviation for each class.
   (b) Use the means and standard deviations to compare the marks of these classes.

4. Philippa collected data, on weekly pocket money, from the Year 5 classes in a neighbouring primary school. Her data is shown.

   | Pocket Money | Number of Boys | Number of Girls |
   |--------------|----------------|-----------------|
   | 0 – 49p      | 4              | 3               |
   | 50 – 99p     | 16             | 8               |
   | 100 – 149p   | 25             | 13              |
   | 150 – 199p   | 14             | 25              |
   | 200 – 249p   | 26             | 30              |
   | 250 – 299p   | 18             | 24              |
   | 300 – 399p   | 3              | 3               |
   | 400 – 999p   | 4              | 1               |

   (a) What is the mid-point of the class interval 0–49p?
   (b) What is the mid-point of the class interval 400–999p?
   (c) Calculate the mean and standard deviation of the boys' pocket money. Round your answers sensibly.
   (d) Calculate the mean and standard deviation of the girls' pocket money. Round your answers sensibly.
   (e) Explain what the difference in the means tells you.
   (f) Explain what the difference in the standard deviations tells you.

5. The following tables give the heights of 100 sunflower plants and 100 dahlia plants, 4 weeks after germination.

| Dahlia height (mm) | $0 \leq h < 50$ | $50 \leq h < 75$ | $75 \leq h < 100$ | $100 \leq h < 125$ | $125 \leq h < 150$ | $150 \leq h < 200$ |
|---|---|---|---|---|---|---|
| Number of plants | 11 | 27 | 35 | 18 | 5 | 4 |

| Sunflower height (mm) | $0 \leq h < 50$ | $50 \leq h < 100$ | $100 \leq h < 200$ | $200 \leq h < 300$ | $300 \leq h < 400$ | $400 \leq h < 500$ | $500 \leq h < 600$ |
|---|---|---|---|---|---|---|---|
| Number of plants | 5 | 1 | 12 | 34 | 23 | 16 | 9 |

(a) Find the mid-point of each class interval for the distribution of the heights of the dahlia plants. Use these mid-points to estimate the mean height and the standard deviation.

(b) Estimate the mean height and the standard deviation of the sunflower plants.

(c) Compare the distributions of the heights of the dahlia and sunflower plants. Use the means and standard deviations.

6.

### Age distribution of estimated resident population at 30 June 1989

Thousands

| | England and Wales | | Wales | | Scotland | | Northern Ireland[1] | | United Kingdom | | |
|---|---|---|---|---|---|---|---|---|---|---|---|
| | Males | Females | Males | Females | Males | Females | Males | Females | Males | Females | Persons |
| 0-4 | 1 713.8 | 1 632.4 | 97.2 | 92.5 | 166.7 | 158.6 | 69.5 | 65.7 | 1 950.7 | 1 857.0 | 3 807.7 |
| 5-9 | 1 629.4 | 1 548.4 | 93.8 | 89.0 | 164.7 | 157.1 | 68.2 | 65.2 | 1 862.0 | 1 770.7 | 3 632.7 |
| 10-14 | 1 517.1 | 1 434.1 | 88.6 | 83.3 | 158.1 | 149.7 | 64.8 | 62.4 | 1 739.3 | 1 645.2 | 3 384.5 |
| 15-19 | 1 830.1 | 1 739.0 | 105.1 | 100.6 | 190.1 | 183.5 | 70.0 | 63.5 | 2 091.2 | 1 987.8 | 4 079.0 |
| 20-24 | 2 077.5 | 2 010.1 | 113.0 | 110.6 | 217.8 | 208.4 | 71.8 | 63.8 | 2 367.9 | 2 282.8 | 4 650.7 |
| 25-29 | 2 058.9 | 2 023.2 | 113.1 | 114.2 | 210.8 | 201.8 | 64.8 | 60.6 | 2 333.5 | 2 285.1 | 4 618.7 |
| 30-34 | 1 761.4 | 1 737.0 | 93.4 | 91.2 | 184.2 | 182.1 | 54.3 | 55.3 | 1 998.2 | 1 972.9 | 3 971.1 |
| 35-39 | 1 682.8 | 1 681.4 | 92.2 | 92.6 | 167.8 | 168.1 | 47.5 | 48.7 | 1 898.1 | 1 897.4 | 3 795.6 |
| 40-44 | 1 821.8 | 1 812.7 | 98.8 | 99.6 | 172.6 | 172.8 | 47.0 | 47.9 | 2 041.4 | 2 033.4 | 4 074.5 |
| 45-49 | 1 466.6 | 1 454.9 | 83.0 | 82.8 | 144.0 | 149.1 | 43.1 | 44.6 | 1 652.6 | 1 647.2 | 3 299.9 |
| 50-54 | 1 367.3 | 1 367.4 | 77.1 | 77.6 | 136.9 | 145.7 | 37.7 | 39.4 | 1 541.5 | 1 552.2 | 3 093.7 |
| 55-59 | 1 293.7 | 1 323.7 | 74.1 | 77.3 | 131.2 | 144.3 | 34.0 | 37.2 | 1 458.8 | 1 505.4 | 2 964.2 |
| 60-64 | 1 245.2 | 1 333.3 | 74.2 | 81.5 | 123.1 | 141.1 | 31.3 | 36.5 | 1 399.7 | 1 510.8 | 2 910.4 |
| 65-69 | 1 215.0 | 1 422.9 | 73.3 | 86.2 | 113.2 | 142.0 | 28.0 | 35.1 | 1 356.6 | 1 600.6 | 2 957.1 |
| 70-74 | 784.9 | 1 050.7 | 48.3 | 65.4 | 73.2 | 106.3 | 20.6 | 29.2 | 878.4 | 1 185.9 | 2 064.2 |
| 75-79 | 648.3 | 1 022.9 | 37.1 | 60.2 | 59.1 | 99.6 | 15.5 | 25.4 | 723.1 | 1 147.8 | 1 870.9 |
| 80-84 | 365.7 | 734.1 | 20.5 | 43.0 | 31.9 | 70.1 | 8.5 | 17.3 | 405.9 | 820.9 | 1 226.8 |
| 85 and over | 189.3 | 565.2 | 10.6 | 31.9 | 15.0 | 50.3 | 3.8 | 11.3 | 208.1 | 626.6 | 834.7 |
| 0-14 | 4 860.4 | 4 614.8 | 279.6 | 264.7 | 489.5 | 465.3 | 202.5 | 193.3 | 5 552.0 | 5 272.9 | 10 824.9 |
| 15-64 | 16 605.4 | 16 482.8 | 924.1 | 928.1 | 1 678.4 | 1 696.8 | 501.5 | 497.4 | 18 782.6 | 18 675.0 | 37 457.6 |
| 65 and over | 3 203.3 | 4 795.8 | 189.8 | 286.7 | 292.4 | 468.2 | 76.4 | 118.3 | 3 572.0 | 5 381.8 | 8 953.8 |
| All ages | 24 669.1 | 25 893.4 | 1 393.5 | 1 479.6 | 2 460.4 | 2 630.3 | 780.4 | 809.0 | 27 906.5 | 29 329.7 | 57 236.2 |

Figures may not add due to rounding.
1 For Northern Ireland: population at June 1990.

***Source: Key Data 1992/93***

*From: Monthly Digest of Statistics, June 1992, Tables 2.1 and 2.2*

(a) The mid-point of the interval 60-64 years is 62·5 years. What is the mid-point of the interval 65-69 years?

(b) Some research is being done on Welsh people aged between 60 and 84. As part of this research, the mean age and standard deviation for women is compared with the mean age and standard deviation for men. Calculate these means and standard deviations. What might be written in the comparison.

7.  X is the set of data   3, 4, 7, 7, 9, 12, 15, 15.   Y is the set of data   6, 7, 10, 10, 12, 15, 18, 18.
    (a) Calculate the mean and standard deviation of X.
    (b) How is the data in Y related to the data in X?
    (c) What is the relationship between the mean of Y and the mean of X?
    (d) Explain why X and Y have the same standard deviation.
    (e) Z is the set of data 300, 400, 700, 700, 900, 1200, 1500, 1500. How are the mean and
        standard deviation of Z related to the mean and standard deviation of X?

8.

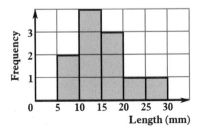

These distributions have   A.  The same mean and standard deviation.
                           B.  The same mean but different standard deviations.
                           C.  The same standard deviation but different means.
                           D.  Different means and different standard deviations.

9.

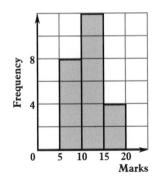

If the mean of the distribution shown at the left is  x  and the standard deviation is  y,  find in
terms of  x  and  y  the mean and standard deviation of the distribution shown at the right.

10. Which of the following distributions has the greater standard deviation?

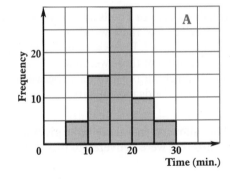

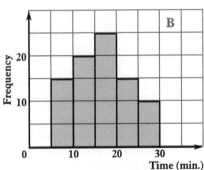

11. Sarah spent her summer holiday in France; Daniel spent his in Switzerland. Each gathered data on the rainfall. This is shown in the following tables.

**Sarah**

| mm of rain | 0 – | 5– | 10– | 15– | 20– | 25– | 30– | 35– 40 |
|---|---|---|---|---|---|---|---|---|
| Number of days | 1 | 4 | 5 | 3 | 6 | 0 | 2 | 3 |

**Daniel**

| mm of rain | 0 – | 5– | 10– | 15– | 20– | 25– | 30– | 35– 40 |
|---|---|---|---|---|---|---|---|---|
| Number of days | 2 | 3 | 2 | 6 | 5 | 4 | 3 | 1 |

(a) Draw frequency diagrams for Sarah's data and Daniel's data.
(b) Use the frequency diagrams to compare the mean rainfall each day that it rained and the standard deviations.

12.

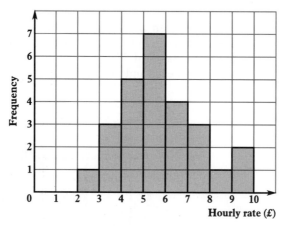

This frequency diagram shows the distribution of the amount earned per hour by the workers in an office.

(a) Calculate the mean hourly rate and the standard deviation.
(b) The workers all get an increase of 50p per hour. Explain how the frequency diagram for the new distribution can be drawn from the above frequency diagram.
(c) Instead of getting an increase of 50p per hour, the workers get an increase of 20%. Explain how the new mean and standard deviation can be found from the mean and standard deviation of the original distribution.

Review 1  (a) The weights (in grams) of 10 muesli bars made by Health Foods are 46, 46, 48, 49, 51, 50, 52, 47, 50, 51. Calculate the standard deviation of these weights.
   (b) The weights (in grams) of 10 muesli bars made by Snack Foods are 46, 48, 44, 53, 57, 49, 50, 56, 43, 52. Calculate the standard deviation of these weights.
   (c) Explain what the two standard deviations tell you about the difference between the 10 Health Foods muesli bars and the 10 Snack Foods muesli bars.

Review 2  (a) Karen works part-time in a florist shop. The following frequency table gives the number of flower buds on each stem of orchids that were delivered to this shop one Monday.

| Buds | 10 | 11 | 12 | 13 | 14 | 15 | 16 | 17 | 18 | 19 | 20 |
|---|---|---|---|---|---|---|---|---|---|---|---|
| Number of stems | 2 | 1 | 3 | 5 | 5 | 6 | 4 | 5 | 4 | 2 | 3 |

Calculate the mean number of buds per stem and the standard deviation.

(b) The mean and standard deviation of the number of flower buds per stem of an earlier delivery of orchids was: mean = 13, s.d. = 3·6. Use the means and standard deviations to compare these two deliveries.

**Review 3** As part of a statistical investigation Barbara gave each student in her class practice at estimating a time of 1 minute. The tables show the results before and after practice.

**Before Practice**

| Estimate (seconds) | $40 \leq t < 45$ | $45 \leq t < 50$ | $50 \leq t < 55$ | $55 \leq t < 60$ | $60 \leq t < 65$ | $65 \leq t < 70$ |
|---|---|---|---|---|---|---|
| Number of students | 2 | 5 | 6 | 5 | 4 | 3 |

**After Practice**

| Estimate (seconds) | $45 \leq t < 50$ | $50 \leq t < 55$ | $55 \leq t < 60$ | $60 \leq t < 65$ | $65 \leq t < 70$ | $70 \leq t < 75$ |
|---|---|---|---|---|---|---|
| Number of students | 1 | 2 | 9 | 7 | 4 | 2 |

Use the means and standard deviations to compare these distributions.

**Review 4**

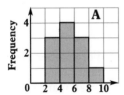
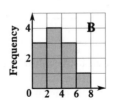
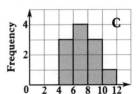

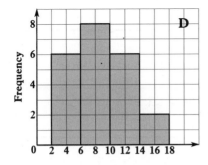
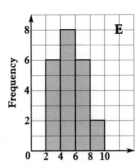

(i) Name the distributions which have (a) the same mean as A
(b) the same standard deviation as A.

(ii) If the mean of A is x and the standard deviation is y, express in terms of x and y
(a) the mean of C
(b) the standard deviation of D.

## PRACTICAL EXERCISE 25:10

1.  Collect two sets of related data. Analyse the data. As part of this analysis, calculate and compare means and standard deviations. If you collect your data from a sample, use one of the sampling techniques from the previous chapter.

    *Suggestions*   Data to compare performance before and after practice at some skill.
    Data to compare plant growth under varying conditions.
    Data on the time boys and girls spend on homework.

2.  Collect published data in table form. Some suggestions follow. As part of your analysis of this data, calculate and compare means and standard deviations.

    *Suggestions*   Data on driving licence holders.
    Data on age of workforce.
    Data on unemployment.
    Data on incomes.
    Data on climate.

3.  Collect published histograms of related data. Use these histograms to compare and contrast the data. You could collect data from the newspaper or from statistical publications.

## INVESTIGATION 25:11

**Combining Data**

For one maths. test the mean is 58 and the standard deviation is 8. For another maths. test the mean is 62 and the standard deviation is 7.

If the marks from both tests are given as one list, is it true that the mean mark is 60 and the standard deviation is 7·5? **Investigate.**

As part of your investigation, write down two lists of data. Find the means and standard deviations of these individual lists of data and the mean and standard deviation of the combined list.

## RESEARCH PROJECT 25:12

**Coefficient of Variation**

When we are comparing two sets of data we can consider the means and standard deviations. If the sets of data are quite different, for instance the weight of cereal in packets and the prices of these cereals at different shops, they can be compared using the **coefficient of variation.**

Research the coefficient of variation.

## CHAPTER 25   REVIEW

1.  The table below shows the time, to the nearest minute, taken by Tony to complete his journey to work for a single week.

| | Monday | Tuesday | Wednesday | Thursday | Friday |
|---|---|---|---|---|---|
| Time (minutes) | 34 | 40 | 32 | 35 | 37 |

Find the mean and standard deviation of the time, in minutes, taken by Tony to travel to work for this week.                                                                **WJEC**

2.  In a survey on examination qualifications, 50 people were asked 'How many subjects are listed on your GCSE certificate?' The frequency distribution of their responses is recorded in the table below.

| Number of subjects | Number of people (frequency) |
|---|---|
| 1 | 5 |
| 2 | 3 |
| 3 | 7 |
| 4 | 8 |
| 5 | 9 |
| 6 | 10 |
| 7 | 8 |

Calculate the mean and standard deviation of the distribution.                    **MEG**

3.  Mary thinks that girls are better than boys at estimating volumes.
She decides to carry out an experiment.
She pours 120ml of water into a glass.
She asks 20 girls and 20 boys to each estimate the volume of water in the glass.

The boys' estimates, in millilitres, are:

140  100  120  125  120  123  135  130  100  115
127  136  132  120  117  110  112  116  110  108

(a) Calculate the standard deviation of the boys' estimates.
Write your result in the table below.

| | Mean | Standard deviation |
|---|---|---|
| Girls | 124·1 | 5·86 |
| Boys | 119·8 | |

**(b)** Interpret these results in order to compare the girls' and the boys' ability to estimate volume.

**NEAB**

4. Ten students sat a test in Mathematics, marked out of 50.
   The results are shown below for each student.

   |     |     |     |     |     |     |     |     |     |     |
   |-----|-----|-----|-----|-----|-----|-----|-----|-----|-----|
   | 25  | 27  | 35  | 4   | 49  | 10  | 12  | 45  | 45  | 48  |

   **(a)** Calculate the mean and standard deviation of the data.

   The same students also sat an English test, marked out of 50.
   The mean and standard deviation for these data are given by
   mean = 30, standard deviation = 3·6.

   **(b)** Comment on and contrast the results in Mathematics and English.

   **SEG**

5. The data below for 1989-90 shows the efficiency of the delivery of FIRST class letters for ten Sorting Offices. It gives the percentage of letters delivered the next day in three categories: Within District, Neighbouring District, Distant District.

   | Letters posted | District | | |
   |----------------|----------|--------------|---------|
   | in | Within | Neighbouring | Distant |
   | Brighton | 92 | 78 | 73 |
   | London | 86 | 80 | 70 |
   | Guildford | 87 | 75 | 74 |
   | Oxford | 81 | 68 | 65 |
   | Reading | 85 | 67 | 65 |
   | Exeter | 95 | 89 | 67 |
   | Milton Keynes | 84 | 70 | 62 |
   | Leeds | 93 | 88 | 70 |
   | Glasgow | 93 | 83 | 67 |
   | Inverness | 83 | 79 | 40 |

   **(a)** Complete the table to show the mean and standard deviation of the data for each of the Within, Neighbouring and Distant districts.

   | | District | | |
   |---|----------|--------------|---------|
   | | Within | Neighbouring | Distant |
   | **Mean** | 87·9 | | |
   | **Standard Deviation** | 4·68 | | |

   **(b)** What conclusions can you draw from the values obtained in **(a)**?

   **SEG**

6. There are twenty pupils in class *A* and twenty pupils in class *B*.
   All the pupils in class *A* were given an I.Q. test.
   Their scores on the test are given below.

   100, 104, 106, 107, 109, 110, 113, 114, 116, 117,
   118, 119, 119, 121, 124, 125, 127, 127, 130, 134.

   **(a)** The mean of their scores is 117.
   Calculate the standard deviation.

**(b)** Class $B$ takes the same I.Q. test.
They obtain a mean of 110 and standard deviation of 21.
Compare the data for class $A$ and class $B$.

**(c)** Class $C$ has only 5 pupils.
When they take the I.Q. test they all score 105.
What is the value of the standard deviation for class $C$?   **SEG**

7. Twenty Adult Education students are comparing the number of hours that they spent on their homework last week. The results, rounded to the nearest half hour, are as follows.

| 2 | 3·5 | 2 | 4 | 8 | 3 | 5·5 | 3 | 4·5 | 4·5 |
|---|-----|---|---|---|---|-----|---|-----|-----|
| 4 | 3·5 | 2·5 | 5 | 4 | 3 | 4 | 4·5 | 4·5 | 5 |

**(a)** Calculate the mean and standard deviation.
You may wish to use the following formula $S^2 = \dfrac{\Sigma x^2}{n} - m^2$ where $m$ is the mean and $S$ is the standard deviation.

**(b)** An additional student arrives just after the mean and standard deviation have been worked out. He says that he spent about 4 hours on his homework.
State what effect the inclusion of this student would have on
  **(i)** the mean,    **(ii)** the standard deviation.   **SEG**

8. At Parker High School, the Mathematics and Geography tests were each marked out of 80.
The marks the students scored, out of 80, are called **raw scores.**
For reports, the Mathematics and Geography teachers have to change the raw scores to marks out of 100.
The marks out of 100 are called **reported marks.**
Five students were given the same **reported mark** for both their Mathematics and Geography tests. The **reported marks** for each student were

  60    80    30    70    35

**(a)** Calculate the standard deviation of these five marks. Give your answer to 3 significant figures.

To find the **reported mark** the Geography teacher had added 20 marks to each **raw score.**
**(b)** Write down the mean and standard deviation of the five Geography **raw scores.**

The Mathematics teacher had used a different method to change the **raw scores** to **reported marks.** The mean of the five Mathematics **raw scores** (out of 80) was 44.
**(c)** Find the standard deviation of the five Mathematics **raw scores.**   **ULEAC**

9. **(a)** Calculate the standard deviation of the numbers 3, 4, 5, 6, 7.

**(b)** Show that the standard deviation of **every** set of five consecutive integers is the same as the answer to part **(a)**.   **ULEAC**

**Chase The Ace: a game for a group.**

**Note** This game can be played with as few as 4 players and as many as 51.

**Equipment** A pack of cards.

**Aim of the Game** Each player aims not to have the lowest card. Ace is lowest, then 2 etc.

**The Play** The players sit in a circle.

The players take it in turn to be the dealer.

One card is dealt to each player. The players secretly look at their cards before they place them face down on the table.

Beginning with the player on the dealer's right, players take it in turns to either swap their card with the next player or to say **"sit"**. The dealer is the last player to decide whether to swap his or her card or to **"sit"**. If the dealer swaps, he or she swaps for the card on top of the remaining pack.

Once the dealer has had his or her turn, the round is finished. The player who now has the lowest card is out of the game. The second round is now played. The winner is the only person remaining in the game at the end.

A **sample round** with 7 players is shown below.

**The beginning of the round.**

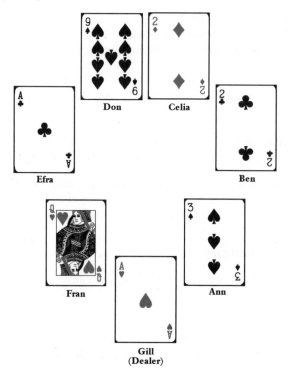

*continued . . .*

. . . *from previous page*

**The end of the round.**

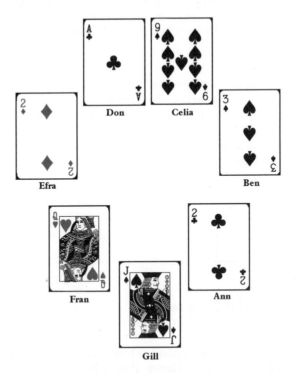

In this sample round, Ann begins first. Ann believes her 3 is too low to keep, so she swaps with Ben. To her horror, she gets a 2 in return for her 3.

It is now Ben's turn. He is quite happy with the 3 Ann has given him as he knows Ann now has a lower card. Ben says "sit".

It is now Celia's turn. She swaps with Don, getting a 9 in return for her 2.

It is now Don's turn. He is most unhappy with the 2 Celia has given him so he swaps with Efra. In return for the 2, he now has an Ace!

It is now Efra's turn. She is happy with the 2, so says "sit".

It is now Fran's turn. She says "sit" as she is happy with a Queen.

It is now Gill's turn. She swaps her card with the card on top of the remaining pack. In return for her Ace she gets a Jack.

Now everyone turns their cards face up. Since Don has the lowest card, he is out of the game.

**Things to Consider**   What is the lowest card you will "sit" with? Does this depend on the number of players left in the game?

How much skill and how much chance is involved in this game? Are there factors other than skill or chance involved?

**Variations**   1. If a player is dealt a King, this card is placed face up on the table. The left-hand opponent of this player cannot take this card and must "sit".

2. A player is out of the game when he or she has lost 3 rounds.

## NON-MUTUALLY-EXCLUSIVE EVENTS

Events which cannot happen at the same time are mutually exclusive. For instance, when a die is tossed the events "a five", "a multiple of 3" are mutually exclusive.
The events "a six", "a multiple of 3" could happen at the same time. These events are not mutually exclusive.

*Example*   In Alice's group of friends, 14 play netball, 12 play badminton, 3 play both netball and badminton and 2 play neither. To find the probability that one of these people, chosen at random, plays netball or badminton we cannot use P(N or B) = P(N) + P(B) since the events are not mutually exclusive.
We can draw a diagram to represent the given information, then use the diagram to find the required probability.

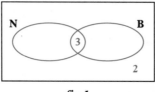

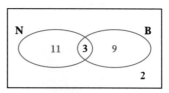

*fig 1*                          *fig 2*

*fig 1*   3 play both N and B, 2 play neither.
*fig 2*   Since 14 play N, 11 is filled in as shown. Since 12 play B, 9 is filled in as shown.
From *fig 2*,  11 + 3 + 9 = 23 play netball or badminton. There are 11 + 3 + 9 + 2 = 25 friends altogether.     Hence  P(N or B) = $\frac{23}{25}$.

## DISCUSSION EXERCISE 26:2

In the previous example  P(N) = $\frac{14}{25}$,  P(B) = $\frac{12}{25}$,  P(N and B) = $\frac{3}{25}$,
P(N or B) = P(N) + P(B) – P(N and B).  Think of other non mutually exclusive events, X and Y.
Is  P(X or Y)  always equal to  P(X) + P(Y) – P(X and Y)?  Why? **Discuss.**

If events A and B are mutually exclusive then  P(A or B) = P(A) + P(B).  If events A and B are not mutually exclusive then  P(A or B) = P(A) + P(B) – P(A and B).

*Worked Example*  If one card is drawn at random from a full pack of cards find the probability that this card is either an Ace or a heart.

*Answer*   The events "Ace", "heart" are not mutually exclusive since if the Ace of hearts is drawn both events have happened.
P (A or H) = P(A) + P(H) – P(A and H)
$$= \frac{4}{52} + \frac{13}{52} - \frac{1}{52}$$
$$= \frac{16}{52}$$
$$= \frac{4}{13}$$

## EXERCISE 26:3

1. A die is tossed. Find the probability of getting a multiple of 2 or a number greater than 3.

2. Two dice are tossed.
   (a) Find the probability of getting a total of more than 8.
   (b) Find the probability of getting the same number.
   (c) Use your answers to (a) and (b) to find the probability of getting a total of more than 8 or the same number.

3. A card is drawn at random from a full pack. Find the probability of this card being a spade or a King.

4. David gathered the following data.
   68% of families who live in Shirley Road have a dog, 42% have a cat and 15% have both a dog and a cat.
   Copy and complete this diagram of probabilities.
   Hence, or otherwise, find the probability of a family from Shirley Road, chosen at random, having
   (a) neither a dog nor a cat
   (b) at least one of these pets.

5. Of 150 houses advertised for sale, 32 have double garages, 40 have four bedrooms and 12 have both double garages and four bedrooms.
   If one of these houses is chosen at random find the probability that it has either a double garage or four bedrooms.

6. Statistics for A level students from Milton High School who take both physics and chemistry show that the probability of a student passing physics is 0·72, of passing chemistry is 0·83 and of passing both is 0·59.
   What is the probability that a student, chosen at random from those who take physics and chemistry, will pass at least one of these subjects?

7. 16 men and 12 women members of a rambling club went hiking on the Cotswold Way. Of the 7 who got blisters, 2 were women.
   Find the probability that one of these hikers, chosen at random, is either a woman or a person with blisters.

Review 1    In a pack of cards, the face cards are Kings, Queens and Jacks.
What is the probability that a card, chosen at random from a full pack, is a face card or a diamond?

Review 2    Of the 138 students in Year 10 at Cashmere School, 72 are girls. Of the 98 students in this year group who have weekend jobs, 54 are girls.
(a) Copy and complete this diagram.
(b) If one student is chosen at random from the Year 10 students, find the probability that this student is a girl or has a weekend job.

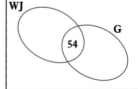

## NON-INDEPENDENT EVENTS

---

### DISCUSSION EXERCISE 26:4

---

**Experiment 1** Each of the 5 letters in the word MATHS is written on a small card. These 5 cards are then placed in a bag. Two cards are chosen at random. The first card is replaced before the second card is chosen.

**Experiment 2** Each of the 5 letters in the word MATHS is written on a small card. These 5 cards are then placed in a bag. Two cards are chosen at random. The first card is not replaced before the second card is chosen.

**Discuss** the above experiments. What does "replacement" mean? Which experiment concerns independent events and which concerns non-independent events? Is the probability of getting an M and an H the same in both experiments?

Think of some other experiments where the events are non-independent. **Discuss.**

## TREE DIAGRAMS for NON-INDEPENDENT EVENTS

When events are not independent, the outcome of earlier events affects the outcome of later events. Tree diagrams are an efficient way of illustrating the combined probability of several events which are not independent. The probabilities at each level, on the tree diagram, will be different. This is shown in the following worked example.

*Worked Example* There are 12 girls and 8 boys in an A-level physics class. Two of these students are to go to a workshop at the local University. These two students are to be chosen randomly by putting all 20 names in a hat. Their physics teacher is to draw the names out, one at a time.
(i) Draw a tree diagram to show all the possible outcomes for the gender of the students chosen.
(ii) Find the probability that
    (a) both the chosen students are girls
    (b) at least one of the chosen students is a girl.

*Answer*  (i)  For the first draw there are 20 students, 12 girls and 8 boys, to choose from.
Hence  $P(G) = \frac{12}{20}$, $P(B) = \frac{8}{20}$. *fig 1* shows the probabilities for the first draw.

The outcome of the first draw affects the probabilities $P(G)$ and $P(B)$ for the
second draw. For the second draw there are 19 students to choose from.
*If a girl is chosen on the first draw*, the probabilities for the second draw are:
$$P(G) = \tfrac{11}{19} \text{ (11 of the 19 left are girls)}$$
$$P(B) = \tfrac{8}{19} \text{ (8 of the 19 left are boys).}$$
*If a boy is chosen on the first draw*, the probabilities for the second draw are:
$$P(G) = \tfrac{12}{19} \text{ (12 of the 19 left are girls)}$$
$$P(B) = \tfrac{7}{19} \text{ (7 of the 19 left are boys).}$$

*fig 2* shows the probabilities for the first and second draws.

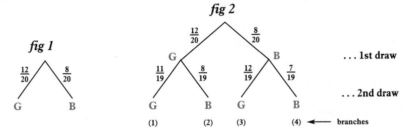

*fig 2*

*fig 1*

(ii) (a)  Branch 1 gives the probability that both the chosen students are girls.
$$P(\text{both girls}) = \tfrac{12}{20} \times \tfrac{11}{19}$$
$$= \tfrac{33}{95} .$$

(b)  Branches 1, 2, 3 give the probability that at least one is a girl.
The probability that at least one is a girl is found by adding the probabilities of
branches 1, 2, and 3.
$$P(\text{at least one girl}) = \tfrac{12}{20} \times \tfrac{11}{19} + \tfrac{12}{20} \times \tfrac{8}{19} + \tfrac{8}{20} \times \tfrac{12}{19}$$
$$= \tfrac{81}{95} .$$

*Note*  It is quite acceptable to give the probability as a decimal. We could have given the
answers as  **(a)** 0·347 (3 d.p.)  **(b)** 0·853 (3 d.p.).

## DISCUSSION EXERCISE 26:5

- Beth claimed that the answer to **(b)** of the previous worked example could be found more
efficiently as follows:  $P(\text{at least one girl}) = 1 - P(\text{no girls})$
$$= 1 - P(\text{both boys})$$
$$= 1 - \tfrac{8}{20} \times \tfrac{7}{19}$$
$$= \ldots$$

Discuss Beth's claim.

- Draw a tree diagram to show all the possible outcomes if three students are to go to the
workshop. What questions could you answer from this tree diagram? Discuss efficient
solutions for your questions.

## EXERCISE 26:6

1. There are 3 boys and 2 girls in a PSE group. Two of these students are chosen at random to lead a discussion.
   Draw a tree diagram to find the probability that    (a) two girls lead the discussion
        (b) a boy and a girl lead the discussion
        (c) at least one boy leads the discussion.

2. The Kings and Queens are taken from a pack of cards and laid face down on the desk. Two of these cards are then chosen at random, one after the other. The first card is not replaced before the second is chosen.
   Draw a tree diagram to show all the possible outcomes.
   Find the probability that    (a) both the chosen cards are Queens
        (b) only one of the chosen cards is a Queen
        (c) at least one of the chosen cards is a Queen
        (d) neither chosen card is a King.

3. Of the 10 smarties left in a bag, 6 are red and the rest are white. Anna chooses two of these at random, one after the other.
   Draw a tree diagram to find the probability that Anna chooses    (a) one of each colour
        (b) both red
        (c) at least one white
        (d) both the same colour.

4. Five fiction and three non-fiction books are in the "Returns Box" outside the library door. The duty librarian takes out 3 of these books, one after the other.
   Find the probability that, of the books this librarian takes out
        (a) all three are fiction
        (b) just two of them are fiction
        (c) at least two of them are non-fiction.

5. Of the 20 householders in Elm Grove, 14 have decided which party they will vote for in the next election. The remaining 6 are undecided. A canvasser hopes that, by interviewing just three of the householders in Elm Grove, he will manage to interview at least one that is undecided.
   Draw a tree diagram to show all the possible outcomes for the three householders chosen at random. Use your tree diagram to find the probability that of the householders interviewed
        (a) just one was undecided
        (b) all were undecided
        (c) at least one was undecided.

6. A box contains 9 tickets, labelled from 1 to 9. Three tickets are taken at random from this box, one after the other. Find the probability that
        (a) all three have even numbers
        (b) two have even numbers
        (c) at least two have even numbers
        (d) at least one has an even number
        (e) they are alternately even and odd.

**Review 1** There are 10 socks in a drawer, 5 grey and 5 white.
In the dark, Alex chooses two of these socks. What is the probability that Alex chose
(a) both grey socks    (b) one of each colour    (c) at least one grey sock
(d) both socks the same colour.

**Review 2** The labels have come off some tins of apricots and peaches.
There are 20 tins altogether, 15 of which are apricots and 5 peaches. These 20 tins are
in a "lucky-dip" bin at the supermarket. Yasmin buys three of these tins, hoping to
get at least two tins of apricots.
Draw a tree diagram to show the possible outcomes for the contents of the tins that
Yasmin chose.
Find the probability that Yasmin chose at least two tins of apricots.

Sometimes, not all branches of a tree diagram are the same length i.e. the branches stop at
different levels. Tree diagrams illustrating success or failure are often like this.

*Worked Example* The first time an operation is attempted the success rate is 70%. If it is
unsuccessful it can be repeated, but this time the success rate is reduced to
40%. Find the probability that the operation will fail twice.

*Answer* The tree diagram for this situation is shown below.

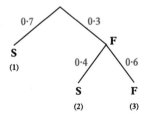

**S** is success, **F** is fail.

Notice that branch 1 stops at the first level since, if
the operation is successful, it is not repeated.

Branch 3 gives the operation failing twice.
$$P(\text{fails twice}) = 0.3 \times 0.6$$
$$= 0.18$$

## EXERCISE 26:7

1. The Aces and Jacks are taken from a pack of cards and put face down on the desk. Carmelo
picks up cards from this desk, one at a time. He hopes to pick up two Aces.
He is allowed to pick up a maximum of 3 cards.
Draw a tree diagram to show the possible outcomes. (Some branches will be shorter than
others).
Find the probability that Carmelo succeeds in picking up two Aces.

2. The five Habib children draw straws to decide which two of them are to do the dishes. There
are 2 short straws among the 5 they use. The children who draw the short straws, do the dishes.
Draw a tree diagram to show all the possible outcomes after just three of the children have
chosen straws.
Find the probability that it takes no more than three children to draw straws to decide who is
to do the dishes.

3. 60% of elderly people have a flu vaccination. Of those who do not have the vaccination, 80% get the flu. Find the probability that an elderly person will get the flu. (Assume that no one who has the vaccination gets the flu.)

4. Of the students who sit a test, 75% will pass. Those who do not pass, may do the test again at a later date. There is an 80% pass rate for those students who sit the test again.
    (a) What is the probability that a student fails twice?
    (b) Out of 200 students, how many do you expect to pass the test at the first or second attempt?

**Review**

The Kings and Jacks are taken from a pack of cards and laid face down on the desk. Mai-Ling picks up cards from this desk, one at a time. She has to pick up a pair i.e. either two Kings or two Jacks. Draw a tree diagram to show the possible outcomes.
Find the probability that Mai-Ling has to pick up 3 cards to get her pair.

Problems concerning events which are not independent can be solved without using tree diagrams.

*Worked Example*   Two cards are chosen at random from a full 52 card pack. The first card is not replaced. Calculate the probability that
 (a) both cards are spades
 (b) the second card is a heart
 (c) at least one card is a Queen
 (d) the second card is a King, given that the first card is a Jack.

*Answer*  (a) $P(S \text{ and } S) = P(S) \times P(S)$
$$= \tfrac{13}{52} \times \tfrac{12}{51}$$
$$= \tfrac{1}{17}$$

(b) If the first card is a heart, the probability of the second card being a heart is $\tfrac{12}{51}$ whereas if the first card is not a heart, the probability of the second being a heart is $\tfrac{13}{51}$.
We require $P(H \text{ and } H \text{ or } \text{not } H \text{ and } H)$.
$$P(H \text{ and } H \text{ or } \text{not } H \text{ and } H) = \tfrac{13}{52} \times \tfrac{12}{51} + \tfrac{39}{52} \times \tfrac{13}{51}$$
$$= \tfrac{1}{4}$$

(c) $P(\text{at least one card a Queen}) = 1 - P(\text{no queen})$
$$= 1 - P(\text{not } Q \text{ and not } Q)$$
$$= 1 - \tfrac{48}{52} \times \tfrac{47}{51}$$
$$= \tfrac{33}{221}$$

(d) If the first card is a Jack there are 4 Kings left out of 51 cards.
$$P(\text{second a King, given first a Jack}) = \tfrac{4}{51}$$

## EXERCISE 26:8

1. Jim has 4 keys of a similar type on his key-ring. Only one of these will open the boot of his new car. If he tries these keys one after the other, find the probability that Jim opens the boot on his third attempt.

2. In a lucky-dip box there are 10 wrapped gifts, all of the same size and weight. Eight of these are worth less than £1, two are worth at least £1. Meg chooses two of these gifts.
   Find the probability that Meg chooses the two which are worth at least £1.

3. Three red and two blue balls are placed in a container. Balls are drawn at random, one after the other until a blue ball appears. Calculate the probability that exactly two balls are drawn.

4. Two letters are chosen at random, one after the other, from the 11 letters of the word PROBABILITY. Find the probability that the chosen letters are
   (a) the letters P and B, in that order
   (b) the letters L and A in any order
   (c) both vowels
   (d) the same letter
   (e) not the same letter.

5. 

These cards are shuffled and placed face down on the desk. Tung and Andrea play a game in which they take it in turn to choose a card at random. The first to choose a Queen wins. Tung has the first turn.
   (a) Explain why the events "Tung chooses a King on his first turn" and "Andrea chooses a King on her first turn" are not independent.
   (b) Find the probability that Andrea wins on her first turn.
   (c) If Andrea and Tung toss a coin to decide who has the first turn, find the probability that Andrea wins on her first turn.

6. A bag contains 2 white counters and 3 coloured counters. The counters are drawn out at random, one at a time.
   (a) Find the probability of drawing out coloured and white counters alternately.
   (b) What if there were 2 white counters and 2 coloured counters?

7. Danny and William are opponents in a darts competition. They play until one of them has won 2 games. The probability that Danny wins the first game is 0·6. If William wins a game he gains in confidence and his probability of winning the next game is increased by 25%. A game cannot result in a draw.
   (a) Show that if William wins the first game, Danny's probability of winning the second game is reduced to 0·5.
   (b) Find the probability that Danny and William will play three games.

Review 1    A committee consists of 2 men and 4 women. A chairperson and a secretary are to be chosen at random from this committee.
   Find the probability that    (a) both the chairperson and the secretary are men
                                (b) just one of them is a woman
                                (c) at least one of them is a man.

Review 2    Two dice are tossed. What is the probability that if the numbers obtained add to less than 6, they are the same?

## CONDITIONAL PROBABILITY

*Worked Example*

|        | Under 20 | Over 20 |
|--------|----------|---------|
| Male   | 75       | 124     |
| Female | 188      | 43      |

This table shows the number of people who have enrolled for computing night classes at the Polytechnic.
   (a) How many people enrolled?
   (b) How many were male?
   (c) If one person is chosen at random, what is the probability that this person is under 20?
   (d) One of the males is chosen at random. What is the probability that he is under 20?

*Answer*    (a) We add all the figures in the table to get 430.
   (b) We add the figures for the males to get 199.
   (c) Adding the under 20 figures, we get 263. The total number of people is 430.
      P(under 20) = $\frac{263}{430}$ or 0·61 (2 d.p.)
   (d) The number of males is 199. Of these, 75 are under 20.
      P(under 20, given a male) = $\frac{75}{199}$ or 0·38 (2 d.p.)

## EXERCISE 26:9

1.

|  | Smokers | Non-smokers |
|---|---|---|
| Drinkers | 35 | 120 |
| Non-drinkers | 20 | 25 |

This table shows the drinking and smoking habits of those admitted to a hospital. If one of these patients is chosen at random find the probability that this patient
  (a) both drinks and smokes
  (b) neither smokes nor drinks
  (c) is a non-smoker
  (d) does not drink
  (e) is a smoker, given that this patient is a non-drinker
  (f) does not smoke, given that this patient drinks.

2. Diners in a restaurant drink either wine or water. This table shows the results of a survey of a number of diners. What is the probability that one of those surveyed is
  (a) female
  (b) a wine drinker
  (c) a female wine drinker
  (d) a wine drinker, given that this diner is male?

|  | Wine | Water |
|---|---|---|
| Male | 48 | 14 |
| Female | 49 | 29 |

3.

|  | Female | Male |
|---|---|---|
| Conservative | 222 | 208 |
| Labour | 204 | 289 |
| Liberal | 35 | 42 |

This table shows the way a sample of voters said they intended to vote at the next election. Find the probability that one of these voters, chosen at random
  (a) is male
  (b) intends to vote Liberal
  (c) is female, given that this voter intends to vote Labour
  (d) is a male Conservative voter
  (e) intends to vote Conservative, given that this voter is female.

4. This table shows the age group of those Conservative voters we talked about in the previous question. Find the probability that one of these voters, chosen at random
  (a) is female
  (b) is a female over 40
  (c) is over 40, given that the voter is female
  (d) is under 40.

|  | Under 40 | Over 40 |
|---|---|---|
| Male | 108 | 100 |
| Female | 81 | 141 |

Review   A survey was made of the cars that were for sale in one area of Manchester. This table shows the results of this survey. If one of these cars is chosen at random, find the probability that it is

|        | British | Non-British |
|--------|---------|-------------|
| New    | 86      | 24          |
| Used   | 64      | 120         |

(a) a British car
(b) a new car
(c) a non-British car, given that it is used.

---

In (d) of the Worked Example on Page 544 we were asked to find the probability that a person is under 20, given that the person is male. In this case, the event "under 20" is dependent on the event "being male". We say that the probability of the event "under 20" is **conditional** on the event "being male".

---

## DISCUSSION EXERCISE 26:10

- At least one part of each question in Exercise 26:9 involves conditional probability. Which parts? **Discuss.**

- Adrian found the answer to (d) of the Worked Example on Page 544 as follows.

$$P \text{ (under 20, given male)} = \frac{P(\text{under 20 } \textbf{and} \text{ male})}{P(\text{male})}$$

$$= \frac{\frac{75}{430}}{\frac{199}{430}}$$

$$= \frac{75}{199}$$

**Discuss** Adrian's method. As part of your discussion find the answer to the conditional probability questions in Exercise 26:9 using this method.

---

To find the probability of event A occurring given that event B has occurred we can use the following formula.

$$P(A, \text{ given } B) = \frac{P(A \textbf{ and } B)}{P(B)} .$$

*Example*

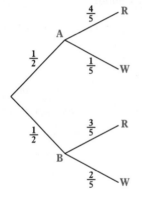

Two bags, A and B, contain some red and some white counters. Bag A contains 20 red and 5 white counters; bag B contains 18 red and 12 white counters.
A student chooses one of the bags at random then chooses a counter at random.

The first level of the tree diagram shows that P(bag A chosen) = $\frac{1}{2}$, P(bag B chosen) = $\frac{1}{2}$.
The second level of the tree diagram shows that if bag A is chosen then
P(red counter chosen) = $\frac{4}{5}$ and P(white counter chosen) = $\frac{1}{5}$ whereas if bag B is chosen then
P(red counter chosen) = $\frac{3}{5}$ and P(white counter chosen) = $\frac{2}{5}$. In other words, the second level
shows the following:

P(red, given bag A) = $\frac{4}{5}$

P(white, given bag A) = $\frac{1}{5}$

P(red, given bag B) = $\frac{3}{5}$

P(white, given bag B) = $\frac{2}{5}$

*Worked Example*    For the previous example find the probability of
        (a) a red counter being chosen
        (b) a red counter being chosen, given that bag A is chosen
        (c) bag A being chosen, given that a red counter is chosen.

*Answer*    (a) P(red) = $\frac{1}{2} \times \frac{4}{5} + \frac{1}{2} \times \frac{3}{5}$

           = $\frac{7}{10}$

(b) P(red, given A) = $\dfrac{\text{P(red and A)}}{\text{P(A)}}$

             = $\dfrac{\frac{1}{2} \times \frac{4}{5}}{\frac{1}{2}}$

             = $\frac{4}{5}$

(c) P(A, given red) = $\dfrac{\text{P(A and red)}}{\text{P(red)}}$

             = $\dfrac{\frac{1}{2} \times \frac{4}{5}}{\frac{1}{2} \times \frac{4}{5} + \frac{1}{2} \times \frac{3}{5}}$

             = $\dfrac{\frac{4}{10}}{\frac{7}{10}}$

             = $\frac{4}{7}$

## DISCUSSION EXERCISE 26:11

Carol claims that the answers to **(b)** and **(c)** of the previous worked example can be found from
the given information without using the conditional probability formula. Carol wrote:

**(b)** P(red, given A) = $\frac{20}{25}$    **(c)** P(A, given red) = $\dfrac{\frac{20}{25}}{\frac{20}{25} + \frac{18}{30}}$

What reasons might Carol have given for her working? Could Carol have found the answers from
the tree diagram instead of from the given information? **Discuss.**

Suppose the probability of choosing bag A is $\frac{1}{3}$ and the probability of choosing bag B is $\frac{2}{3}$.
Could the answers to **(b)** and **(c)** be found without using the conditional probability formula?
**Discuss.**

**Example**

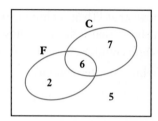

This diagram shows the number of students in a Year 11 class who take French (F) or Chemistry (C) or both.

This diagram shows that of the 20 (5 + 2 + 6 + 7) students in this class 5 take neither French nor Chemistry, 8 (2 + 6) take French, 13 (7 + 6) take Chemistry and 6 take both French and Chemistry.

We can draw a tree diagram as follows. (F is French, NF is not French, C is Chemistry, NC is not Chemistry.)

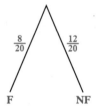

8 of the 20 take French. $P(F) = \frac{8}{20}$

12 of the 20 do not take French. $P(NF) = \frac{12}{20}$

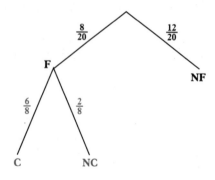

Of the 8 who take French, 6 take Chemistry and 2 do not take Chemistry.

$P(C, \text{given } F) = \frac{6}{8}, \ P(NC, \text{given } F) = \frac{2}{8}.$

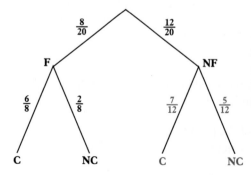

Of the 12 who do not take French, 7 take Chemistry and 5 do not take Chemistry.

$P(C, \text{given } NF) = \frac{7}{12}, \ P(NC, \text{given } NF) = \frac{5}{12}.$

*Worked Example*  (i)  Use the tree diagram in the previous example to find the probability that a student chosen at random
   (a) does not take Chemistry, given that the student takes French
   (b) takes just one of the subjects Chemistry or French.
(ii) Explain how you can use the diagram at the beginning of the previous example to check the answers to **(i)**.

*Answer*  (i)  (a)  P(NC, given F) = $\frac{2}{8}$
   (b)  P(F and NC **or** C and NF) = P (F and NC **or** NF and C)
$$= \frac{8}{20} \times \frac{2}{8} + \frac{12}{20} \times \frac{7}{12}$$
$$= \frac{9}{20}$$

   (ii) (a)  From the diagram, 2 of the 8 students who take F do not take C. Hence P(NC, given F) = $\frac{2}{8}$.
   (b)  From the diagram, there are 20 students altogether. Of these, 2 take F but not C and 7 take C but not F. Hence P (just one of F or C) = $\frac{9}{20}$.

*Worked Example*  Alexander's alarm usually wakes him. Even if it does, he can still be late for school. The probability that Alexander's alarm fails to wake him is 0·1. If the alarm does wake him, the probability he will be late for school is 0·05. If the alarm doesn't wake him, the probability that he will be late for school is 0·6.
   (a)  Draw a tree diagram for this.
   (b)  Find the probability that Alexander will be late for school.
   (c)  Find the probability that Alexander's alarm woke him, given that he is late for school.

*Answer*  (a)

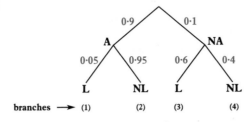

A – alarm wakes Alexander
NA – alarm does not wake him
L – Alexander is late
NL – Alexander is not late

branches → (1)  (2)  (3)  (4)

   (b)  Branch 1 or branch 3 gives Alexander being late.
P(L) = 0·9 × 0·05 + 0·1 × 0·6
   = 0·105

   (c)  We need P(A, given L) = $\dfrac{P(A \text{ and } L)}{P(L)}$

$$= \frac{0.9 \times 0.05}{0.105}$$
   = 0·43 to 2 d.p.

## EXERCISE 26:12

1. The probability that Kay goes home for lunch is 0·2. If she goes home for lunch, the probability that her younger brother, Brett, goes home also is 0·9. Even if Kay does not go home for lunch, Brett sometimes still does. The probability of Brett going home when Kay doesn't is 0·1.
   Draw a tree diagram for this situation. Use your tree diagram to find the probability of Brett going home for lunch.

2. The probability that any best-selling spy thriller will be published as a paperback is 0·9. If it is published as a paperback, the probability that it will be made into a movie is 0·2. The probability that it will be made into a movie even although it wasn't published as a paperback is 0·05.
   Draw a tree diagram to illustrate. Find the probability that a best-selling spy thriller will be made into a movie.

3. The probability of Kenji's family taking a summer holiday is 0·85. If they do take a summer holiday, the probability of this family taking a winter holiday is 0·35, while the probability of them taking a winter holiday if they don't take a summer one is 0·7. Find the probability that Kenji's family will take a holiday next year. Use a tree diagram.

4.

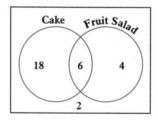

For dessert, at a party, there were various kinds of cake and a bowl of fruit salad. This diagram shows which desserts the guests ate.
   (a) How many guests were at the party?
   (b) What is the probability that a guest, chosen at random, ate fruit salad?
   (c) Copy and complete this tree diagram.

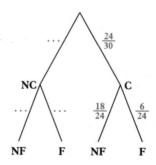

C – cake
NC – not cake
F – fruit salad
NF – not fruit salad

   (d) Use the tree diagram to calculate the probability that a guest, chosen at random, ate just one of the desserts.

5. Morag surveyed 50 students in her year group about where they had eaten out in the last month. The table and diagram show some of her results.

| Restaurant | Number |
|---|---|
| McDonalds | 20 |
| Pizza Hut | 12 |
| Both McDonalds and Pizza Hut | 4 |
| Neither McDonalds nor Pizza Hut | 22 |

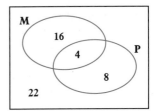

(a) Use the diagram, above, to find the probability that a student, chosen at random, ate at either McDonalds or Pizza Hut but not at both.

(b) Copy and complete this tree diagram.

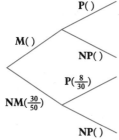

M – McDonalds
NM – not McDonalds
P – Pizza Hut
NP – not Pizza Hut

(c) Use the tree diagram to calculate the probability that a student, chosen at random, ate at McDonalds but not at Pizza Hut.

(d) Suppose Morag had displayed her results on the tree diagram rather than in the table and diagram at the beginning of the question. Explain how you could find the answer to (a) using the tree diagram.

6. This diagram shows the number of students in a class who got 80% or more on two maths. tests.

(i)   How many students are in this class?

(ii)  A student is chosen at random from this class.
Find the probability that this student
(a) scored 80% or more on both tests
(b) scored less than 80% on Test 1
(c) scored less than 80% on both tests.

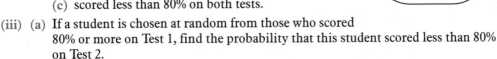

(iii) (a) If a student is chosen at random from those who scored 80% or more on Test 1, find the probability that this student scored less than 80% on Test 2.
(b) Find the probability of a student scoring 80% or more on Test 2, given that this student scored less than 80% on Test 1.

7. Die A has three red faces, two green faces and one white face. Die B has two red faces, two green faces and two white faces. One of these dice is chosen at random, then tossed.
(a) Draw a tree diagram. Use the tree diagram to answer the following questions.
(b) What is the probability of getting a white face?
(c) Given that die A has been chosen, what is the probability of getting a white face?
(d) What is the probability that die A was tossed given that a white face is obtained?

8. X, Y and Z are three bags which contain coloured balls of the same size and weight.
   X contains 2 blue balls and 8 green balls, Y contains 5 blue balls and 3 red balls, Z contains 6 red balls and 6 green balls.
   A bag is chosen at random, then a ball is chosen from this bag.
   (i) Copy and complete this tree diagram.

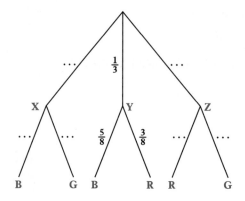

   (ii) Find the probability of choosing (a) a green ball
                                         (b) a blue ball if bag X is chosen.
   (iii) If a blue ball is chosen what is the probability that it came from bag X?

**Review 1**  Three times out of every ten, Megan uses the calculator for a calculation. If she uses the calculator, the probability of Megan getting the correct answer is 0·95. If she does not use the calculator, this probability is 0·8.
   (a) Draw a tree diagram.
   (b) Use the tree diagram to calculate the probability of Megan getting her next calculation correct.

**Review 2**  Twenty-two different models of microwave ovens were tested for how well they cooked chicken and fish. The results are given in the table.

| Cooked chicken well | 17 |
|---|---|
| Cooked fish well | 8 |
| Cooked both chicken and fish well | 6 |
| Cooked neither chicken nor fish well | 3 |

   (a) Copy and complete this diagram.
   (b) Use the diagram to find the probability of a microwave oven, chosen at random, cooking either chicken or fish well but not both.

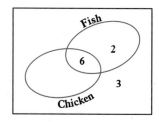

**Review 3** Two jars contain counters. Jar A contains 4 red counters, 9 blue counters and 7 white counters. Jar B contains 4 red counters and 11 white counters.

One of these jars is chosen at random, then a counter is chosen.

(a) Draw a tree diagram.

(b) Find the probability of choosing a red counter.

(c) If a blue counter is chosen, what is the probability it came from jar A?

(d) Find the probability of choosing a white counter, given that jar B was chosen.

(e) Given that a red counter is chosen, what is the probability it came from jar A?

---

## INVESTIGATION 26:13

**The Winning Chance**

1.

A bag contains six red balls, four black balls and five white balls. Two students take it in turns to take a ball, at random, from the bag. The first student to have taken two balls of the same colour is the winner.

Do both students have the same chance of winning if each ball is replaced after each turn? What is the probability of the first student winning on his or her second turn? **Investigate** the probabilities of each student winning.

**What if** the balls are not replaced after each turn?
**What if** the bag contained equal numbers of balls of just two colours?
**What if** . . .

*continued . . .*

*. . . from previous page*

2. Vusi chooses 2 balls, at random, from this
   bag. He chooses them one by one, without
   replacement.
   What is the probability that Vusi chooses
   2 red balls?

   Will Vusi improve his chances of getting
   exactly 2 red balls if he chooses three balls from
   the bag? What if he chose seven balls?

   **Investigate** to find the number of balls Vusi should choose to have the greatest chance of
   getting exactly 2 red balls.

3. Andrea and Hamish each have a bag with six balls. Three are numbered 4, two are
   numbered 5 and one is numbered 6. They play a game in which each chooses, at
   random, a ball from his or her bag. If the balls are the same number there is no winner,
   otherwise 6 beats 5, 5 beats 4 and 4 beats 6. Show that the probability of Hamish
   winning is $\frac{11}{36}$ .

   Hamish decides to improve his chances of winning by changing the number on one of
   his balls. Which of his balls should he change to give himself the greatest chance of
   winning? **Investigate.**

## PROBABILITY of ANY TWO EVENTS

In the following exercise some questions concern mutually exclusive events, some concern non-
mutually exclusive events, some concern independent events, some concern non-independent
events. In some, conditional probability is involved.
Use tree diagrams or other diagrams if you wish.

Remember that choosing **with replacement** gives rise to independent events while choosing
**without replacement** gives rise to non-independent events.

### EXERCISE 26:14

1. In a secondary school's athletics competition, the first three in each heat go into the final.
   The probability that Barbara is placed in the first three in her heat is 0·8. If she gets into the
   final, the probability that she wins this race is 0·2.
   Find the probability that Barbara wins the final.

2. A bag contains 5 red balls, 4 black balls and 3 green balls. Two balls are drawn at random, one after the other.
   (a) What is the probability that if the first ball is red, the second ball is green?
   (b) What is the probability that the balls drawn are the same colour?
   (c) What is the probability that the two balls are different colours?

3. At an athletics competition, Daniel represents his school in the 100m and 200m races. The probability that he wins the 100m race is $\frac{2}{5}$; the probability that he wins the 200m race is $\frac{1}{4}$. Find the probability that Daniel  (a) wins both races
   (b) wins just one race
   (c) wins at least one race.

4. In a survey on opinions about beginning the school day at 0815 it was found that 3 out of 5 students were in favour. What is the probability that the next two students who are interviewed will be in favour?

5. Each of the 12 letters in the word EXAMINATIONS is written on a small card. Justin chooses two of these cards at random, without replacement.
   Find the probability that Justin chooses  (a) the letters M and A in that order
   (b) the letters A and N in either order
   (c) two letters the same.

6. Experience has shown that if a pair of jeans is sewn by an apprentice, there is a probability of 0·1 that a pair will be classified as "seconds". Two pairs of jeans are chosen at random from those sewn by apprentices. Find the probability that  (a) neither is a "second"
   (b) just one is a "second"
   (c) at least one is a "second"
   (d) both are "seconds".

7. In an experiment, Nicola gathered 20 daisy seeds; 12 from a white daisy and 8 from a yellow daisy. She planted these in a tray. It is known that the probability of a white daisy seed germinating is $\frac{3}{4}$ while that of a yellow daisy seed is $\frac{3}{5}$.
   (a) Copy and complete this tree diagram.

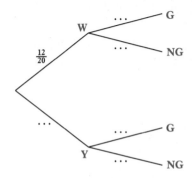

W – white daisy seed
Y – yellow daisy seed
G – germinates
NG – does not germinate

   (b) If one of these seeds is chosen at random, what is the probability that it will not germinate?
   (c) Given that a seed has germinated, what is the probability that it is a yellow daisy seed?

8. Kevin tossed a coin and a die together. What is the probability that he gets either a "four" or a "tail" or both?

9. The probability that an apprentice baker passes a theory exam. is $\frac{5}{8}$. If the exam. is failed it may be retaken later. The probability of passing at the second attempt is $\frac{2}{3}$.
   (a) Draw a tree diagram to show the probability of an apprentice baker passing and failing at these two attempts.
   (b) Find the probability that an apprentice baker passes on the first or second attempt.

10. Two dice are tossed.
    (a) Find the probability of getting a total of less than 5.
    (b) What is the probability of getting just one odd number?
    (c) Explain how you can use the answers to (a) and (b) to find the probability of getting a total of less than 5 or just one odd number. Find this probability.

11. Linda is very confident about her work on iteration and graphs of related functions. She hopes the exam. will have questions on these topics.
    If the probability of a question on iteration is 0·8 and on graphs of related functions is 0·3, what is the probability that an exam. will have questions on (a) both these topics
    (b) just one of these topics?

12. Anna always parks on the block beside her office. If no park is available the first time she drives around the block, she continues to drive around the block. The probability of Anna finding an available park, on any circuit of this block, is 0·7. It takes her 5 minutes to drive around this block.
    Find the probability of (a) Anna finding a park on her second circuit
    (b) Anna finding a park within 10 minutes.

13. There is a probability of 0·3 that it will rain on Easter Saturday. If it rains on the Saturday, the probability that it rains on Easter Sunday is 0·7. If it does not rain on the Saturday, there is a probability of 0·2 that it will rain on the Sunday.
    Find the probability of rain sometime during Easter Saturday or Sunday.

14. The five Smith children are going to draw straws to decide which two are to do the dishes. Sam is to be the third to draw a straw. Find the probability that Sam needs to draw a straw.

15. Alan selected a random sample of students to interview about their TV viewing habits. Some of the results of Alan's survey are shown in the table and in the diagram.

| ITV | 63 |
|---|---|
| BBC 2 | 49 |
| ITV and BBC 2 | 15 |
| Neither ITV nor BBC 2 | 3 |

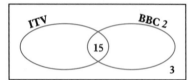

(a) Copy and complete the diagram.
(b) How many students did Alan interview?
(c) Use the diagram to find the probability that one of these students, chosen at random, watched just one of ITV or BBC 2.

16. A box contains 4 red balls and 5 black balls. A second box contains 3 red balls and 4 black balls. One ball is chosen at random from the first box and placed in the second. A ball is now chosen at random from the 8 balls in the second box. What is the probability that this ball is red?

17. 85% of the students interviewed by Judy said they enjoyed maths., 64% enjoyed economics, 52% enjoyed both maths. and economics.
    If one of these students is chosen at random, what is the probability that this student does not enjoy either maths. or economics?

18. Eight of the questions in a science exam. have true/false answers. Brent knows the answers to 3 of these questions and guesses the answers to the other 5.
    Find the probability that Brent gets at least 5 of the questions in this true/false section correct.

19. A maths. teacher knows, from past experience, that a GCSE student who does homework regularly has a probability of 0·9 of passing the exams. whereas a student who does not do homework regularly has only a probability of 0·2. Last year, 80% of this teacher's students regularly did their homework. What is the probability that one of the students who passed did homework regularly?

20. Elizabeth and Jenny are playing a card game. They take the face cards (Kings, Queens and Jacks) from a pack and put these face down on the desk.
    Elizabeth takes a card at random. Each time she picks up a Queen she has another turn. When Elizabeth picks up a card other than a Queen it becomes Jenny's turn. Jenny is also allowed another turn every time she picks up a Queen.
    If the cards are not replaced, what is the probability that the third card is picked up by Elizabeth?

21. Dina asked 50 students about the countries they had visited. Some of her results are shown.

| Wales | 32 |
| Scotland | 20 |
| Wales and Scotland | 8 |
| Neither Wales nor Scotland | 6 |

(a) Copy and complete this diagram.

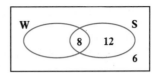

(b) Copy and complete this tree diagram.

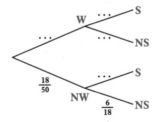

W – Wales
NW – not Wales
S – Scotland
NS – not Scotland

(c) Find the probability that one of these students, chosen at random, had visited either Wales or Scotland but not both.

(d) Two students are chosen at random from those who had visited Wales. Calculate the probability that just one of these had also visited Scotland.

**Review 1**  A card is drawn at random from a full pack. Find the probability of this card being either a club or a Jack.

**Review 2**  On any one day, the probability that Jason is early for school is 0·2; the probability that Erica is early is 0·15. Assuming that the events "Jason is early" and "Erica is early" are independent, find the probability that on any one day
(a) both Jason and Erica are early
(b) neither Jason nor Erica is early
(c) at least one of Jason or Erica is early
(d) either Jason or Erica is early.

**Review 3**  On a multiple choice test there are 10 questions each with five choices. Angela knows the answers to 8 of the questions and guesses the answers to the other 2.
What is the probability that Angela answers all 10 questions correctly?

**Review 4**  There are 5 black balls and 3 red balls in bag A. In bag B there are 3 black, 2 red and 3 white balls.
(i) Two balls are chosen without replacement from bag A. Find the probability that at least one of these balls is black.
(ii) Calculate the probability that of two balls chosen from bag B, one after the other, exactly one of them will be black.
(iii) Kate chooses one of the bags A or B at random, then chooses a ball from that bag.
   (a) What is the probability that Kate chooses a black ball?
   (b) What is the probability that Kate chose bag A given that the ball chosen was white?
   (c) Given that Kate chose a red ball, what is the probability that it came from bag B?

**Review 5**  Two new drugs are available for migraines. Three out of five migraine sufferers who are treated with drug X get relief while four out of five of those treated with drug Y do. One migraine sufferer, selected at random, is given drug X and another is given drug Y. Find the probability that
(a) both these people get relief
(b) just one of them gets relief
(c) if just one gets relief it is the one treated with drug X.

## INVESTIGATION 26:15

**Birthdays**

Would you think it most unlikely that two students in a class of 20 have their birthday on the same day? You may be surprised. **Investigate.**

## INVESTIGATION 26:16

### Analysis of Games

Many **games of chance** have an element of skill. This applies in particular to most card games. It also applies to most board games. Often, by analysing a game of chance i.e. by working out the probability of particular outcomes, we can improve our chances of winning.

An analysis of a move in backgammon follows.

**Backgammon**

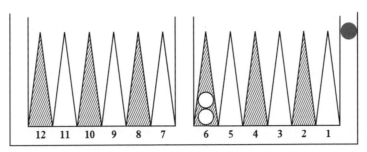

In the game of Backgammon two dice are thrown together. On the section of board shown, the white counters move to the right and the red counter moves to the left. If the red counter lands on a point where there is just one white counter, the white counter is removed from the board. Suppose it is white's turn to throw the dice and white gets a 2 and a 3 and must move either one of the counters 5 places or one of them 2 places and the other 3 places. The possible new positions of the white counters would be:

**Case 1**  One on the 6 point and the other on the 1 point (one counter moved 5 places).

**Case 2**  One on the 4 point and the other on the 3 point (the 2 and 3 moved by different counters).

We want to find the best possible move for the white counters. This will be the move that gives them the least chance of being removed at red's next throw.

**Analysis**  Remember that there are 36 possible outcomes when 2 dice are thrown.

**Case 1**  (a)  Both counters will be removed if red throws 1 and 5, or 5 and 1. Then the probability of both counters being removed is $\frac{2}{36}$.

(b)  Just the counter on the 1 point will be removed if red throws 1 and a number other than 5. There are 9 ways of this happening. Hence the probability of just the counter on the 1 point being removed is $\frac{9}{36}$.

(c)  Just the counter on the 6 point will be removed if red throws 6 and any other number; or a total of 6 consisting of 4 and 2, or 2 and 4, or 3 and 3 (remember 1 and 5, or 5 and 1 would have removed both counters). There are 11 ways of throwing a 6 and any other number. There are 3 ways of throwing a total of 6 consisting of 4 and 2, or 2 and 4, or 3 and 3. Hence there are 14 outcomes that would remove just the counter on the 6 point.

The probability of this happening is $\frac{14}{36}$.
Hence   probability of both counters being removed is $\frac{2}{36}$,

probability of just one counter being removed is $\frac{9}{36} + \frac{14}{36} = \frac{23}{36}$.

*continued . . .*

**Case 2** (a) Both counters will be removed if red throws 3 and 1, or 1 and 3. Hence the probability of both counters being removed is $\frac{2}{36}$.

(b) Just the counter on the 3 point will be removed if red throws 3 and a number other than 1; or a total of 3. There are 9 ways of throwing 3 and a number other than 1. There are 2 ways of throwing a total of 3 (2 and 1, or 1 and 2). Hence the probability of just the counter on the 3 point being removed is $\frac{11}{36}$.

(c) Just the counter on the 4 point will be removed if red throws 4 and a number other than 3; or a total of 4 consisting of 2 and 2. There are 9 ways of throwing a 4 and a number other than 3. There is 1 way of throwing a total of 4 consisting of 2 and 2. Hence the probability of just the counter on the 4 point being removed is $\frac{10}{36}$.

Hence    probability of both counters being removed is $\frac{2}{36}$,

probability of just one counter being removed is $\frac{11}{36} + \frac{10}{36} = \frac{21}{36}$.

**Conclusion** In both cases the probability of both counters being removed is the same. The probability of just one counter being removed in Case 2 is less than in Case 1. So the best possible move for the white counters will be to move both of them, one of them 3 and the other 2.

**Analyse** other possible positions in backgammon or **analyse** another board game involving dice or analyse a card game.

## CHAPTER 26  REVIEW

1. A bag contains 2 red, 4 green and 6 white sweets. The sweets are identical apart from colour and flavour. Jill randomly chooses a sweet from the bag, then Jack randomly chooses a sweet from those remaining in the bag.

   (a) Complete the tree diagram below.

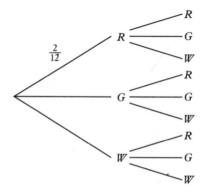

   (b) Find the probability that they choose sweets of the same colour.         **WJEC**

2.  In a group of students there are five girls and four boys.
    Two of these students are chosen at random.
    Find the probability that both of these students will be boys.  **ULEAC**

3.  

The diagram shows a card used to play a game.

The nine circled numbers are covered and cannot be seen until the covering is removed.

The game is played by removing at random the covering from any two of the numbers and the score is the sum of the two numbers revealed.

(a) Calculate the probability that exactly 2 will be scored.

(b) Calculate the probability that exactly 3 will be scored.

(c) Calculate the probability that 4 or more will be scored.  **ULEAC**

4.  The probability that a randomly chosen pupil will be **absent** from school on any one particular day is 0·6 if the pupil was absent the day before.

    This probability is only 0·1 if the pupil was **not absent** the day before.

    Today is Monday and Claire is **absent** from school.

    (a) Draw a tree diagram to show all the possible outcomes in Claire's attendance for Tuesday and Wednesday.

    Write the probabilities on the branches.

    (b) Use your diagram to calculate the probability that Claire will be **absent** on Wednesday.  **SEG**

5.  A bag contains eight counters. Five of the counters are green and three are red. A counter is taken at random from the bag and its colour is noted. The counter is not replaced. A second counter is then taken from the bag.
    Calculate the probability that

    (i) the first counter is green and the second is red;

    (ii) the counters are of the same colour.  **NEAB**

**6.** Of 50 pupils, 30 pass the Maths exam at the first attempt. From past performance it is known that, if a pupil fails at the first attempt, the probability of passing at the second attempt is 0·7. Calculate the probability that a pupil, chosen at random from the 50 pupils, will pass the Maths exam at either the first or second attempt. **MEG**

**7.** The fast food chain, Macduff's, is running a competition.

You obtain a card with 12 circles covered up.

You are allowed to scratch off up to three circles.

You win if 2 or more PALM TREES are revealed.

You lose if 2 or more CRABS are found.

If you win, you scratch off one of the three squares to show your prize.

One of the cards is illustrated above, with all the circles and squares revealed. The ratio of PALM TREES to CRABS is always 2:1 but their positions can change.

**(a)** The first circle you scratch off reveals a PALM TREE. What is the probability that the second circle reveals a PALM TREE?

**(b)** Complete the tree diagram for all the winning combinations.

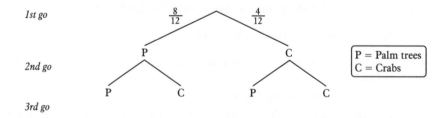

**(c)** List the possible winning combinations.
**(d)** What is the probability of winning? **SEG**

**8.** A tube of fruit gums contains 3 red gums, 4 black gums and 3 green gums. Two gums are chosen, at random, and not replaced.
What is the probability that they are both the same colour? **SEG**

9. Of a pack of 45 identical white cards, 20 are marked with an A, the remaining 25 with an X. Cards are drawn at random and are not replaced. Find the probability that

    (a) the first card drawn is marked A and the second is marked X,

    (b) the first two cards drawn are both marked X,

    (c) the second card is marked X,

    (d) the first three cards are marked A, X, X in that order.          **MEG**

10. A bag contains 4 RED and 6 BLUE balls. One ball is chosen and its colour noted. It is **not** put back into the bag. A second ball is chosen and its colour noted.

    (a) Draw a tree diagram to represent this situation.

    (b) (i) Find the probability of obtaining **two** RED balls.

        (ii) Find the probability of obtaining **one** RED and **one** BLUE ball in either order.   **SEG**

11. On a production line at the SMP chocolate factory, the chocolates are made by two machines. The first moulds the centre and the second coats the centre with chocolate.

    Dipti works for the quality control section. Some of the chocolates are faulty. She estimates that the first machine makes a misshapen centre with probability 0·05 and that the second machine fails to coat a centre with probability 0·02.

    (a) What is the probability that a chocolate picked at random
        (i) is coated,          (ii) is not faulty?

    However, Dipti had not noticed that misshapen centres were less likely to be coated than correct shape centres. She estimated these new probabilities:

    | | |
    |---|---|
    | Probability centre misshapen | 0·05 |
    | Probability misshapen centre not coated | 0·75 |
    | Probability correct shape centre not coated | 0·015 |

    (b) (i) Complete the tree diagram to show the probabilities of all possible outcomes:

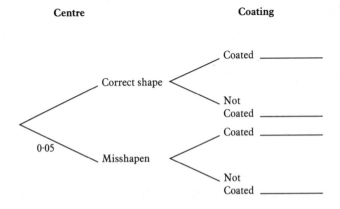

        (ii) Find the probability that a chocolate picked at random is faulty.          **MEG**

12. There are 8 balls in a box. 7 of the balls are yellow and 1 ball is red.
Jean selects balls at random, without replacement, from the box until she obtains the red ball.

When she obtains the red ball, then she stops selecting.

By extending the tree diagram shown below, or otherwise, calculate the probability that Jean selects the red ball on one of her first three selections.

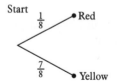

ULEAC

13. Brian enjoys swimming.

If it is a sunny day the probability that he swims is 0·9.

If the day is not sunny, the probability that he swims is 0·65.

The probability that tomorrow will be sunny is 0·8.

(a) Draw a tree diagram to illustrate this information.
(b) Calculate the probability that Brian will not swim tomorrow.       **MEG**

14. Wes gives Bronwen a box of 25 mixed sweets.

12 of them have soft centres, 8 have toffee centres and 5 have hard centres.

All of the sweets have identical wrappers.

Bronwen chooses 2 sweets at random.

(a) What is the probability that Bronwen will choose 2 toffee centred sweets?

After they have eaten 3 soft centred sweets and 2 toffee centred sweets, Wes chooses 3 sweets at random from the 20 sweets that are left.

(b) What is the probability that Wes will choose a soft centred sweet, followed by a toffee centred sweet, followed by a hard centred sweet?

When there are only 10 sweets left, 3 have soft centres, 4 have toffee centres and 3 have hard centres.

Bronwen chooses two sweets at random.

(c) What is the probability that neither of the sweets will have a hard centre?       **ULEAC**

15. Alex takes a driving test. The probability that he will pass on his first attempt is 0·4. If he fails his first test then the probability that he will pass the test on any subsequent attempt is 0·7.

(a) Complete the tree diagram to show all the possible outcomes for his first two attempts.

1st
ATTEMPT

PASS

FAIL

**(b)** Calculate the probability that Alex needs two attempts, and passes on his second attempt.

**(c)** Calculate the probability that he passes the test after three or four attempts.　　　　**SEG**

16. A squirrel feeder in a garden is on the right hand branch of a tree.

    When the squirrel first runs up the tree, the probability that it will turn **right** is 0·5.

    For each time the squirrel turns **right** as it runs up the tree, the probability that it will turn **right** next time **increases** by 20%.

    For each time the squirrel turns **left** as it runs up the tree, the probability that it will turn **left** next time **decreases** by 10%.

    **(a)** Work out the probability that the squirrel will turn left on both of the first two runs up the tree.

    **(b)** Using a tree diagram, work out the probability that the squirrel will have turned right exactly twice after three runs up the tree.　　　　**NEAB**

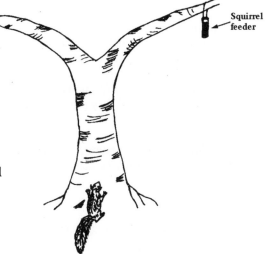

Squirrel feeder

17. Frankie has been keeping a check on the weather. She has found that
    • if it rains on one day, the probability of rain on the next day is 0·4.
    • if it is fine on one day, the probability of rain on the next day is 0·1.

    On the Thursday before the fete, it rains.
    The fete is on the Saturday.

    Use Frankie's information to find the probability that it will rain on the Saturday.　　　　**NEAB**

18. Ahmed stores three different sized bolts in a plastic 'tidy box'.

    The box is known to contain　　**6** bolts of $\frac{3}{8}$ inch size,

    　　　　　　　　　　　　　　　**3** bolts of $\frac{1}{2}$ inch size and

    　　　　　　　　　　　　　　　**1** bolt of $\frac{5}{8}$ inch size.

    In order to complete a particular job, Ahmed needs two bolts of **different sizes**.
    He randomly takes two bolts out of the box.
    Calculate the probability that Ahmed obtains two bolts **of different sizes**.　　　　**SEG**

565

**19.** Jasmin and Carl are playing a game with twenty numbered cards.

The cards are numbered from 1 to 5.

There are four cards of each number.

> Rules:
> - One player turns over two cards.
> - If both cards have the same value (e.g. two 5s), the player keeps these cards and turns over another two cards.
> - The player goes on doing this until he turns over two cards which do not have the same value.
> - These two cards are then turned face down again, and it is the other player's go.

**(i)** Jasmin goes first.
Calculate the probability that she turns over two 4s.
**(ii)** In fact, Jasmin turns over a 4 and a 2. The cards are replaced, face down. Carl remembers the positions of these cards.
He knows he can find them again if he turns over one of the other 4s or 2s.
What is the probability that Carl's first card will be *either* one of the other 4s *or* one of the other 2s?
Show your working.
**(iii)** John and Sue are playing the game. John goes first.
  **(a)** Complete the tree diagram by writing a probability in each box and some words on the dotted line.

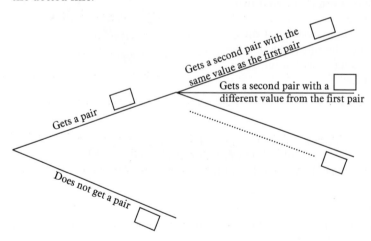

  **(b)** Use the tree diagram to calculate the probability that John gets only one pair on his first go. **NEAB**

**20.** John has 8 red socks and 6 white socks all mixed up in his sock drawer. He takes 2 socks at random from the drawer.

  **(a)** If the first sock that John takes is red, what is the probability that the second sock will also be red?
  **(b)** What is the probability that John will take 2 socks of the same colour? **ULEAC**

21. When there are no darts in the 20 sector of the darts
    board, a darts player estimates the probability of hitting
    the 20 sector as being 30%. When she hits a 20 sector with
    one of her darts, her estimate of the probability of hitting
    the 20 sector changes to 15%.

    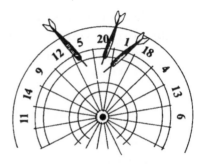

    She throws three darts one after the other.
    Calculate an estimate of the probability that she will hit a
    sector other than 20 with her first dart, the 20 sector with
    her second dart and the 20 sector with her third dart.

    ULEAC

22. Girls and boys in Form 5A can all be classified as having either dark or fair hair. The table
    shows the numbers in each group.

    | FORM 5 A | DARK HAIR | FAIR HAIR |
    |---|---|---|
    | GIRLS | 4 | 10 |
    | BOYS | 9 | 5 |

    What is the probability that
    (a) a pupil chosen at random from Form 5A
        (i) is a girl,        (ii) has fair hair,        (iii) is a boy with dark hair?
    (b) a pupil chosen at random from the *girls* in Form 5A has fair hair?
    (c) two pupils chosen at random from Form 5A both have dark hair?
    (d) three pupils chosen at random from Form 5A include at least two with fair hair?

    In Form 4A the ratio of girls to boys is 3:2. These pupils can all be classified as having either
    dark or fair hair.
    The probability of choosing at random a pupil with fair hair from the girls is $\frac{2}{3}$. The
    probability of choosing at random a pupil with fair hair from the boys is $\frac{1}{4}$.
    (e) Show that the probability of choosing at random a pupil with fair hair from Form 4A
        is $\frac{1}{2}$.

    NICCEA

23.

The letters of the word PROTRACTOR are written on ten cards, one letter on each card. The
cards are shuffled and placed face down.
(a) One card is chosen at random.

    What is the probability that the letter on the card is
    (i) T,     (ii) a vowel, (vowels are A, E, I, O, U, the rest are consonants)     (iii) M?

The card is replaced and all the cards reshuffled.

**(b)** Two cards are now chosen at random, one after the other without replacement.

What is the probability that the letters on the two cards are
**(i)** a vowel and a consonant,     **(ii)** the same as each other?

**(c)** Another word contains five vowels. As before, the letters of the word are written on cards and two cards are chosen at random without replacement from this new set.

The probability of obtaining two consonants is $\frac{1}{6}$.

**(i)** Letting $x$ equal the number of consonants in the word, form an equation involving $x$ and show that it simplifies to $x^2 - 3x - 4 = 0$.

**(ii)** Hence calculate the number of letters in the word.          **NICCEA**

1.

| | Maths. | Science |
|---|---|---|
| Public sector school | 189 | 208 |
| Independent school | 110 | 96 |

At a conference of maths. and science teachers there are teachers from public sector schools and from independent schools. This table shows the number who teach mostly maths. and the number who teach mostly science.

Find the probability that one of these teachers, chosen at random

(a) teaches mostly maths.

(b) teaches at an independent school

(c) teaches mostly science at a public sector school

(d) teaches mostly maths., given that the teacher is from an independent school.

2. To survey opinions about the school shop, a sample of 30 students was asked to complete a questionnaire. The 30 students chosen were the first 30 to be served in the school shop one day.

(a) Explain why this sample is not likely to be representative?

(b) Suggest a way of choosing a more representative sample.

3. Die A has faces numbered 1, 1, 2, 3, 4, 4. Die B has faces numbered 1, 2, 3, 4, 4, 4. One of these dice is chosen at random, then tossed.

(a) What is the probability that die A is tossed?

(b) Copy and complete this tree diagram to show the probability of getting a "4".

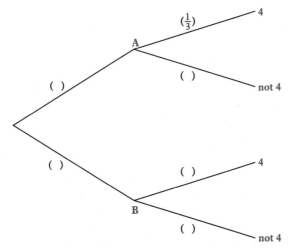

(c) Find the probability of tossing a "4".

(d) If a "4" was tossed, what is the probability that die B was tossed?

**4.**

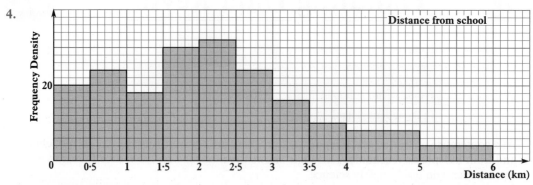

This histogram shows the distance the Year 11 students at Cranford High School live from school.

(a) Show that 10 students live less than 0·5km from school.

(b) How many students are there in Year 11 at this school?

**5.** A class is divided into groups to conduct a statistical investigation. In Jill's group there are 3 girls and 2 boys. From this group, two students are chosen at random, to report the results to the class. Draw a tree diagram to find the probability that

(a) both of these students are boys

(b) one is a boy and the other is a girl

(c) at least one is a girl.

**6.** Within a 10km radius of Amanda's home there are 5 state secondary schools. The number of students in each is given in the list.

A stratified sample of size 60 is to be chosen from these schools. How many students are chosen from each school?

| Aviemore School | 784 |
| Briarhill High School | 625 |
| Hillsborough School | 526 |
| Surden High School | 809 |
| Winthrop School | 1054 |

**7.** Of the students who are trialled for an A sports team, 30% will be successful. Those who do not gain a place in the A team are then trialled for the B team. 43% of those who trial for the B team are successful. Tim is one of the students trialled for the A team.

(a) Draw a tree diagram to show the possible outcomes for Tim.

(b) Use the tree diagram to find the probability that Tim does not get into either of the teams.

**8.** (i)

| 17 | 24 | 9 | 31 | 23 | 8 | 4 | 15 | 18 | 22 | 20 | 41 | 39 | 43 | 4 |
| 10 | 27 | 23 | 32 | 15 | 31 | 21 | 30 | 11 | 18 | 29 | 36 | 31 | 12 | 26 |
| 30 | 17 | 13 | 33 | 11 | 29 | 25 | 19 | 14 | 34 | 11 | 24 | 32 | 15 | 49 |
| 21 | 31 | 26 | 1 | 17 | 32 | 37 | 29 | 20 | 14 | 33 | 32 | 39 | 27 | 3 |
| 11 | 14 | 11 | 34 | 22 | 26 | 26 | 10 | 40 | 19 | 7 | 25 | 12 | 34 | 20 |
| 6 | 24 | 17 | 16 | 14 | 33 | 23 | 16 | 27 | 34 | 28 | 21 | 33 | 26 | 29 |
| 26 | 30 | 44 | 30 | 10 | 34 | 36 | 31 | 12 | 25 | | | | | |

Jan chose a sample of 100 novels from the library. She recorded the number of times these had been issued in the last year. Jan's data is shown above.

Jan grouped her data into the categories 0–4, 5–9, 10–14, 15–19, . . . 45–49.

(a) Write a frequency table for the data, using Jan's categories.

(b) Regroup the data into 7 class intervals, none of which has fewer than 6 data values.

(c) Draw a histogram for the regrouped data.

(ii) Explain how Jan might have chosen a representative sample of 100 novels.

9.

| Estimated length (cm) | 70– | 80– | 85– | 90– | 95– | 100– | 105– | 110– | 115– | 120–150 |
|---|---|---|---|---|---|---|---|---|---|---|
| Frequency | 2 | 2 | 3 | 4 | 3 | 4 | 2 | 2 | 3 | 3 |
| Frequency density | | | | | | | | | | |

This frequency table gives the results of an experiment in which students estimated the length of a desk. (The desk was 1 metre long!)
(a) Copy the table. Complete the frequency densities.
(b) Draw a histogram for this data.
The experiment was repeated with different students. The histogram below shows the results.
(c) Use this histogram and the histogram drawn in (b) to compare the distributions of the estimated lengths.

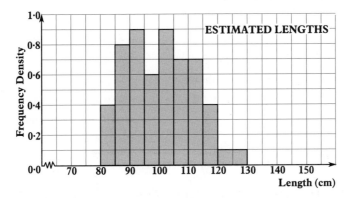

10. Atique, Ellena and Susan are going to interview students about their use of the gymnasium. They each use the school roll to choose samples of size 50. There are 554 names on the school roll.
   (a) Explain how Atique could use a random number table to choose a simple random sample of size 50.
   (b) Ellena chooses every 11th student on the roll for her sample. Susan chooses the 38 students whose surnames begin with A and the 12 students whose surnames begin with W. Who has taken a systematic sample, Ellena or Susan? Who has taken a cluster sample, Ellena or Susan?
   (c) Give a reason why Susan's sample may not be as representative as Atique's or Ellena's.

11. Tina's statistical investigation compared the sports watched on TV by 11-year-old boys and 16-year-old boys. Some of the data from Tina's survey of 16-year-old boys is shown on the table and diagram below.

| Sport | Number |
|---|---|
| Football | 76 |
| Cricket | 56 |
| Both football and cricket | 41 |
| Neither football nor cricket | 9 |

Football   Cricket
35   41   15
9

   (a) How many 16-year-old boys did Tina survey?
   (b) Use the diagram to find the probability that one of these boys, chosen at random, watched football or cricket but not both.

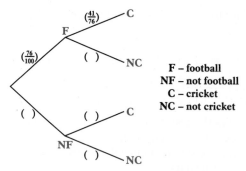

F – football
NF – not football
C – cricket
NC – not cricket

(c) The probability $\frac{76}{100}$, written on this tree diagram, shows that 76 of the 100 boys watched football.
Explain what the probability $\frac{41}{76}$ shows.

(d) Copy and complete this tree diagram.

12. The previous question showed some of the results for 16-year-old boys. This table shows some of the results for 11-year-old boys.

| Sport | Number |
|-------|--------|
| Football | 69 |
| Cricket | 27 |
| Both football and cricket | 11 |
| Neither football nor cricket | 15 |

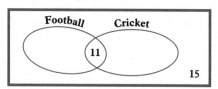

(a) Copy and complete this diagram.
(b) How many 11-year-old boys were surveyed?
(c) Find the probability that two of these 11-year-olds, chosen at random, watch both football and cricket.
(d) From the 11 and 16-year-old boys who watch football, two boys are chosen at random.
Show that the probability that just one of these boys watches cricket is $2 \times \frac{52}{145} \times \frac{93}{144}$.

13. (i) The time it took the students in Andrew's class to complete a maths. test is shown in the table.

| Time (minutes) | $15 \leq t < 18$ | $18 \leq t < 21$ | $21 \leq t < 24$ | $24 \leq t < 27$ | $27 \leq t < 30$ | $30 \leq t < 40$ |
|----------------|------|------|------|------|------|------|
| Number of students | 2 | 3 | 5 | 8 | 3 | 2 |

(a) What is the mid-point of the interval $15 \leq t < 18$?
(b) What is the mid-point of the interval $30 \leq t < 40$?
(c) Calculate approximate values for the mean and standard deviation.

(ii) Jason's class also sat this test. The times for the students in this class had mean 26·8 and standard deviation 3·6.
(a) What does the difference in means tell you?
(b) What does the difference in the standard deviations tell you?

14. Robbie tossed two dice together 36 times. The list gives the totals.

| 2 | 5 | 7 | 6 | 12 | 9 | 11 | 8 | 7 | 3 | 8 | 11 |
| 7 | 8 | 4 | 12 | 6 | 2 | 3 | 9 | 6 | 5 | 12 | 7 |
| 9 | 5 | 2 | 4 | 10 | 10 | 8 | 11 | 2 | 5 | 4 | 12 |

(a) Calculate the mean and standard deviation of Robbie's totals.

(b) When two dice are tossed, a total of 6 can be obtained in five ways: 3 and 3 or 4 and 2 or 2 and 4 or 5 and 1 or 1 and 5.

Hence $P(6) = \frac{1}{6} \times \frac{1}{6} + \frac{1}{6} \times \frac{1}{6} + \frac{1}{6} \times \frac{1}{6} + \frac{1}{6} \times \frac{1}{6} + \frac{1}{6} \times \frac{1}{6}$
$= \frac{5}{36}$

Out of 36 tosses we expect to get a total of 6 on $36 \times \frac{5}{36} = 5$ occasions.
Copy and complete the following table for the number of times we expect to get totals of $2, 3, 4, \ldots 12$.

| Total | 2 | 3 | 4 | 5 | 6 | 7 | 8 | 9 | 10 | 11 | 12 |
|---|---|---|---|---|---|---|---|---|---|---|---|
| Frequency | | | | | 5 | | | | | | |

Calculate the mean expected total and the standard deviation of this total.

(c) Use the means and standard deviations to compare Robbie's distribution with the expected distribution. Comment.

15. The probability that Robyn wins the rally for service and begins serving in a tennis match is 0·6. If she begins serving, the probability that she wins the first game is 0·7. The probability that Robyn wins the first game if she does not begin serving is 0·5.
Calculate the probability that Robyn loses the first game of her next tennis match.

16. The probability that a woman passes her driving test at the first attempt is $\frac{3}{4}$ whereas the probability that a man passes at the first attempt is $\frac{3}{5}$. On the second attempt these probabilities increase to: woman $\frac{7}{8}$, man $\frac{3}{4}$.

(a) Copy and complete this tree diagram for women.

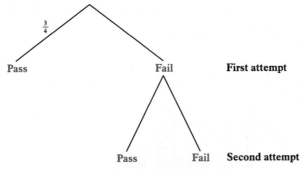

(b) Find the probability that a woman, chosen at random, needs more than two attempts to pass her driving test.

(c) Of 100 men, how many do you expect to need no more than two attempts to pass their driving test?

(d) Both Linda and Steven are learning to drive. Find the probability that just one of them passes the driving test at the first attempt.

17. A survey at a service station finds that the probability of a car needing oil is 0·1, the probability of a car needing water is 0·06 and the probability of a car needing both oil and water is 0·02. Calculate the probability that the next car to stop at this service station needs water or oil.

18. Jeanette gathered data on the number of runs the players in her school cricket team made in their matches during one season. She organised this data onto the table.

| Runs made | 0–9 | 10–19 | 20–29 | 30–39 | 40–49 | 50–59 | 60–69 | 70–79 | 80–99 |
|---|---|---|---|---|---|---|---|---|---|
| Frequency | 11 | 44 | 52 | 38 | 25 | 6 | 7 | 5 | 2 |
| Mid-point of class interval | 4·5 | | | | | | | | |

   (a) Copy and complete the table.
   (b) Calculate the mean and standard deviation of this data.
   (c) Draw a histogram for this data.

19. In container A there are 7 black and 3 red counters. In container B there are 5 black, 3 red and 2 white counters. In container C there are 3 black, 3 red and 4 white counters. Tracey chooses a container at random then chooses, at random, one of the counters from that container.
   (a) Find the probability that Tracey chooses a red counter.
   (b) Given that Tracey chose a white counter, what is the probability that she chose container A?
   (c) Brian chooses two counters, without replacement, from container B. Find the probability that Brian chooses just one red counter.

20.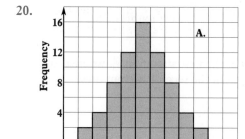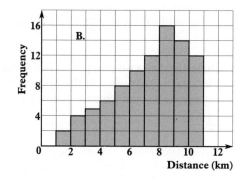

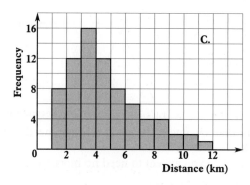

   Which of these distributions  (a) has the greatest mean
                                  (b) has the smallest standard deviation?

21.

P A V E A A K

In a game of scrabble, these tiles are left. Colin chooses two of them, one after the other.
(i) Find the probability that the tiles Colin chooses have a total of
    (a) 4      (b) more than 4    (c) 3.
(ii) Find the probability that  (a) the first tile chosen is an A
                           (b) the second tile chosen is an A
                           (c) both tiles chosen are A
                           (d) an A and an E are chosen
                           (e) the second tile chosen is A, given that the first tile chosen
                               is E.

22.    A is the set of data  11, 12, 14, 15, 16, 19, 25.
      B is the set of data  1, 2, 4, 5, 6, 9, 15.
      C is the set of data  2, 4, 8, 10, 12, 18, 30.
(a) Explain why the mean of A is 10 more than the mean of B.
(b) Explain why A and B have the same standard deviation.
(c) What is the relationship between the standard deviation of B and the standard deviation of C?
(d) What is the relationship between the mean of B and the mean of C?
(e) Write down a set of data which has the same mean as B but twice the standard deviation.

23. Laurie is designing a survey to find out about people who use a superstore near her home.

One of the things Laurie wants to find out is how far people have travelled to get to the superstore.

(a) Decide which question below is best to ask. Give **two** reasons for your decision.

    [A] How far have you travelled to get here today?
    [B] Where do you live?
    [C] Do you live far from here?
    [D] Please show me on this map where you have travelled from.

Laurie decides to do her survey one Friday evening outside the superstore.
(b) Give **one** reason why this would give a biased sample.        **ULEAC**

24. A box contains 10 discs. 4 of the discs are green and 6 are red.
2 discs are removed at random from the box.
By drawing a diagram, or otherwise,
(i) find the probability that both discs will be red
(ii) find the probability that the discs will be one of each colour.      **ULEAC**

25. The marks obtained by 10 pupils in an English Language GCSE examination were as follows:    73, 70, 62, 67, 69, 76, 55, 65, 61, 82
(a) Calculate the standard deviation of these marks.

All the ten pupils had their marks increased by 3 for good spelling.
(b) Write down for the **new** set of marks
    (i) the mean         (ii) the standard deviation        **ULEAC**

26. In a survey on October 1st, pupils present at Bank school were asked how long they had taken to go from home to school that morning. Each pupil present ticked one and only one of the following responses:

| | |
|---|---|
| 0 minutes up to but not including 5 minutes | |
| 5 minutes up to but not including 15 minutes | |
| 15 minutes up to but not including 25 minutes | |
| 25 minutes up to but not including 40 minutes | |
| 40 minutes up to but not including 70 minutes | |
| 70 minutes and over | |

**Exactly** 96 pupils ticked the "5 minutes up to but not including 15 minutes" response.
No pupil ticked the "70 minutes and over" response.
The histogram shows the result of the survey.

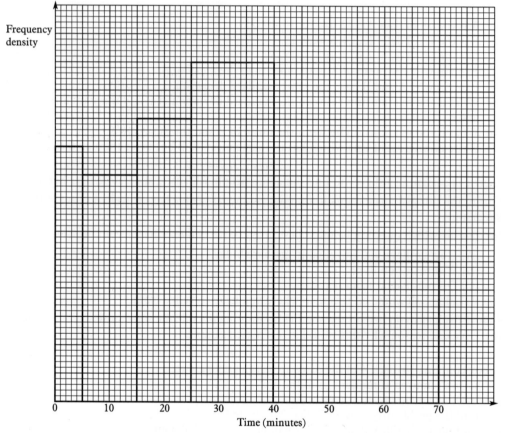

Calculate the number of pupils who were absent on October 1st given that the total number of pupils at the school is 726.

ULEAC

27. There are 15 tracks on a compact disc. The tracks are numbered from 1 to 15. The shuffle program on a compact disc player plays the tracks in random order. Each track is equally likely to be chosen; each track is played once only.
    (a) Calculate the probability that the first two tracks played will both be even numbered tracks.

**(b)** Calculate the probability that the first two tracks played will be an odd numbered and an even numbered track in either order. **ULEAC**

28. Sanjay has four possible ways home from school.
    From school he takes either a bus or a train.
    The probability that he will go by train is $\frac{3}{5}$.

    If he goes by train, he completes the journey by walking or by getting a lift.
    The probability that he gets a lift is $\frac{1}{5}$.

    If he catches the bus, the second part of his journey can be completed by catching another bus or he can walk.
    The probability that he will walk is $\frac{7}{8}$.

    What is the probability that Sanjay
    **(a)** catches a bus from school and then walks?
    **(b)** walks for part of his journey home? **NEAB**

29. There are three secondary schools in a large town.
    The number of pupils in each school is given in the table.

    | Albert High School | 570 |
    |---|---|
    | St Joseph's High School | 965 |
    | London Road School | 1015 |

    A researcher wishes to find out what secondary school pupils feel about the standard of education in the town.
    She chooses a representative sample of total size 50.
    How many pupils should be chosen from each school? **ULEAC**

30. Ann weighed 21 individual biscuits from a 300g packet.
    For this packet of biscuits:
    the sum of the individual weights of the biscuits $= 312$g
    the sum of the squares of these weights $= 4636$g$^2$
    Calculate the standard deviation of the weights.
    You should work to as many decimal places as your calculator will allow. **NEAB**

31. The probability that Simon passes his driving test at the first attempt has been estimated to be about $\frac{1}{3}$.
    If a test is failed, the probability of passing at the next attempt is $\frac{7}{12}$.
    Calculate the probability that Simon passes his driving test at his third attempt. **SEG**

**32.** Last year, Geraint carried out a survey of the weather in which he noted the number of hours of sunshine each day. His results for the month of June are summarised in the following grouped frequency distribution.

| Hours of sunshine, $h$ | Number of days | Frequency density |
|---|---|---|
| $0 \leq h < 4$ | 4 | |
| $4 \leq h < 6$ | 6 | |
| $6 \leq h < 8$ | 7 | |
| $8 \leq h < 9$ | 4 | |
| $9 \leq h < 11$ | 6 | |
| $11 \leq h < 13$ | 2 | |
| $13 \leq h < 17$ | 1 | |

(a) Complete the above table.

(b) Draw a histogram to illustrate the above distribution.

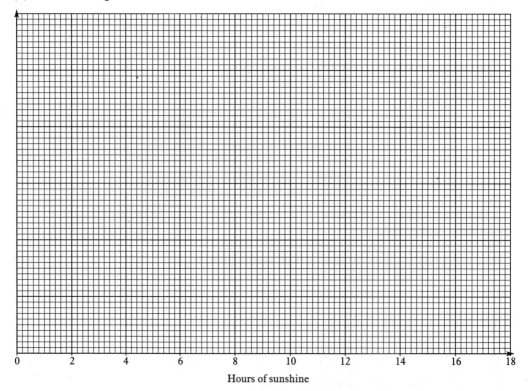

Hours of sunshine

(c) Geraint uses his data to calculate the mean and standard deviation of the number of hours of sunshine per day for the month of June. He compares these values with his corresponding values for May. His results are shown below.

| Hours of sunshine per day | May | June |
|---|---|---|
| Mean (hours) | 9·2 | 7·3 |
| Standard deviation (hours) | 1·2 | 3·1 |

By comparing the values for the mean and standard deviation of the number of hours of sunshine per day for May with the values for June, describe **two** ways in which the number of hours of sunshine per day in May was different from that in June.          **WJEC**

**33.** Boris and John play three sets of tennis.
The probability of Boris winning the first set is 0·4.
If Boris wins a set the probability of his winning the next set is 0·7.
If John wins a set the probability of his winning the next set is 0·8.

(a) Complete the tree diagram to show all the possible outcomes of winning.
Label each branch with its probability.

1st set

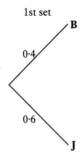

(b) Calculate the probability that John wins all **three** sets.
(c) Calculate the probability that Boris wins **at least** two sets.          **SEG**

**34.** Flyway Tours decide to conduct a survey of last year's customers to obtain information on what customers thought about their holidays.

A representative sample of 10% of the customers is to be used for the survey.

Questionnaires will be sent out to last year's customers, 60% of which were male and 40% female.

(a) Explain why it would be wrong to use a 10% random sample taken from all customers who booked a holiday last year.

(b) Describe a better way of obtaining a representative sample of 10% of customers.          **SEG**

**35.** A bag contains two black discs and three white discs.
Three children play a game in which each draws a disc from the bag.
Parveen goes first, then Seema, and Jane is last.
Each time a disc is withdrawn it is not replaced.
The first child to draw a white disc wins the game.

(a) In a game, calculate the probability that
   (i) Parveen wins,          (ii) Seema wins.

They replace the discs and play the game a second time.

(b) Calculate the probability that
   (i) Parveen wins neither the first nor the second game.
   (ii) Jane wins both games.          **NEAB**

**36. (a)** The cumulative frequency graphs show the distribution of workers in the Boot, Shoe and Clog industry in 1937:

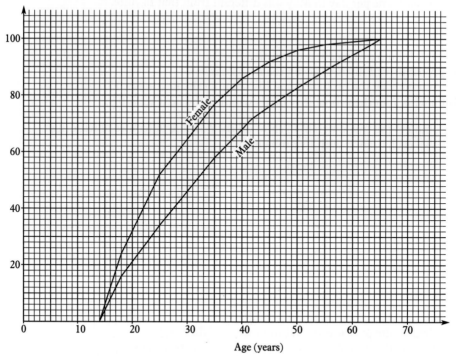

Age (years)

Find the median ages of    **(i)** females,
                        **(ii)** males.

The table shows the percentage frequencies for the same data:

| Age | % Female | % Male |
|-----|----------|--------|
| 14 – | 11·0 | 7·2 |
| 16 – | 13·2 | 8·7 |
| 18 – | 11·7 | 7·8 |
| 21 – | 15·4 | 10·7 |
| 25 – | 13·7 | 11·4 |
| 30 – | 12·3 | 12·2 |
| 35 – | 8·5 | 9·6 |
| 40 – | 5·9 | 7·8 |
| 45 – | 4·2 | 7·0 |
| 50 – | 2·3 | 6·7 |
| 55 – | 1·2 | 5·6 |
| 60 – | 0·6 | 5·3 |
| 65+ | 0·0 | 0·0 |

For males the mean age = 33·9 years and the standard deviation = 14·2 years.

**(b)** Calculate estimates of the mean and standard deviation of the ages of females.

$$\left[\text{Standard deviation} = \sqrt{\frac{1}{n}\Sigma fx^2 - m^2} \quad \text{where } m = \text{mean}\right]$$

**(c)** Using all the information, compare the female and male distributions.

(d) Re-group these data for females with classes:

14 –
21 –
40 –
60 –
65 +

Draw a histogram, on graph paper, to represent this distribution.      **MEG**

37. A street contains 36 houses.
    (a) The income earned in each house is as follows

| House Number | £ | House Number | £ | House Number | £ |
|---|---|---|---|---|---|
| 1 | 10 400 | 13 | 4250 | 25 | 6200 |
| 2 | 11 500 | 14 | 19 700 | 26 | 9800 |
| 3 | 11 200 | 15 | 5750 | 27 | 8700 |
| 4 | 5750 | 16 | 47 500 | 28 | 9300 |
| 5 | 4250 | 17 | 75 600 | 29 | 12 700 |
| 6 | 32 500 | 18 | 77 500 | 30 | 6800 |
| 7 | 17 500 | 19 | 47 500 | 31 | 8500 |
| 8 | 20 400 | 20 | 79 400 | 32 | 4200 |
| 9 | 16 540 | 21 | 28 500 | 33 | 4200 |
| 10 | 36 500 | 22 | 67 500 | 34 | 5200 |
| 11 | 4250 | 23 | 48 500 | 35 | 5800 |
| 12 | 4750 | 24 | 36 200 | 36 | 10 900 |

Houses numbered 1–15 belong to a Housing Association.
Houses numbered 16–24 belong to a Private Development of large houses.
Houses numbered 25–36 are Sheltered Housing for old age pensioners.
A sample of 12 houses is chosen to estimate the mean income, per house, for the whole street.
The sample is chosen by selecting the first four in each column.

(i) Why is this sample of 12 not suitable?

(ii) Fill in this table to show how many houses, from each type of housing, you require for a stratified sample of 12.

| Type of Housing | Number Required |
|---|---|
| Housing Association | |
| Private Development | |
| Sheltered Housing | |

(b) (i) The incomes for the houses in the Private Development are as follows
47 500, 75 600, 77 500, 47 500, 79 400, 28 500, 67 500, 48 500 and 36 200.

Calculate the standard deviation of these incomes.

**(ii)** These numbers are the values of the other standard deviations.
2602, 9910 and 22 735.

Use these figures to complete this table.

|  | Standard deviation |
|---|---|
| **Whole street** |  |
| **Housing Association** |  |
| **Sheltered Housing** |  |

**(iii)** Explain how you arrived at your answer to part **(ii)**. **SEG**

38. Joe devises a stall for his school's summer fair.

## LUCKY MONEY DIP
## 10p A GO

Each barrel contains some boxes.

In each box is a single coin.

You take one box from each barrel and win the total amount of money in the boxes.

The boxes containing the money are replaced after each turn.

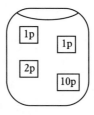

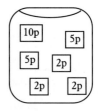

**(i)** Collette has a go. She takes out a box from each barrel.

The probability that she gets a total of 3p is $\frac{1}{4}$.

The probability that she gets a total of 4p is $\frac{1}{8}$.

What is the probability that she gets a total of less than 5p?

**(ii) (a)** Complete this tree diagram to show all the possible outcomes.
Write the correct probability on each branch of the tree.

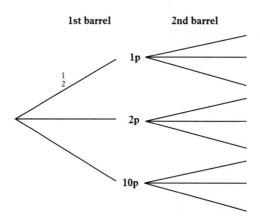

**(b)** What is the probability that she will take out 15p?

**(c)** What is the probability that she will take out at least 10p?

**(iii)** Joe decides he will make more money on the stall if he puts all the boxes into one barrel and the players draw two boxes from this barrel.

**(a)** Collette plays this new game.
What is the probability that she will take out exactly 15p?

**(b)** What is the probability that she will take out at least 10p?

**(c)** Is Joe likely to make more money with the new game than the old?
Explain your reasoning.

**(iv)** In the new game, what is the probability of taking out two boxes containing the same value coins?

**(v)** Joe has collected about 500 coins to be sure of having enough change to give to his customers.
He has a mixture of 1p, 2p, 5p and 10p coins.
He puts all the coins in a bag and takes out a handful.
This is what he gets.

He is worried because there are no 5p coins in this sample.

**(a)** Is he right to be worried?
Explain your answer.

**(b)** Describe a method of sampling the coins in the bag that will give him a reasonable estimate of the numbers of each value coin that he has.

**NEAB**

# ANSWERS

# ANSWERS

## Number Revision

**Revision Exercise**

1. £1465   2. (a) $2^4 \times 5$  (b) 16   3. (a) £5600  (b) 5%  4. (a) $-6$  (b) 8  (c) $-11$  (d) 15  (e) $-6$  (f) $-24$  (g) $-8$
(h) $-46$  (i) 2   5. 44   6. 2·7m   7. (a) $1·58 \times 10^1$  (b) $8·0 \times 10^0$  (c) $4·1 \times 10^{-4}$  (d) $3·4859 \times 10^8$   8. Aaron
9. (a) 5 : 1  (b) 9 : 28   10. (ii) (a) 160 (2 s.f.)  (b) 2800 (2 s.f.)  (c) 3·3 (2 s.f.)  (d) 1·4 (2 s.f)   11. (a) Belinda won,
Carmen lost  (b) 75   12. (i) (a) $\frac{3}{25}$  (b) $\frac{3}{100}$  (c) $\frac{1}{2}$  (ii) (a) 42·5%  (b) 0·23%  (c) 20%  (iii) (a) 0·003
(b) 0·5  (c) 3·1875   13. 21000m   14. (a) $\frac{3}{20}$  (b) 9  (c) 6  (d) $\frac{4}{5}$  (e) $1\frac{4}{5}$  (f) $\frac{1}{9}$  (g) $6\frac{1}{3}$  (h) $\frac{7}{20}$  (i) $2\frac{5}{6}$
(j) $1\frac{1}{18}$  (k) $8\frac{7}{9}$   15. (a) $2·58 \times 10^9$  (b) $2·06 \times 10^6$  (c) $4·74 \times 10^4$   16. (a) 48% (2 s.f.)  (b) 2·3% (2 s.f.)
(c) 1935 and 1945  (d) 1931 and 1935   17. (a) $1·68 \times 10^{18}$  (b) $1·07 \times 10^2$  (c) 0·04   18. 5209   19. (a) 9
(b) 8·6   20. 3; $3\frac{3}{4}$ cups   21. $4\frac{11}{40}$   22. Option 2   23. (a) 6  (b) B: $\frac{2}{5}$, A: $1\frac{1}{5}$   24. 11   25. (a) 1·2 and $\frac{4}{5}$
(b) 0·4 and $\frac{5}{8}$   26. (a) (i) 5m  (ii) 16cm  (b) about 8 feet   27. (a) 45p  (b) $\frac{1}{30}$   28. £53·14
29. (a) h $= 8·0 \times 10^2$mm, $l = 2·0 \times 10^3$mm  (b) $2·01 \times 10^9$mm³   30. 60%   31. £106 to £110   32. (a) $1·47 \times 10^8$
(b) $2·1 \times 10^3$  (c) £$7·0 \times 10^4$   33. (a) 28·9%  (b) £7·99   34. (a) 97·5cm³  (b) A $\approx 6^2 + 6\sqrt{4 \times 5^2 - 6^2}$  which
gives A $\approx$ 84cm²   35. 3·63 and 6·17   36. (a) $9·4608 \times 10^{12}$km  (b) 4·2 light years (2 s.f.)  (e) $1·875 \times 10^5$
miles per second   37. $3·96 \times 10^8$   38. (a) 22 minutes  (b) 9.32am  (c) (i) £13  (ii) a possible keying
sequence is  $\boxed{5}\boxed{\times}\boxed{(}\boxed{26}\boxed{\text{SHIFT}}\boxed{x^2}\boxed{\div}\boxed{100}\boxed{)}\boxed{\sqrt{}}\boxed{=}$   39. (i) 7000  (ii) (a) $1·4 \times 10^7$  (b) £41·67 to the
nearest penny   40. (a) $100p + 10q + r$  (b) The expression simplifies to 99 (p – r) which is divisible by 11
41. 57 and 117

## Chapter 1   Approximation. Accuracy. Errors

**Exercise 1:2**

1. 27·3m is correct to the nearest tenth of a metre; 27·30m is correct to the nearest hundredth of a metre   2. C
3. B   4. C   5. (a) 1·45kg  (b) 1·35kg   6. (a) 50·725seconds  (b) $50·725 \text{ sec} \leq t < 50·735$ sec   7. (a) 260g
(b) 240g   8. between 45·55°C and 45·65°C   9. $46·8 \pm 0·05$cm   10. (a) 25·05cm  (b) 24·95cm
(c) $2·85\text{cm} \leq w < 2·95$cm   11. C   12. lower bound = 1015m$l$, upper bound = 1025m$l$
13. (a) greatest number = 262449, least number = 262350  (b) upper bound = 262405, lower bound = 262395
14. (a) $90·5\text{m} \leq l < 91·5$m  (b) upper bound = 55·5m, lower bound = 54·5m   15. upper bound = 42·75m,
lower bound = 42·25m   **Review 1** (a) upper bound = 1·2345m, lower bound = 1·2335m  (b) C
(c) $1·705\text{m} \leq \text{Height} < 1·715$m  (d) between 0·355kg and 0·365kg   **Review 2** $28·595\text{g} \leq m < 28·605$g
**Review 3** 26·5 min. $\leq t < 27·5$ min.

**Exercise 1:5**

1. 650mm   2. (a) 18·4m  (b) 18·0m  (c) $18·815\text{m}^2 \leq \text{area} \leq 19·71\text{m}^2$   3. (a) upper bound = 6905m², lower
bound = 6895m²  (b) 100·5m  (c) 68·6m (3 s.f.)   4. (a) length = 38mm, breadth = 17mm
(b) upper bound = 673·75mm², lower bound = 618·75mm²  (c) lower bound = 108mm, upper bound = 112mm
5. to 4 s.f., $2·560 \leq r < 2·561$   6. (a) $6·825\text{cm}^2 \leq \text{area} < 7·585\text{cm}^2$  (b) 62·1cm³ (3 s.f.)
7. (a) maximum value = 1·77 (3 s.f.), minimum value = 1·70 (3 s.f.)  (b) to 3 s.f., $11·1 \leq p < 11·8$
8. (a) 47·4 (3 s.f.)  (b) 44   9. 3·66cm (3 s.f.)   10. (i) 9·95  (ii) (a) upper bound = 53, lower bound = 51
(b) upper bound = 15·55, lower bound = 14  (c) upper bound = 28·5, lower bound = 25·5
(d) upper bound = 267·75, lower bound = 243·775  (e) upper bound = 3·47 (3 s.f.), lower bound = 3·19 (3 s.f.)
(f) upper bound = 342·25, lower bound = 306·25  (g) upper bound = 4·42 (3 s.f.), lower bound = 4
(h) upper bound = 1·68 (3 s.f.), lower bound = 1·39 (3 s.f.)   **Review 1** (a) $10·965\text{m} \leq w < 10·975$m
(b) 260·93m² (5 s.f.)   **Review 2** (i) (a) $8·15\text{cm} \leq r < 8·25$cm  (b) to 4 s.f., $2268\text{cm}^3 \leq V < 2352\text{cm}^3$
(ii) greatest value = 5·00cm (3 s.f.), least value = 4·97cm (3 s.f.)   **Review 3** (a) 7

## Answers

### Exercise 1:6

1. (a) greatest area = 4415·25m², least area = 4271·25m² (b) 4000m²   2. (a) upper bound = 17·65cm², lower bound = 17·55cm² (b) upper bound = 6·15cm, lower bound = 6·05cm
(c) 5·71cm ≤ length of base < 5·83cm (2 d.p.) (d) 1 since 5·71 and 5·83 only agree to 1 s.f. To 1 s.f. base = 6cm
3. (a) greatest value = 162·5m², least value = 161·5m² (b) upper bound = 9·05m, lower bound = 8·95m
(c) 18m (2 s.f.)   4. (a) 17·75cm ≤ P < 17·85m (b) 2·8cm (2 s.f.)   5. 120cm (3 s.f.)   6. 6·5mm (2 s.f.)
Review (a) greatest time = 12·35 sec., least time = 12·25 sec. (b) 8m/sec (1 s.f.)

### Exercise 1:7

1. (a) 0·05kg (b) 2·1% (1 d.p.)   2. (a) 0·5m*l* (b) 1·8% (1 d.p.)   3. (a) 0·03% (1 s.f.)   4. 0·1% (1 d.p.)
5. 0·2% (1 d.p.)   6. 50·6% (1 d.p.)   7. 2·9% (1 d.p.)   8. (a) greatest speed = 29·00m/s (4 s.f.),
least speed = 28·76m/s (4 s.f.) (b) 0·42% (2 d.p.)   9. (a) maximum area = 63·2cm² (3 s.f.),
minimum area = 61·6cm² (3 s.f.) (b) 1·30%   10. (a) 0·3431 ohms (4 s.f.) (b) 0·3448 ohms (4 s.f.)
(c) 0·26% (2 d.p.)   Review 1 0·3% (1 d.p.)   Review 2 (a) 3033cm³ (4 s.f.) (b) 4052cm³ (4 s.f.) (c) 25% (2 s.f.)
Review 3 (a) 0·45 hour ≤ time < 0·55 hour. (b) 39·5mph ≤ speed < 40·5mph (c) 12·5% (1 d.p.)

### Chapter 1 Review

1. (a) 29·5cm (b) maximum length = 18·45cm, minimum length = 18·35cm   2. Anita's handspan is between
15·5cm and 16·5cm. Julie's handspan is between 15·75cm and 15·85cm. Yes it is possible.   3. 9·9 is given to
1 d.p. while 9·90 is given to 2 d.p. A measurement given as 9·9 could be between 9·85 and 9·95 while a
measurement given as 9·90 could be between 9·895 and 9·905. The measurement 9·90 has a much smaller range
of possible values than the measurement 9·9.   4. (a) 2·4735kg (b) upper bound = 1·62805kg, lower bound = 1·62795kg
5. (a) upper bound = 2·65cm, lower bound = 2·55cm (b) the upper and lower bounds are not the same as for
the bolt. The gauge measures diameters between 2·5cm and 2·7cm (c) 2·6 ± 0·05cm
(d) upper bound = 2·605cm, lower bound = 2·595cm   6. 9·37m/s (2 d.p.)   7. (a) The 3m tape. Any error with
the 15cm tape could be compounded 80 times (12m ÷ 15cm = 80) whereas any error with the 3m tape could be
compounded just 4 times (12m ÷ 3m = 4). (b) (i) 50·5cm (ii) 14·5cm (iii) 36cm. This gives the greatest
possible remaining length.   8. maximum current = 2·96 amps, minimum current = 2·50 amps
9. lower bound = 49·5kg, upper bound = 50·5kg   10. (a) 11·5mm ≤ length < 12·5mm
(b) 74·75mm² ≤ area < 93·75mm² (c) 10   11. (a) £625 (b) £0   12. (a) lower bound = 15·94m²
(b) The maximum possible volume = 70·66m³ (4 s.f.). Hence the volume could exceed 70 cubic metres.
13. 4·98cm ≤ r < 5·03cm (3 s.f.)   14. No. Upper bound of weight = 25 × 25·5 + 120 × 3·005kg = 998·1kg
15. (a) 68·25 seconds (b) 68·20 seconds implies Damian's time was between 68·195 and 68·205 seconds when it
is in fact between 68·15 and 68·25 seconds. (c) maximum speed = 5·87m/s (2 d.p.),
minimum speed = 5·86m/s (2 d.p.) (d) 57·0 seconds   16. (a) 17·15 metres (b) (i) 3·25km (ii) 0·3km²
17. maximum a = 2·89m/s² (2 d.p.), minimum a = 2·67 m/s² (2 d.p.)   18. 1362m ≤ s < 1698m (4 s.f.)
19. (a) 176·5 metres ≤ length < 178·3 metres (4 s.f.) (b) 2   20. (a) 3·65cm (b) greatest perimeter = 15cm,
least perimeter = 14·6cm (c) (i) 2 (ii) 15 and 14·6 agree to 2 s.f. since to 2 s.f. 14·6 is 15. (d) No. The
perimeter could be between 29·2cm and 30cm. These figures agree to only 1 s.f.   21. (a) (i) 815 (ii) 805
(b) (i) 2·935 (ii) 2·925 (c) (i) 278·63248 (ii) 274·27598 (d) 300   22. (a) (i) 292·5 miles (ii) 192·5 miles
(b) 24·7% (1 d.p.)

## Chapter 2  Proportion

### Exercise 2:2

1. (a) If C ∝ N, then C = kN (b) k = 4·5 (c) C = 4·5N (d) £85·50 (e) 34
2. (a) k = 6

| x | 3 | 5 | 9 | 20 |
|---|---|---|---|---|
| y | 18 | 30 | 54 | 120 |

(b) k = 3·5

| x | 2 | 10 | 16 | 35 |
|---|---|---|---|---|
| y | 7 | 35 | 56 | 122·5 |

(c) k = 0·4

| x | 1 | 3 | 5 | 7 |
|---|---|---|---|---|
| y | 0·4 | 1·2 | 2 | 2·8 |

3. (a) m ∝ g (b) m = 0·4g (c) 4·8mm (d) 17·5km   4. (a) s = kr (b) s = 2·4r (c) 288m (d) 50
5. (a) e = 2·5m (b) 1·6kg   6. (a) a = 0·12F (b) 37·5 Newton (c) 24m/sec²   7. e, since this is the only
straight-line graph with equation y = mx.   8. If u = 0, v is proportional to t. The equation then becomes
v = at, where a is a constant.   Review 1 (a) s ∝ t (b) s = kt (c) s = 80t (d) s = 180km (e) 3½ hours
Review 2 (a) C = kW (b) £16·20

*Answers*

**Page 49**

### Exercise 2:3

1. (a) $A = kl^2$ (b) $V = kr^3$ (c) $P = kn$ (d) $A = kl^2$ (e) $T = k\sqrt{l}$ (f) $r = kv^2$  2. (a) $k = 0.5$
(b) $a = 0.5n^2$ (c)

| n | 2 | 4 | 5 | 8 | 20 |
|---|---|---|---|---|----|
| a | 2 | 8 | 12.5 | 32 | 200 |

3. 125g  4. 14m/sec (2 s.f.)  5. (a) $m = kl^3$
(b) $k = 3.2$ (c) 1600g (2 s.f.)  6. (a) $32ml$ (b) 6cm (1 s.f.)
7. (b) 30.4 (1 d.p.) (c) 4.9 (1 d.p.)  8. 3.2 seconds (1 d.p.)

Review 1 (a) $E = ke^2$ (b) 20 (c) 80 joules  Review 2 (a) 250 (b) 15  Review 3 4.2 amps

**Page 54**

### Exercise 2:7

1. (a) $m = \frac{k}{n}$ (b) $x = \frac{k}{y^2}$ (c) $b = \frac{k}{d^2}$ (d) $l = \frac{k}{P}$ (e) $T = \frac{k}{\sqrt{u}}$ (f) $a = \frac{k}{h^3}$  2. (a) $h = \frac{k}{T}$ (b) 40
(c) 16cm  3. 1.29m (3 s.f.)  4. (a) $y = \frac{k}{x^2}$ (b) 2 (c) 0.5  5. 0.125 ohms  6. (a) 25.5 units (1 d.p.)
(b) 18mm (to the nearest mm)  7. (a) $7.84 \times 10^5$ cycles per second (3 s.f.) (b) 486m (to the nearest metre)
8. 125N/m²  Review 1

| m | 0.5 | 2 | 5 | 10 | 20 |
|---|-----|---|---|----|----|
| n | 100 | 25 | 10 | 5 | 2.5 |

Review 2 8 units

**Page 59**

### Chapter 2 Review

1. (a) $C = 7.5Z$ (b) (i) £30 (ii) £22.50  2. (a) $d = kt^2$ (b) 5 (c) 80 metres (d) 10 seconds  3. $T = 0.2\sqrt{L}$
4. (a) $y = \frac{80}{x^2}$ (b) 3.2  5. (a) 31250 (b) 7812 (c) $d = \sqrt{\frac{k}{N}}$ (d) 3.95cm (2 d.p.)  6. (i) b (ii) c (iii) e (iv) d
7. (a) y varies directly as $l$ and inversely as the square of t. (b) 0.8

## Chapter 3 Rational and Irrational Numbers

**Page 62**

### Exercise 3:3

1. a, d, e, f  2. b, e, g  3. (a) irrational (b) irrational (c) rational, $\frac{2}{5}$ (d) irrational (e) rational, $\frac{49}{50}$
(f) rational, $\frac{2}{45}$ (g) rational, $\frac{125}{99}$  4. (a) $\frac{9}{25}$ (b) $\frac{2}{5}$ (c) irrational (d) $\frac{7}{2}$ (e) $\frac{7}{9}$ (f) $\frac{34}{999}$ (g) irrational
(h) $\frac{23}{90}$ (i) $\frac{169}{495}$ (j) irrational (k) irrational (l) $\frac{259}{99}$  5. Possible answers are: (a) $\frac{3}{4} = 0.75$
(b) not possible (c) $\frac{1}{3} = 0.\dot{3}$ (d) $\sqrt{2}$ (e) $\frac{7}{55} = 0.12\dot{7}$  Review 1 (a) rational (b) irrational (c) rational
(d) rational (e) irrational (f) rational (g) irrational  Review 2 Possible answers are: (a) 3.6, $3\frac{5}{8}$, 3.92
(b) π, $\sqrt{10}$, $\sqrt{12.78}$  Review 3 (a) $\frac{4}{75}$ (b) $\frac{169}{330}$ (c) $\frac{13093}{9999}$ (d) $\frac{8}{33}$

**Page 66**

### Exercise 3:7

1. (a) $\frac{\sqrt{2}}{2}$ (b) $2\sqrt{3}$ (c) $\sqrt{5}$ (d) $\frac{\sqrt{6}}{3}$ (e) $\frac{2\sqrt{3}}{3} - \frac{\sqrt{6}}{3}$ (f) $1 + \frac{\sqrt{6}}{3}$  2. (a) $3\sqrt{2}$ (b) $2\sqrt{3}$ (c) $5\sqrt{3}$
(d) $6\sqrt{2}$ (e) $6\sqrt{2}$ (f) $15\sqrt{3}$  3. (a) 6 (b) 9 (c) $2\sqrt{10}$ (d) $16\sqrt{3}$ (e) $6\sqrt{6}$ (f) $24\sqrt{3}$ (g) $75\sqrt{15}$
4. (a) $5\sqrt{5}$ (b) $2\sqrt{2}$ (c) $4\sqrt{3}$ (d) $-\sqrt{2}$ (e) $8\sqrt{3}$ (f) 0 (g) $2\sqrt{2}$  5. (a) $11 + 6\sqrt{2}$ (b) $6 - 2\sqrt{5}$
(c) $5 + 2\sqrt{6}$ (d) $5 - 2\sqrt{6}$ (e) $1 - 2\sqrt{2}$ (f) $4 - \sqrt{6} + \sqrt{3} - 4\sqrt{2}$ (g) 2  6. (a) $\frac{11\sqrt{3}}{3}$ (b) $\frac{7\sqrt{2}}{2}$ (c) $\frac{13\sqrt{3}}{6}$
(d) $\frac{12\sqrt{5}}{5}$  Review 1 (a) $2\sqrt{15}$ (b) $4\sqrt{3}$ (c) $6\sqrt{5}$ (d) $3\sqrt{10}$ (e) $10\sqrt{10}$ (f) $30\sqrt{10}$ (g) $4\sqrt{2}$
(h) $3\sqrt{2}$  Review 2 (a) $28 + 10\sqrt{3}$ (b) $7 - 2\sqrt{10}$ (c) 4  Review 3 (a) $\frac{8\sqrt{3}}{3}$ (b) $\frac{5\sqrt{2}}{2}$

**Page 67**

### Chapter 3 Review

1. (a) it is a repeating decimal and can be written in the form $\frac{a}{b}$ where a and b are whole numbers
(b) $\sqrt{1}$, $\sqrt{4}$, $\sqrt{9}$  2. (a) $\frac{7}{3}$ is rational, π and $4\sqrt{2}$ are irrational (b) a possible number is $\sqrt{37}$
(c) (i) irrational (ii) irrational  3. (a) a possible example is $\sqrt{2} \times \sqrt{8} = 4$ (b) a possible example is $\frac{\sqrt{2}}{\sqrt{8}}$
4. (a) (i) always rational (ii) possibly rational (iii) possibly rational (iv) always rational (b) possible examples
for (iii) are: $\sqrt{4}$ rational, $\sqrt{3}$ irrational  5. $\frac{2}{7}$, $\frac{1}{17}$, $\frac{6}{47}$ can be written as recurring decimals. π and $\sqrt{7}$ can
be written as non-recurring decimals.  6. (a) $\frac{1}{2}$ (terminating decimal), $\sqrt{3}$ and $\sqrt[3]{3}$ (non-terminating and
non-recurring) (b) a possible example is $\sqrt{2}$ and $\sqrt{8}$ (c) $2 + \sqrt{3}$ is irrational as is $2\sqrt{3}$. $\left(\sqrt{3}\right)^2$ is rational
7. (a) $\frac{17}{33}$ (b) Yes. At step 1, multiply by 1000 to get 1000x = 123. 123123... Step 3 will be 999x = 123 to give
answer $\frac{41}{333}$.  8. (a) (i) a possible number is 4 (ii) a possible number is $\sqrt{26}$. (b) (i) possible numbers are $\frac{1}{3}$
(recurring decimal) and $\frac{1}{2}$ (a terminating and hence a non-recurring decimal) (ii) For the given examples,
sum = $\frac{5}{6}$ which is of the form $\frac{a}{b}$, where a, b are whole numbers, and hence is rational. (c) A possible
example is $\sqrt{2}$ and $\sqrt{8}$.  9. (a) a possible number is 1.24 (b) a possible number is $\sqrt{1.5}$

587

*Answers*

10. **(a) (i)** An example is $0.6666\ldots = \frac{2}{3}$ which is rational. **(ii)** The words non-repeating must be inserted.
**(b)** $\sqrt{6\frac{1}{4}}$ and $\left(\frac{1}{3}\sqrt{3}\right)^2$ are rational. $\sqrt{4\frac{1}{4}}$ and $\frac{1}{3}+\sqrt{3}$ are irrational. $\sqrt{6\frac{1}{4}}=\frac{5}{2}$, $\left(\frac{1}{3}\sqrt{3}\right)^2=\frac{1}{3}$    11. $\frac{35}{99}$
12. **(a)** possible points are $(7, 4), (14, 8)$ **(b)** because $\sqrt{2}$ multiplied by an integer (other than 0) is not an integer
**(c)** The only integer value of y is when $x = 0$, then $y = K$.    13. **(a)** a possible number is $\sqrt{17}$ **(b)** If N is a rational number other than 0 then $N = \frac{a}{b}$ and neither a nor b is zero. Then $\frac{1}{N} = \frac{b}{a}$ (with $a \neq 0$) which is also rational.    14. **(a) (i)** A possible value is 238. **(ii)** because n is not a square number **(b)** 10·24
15. **(i)** 24cm **(ii)** Irrational. Since area of square D is 18cm², then the length of a side is $\sqrt{18} = 3\sqrt{2}$ and the perimeter is $12\sqrt{2}$.    16. **(a) Stage 1** $\sqrt{2} < 1\frac{1}{2}$ since 1 is the nearest integer to $\sqrt{2}$. $\sqrt{2} < 1\frac{1}{2}$ can be written as $\sqrt{2} < 1 + \frac{1}{2}$ or $\sqrt{2} - 1 < \frac{1}{2}$.   **Stage 2** $(\sqrt{2} - 1)^2 = (\sqrt{2} - 1)(\sqrt{2} - 1) = 2 - 2\sqrt{2} + 1 = 3 - 2\sqrt{2}$
**Stage 3** $(3 - 2\sqrt{2})^2 = (3 - 2\sqrt{2})(3 - 2\sqrt{2}) = 9 - 12\sqrt{2} + 4\sqrt{2}\sqrt{2} = 9 - 12\sqrt{2} + 8 = 17 - 12\sqrt{2}$
**Stage 4** $12\sqrt{2} > 17 - \frac{1}{16} \approx 17$ so $\sqrt{2} \approx \frac{17}{12}$ **(c)** The nearest integer to $\sqrt{3}$ is 2. Hence $\sqrt{3} < 2\frac{1}{2}$ or
$\sqrt{3} < 2 + \frac{1}{2}$ or $\sqrt{3} - 2 < \frac{1}{2}$    17. **(a)** $\frac{7}{9}$ **(b) (i)** $0.8\dot{3}$ **(ii)** $\frac{209}{600}$ $(0.348\dot{3} = 0.34 + 0.008\dot{3} = 0.34 + \frac{0.8\dot{3}}{100} = \ldots$
18. **(a)** $12\sqrt{2}$ **(b)** $\frac{3\sqrt{2}}{2}$ **(c)** $3\sqrt{2}$ **(d)** $7 - 2\sqrt{6}$ **(e)** $\frac{5\sqrt{2}}{2}$

## Chapter 4    Number Review

1. 59 seconds is given correct to the nearest second while 59·0 seconds is given correct to the nearest tenth of a second. A time of 59 seconds means the time was between 58·5 seconds and 59·5 seconds while the time of 59·0 seconds means the time was between 58·95 seconds and 59·05 seconds, a much smaller time interval.
2. **(a)** irrational **(b)** rational; $\frac{19}{50}$ **(c)** rational; $\frac{221}{90}$ **(d)** irrational **(e)** rational; $\frac{83}{99}$ **(f)** rational; $\frac{3}{2}$
**(g)** rational; $\frac{167}{333}$    3. greatest distance = 83·5m; least distance = 82·5m    4. lower bound = 0·445*l*;
upper bound = 0·455*l*    5. **(a)** rational, non-terminating decimal expansion, 1-digit recurring cycle
**(b)** rational, non-terminating decimal expansion, 1-digit recurring cycle after 1 non repeating digit
**(c)** rational, non-terminating decimal expansion, 2-digit recurring cycle **(d)** rational, terminating decimal expansion **(e)** rational, non-terminating decimal expansion, 3-digit recurring cycle **(f)** rational, non-terminating decimal expansion, 6-digit recurring cycle **(g)** rational, terminating decimal expansion
6. **(a)** 8·2cm (2 s.f.) **(b)** 65cm³ (2 s.f.)    7. B    8. **(a)** A possible example is $\sqrt{2}$. **(b)** Not possible since no irrational number is a repeating decimal. **(c)** Not possible since no irrational number is a terminating decimal.
9. **(a)** $6.25\text{kg} \leq m < 6.35\text{kg}$ **(b)** $3750\text{g} \leq m < 3850\text{g}$ **(c)** $0.0955t \leq m < 0.0965t$    10. **(a)** 3 hours
**(b)** 60km/h    11. **(a)** No. If length = $\sqrt{8}$ and width = $\sqrt{2}$ then area = $\sqrt{8} \times \sqrt{2} = \sqrt{16} = 4$ which is rational.
**(b)** If length = $5 + \sqrt{3}$ and width = $2 - \sqrt{3}$ then perimeter = 14 which is rational. If length = $\sqrt{5}$ and width = $\sqrt{2}$ then perimeter = $2\sqrt{5} + 2\sqrt{2}$ which is irrational.    12. upper bound = 651·5km; lower bound = 648·5km.    13. 20 units    14. to 3 s.f., $535\text{m} \leq \text{height} < 554\text{m}$    15. to 1 d.p., greatest width = 10·4m, least width = 9·6m    16. **(a)** to 1 d.p., upper bound = 23·5, lower bound = 22·6
**(b)** upper bound = 2, lower bound = 1·8 **(c)** to 2 d.p., upper bound = 0·48, lower bound = 0·45 **(d)** to 2 d.p., upper bound = 0·92, lower bound = 0·84    17. **(a)** The figures on the left of each column are in metres; those on the right are in feet. **(c)** 30 metres **(e)** 45 feet (to the nearest foot)    18. **(i) (a)** $4\sqrt{6}$ **(b)** $\frac{4}{7}\sqrt{7}$ **(c)** $2\sqrt{21}$
**(d)** $16\sqrt{2}$    19. **(a)** $1.42\text{cm} \leq r < 1.43\text{cm}$, to 2 d.p. **(b)** 1·4cm    20. 0·25%    21. **(a)** $7.5\text{cm} \leq h < 8.5\text{cm}$
**(b)** $1.55\text{m} \leq r < 1.65\text{m}$    22. **(a)** $60\sqrt{13}$ is an irrational number which cannot be written in the form $\frac{a}{b}$ where a and b are whole numbers. **(b)** $215.5\text{cm} \leq \text{diameter} < 216.5\text{cm}$    23. $\sqrt{6}$ and $2\pi$    24. **(a)** between 13·95cm and 14·05cm **(b)** between 13·995cm and 14·005cm **(c)** to the nearest 10 grams    25. **(a) (i)** $h = 0.08d^2$
**(ii)** 25·92m **(b) (i)** $d = \sqrt{\frac{h}{0.08}}$ **(ii)** 17km    26. **(a)** $\sqrt{85}$, irrational **(b)** $\sqrt{5}$, irrational **(c)** $\sqrt{16}$, rational
27. **(a)** between 5·65cm and 5·75cm **(b)** between 33·9cm and 34·5cm **(c)** The width of Box A is between 33·5cm and 34·5cm. If the width is from 33·5cm to 33·9cm the cubes won't fit. The width of Box B is between 34·5cm and 35·5cm so the cubes will always fit.    28. **(a)** A possible number is $\sqrt{5}$. **(b)** A possible number is $\sqrt{2}$.
29. **(a) Height** lower bound = 0·645m, upper bound = 0·655m **Radius** lower bound = 2·155m, upper bound = 2·165m **(b)** upper bound = 9·645m³ (4 s.f.), lower bound = 9·410m³ **(c) (i)** 752·8 minutes (1 d.p.) **(ii)** 838·7 minutes (1 d.p.)    30. **(a) (i)** 2 **(ii)** $\frac{2}{99}$ **(b)** $\frac{41}{333}$    31. **(a)** Yes. Each of the 233 pieces could be up to 0·5kg more than recorded so the total weight could be as great as $6896 + 233 \times 0.5$ kg $= 7012.5$ kg
**(b)** No. We would expect some of the 233 pieces to weigh up to 0·5kg less than recorded.
32. **(a)** between 8 450 000km² and 8 550 000km² **(b)** maximum = 17·1 (1 d.p.), minimum = 16·8 (1 d.p.)
33. **(a)** 28000 **(b) (i)** 0·3 **(ii)** 0·6    34. **(a)** largest possible value = 6·0025, smallest possible value = 5·5225
**(b)** largest possible value = 4·82 watts, smallest possible value = 4·40 watts    35. **(i)** 380cm² **(ii)** 460cm²
36. **(a) (i)** $\sqrt{2}$m, irrational **(ii)** 1m, rational **(iii)** $\pi\sqrt{2}$ m, irrational **(iv)** 1m², rational **(b)** A possible value is 8.
**(c)** $\frac{3}{11}$    37. **(a) (i)** 159·2m **(ii)** 157·9m **(b)** 2    38. **(a) (i)** 2cm **(ii)** 15cm **(b) (i)** 1·803cm **(ii)** 1·752cm **(iii)** 1·47%

Revision Exercise

1. **(a)** 10km  **(b)** Marise, then Jan, then Olga  **(c)** 5 minutes  **(d)** after about 18·5 minutes  **(e)** about 2·5km
**(f)** about 17 minutes  **(g)** about 5·5km    2. A : 3, B : 2, C : 4, D : 1    3. **(a)** 3, 4, 6, 7  **(b)** If $n = 1$, $n^3 - n = 0$
which is not divisible by 3.  **(c)** "the expression $n^3 - n$, where n is a whole number greater than 1, always gives
numbers divisible by 3".  **(d)** 2 and 6  4. **(a)** 3, 2, $1\frac{2}{3}$, $1\frac{1}{2}$, $1\frac{2}{5}$, $1\frac{1}{3}$, $1\frac{2}{7}$  5. **(i) (a)** $8a^6b^3$  **(b)** $3xy$  **(c)** $5n - 2$
**(ii) (a)** $3^2$  **(b)** $3^{-6}$  **(c)** $3^{3x}$  6. 7  7. **(i) (a)** 1·25  **(b)** 1·5  **(c)** $-4$  **(d)** $0·\dot{6}$  **(e)** 6  **(ii)** $x > 7$  **(iii)** $-3, -2, -1, 0, 1, 2$
**(iv)** $n < -3$ or $n > 3$  8. **(i) (a)** 16km  **(b)** A possible expression is $6 + 2n$.  **(c)** 30km  **(d)** A possible equation is
$6 + 2n = 50$; $n = 22$ days  **(ii) (a)** 60, 78, 98  **(b)** 98km  **(c)** $n^2 + 7n$. Since the 2nd differences are constant the
highest power of n is 2.  **(d)** 588km    9. **(i) (a)** $y = \frac{1}{2}x - 2$  **(b)** $y = -\frac{4}{5}x + 2$  **(c)** $y = \frac{1}{2}x$  **(ii) (a)** 700
**(b)** $\frac{5}{2}$  **(c)** $2y = 5x + 1400$  **(d)** 1950mm Hg
10. **(a)**              **(b)** $C_n H_{2n+2}$
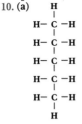
      **(c)** Since $2n + 2 = 2(n + 1)$, $2n + 2$ is always divisible by 2. That is, $2n + 2$ is always even.

11. **(a)**              **(b)**

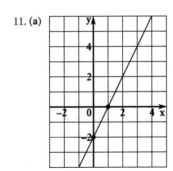    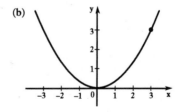

12. **(i) (a)** $3 - 11a - 2a^2$  **(b)** $2x^2 - 7x - 15$  **(c)** $9p^2 - q^2$  **(ii) (a)** $6(p + 3)$  **(b)** $x(3x - 4)$  **(c)** $ac(a + b)$
13. **(a)** $96 = 82a + b$  **(b)** $a = 2, b = -68$  **(c)** Ben  **(d)** The line $y = 2x - 68$ could be drawn then the y-value
(the scaled mark) read off for any given x-value (the original mark).    14. **(a)** 23cm  **(b)** $h = \frac{10f + 256}{3}$
**(c)** 1·72 metres    15. **(i) (a)** $(x - 4)(x + 3)$  **(b)** $(x - 4)(x - 3)$  **(ii) (a)** 2, $-3$  **(b)** $-1, -6$  **(c)** 4, $-3$
17. **(a)**                             **(b)** $y \geq 0, y < 3x - 2$  18. **(i) (a)** $n - 2$  **(b)** $n(n - 2)$  **(iii)** If $n = 6$,
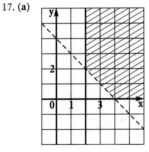                     $n^2 - 2n = 24$; if $n = 7$, $n^2 - 2n = 35$. Since 30 is between 24 and 35,
                                        a solution of the equation $n^2 - 2n = 30$ is between 6 and 7.
                                        **(iv)** 6·6  **(v)** 6·57 metres    19. **(a)** 17  18  19  20  21  22  23  24  25
                                        **(b)** $n = 2r - 1$ or $r = \frac{1}{2}(n + 1)$  **(c)** 39  **(d)** 11th row  **(e)** 21
                                        **(f)** average $= 31$; 31 is the next number in the sequence
                                        $1, 3, 7, 13, 21, \ldots$; sum $= 11 \times 31 = 341$    20. **(a)** $x = 0·5, y = -1·5$
                                        **(b)** $a = 2, b = -1$

**21. (i) (a)** 1 **(b)** 2 **(c)** 1 **(d)** 2 **(ii)** The pattern 1, 2, 1, 2, 1, 2, . . . emerges as more cubes are added.
If an odd-numbered cube is last, the remainder is 1; if an even-numbered cube is last, the remainder is 2.
**22. (a)** A : 3, B : 1, C : 2 **(b)** A possible container is shown.
**23.** $t_n = n^2 + n$ **24. (a)** x (x + 2) = 80

**(b)** x = 8cm **(c)** 36cm

**25. (a)**

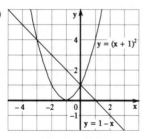

**(b)** $-3 \leq x \leq 0$

**26.** 50x − 20 (10 − x) = 290; 7 questions **27. (a)** Possible examples are: if n = 0, 6n + 5 = 5; if n = 2,
6n + 5 = 17; if n = 7, 6n + 5 = 47 **(b)** A possible example is: if n = 5, 6n + 5 = 35 **(c)** Apart from 2 and 3
every prime number is either one less than or one more than a multiple of 6. This relationship is true for all
prime numbers. **(d)** $\frac{5n-20}{2} > n$; 7 **28. (a)** $\frac{5}{6}$ **(b)** $t_n = \frac{n}{n+1}$ **(c)** $\frac{71}{42}$ **(d)** $\frac{241}{132}$ **29. (a)** 9·55a.m.

**(b)** 52·5km **30. (b)**

| x | 0·5 | 1·0 | 1·5 | 2·0 | 2·5 | 3·0 | 3·5 | 4·0 | 4·5 | 5·0 |
|---|-----|-----|-----|-----|-----|-----|-----|-----|-----|-----|
| A | 4·5 | 8·0 | 10·5 | 12·0 | 12·5 | 12·0 | 10·5 | 8·0 | 4·5 | 0 |

**(c)**

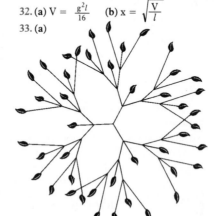

**(d)** 1·4m or 3·6m (to 1 d.p.) **(e)** width 2·5m and length 5m
**31. (i) (a)** 40 **(b)** $-9\frac{1}{2}$ **(c)** $-4 < x < 4$ **(ii) (a)** 8 **(b)** −1
**32. (a)** $V = \frac{g^2 l}{16}$ **(b)** $x = \sqrt{\frac{V}{l}}$
**33. (a)**

**33. (b)** In Year 5, the plant has twice as many new leaves as it had in Year 4. Since it develops 24 new leaves in
Year 4 it develops 48 new leaves in Year 5. Hence total number of leaves in Year 5 = 45 + 48 = 93.
**34.** The only possible answer is £31·63. **35. (i) (a)** $p^9 - p$ **(b)** $p^8 + 1$ **(c)** $p + p^8$ **(ii)** largest is $p^9 - p$, smallest
is $p^8 + 1$ **36.** 2·1 metres

**37. (a)**

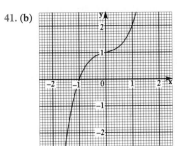

**38. (a)** $4n - 1$ **(b)** $n^2 + 2$ **39.** $x = 0.5, y = 2.5$ **40. (a) (i)** $x \le 4$
**(ii)** $x > 2$ **(b)** 3 and 4 **41. (a) (i)** $y = 1 - x^2$ **(ii)** $2y = 2 + x$ **(iii)** $y = x^2$
**(iv)** $xy = 1$

**41. (b)**

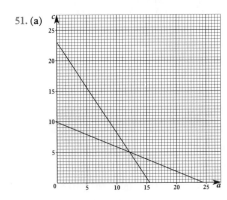

**42.** $-21.7°C$ (1 d.p.) **43. (a)** $(5, 1)$ **(b)** The hole labelled T is the 3rd
from the top on the right-hand column of holes **(c)** $y = x$

**44. (a)**

| 16 | | 18 |
|---|---|---|
| | 22 | |
| 26 | | 28 |

**(b)**

| $n$ | | $n+2$ |
|---|---|---|
| | $n+6$ | |
| $n+10$ | | $n+12$ |

**45. (a)**

| Time, $t$ | 0 | 1 | 2 | 3 | 4 | 5 | 6 | 7 | 8 |
|---|---|---|---|---|---|---|---|---|---|
| Distance, $d$ | 0 | 2·5 | 10 | 22·5 | 40 | 62·5 | 90 | 122·5 | 160 |

**(b)**

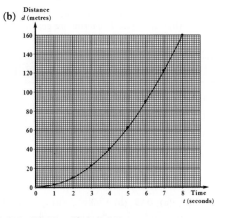

**(c)** about 106m **(d)** about 4·5 sec
**46. (a) (i)** –5 **(ii)** 1 **(b) (i)** $x \ge 2$
**(ii)** $x > 3$ **(iii)** $-5 < x < 5$
**47. (a)** $n^3$ **(b)** $n^{-1}$ **48. (a) (i)** $C = 10, F = 50$
**(ii)** These rules give the same answer only if
$C = 10$ (or $F = 50$)
**(b) (i)** $F = 1.8C + 32$
**(ii)** $1.8 \approx 2, 32 \approx 30$
**49.** 3  4  7  12 19 $\boxed{28}$     **50.** 2·9
     1  3 $\boxed{5}$  7
     $\boxed{2}$  2  2

**51. (a)**

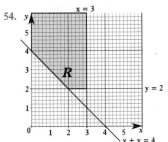

**(b) (i)** £12 **(ii)** £5 **52.** 1, 2, 3, 4
**53. (a)**

| $a + b$ | = | $c$ |
|---|---|---|
| $c - a$ | = | $b$ |
| $a + b + c$ | = | $d$ |

**(b)**

triangle with $x$, $2x+12$, $x + 6$, 6

**(c) (i)** $4x + 24 = 60$ **(ii)** 9

**54.**

graph with $x = 3$, $y = 2$, $R$, $x + y = 4$

**55. (i)** c **(ii)** d **56. (a)**

| Octagon | Perimeter of octagon | Cumulative length |
|---|---|---|
| 1 | 32 | 32 |
| 2 | 64 | 96 |
| 3 | 96 | 192 |
| 4 | 128 | 320 |

**(b)** $P = 32n$
**(c)** $B = 16n^2 + 16n$
**57.** 7·3 **58. (a)** $3a$
**(b)** $a = 5, b = 3, c = 1$ **(c)** $a = 7, b = 2$ **(d) (i)** 3
**(ii)**

| 9 | 8 | 4 |
|---|---|---|
| 2 | 7 | 12 |
| 10 | 6 | 5 |

**59. (b) (i)** $73\frac{1}{3}$ miles **(ii)** $8\frac{1}{3}$ miles

## Chapter 5    Sequences

**Page 109**

Exercise 5:3

1. (a) $0, 3, 6, 9, 12$  (b) $\frac{1}{2}, 1, 2, 4, 8$  (c) $3, 11, 27, 59, 123$  (d) $2, 4, 16, 256, 65536$  (e) $1, 3, 9, 27, 81$
(f) $4, -4, 4, -4, 4$    2. (a) $0.0625$  (b) $-1.585$ (4 s.f.)  (c) $3$  (d) $0.9091$ (4 s.f.)  (e) $-5$    3. (a) the roll this year
(b) $368$    4. £1000    5. (a) $3, 1, -2, -3, -1, 2, 3$  (b) $2, 3, 6, 18, 108, 1944, 209952$  (c) $2, 6, 3, \frac{1}{2}, \frac{1}{6}, \frac{1}{3}, 2$
(d) $1, 1, 3, 7, 17, 41, 99$    6. (a) $2, 6, 18, 54, \ldots$  (b) $t_n = 2 \times 3^{n-1}$ which is always even since it is a multiple of 2.
Review 1 (a) $4, 6.5, 11.5, 21.5, 41.5, 81.5$  (b) $1, 2, 5, 26, 677, 458330$    Review 2 $764$
Review 3 (a) $4.65$ (3 s.f.)  (b) $84$

**Page 111**

Exercise 5:6

1. divergent    2. convergent; 3    3. divergent    4. convergent; 0    5. divergent    6. divergent    7. divergent
8. convergent; 1    9. divergent    10. divergent    11. divergent    12. convergent; 0    13. convergent; 0
14. divergent    15. convergent; 1    16. convergent; 6    Review 1 convergent; 5    Review 2 convergent; 0
Review 3 divergent    Review 4 convergent; 1

**Page 113**

Chapter 5 Review

1. (a) $a = 1, b = 5$  | 1 | 5 | 6 | 11 | 17 | 28 |    2. (a) $47, 76$  (b) (i) $1.64, 1.61, 1.62$  (ii) The sequence converges.
By taking further terms it seems the sequence converges to $1.68$ (2 d.p.)    3. (a) $\frac{n}{2n+1}$  (b) (i) $0.32$  (ii) $0.5$
4. (a) $x_1 = 1$, $x_2 = 1.414$, $x_3 = 1.307$, $x_4 = 1.329$, $x_5 = 1.324$, $x_6 = 1.325$
(b) Converges. The terms are getting closer together.

## Chapter 6    Graphical Solution of Equations

**Page 118**

Exercise 6:1

**Unless otherwise stated, approximate answers are rounded to 1 d.p.**
1. (e) $-1.8$    2. (d) $-1.2, 0.4, 1.8$    3. (b) $-1.8, 3.8$    4. (ii) (a) $-2.2, 2.2$  (b) $-1.3, 2.3$  (c) $0.4, -2.4$
5. (b) $0.45$ (2 d.p.), $-0.6, -1.85$ (2 d.p.)  (c) $y = 0.5$; $x = 1.4, x = -1.4$    6. (a) $y = 2$  (b) $y = -3$  (c) None. The
line $y = 0$ is already drawn.  (d) $y = -x$  (e) $y = 2x + 4$  (f) $y = 3 - 2x$    7. (ii) (a) $0, 3$  (b) $3.2$  (c) $-0.7, 1, 2.7$
(d) $-0.8, 0.8, 3.1$  (e) $2.9$    8. (d) $2.1$    Review 1 (b) $4.6$    Review 2 (i) $-2.4, 0, 2.4$  (ii) (a) $y = 4$  (b) $y = -3$
(c) $y = 2x - 5$    Review 3 (b) $-2.3, 4.3$  (c) $y = 2x - 3$

**Page 123**

Exercise 6:3

1. (a) $-0.88$  (b) $0.768$    2. (b) $1, -2$  (c) $1.302$  (d) $-2.3027$    3. (a) $3$  (b) $3.129$    4. (a) $y = 1 - 3x$  (b) $0$
(c) $0.312$    5. (b) $3$  (c) $0.125$  (d) $2.763$  (e) $-2.8889$    Review (a) $y = 3$  (b) $-0.732$  (c) $x_2 = 1, x_3 = 1$,
$x_4 = 1$ etc. A solution is $x = 1$.  (d) $2.732$

**Page 125**

Chapter 6 Review

1. (a) $3.3$  (b) $x^2 - 3x - 0.99$  (c) (ii) about $-0.3$ and $3.3$    2. x is about $1.3$    3. (a) about $0.25$ and $1.85$
(b) (i) about $-1.8$ and $-0.25$  (ii) about $0.65$ and $1.85$    4. (a) about $1.2$  (c) $1.174$ to 3 correct decimal places or
$1.175$ correct to 3 decimal places.

## Chapter 7    Indices

**Page 131**

Exercise 7:3

1. (a) $\frac{1}{2}$  (b) $\frac{1}{2}$  (c) $\frac{1}{2}$  (d) $\frac{1}{3}$  (e) $\frac{1}{3}$  (f) $\frac{1}{4}$  (g) $\frac{1}{7}$    2. (a) $2$  (b) $4$  (c) $3$  (d) $8$  (e) $10$  (f) $2$  (g) $2$
(h) $5$  (i) $2$  (j) $3$  (k) $2$    3. (a) $16$  (b) $\frac{1}{4}$  (c) $\frac{1}{16}$  (d) $\frac{1}{27}$  (e) $1$  (f) $3$  (g) $5$  (h) $2$  (i) $8$  (j) $4$  (k) $\frac{1}{2}$  (l) $2$
(m) $\frac{1}{2}$  (n) $\frac{1}{4}$  (o) $\frac{1}{32}$  (p) $\frac{1}{27}$  (q) $\frac{1}{4}$  (r) $\frac{1}{243}$    4. (a) $2.34$ (2 d.p.)  (b) $2.37$ (2 d.p.)  (c) $3.16$ (2 d.p.)
(d) $2.15$ (2 d.p.)  (e) $2.61$ (2 d.p.)    5. (a) $x^2$  (b) $x^2$  (c) $\frac{1}{x^2}$  (d) $x$  (e) $\frac{1}{x}$  (f) $x^2$  (g) $\frac{1}{x^5}$  (h) $x^{3.5}$  (i) $x$
6. (a) $12x^3y^2$  (b) $12x^3y^5$  (c) $9n^2m^6$  (d) $4n^8m^2$  (e) $\frac{3m^2}{n}$  (f) $\frac{b^2}{3a}$  (g) $\frac{n}{4}$    7. (a) $7x^3$  (b) $3n^2$  (c) $2y^4$
(d) $10a^4$  (e) $6n^3$  (f) $20m^2$  (g) $\frac{1}{4n}$  (h) $\frac{6a^3}{b}$  (i) $3xy^2$  (j) $\frac{a^3b^2}{2}$  (k) $\frac{1}{16n^6}$    8. (a) $\sqrt{x}$  (b) $\sqrt{x^7}$  (c) $\frac{1}{\sqrt{x^3}}$
(d) $\frac{1}{\sqrt{x^3}}$    9. (a) $\frac{3}{5}$  (b) $\frac{3}{4}$  (c) $\frac{3}{2}$  (d) $32$  (e) $\frac{64}{27}$  (f) $\frac{9}{4}$  (g) $0.3$  (h) $\frac{1}{2}$    Review 1 (a) $1$  (b) $\frac{1}{16}$  (c) $7$
(d) $\frac{1}{3}$  (e) $\frac{1}{3}$  (f) $2.19$ (2 d.p.)    Review 2 (a) $n^6$  (b) $n^5$  (c) $\frac{1}{x^3}$  (d) $4a^6$  (e) $15x^5y^3$  (f) $\frac{x}{2y}$  (g) $\frac{1}{4n^6}$
(h) $\frac{3}{nm^2}$  (i) $\frac{1}{\sqrt{x}}$    Review 3 (a) $\frac{1}{64}$  (b) $\frac{2}{3}$  (c) $\frac{3}{5}$  (d) $32$  (e) $\frac{3}{2}$  (f) $\frac{4}{5}$

*Answers*

Page 134

## Exercise 7:4

1. (a) 0·3 (b) 0·6 (c) 0·1 (d) 1·2 (e) 0·5 (f) 1·5  2. (a) 2·5 (b) 3·5 (c) 4·5 (d) 4 (e) 16 (f) 9  3. (a) x = 3
(b) n = 4 (c) y = 2 (d) x = 0 (e) y = 3 (f) n = 3 (g) x = 0 (h) x = 5  4. (a) −2 (b) −$\frac{1}{2}$ (c) $\frac{1}{3}$ (d) −2
(e) $\frac{5}{2}$ (f) $\frac{3}{2}$ (g) −$\frac{3}{2}$ (h) $\frac{1}{4}$ (i) 3 (j) −4 (k) −5  5. (a) 3 (b) $\frac{5}{2}$ (c) 4 (d) 9 (e) 6 (f) 2 (g) 1·5 (h) −2
(i) 1·5  6. (a) 65536 (b) 3 hours (c) 2$\frac{1}{2}$ hours (d) 1  Review 1 (a) x = 0·2 (b) x = 0 (c) n = 6 (d) y = 3
(e) x = $\frac{1}{2}$ (f) x = −2 (g) x = $\frac{1}{2}$ (h) x = $\frac{2}{5}$ (i) y = $\frac{3}{2}$ (j) n = $\sqrt{3}$  Review 2 1·5  Review 3 (a) −2
(b) −1 (c) 6 (d) 4  Review 4 (a) 4 (b) 7 days (c) 6

Page 135

## Exercise 7:5

**The answers read from graphs are approximate.**

1. For the graph, the points plotted are (−2, $\frac{1}{9}$), (−1, $\frac{1}{3}$), (0, 1), (1, 3), (2, 9). (a) 1·9 (b) 1·4
2. For the graph, the points plotted are (−3, 8), (−2, 4), (−1, 2), (0, 1), (1, $\frac{1}{2}$), (2, $\frac{1}{4}$) (a) −2·6 (b) −1·8
3. (a) y = x + 3 (b) y = −2x + 2  4. (a) 0·6 (b) 1·6  5. The line y = −2 does not meet the graph of y = 2$^{-x}$.
6. (a) £5000 (b) £3200 (c) The points plotted are (0, 5000), (1, 4000), (2, 3200), (3, 2560), (4, 2048), (5, 1638),
(6, 1311), (7, 1049), (8, 839), (9, 671), (10, 537). (d) just over 3 years.

Review (i)

| x | −1·0 | −0·8 | −0·6 | −0·4 | −0·2 | 0 | 0·2 | 0·4 | 0·6 | 0·8 | 1·0 |
|---|------|------|------|------|------|---|-----|-----|-----|-----|-----|
| y | 0·1 | 0·16 | 0·25 | 0·40 | 0·63 | 1 | 1·58 | 2·51 | 3·98 | 6·31 | 10 |

For the graph the points plotted are (−1, 0·1), (−0·8, 0·16), (−0·6, 0·25), (−0·4, 0·4), (−0·2, 0·63), (0, 1), (0·2, 1·58),
(0·4, 2·51), (0·6, 3·98), (0·8, 6·31), (1, 10). (ii) (a) 0·89 (2 d.p.) (b) 0·65 (2 d.p.) (c) 0·48 (2 d.p.)

Page 137

## Chapter 7 Review

1. (a) 2 (b) −1  2. (a) 1 (b) $\frac{1}{8}$  3. (a) x$^{-3}$ (b) x$^5$ (c) x$^7$  4. (a) 2 (b) $\frac{1}{16}$ (c) $\frac{1}{3}$  5. (a) n = 7 (b) p = 0
(c) q = $\frac{5}{2}$  6. (a) x$^7$ (b) 5  7. (a) p = 3 (b) q = 0 (c) r = −2  8. (a) $\frac{9}{1}$ (b) a$^8$ (c) $\frac{5}{2}$
9. (a)

| t(minutes) | 0 | 1 | 2 | 3 | 4 |
|---|---|---|---|---|---|
| T(°C) | 14 | −2 | −10 | −14 | −16 |

(b)
(c)

T (°C) / t (minutes)

(d) about 2·7 minutes

10. (a)

| t | 0 | 1 | 2 | 3 | 4 | 5 | 6 |
|---|---|---|---|---|---|---|---|
| v | 1 | 2 | 4 | 8 | 16 | 32 | 64 |

(b) For the graph of V = 2$^t$ the points plotted are
(0, 1), (1, 2), (2, 4), (3, 8), (4, 16), (5, 32), (6, 64).
(c) The graph of P = 30 + 4t goes through the points
(0, 30), (3, 42), (6, 54). (d) 5·7 days

11. (a)

| t | 0 | 2 | 4 | 6 | 8 | 10 | 12 | 14 | 16 | 18 |
|---|---|---|---|---|---|----|----|----|----|----|
| P | 1·3 | 1·43 | 1·58 | 1·74 | 1·92 | 2·12 | 2·33 | 2·57 | 2·84 | 3·13 |

(b) The points plotted are (0, 1·3), (2, 1·43), (4, 1·58),
(6, 1·74), (8, 1·92), (10, 2·12), (12, 2·33), (14, 2·57),
(16, 2·84), (18, 3·13). (c) 1·5 million
(d) just after 1st Jan 2010  12. (a) 42875
(b) a = 35, n = $\frac{2}{3}$

---

# Chapter 8  Expressing Laws in Symbolic Form

Page 141

## Exercise 8:2

**The answers given in this exercise are approximate answers.**
1. (b) a = 2·5, b = −1·3; y = 2·5x − 1·3  2. (b) a = 0·02, b = 5; R = 0·02t + 5 (c) 5·76 ohms
3. (b) q = 1·5n + 200 (c) £650 (d) This data is exact, not experimental.  4. (b) t = 20, v = 30 (d) v = 3 + 2t
Review (b) a = 0·1, b = 3·4; *l* = 0·1m + 3·4 (c) 5·9cm

### Exercise 8:4

**The answers given in this exercise are approximate answers.**

1. Acceleration is constant; 4·5.　2. $P = \frac{15}{V}$　3. (b) $F = v^2 + 45$　4. $P = 0.5x^3 + 45$　5. (b) $R = \frac{8}{I} - 0.6$

6. $I = \frac{8}{d^2} + 5$　7. $T = 2\sqrt{l}$　8. (a) $y = x^2 - 2.6$　(b) $y = 1.5x + 2.2$　(c) $y = \frac{2}{x} + 4.8$　(d) $y = 1.8x - 1.4$

(e) $y = 0.4x^2 + 1$　(f) $y = \frac{8.8}{x} + 0.4$　(g) $y = 0.2x^3 - 1.4$　**Review 1** (c) $a = 0.05$, $b = 5$; $I = 0.05d^2 + 5$

**Review 2** (a) $y = \frac{25}{x} + 4$　(b) $y = 0.2x^2 - 4$

### Chapter 8 Review

**The answers read from graphs are approximate.**

1. (b) A line can be drawn to fit the data quite well.　(c) $a = 0.8$, $b = 0.35$　2. (a) when d is plotted against $\frac{1}{t}$, a line can be drawn to fit the data quite well.　(b) $a = 20$, $b = 24$

3. (a) (i)

| d | 0·50 | 0·75 | 1·00 | 1·25 | 1·50 |
|---|---|---|---|---|---|
| t | 1·32 | 1·60 | 1·83 | 2·05 | 2·25 |
| $t^2$ | 1·74 | 2·56 | 3·35 | 4·20 | 5·06 |

The points plotted are (1·74, 0·5), (2·56, 0·75), (3·35, 1), (4·2, 1·25), (5·06, 1·5)
(b) A line, which passes through the origin, can be drawn to fit the data quite well.　(c) 0·3

## Chapter 9　Graphs: Gradient, Area

### Exercise 9:2

**Answers read from graphs are approximate.**

1. (a) (0, 80), (5, 72), (10, 66), (15, 62), (20, 58), (25, 56), (30, 54)　(c) –0·6 (1 d.p.)　(d) At t = 20 min. the temperature is falling at the rate of 0·6°C per minute.　2. (i) (a) 6　(b) 10　(ii) during the first 2 minutes; this is where the graph is steepest　(iii) 2 minutes; for 2 minutes, between t = 6 and t = 8 minutes the gradient of the graph is zero.　(iv) 45 beats per minute$^2$　(v) 12·5 minutes; at t = 12·5 min. and t = 9·5 min. the tangents are parallel.　3. (b) –0·3 (1 d.p.)　(c) 1 metre per minute　4. (i) (a) –7　(b) 11　(ii) 1

5. (a)

| x | –2·5 | –2·0 | –1·5 | –1·0 | –0·5 | 0 | 0·5 | 1·0 | 1·5 | 2·0 | 2·5 | 3·0 | 3·5 | 4·0 | 4·5 |
|---|---|---|---|---|---|---|---|---|---|---|---|---|---|---|---|
| y | 8·25 | 5·0 | 2·25 | 0 | –1·75 | –3 | –3·75 | –4 | –3·75 | –3 | –1·75 | 0 | 2·25 | 5·0 | 8·25 |

(c) 4　(d) (1, –4); the gradient changes from negative to positive.　6. Gradient = 1·6 (1 d.p.); when the depth of water is 10cm the diameter is increasing at the rate of 1·6cm for every 1cm increase in depth.

**Review**　Gradient = 0·6 (1 d.p.); when the length is 50cm, the rate of change of the tension is 0·6 Newtons for every cm increase in the length.

### Exercise 9:5

**The answers are approximate.**

1. 800 (2 s.f.)　2. 78 (2 s.f.)　3. 240 (2 s.f.)　4. 120

5. (a)

| x | –3 | –2 | –1 | 0 | 1 | 2 | 3 | 4 | 5 | 6 | 7 |
|---|---|---|---|---|---|---|---|---|---|---|---|
| y | –9 | 0 | 7 | 12 | 15 | 16 | 15 | 12 | 7 | 0 | –9 |

(c) 72　6. (b) 5·5 (2 s.f.)　(c) 11 (2 s.f.)　7. (a) 330 (2 s.f.)　(b) 330 litres of water flowed from the pipe in the 30 minutes.　**Review 1** 2100 (2 s.f.)

**Review 2** (a)

| x | 0 | 0·5 | 1 | 1·5 | 2 | 2·5 | 3 | 3·5 | 4 | 4·5 | 5 | 5·5 | 6 |
|---|---|---|---|---|---|---|---|---|---|---|---|---|---|
| y | –6 | –2·75 | 0 | 2·25 | 4 | 5·25 | 6 | 6·25 | 6 | 5·25 | 4 | 2·25 | 0 |

(b) 20 (1 s.f.)

### Exercise 9:8

**The answers are approximate.**

1. Gradient = 4·5 (1 d.p.); at t = 20 seconds, Ben's speed was 4·5m/s　2. Velocity when t = 4 sec. is found by finding the gradient of the tangent to the curve at t = 4; 2m/s　3. (b) between 0 and 10 seconds; 1·75ms$^{-2}$
4. 1·025km　5. distance travelled = 180m (2 s.f.); since seconds is the unit of time on the horizontal axis, seconds should be part of the unit for velocity on the vertical axis.　6. (a) 35m/s　(b) 30 seconds
(c) at t = 12 seconds; this is where the curve is steepest.　7. (a) 1300 (2 s.f.); the distance in metres, travelled.
(b) 22m/s (2 s.f.)　8. The points in the table give velocity in km/h; we need velocity in m/s since the times are given in seconds. Should plot (0, 0), (2, 10·6), (4, 18·6), (6, 25), (8, 30·6), (10, 35), (12, 38·1), (14, 41·1), (16, 42·5).
When t = 10 seconds, acceleration = 1·9m/s$^2$ (1 d.p.)　9. (a) 900m　(b) 27·5 sec

10. (a)

| t | 0 | 1 | 2 | 3 | 4 | 5 |
|---|---|---|---|---|---|---|
| v | 5 | 9 | 15 | 23 | 33 | 45 |

(c) 31 metres

**Review 1** (a) about 42 seconds　(b) about 43 seconds　(c) about 0·3ms$^{-2}$　**Review 2** 1·3km (2 s.f.)
**Review 3** (a) 16·6　(c) 1·7m/s$^2$ (1 d.p.)　(d) 0·6m/s$^2$ (1 d.p.)　**Review 4** (a) 1·6 km　(b) after 55 seconds　(c) 50 km/h

## Chapter 9 Review

**Answers read from graphs are approximate.**

1. about 3cm per minute   2. (a) The graph of $y = x - 2$ goes through the points $(-2, -4), (1, -1), (5, 3)$
(b) 0 or 4  (c) 2   3. (a) (i) 12 seconds  (ii) 0 cm per second  (b) 10 cm per second   4. (b) $-0.2$   5. (a) 1500m
(b) 100 seconds   6. (a) about $0.08 \text{m/s}^2$  (b) about 1460m   7. (a) $46\text{m}^2$  (b) $9.2\text{m}^3$   8. (a) (ii) about $2\text{m/s}^2$
(iii) the acceleration at $t = 5$ seconds  (b) about 83m   9. (a) (i) about $80 \text{ m/s}^2$  (ii) the acceleration at
$t = 160$ seconds  (b) (i) about $151, 600$m  (ii) the distance travelled between $t = 20$ and $t = 100$ seconds
10. (a) At A, the car stops accelerating. At B, the car begins to decelerate at a constant rate.  (b) about $10\text{m/s}^2$
(c) about 315m   11. (a) $v = 2t$  (b) about $19.5$ seconds  (c) (i) 10 seconds (and also after about $20.5$ seconds)
(ii) $2\text{m/s}^2$  (d) (i) about 380 feet  (ii) about 260 feet (after $19.5$ seconds)

## Chapter 10    Expressions and Equations

### Exercise 10:2

1. $(a + b)(c + d)$
2. $(x + z)(y + w)$
3. $(c + d)(y - z)$
4. $(p - q)(r - s)$
5. $(p + r)(q - r)$
6. $(p - z)(q + z)$
7. $(a + x)(b + y)$
8. $(a + b)(c - d)$
9. $(x - y)(z - w)$
10. $(x - y)(w + y)$
11. $(a + x)(b - x)$
12. $(x + 1)(a - 3)$
13. $(x + 3a)(y - 4b)$
14. $(b^2 + 1)(a - 1)$
15. $(z - a)(5y - x)$

Review 1 $(p + a)(p + q)$     Review 2 $(a - b)(x - y)$    Review 3 $(p - 2)(x - 1)$

### Exercise 10:4

1. (a) $(x + 5)(x - 1)$  (b) $(x + 3)(x + 2)$  (c) $(x + 3)(x - 4)$  (d) $(x - 7)(x + 4)$
(e) $(a - 1)(a - 9)$  (f) $(a - 5)(a + 3)$  (g) $(a + 7)(a - 5)$  (h) $(a - 4)(a - 4)$
(i) $(2x + 1)(x + 3)$  (j) $(3x + 2)(x + 1)$  (k) $(2x - 1)(x + 3)$  (l) $(2x - 1)(3x + 2)$
(m) $(4n - 1)(n + 3)$  (n) $(2n - 1)(6n - 5)$  (o) $(6n + 5)(n - 2)$  (p) $(5n - 4)(2n + 1)$
(q) $(5y + 2)(4y - 3)$  (r) $(3y + 2)(3y + 2)$  (s) $(3y - 10)(2y + 1)$  (t) $(4y - 3)(y + 2)$
(u) $(8n + 15)(n - 1)$  (v) $(4n - 1)(3n - 2)$  (w) $(n - 12)(n + 3)$  (x) $(x - 9)(x + 4)$
(y) $(3y - 2)(2y - 3)$  (z) $(4a - 1)(3a + 4)$

2. (a) $3(a - 2)(a + 2)$  (b) $(n - 4)(n + 4)$  (c) $2(2x - 1)(x - 2)$  (d) $(2x + 5)(x - 2)$
(e) $(2x - 3)(x + 1)$  (f) $x(x - 5)$  (g) $(a + 5)(a - 5)$  (h) $2(x + 1)(x - 1)$
(i) $5(2 - x^2)$  (j) $2(2n + 1)(2n - 1)$  (k) $2(y - 1)(y - 2)$  (l) $5(a + 4)(a - 1)$
(m) $3(4n + 1)(n + 3)$  (n) $3n(n + 3)$  (o) $2(5 + n)(5 - n)$  (p) $(10 + x)(10 - x)$
(q) $5(a^2 + 3)$  (r) $(3n + 4)(n - 1)$  (s) $2(x + 1)(x + 1)$  (t) $2(2x - 1)(2x - 1)$
(u) $2x(x + 2)$  (v) $x(x + 4)(x - 1)$  (w) $(3n - 1)(n - 1)$  (x) $(2p + q + r)(q - r)$

3. (a) Area $= \pi n^2$   4. (a) 115  (b) 40609  (c) 272  (d) 2  (e) $9\frac{6}{7}$   5. Answer should be $(1 - 2x)(3 + x)$
7. (a) $5 \times 29$  (b) $73^2 - 72^2$ or $17^2 - 12^2$   8. (a) $(5n + 3)(n + 9)$  (b) $54827 = 503 \times 109$; if n = 100 then
$5n^2 + 48n + 27 = 5 \times 10\,000 + 48 \times 100 + 27 = 54827$  (c) $4n^2 + 13n + 9$; $409 \times 101$
Review (a) $(x + 3)(x + 2)$  (b) $(3x + 4)(2x - 5)$  (c) $(2p + 3)(2p - 3)$  (d) $2(2n - 3)(n - 7)$  (e) $a(5a - 3)$
(f) $(5n - 4m)(3n + 2m)$  (g) $\pi(x + y)(x - y)$  (h) $2(3 + 2x)(3 - 2x)$  (i) $(5y - 2)(5y - 2)$  (j) $(1 - 3x)(2x - 3)$ or
$(3x - 1)(3 - 2x)$  (k) $(6n + 1)(4n + 3)$

### Exercise 10:6

1. (a) $x + 2$  (b) $\frac{1}{3 - x}$  (c) $\frac{a - 2b}{4ab}$  (d) $\frac{2a}{b}$  (e) $\frac{x}{y}$  (f) $\frac{3}{2}$  (g) 5  (h) $x - 5$  (i) $\frac{1}{x + 3}$  (j) $\frac{4}{x + 3}$  (k) $\frac{x - 1}{2}$
(l) $\frac{3x - 1}{3}$  (m) $\frac{3}{2}$  (n) $\frac{a + 2}{a - 5}$  (o) $\frac{x}{x - y}$  (p) $\frac{a}{2b}$  (q) $-3$  (r) $-2$  (s) $-\frac{a}{b}$  (t) $\frac{2(x + 1)}{x - 1}$   2. (a) $2(x + 1)$
(b) $\frac{2}{3(a + 1)}$  (c) $\frac{a - 1}{2a}$  (d) $3 - 2n$  (e) $\frac{x}{6(x - 1)}$  (f) $\frac{x - 1}{x + 1}$  (g) $\frac{y - 2}{y(y + 2)}$   3. (a) $\frac{x}{12}$  (b) $\frac{13a}{15}$  (c) $\frac{3}{10a}$
(d) $\frac{7}{2n}$  (e) $\frac{11x - 3y}{30}$  (f) $-\frac{8a + 15b}{10}$  (g) $\frac{56 - 12x}{15}$  (h) $\frac{5x + 1}{(x + 1)(x - 1)}$  (i) $\frac{2a - 7}{(2a - 1)(a - 2)}$  (j) $\frac{n + 27}{(n - 3)(n + 2)}$  (k) $\frac{1}{x - 2}$
(l) $\frac{9 - x}{x(x + 3)}$  (m) $\frac{an - bm}{mn}$  (n) $\frac{5}{m - n}$  (o) 1  (p) $\frac{5a + 1}{a(a + 1)(a - 1)}$  (q) $\frac{4 - 3x}{2(x - 1)(x + 1)}$   5. (a) OD $= r - h$
6. $u = \frac{fv}{v - f}$   Review (a) $\frac{3}{x - 2}$  (b) $-5$  (c) $\frac{a + 3}{2a + 1}$  (d) $\frac{5a}{12}$  (e) $\frac{n + 2m}{mn}$  (f) $\frac{2}{(x - 1)(x - 3)}$  (g) $\frac{2(3x - 1)}{(x - 3)(x + 1)}$
(h) $-\frac{(x + 4y)}{6}$  (i) $-x$  (j) 2

**Exercise 10:8**

1. a, d, e, h, i   2. (a) 36   (b) $\frac{49}{4}$   (c) $\frac{1}{4}$   (d) 2 or $-2$   (e) 12 or $-12$   (f) 4 or $-4$   3. (a) 16   (b) 1   (c) 49

(d) $\frac{49}{4}$   (e) $\frac{25}{4}$   (f) $\frac{81}{4}$   4. (a) $(x+1)^2+2$   (b) $(x+3)^2-10$   (c) $(x-1)^2+1$   (d) $(x-2)^2-6$

(e) $(x+\frac{1}{2})^2+\frac{3}{4}$   (f) $(x+\frac{3}{2})^2-\frac{17}{4}$   (g) $(x-\frac{1}{2})^2+\frac{3}{4}$   (h) $(x-\frac{5}{2})^2-\frac{25}{4}$   5. (b) 0   (c) 15   (d) 5

(e) no   6. (a) $a=4, b=3, c=-35$   (b) $a=4, b=3, c=-8\frac{3}{4}$   (c) $a=2, b=6, c=-35$

Review 1 (a) $(x+2)^2-6$   (b) $(x-1)^2+5$   (c) $(x-\frac{5}{2})^2-7\frac{1}{4}$   Review 2 $-7$

**Exercise 10:9**

1. (a) 2, 5   (b) $-2$, 1   (c) $-4$, $-5$   (d) 0, $-6$   (e) $-\frac{1}{2}$, 4   (f) $1\frac{1}{2}$, $\frac{1}{2}$   (g) $-2$, $1\frac{1}{4}$   (h) $-1\frac{1}{4}$, $-1\frac{1}{2}$   (i) 0, $\frac{3}{4}$

(j) $-2\frac{1}{2}$, $\frac{2}{3}$   2. (a) $-1$, $-2$   (b) $-3$, 2   (c) 1   (d) $-2$, 4   (e) $-1$, 4   (f) $-5$, 1   (g) $-3$, 5   (h) $-5$, $-4$   (i) $-\frac{1}{2}$, 3

(j) $-\frac{1}{3}$, $-1$   (k) $-\frac{1}{3}$, $\frac{1}{2}$   (l) $-\frac{1}{2}$, $1\frac{1}{3}$   (m) $-4$, $-\frac{2}{3}$   (n) $-1\frac{1}{2}$, $\frac{3}{4}$   (o) $-1\frac{1}{3}$, $\frac{3}{4}$   (p) $2\frac{1}{2}$   (q) $\frac{3}{4}$, 4   (r) $-4$, 4

(s) $-1\frac{1}{2}$, $1\frac{1}{2}$   (t) 0, 9   (u) 0, $-\frac{1}{4}$   3. (a) $-6$, 1   (b) 4, 7   (c) $-7$, 5   (d) $\frac{3}{4}$, 2   (e) 0, 1   (f) $-\frac{1}{2}$, $2\frac{1}{3}$   (g) $-3$, $-1$

(h) $-2$, 2   (i) $-2$, $\frac{1}{3}$   (j) $-4$, 3   (k) $-2\frac{1}{2}$, $2\frac{1}{2}$   (l) $-2$, 5   (m) 0, 4   (n) 1, 2   (o) $-10$, 6   (p) $-4$, 5   (q) $-\frac{5}{6}$, 1

4. (a) $x(2x+3)$   (b) $2x^2+3x-90=0$   (c) $x=6$ metres   (d) $54m^2$   5. $x^2+10x=39$;

length of square = 3 units   6. 10   7. $-8$ and $-7$ or 7 and 8   8. 25   9. 2·5 units or 1 unit   10. 12km

11. 5cm   12. (i) (a) $x+5$   (b) $x-7$   (c) $x-12$   (iii) 27cm   13. 7cm from one end   Review 1 (a) $-4$, 7

(b) 0, $\frac{1}{4}$   (c) $-3$, 5   (d) $-5$, $\frac{1}{2}$   (e) $-5$, 0   (f) $-1\frac{1}{2}$, $1\frac{1}{4}$   (g) $-5$, 5   (h) $\frac{3}{4}$, 6   (i) $-6$, 4   Review 2 (b) 4, $-11$

(c) 11m   Review 3 $7\frac{1}{2}$, 8   Review 4 (b) $x^2+22x$   (c) 4 metres   Review 5 $n^2+(51-n)^2=39^2$;

length is 36cm

**Exercise 10:11**

1. $-5·2$, 1·2   2. $-3·2$, 1·2   3. 2·7, $-0·7$   4. 6·5, 0·5   5. $-2·6$, 1·6   6. $-1$, $-2$   7. 2·4, 0·6   8. $-2·8$, 1·3   9. $-1$, 0·8

10. 1·4, 0·4   Review 1 4·6, $-0·6$   Review 2 $-5·2$, 0·2   Review 3 $-2·9$, 0·9

**Exercise 10:13**

1. (a) $a=1, b=2, c=4$   (b) $a=1, b=3, c=-1$   (c) $a=2, b=-1, c=-7$   (d) $a=3, b=-5, c=2$   (e) $a=1$,
$b=4, c=-1$   (f) $a=5, b=7, c=-4$   (g) $a=6, b=0, c=-5$   (h) $a=2, b=-3, c=0$   2. (a) 4·56, 0·44
(b) $-1·78$, 0·28   (c) 1·15, $-0·35$   (d) $-0·77$, 0·43   (e) 0·84, $-0·59$   (f) 1, 3   (g) $-3·56$, 0·56   (h) $-0·87$, 2·87
(i) $-3·45$, 1·45   (j) $-1·79$, 2·79   3. (a) $x^2+(x+50)^2=650^2$   (c) $x=434$ metres (to the nearest metre)
(d) 268 metres (to the nearest metre)   4. 0·98 sec, 2·08 sec (2 d.p.)   5. (i) (a) $n+1$   (b) $n+2$   (c) $(n+1)^2$
(ii) $n^2+(n+1)^2+(n+2)^2$   (iii) 2·5cm   6. 3·8cm (1 d.p.)   7. $4\frac{1}{6}$cm   Review 1 (a) $-7·4$, $-1·6$   (b) $-1·1$, 3·6
(c) $-0·3$, 3·3   (d) $-5·7$, 0·7   Review 2 (a) one possible expression is $2w(30+2w)+60w$   (b) $900=120w+4w^2$
(d) 6·2cm

**Exercise 10:14**

1. (b) 1·30   (c) $-2·30$   2. (b) $-1·79$   (c) The sequence of values $x_1, x_2, x_3, \ldots$ diverges.   (e) 2·79   3. (b) 1·35
(c) $-1·85$   4. (b) $-1·56$   (c) $x_{n+1}=-\sqrt{4+x_n}$   Review (b) 0·27   (d) 2·38

**Exercise 10:16**

1. (a) $-4$, 3   (b) 4·3, 0·70 (2 s.f.)   (c) $-3·9$, 3·9 (2 s.f.)   (d) $-2\frac{1}{2}$, $\frac{2}{3}$   (e) $-6$, $\frac{1}{2}$   (f) 2·3, 0·69 (2 s.f.)
(g) $-4·3$, 2·3 (2 s.f.)   (h) 0·74, $-0·54$ (2 s.f.)   2. $n^2+n=20$; $-5$ or 4   3. 2 seconds   4. $860m^2$ (2 s.f.)
5. 9   6. (a) $x^2+3x-2=0$   (b) 0·56 (2 s.f.)   7. (a) A(2, 0), B(4, 0)   (b) $x^2-6x+8=4$; C(0·8, 4), D(5·2, 4)
(c) $(x-3)^2-1$; E(3, $-1$)   (d) 6·4, 0·63 (2 s.f.) The solutions give the x-coordinates of the points of intersection.
Review 1 (a) 2·4, $-0·85$ (2 s.f.)   (b) $-1\frac{1}{2}$, 1   (c) 0, 5   Review 2 (a) one possible expression is
$4x^2+2x(30-2x)+2x(20-2x)$   (c) 3·5m

**Exercise 10:19**

1. **(a)** $\frac{10}{27}$ **(b)** $-34$ **(c)** $-3\frac{1}{20}$ **(d)** $\frac{5}{8}$ **(e)** 5 or $-\frac{1}{3}$ **(f)** 4·4 or $-1·4$ (1 d.p.) **(g)** 1·7 or $-1·7$ (1 d.p.)
**(h)** 0·7 or $-2·2$ (1 d.p.) **(i)** $\frac{5}{13}$ **(j)** 1·8 or 0·2 (1 d.p.) **(k)** 2 or $-6\frac{1}{3}$   2. **(a)** $-1$ or 2 **(b)** $(-1, -2)$, $(2, 1)$

3. $\frac{29}{32}$ 4. **(a)** $\frac{500}{x}$ **(b)** $\frac{500}{x+10}$ **(d)** 95km/h (to 2 s.f.) 5. **(b)** $\frac{36}{n(n-1)} = 3$; n = 4 6. 34cm 7. **(a)** $\frac{1200}{x} + 1$
**(b)** $\frac{1200}{x+2} + 1$ **(c)** $\frac{2400}{x(x+2)}$ **(d)** 48 metres 8. 7 Review 1 **(a)** $2\frac{2}{3}$ **(b)** 1·7, $-0·1$ (1 d.p.) **(c)** $1\frac{5}{13}$
**(d)** 5 or $-4·5$ **(e)** 6·2 or $-0·9$ (1 d.p.) Review 2 **(a)** $\frac{50}{200+w}$ **(b)** $\frac{40}{200-w}$
**(c)** $\frac{50}{200+w} = \frac{40}{200-w}$ ; w = 22mph (2 s.f.) Review 3 **(a)** $\frac{225}{n+1} - \frac{184}{n} = 2$ **(b)** 8

**Chapter 10 Review**

1. **(a)** $3(d + 2e)$ **(b)** $4x(x + 2y)$ **(c)** $(x - 5)(x - 6)$ **(d)** $(5x + 1)(5x - 1)$ 2. **(a)** $x^2 - 4x + 2 = (x - 2)^2 - 2$.
a $= -2$, b $= -2$. Minimum value $= -2$. **(b)** 3·41, 0·59 3. **(a)** after 5 seconds **(b)** 50 metres 4. $\frac{2(x-1)}{(x+3)(x-5)}$
5. **(b)** 23·7m (1 d.p.), 6·3m (1 d.p.) 6. **(a)** $3x^2 + y^2$ **(b)** $(a + b)(a - b)$ 7. **(a)** $L = \frac{2V}{W(E+R)}$ **(c)** 5, 10
8. **(a)** $x_2 = 3·3166248$, $x_3 = 3·21195031$, $x_4 = 3·1956142$ **(b)** 3·193 correct to 3 decimal places (or 3·192
to 3 correct decimal places) 9. **(a)** $S = 20 + 4n$ **(b)** 40 **(c)** $4n - \frac{n^2}{10}$ As n increases this difference becomes
larger. 10. **(a)** 75 **(b)** 175cm **(c)** $M = \sqrt{\frac{P}{a}} + b$ 11. **(a) (i)** about 0·7 seconds **(ii)** 20m **(b)** about 13m/s
**(c)** 3·26 seconds 12. **(a)** $\frac{20}{x} + \frac{20}{x-2} = 4$ **(c)** 11·1, 0·9 **(d)** If x = 0·9km per hour then Fred's speed is
$-1·1$km per hour on the way back. A negative value is not possible. Hence the only answer for Fred's speed is
11·1km per hour (1 d.p.) 13. **(a)** The points are clustered about the line n = 60 − 6x. **(c)** £6·70 or £3·30
**(d)** 40 people at £3·30 or 20 at £6·70 14. 4·14cm (2 d.p.) 15. $x(x + 2)(x - 2)$ 16. **(a) (ii)** $-1·5$ accurate to 1 d.p.
(or $-1·4$ to 1 correct d.p.) **(b) (i)** 5·5 (1 d.p.), $-1·5$ (1 d.p.) **(ii)** The smaller solution can be found accurately
by using the iterative formula given in (a). 17. **(a)** $(m + n)(m - n)$ **(b)** $9991 = 100^2 - 3^2$. Prime factors are
$100 + 3$ and $100 - 3$; i.e. 103 and 97.

# Chapter 11   Graphs of Related Functions

**Exercise 11:2**

1. **(a)**

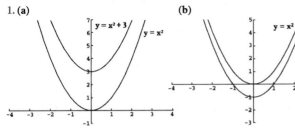

**(b)**

**(c)**

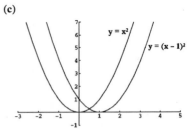

**(d)**

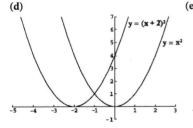

**(e)**

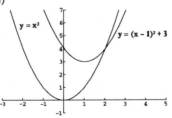

**(f)**

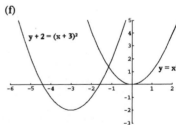

Answers

**2. (a)**

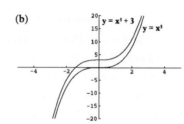

**(b)**

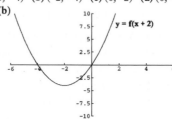

**(c)**

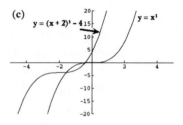

3. Coordinates of lowest point are: **(a)** $(0, -4)$ **(b)** $(-2, -4)$ **(c)** $(0, -2)$ **(d)** $(0, -4)$ **(e)** $(0, -8)$

**(a)**

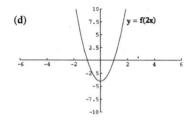

**(b)**

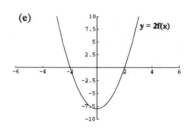

**(c)**

**(d)**

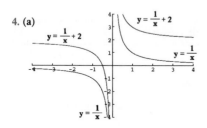

**(e)**

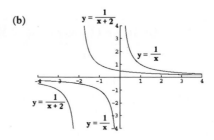

**4. (a)**

**(b)**

5. **(a)** Crosses x-axis at $x = 0$ and $x = 8$; highest point is $(4, 8)$. **(b)** Crosses x-axis at $x = 0$ and $x = 16$; highest point is $(8, 16)$

**(a)**

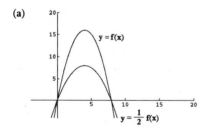

**(b)**

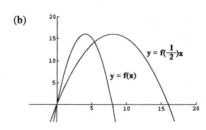

6. **(i)** a = 2, b = –1  **(ii)** (–2, –1)  **(iii) (a)**

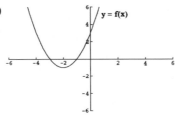

**(b)**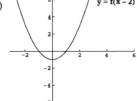

**(c)**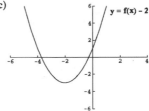

**(d)**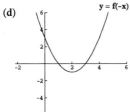

**(e)**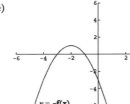

7. **(a)** a = 2, b = –5  **(b)** The graph of y = g(x) may be obtained by translating the graph of y = f(x) by the vector $\left(\begin{smallmatrix}-2\\-5\end{smallmatrix}\right)$.

8. **(a)** By translating y = f(x) by the vector $\left(\begin{smallmatrix}-2\\0\end{smallmatrix}\right)$.  g(x) = f(x + 2)

**(b)** By translating y = f(x) by the vector $\left(\begin{smallmatrix}0\\-2\end{smallmatrix}\right)$.  g(x) = f(x) – 2

**(c)** By translating y = f(x) by the vector $\left(\begin{smallmatrix}2\\1\end{smallmatrix}\right)$.  g(x) = f(x – 2) + 1

**(d)** By multiplying each x-coordinate on y = f(x) by $\frac{1}{2}$.  g(x) = f(2x)

**Review 1** Coordinates of highest or lowest points are: **(a)** (0, – 4)  **(b)** (2, –2)  **(c)** (2, –2)  **(d)** (4, – 4)
**(e)** (–2, – 4)  **(f)** (2, 4)

**(a)**
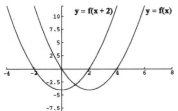

**(b)**
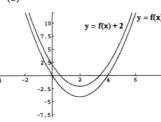

**(c)**
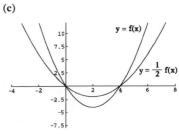

**(d)**

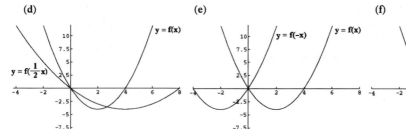

**(e)**

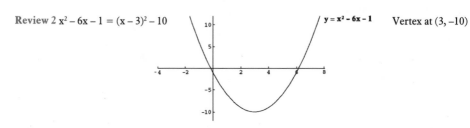

**(f)**

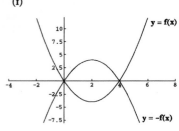

Review 2 $x^2 - 6x - 1 = (x - 3)^2 - 10$

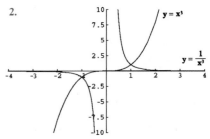

$y = x^2 - 6x - 1$    Vertex at $(3, -10)$

Page 222    **Exercise 11:5**

1.

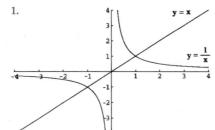

$y = x$

$y = \dfrac{1}{x}$

2.

$y = x^3$

$y = \dfrac{1}{x^3}$

3.

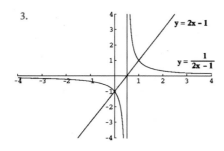

$y = 2x - 1$

$y = \dfrac{1}{2x - 1}$

4. **(b)** $(0, 1)$   **(d)** $(0, 1)$
**(a)**
**(c)**

$y = x^2 + 1$

$y = \dfrac{1}{x^2 + 1}$

5. **(ii)**

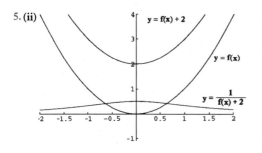

$y = f(x) + 2$

$y = f(x)$

$y = \dfrac{1}{f(x) + 2}$

6.

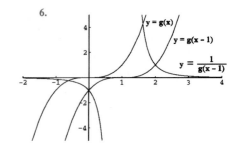

$y = g(x)$

$y = g(x - 1)$

$y = \dfrac{1}{g(x - 1)}$

Review 1

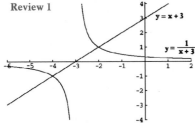

Review 2

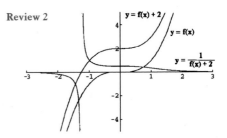

Review 3

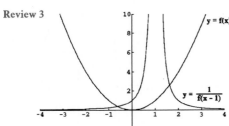

Page 224

**Exercise 11:7**

1. (a)

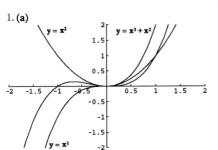

(b)

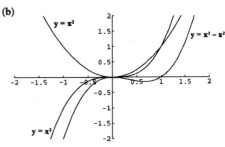

2. We add the y-coordinate of each point on $y = x^3$ to double the y-coordinate on $y = x^2$.

3. Possible answers are: $y = x^2$ and $y = -2x + 6$; $y = x^2 + 6$ and $y = -2x$; $y = x^2 - 2x$ and $y = 6$.

4.

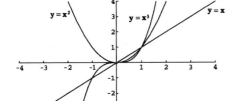

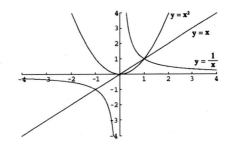

Review 1 (a)

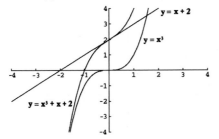

(b)

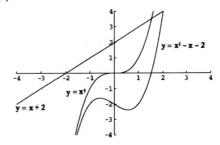

Answers

Review 2 Since $x^2 - 4x = x(x - 4)$ the graph of $y = x^2 - 4x$ may be obtained by multiplying the y-coordinates of each point on the graphs of $y = x$ and $y = x - 4$.

Page 224

**Chapter 11   Review**

1.

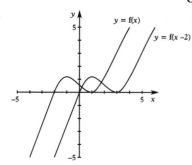

2. (a)

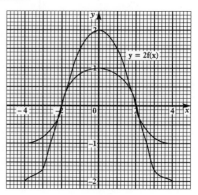

(b)

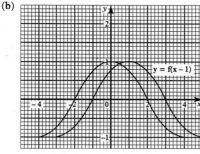

3. (a)

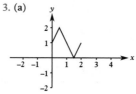

(b)

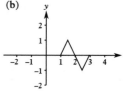

(c)

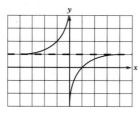

4. (a)

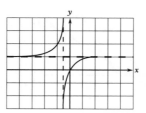

(b)

5.

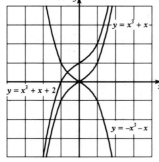

6. (a) $1\cdot47, -7\cdot47$  (b) $p = 3, q = -20$
(c) (i)

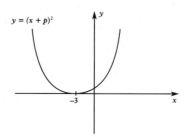

602

(ii)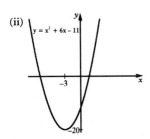

7. (a) 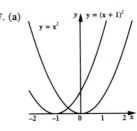  (b) $-\frac{1}{2}$

(c) 2 and −4

8.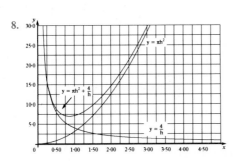

# Chapter 12   Linear Programming

Page 231

**Exercise 12:1**

1. (a) $x \geq 2, y \leq 8, y \geq 4, x + y \leq 12$

(b)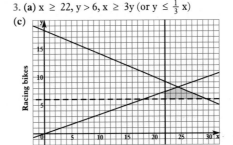

(c) In the following the first figure gives the number of 3-seat couches and the second figure gives the number of 2-seat couches:
2 and 4, 2 and 5, 2 and 6, 2 and 7, 2 and 8, 3 and 4, 3 and 5, 3 and 6, 3 and 7, 3 and 8, 4 and 4, 4 and 5, 4 and 6, 4 and 7, 4 and 8, 5 and 4, 5 and 5, 5 and 6, 5 and 7, 6 and 4, 6 and 5, 6 and 6, 7 and 4, 7 and 5, 8 and 4.

The region which is wanted is unshaded.

2. (b) $x \geq 50, y \geq 70, y - x \leq 40.$

(c)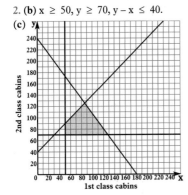

The shaded region gives all the possible values of x and y.

3. (a) $x \geq 22, y > 6, x \geq 3y$ (or $y \leq \frac{1}{3}x$)

(c)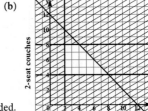

The required region is shaded.

22 mountain and 7 racing bikes, 23 mountain and 7 racing bikes, 24 mountain and 7 racing bikes, 24 mountain and 8 racing bikes, 25 mountain and 7 racing bikes, 25 mountain and 8 racing bikes, 26 mountain and 7 racing bikes, 27 mountain and 7 racing bikes.

603

*Answers*

**Review (a)** x < 300, y ≤ 140, x + y ≤ 400   **(b)** 20x + 25y ≥ 5000

**(c)**

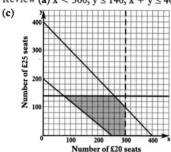

The required region is shaded

Page 235

**Exercise 12:3**

1. **(i)** (3, 2), (3, 5·5), (6, 7), (11, 2)   **(ii) (a)** 20   **(b)** 7   **(c)** 24   **(d)** 8   **(e)** –9   **(f)** 2   2. **(a)** x = 89, y = 64; greatest value is 1530   **(b)** x = 60, y = 0; minimum value is 120.   3. **(a)** y ≥ 0, y ≤ 8   **(b)** x + y ≤ 15

**(c)**

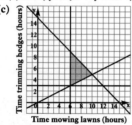

**(d)** 50x + 40y = R; greatest amount = £700.

4. **(a)** x + y ≤ 12
**(c)** 300x + 100y = C
**(d)** 4 weeks for Robbie's and
8 weeks for Deborah's;
minimum cost is £2000

**(b)**

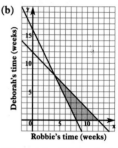

The required region is shaded.

The unshaded region gives
all the possible values of x and y.

5. **(a)** x ≥ 6, y ≥ 2, x + y ≤ 15   **(b)** x ≤ 2y (or y ≥ $\frac{1}{2}$ x)

**(c)**

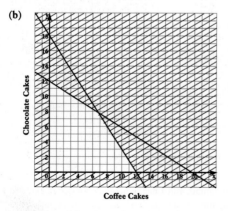

All possible values of x and
y are in the shaded region.
**(d)** £39   6. **(a)** 3x + 2y ≤ 36, 150x + 250y ≤ 3000

**(b)**

All possible values of x and y are in the unshaded region.

(c) Lisa can make either 6 coffee cakes and 8 chocolate cakes or 7 cofee cakes and 7 chocolate cakes.
Review 1 (a) (7, 6), (10, 10), (16, 4), (8, 4)  (b) $x = 16$, $y = 4$; least value is $-12$  (c) 88
Review 2 (a) $x \le 1000$, $y \ge 200$, $y \le 400$, $x + y \le 1000$
(b)

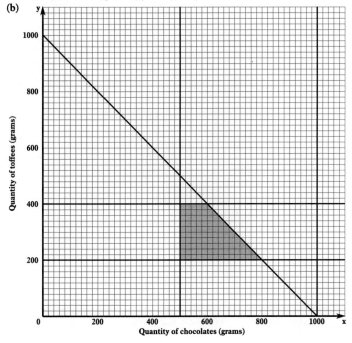

All the possible values of x and y are in the shaded region.  (d) £3·40

Page 238

**Chapter 12   Review**

1. (b)

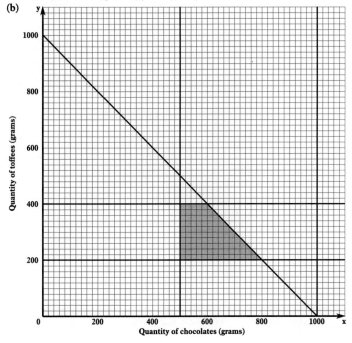

(c) 67 at £2 and 133 at £3

2. (a) $x + y \le 40$  (b) Jack works at least 12 hours each week in the newsagent's.
(d)

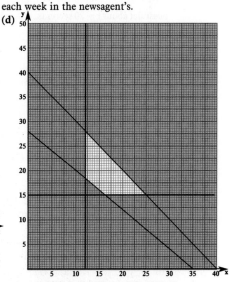

(e) (i) £162  (ii) 31  (iii) £157·50
(iv) 36 (20 at newsagents' and 16 at filling station).

3. **(a)** $x < 250$, $x + y \leq 300$, $x \geq 2y$  **(b)**
**(c)** £1000  **(d)** 120
4. **(a)** 120 hours
**(b) (i)** $C = 50x + 20y$  **(ii)** £29

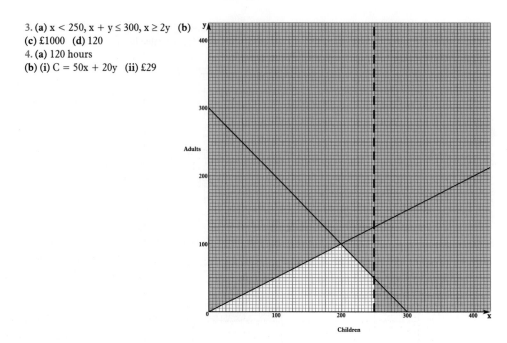

## Chapter 13    Algebra Review

**1. (i) (a)** $y = 2$  **(b)** $y = 8$  **(c)** $y = 2x$  **(d)** $y = 3 - x$  **(e)** None, since the line $y = 0$ (the x-axis) is already drawn.
**(ii) (a)** 1  **(b)** 3  **(c)** 3  **(d)** 1  **(e)** 1    **2. (i) (a)** $n$  **(b)** $n^6$  **(c)** $\frac{8}{n^6}$  **(d)** $n^4$  **(e)** $\frac{4n^3}{m^2}$  **(ii) (a)** $\frac{1}{2}$  **(b)** $-2\cdot5$  **(c)** 0
**(d)** $\frac{1}{2}$  **(iii)** Rewrite as $\frac{1}{\sqrt{9}}$ to get $\frac{1}{3}$.  **(iv)** $2\cdot01$ (2 d.p.)    **3. (b)** gradient is $0\cdot3$ (1 d.p.); rate is $0\cdot3$cm/sec
**(c)** $0\cdot3$ cm/sec (1 d.p.)  **(d)** We find the time when the gradient of the tangent is positive and as close to zero as
possible; about $t = 20$ seconds.    **4. (b)** An approximate relationship is $E = 0\cdot5W + 1\cdot8$.

**5. (i)**

| x | −3·0 | −2·5 | −2·0 | −1·5 | −1·0 | −0·5 | 0 | 0·5 | 1·0 | 1·5 | 2·0 |
|---|------|------|------|------|------|------|---|-----|-----|-----|-----|
| y | 27 | 15·6 | 9 | 5·2 | 3 | 1·7 | 1 | 0·6 | 0·3 | 0·2 | 0·1 |

**(iii) (a)** $-1\cdot6$ (1 d.p.)  **(b)** $-2\cdot1$ (1 d.p.)  **(c)** $-2\cdot7$ (1 d.p.)    **6. (a)** Graph y against $x^2$. The gradient of this graph
gives a; b is where this graph crosses the y-axis.  **(b)** An approximate relationship is $y = 9\cdot2 - 0\cdot1x^2$  **(c)** $9\cdot6$m
(to the nearest tenth of a metre)

**7. (a)**

| x | −6 | −5 | −4 | −3 | −2 | −1 | 0 | 1 | 2 | 3 | 4 |
|---|----|----|----|----|----|----|---|---|---|---|---|
| y | −16 | −7 | 0 | 5 | 8 | 9 | 8 | 5 | 0 | −7 | −16 |

**(b)** $0\cdot7$ and $-2\cdot7$ (1 d.p.)  **(c)** Yes. We find where the graph $y = (2 - x)(4 + x)$ meets the line $y = 1 - 2x$.
**8. (a)** $(4, 2), (16, 8), (28, 5), (28, 2)$  **(b)** $x = 28$, $y = 5$. Greatest value is 33.  **(c)** $-20$    **9.** At about $t = 10$ seconds
and $t = 27$ seconds since at these times the gradients of both graphs are the same.    **10. (a)** If the correct
value has been chosen for n the graph should be a straight line.  **(b)** A: $y = 5x - 3$  B: $y = \frac{2}{x} - 1$  C: $y = 0\cdot01x^3 + 2\cdot5$
D: $y = 0\cdot5x^2 + 3$    **11. (a)** $0\cdot14$ (2 d.p.); the acceleration at $t = 14$ seconds is $0\cdot14$m/s².
**(b)** at about $t = 73$ seconds  **(c)** during the first 10 seconds    **12. (a)** $n(n - 4)$  **(b)** $(n - 6)(n + 2)$ **(c)** $(n - 2)(n + 2)$
**(d)** $8(n - 2)$  **(e)** $(n - 5)(n + 2m)$    **13. (a)** D  **(b)** Giving the terms to the nearest penny: £66, £69·30, £72·77,
£76·40, £80·22, £84·23    **14.** The mistake is in the last line. We cannot divide both sides of $x(x - 2) = 4(x -$
$2)$ by $x - 2$ as $x = 2$; we cannot divide by zero.    **15.** 150m    **16.** 17    **17. (a)** $\frac{x-1}{x-3}$  **(b)** $-\frac{x}{x+y}$  **(c)** $\frac{x}{x+1}$
**(d)** $\frac{x-4}{(x-2)(x-3)}$    **18. (a)** $(x - 1)^2 + 4$  **(b)** 4  **(c)** 1  **(d)** No; the square $(x - 1)^2$ can take values as large
as we please.    **19. (i) (a)** $2, 1\cdot5, 1\cdot\dot6, 1\cdot6, 1\cdot625$  **(b)** $2, 0\cdot3, 0\cdot75, 0\cdot57$ (2 d.p.), $0\cdot\dot6\dot3$  **(ii) (a)** divergent
**(b)** convergent  **(c)** convergent  **(d)** convergent  **(e)** convergent  **(f)** convergent  **(iii) (b)** 0  **(c)** 0  **(d)** $2\cdot3$
**(e)** 0  **(f)** $0\cdot618$ (3 d.p.)    **20. (a)** 41  **(b)** 35 and 44    **21. (a)** $(x - 1)^2 + 1$

**(b)** 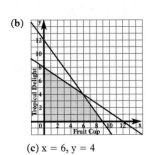 **(c)**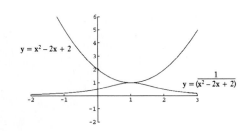

22. **(b)** 2·70  **(c)** The sequence of values diverges.  **(d)** Yes. The sequence of values converges more quickly.
**(e)** $x_{n+1} = -\sqrt{10 - x_n}$ ; –3·70   23. **(a)** $(3x + 4)(2x + 6) = 130$  **(c)** To the nearest millimetre,
length = 11·686m and width = 11·124m   24. Distance is approximately 29 metres.   25. **(b)** 1  **(d)** 1·174
26. **(a)** $x + 1\cdot5y \le 12$

**(b)**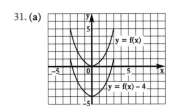

**(c)** x = 6, y = 4

27. **(a)** $\frac{50}{x-2} - \frac{50}{x} = \frac{1}{3}$  **(c)** 18·3km/h (3 s.f.)   28. Each graph is obtained
from y = f(x) as follows: **(a)** reflection in the x-axis  **(b)** reflection in the y-axis
**(c)** translation by the vector $\binom{-2}{0}$  **(d)** translation by the vector $\binom{0}{4}$
**(e)** translation by the vector $\binom{2}{-1}$  **(f)** enlarged by a factor of $\frac{1}{2}$ in the x-direction
**(g)** enlarged by a factor of 2 in the y-direction  **(h)** enlarged by a factor of 2
in the x-direction  **(i)** enlarged by a factor of $\frac{1}{2}$ in the y-direction
29. **(a)** $\frac{n}{n+1}$  **(c)** n = 8. The sum of the 8th and 9th terms of the sequence
$\frac{1}{2}, \frac{2}{3}, \frac{3}{4}, \frac{4}{5}, \ldots$ is $\frac{161}{90}$. The denominators of the terms in the sequence.
$\frac{7}{6}, \frac{17}{12}, \frac{31}{20}, \frac{49}{30}, \ldots$ are $2 \times 3, 3 \times 4, 4 \times 5, 5 \times 6, \ldots$; the term with
denominator 90 ($9 \times 10$) is the 8th term which is the sum of the 8th and 9th
terms of the original sequence.   30. **(a)** $(p - q)(p + q)$  **(b)** $91 = 10^2 - 3^2$;
prime factors are 7, 13

31. **(a)** **(b)**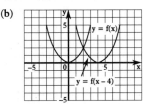

32. **(a)** m = 2, c = 3  **(b)** **(i)** about 2
**(ii)** 0  **(c)** about –0·7 and 2·7
33. **(a)** $2x^2 - 5x - 12$ **(b)** $5x(2x - 1)$
**(c)** –2·5   34. **(a)** **(i)** $(x + 1)(x + 2)$
**(ii)** $(2x - 5)(x + 2)$  **(b)** $\frac{3}{(2x+1)(x+1)}$
35. **(a)** $8^{\frac{1}{3}} = \sqrt[3]{8} = 2$  **(b)** 0·2

36. **(a)**

| T hours | 1·70 | 1·38 | 1·00 | 0·84 | 0·63 |
|---|---|---|---|---|---|
| V km/h | 36 | 45 | 67 | 83 | 120 |
| $\frac{1}{V}$ | 0·028 | 0·022 | 0·015 | 0·012 | 0·008 |

**(b)** The points plotted are (0·028, 1·7), (0·022, 1·38),
(0·015, 1), (0·012, 0·84), (0·008, 0·63).  **(c)** The graph of
T against $\frac{1}{V}$ is a straight line.  **(d)** a = 54, b = 0·20
**(e)** **(i)** about 1·2 hours  **(ii)** about 67km/h

37. **(a)** **(i)** $3^4 + 4^4 + 5^4 + 6^4 = 7^4$  **(ii)** The answer given to (i) is not correct. **(b)** **(ii)** The sum of three odd
numbers and two even numbers is odd. $8^5$ is even.
38. **(a)**

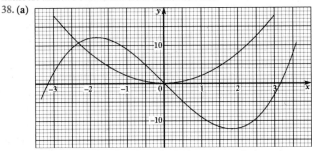

**(b)** 0 and –2·3  **(c)** **(i)** 4·2426407  **(ii)** $x_3 = 4\cdot2994513$, $x_4 = 4\cdot3126445$, $x_5 = 4\cdot3157026$   39. about 0·5m/s²

40. **(a)** $60x + 160y \leq 640$

**(b)**

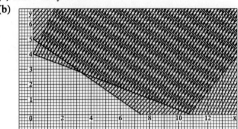

**(c)** $x = 4\cdot5$, $y = 2$ giving 68 grams of protein

41. **(a) (i)** $x_2 = 1\cdot714$ (3 d.p.), $x_3 = 2\cdot1$, $x_4 = 1\cdot967$ (3 d.p.) **(ii)** 2 **(b) (ii)** $-6, 2$

42. **(b)** $x = 0\cdot697$m  43. **(a)** about 9cm **(b)** The amount of rain which fell.

44. **(a) (i)** 1 **(ii)** 9 **(b) (i)** 4 **(ii)** 1

45. **(a)**

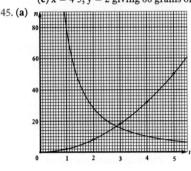

**(b) (i)** about $2\cdot85$ **(ii)** $40 = t^{3\cdot5}$
**(c)** about 20 **(d)** about 16
47. **(a)** $\frac{16}{81}$ **(b)** $0\cdot25$

48. **(a)**

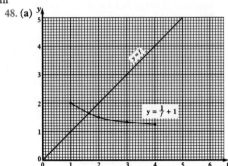

An approximate solution is $1\cdot6$.
**(b)** Equation is $f^2 - f - 1 = 0$.
Solution is $1\cdot618$ (4 s.f.)

## Shape, Space and Measures Revision

Page 268  **Revision Exercise**

1. **(a)** $a = 64°$, $b = 64°$, $c = 52°$, $d = 64°$, $e = 64°$ **(b)** $\angle ABC = \angle ACB$  2. $\frac{6}{7}$  3. **(i) (a)** 3, 7, 12 **(b)** 1, 10, 11 **(c)** 5, 8, 9 **(ii)** 30m and 41m; 615m² **(iii)** 740m² (3 s.f.) **(iv)** $1\cdot04$ha  5. **(a)** kite, rhombus **(b)** kite **(c)** parallelogram, rhombus **(d)** trapezium **(e)** none of these shapes  6. **(a)** $12\cdot35$cm **(b)** $12\cdot25$cm 7. **(a)** B : 2 axes, C : 6 axes, D : 2 axes **(b)** A : order 4, B : order 2, C : order 6, D : order 2  8. **(a)** $13\cdot6$cm (3 s.f.) **(b)** 37° (to the nearest degree) **(c)** $9\cdot7$mm (2 s.f.)  9. **(a)** C **(b)** B **(c)** C **(d)** D **(e)** A : 6, B : 4, C : 2, D : 0 10. $\frac{d}{100} = \tan 34°$, $d = 67$m (2 s.f.)  11. **(a)** 149 600 000km **(b)** 500 sec $= 8\cdot3$ min  12. **(a)** a reflection in the line $x = 1$ **(b)** 90° about centre $(-1, 1)$ **(c)** $(1, 2), (3, 3), (3, 4), (1, 7)$  13. **(a)** dimension of area is $L^2$, dimension of given formula is $L^3$ **(b)** A, C, E, F **(c)** B, D, H  14. $\angle AWT = 9°$, $\angle AWB = 6°$ **(b)** Use $\triangle TAW$ to find TA, use $\triangle BAW$ to find BA, add TA and BA. 13m (to the nearest metre) 15. **(e)** 19 metres  16. **(a)** they are equiangular **(b)** AC **(c)** $13\cdot31$m  17. **(a)** 180° **(b)** F **(c)** E **(d)** C (D is a combination of a reflection and a translation)  18. **(a)** 129cm² (3 s.f.) **(b)** $42\cdot8$cm (3 s.f.) 19. **(a)** 42° **(b)** $7\cdot2$km (2 s.f.) **(c)** 14:53 (to the nearest minute)  20. **(a)** a parallelogram (or a triangle) **(b)** translation, reflection  21. **(a)** $40l$ **(b)** about £30  22. **(a)** 45° **(b)** 135°  23. **(a)** parallelogram **(b)** $\angle DCE = 52°$ (angle sum of triangle), $\angle DCB = 128°$ (adjacent angles on straight line), $\angle ADC = 52°$ (interior angles, parallel lines) **(d)** $AX = 0\cdot12$m (2 s.f.); $AB = 4\cdot38$m (2 s.f.) **(e)** $XD = 0\cdot16$m (2 s.f.), area ABCD $= 0\cdot7$m² (1 s.f.) 24. **(a)** $a = 12$cm, $b = 20$cm, $c = 12$cm, $d = 20$cm **(b)** 6 **(c)** prism (or triangular prism) **(d)** $0\cdot96$ litres **(e)** 672cm³ **(f)** 250cm³ (2 s.f.) **(g)** $2\cdot9$cm (2 s.f.) **(h)** $3\cdot9$cm  25. $2\cdot6$m  26. **(b) (ii)** 120° clockwise or 240° anticlockwise **(c) (i)** 2 **(ii)** 6 **(d)** cube  27. **(a)** $8\cdot8$m (1 d.p.) **(b)** to the nearest tenth of a metre since $13\cdot6$m is given to this degree of accuracy  28. **(a)** 34cm **(b)** 44cm² **(c)** A possible answer is: **(d)** 4cm, 2cm, 3cm, **(f)** **(e)** 24cm³

29. 4·5cm   30. Those circled are 3·15km, 3·16km, 3·18km, 3·20km, 3·24km   31. (a) ∠DAB = 62°, ∠ABD = 59°, ∠ADB = 59°, ∠BDC = 59°, ∠BCD = 59° (i) False (ii) True (iii) True (b) One possible reason is: alternate angles ABD and DBC are not equal   32. (a) 22·6° (b) 22·6°   33. 150km/h   34. (a) (i) d (ii) e (iii) g (iv) b (v) a (vi) c (vii) h (b) (i) (−2·2, 1·4) (ii) 2·5   35. (a) (i) 1·35m² (ii) 1·62m³ (b) 4   36. (a) 055° (b) 345° (c) 235°

37.

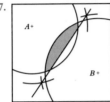

38. (a) 188cm (3 s.f.) (b) 531   39. (a) abh, a²b (b) dimension of 2π(R − r) is Length, dimension of area is (Length)²   40. (a) (i) 3·1cm (1 d.p.)
(ii) 26·4cm (1 d.p.) (b) (i) 6·75m (ii) 70°   41. (b) (i) about 13·9km (ii) 137°
(c) (ii) 302°   42. (a) (i) 80cm (ii) 50cm (b) 5040cm²
(c) 67° (to the nearest degree)   43. (a) 175·4cm² (b) 26·8cm to 27·0cm
(c) 37·4° (1 d.p.)   44. (a) (i) 120° (ii) 108° (iii) 24° (b) exterior angle would be 48° which does not divide into 360° exactly.

## Chapter 14   Similar Shapes. Congruent Triangles. Proofs

Page 287                                    **Exercise 14:2**

1. 51·2cm²   2. (a) The triangles are equiangular. (b) 0·45 square units   3. 250cm²   4. 3·7*l* (2 s.f.)
5. £40·50   6. 350g (2 s.f.)   7. ⅞ : 1   8. (a) 32 cubes (b) Number of cubes = 2³ × 4 (c) 72cm² (d) 288cm²
(ii) (a) 40 (b) 135 (c) 320 (d) 1080   9. 5cm: £1·45; 7cm: £3·95   10. 37 litres (2 s.f.)   11. (a) 26cm² (2 s.f.)
(b) 59cm² (2 s.f.)   12. (a) Yes (b) No (c) 4 : 25   13. 4 times as much   14. 24cm × 16cm × 3cm
15. 44mm (2 s.f.)   16. 76mm (2 s.f.)   17. d = 5·5cm (2 s.f.); h = 6·6cm (2 s.f.)   18. 1cm²   Review 1 (a) 3
(b) 9 (c) 45cm² (d) 27 (e) 4·2cm³ (2 s.f.)   Review 2 6kg   Review 3 (a) The triangles are equiangular.
(b) 6·4cm²   Review 4 (a) 216 (b) surface area of shape shown = 34cm², surface area of new shape = 306cm²
Review 5 20m²   Review 6 16cm.

Page 294                                    **Exercise 14:5**

1. (a) Δs $\frac{PQR}{CAB}$, Δs $\frac{PQR}{XYZ}$, Δs $\frac{PQR}{NML}$ (b) ∠B, ∠Z, ∠L (c) AB, YZ, ML   2. (a) Δ ABC (SSS); Δ XYZ (SAS)
3. Triangles ABC, RQP, UST   4. (a) RHS (b) SAS (d) SSS (f) AAS (g) AAS (j) AAS   7. Δs ABD and CBD; Δs ABX and CBX; Δs AXD and CXD   11. No   14. (c) The line joining the centres is the perpendicular bisector of the common chord.   Review 1 Yes.

Page 300                                    **Exercise 14:6**

6. Proves the sum of the interior angles of a parallelogram is 360°. Possible reasons are: line 1 – alternate angles, parallel lines; line 2 – corresponding angles, parallel lines; line 3 – interior angles, parallel lines; line 4 – adjacent angles on straight line.

Page 303                                    **Chapter 14   Review**

1. (a) 6·75cm (b) they are equal (c) 144cm²   2. 356cm³ (3 s.f.)   3. (a) 56·25cm³ (b) 4 : 1 (c) 3600cm³
4. (a) 3·44cm (2 d.p.) (b) 41° (to the nearest degree) (c) (i) 104° (to the nearest degree) (ii) 18cm   5. 8 oz
6. (a) about 1·63 : 1 (b) about 2·08 : 1 (c) Yes. It is just a little less than ½ a bottle – it is about 0·48 of the standard bottle   7. 10·1cm   9. 39cm³ (2 s.f.)

## Chapter 15   Perimeter. Area. Volume

Page 309                                    **Exercise 15:2**

1. (a) 29cm² (2 s.f.) (b) 2480mm² (3 s.f.)   2. (a) 9·7cm (2 s.f.) (b) 80mm (2 s.f.)   3. (a) 36·7cm² (3 s.f.)
(b) 410cm (3 s.f.)   4. 0·30 square metres (2 s.f.)   5. (a) 179° (3 s.f.) (b) 9·3cm (2 s.f.)   6. 13cm (2 s.f.)
7. (a) 100° (3 s.f.) (b) 550m² (2 s.f.)   8. (a) CB = 45cm, OC = 19cm (b) area ΔOCB = 427·5cm²; area ΔOAB = 855cm² (c) θ = 66·7° (3 s.f.); ∠AOB = 133° (3 s.f.) (d) 2795cm² (4 s.f.) (e) 1940cm² (3 s.f.)
9. (a) AB = BC and AC = AB. Hence AB = BC = AC. Hence ΔABC is equilateral.   Review 1 (a) 350cm² (2 s.f.)
(b) 75cm (2 s.f.)   Review 2 (a) 207cm² (3 s.f.) (b) 73·1cm (3 s.f.)   Review 3 (a) radius = 11·5cm (3 s.f.); area of sector = 100cm² (2 s.f.) (b) OP = 8·3cm (2 s.f.); area ΔOAB = 66cm² (2 s.f.) (c) 34cm² (2 s.f.)
Review 4 (a) AB = AC and CB = CA. Hence AB = AC = CB. Hence ΔABC is equilateral. Hence θ = 60°.

### Exercise 15:5

1. 245cm² (3 s.f.)   2. 1·96m² (3 s.f.)   3. 37m² (2 s.f.)   4. 129cm² (3 s.f.)   5. 237·5mm × 115mm
6. (a) 94cm² (2 s.f.) (b) 148mm² (3 s.f.)   7. 152000mm² (3 s.f.)   8. 156cm² (3 s.f.)   9. 120cm² (2 s.f.)
10. A   11. (a) 377cm² (3 s.f.) (b) 1710mm² (3 s.f.) (c) 479cm² (3 s.f.)   12. 2·4m² (2 s.f.)   13. (a) 3·0cm (2 s.f.) (b)
1·8m (2 s.f.) (c) 13cm (2 s.f.) (d) 1·78cm (3 s.f.)   14. 1·78cm (3 s.f.)   15. (a) h = $\frac{A - 2\pi r^2}{2\pi r}$   (b) 0·87m (2 s.f.)
16. (b) 1·2m (2 s.f.)   Review 1 (a) 9550mm² (3 s.f.) or 95·5cm² (3 s.f.) (b) 115cm² (3 s.f.)
Review 2 117cm² (3 s.f.)   Review 3 3·43m² (3 s.f.)   Review 4 0·6m (1 d.p.)   Review 5 Floyd's hat has about
1360cm² more surface area than Ann's.

### Exercise 15:7

1. (a) 11300cm³ (3 s.f.) (b) 1280cm³ (3 s.f.) or 128000mm³ (3 s.f.) (c) 8·5m³ (2 s.f.) (d) 270cm³ (2 s.f.)
(e) 0·90m³ (2 s.f.) (f) 8580mm³ (3 s.f.)   2. (a) 4540cm³ (3 s.f.) (b) 4·7m³ (2 s.f.)   3. 22400mm³ (3 s.f.)
4. 1·1 litres (2 s.f.)   5. (a) 59cm³ (2 s.f.) (b) 640cm³ (2 s.f.) (c) 6300mm³ (2 s.f.) (d) 840cm³ (2 s.f.)   6. 60
7. 2cm   8. 48% (2 s.f.)   9. 17   10. (a) calculate the radius using C = 2πr, use Pythagoras' Theorem to find the
height, calculate the volume (b) 3·71m³ (3 s.f.)   11. the one gold sphere of radius 3mm   12. 2500kg (3 s.f.)
13. 1mm (to the nearest mm)   14. 0·2 litres   15. (a) 3cm (b) 18πcm³ (c) 512 : 27   16. (a) 2 : 3 (b) 2 : 1
17. 5·4cm (2 s.f.)   Review 1 (a) 280cm³ (2 s.f.) (b) 7·2m³ (2 s.f.) (c) 1·7m³ (2 s.f.) (d) 96m³ (2 s.f.)
Review 2 2970   Review 3 67 grams (2 s.f.)   Review 4 2 : 1

### Chapter 15   Review

1. 216m² (3 s.f.)   2. (a) 424cm³ (3 s.f.) (b) 283cm² (3 s.f.)   3. Taking π = 3·14   (a) 703cm² (3 s.f.)
(b) 202·6cm (1 d.p.)   4. (a) 497cm³ (3 s.f.) (b) 319cm² (3 s.f.)   5. (a) 12·9m (3 s.f.) (b) 14·0m (3 s.f.)
(c) 69·8m² (3 s.f.)   6. (a) (i) 10·5m (ii) 20m (b) 43·6° (1 d.p.) (c) 55m² (2 s.f.)   7. (a) 1357cm³ (4 s.f.)
(b) 371cm³ (3 s.f.) (c) 823cm³ (3 s.f.) (d) 1 : 6   8. (a) 1·43m (3 s.f.) (b) 3·82m² (3 s.f.) (c) 6·75m² (3 s.f.)
(d) 10·0m (3 s.f.)   9. (a) 22·45cm³ (2 d.p.) (b) 1·92cm³ (2 d.p.) (c) 9·31cm³ (2 d.p.) (d) 74·48cm³ (2 d.p.)
10. 743m² (3 s.f.)

## Chapter 16   Angle and Tangent Properties of Circles

### Exercise 16:2

1. (a) ∠FAC, ∠FBC, ∠FDC, ∠ECB   (b) ∠FAE, ∠FCE, ∠FDE   (c) ∠EFD, ∠EAD, ∠EBD, ∠ECD
(d) ∠AEC   2. (a) 148° (b) 108° (c) 112° (d) 90°   3. (a) α = 35°, β = 110°, θ = 55° (b) α = 35°, β = 47°,
θ = 82° (c) α = 40°, β = 50°, θ = 100°   4. (i) (a) 70° (b) 55° (c) 35° (d) 70° (ii) (a) 28° (b) 52° (iii) (a) 90°
(b) 106°   5. p = 32°, q = 41°, r = 42°   6. (i) (a) 108° (b) 54° (ii) 69° (iii) (a) 128° (b) 124°   7. (i) (a) 49°
(b) 41° (c) 140° (d) 21° (ii) 26°   8. No. One reason is that ∠QRS = 80°.   10. (a) 20° (b) 25° (c) 55°   11. 36
12. 90°; No (angle in a semicircle = 90°).   Review 1 p = 53°, q = 37°, r = 37°, s = 74°, θ = 22°, α = 30°

### Exercise 16:4

1. (a) r (b) q (c) s   2. (a) 112° (b) 68° (c) 112°   3. (a) 82°, b = 88°, c = 104°, d = 74°, e = 74°
4. θ = 168°, α = 88°, β = 17°   5. p = 130°, q = 73°, r = 82°   6. (a) 66° (b) 26° (c) 114°   7. (i) (a) 104°
(b) 104° (c) 76° (ii) They are parallel.   8. (a) 20° (b) 40°   Review 1 (a) 80° (b) 121° (c) 25°
Review 2 (a) 128° (b) 41°

### Exercise 16:7

1. ∠AQO, ∠BQO, ∠FPO, ∠EPO, ∠DRO, ∠CRO, ∠QPS, ∠QRS   2. (a) b (b) c (c) a   3. (a) 80°
(b) p = 70°, q = 70°   4. (a) 35° (b) 50°   5. (a) α = 28°, β = 59° (b) ∠ADB = 76°, ∠BFD = 76°, ∠BDO = 14°
6. a = 40°, b = 40°, c = 40°, d = 44°, e = 60°, f = 25°, g = 85°, h = 25°, i = 70°, j = 25°, k = 68°, m = 21°.
7. (i) (a) ∠QSB = 90° (radius perpendicular to tangent) and ∠ACB = ∠QSB (corresponding angles, parallel lines)
(b) 79·2cm (1 d.p.) (ii) (a) ∠ABC = 82°; θ = 196° (b) 68·4cm (1 d.p.) (c) 253cm (to the nearest cm)
Review 1 (a) ∠ABC = 62°, ∠OCA = 28° (b) ∠DCB = 88°, ∠BDC = 46°, ∠BCF = 46°   Review 2 a = 28°,
b = 62°, c = 62°, d = 56°   Review 3 Possible reasoning is: ∠ABC = 90° (radius perpendicular to tangent),
∠BCD = 90° (given), BC = CD (equal tangents from C).

**Chapter 16    Review**

1. (a) 66° (tangent ⊥ radius) (b) 66° (∠ in alt. segment)   2. x = 94°,
y = 28°, z = 19°   3. (i) 20° (ii) 120° (iii) 10°   4. x = 65°, y = 130°,
z = 50°   5. (a) (i) ∠BOC = 2 (p + q) (ii) ∠BOC = 2 ∠BAC
6. (a) (i) 112° (ii) 136° (c) One possible way is:  ∠PRS = 58°
(∠ sum of ΔPRS). ∠TSP = ∠PRS (∠ in alt. segment) (c) 36°

8.

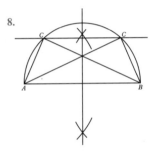

---

# Chapter 17    Trigonometrical Ratios and Graphs

**Exercise 17:3**

2. (a) negative (b) positive   3. (a) True (b) True (c) True   4. C   5. C   6. (a) B   (b) A (c) D (d) D (e) B
(f) D (g) B (h) C (i) D   7. (a) 0·5 (b) – 0·5 (c) – 0·5 (d) – 0·5   8. (a) –5·7 (2 s.f.) (b) –5·7 (2 s.f.)
(c) 0·18 (2 s.f.) (d) 0·18 (2 s.f.)   9. (a) –sin 40° (b) –cos 60° (c) –tan 40° (d) –tan 10° (e) sin 10° (f) –tan 40°
(g) –cos 85° (h) sin 40° (i) tan 30° (j) –sin 30° (k) tan 30° (l) tan 60° (m) sin 85° (n) cos 70° (o) cos 60°
(p) –cos 20° (q) –sin 20°   10. (a) –340°, –20°, 20°, 340°, 380°, 700° (b) –280°, –100°, 80°, 260°, 440°, 620°
(c) –310°, –230°, 50°, 130°, 410°, 490°   Review 1 C   Review 2 E   Review 3 (a) B (b) D (c) A (d) B
(e) B   Review 4 (a) –tan 55° (b) sin 20°

**Exercise 17:6**

1. (a) Graph 1 has equation y = tan x, graph 2 has equation y = sin x, graph 3 has equation y = cos x.
(b) A (90°, 0), B (–180°, 0), C (360°, 0), D (90°, 1), E (180°, 0), F (360°, 0), G (–90°, –1), H (–180°, 0), I (–270°, 1),
J (360°, 1), K (–360°, 1), L (–180°, –1), M (–90°, 0), N (90°, 0), P (270°, 0), Q (540°, –1), R (630°, 0)   2. (a) D
(b) C, G   3. (i) (a) y = cos x (b) none (c) y = cos x (d) none (e) y = sin x and y = tan x (f) none
(g) y = cos x (ii) (a) y = tan x (b) y = sin x and y = cos x
4. (i) (b)

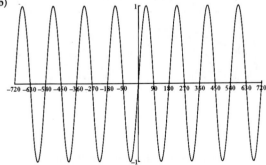

(c) y = sin 2x is the same as y = sin x enlarged in the x-direction by a factor of $\frac{1}{2}$.
(ii) (a)

(b) y = sin $\frac{1}{2}$ x is the same as y = sin x enlarged in the x-direction by a factor of 2.

**(iii) (a)**

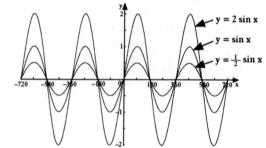

**(b)** y = 2sin x is the same as y = sin x enlarged in the y-direction by a factor of 2. y = $\frac{1}{2}$ sin x is the same as y = sin x enlarged in the y-direction by a factor of $\frac{1}{2}$.

**(iv) (a)**

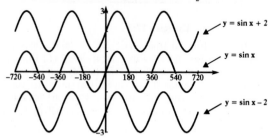

**(b)** y = sin x + 2 is the same as y = sin x translated 2 units in the y-direction. y = sin x – 2 is the same as y = sin x translated –2 units in the y-direction.

**(v) (a)** y = –sin x is the reflection of y = sin x in the x-axis.  **(b)** y = sin (–x) is the reflection of y = sin x in the y-axis.

**(iv)** a = 4, b = 3

**5. (a)**  

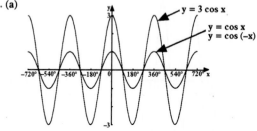

**(b)**

**(c)** y = – cos x is the reflection of y = cos x in the x-axis.  **(d)** A (–360°, 0), B (180°, 2)  **6.(a)** 3m  **(b)** 5m
**(c)** 3m  **7.** – 0·10m (2 s.f.) The water is below the base of the boatshed.

**8. (a)**

| t | 0 | 1 | 2 | 3 | 4 | 5 | 6 | 7 | 8 | 9 | 10 |
|---|---|---|---|---|---|---|---|---|---|---|----|
| d | 9 | 11 | 12·46 | 13 | 12·46 | 11 | 9 | 7 | 5·54 | 5 | 5·54 |

**(b)** 9a.m.; 5 metres

**(c)**

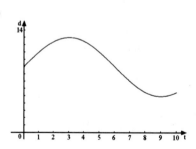

**(d)** 3 $\frac{1}{2}$ hours.

**9. (a)** OP $= 10 \cos \theta$

**(c)**

| $\theta$ | $-180°$ | $-135°$ | $-90°$ | $-45°$ | $0°$ | $45°$ | $90°$ | $135°$ | $180°$ | $225°$ | $270°$ | $315°$ | $360°$ |
|---|---|---|---|---|---|---|---|---|---|---|---|---|---|
| h | 22 | 19·1 | 12 | 4·9 | 2 | 4·9 | 12 | 19·1 | 22 | 19·1 | 12 | 4·9 | 2 |

**(d)**

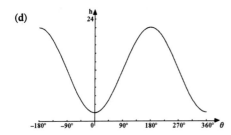

**(e)** 253° **(f)** *fig (ii)* at t = 3 sec, *fig (iii)* at t = 6 sec, *fig (iv)* at t = 9 sec, *fig (v)* at t = 12 sec. At t = 3 sec, h = 6m; at t = 6 sec, h = 11m; at t = 9 sec, h = 6m; at t = 12 sec, h = 1m.

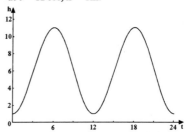

**10. (a)**

| x | $-180$ | $-150$ | $-120$ | $-90$ | $-60$ | $-30$ | 0 | 30 | 60 | 90 | 120 | 150 | 180 |
|---|---|---|---|---|---|---|---|---|---|---|---|---|---|
| $\cos x°$ | $-1$ | $-0·87$ | $-0·5$ | 0 | 0·5 | 0·87 | 1 | 0·87 | 0·5 | 0 | $-0·5$ | $-0·87$ | $-1$ |
| $\dfrac{x}{100}$ | $-1·8$ | $-1·5$ | $-1·2$ | $-0·9$ | $-0·6$ | $-0·3$ | 0 | 0·3 | 0·6 | 0·9 | 1·2 | 1·5 | 1·8 |

**(b)**

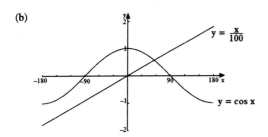

**(c)** x = 60 (1 s.f.) **(d)** y = 0·6; 2 solutions **(e)** The line $y = \frac{x}{100}$ meets the curve y = cos x only once, no matter how far both graphs are extended whereas the line y = 0·6 meets y = cos x an infinite number of times.

**11. (a)**

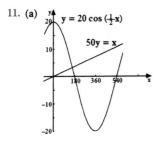

**12. (a)**

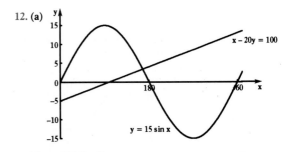

**(b)** x = 160 (2 s.f.) **(c)** y = 16

**(c)** x = 170 (2 s.f.)

**Review 1 (c)** translated 90° in the x-direction i.e. translated by the vector $\begin{pmatrix} 90° \\ 0 \end{pmatrix}$

**Review 2 (a)**

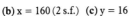

| t | 0 | 1 | 2 | 3 | 4 | 5 | 6 | 7 | 8 | 9 | 10 |
|---|---|---|---|---|---|---|---|---|---|---|---|
| d | 8 | 7·73 | 7 | 6 | 5 | 4·27 | 4 | 4·27 | 5 | 6 | 7 |

**(b)**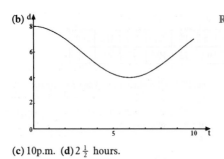

Review 3 **(a) (b)**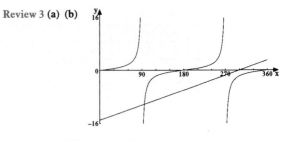

**(c)** 10p.m. **(d)** $2\frac{1}{2}$ hours.

**(d)** x is about 95.

**Chapter 17   Review**

1. **(a) (i)** 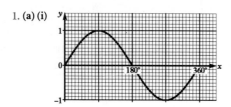    **(ii)**

**(iii)**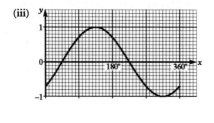

**(b)** 350°

2. **(a) (i)** 90

**(ii)**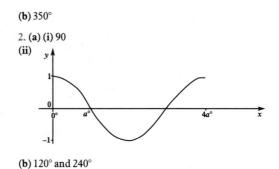

**(b)** 120° and 240°

3. **(a)** 44° and 136° (to nearest degree)  **(b)** 135° and 315°  4. **(a)** a = 2, b = 1  **(b)** 60° and 300°
5. **(a)** 330°

**(b)**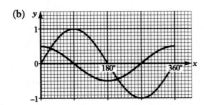

**(c)** about 27° and 207°

6. **(a)**

| $x$ | 0 | 30 | 60 | 90 | 120 | 150 | 180 | 210 | 240 | 270 | 300 | 330 | 360 |
|---|---|---|---|---|---|---|---|---|---|---|---|---|---|
| $y = \sin x°$ | 0 | 0·5 | 0·866 | 1 | 0·866 | 0·5 | 0 | −0·5 | −0·866 | −1 | −0·866 | −0·5 | 0 |

(ii)
(c)
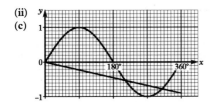

(d) x is about 215 or 310   7. 30° and 150°

8. (a) (i) Maximum range is 14·4m and occurs when x = 45°.

(ii)
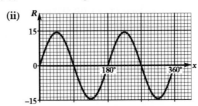

## Chapter 18   3-D Shapes. Calculations with Right-Angled Triangles.

Page 369

### Exercise 18:2

1. (a) HF = 5m; AF = 5·4m (1 d.p.) (b) x = 11·7m (1 d.p.), y = 12·0m (1 d.p.)   2. 35·2cm (to the nearest mm)   3. 17·3cm (to the nearest mm)   4. (a) FP = 4cm, AF = 12·6cm (1 d.p.) (b) QR = 9·4m (1 d.p.), height = 28·5m (1 d.p.)   5. 18cm   6. about 102 seconds   7. 1·44m (to the nearest cm)   8. (a) 4 (b) 3 (c) 5 (d) 7·2 (1 d.p.) (e) 7·8 (1 d.p.)   Review 1 (a) 20m (b) 20·4m (1 d.p.)   Review 2 2·21m (to the nearest cm) Review 3 3·4m (1 d.p.)

Page 373

### Exercise 18:3

1. (a) 16·3cm (1 d.p.) (b) 37° (to the nearest degree)   2. (a) 18·8cm (1 d.p.) (b) 51° (to the nearest degree) (c) 29·2cm (1 d.p.)   3. (a) 2·5m (b) 2·7m (1 d.p.) (c) 37° (to the nearest degree) (d) 22° (to the nearest degree) 4. 19·2cm (1 d.p.)   5. (a) 3·1cm (1 d.p.) (b) 110cm³ (2 s.f.)   6. (a) 23° (to the nearest degree) (b) Use $\triangle$CBF to find BF then use $\triangle$BDF to find $\beta$; 9° (to the nearest degree)   7. (a) QS = 42·4cm (1 d.p.) (b) 67° (to the nearest degree)   8. (a) EK = KB (b) 15cm, 15cm, 17·0cm (1 d.p.) (b) To the nearest degree the angles are 56°, 56°, 69°.   Review 1 (a) 4·1cm (1 d.p.) (b) Possible steps are: In $\triangle$TBM use trigonometry to find TM then use Pythagoras' Theorem in $\triangle$TMQ; 5·9cm (1 d.p.)   Review 2 (a) 17cm (b) 28° (to the nearest degree) (c) 30° (to the nearest degree) (d) 19·7cm (1 d.p.) (e) 34° (to the nearest degree)

Page 376

### Exercise 18:4

1. (a) ∠HEG (b) ∠EGH (c) ∠EDH (d) ∠DEH (e) ∠FEA or ∠GHD (f) ∠EHD or ∠FGC   2. (a) ∠VQU (b) ∠QVU (c) ∠QWP (d) ∠PWT or ∠QVU (e) ∠SWT or ∠RVU   3. (a) ∠VSB (∠VSQ) (b) ∠VPB (∠VPR) (c) ∠VNB (d) ∠VMB   4. (a) ∠FBC (b) ∠BFC or ∠AED (c) ABFE and ABCD 5. (a) ∠QDY (b) ∠PAD or ∠QBC   Review 1 (a) ∠AQB (b) ∠ANB (c) ∠AMB   Review 2 (a) ∠BHC (b) ∠BAE or ∠BAD (c) BH is not perpendicular to the line of intersection, DH. (d) ∠BDC

Page 379

### Exercise 18:5

1. (a) 10m (b) 50° (to the nearest degree) (c) ∠AGE; 27° (to the nearest degree)   2. (a) 8cm (b) 59° (to the nearest degree) (c) 48° (to the nearest degree)   3. (a) 9m (b) 17m (c) 12·0m (1 d.p.) (d) 53° (to the nearest degree) (e) 42° (to the nearest degree)   4. (a) 35cm (b) 63° (to the nearest degree) (c) 27° (to the nearest degree) 5. (a) 21·2cm (1 d.p.) (b) 17·0cm (1 d.p.) (c) ∠PDO; 58° (to the nearest degree) (d) 66° (to the nearest degree) 6. (a) 7·1cm (1 d.p.) (b) 35° (to the nearest degree)   7. (a) 24mm (2 s.f.) (b) 37mm (2 s.f.)   8. (a) 51° (b) 7·77m (c) 23° (to the nearest degree)   9. (a) 78° (to the nearest degree) (b) 28·8cm (1 d.p.) 10. ∠PMN; 63° (to the nearest degree)   Review 1 (a) 12·8cm (1 d.p.) (b) 13·4cm (1 d.p.) (c) 27° (to the nearest degree) (d) 37° (to the nearest degree) (e) 39° (to the nearest degree)   Review 2 (a) BD = 9·2m (1 d.p.), OB = 4·6m (1 d.p.), PB = 10·1m (1 d.p.) (b) 72° (to the nearest degree) (c) Because the perpendicular distance from DC to O is not the same as the perpendicular distance from BC to O. Review 3 (a) 7·1cm (1 d.p.) (b) ∠RST; 61° (to the nearest degree) (c) 74° (to the nearest degree)

## Chapter 18   Review

1. **(a) (i)** 36·8mm (3 s.f.)  **(ii)** 51° (to the nearest degree)  **(iii)** 44·8mm (3 s.f.)  **(b)** 60° (to the nearest degree)
2. 25° (to the nearest degree)    3. **(i)** 6° (to the nearest degree)  **(ii) (b)** 3·49m (2 d.p.)  **(c)** 3·69m (2 d.p.)
4. 61° (to the nearest degree)

## Chapter 19   Vectors

**Exercise 19:1**

1.
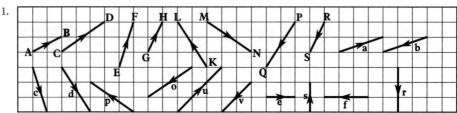

2. $\overrightarrow{PQ} = \binom{2}{1}$, $\overrightarrow{AB} = \binom{2}{2}$, $\overrightarrow{RS} = \binom{-2}{-3}$, $\overrightarrow{EF} = \binom{1}{-2}$, $\overrightarrow{GH} = \binom{-2}{3}$, $\overrightarrow{PQ} = \binom{3}{0}$, $\overrightarrow{MN} = \binom{0}{-2}$, $\overrightarrow{VW} = \binom{4}{1}$,
$\mathbf{a} = \binom{-1}{2}$, $\mathbf{b} = \binom{1}{1}$, $\mathbf{c} = \binom{2}{0}$, $\mathbf{d} = \binom{0}{3}$, $\mathbf{e} = \binom{-4}{-1}$, $\mathbf{f} = \binom{3}{2}$, $\mathbf{p} = \binom{6}{2}$, $\mathbf{q} = \binom{-5}{1}$    3. **(a)** twice

4. **(a)** $\overrightarrow{PQ} = \binom{1}{2}$   **(b)** $\overrightarrow{PQ} = \binom{6}{1}$   **(c)** $\overrightarrow{PQ} = \binom{-3}{0}$   **(d)** $\overrightarrow{PQ} = \binom{2}{-3}$   **(e)** $\overrightarrow{PQ} = \binom{-2}{-4}$

**Review (i)** Simon's group and Bik's group  **(ii) (a)** $\binom{8}{-1}$,  **(b)** $\binom{5}{13}$,  **(c)** $\binom{-4}{-5}$,  **(d)** $\binom{6}{-5}$,  **(e)** $\binom{-6}{5}$

**Exercise 19:3**

1. **(a)** c  **(b)** h  **(c)** f  **(d)** b  **(e)** q  **(f)** e  **(g)** b  **(h)** a  **(i)** h

2.
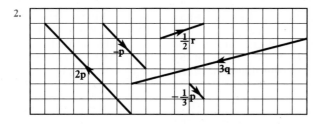

3. **(a)** $\binom{-5}{-2}$

   **(b)** $\overrightarrow{QP} = -\overrightarrow{PQ}$

4. **(a)** $\overrightarrow{CK} = -\overrightarrow{KC}$  **(b)** $\overrightarrow{AB} = 2\overrightarrow{ED}$  **(c)** $\overrightarrow{AF} = 2\overrightarrow{IG}$  **(d)** $\overrightarrow{AB} = -2\overrightarrow{CK}$  **(e)** $\overrightarrow{LM} = \frac{1}{3}\overrightarrow{CK}$

   **(f)** $\overrightarrow{DC} = -\frac{1}{2}\overrightarrow{AF}$  **(g)** $\overrightarrow{LM} = -\frac{1}{3}\overrightarrow{ED}$    **Review 1 (a)** g  **(b)** b  **(c)** c  **(d)** d  **(e)** h  **(f)** f  **(g)** f  **(h)** n

**Review 2**

*Answers*

## Exercise 19:7

1. (a) $\begin{pmatrix} 5 \\ 1 \end{pmatrix}$  (b) $\begin{pmatrix} 2 \\ -1 \end{pmatrix}$  (c) $\begin{pmatrix} 6 \\ -1 \end{pmatrix}$  (d) $\begin{pmatrix} 4 \\ -2 \end{pmatrix}$  (e) $\begin{pmatrix} 6 \\ -1 \end{pmatrix}$  (f) $\begin{pmatrix} 1 \\ 3 \end{pmatrix}$  (g) $\begin{pmatrix} -1 \\ -3 \end{pmatrix}$  (h) $\begin{pmatrix} 5 \\ 3 \end{pmatrix}$  (i) $\begin{pmatrix} 6 \\ -3 \end{pmatrix}$  (j) $\begin{pmatrix} 2 \\ 0 \end{pmatrix}$

(k) $\begin{pmatrix} 9 \\ -1 \end{pmatrix}$  (l) $\begin{pmatrix} -3 \\ -3 \end{pmatrix}$  (m) $\begin{pmatrix} 7 \\ 7 \end{pmatrix}$

2.

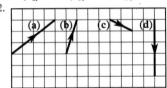

3. (a) p  (b) e  (c) h  (d) b  (e) $l$  (f) q  (g) k    4. (a) $\begin{pmatrix} 4 \\ 2 \end{pmatrix}$  (b) $\begin{pmatrix} -4 \\ -2 \end{pmatrix}$  (c) $\begin{pmatrix} -1 \\ 3 \end{pmatrix}$  (d) $\begin{pmatrix} 3 \\ 5 \end{pmatrix}$  (e) $\begin{pmatrix} 5 \\ -1 \end{pmatrix}$

5. (a) $\overrightarrow{AB}$  (b) $\overrightarrow{CD}$  (c) $\overrightarrow{CE}$  (d) $\overrightarrow{CB}$  (e) $\overrightarrow{CD}$  (f) $\overrightarrow{AB}$    Review 1 (a) $\begin{pmatrix} -2 \\ -3 \end{pmatrix}$  (b) $\begin{pmatrix} 6 \\ -2 \end{pmatrix}$  (c) $\begin{pmatrix} 8 \\ -4 \end{pmatrix}$

(d) $\begin{pmatrix} -8 \\ 1 \end{pmatrix}$  (e) $\begin{pmatrix} 4 \\ -2 \end{pmatrix}$

Review 2

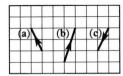

Review 3 (a) $\overrightarrow{BC}$  (b) $\overrightarrow{CD}$  (c) $\overrightarrow{ED}$  (d) $\overrightarrow{CA}$  (e) $\overrightarrow{BE}$ (or $\overrightarrow{ED}$)  (f) $\overrightarrow{AE}$ (or $\overrightarrow{EC}$)

## Exercise 19:8

1. (a) a + b  (b) c − a    2. (a) p + r  (b) p + q + r  (c) −p − q    3. (a) $\overrightarrow{BM} = -a$, $\overrightarrow{MC} = a + b$
4. (a) $\overrightarrow{TR} = \overrightarrow{QR} - \overrightarrow{QT}$, $\overrightarrow{PS} = 4(\overrightarrow{QR} - \overrightarrow{QT})$  (b) Since $\overrightarrow{PS} = 4\overrightarrow{TR}$ then the sides PS and TR are parallel.
5. (a) $\overrightarrow{QP} = -r$, $\overrightarrow{RP} = p - r$, $\overrightarrow{PT} = -r$,  (b) Since $\overrightarrow{QP} = \overrightarrow{PT}$ then P is the mid-point of QT.
7. (a) $\overrightarrow{AB} = \overrightarrow{DC}$, $\overrightarrow{DP} = \frac{1}{2}(\overrightarrow{DA} + \overrightarrow{DC})$, $\overrightarrow{MP} = -\frac{1}{2}\overrightarrow{DC}$, $\overrightarrow{PN} = -\frac{1}{2}\overrightarrow{DC}$  (b) They are on same straight line.
(Since $\overrightarrow{PN} = \overrightarrow{PD} + \overrightarrow{DN} = -\frac{1}{2}\overrightarrow{DA} - \frac{1}{2}\overrightarrow{DC} + \frac{1}{2}\overrightarrow{DA} = -\frac{1}{2}\overrightarrow{DC}$ then $\overrightarrow{PN}$ and $\overrightarrow{MP}$ are parallel).
8. (a) c − b  (b) c − b − a  (c) $\frac{1}{2}(c - b - a)$  (d) $\frac{1}{2}(a - b + c)$   9. (a) $\overrightarrow{CB} = q - p$, $\overrightarrow{CX} = \frac{1}{5}(q - p)$,
$\overrightarrow{AX} = \frac{1}{5}(q - 4p)$   10. (i) (a) $\overrightarrow{CD} = r$, $\overrightarrow{BF} = q + r$, $\overrightarrow{BD} = p + r$, $\overrightarrow{CA} = q - p$  (b) $\overrightarrow{DF} = -\overrightarrow{BD} + \overrightarrow{BF}$
(ii) (b) B (4, 0), A (3, $\sqrt{3}$)   Review 1 $\overrightarrow{PQ} = b - a$, $\overrightarrow{RD} = a$, $\overrightarrow{SP} = a + b$   Review 2 (a) $\overrightarrow{QR} = a - b$,
$\overrightarrow{QM} = \frac{1}{2}(a - b)$, $\overrightarrow{PM} = \frac{1}{2}(a + b)$, $\overrightarrow{QN} = \frac{1}{2}a - b$

## Exercise 19:10

1. (b) 7·2 m/s (1 d.p.)  (c) 56° (2 s.f.)   2. (a) 63° (2 s.f.)  (b) 2·2 km/h (2 s.f.)   3. Speed = 310 km/h (2 s.f.),
direction: bearing of 015°   4. 160km/h (2 s.f.) on a bearing of 072° (2 s.f.)   5. 73° (2 s.f.) to the direction of the
current   6. direction: bearing of 160° (3 s.f.), speed = 117km/h (3 s.f.)   7. (a) 9·4N (2 s.f.) at an angle
of 58° (2 s.f.) to the 5N force.  (b) 18N (2 s.f.) at an angle of 56° (2 s.f.) to the 10N force  (c) 19·2N (3 s.f.)
at an angle of 51° (2 s.f.) to the 12N force   8. 31 knots (2 s.f.) on a bearing of 165° (3 s.f.)   9. (a) 35·2N (3 s.f.) (b)
25° (2 s.f.)   10. (a) 20N  (b) 53° (2 s.f.)   11. 15 metres   12. (a) 0·45 m/s (2 s.f.)  (b) 336° (3 s.f.)
(c) 3 min. 42 sec. (to the nearest second)   13. $T_1$ = 46N (2 s.f.), $T_2$ = 39N (2 s.f.)   Review 1 (a) on a bearing of
256° (2 s.f.)  (b) 770km (2 s.f.)   Review 2 (a) 9·6N (2 s.f.)  (b) 36° (2 s.f.)   Review 3 (a) 16·2ms⁻¹ (3 s.f.)
(b) on a bearing of 113° (3 s.f.).

## Chapter 19   Review

1. (b) 2 : 1   2. 0·64m/s (2 s.f.)   3. 93·75m   4. (a) (i) b − a  (ii) 2 (b − a)  (b) AB and FC are parallel
5. (b) (i) 23·8km/h  (ii) 262° (or 261°)   6. (a) (i) 2 cos α  (ii) 1 − 2 sin α  (b) 30°   7. (a) 2p + 8q
8. (a) (i) 48° (to the nearest degree)  (b) 46 sec (to the nearest sec)

617

## Chapter 20 Calculations with Non Right-Angled Triangles

**Page 411**

**Exercise 20:2**

1. **(a)** D **(b)** C **(c)** B **(d)** A **(e)** C   2. **(a)** 3·2m (2 s.f.) **(b)** 3·6m (2 s.f.) **(c)** 33·9mm (3 s.f.) **(d)** 3·3m (2 s.f.)
**(e)** 8·4cm (2 s.f.)   3. To the nearest degree the answers are **(a)** 37° **(b)** 36° **(c)** 47° **(d)** 47°
**Review** angle P = 46·7° (1 d.p.), angle T = 68·7° (1 d.p.), 7·4cm (1 d.p.).

**Page 414**

**Exercise 20:4**

1. **(a)** 4·4cm (2 s.f.) **(b)** 10m (2 s.f.) **(c)** 78mm (2 s.f.)   2. To the nearest degree the answers are: **(a)** 47°
**(b)** 122° **(c)** 77°   3. angle P = 90°   4. **(a)** 5·1cm (2 s.f.) **(b)** 84° (to the nearest degree)
**(c)** To the nearest degree the angles are 48°, 78°, 55°. These angles add to more than 180° because of rounding.
5. **(a)** Yes **(b)** The smallest angle is opposite the smallest side. **(c)** 41° (to the nearest degree)
**(d)** 85° (to the nearest degree)   **Review (a)** 107° (to the nearest degree) **(b)** 58·7cm (1 d.p.) **(c)** 2·1m (1 d.p.)

**Page 418**

**Exercise 20:5**

1. To the nearest degree **(a)** 76° **(b)** 46° **(c)** 58°   2. **(a)** 6·1cm (1 d.p.) **(b)** 28° (to the nearest degree)
**(c)** 44°   3. 33m (2 s.f.)   4. 64m (2 s.f.)   5. T; 2·7km (1 d.p.)   6. **(a)** 105° (to the nearest degree) **(b)** 10m
7. 116m (to the nearest metre)   8. 3·84km (3 s.f.)   9. **(a)** 40km (to the nearest km) **(b)** 008°   10. **(a)** 58° (to
the nearest degree) **(b)** 328°   11. **(a)** 225m (to the nearest metre) **(b)** 156m (to the nearest metre)
12. 16km (to the nearest km)   13. 006°   14. 250°   15. **(a)** 362m (to the nearest metre) **(b)** 500m
16. AG = 19m (to the nearest metre), h = 8m (to the nearest metre)   17. **(a)** ∠YAB = 74°, ∠XAB = 59°
**(c)** 150m (2 s.f.) **(d)** 310m (2 s.f.) **(e)** ∠YBX = 36°, distance = 210m (2 s.f.)   18. **(a)** ∠BQT **(b)** 70°
**(d)** 26° (to the nearest degree)   19. 12·6cm (1 d.p.)   20. 14·2km (3 s.f.)   21. **(a)** 15km (to the nearest km)
**(b)** 11km (to the nearest km)   **Review 1** 22cm   **Review 2 (a)** 76m (to the nearest metre)
**(b)** 72m (to the nearest metre)   **Review 3** 8·7km (2 s.f.)   **Review 4 (a)** 154m (to the nearest metre)
**(c)** 153m (to the nearest metre) **(d)** ∠XMY;83° (to the nearest degree)

**Page 423**

**Investigation 20:6**

b sin A < a < b

**Page 425**

**Exercise 20:8**

1. **(a)** 26cm² (2 s.f.) **(b)** 17·3m² (3 s.f.) **(c)** 1480m² (3 s.f.)   2. 50m² (2 s.f.) **(b)** 21cm² (2 s.f.)
3. **(a)** 55° **(b)** 82° (to the nearest degree) Area = 15cm² (2 s.f.)   4. **(a)** 800m² (2 s.f.) **(b)** 2700m² (2 s.f.)
5. **(a)** 152cm² (3 s.f.) **(b)** area of sector = 198cm² (3 s.f.); area of segment = 46cm² (2 s.f.)   6. 10m³ (2 s.f.)
7. 42930m²   8. 7890m² (3 s.f.)   9. **(a)** 180° − θ **(b)** Area △ PQR = $\frac{1}{2}$ pr sin θ;
Area △ BQC = $\frac{1}{2}$ bc sin (180° − θ) = $\frac{1}{2}$ pr sin θ since b = p and c = r and sin (180° − θ) = sin θ.
10. **(a)** 34° (to the nearest degree) **(b)** 245cm² (3 s.f.) **(c)** radius perpendicular to tangent **(d)** 6·1cm (2 s.f.)
11. $\frac{1}{2}$ ac sin θ + $\frac{1}{2}$ cb sin θ + $\frac{1}{2}$ bd sin θ + $\frac{1}{2}$ ad sin θ = $\frac{1}{2}$ sin θ (ac + cb + bd + ad)
= $\frac{1}{2}$ sin θ ([ac + ad] + [cb + bd] ) = $\frac{1}{2}$ sin θ (a [c + d] + b [c + d] ) = $\frac{1}{2}$ sin θ (c + d)(a + b)
**Review 1 (a)** 400m² (2 s.f.) **(b)** 8·6cm² (2 s.f.) **(c)** 63 mm² (2 s.f.)   **Review 2** 3200m² (2 s.f.)

**Page 428**

**Chapter 20 Review**

1. **(a)** 23·3cm (1 d.p.) **(b)** 63° (to the nearest degree)   2. **(a)** 48·5° (1 d.p.) **(b)** 15·0m² (1 d.p.)
3. 135·2° (1 d.p.)   4. **(a)** 12·6m (1 d.p.) **(b)** 35·3° (1 d.p.)   5. 303°   6. 13·2 miles   7. **(a)** 36·9° (1 d.p.)
**(b)** 123·9° (1 d.p.) **(c)** upper bound = 7·25m, lower bound = 7·15m **(d)** 2·0m   8. 6·9km (1 d.p.)
9. **(a) (i)** 80° **(ii)** 7·0cm (2 s.f.) **(b) (i)** 79° **(ii)** maximum = 7·09cm (2 s.f.), minimum = 6·90cm (2 s.f.)
10. 66m ( 2 s.f.)   11. **(a)** 1260m² (4 s.f.) **(b)** 116·4m (4 s.f.)

618

## Chapter 21   Transformations

### Exercise 21:2

1. A′ (9, –1), B′ (5, –1), C′(5, 3)   2. P′ (0, –1), Q′ (–2, –1), R′ (–2, –2)   3. centre of enlargement (3, 4), scale factor –1
4. (a) P′ (0, –3), Q′ (0, –7), R′ (–8, –7), S′ (–8, –3) (b) P′ (19, 0), Q′ (19, – 6), R′ (7, –6), S′ (7, 0) (c) P′ (11, 4),
Q′ (11, 2), R′ (7, 2), S′ (7, 4) (d) P′ (–3, 6), Q′ (–3, 5), R′ (–5, 5), S′ (–5, 6) (e) P′ (9, 6), Q′ (9, 2), R′ (1, 2),
S′ (1, 6) (f) P′ (7, 4), Q′ (7, –2), R′ (–5, –2), S′ (–5, 4) (g) P′ (9, 3), Q′ (9, 2), R′ (7, 2), S′ (7, 3)
Review (a) A′ (13, –2), B′ (5, 10), C′ (13, 10) (b) A′ (1, –14), B′ (–7, –2), C′ (1, –2) (c) A′ (1, – 6), B′ (–3, 0),
C′ (1, 0) (d) A′ (7, –5), B′ (5, –2), C′ (7, –2)

### Exercise 21:6

1. (a) enlargement, centre (–1, 2), scale factor –1  (b) translation by the vector $\binom{8}{2}$   2. (a) X′(–1, 0), Y′ (0, –1),
Z′ (–3, –3) (b) X″ (–1, 0), Y″ (–2, –1), Z″ (1, –3) (c) reflection in line  y = x + 3  3. (a) reflection in the
line y = –x + 2 (b) a possible answer is: enlargement, centre (0, 3), scale factor $-\frac{1}{2}$ then reflection in the
line y = –x + 2  4. (a) A′ (4, 3), B′ (2, 3), C′ (2, 6), D′ (5, 6) (b) reflection in the line x = 2  5. a possible answer
is: anticlockwise rotation through 90° about (1, 5) followed by translation by the vector $\binom{3}{2}$   6. (a) angle is
90° anticlockwise, centre is (1, 4) (b) $\binom{-2}{6}$ (c) centre is (–1, 3), angle is 180°  8. centre (0, 1), scale factor –1
9. (a) translation by the vector $\binom{-2}{-1}$ (b) rotation through 180°, about (1, 0)  10. $\binom{3}{-2}$   Review 1 one
possible answer is: translation by the vector $\binom{3}{3}$ followed by reflection in the line y = 4  Review 2 one
possible answer is: enlargement, centre (–1, 3), scale factor –2, followed by reflection in the line y = 1.

### Chapter 21   Review

1. (a) (i) reflection in y-axis (ii) reflection in the line y = x (iii) clockwise rotation through 90°, about (0, 0)
(b) (i) rotation through 180°, centre (0, 0) (ii) a possible answer is: enlargement, centre (0, 0), scale factor –1
(c) a possible answer is: clockwise rotation through 90° about (0, 0) followed by reflection in y-axis (d) (ii) $\frac{9}{4}$
2. (a) (i) 90° (ii) $\binom{0}{-4}$ (b) (2, –2) (c) reflection in the line y = –x   3. (b) reflection in line x = 6
(c) (i) translation by the vector $\binom{3n}{0}$ (ii) reflection in line x = 1·5n + 1·5   4. a possible answer is: rotation
through 180° about (0, 0) followed by enlargement, centre (0, 0), scale factor 1·5

## Chapter 22   Shape, Space and Measures Review

1. ΔABC and ΔRPQ are congruent (AAS), ΔABC and ΔTUS are congruent (SSS), ΔABC and ΔNLM are
congruent (SAS)  2. (a) $\binom{5}{-4}$ (b) $\binom{-3}{1}$ (c) $\binom{0}{-3}$ (d) $\binom{22}{-26}$   3. 110 metres (2 s.f.)
4. 50cm (to the nearest cm)  5. (a) q (b) p (c) e (d) e (e) t (f) d or a   6. Not necessarily. They are only
congruent if the equal angles are between equal sides.   7. (a) C (b) B (c) D (d) A (e) C (f) B
8. (a) 125cm (3 s.f.) (b) 109cm (3 s.f.) (c) 49° (to the nearest degree)  10. (a) A : y = cos x, B : y = sin x
(b) C   11. 8·7 litres (2 s.f.)   12. (a) $\overrightarrow{BD} = \binom{-2}{-5}$, $\overrightarrow{DC} = \binom{3}{4}$, $\overrightarrow{CB} = \binom{-1}{1}$, $\overrightarrow{DA} = \binom{-1}{1}$ (b) 5 units and 5·4
units (2 s.f.)   13. 29° (to the nearest degree)   15. 95km/h (2 s.f.) on a bearing of 342° (to the nearest degree)
16. 304cm² (3 s.f.)   17. (b) 47cm (2 s.f.)  (c)

| θ | 0° | 30° | 60° | 90° | 120° | 150° | 180° | 210° | 240° | 270° | 300° | 330° | 360° |
|---|----|-----|-----|-----|------|------|------|------|------|------|------|------|------|
| h | 45 | 47 | 52·5 | 60 | 67·5 | 73 | 75 | 73 | 67·5 | 60 | 52·5 | 47 | 45 |

(d)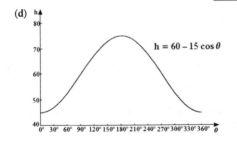
h = 60 – 15 cos θ

(e) 130° or 230°   18. 7·8cm (to the nearest mm)
19. (a) ∠BCQ = ∠QCA + ∠ACB = 90° + ∠ACB,
∠ACR = ∠RCB + ∠ACB = 90° + ∠ACB
20. (a) 37° (to the nearest degree)  (b) 150N
21. 400cm²  22. (a) at an angle of 53° (2 s.f.) to the
direction of the current  (b) 18 seconds
23. (a) $\overrightarrow{MN} = \overrightarrow{MP} + \overrightarrow{PN}$   25. (a) ∠ABE = 24° (to the
nearest degree)  (b) 66° (to the nearest degree)
(c) ∠BHF = 23° (to the nearest degree)

26.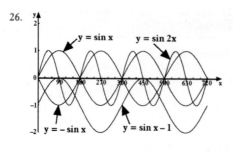

28. (a)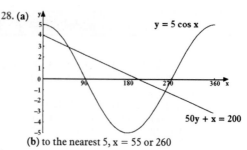

(b) to the nearest 5, x = 55 or 260

27. (a) $\overrightarrow{BC}$ = –a, $\overrightarrow{CA}$ = a – c, $\overrightarrow{CQ}$ = $\frac{1}{3}$(a – c) (c) $\overrightarrow{PD}$ = –$\frac{1}{3}$(c + 2a) (d) Since $\overrightarrow{BQ}$ = $\overrightarrow{PD}$ a pair of opposite sides of BQDP is both parallel and equal.  29. 11·9cm (to the nearest mm)  30. (a) 11cm (2 s.f.)
(b) ∠VCX = 57° (2 s.f.)  (c) ∠VMX = 65° (2 s.f.)  (d) a, b, c, $l$, d, e, f  (e) k, j, i, h, g  (h) to 2 s.f. the dimensions are 35cm × 13cm  31. (a) QT = 0·32m (2 s.f.), PT = 1·16m (3 s.f.)  (b) 0·37m² (2 s.f.)  (c) area of segment = 0·73m² (2 s.f.)  32. (a) One possible answer is: reflection in y-axis then reflection in y = –x
(b) $S_5$  (c) enlargement, centre (0, 0), scale factor – 1  33. ∠ROQ = 90°, a = 36°, b = 54°, $\theta$= 152°
34. PR = 58m (2 s.f.), w = 50m (2 s.f.)  35. ∠QPO = 54°, ∠SPO = 21°, ∠SRQ = 105°, ∠ABE = 48°
36. (a)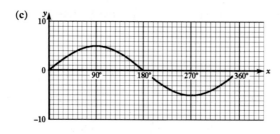
(b) about 70°  37. (a) 9m  (b) 16m (2 s.f.)  (c) 11m (2 s.f.)  (d) 53° (2 s.f.)
(e) 34° (2 s.f.)  (f) 49° (2 s.f.) using the values for AC and AD from (b) and (c)
39. p = 65° (angle in alternate segment), q = 42° (angle in same segment), r = 50° (angle sum of isosceles triangle formed with equal tangents), a = 44° (radius perpendicular to tangent), b = 46° (angle in alternate segment), c = 20° (angle at centre), d = 20° (angle in alternate segment), e = 48° (interior angles of quadrilateral)
40. (a) centre (4, 6), scale factor $-\frac{1}{2}$  (b) (0, 4), (0, 7), (2, 4), (2, 7)  42. (a) 27m (2 s.f.)  (b) 22m (2 s.f.)
43. (a) radius perpendicular to tangent  (b) 75° (2 s.f.)  (c) 46cm (2 s.f.)  44. (a) ∠QRP = 60°, ∠RPS = 30°, ∠RSP = 60°, ∠SRQ = 30°  (b) Since ∠SRP = 90°, then ∠SRP is the angle in a semicircle. Hence PS is a diameter.  45. (a) radius perpendicular to tangent  (b) 19·8cm (to the nearest mm)  46. (a) angle in alternate segment  (b) They are equiangular since ∠DAC = ∠BDC, ∠ACD = ∠DCB (same angle) and ∠CDA = ∠CBD (third angle of the triangles).  (c) $\frac{AC}{DC} = \frac{DC}{BC}$  (d) 12cm  47. 1750m² (3 s.f.)
48. (a) 17km (to the nearest km)  (b) 136°  49. (a) ∠TAC = 90° since radius ⊥ tangent, ∠ABC = 90° since this is an angle in a semicircle  (b) (i) 32° (tgt. ⊥ rad.)  (ii) 58° (∠in alt. seg.)  (iii) 58° (∠s in same seg.)
(iv) 122° (opp.∠s of cyclic quad.)  50. ∠BLR = 56° (to the nearest degree) Bearing = 319°  51. (i) ∆OAB
(ii) $\frac{XY}{AB} = \frac{OY}{OB} = \frac{1}{2}$  (iii) $\frac{1}{4}$  52. (a) (iii) reflection in line y = x  (b) (ii) translation by the vector $\binom{0}{4}$
(c) (i) a possible answer is: rotation about (0, 0) through 180° followed by translation by the vector $\binom{0}{-4}$
53. 3·2cm  54. (a)

| x | y = 4sin x |
|---|---|
| 0° | 0 |
| 30° | 2 |
| 60° | 3·5 |
| 90° | 4 |
| 120° | 3·5 |
| 150° | 2 |
| 180° | 0 |

(b) about 20° and 160°  55. (a) 4·9cm (1 d.p.)  (b) 56° (to the nearest degree)  (c) 49° (to the nearest degree)  56. (a) 7·57cm
(b) 59°  57. (a) 37·5m  (b) 49° (to the nearest degree)
58. (a) 81cm³  (b) 4·5cm  59. (a) 71·8° and 108·2°
(b) 2560cm² (3 s.f.)  (c) 4·0m² (2 s.f.)  60. (a) (i) –3y  (ii) x – y
(iii) 2x – 3y  (b) (i) x + y  (ii) 2 (x + y)  (iii) EH//DB and EH is twice the length of DB  61. 26·8m (1 d.p.)  62. (a) 60° and 300°
(b) 330°

(c)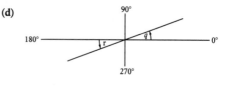

(d)

63. (a) (i) 57·7cm³ (3 s.f.)  (ii) 92·3cm (3 s.f.)  (b) 12·7cm³ (3 s.f.)  64. velocity is about 490km/h on a bearing of about 50°  65. (a) (i) 50°  (ii) 65°  (iii) 25°  (iv) 65°  (v) 25°  66. 45·1° (1 d.p.)

## Handling Data Revision

**Revision Exercise**

1. **(a)** 17·4 (1 d.p.)  **(b)** B and D have the highest median of 18.  **(c)** upper quartile = 18, lower quartile = 15
**(d)** Since the interquartile range of C is 3 years and the interquartile range of D is 2·5 years then the
interquartile range of C is 0·5 years greater than that of D.  **(e)** Since the range of C is 5 years and the range of
D is 6 years, the range of C is 1 year less than that of D.

**(f)**

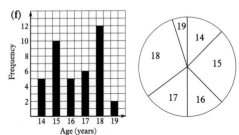

**(g)** The pie graphs clearly show the proportion of each age.
**(h)** The bar graphs clearly show the number of each age.

2. How old are you?     less than 13 ☐     13 ☐     14 ☐     Older than 14 ☐
I enjoyed the evening activities. All of them ☐     Most of them ☐     Some of them ☐
None of them ☐     Did you prefer the evening or the daytime activities? Evening ☐     Daytime ☐
3. **(i)** Christine used the unbiased die: she got approximately equal numbers of E and O. Nicholas used the
biased die: he got many more Es than Os. Lucinda made hers up: it is highly unlikely to get alternate Es and
Os when a die is tossed.  **(ii) (a)** $\frac{3}{20}$  **(b)** $\frac{3}{20}$  **(iii) (a)** $\frac{3}{100}$  **(b)** $\frac{21}{200}$  **(c)** $\frac{91}{400}$
4. median    5. **(a)** They can occur at the same time since if two heads are tossed we have both event A and
event B.  **(b)** They are independent since event A happening or not happening has no influence on whether
event B happens.  **(c)** H1, H2, H3, H4, H5, H6, T1, T2, T3, T4, T5, T6; P(H or even number) = $\frac{3}{4}$ .
**(d)** They are not exhaustive since they do not account for all possible outcomes: the arrow may stop in the
grey sections marked A.  **(e)** Since the events "Grey", "B" are not mutually exclusive the probabilities of
these events cannot be added.  6. **(a)** no correlation  **(b)** positive correlation  **(c)** no correlation  **(d)** negative
correlation  **(e)** positive correlation  **(f)** negative correlation  7. **(a)** (174·5, 5), (224·5, 6), (274·5, 4),
(324·5, 3), (374·5, 4), (424·5, 5), (474·5, 0)

**(b)**
**(c)**

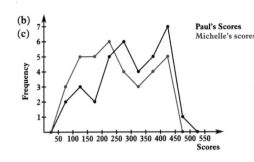

Paul's Scores
Michelle's scores

8. **(i) (a)** about 51 million  **(b)** about 64
million  **(ii) (a)** 1989  **(b)** 1985  **(c)** 1986
**(iii)** about 20 million
9. **(a)**

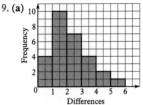

9. **(b)** median = 2m, upper quartile = 3m, lower quartile = 1·4m, interquartile range = 1·6m
10. Three possible questions are:
What time do you think the dance should finish?     9p.m. ☐    10p.m. ☐    11p.m. ☐    12p.m. ☐
Do you think snacks and drinks should be included in the price?     Yes ☐    No ☐
Rank the following types of music in order of preference using the
numbers 1, 2, 3, 4 with 1 the most preferred and 4 the least preferred.

Disco                          ☐
Guitarist & Vocalist           ☐
Jazz Band                      ☐
Rock and Roll Band             ☐

*Answers*

**11.** Equally likely outcomes: C; Relative frequency: A, B, E   **12. (a)** 5·6 (1 d.p.)  **(b)** 3

**13. (i) (a)**

| Time Taken (min.) | <6·0 | <7·0 | <8·0 | <9·0 | <10·0 | <11·0 | <12·0 | <13·0 |
|---|---|---|---|---|---|---|---|---|
| Cumulative Frequency | 1 | 4 | 9 | 15 | 24 | 37 | 41 | 43 |

**(b)**

| Length (mm) less than | Cumulative Frequency |
|---|---|
| 125 | 3 |
| 130 | 9 |
| 135 | 16 |
| 140 | 27 |
| 145 | 40 |
| 150 | 55 |
| 155 | 60 |
| 160 | 62 |

**(ii) (a)** (8·0, 9), (9·0, 15), (10·0, 24), (11·0, 37), (12·0, 41), (13·0, 43)

**(b)** (120, 0), (125, 3), (130, 9), (135, 16), (140, 27), (145, 40), (150, 55), (155, 60), (160, 62)

**(iii) (a)**

| Score | ≤40 | ≤50 | ≤60 | ≤70 | ≤80 | ≤90 | ≤100 |
|---|---|---|---|---|---|---|---|
| Cumulative Frequency | 2 | 7 | 20 | 31 | 40 | 46 | 50 |

**(b)** (30, 0), (40, 2), (50, 7), (60, 20), (70, 31), (80, 40), (90, 46), (100, 50)

**(iv) (a)**

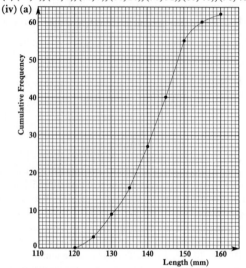

**(b)** median = 142mm, upper quartile = 147mm lower quartile = 134·5mm, interquartile range = 12·5mm

**14. (a)**

**(b)**

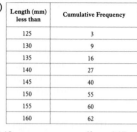

**(c)** The data has positive correlation since it is clustered around a line with positive gradient.
**(d)** 8  **(e)** 17

**15. (i)**

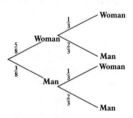

**(ii) (a)** $\frac{1}{4}$  **(b)** $\frac{19}{24}$   **16.** More than one answer is possible. Two possible answers with possible justifications are: Aerobics, Pool/Snooker, Weight training as more students ranked these as their 1st, 2nd or 3rd choice than badminton or table tennis; Aerobics, Pool/Snooker, Table tennis since these three have the lowest totals when the 1st preferences are given 1 point, the 2nd preferences 2 points and so on.

**17.**

| M's die \ J's die | 1 | 2 | 3 | 4 | 5 | 6 |
|---|---|---|---|---|---|---|
| 1 | 0 | 1 | 2 | 3 | 4 | 5 |
| 2 | 1 | 0 | 1 | 2 | 3 | 4 |
| 3 | 2 | 1 | 0 | 1 | 2 | 3 |
| 4 | 3 | 2 | 1 | 0 | 1 | 2 |
| 5 | 4 | 3 | 2 | 1 | 0 | 1 |
| 6 | 5 | 4 | 3 | 2 | 1 | 0 |

**(b)** $\frac{2}{3}$  **(c)** Matthew and Julia do not have the same chance of scoring a point each time the die is tossed: P(M scores) = $\frac{2}{3}$, P(J scores) = $\frac{1}{3}$.
**(d)** The game is now fair.  **(e)** The game is now fair.  **(f)** One way is: M could score a point for 0, 3, 4 or 5; J could score a point for 1 or 2.
**18. (a)** 2  **(b)** 12·2  **(c)** 10–14  **(d)** 5–9
**(e)**

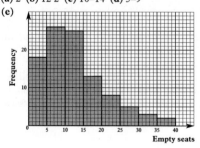

19. (i) (a) $\frac{7}{20}$ (b) $\frac{3}{4}$ (c)

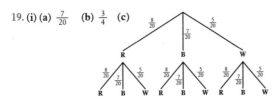
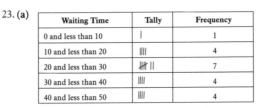

(ii) $\frac{123}{200}$   21. (a) $\frac{1}{6}$ (b) There are too few 2's and too many 5's. (c) $\frac{1}{3}$   22. A allows for any answer. B is easier to answer.

23. (a)

| Waiting Time | Tally | Frequency |
|---|---|---|
| 0 and less than 10 | I | 1 |
| 10 and less than 20 | IIII | 4 |
| 20 and less than 30 | HH II | 7 |
| 30 and less than 40 | IIII | 4 |
| 40 and less than 50 | IIII | 4 |

(b)
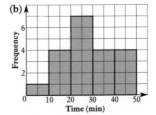

24. $\frac{29}{48}$   25. (a) range for both is $18 - 3 = 15$ (b) mean for A = 9, mean for B = 9 (c) scores for B are more closely clustered around the mean   26. 0·6

27. (a)

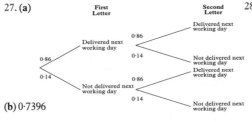

(b) 0·7396

28. (a) (i)
(b)

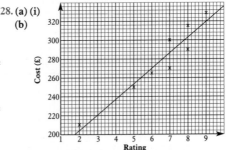

(ii) There is positive correlation between cost and rating. The higher the cost, the higher the rating.
(c) (i) about £236 (ii) the correlation isn't very strong   29. (a) P(Green) = 0·2 (b) 0·7 (c) 20

31. (a)

| Throw Number | 1 | 2 | 3 | 4 | 5 | 6 | 7 | 8 | 9 | 10 | 11 | 12 |
|---|---|---|---|---|---|---|---|---|---|---|---|---|
| Letter on bottom | B | A | B | C | D | A | B | A | B | C | D | A |
| Number of A's so far | 0 | 1 | 1 | 1 | 1 | 2 | 2 | 3 | 3 | 3 | 3 | 4 |
| Proportion of A's so far | 0 | $\frac{1}{2}$ | $\frac{1}{3}$ | $\frac{1}{4}$ | $\frac{1}{5}$ | $\frac{2}{6}$ | $\frac{2}{7}$ | $\frac{3}{8}$ | $\frac{3}{10}$ | $\frac{3}{10}$ | $\frac{3}{11}$ | $\frac{1}{3}$ |

(b) $\frac{1}{3}$ (c) will get close to $\frac{1}{4}$   32. (a) 70·2 (b) 60–
(c) mean since it takes account of all the weights
33. (a) heads and tails have the same chance of occurring
(b)

| 4 | 7 | 1 | 8 | 1 | 3 | 6 | 6 | 4 | 3 | 0 | 2 | 5 | 9 | 2 | 7 | 8 | 4 | 6 | 3 |
|---|---|---|---|---|---|---|---|---|---|---|---|---|---|---|---|---|---|---|---|
| H | T | T | H | T | T | T | H | H | H | T | H | H | T | T | H | T | H | H | T |

(c) $\frac{11}{20}$ (d) would get closer to $\frac{1}{2}$   34. (a) (i) $\frac{1}{6}$ (ii) $\frac{1}{36}$ (b) $\frac{13}{36}$   35. (ii) (a) 10 (b) 4 (c) Bran Flakes. Equal last for 1st choice, almost last for 2nd and 3rd choices. (d) Cornflakes. Equal 2nd for 1st choice, first for 2nd choice (twice as popular as any other), equal first for 3rd choice. (iii) A, E

36. (i)

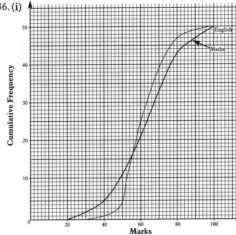

(ii)

| | English | Maths |
|---|---|---|
| Median | 60 | 62 |
| Inter-quartile Range | 14 | 12 |

(iii) The average maths mark is higher. The maths marks are less variable.   37. (a) $\frac{9}{25}$ (b) $\frac{12}{25}$
38. (a) (i) 0·25 (ii) 0·75 (b) (i) 0·4 (ii) events are not mutually exclusive.
39. (a)

| Height (Inches) | Class mid-point | Frequency |
|---|---|---|
| 54·5 – 59·5 | 57 | 1 |
| 59·5 – 64·5 | 62 | 115 |
| 64·5 – 69·5 | 67 | 380 |
| 69·5 – 74·5 | 72 | 4 |

(b) 65·87 inches

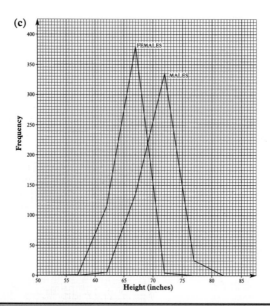

(c)

Chapter 23   Histograms. Representing and Analysing Data

Page 493                                              Exercise 23:2

1. (a)

| Time, in minutes | 40 ≤ t <60 | 60 ≤ t <70 | 70 ≤ t <80 | 80 ≤ t <90 | 90 ≤ t <100 | 100 ≤ t <120 |
|---|---|---|---|---|---|---|
| Number of students | 28 | 43 | 58 | 40 | 34 | 18 |
| Frequency density | 1·4 | 4·3 | 5·8 | 4·0 | 3·4 | 0·9 |

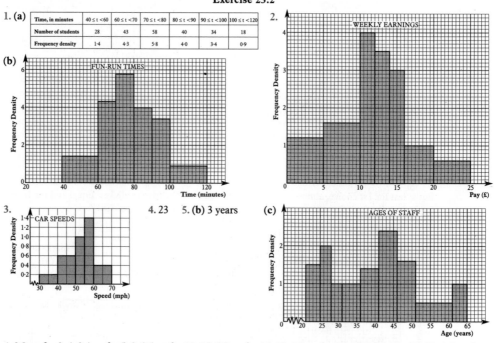

(b)  FUN-RUN TIMES

2.  WEEKLY EARNINGS

3.  CAR SPEEDS     4. 23     5. (b) 3 years     (c) AGES OF STAFF

6. 2·8cm for 0–4, 3·4cm for 5–9, 3·5cm for 10–15, 5·3cm for 16–18, 4·7cm for 19–21, 3·5cm for 22–29, 3·6cm for 30–39, 2·4cm for 50–59, 0·3cm for 60–84.     7. (b) 23·5 minutes  (c) 17·5 minutes

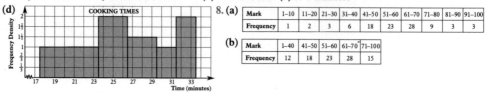

(d)  COOKING TIMES

8. (a)

| Mark | 1–10 | 11–20 | 21–30 | 31–40 | 41–50 | 51–60 | 61–70 | 71–80 | 81–90 | 91–100 |
|---|---|---|---|---|---|---|---|---|---|---|
| Frequency | 1 | 2 | 3 | 6 | 18 | 23 | 28 | 9 | 3 | 3 |

(b)

| Mark | 1–40 | 41–50 | 51–60 | 61–70 | 71–100 |
|---|---|---|---|---|---|
| Frequency | 12 | 18 | 23 | 28 | 15 |